W. S. B. (William Smythe Babcock) Mathews

Music - A Monthly Magazine

Volume VII.

W. S. B. (William Smythe Babcock) Mathews

Music - A Monthly Magazine
Volume VII.

ISBN/EAN: 9783742831408

Manufactured in Europe, USA, Canada, Australia, Japa

Cover: Foto ©Angelika Wolter / pixelio.de

Manufactured and distributed by brebook publishing software (www.brebook.com)

W. S. B. (William Smythe Babcock) Mathews

Music - A Monthly Magazine

MUSIC.

A MONTHLY MAGAZINE

DEVOTED TO THE ART, SCIENCE, TECHNIC AND LITERATURE OF MUSIC.

W. S. B. MATHEWS, *Editor.*

VOLUME VII.

NOVEMBER, 1894, TO APRIL, 1895.

CHICAGO:
THE MUSIC MAGAZINE PUBLISHING COMPANY
1402-1405, AUDITORIUM TOWER.

1895

INDEX TO VOLUME VII.

INDEX BY AUTHORS.

Blue Delft Portrait by Miss Magda M. Heinemann. Medal awarded by Columbian Exhibition, 1894.

GENERAL VIEW OF THE MT. BLANC RANGE.

From the Cross of Flegère. The four peaks at the extreme right belong to Mt. Blanc proper, Mt. Blanc itself being the third peak from the right. The fifth peak from the right is the Aiguille du Midi. Upon the extreme right is the Glacier des Bossons. That in the immediate front of the beholder is the Mer de Glace. The Cross of Flegère is upon the hither side of the valley, at an elevation of about 1,000 ft. above that of the Mer de Glace.

MUSIC

NOVEMBER, 1894.

NOTES OF A SUMMER TOUR.

Lucerne, Switzerland, Sep. 10, 1894.

THE Philadelphia summer school deserved considerably more notice than I gave it, but the time is so long ago that it is hardly worth while to go back now and try and pick up any of the loose ends. I meant to have mentioned the interesting lectures of Mr. L. C. Elson, which like all his writings on musical subjects were full of good matter, and were delivered with that pleasing good humor and readiness of speech which characterizes the thorough man of the world—who happens also to be well informed. There were many other lectures there, but I attended none of them, inasmuch as, having all I could possibly stand of teaching, I felt obliged to take the evenings to recreate.

The advantages of the university extension lectures were availed of to some extent by our pupils, but the only lecture I heard was a very interesting one by that great Boston citizen, Rev. Edward Everett Hale, whose subject was one connected with colonial history—the exact topic I do not at the moment remember.

* * *

I took the Allan line for Liverpool, led to do so by several considerations; first a feeling that five days outside was all the ocean a poor sailor need desire; and then also by a longing for the pleasant ride down the majestic St. Lawrence, and through the gulf. And more by the fact that I had crossed twice by this line before and found everything very pleasant. The steamer this time was the Parisian, the best of the line. She is not a greyhound in the modern sense, but a good reliable boat built about twelve years ago, well made in every respect, a remarkably steady sea boat, and well manned. On her we found every comfort that sea going could permit, and leaving Quebec Sunday morning at nine o'clock we passed the custom house at Liverpool Monday afternoon just before dinner time. While this is not a record breaking speed, it is practically as quick as most of the passages are made by any of the lines, and of this time we were out on the broad Atlantic only from Tuesday afternoon to Sunday afternoon, passing around the coast of Ireland Sunday evening.

* * *

The early part of our tour was the usual one. A short stop at the city of Chester near Liverpool, in order to see the walls and the old Cathedral, and then a trip across green England to London. There about five or six days, doing the principal sights, and then to the continent. We selected the New Haven and Dieppe route—never having tried that way before. To any others similarly tempted my advice is, don't yield. It is a very unpleasant way. The channel trip lasts nearly five hours, and all the way we sat on deck because it was less miserable there than below—where everybody was sick, and where the air was something to be appreciated by those only who have "been down on the sea in ships;" to quote the Psalmist's expression. I fancy that most landsmen are "down on" the sea when once they have been in a ship. All things end, and so did this passage, and we landed in Paris in due time, after a ride across a lovely farming country—which however is not so well kept as England, nor so prosperous looking. It was Sunday morning but the men were at work in the fields just the same as any other day. I failed to preach any sermons on the subject, as we were also travelling on that day.

Then followed abut five days in Paris. We spent some time in the Louvre, and the Luxembourg (from which many of the best pictures were loaned to the French exhibit at the Columbian Exposition), and did the sights generally, not forgetting Versailles and Fontainbleau. The most interesting sight we did at Paris was perhaps the exhibition at Sevres, where the finest pottery in the world is produced.

From Paris to Geneva, and again a day or two in a pretty and interesting city, and upon the charming lake, where we were fortunate enough to have perfect weather. Speaking of weather I may mention that the heat failed us soon after leaving Quebec, and we were not again too warm for comfort (except through violent exercise) until we

CASTLE OF CHILLON, LAKE GENEVA.

reached Italy—and there by no means so hot as we had been in America.

* * *

The great object of the trip had been to get to Switzerland and to do there some walking among the mountains. This we had intended to do from Lucerne, passing through the country and coming out by way of Geneva, in order to have Mt. Blanc and beautiful Chamounix last. But inasmuch as certain of the party were on the road to Leipsic, we changed our order and began at Chamounix, which was not so well, since besides bringing all the grandest mountains before the comparatively low ones of Lucerne, it also gave us the longest walks first, and walks also which there was very little possibility of dividing, as will appear later in the narrative.

So when we took the train out of Geneva for Chamounix we felt that now the trip was about beginning. The railway runs to Cluses, half way to Chamounix, where the diligence connects with it. Ill advised, we had taken tickets from Gaze for this trip with the other railway part of our journey. This was a mistake, for when there are four or more in a party it is usually quite as cheap and far pleasanter to take a carriage instead of the diligence, in which one gets a place somewhat by lot and in whatever kind of position it

THE MT. BLANC RANGE FROM GENEVA.
(The snow peaks in the distance.)

pleases the Cook interpreter to place you. This ride in an open carriage would be as pleasant a one as could be found —having most of the latter part of it a view of Mt. Blanc as background to whatever romantic scenery the road might for the moment afford.

* * *

At Chamounix we remained four or five days. Our first walk was to the Montanvert, across the Mer de Glace to the Chapeau, and down to the valley. This little exposition reads easily upon paper. Baedecker calls the ascent a matter of three and a half hours. The trip across the glacier takes about an hour or a little more, and the walk down the lateral moraine takes more than two hours, in which the Mauvais Pas is not the most pleasing incident. I had been over this route before, ten years ago, but had forgotten how bad this walk was. Instead of the three hours of Baedecker we made it four going up, but the trip was very pleasant in spite of its fatigue. Also was the passage of the glacier, the only difficulty of which consists in the hilly nature of the ice, where the pressure has bulged it up in various directions, making footing a matter of considerable care, not to say difficulty. In this walk as in all others the question of elevation cuts a very important figure. The valley of Chamounix is at an elevation of 3445 ft. The Montanvert is a hotel upon the side of the Mt. Blanc range, near the Aiguille of Charmoz, at an elevation of 6303 feet. This gives one nearly 3000 feet elevation to overcome. Then in coming down after crossing the glacier the distance is apparently increased by the walk following along the lateral moraine of the glacier. A moraine is simply a hill or continuous ridge of gravel and bowlders of all sizes which the glacier has brought down from the higher peaks, and at length has worked off to one side and deposited as before described. The lateral moraine of the Mer de Glace may be anywhere from twenty to fifty feet thick, and about twice as wide at the base. As boulders of from ten to twenty or even thirty feet through are by no means unusual incidents, it may be imagined that the walking is far from pleasant, and the path any thing but straight and well made.

The walk up was through a forest of fir trees, with occasional views out to the other side of the valley, and although getting more and more steep towards the last was not really difficult. But a steady going up hill for three or four hours on foot, along a path which while not steep for a mountain trail is nevertheless much too steep for wheeled vehicles, is not a form of exercise conducing to stagnation, and the longer the path grew the more we wished for the ending of it. At length we reached the Montanvert, the particular office of which is to afford a good view of the Mer de Glace, and to sell trinkets to travellers, and incidentally to feed them. The latter office as well as the one first named it does very well, and so after a rest of a couple of hours we found ourselves more reconciled to the world. From the Montanvert none of the peaks of Mt. Blanc are visible. The main features there are the great Aiguilles of Charmoz, Dru and the Grandes Jorrasses—which are sufficiently respectable in point of magnitude and presence. Nor does the walk down give much in the way of view that is of the first importance, since this also lies most of the way, as soon as the glacier is left, through the fir forest. Nor is the walk down materially easier than that in ascending. The path is rougher, and the continual going down in time tires the knees to such a point that one dislikes it about as much as the continual ascending. Still at last we reached home after a walk covering about eight hours of continual work. This was our initiation, and it may well be supposed that the passengers found the ensuing day better suited for repose than for more rapid duties. Such was indeed the case. We took a few looks through the great telescope at Mt. Blanc, where there was the usual ascent going on, and occupied ourselves in viewing at our leisure this, the most beautiful of all mountains.

* * *

Chamounix well deserves its fame. It is a valley about twelve miles long, with the Col de Balme at one end and some hills the name of which I do not know at the other; the wall on the Mt. Blanc side rises to a height of from 12,500 feet to 15,000 feet, the saddles between the peaks being generally from 11,500 feet and upwards. Meanwhile the valley is only at an elevation of 3445 feet, making more than two miles vertical of mountain side set up for beholding.

And what a mountain side! Between the Col de Balme ten miles away, and Chamounix, there are no less than five glaciers which come down well towards the valley. Some of these, indeed, are not visible from Chamounix, but the great glacier des Bossons, which takes the largest part of the snow drainage of Mt. Blanc proper, on this side, comes down the valley in a very prominent position, and constitutes a notable feature in the landscape. Indeed I have always thought of this great snow white glacier, coming so low down on the front of Mt. Blanc, as taking the character of a well polished shirt bosom, giving Mt. Blanc from this side the air of being in evening dress, for the delectation of beholders. In this respect there is no other mountain side that I have seen comparing with it. Nor is the mountain interest confined to the Mt. Blanc side. The Aguilles Rouges on the other side are indeed not very high, but even 8,000 feet is not to be despised, and they make a very telling offset to the brilliant mountain display in the foreground, besides affording many points of view from which the whole magnificent mountain side can be seen to advantage.

* * *

Our next walk was to the Brevent, the highest of the peaks of the Aguilles Rouges, its elevation being 8385 feet. An arithmetical exercise will convince the most incredulous that between the elevation of Chamounix and the Brevent there is nearly 4,000 feet vertical to be overcome by the diligent foot passenger. And the walk is something memorable. Beginning innocently, along fields and through fir woods it presently after about an hour and a half emerges at a little way side hotel, Plan Achat, about 1,000 feet up the side of the hill. We come there upon open ground, and the path lies in zig-zag along the exceeding steep hill side, where outside the path a man could scarcely hold a footing but would slide to the bottom. The next landing place is 2,000 feet farther up, on the top of one of the lower parts of the range, and all the walk is in full view of the grand mountain side already mentioned, the whole valley of Chamounix being visible nearly every step of the way. At Bel Achat the view is splendid, but this is not the end. After fifteen minutes rather hard ascent one comes out on the very top of the crest, the narrow crest of the ridge, from which one has not alone the valley of Chamounix on one side, with the magnificent range of Mt. Blanc for a background, but on the other side still other ranges, and a richly tilled farming country. Then after about thirty minutes along the ridge of as pretty walk as I ever saw, we begin again another ascent, which in twenty minutes or so brings us to the top of the Brevent—the highest peak of the Aiguilles Rouges. Here the view is magnificent. Not

MT. BLANC FROM THE BREVENT.

alone the Mt. Blanc range, but glimpses of the Bernese Alps and the snow peaks of the Pourraine are seen. There is no hotel at the top—only, an attendant, a little tent about six feet in diameter, a bottle of wine or so (very poor wine) water, etc., in order that the weary passenger may not fail of due refreshment. All this in four hours. Then the come-down, which again is lovely, the view diminishing in grandeur by a gradual decrescendo as one retraces the path. And so the end—a view to be always remembered;

and from a pathological point of view an exercise of muscles extending over the greater part of nine solid hours; and a pumping of air and of perspiration worthy a first class machine.

Again a day of rest. Nine hours for a greenhorn is rather too much. Again small walks in the valley, coquetting with the shop keeping exhibits of notions, and at length we feel that we have done Chamounix. Now begins the "piece de resistance" of all our vacation, the trip around Mt. Blanc. We began our walk easily, after the Mark Twain recipe, by taking a carriage for Contamines, a village on the west side of the Mt. Blanc range. This great range is

CABIN OF THE GRAND MULETS.
(Here those intending to make the ascent of Mt. Blanc spend the first night.)

a diamond shaped paralellgram, the long sides running north east and south west, the short sides about straight north and south. The east short side is the valley of the Trient or the Great St. Bernard pass. The west is the valley of Montjoie. The north is the valley of Chamounix; and the south the valley of Aosta, or more properly of the Doire. Thus in order to walk around the mountain at the south west end one must cross the great ridges forming the water sheds, namely, Cols of Bonhomme, Fours, and Seigne, all of which are about 8,000 feet high, and between which in some cases there are deep valleys. In Switzerland the timber ends at about five or six thousand feet. Eternal snow begins at about nine thousand feet, but glaciers often come down permanently to about four or five thousand feet. Thus in order to cross one of the high Cols we have always at least two thousand feet of very desolate and rocky hill, and occasionally snow in the hollows.

Moreover, at an elevation of anything over six thousand feet the difference in weight of atmosphere forms an element in the problem, intensifying the exertion necessary for a given walk. The tour of Mt. Blanc takes three days, even without tying up the end by coming back to Chamonix.

The drive to Contamines was delightful. This is not

AIGUILLE DU MIDI.

(View taken from the Cabin of the Grand Mulets, showing the detail of the rock pinnacles, the ice formations, etc.)

the orthodox way of the tour. One ought to have walked over the hill at the lower end of the valley (which the carriage makes a long detour around) and have gained at the top thereof a magnificent view of the valley of Chamounix, the Mt. Blanc range, etc, with an encouraging outlook into the valley of Montjoie, forming the south end of our province of Mt. Blanc. But we did not. We drove to Contamines. Baedecker, that guide, philosopher and friend of the tourist, says that one ought to go on to Nant Borant, because the night quarters are better there. So after a charming drive down the valley of the Arve for about twelve miles, and a long and rather dusty drive up the valley of the Montjoie, in which we went down from Chamounix more than 1400 feet, and then up to Contamines more than 2000 feet, we found ourselves in one of the most dilapidated looking villages I have ever seen of its size. Without tarrying to test its quality we loaded up with our packs and started upon our walk—not to go around Mt. Blanc that night (for it was now about three in the afternoon) but simply to go on to Nant Borant, were Baedecker had said that the night quarters were better. We still had a carriage road for six or eight miles, ending at Notre Dame de la Gorge, where the gorge of the Bon-Nant ends, and the bridle path ascends steeply, very steeply, through woods, beside the deep gorge of the stream.

The path was extremely steep, and paved with large boulders much of the way, making it not altogether pleasant. Nevertheless the boulders were many of them covered with green moss; as also were the trunks of the trees. The way-side was a tangle of under-brush, ferns, flowers, and the like, the spray in vapor from the fierce torrent of the Bon Nant, coming down from the eternal snows, affording a surplus of moisture in all seasons. The trees of the wood were of good size, many of them sixty feet or more in height. Hence from a picturesque point of view this path, in itself considered, was one of the most beautiful we found in all our walk. And about the time the timber ended (as a consequence of the elevation reached) we came to a stone bridge over the Bon Nant at a point where the gorge was at its best, and the cascades and water-worn rocks made a strong and satisfactory picture. The bridge, also was old, two hundred years or more, as shown by the dates there upon.

At length we reached Nant Borant. It is a small

inn, formly a *chalet.* The quarters for travellers are situated in a new addition built along the hill side, like what is called in New England an "L," one story high, dining room, and sleeping rooms, all opening upon a small gallery or piazza, and in one case at least the room with two beds having no window except the glass in the door, and no way of ventilating the room except by leaving the door ajar. Good beds, a really good dinner, and the best of service put us in good humor for our morning's walk, which was to be very trying.

* * *

For the second day of our trip we had to cross two Cols, that of Bonhomme, 8153, and that of Fours, 8800 feet respectively. Nant Borant is at 4780, thus giving us something more than 4,000 feet elevation to overcome, at a pitch already high enough to make exercise more trying. This was a magnificent walk. The path was steep in places, rocky much of the way, but it afforded views back down the entire valley of the Montjoie, and to the peaks in the rear, while the southern peaks of the Mt. Blanc range made conspicuous features in the foreground at the side. It was also interesting to watch the behavior of the glaciers, which now and then came into view high up the mountain side. At first a mere cornice of snow; then after a half hour, a little more; finally when we were high enough a vast field of ice would come into view, contained within an embracing circle of peaks. In order to describe a walk of this kind one needs the pen of a poet. And this went on all the morning until we reached the Col de Bonhomme. We carried a lunch, as there are no hotels along the route, and ate our hard bread, cheese and red wine by a spring coming out of the rock near the Col de Bonhomme. At the resting place we had a view into a sunny but desolate valley to the south, and as usual some peak of the Mt. Blanc range close at hand upon our left.

The Col de la Fours we found covered with snow. To reach it we had put in about five hours of work. The view from the top was not so grand as that of the next day.

But the route down to our next stopping place, Motets, was exceedingly steep, over slate detritus, and later through pastures, for about three hours, during which we had something more than half a mile vertical to come down.

* * *

The inn at Motets is a thoroughly Swiss establishment, kept by the widow of one Fort—and a capable woman is she. As this is upon the boundary line, we found a station of gend'armes, one of whom was sent for fresh water upon my arrival. The inn is a two story structure, about sixty feet long and two rooms wide. The upper or main floor is devoted to guests; the lower to kitchen, 3d class eating accommodations, and stables for cows, mules, hens etc. The consequence is a pervading odor of fresh cow, an equally pervading buzz of fresh roosters (especially in the morning), and at last some of the most obdurate bread it was ever my lot to tackle. In all these remote inns the larder is limited. What is called coffee, very hard bread of poor quality, and a little fresh meat and vegetables, is all that one can get. Salt meat appears to be unknown, or if known is kept for the family. The usual meat is veal, varied with chicken. And at one place where beefsteak was the subject of negotiation, the landlord honestly confessed that he had none. He said that beefsteaks were there made of veal, as also were mutton cutlets—when ordered by deluded Englishmen or Americans. As for the natives, they partook of the same, but under its zoological name.

The ensuing day was the most arduous of the series. We took a porter for the ascent of the Col de la Seigne, an ascent of only two thousand feet from our inn, but over a steep and trying path. At the top one of the grandest views of the entire trip. Here we were upon the actual boundary between France and Italy. Before us the valley called Allee Blanche, in which the river Doire rises, upon the left the tremendous precipices of the Mt. Blanc range, Mt. Blanc itself being seen exactly from the opposite side as at Chamounix, and a grand array of glaciers and smaller peaks. It was very cold at the Col, so we soon forsook the spirit-stirring view in favor of milder climes. A steep descent brought us presently to some *chalets*, and later along by the terminal moraines of glaciers and along a lateral moraine of the vast glacier of Miage, and so on down and down the magnificent valley Val Veni along by the constantly increasing Doire, to the joining with Val Ferret and the turn South towards Courmayer. All this during a hot afternoon, where the sun had unlimited chance at the tender foot Americans. The valley in the upper parts was entirely desolate; then grass, where the stagnant glacier had left a level deposit, and so later a beautiful meadow; then trees, and at length great fir trees. About two o'clock we reached a cantine where we proposed at length to eat our lunch. It was poor enough, lunch and cantine alike, but the bill was a work of art. For a little water, and milk, (we had bread and cheese with us) and a bottle of ordinary, the bill was seven francs, almost the only time during the trip when we were distinctly swindled. It should have been about three francs.

Along about four o'clock it dawned upon the editorial mind that one of the ladies at least had had enough, and then a looking out for a chalet where a mule might be hired for the remainder of the distance. At length we found a place: but the good humored Italian (who resembled a copy of the smiling Del Puente in plain colors) intimated that he had a chariot affording place for two and all the baggages, which he would make to the distinguished Signor at the same price. This was enough. We ordered the chariot.

The chariot turned out to be a very small cart—rather too large for a child's plaything, a two wheeled affair, with sides, but without ends. This was drawn by a small but amiable donkey, harnessed up with all sorts of rope splices and fastening, and the curious wooden buckle they use in this part of Italy for fastening rope lashing and harnessing. About half way out on the left shaft was the crank for the brake, all the brakes in Switzerland being operated by means of a crank, which when the driver is expected to ride, is just handy for his right hand. But this was a farm wagon, and the driver was expected to walk and lead the donkey, hence the location. Then a well stuffed seat being brought the distinguished Signor and the Signorina were mounted upon it, the "baggages" being duly tied in place below, and then a large hamper of the amiable proprietor himself last of all. And so in grand estate down that steep mountain road, where most of the way there was no room for another team to pass, had the country afforded the luxury of two teams upon a single road at the same time, we made passage into Courmayer. All the way the driver trotted at the donkey's head, loosening and tightening the brake again and again, and cheering the worthy little beast, now with the stick and now with all sorts of Italian diminutives of wholly different temper from the words by means of which American mules are driven.

Courmayer is a fine old Italian village situated exactly south of Mt. Blanc, just a little way down the main valley towards Aosta. The streets are narrow, after the good old fashion. Now and then an aspiring hotel has run a gallery across the street in order to connect with a dependency upon the other side. The widest part of the street proper is not ten feet. There is pavement, and there are carriages now and then—carriages of all sorts, but rarely one provoking more good natured mirth than this cavalcade of ours, which gave itself away as a "tender foot" last resort, at first glance. As for the teams on these narrow streets, the drivers make their way with great cracking of whips and when one hears these sounding explosions ahead of him, he straightway seeks a corner of the wall into which he may in part crowd himself and so a passage by be effected.

There are good hotels in Courmayer and the plain little one which we took by recommendation of an English traveller, whom we had encountered earlier in the day, turned out to be fairly good, and after the hard luck we had been having, it seemed almost like a *palazzo*, which it was not in the least. Two of the ladies had a room upon the third floor overlooking the valley and the mountains upon the other side. The distinguished Signor and lady were lodged more magnificently, if less pleasantly, in a room upon the main street, with sitting room attached, and a queer little dressing room enclosed from what had formerly been a balcony. For all this magnificence we were charged eighty cents per day for two persons, meals not included. There was also the usual supplementary charge of ten cents per day for lights. But America has often done worse for us, so we did not complain.

At Courmayer our tour of Mt. Blanc ended, for we did not mean to complete it by going back to the Rhone valley over the Great St. Bernard—which we would have been more prudent to do.

W. S. B. M.

(TO BE CONTINUED).

THE HARMONIC NATURE OF MUSICAL SCALES.

IV.

POLYTONIC SCALES.

HAVING in the preceding parts of our inquiry endeavored to discover the various causes which by their combined action have ultimately established the succession of tones known as pentatonic and heptatonic scales, we may now enter upon the consideration of the third group, which we have termed Polytonic scales. When speaking of scales of seven tones we have considered them as forms of a higher degree of structural perfection than the scales of only five degrees, and as reasons we have adduced the higher degree of complexity exhibited by the former, and, resulting from this, an increased multiplicity and subtlety of possible inter-relations between the tones. Applying the same criterion when comparing the heptatonic and polytonic scales, the latter, on the strength of greater complexity, might be expected to exhibit a higher degree of structural development than the former. This conclusion will, however, by a closer inspection, prove to be fallacious. In the scales which have been placed in the first two groups, all the degrees have been tacitly assumed as of about equal importance. Accordingly relations might be, and actually are, subsisting between any two degrees of them. In polytonic scales the case is changed; because among the tones we must distinguish between two essentially different constituents: *e. g.*, the *fixed tones* and the *changeable tones*, the former being invariably present, while the latter may be partly present, or entirely absent. In other words, the fixed tones represent the firmly-established groundwork; of the proper scale the changeable notes are in some measure accidental, and altogether merely ornamental, standing much in the same relation to the fixed tones as the ornamentation of an edifice stands to the entire architectural design. The former may be said to correspond to our musical ornamentation, having no independent significance by themselves, being rather a transition between the fixed notes, somewhat similar in their character to the tones which are touched when a violin player or vocal performer slides from one tone into another, only that in polytonic scales these transitional tones are reduced to accurately-defined degrees, and as such have been incorporated into the system as a whole. And accordingly we find the changeable tones governed by rules similar to those which govern our musical ornamentation, and what are known as changing and passing notes. A changeable tone, for instance, cannot progress into another changeable tone, but must pass into the next fixed note. The fixed notes may, for illustration's sake, be compared to our diatonic scale, in which case the entire polytonic scale would correspond to the chromatic scale, only that in the former the chromatic steps are smaller and more numerous than in the modern European chromatic scale.

This being understood we can now easily see that polytonic scales do not represent a higher degree of structural perfection than that represented by heptatonic systems. For, since among the changeable tones no relations can exist, although those between them and the fixed tones might in one sense be considered more subtle, yet this very excess of minor relations of only a slight degree of perceptibility serves to render the relations among the fixed tones weak and ill-defined; and therefore we can understand what might almost seem paradoxical, that this very excessive subtlety of relations not only fails to enhance the structural value of the system in question taken as a whole, but by its very complexity detracts from their intelligibility and lessens their degree of structural perfection. And the inferiority of these changeable intervals is tacitly acknowledged in actual performance, as will best be seen from the manner in which they are produced. In Arabia and East India, the only two countries where polytonic scales are in use, music is performed almost exclusively on numerous-stringed instruments of the lute and violin tribe, which instruments have usually high and immovable frets. The strings, if pressed against these frets and plucked, give the fixed tones of the scale, and the changeable tones are produced by pressing the string down behind the fret, thereby increasing the tension of the string, which thus yields a tone somewhat sharper than before. The same effect is produced on instruments without frets by sliding the finger sideways after pressing the string towards the finger-board, thus again sharpening the tone. That such a crude and uncertain mode of production excludes an accurate rendering of the theoretically fixed values is obvious, and this ambiguity of the changeable tones more than anything else betrays their inferiority as compared to the absolute certainty and accuracy with which the fixed tones can be evoked.

Whether these changeable tones should be considered as a remnant of that mode of passing from one degree to another by a continuous transition which is met with in many forms of primitive music, and as carrying further the subdivision from an internal necessity, admits of conjecture. But the first assumption has more probability for itself, as, if the latter should have been the case, the desire for further subdivision would in all likelihood have gone hand in hand with a tendency to make, by degrees, all the steps of equal importance. The retention of the fixed tones with undiminished importance may, however, serve as an indication that they and their recognition as such have been reached at a later date and will eventually, if the process of development should go on, survive the changeable notes altogether, so that perhaps the number of steps would in the course of time be reduced to the almost universal number of seven. This view is further countenanced by the fact that in ancient times in Arabia there was a system in use carrying the division of the octave much further than the scale in use at present, subdividing, namely, each tone into twelve equal intervals, the octave thus containing one hundred and forty-four degrees. This system however having fallen out of use, seems to indicate that polytonic systems with a smaller number of degrees, and eventually heptatonic scales, are destined to outlive polytonic scales of many degrees. Certain it is that these polytonic systems have been in use and theoretically established as far back as historical record reaches, and if the extremely improbable change from the lesser number of steps to the higher has taken place, it has been in times anterior to those of which we have historical data.

Since, then, as we have seen, the changeable tones are merely a secondary element, and can as such easily be separated from the primary element, it becomes clear that polytonic scales may, by eliminating this non essential element, be reduced to scales of a smaller number of tones. Moreover, we see that there exists no clearly defined boundary line between the heptatonic and polytonic scales, as little as between the pentatonic and the heptatonic scales; in other words, the three groups which we have distinguished at the outset, have points of contact among themselves, and one merges by insensible degrees into the other. This with regard to the second and third group will be more clearly brought out by the Table of Polytonic Scales which appears on the following page, and in which the darker figures represent the fixed tones in the same manner as in the tables previously presented, while the lighter figures give the cent numbers of the changeable intervals.

The first four examples represent polytonic scales of eight degrees. Omitting the one changeable note which each scale shows, we recognize them as ordinary heptatonic scales, numbers 1, 2 and 4 corresponding approximately to our major scale but showing in the first two instances at least, minor sevenths. No. 3 coincides with our modern ascending minor scale. The changeable tones in the first two specimens lie each a little less than a quarter of a semitone below the upper tonic, forming thus a leading note to it, as if the insufficiency of the traditional minor seventh had been felt and this leading note had been added as quasi-compromise between the conventionally established interval and that solicited by the attractive force exerted on the seventh by the tonic. Number 4 shows a similar leading note to the fifth, the interval next in importance to the tonic. The scale number three, which as already said is minor in character, has as a changeable note a minor sixth, besides the major sixth, which is a fixed tone. It may thus be said to be a combination of our harmonic and ascending melodic minor scales, the leading note B tending towards the tonic C, while A♭ would have a downward tendency toward the dominant G. In these scales we can trace most clearly the transition between the heptatonic and the polytonic scales, for they are unmistakably heptatonic, although each shows the admixture of a foreign element in its changeable note. Indeed, if we compare them with the previously examined Arabic heptatonic scales, we find that No. 4 of the polytonic is, omitting the changeable note, identical with No. 6 of the heptatonic scales, while No. 3 of the former and No. 7 of the latter coincide, save a slight disparity in the fifth, and Nos.

TABLE V.
POLYTONIC SCALES.

		C	D	E	F	G	A	B	C
Arabia.	1.	0	24	2	0	24	2	92	0
	2.	0	24	2	0	0	2	92	0
	3.	0	24	92	0	24	2	2	0
	4.	0	24	2	0	0	22	2	0
	5.	0	0	22	0	0	22	2	0
	6.	0	0	22	0	0	22	122	0
India.	7.	0	4	38	2	2	34	88	0
	8.	0	0	0	0	0	22	0	0
	9.	0	0	12	0	17	12	18	0

The dagger † stands for the plus sign.
The dash — stands for the minus sign.

1 and 2 bear a close resemblance with those formerly numbered 1 and 3 respectively.

Examples 5 and 6 are polytonic scales of seventeen degrees, and their structure has given rise to the very general misconception that the Arabian system divides the octave into seventeen equal intervals, each being one third of a tone. This assumption, however, has, by the recent researches of Prof. Land, been proved to be inaccurate, in so far, namely, that although the scales contain seventeen degrees, these are not equal, the scales being in reality heptatonic with additional auxiliary intervals differing from the fixed tones by intervals of ninety or twenty-four cents, as our table shows. These auxiliary notes are not placed at hazard, but are arranged according to some order. The intervals of ninety cents, namely, being nearly equal to a semitone, or more exactly a Pythagorean limma, raise each of the diatonic degrees by a semitone, producing thus a chromatic scale of twelve semitones with the additional intervals of twenty-four cents serving to fill out the gaps arising between the somewhat too small semitones. Here, then, we can trace three different elements which are combined into our scale: first, the basal heptatonic scale; second, the chromatic semitones which constitute it a chromatic scale; and, lastly, the the third and least important element, filling in the discrepancies existing between the chromatic semitones. Thus considered the two scales will be recognized as coinciding in their main constituent very nearly with our equal tempered major scale, to which the chromatic semitones, which have again been subdivided, are superadded. This tonic system, prevailing from the thirteenth to the fifteenth century, has in modern times been partly replaced by another, which, although it carries the subdivision of the octave still farther, or rather carries it through with more regularity and consistency, is a still closer approximation to our modern tone system. The scale represented in our table as number seven shows a division of the octave in twenty-four equal degrees of fifty cents (half of a semi-tone) each. That this division contains in itself our chromatic scale of twelve steps is self-evident, and the table shows also that the fixed notes form a heptatonic scale of seven tones, having an accurate second, fourth and fifth, but a minor seventh, and in addition a third and sixth lying midway between our major and minor third and sixth. The occurrence of these two neutral intervals, especially that of the neutral third, is of great significance; for the scale of twenty-four quarter tones shows among its degrees both the major and minor third and sixth. And yet these intervals have not been selected as fixed tones, but have been assigned the subordinate position of changeable tones, which appears particularly surprising in the case of the major third, which should have been suggested as a fixed tone by the principle of conformity to the physical constitution of sound. And that this principle could thus be violated only confirms what we have formerly found, namely, that, in the case of the major third, this principle has acted with so little certainty and consistency that a deviation from a tone suggested by it has apparently not given rise to a recognition of its non-observance. Incidentally it proves the possibility that the minor third, which also disregards the dictates of this principle, could, by a process already described, be established through the intervention of psychical motives overruling the physical suggestive force.

Not less complicated are the Indian polytonic scales. They embody a division of the octave into twenty-three degrees, and have for their basis heptatonic scales resembling very much our own. Especially is this the case in No. 8, the old Indian scale, which, as the table shows, is based on a scale of pure harmonic intervals, save that of the sixth which is twenty-two cents sharp. The heptatonic scale, however, which forms the foundation of the modern Indian scale shows more considerable disparities, its third as already mentioned being neutral, and the fifth, sixth and seventh also showing sensible deviations. The auxiliary intervals are arrived at by a rather complicated mode of division, the major tone of two hundred and four cents being divided in four, the minor tone into three, and the semi-tone into two degrees. But the resulting values may practically be considered as quarter [illegible] which they are produced offering so [illegible] a constant accurate intonation that this [illegible] will be justified.

[illegible] our survey of the polytonic scales. But [illegible] for on the same principles which we [illegible] govern the selection of the pentatonic and [illegible] Since the fixed tones forming their basis [illegible] recognized as heptatonic scales, and in part [illegible] heptatonic scales formerly presented, the [illegible] that this element at least can be referred to [illegible] presents little difficulty, and has in substance [illegible] given when treating of heptatonic scales. Being [illegible] action of the principle of conformity to the [illegible] constitution of sound, we find the octave, fifth and [illegible] in the Arabian polytonic scales established with [illegible] degree of consistency and accuracy, although [illegible] are in this regard somewhat inferior to the purely [illegible] scales, owing to the fact that the principles of tonal attraction and equal division have asserted themselves in the more complex systems with a more than common degree of strength. The Indian scales, however, singularly enough show in their heptatonic basis a greater degree of perfection than the purely heptatonic scales considered heretofore, the inferiority of the latter in all probability being due to inaccuracies which always accrue to measurements taken from performances, while the value of the polytonic scales are determined with theoretical precision.

As already remarked the principle of equal division has been a very efficient cause in the establishment of polytonic scales, especially in those with a great number of degrees. In the scales Nos. 5 and 6 it may be credited with having determined the insertion of the chromatic semitones of ninety cents and the complementary intervals of twenty-four cents. Scale No. 7, consisting of twenty-four equal degrees of fifty cents, is entirely due to a consistently carried out scheme of equal division, although it may be granted that this division has been accepted not solely for its intrinsic value, but for the coincidence of some of the degrees thus established with the stable intervals of the fifth and, perhaps, the fourth. In the Indian scales the principle of equal division has likewise asserted itself, but less forcibly, by determining the sub-division of the diatonic degrees into the auxiliary tones.

Tonal attraction, however, may be said to be the only principle serving as an explanation for the *raison d'être* of the auxiliary tones. By themselves and among themselves they have no right of existence, and what importance they have is simply acquired by the relations which they sustain to the fixed tones. They may be remnants of a form of primitive music which in its transitional progression and minuteness of intervals may be imagined to have been the first step leading ultimately from speech to music; or they may owe their existence to a desire for enhancing the scanty means of expression offered by the comparatively few steps of the diatonic scale through a variety of smaller degrees making possible a more varied expression, which, in the absence of the resources of harmony, was demanded by the many-sided and active mental life characterising the people of India and Arabia. At any rate the principle of tonal attraction alone, in its widest sense as the selection of tones by strength of their relation to other and previously established tones, can furnish us with a key for a division appearing otherwise so strange to our conceptions of tonal relations.

Having, as far as practicable, concluded our analysis of each of the three individual groups of tone systems, we may now, in order to arrive at a full view of the collective evidence furnished by this analysis, briefly restate the main results of our inquiry, and then proceed to draw a short comparison between the extra-European and our modern European tone system. Summarizing the results, we have found that three principles have conjointly governed the establishment of scale intervals. Of these the principle of conformity to the physical constitution of sound stands first in point of time as well as in its universal application, and through its agency have been established first, the octave, with a high degree of universality and accuracy; second, the fifth, with a moderate degree of consistency and accuracy; and third, the major third, with only a slight degree of unanimity and a corresponding lack of precision; these three intervals forming together the framework of the scale, or, as we have termed it, its stable element. Furthermore, we demonstrated that the remaining degrees of the scales, or the intercalary tones, have been added under the joint influence of the principle of equal division and that of tonal attraction, the former appearing as a tendency to so control the process of selection that the degrees of the scale become approximately equi distant in pitch, the latter resulting from a disposition to induce the selection of such tones as stand in a clearly perceptible relation of proximity to the stable intervals. But notwithstanding the fact that excepting a few isolated instances all these three principles have co-operated in the establishment of scales, we notice between them wide differences, resulting from different combinations of these influences, implying corresponding variations in the final result. In other words, all the tonic systems analyzed are the outcome of a compromise between principles totally unlike in nature and in some measure even antagonistic.

We have until now entirely refrained from speaking of the nature of our Modern European tone system. But at this juncture the question naturally suggests itself: Is our own tone system, which is so remarkably well adapted to musical expression, merely the result of a compromise? I am compelled to answer that its existence in its present form is due to nothing more than a compromise of different tendencies; that like all other tone systems it is the direct outcome of the co-operation of the same active forces, and as such differs from them only in the degree of perfection with which this compromise has been enacted, but not in its essential nature; and that its apparent naturalness is nothing but the consequence of a long continued and firmly established habit.

It is hardly necessary to mention that a system whose ultimate structure has been conditioned by harmony, which in its turn is based on the primary harmonic structure of the major chord contained in the upper partials of every musical sound, conforms to the principle whose very office it is to establish the intervals composing this chord. But it may be worthy of our notice to observe that it does not altogether conform to this principle, but conversely shows very marked deviations from the intervals which are dictated by it, this deviation being, in the case of the major third for instance, no less than 14 cents, while the minor scale, or its characteristic interval, the minor third, can not be reconciliated to its agency at all, but can only be accounted for on psychical grounds as given before. These deviations in themselves would be quite sufficient to deprive our tone system of every semblance as a product of nature, and to maintain it as such is only equalled by the similar inconsistency which considers the sense of harmony as cognate with human nature, based as it is on an altogether artificial and strictly speaking nonharmonic (*e. g.* not accurately conforming to true harmony) tone structure as our equally tempered scale.

But we shall not content ourselves by merely stating the presence of these disparities. After what has been said before it is obvious that we have to find the cause for these deviations from the intervals dictated by the principle of conformity to the physical constitution of sound, in the two remaining principles of equal division and tonal attraction. Of these the first, perhaps, is the most efficient in bringing about this discrepancy. Our scale is divided into 6 equal intervals of a tone, and subdivided into 12 equal semitones, and our major and minor scales differ only in the order with which the whole and half tones succeed each other. And this order has been determined by the exigencies of harmonic progression. Yet strictly speaking it is not this generally assigned reason which demanded an equal division, for harmonic combinations and progressions whether true harmonic intervals are possible and actually in use in "a capella" music as, for instance, that of the tonic-sol-faists. The considerations however, which in reality demanded this equal division are fundamentally of a mechanical nature, connected with the requirements of instrumental execution. On stringed instruments we have seen that the equal division of strings stands in great favor with Eastern peoples, this mode having recommended itself by its concreteness as well as by the facility of its application. On keyed instruments and instruments of percussion such a division was necessitated in order to reduce the keys to a reasonable number, admitting of an adequate ease of performance, especially in rapid passages, in which instrumental music abounds.

The principle of tonal attraction also, but more especially in its more specified application of tonality, has contributed its share in determining the ultimate structure of our modern tone system. To its influence is due in the first place the introduction of our leading note, which plays such an important part in our music. Particularly in the minor mode its action has obviously been felt, not only by the introduction of the major seventh, but in the ascending melodic minor scale, also in that of the major sixth, giving thus rise to the inconsistency of having one scale as the basis of harmony and another as the basis of melody. That this conspicuous incongruity bears the stamp of an artificial contrivance and lacks even the least semblance of a natural product, can hardly fail to be admitted; and the question is only whether the melodic minor scale with two different forms for ascending and descending progression, or the harmonic minor scale with the augmented second, generally condemned as unmelodious is the most unnatural. To the influence of the principle of tonal attraction must also be attributed the fact that in the performances of well trained musicians the same degree of the scale varies somewhat in its intonation according to the nature of the progression in which it forms a link; half steps, when ascending, having a tendency to be slightly sharped; when descending, to be flatted; a phenomenon which bears a close analogy to the minute auxiliary intervals employed in some of the systems above considered.

And now, after the inspection of most of the known tone systems may be supposed to have acquainted us sufficiently with their nature, we may undertake to answer the question wherewith we set out: Is the harmonic principle postulated by some writers an actual reality, a principle cognate with human nature and therefore manifest in the musical utterances of all mankind? This question falls naturally into two divisions; for to answer it efficiently we must first inquire whether the tone systems of the extra-European peoples betray any traces which justify us in assuming the presence of such a law; second, we must ascertain whether its existence as inherent in the nature of Europeans, prior to their objective acquaintance with harmonic combinations, can be demonstrated. In order to find an answer to the first question we have subjected to a somewhat extensive analysis those tone systems of which we have a knowledge sufficiently accurate to justify us in attaching some weight to conclusions drawn from them. That it is perfectly legitimate to test in place of the melodies themselves the scales to which they can be reduced, and that, if there exist any harmonic possibilities in the melodies they also are apparent in the scales, – has already been granted. Before we can, however, apply a test, we must endeavor to clearly define the nature and extent of the thing to be tested, which in this case is the supposed harmonic sense. Now no exact definition of this harmonic sense has thus far come to my knowledge. It has been asserted over and over again that it exists; but as to its precise extent we have been left in the dark. Let us then supply this want. From the assertions made in behalf of this harmonic sense it appears to imply the existence of a sub-conscious harmonic tissue, whose chords, when resolved into melodic steps, determine the order as well as the nature of the intervals composing the musical utterances of all mankind. In other words musical expression, according to this harmonic principle, selects those intervals as melodic steps which are contained in this sub-conscious harmonic structure. Not pressing the test too far, we will assume this harmonic tissue to be the simplest imaginable, consisting of the tonic, dominant and sub-dominant chords, with the provision that, since the harmonic sense can only be rudimentary, and therefore only the most simple harmonic structure can come into consideration,—if our test should yield a negative answer, it must be taken for granted that the more complex and artificial harmonic combinations are altogether out of the question. To still more simplify the test, we may add that the tonic, dominant and sub-dominant chords collectively contain all the tones of our modern scale, and can only be formed within this scale. Melodies, therefore, which move within a scale essentially differing from our own cannot possibly contain these three chords, nor can they be based on them.

Now among all the tone systems examined we have found only one, No. 9 of the Arabian heptatonic scales, which approximates our major scale so closely that these three chords could be formed within its intervals. In most of the other scales only the octave, fifth and to a lesser extent the major third, are so nearly identical with ours that in some cases a major chord of a fair degree of perfection could be constructed! While the remaining degrees are for a rule so ambiguous as to defy any attempt whatever at forming the other two chords. The intervals of which the dominant and the sub-dominant chords should be composed, if this were possible, showing such grave deficiencies, it follows at once that either the chords which are assumed to have suggested them have been in a similar measure deficient, or then, that these degrees have not at all been suggested by these chords and have been selected upon other grounds. Since, however, a chord, and especially one dictated by natural law, must be a combination of perfectly consonant intervals, and therefore perfect in itself, we can not conceive it to suggest other than accurate intervals; and as the intervals have been shown to lack this accuracy we can only conclude that this suggestive force has failed to assert itself. It might be pleaded that it is conceivable that the chords in question should have existed as perfect in consciousness, and that the deficiencies in the corresponding intervals are due to the extreme subtlety of the mental process involved. But, while a reasonable amount of inaccuracy may be thus accounted for, and in fact is noticeable also in the intervals composing the tonic chord, yet this reason cannot be taken to explain the presence of deficiencies which by far exceed those noticeable in the case of the latter, as well as the entire absence of the degree corresponding to the fundamental of the sub-dominant chord, and that coinciding with the third of the dominant chord, as is the case in the most universally accepted of the pentatonic scales which omits the fourth and the seventh. A faint apperception of a tonic chord may and indeed must exist in consciousness; for on this alone rests the perception of the musical quality or timbre of sounds. But to speak of a sub-conscious conception of several different chords is absurd. If co-existing, these chords must be perceived as standing in some relation to each other; and as such a relation cannot exist unless its terms be clearly conceived by the mind, it follows that the several chords themselves must either be clearly perceived or then not at all perceived. A clear perception would, however, undoubtedly have prompted their reproduction, or at least a fairly accurate and constant adoption of their intervals as melodic steps in monophonic music. And since none of these possibilities have been realized, we cannot but conclude that the assumption of such a sub-conscious harmonic tissue is not warranted by actual fact. To make the argument still more conclusive it only remains to mention that in an isolated case, where a scale has been established which allows of harmonic treatment, these harmonic possibilities have never been carried into existence. In other words, this sub-conscious perception has, to speak with the adherents of this harmonic sense, been sufficiently vivid to dictate the tones of these chords as intervals of the melodies, and therefore also of the scales, but the relations which it has itself imposed have subsequently utterly failed to be recognized; and not only this, but their very existence is gainsaid by the well known fact that harmonic combinations are particularly distasteful to the æsthetical sense of the Arabs and most other oriental peoples.

JEAN MOOS.

Ripon, Wis.

(REMAINDER NEXT TIME.)

SINGING AND ELOCUTION.

THE question is often asked, "Does the study of elocution interfere with, or does it aid, the development of the singing voice?" The generally accepted theory is that the two arts are opposed. That the public thinks so, is evident from the fact that surprise is always expressed when a good reader is also found to possess the power of singing creditably: that even eminent vocal masters are of this opinion, is proved by the utter disregard of the art they show in their methods of instruction. Vocal teachers, of great repute in our musical centers, are known to advise their pupils *not* to study elocution by any means.

The purport of this paper is to show that the two arts are closely connected, inter-dependent, and that to the ordinary student of singing elocution is indispensable.

This statement will meet with opposition only from the musical instructor, as the teacher of elocution *never* decries the study of music in conjunction with his art; realizing that the speaking voice must have a musical quality, and that tone placing and building is his aim, as it is also that of the musician.

To digress for a moment. Elocution, as a serious study, is most peculiarly misunderstood and under-valued. It is emphatically the most abused of the arts. There are more charlatans in the ranks as its teachers than there are earnest, capable, educated men and women.

No *polite* words can adequately express the contemptuous disgust with which the public justly receives the elocution so largely in vogue. The throaty tones, the affected articulation and pronunciation, the artificial gesticulation, the absurd facial expression, the unnatural posing, are enough to bring any study into disrepute. Earnest teachers know this, and perceiving that in some way their art is below par, take refuge behind such titles as "School of Oratory," "College of Expression," "Teacher of Delsarte," etc., etc., *ad nauseam*. Schools of Oratory, forsooth! We do not teach our girls oratory. "Expression?" Rather a comprehensive term! What does it mean? "Delsarte?" a system condemned by some of the best educators of the world.

Elocution, in this article, means the attainment of a musical voice, a correct, clear, but unaffected enunciation, a pronunciation with cultured usage as the standard, and the power to interpret to others the whole gamut of human emotion by the *use* of such a voice, applying its modifications of force, time, pitch and stress, so as to accord with the sentiment. Is not this the aim of vocal music to the same extent? But more than this. Not only are they kindred arts; it is to be proved that, if the methods are correct ones, they are one and the same, from start to finish. Moreover, we take this position, that when they vary, the method pursued by the *musical* instructor is at fault.

Let us review the methods, and notice where they are made to diverge. First, breathing—the abdominal system is the fundamental requirement of both arts. There are but two ways to use the breath in either: one to sustain a tone at pleasure, by an even, constant expulsion of the breath; the other to exhale suddenly, as if by a blow. The exercises to attain this power are founded on common sense, and used by both elocutionist and vocalist.

The next step is "tone placing", the one object being to get the tone away from the throat, to 'focus' it just back of the upper front teeth and to throw it out, to make it vocal, round, clear, and, above all, steady. Here again the arts agree.

Next in order is enunciation; the forming of tone, no matter what its pitch, into words. In this department of the sister arts, is there any one so bold as to contend that the singing master is as successful as the elocutionist? How often do you catch the words of a song? Every word? Echo answers "Never!"

Timbre, quality, is to be desired above all else. Granted; but not to the *exclusion* of all else. Every sound in a language has its exact value, and also an exact position of the vocal organs to give it that value. You must sing on the vowel tones; but consonants before or after them must be appreciated—sometimes exaggerated to give them carrying power. Does the singing teacher drill you upon these consonantal positions of the vocal organs? I think not. The elocutionist does.

Our next step is to pronunciation. The experience of our ears in this respect is perennially painful: "tôt" for "taught," "ees" for "is," "lêve" or "lobve" for "love." We need not enumerate; this glaring fault in the singer's art is universally recognized and commented on. Elocution will correct it.

The strongest argument we can bring forward, however, in attempting to show that elocution is indispensable to the singer, is this: that, even when voice, enunciation and pronunciation are perfect, neither composer nor vocal master follows the unalterable laws of expression, in the phrasing or the 'marking' of vocal scores. A bold assertion, but one easily verified. The composer is, ordinarily, the more at fault. He has not learned Wagner's teaching, 'that the accompaniment should be as the wife, the text as the husband.' He works up a motif as if for instrumental interpretation merely, and marks and phrases accordingly, in some cases absolutely irrespective of the words—and this from eminent sources! To illustrate. We go now to our music stand, and select at random some half dozen songs. Here is Dudley Buck's beautiful setting of Tennyson's "Crossing the Bar." "Sunset and evening star;" this passage is marked "*sempre tranquillo*," and accords perfectly with the correct elocution of it. "And one clear call for me." Here the words "one" and "clear" are accented, and that although the words are sung to eighth notes, when a half note with a more important word belonging to it follows. Now elocution would demand that the stronger stress be laid upon the word "call". If the noun is used for the *first time* in a clause, it will be found to contain the most potent *thought* of all the words, and is surely stronger than any of its modifiers—as here, it is the "CALL" for me; not the "one," or the "clear" for me. Accent *one* and *clear* if you will, but the stronger accent belongs to *call*. This is, of course, from the elocutionist's standpoint. Does music contradict it? The remainder of the score is not at all fully marked, but we would call attention to the erroneous marking of the phrase (musical) "I hope to see my pilot, face to face". "Face to face" is marked *piano*. Why? The thought in these words is the poet's climax—the hope, the *sure expectation*, that when his soul has drifted out beyond the "moaning of the bar," he may stand, *face to face*, with his Saviour! This hope is the one thing which makes the poem religious—the expression is triumphant over doubt and death; and the elocutionist would deliver it with strong stress, and at least moderate voice, as follows, "I hope to see my Pilot—*face* to face! when I have crossed the bar." Rendered in this manner, it would then have the author's evident meaning—not that he *perhaps* shall see his Lord, but *surely*, in visible presence, "*face to face*."

Purely by chance, the next composition to come into the discussion is the masterly "Fear not Ye, O Israel," by the same composer. In this song we find the phrase, "Thy sorrows now are ended," marked *p.* and rendered so that the effect is anything but joyful, or assuring to the troubled soul. *En passant* the phrase is in the minor key, and as such suggestive of sorrow rather than joy.

Then comes, "and great shall be thy peace," correctly marked; then "Rejoice! be glad! be glad!" The second "be glad" is marked *rallentando*, which Webster defines as 'a direction to perform a passage with a gradual decrease in time and force.'

Now when words or phrases are repeated, the repetition makes either an ascending or descending climax. Here it is evidently the former that is needed, the Lord saying to the sin laden, weary soul, "Thy sorrows now are ended, and great shall be thy peace, Rejoice! be glad! be *positively* GLAD!" and the *rallentando* does not accord with this effect.

Exactly the same fault is found in the closing passages. "I have redeemed thee, I have redeemed thee." The repetition of the phrase should emphasize the assurance of redemption, and the only way to bring this out is to apply the rules of elocutionary expression, to make the second phrase louder in tone, faster in time, more forceful in enunciation. Yet how is it marked? "*Sempre piu p.*"—and the closing tone is indicated *pp.*

Here we have in one work of our best composer, three elements of elocutionary expression utterly overlooked: quantity (of voice), quality, time, a joyous passage marked soft, placed in a minor phrase and another exultant passage marked *rallentando.*

"*Bleib bei mir,*" by Franz Abt. Op. 72., has this wording frequently recurring in its English translation, "Stay with me, when all the woods are still," and several times it is marked *f.* Now, can either the tender yearning of the lover or the quiet and serenity of the woods be interpreted by a forte delivery? Elocution says "No".

We next pick up a catchy ballad— "The sweetest story ever told"—and find this, "Tell me softly, sweetly, as of old" marked forte, and the like folly repeated in a similar passage later in the song.

As for printing two or more verses of a song under the same marks of expression, that is too absurd to call for more than a passing notice. Yet our best music publishers send forth such editions every day. Look at the markings in the ballad "Out on the Deep," and see if the first and second stanzas can be effectively spoken or read in a similar manner. Why then should they be sung alike?

The subject under discussion is too pregnant an one to exhaust in a single article. We merely wish to assert and prove that composers and vocal teachers alike, are either ignorant of the *natural* laws of elocution, or wilfully disregard them. That the composer frequently does so has been instanced; that the teacher is equally culpable is made manifest by the sluggish enunciation and incorrect expression of pupils. We have heard three pupils, of one of New York's most popular teachers, sing these words, from Tosti's song "Could I,"—"Breathe into your ear," in a moderately loud voice. The elocution of this passage would require a sustained connected, whispered tone. Two of these pupils asked for a criticism upon their "expression"—save the mark! and when attention was called to just this inconsistency, between a soft sentiment and a loud tone, the reply was "Oh, Mr. X. taught me that." Now either Mr. X. is wrong, or the laws of elocution are, for in this teaching he radically opposes one of its fundamental mandates.

The long suffering public will decide in favor of elocutionary expression, as soon as it learns that its laws are founded on nature, and not originated by an arbitrary art.

If music is to be merely melodic or harmonic tone, play it on an instrument. But if it is to come to the aid of beautiful, ennobling, uplifting *thought*, then pray let it be really a helpmeet, 'the wife, not the husband'. Let it follow, not dictate, the laws of expression—the true elocution, an art which controlled, electrified, humanized the race, before music was—the laws of which are universal and not to be gainsaid.

HENRY GAINES HAWN.

MR. STERNBERG ON THE PRACTICE CLAVIER.

Just returning from Europe, I find your communication asking for my humble opinion in regard to the use of mechanical aids towards the acquirement of technique on the piano. Had I been at home I should have answered long ago, but I will do so now, at the risk of coming post festum. I have seen some of the opinions expressed on the subject, and cannot help acknowledging that in every argument that has been brought to bear for or against mechanical aids, there was some good reason. One point seems to me to have been overlooked, however, and it appears to me that this is the very point which alone can decide the question. Every one who teaches and combines a higher purpose with his teaching than the mere eating of his bread and butter, will know that all classes and all kinds of pupils have one difficulty in common, it is the difficulty to understand what they are expected to do; after they once understand this, one-half, nay, nine-tenths of their task is as well as done. The cause of this difficulty is not necessarily attributable to the pupil's slowness of mind, nor to the teacher's lack of knowledge; both may have their share in it. The principal difficulty in all teaching is "*how to reach the pupil's mentality.*" Now, if to this end mechanical devices suggest themselves, I should advise using them, no matter if the particular "method" of the teacher is against it, and no matter how high or how many authorities expressed themselves against it; for we are working for *results*, and if we fail to attain them, these high authorities will not make up or console us. Aside from this, there is undeniably such a thing as pure handicraft connected with every art, and if by the aid of mechanical contrivances we can acquire it quicker, (and the Virgil Practice Clavier answers this purpose to perfection), I see no particular reason why we should not use it. Of course, there is one degree of microscopic exactness that is to be avoided. The pupil does not only *not* need to know all about his flexors and tendons, but he *ought* not to know it (in my opinion) any more than the singer ought to know anything about his epiglottis. The singers who have sung best never knew they had such a thing, and I am speaking knowingly when I say that our best pianists have only a few very hazy ideas of the nature of a flexor. I shall never forget one of my former pupils, who being a physician was all the time referring to the muscles which were to be employed in this or that touch. He never acquired more than the automatism for one piece, and in this one piece he came only so far as to know exactly what muscles to employ, without being able to play the piece; he expected that from the future. Strange to say, he was satisfied with his results, and wondered why I was not. Being as staunch a Virgil man as I am, I feel at liberty to point out the danger in the use of the Clavier. That danger lies in using it too long *exclusively*, and here I approach Mr. Liebling's view. There are fanatics on every subject, and there are such on the subject of the V. P. C. who seem to think that we can make a complete musical pianist of a pupil without ever putting him to the piano. This, of course, is a mistake. For preparing the technique and as an *adjunct* to the piano, I advocate the Virgil Practice Clavier and only the Virgil Practice Clavier; and in compliance with the principles of practicing what I preach, I have established regular Virgil classes in my school, and have a Virgil Clavier at my home, where I use it myself prior to studying new works.

Yours very truly,

CONSTANTIN STERNBERG.

THE ELOCUTIONARY ELEMENT IN VOCAL MUSIC.

THE first duty of the singer to an audience is so to render the work in hand that the poem or text of the composition shall ever be uppermost. In fact, if this be not the end and aim of the effort it were better to remain silent.

You may say, "Why, of course;" but I do not intend to let you dismiss the matter so easily. You have only to listen to some of our singers, even our best, to realize that it is decidedly *not* a matter of course.

There are many things that make it difficult to carry out such a proposition, but the painstaking conscientious singer, whose determination is to be truly artistic, and not to sacrifice everything to a display of his or her best "tones," will find the obstacles encountered yield readily to a little good judgment and earnest thought. Let us speak of the two most prominent difficulties.

First, the composer. Too many merely fit a melody with a certain rhythm to a poem based upon the same rhythm, and overlook the important fact that the elementary rendering of the poem or text should be first and the melody second, since, unless they truly mean to add to the force of the poet's text, they had better leave it unmutilated by compelling false accent.

For illustration; read the following lines, giving to each syllable the value of the note placed above it. We will take at random a few examples from well known sacred songs. The notes are not given absolutely, but the values and the intervals before and after the false accent are.

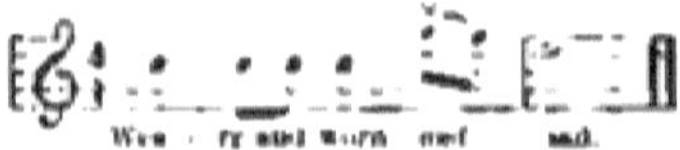

You see how false the accent upon the word "and"

becomes, first, by having two notes allotted to it (more than its relative value to the word "worn," and second, by reason of the pitch of these notes as compared with the rest of the phrase. I claim that in such a case the singer in giving the poet the preference over the musician and simply making this change— Wea - ry and worn and sad, is not injuring the composer, but rather rendering him a service.

Here is another example from the same song:

In this case, not only by its relative value, but by its position as accented beat, the word "and" rises into more importance than any of the other words. Would it be so if you were reading the poem? The word "of" in bar three is in the same manner made to sound out of all proportion to the rest of the phrase. Do we harm the composer if we merely change his values in this way?

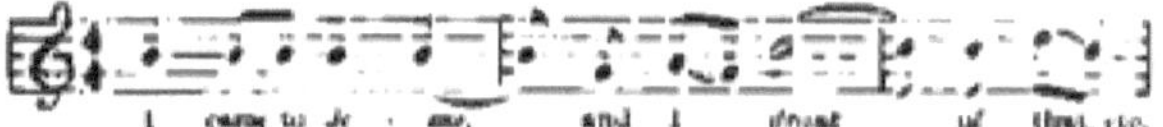

Such a change, far from harming his work, adds strength. If our composers would only try to follow the elocutionary accent more closely, we should have no need of such tampering; but, as it is not in any sense touching their actual work, I claim that it is justifiable. Will it not make the same difference in the effect of the poem upon the auditor when sung as would be felt between the school-boy manner of recitation and the more intelligent reading of the lines?

Here is another!

Is this not better?—

And this from the same song:

How easy to make it natural:—

Again, the same song:

It makes a better effect to sing.

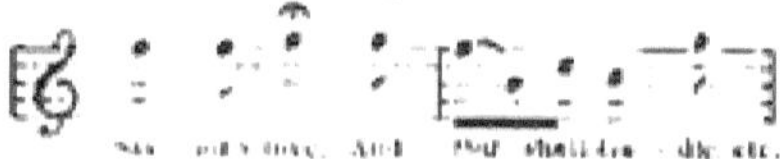

The second difficulty will be found in translations made from other languages, which abound in such instances.

A poem in one language properly set to music can hardly be so translated that the accents in the original will fall upon points of accent in the translation; yet our publishers are most careless in this matter and many false effects creep in which could easily be kept out.

Here is one instance: Saint Saens—Ps. xix.

With the Latin a bar rest after "Domine" but adds force to the "Adjutor" (although, even in this instance, note the double accent upon the word "et," accented beat and two quarters); but why did the translator put the weak word "art" in such a forceful position? He could so easily have written it thus:

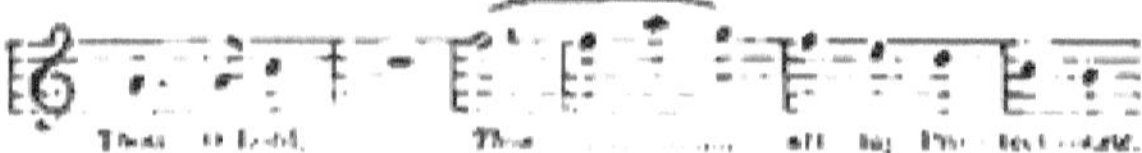

But even that is artistic compared to the following extracts from Liszt's beautiful song, published with English translation by one of our largest and best houses:

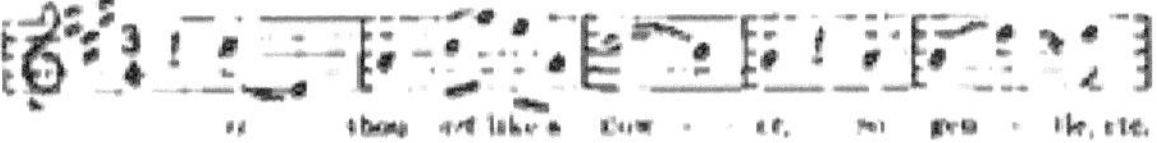

The German "Du" may well have two quarters allotted to it in this connection, but should the translator have put the English "O" in a position to receive such marked accent? "O" and "art" receive all the force of this phrase. But this is not all. Look at the word "gentle" with a rest *between the two syllables.*

You can multiply these examples by the hundred if you will simply take up at random such publications as lie at your hand.

Therefore I say, whenever a word that in a proper reading of the poem has no accent is so placed as to receive a marked one in its musical setting, the poet and not the musician should receive our first consideration, and the false accent given should be overcome by one of the many means at our command, as shown in the above examples, or by *accelerando*, *ritard*, or some equally simple change. The way will readily appear to the thinking person earnestly desiring properly to interpret the *poet's* meaning.

A *lack* of accent in the parts of secondary importance, even rather than force of accent in the parts needing prominence, will give the best results. The elocution does not consist in elevating the voice, straining the muscles, and making a supreme effort, but rather in the repression of all but the salient points.

Mind your poet's punctuation marks first, and your musician's phrases next, but if they conflict, give the right of way to the poet *always*.

If a phrase is in parenthesis in the poem make it so in your singing of it. Do not be afraid of pauses. Silence at the proper time is perhaps the most striking effect within the singer's grasp.

Always read your poem, *know* it, *feel* it, before you try to sing it, and know your music so well that all your thought can be upon the lines and their proper elocution. If you cannot feel or understand the poet, do not attempt to *sing* the selection, any more than you would attempt to *read* it before an audience. Carefully draw the distinction in your own mind between the explanatory and the descriptive lines, and make them natural and evident. These parts of a work are of course more difficult to render than those containing actual quotations. It is for instance, much easier to make your audience feel the cry, "My God, my God, why hast Thou forsaken me!" than to touch them with "Now about the ninth hour with a loud voice He cried."

Again, and yet again, always have a reason for every accent that shall be based *upon the poem alone.* Carefully calculate your climax, and never anticipate it. To do this, you can readily see how necessary is *repression* of accent in the parts leading up to your final effect.

With these few suggestions I will leave the subject for the present. In succeeding talks, I shall hope to treat it in its broader aspects, which, acceptably presented, should produce a larger benefit.

W. H. NEIDLINGER.

THE LIMITS OF PERSONAL RIGHTS IN PIANOFORTE PERFORMANCE.

EVEN since the days when Coleridge, as Carlisle says, "sang sweetly through his nose his endless monologues about the *omjective* and the *sumjective*," the philosophical world has been hard at it trying to distinguish between the ego and the nonego. Long before that, indeed, the metaphysicians had debated the matter, and every one knows the anecdote of Jean Paul, who, at six years old, catching as by a flash the thought that he was different from the pile of kindling wood which he was sent to carry, exclaimed "Ich bin ich."

Aesthetics, that is the philosophy of works of art, is a new science in the world; and Lessing in the 13th century and Vischer in ours are its great exponents. Aesthetics must be clearly separated in the mind from Aestheticism. The one is deep, noble and earnest: a crystal well springing from the mysterious darkness of man's inmost being, and glimpsing the farthest sky. Aestheticism is a mere shallow, brawling brook, doing little but feed the gaudy weeds and sing loudly of its own presence and futile doings. Gilbert and Sullivan have done well to burlesque, in their comic opera "Patience," the silly extravagance of this passing fever—a kind of spurious "Ruskinism" and insincere worship of beauty, used only as another name for fashion.

The love of the beautiful, next to the spiritual perception of God and eternal relationships, must be admitted to be man's crowning distinction. What the rainbow is to the light, beauty is to truth. There has been much debate as to the standard of beauty. Some philosophers derive it purely and directly from experience, others seek to find for it a corner-stone in man's inmost intuitions. The materialists find beauty to be only an echo of sensuous pleasure, and that the mere signature of sensual utility. The intuitional schools hold that the beautiful is the reflection, or rather say the refraction, of God;—that the beautiful is God coming to us, not directly like the mysterious wind that "bloweth where it listeth," nor speaking to us as he did to the prophet on Horeb in "the still small voice" heard in the soul itself, but reflected or illustrated to us by the sublime and the beautiful works of physical nature. Whether the beautiful be derived directly from either of these opposite poles, or whether, as is most likely, it be the confluence of the two, one thing cannot be doubted or disputed, whatever rays of light join to make the conception of beauty, the lens through which they pass must be the human soul. Nothing has any great charm of beauty to man except what is human. A picture of the early fern-age of the world would have little beauty to our eyes, since it would be so remote from human relations and interests. That which makes beauty the transcendent power of the awful sublimity of the Bible is the intense humanity, which quivers through every word. This importance of the individual man gives us a pedestal on which to erect our philosophizings and make firm our conception of art.

In proportion as art draws near to truth of man's nature, or deflects widely from that truth, in that proportion it is beautiful and affecting, or ugly and nugatory. Goethe, whose intellect overarched all things, like the sky, caught a glimpse of the truth of the supremacy of music, though with his ultra Greek love of form, symmetry, intellectual balance and perspicuity, he esteemed the works of the severe fugal school at more than their relative value. He and all subsequent philosophers, who have attempted at all to unravel the mystic skein of musical influences, have admitted its profound significance, its far reaching power, its ideal beauty.

Music is in one sense the most definite, in another the most vague of arts. It closes down upon the individual mood and clasps it close as the calyx of the rose holds in is tresinous embrace the germ of the future flower; and yet no one can say just what any given piece of music intends to represent. Oft times when we are most positive of the composer's intention, could he hear our philosophizings he would tear his hair in distraction, perhaps clothe himself in sackcloth and ashes, or sprinkle dust on his head, or more likely would imitate the worthy example of Bach, who used to jerk off his wig and say to a clumsy pupil: "Go, and be a shoemaker." Or perhaps, like Beethoven when importuned about his "Fidelio," the misrepresented composer would rather burn his work than see it tortured into a caricature of his meaning.

It is impossible to play without being subjective; it is impossible to play being wholly subjective and not make a caricature of the music. A man, in other words, can no more escape from his personal qualities, character and proportion of faculties, when reproducing music, than an actor can escape from his natural appearance and the peculiarities of his voice. A certain amount of disguise may be reached, but pressed beyond a narrow limit it becomes caricature. What the pianist must strive to do is to establish himself firmly on two solid rocks. That is, an intelligent conception of the composer's meaning, attainable only by wide reading and thorough, searching analysis; secondly, by standing on a well considered and predetermined personal conception.

The emotional range which personality may take is illustrated by the two supreme masters Bulow and Rubinstein. It would be mere captiousness for an impulsive and nervous musician to apologize for insane readings and slovenly technique by hiding beneath the supposed wings of Rubinstein; and again it would be mere stupid pedantry for the dull scholastic, devoid of heart and fancy, to claim honor for his mechanical thumpings by comparing them to the divine exactness of Bulow.

Rubinstein is subjective, but he does not crush the composer's conception out of all proportions; on the contrary, no pianist living or dead can surpass him in the perfect mimicry of styles. Mendelssohn he plays as gently and tenderly as if it were some quiet and sweet tempered gentleman suavely uttering noble and temperate sentiments amidst the elegancies of a drawing-room; Chopin he plays like a fierce-hearted, though refined and sensitive, poet; Beethoven roars and storms beneath his hands, and yet it is always an emotional sound; Liszt glitters and dazzles like a shower of fire; through all you feel Rubinstein, but you also feel the composer.

In certain grand emotional qualities Bulow was doubtless lacking, but the omnipresence of his intellectual purpose caused a work, under his hands, to glow and flash with living light, like a prism or a many-angled gem, revealing to the astonished eye its wealth of occult beauty.

The musician is subjected to many of the same laws as the literary artist. Just as the poet must reveal in outward form the inmost fleeting ideas of the soul, so the musician when composing must find such sounds as striking on the ear will perforce reconstruct in the receiver's mind the same, or approximately the same, emotions and pictures as were in his own mind. Always remember that the picture-suggesting power of music is very faint, very illusory and wholly secondary. Its prime business is to ensphere the soul with moods, as the globe of the earth is wrapt in the azure envelop of atmospheric air.

The literary artist may be creative, that is, a poet; or reproductive, that is, an actor or elocutionist. So in music the composer constructs an ideal form, and the performer gives it material existence. The same mechanical preparations are necessary for the reproductive artist, in each case. Certain things are taken for granted in an elocutionist, and we do not praise him for their presence, however severely we may condemn him should they be absent. Thus, a man must pronounce the words correctly, and while occasionally in doubtful or mutable words there is room for taste and for difference of opinion, nevertheless in the main the words pronounced by an elocutionist will be precisely the same as if they were uttered non-artistically by an ordinary reader. An elocutionist may choose, for instance, to give the poetic sound to the word w-i-n-d and say not wind but winde; again he may be a stickler for accuracy, and pronounce the word tune as if it were "chune," and dew "dyew." In the former case he would exercise a license cognate to that of the poet who places wind to rhyme with blind: in the words tune and dew he would simply show himself more minutely accurate than the ordinary speaker. Despite these liberties and refinements, however, the elocutionist would be confined strictly to the pronunciation authorized by the dictionary, and any wide departure, either in the sounds or the accents of the words, subjects him to censure, and perhaps makes him unintelligible. Anyone who would realize how great is the change wrought in a familiar word by a shift of accent, need only read the old English ballads, where such words as window and father receive the stress not upon the first but upon the second syllable. More ridiculous still is the mispronouncing of Latin words. It is said that the Poles have even less sense of rhythm, accent, and quantity in their words than the French and a certain professor, who had a number of Polish boys studying Latin under his tuition, used to ridicule them by accenting the following Latin sentence after their reckless manner:—"Nos poloni non curamus quantitatem syllaborum," which was accented thus, in wild disregard of Latin quantity:—"Nos pol'loni non cu'ramus quantitatum sylla'borum."

The first thing a poetaster does, when he strives to imitate a great model, is to catch, reproduce, amplify eccentricities. So the pianist who would ape Rubinstein out Rubinsteins Rubinstein till what was a world of tumultuous life in the great pianist becomes a weltering chaos of insane vehemence in the little one. Perhaps no restraints are more needed by the living army of pianoforte players than those which stare them coldly in the face whenever they open the pages of their books. There the notes are; they have been counted and conned, composed, compelled, ordered and arranged by imaginative brain, mathematical thought and mechanical skill. What right has the player to deviate from ideas so definitely expressed. "Ah, but" he says "the notes are cold and dead till I breathe into them my living soul, and when my emotions are in flood I cannot help rushing beyond the rigid banks of that which is strictly written." Yes, you do rush beyond the rigid banks of strict prescription and, like other rivers, you bring a vast deal of destruction, distress and obliteration along with you. I have often listened to performances of serious and carefully wrought works, where, had I not the notes distinctly in my memory, it would have been an utter impossibility to divine, from the vast monotonous expanse of confused sound, just where the composer's ideas lay buried, and what might be the configuration of his phrases. No musicians are such constant, willful, red-handed sinners as pianists. They have it dinned into their ears that their instrument is cold, that it is mechanical, that because, forsooth, its tempered scale lies there, already fixed, the learning of it is the task of a mere bungler and a mechanical pedant. It is often said by a class of wiseacres, who would have us to think them super exquisite in their musical taste that the piano is too mechanical an instrument, too imperfect, too raw for them. Stung and annoyed by these exaggerated criticisms, the pianist, irritated by gad flies, plunges into wild excesses, in the determination to force his listeners into sympathy with the burning thoughts, which he distinctly feels throb within his instrument. The result is lamentable. Instead of orderly self-restraint and the noble reserve of true art, we have pianissimos fainter than the laziest breeze, fortissimos that make the thunder puny, scrambles of speed that would require an electrical apparatus to register them, melodies that come booming out as if the Ghouls, of which Poe sings, were thumping and banging and crashing with the rapture of "so rolling on the human heart a stone."

Mere intensity of tone is not legal tender on all occasions for intensity of feeling, neither is rough-shod, rattling speed proof positive of a virtuoso. It may seem like an eccentric assertion, but I am convinced that the lack of scrupulous detail and photographic finesse in pianoforte performances, far more than lack of so called expression or soul, will account for the dislike or the dreary toleration with which the pianoforte is often received. It is because our pianists do not play their instrument, do not touch its delicate stops to any divine results; but because they belabor it, they ride it like those iron horses or magic "steeds of brass," so famous in the romances of chivalry.

A piano may be made of steel, but it must not be treated like an iron steed. It is rather an Ariel, imprisoned in a box, fastened in wood, but capable of much wonderful spiriting. The first thing which, I should say, no pianist has a right to alter, is the actual text written; except in cases where there is an obvious misprint (cases, alas, by no means rare in our day of cheap reprints); or such instances as we frequently find in the Beethoven sonatas, where the idea runs up abruptly against a granite wall of mechanical limitation. In illustration of the first point --should I find, in some slovenly reprint, a Chopin passage where an E was marked flat in the right hand and natural in the left, unless the tonal connection indicated that he meant a diminished octave, I should, of course, reject it as a false and barbarous reading, a mere blunder of the ink machine.

Of the second point the illustrations are numerous in all Beethoven's pianoforte writings, especially in the "Tempest" sonata, where a phrase of unison has a form which would require it to descend to the E, D or C sharp below the fourth space F, in the bass staff. Now it is perfectly obvious here that the reason why Beethoven did not write these Es, Ds, and C sharps, was that his piano stopped at F. In his mind he heard the extreme tones, to-day we have an instrument that can execute them. Therefore, in playing them in the low octave where they are spiritually indicated rather than in the high octave where they are actually printed, we are not violating, but more perfectly obeying, Beethoven's directions. His piano was tongued-tied. Shall we continue to lisp after the impediment has been removed? In Bulow's edition such filling out of the idea is very frequent, and I, for one, make a uniform practice of playing the compositions with Bulow's additional tones.

In the second place every pianist should adhere with the fidelity of bigotry to the phrasing of the music. Occasional slips and inaccuracies in the printed phrasing we may find but, wherever the idea is thus badly outlined, aglutinated to ideas distinct from it and segregated from those which are cognate, any musician, with a rudimentary knowledge of form and formal development, will be able to supply the correction. But, fundamental as the ideas of legato and staccato are, thousands, yes tens of thousands, of students in this country have pecked and pounded and persistently perplexed their patient pates, vainly deluded into the thought that when they had hit nearly all the notes in tolerable rhythm the task of the executant was accomplished. There is a better state of things coming about in our country but still pupils are not taught, from the first, to group and divide their tones into intelligible forms, as they are taught to punctuate the books they read.

Phrasing is musical punctuation, and Shakespeare has given us, in the Pyramis and Thisby episode of the prologue to "Midsummer Night's Dream", a broadly ludicrous illustration of the nonsense produced by over-riding commas. Such nonsense, alas, is not an absurd exception but the rule, in the pianoforte playing we hear. It requires, no doubt, close and patient attention to fix the tones in the mind with strict reference to their grouping, but this is fully as important as correct fingering, and he would be a charlatan, indeed, who never told his pupils anything about the choice of fingers or the underlying mechanical laws which should direct their selection.

A slavish adherence to the printed text may not be always required of a great virtuoso—indeed there are passages in the works of all great masters where the intuitions of the artist would suggest changes from the printed text, changes, however, in the direction of clearer unfolding of the radical ideas. No intelligent connoisseur would unduly criticize such modifications, if they were sufficiently distinct and consistent, showing a purpose, and if there were any underlying and discoverable reason for their being made. In certain details of phrasing, but more especially of shading and tempo, of accentuation, of touch, do we find the difference of great artists and their reading of great works. Thus, the Sixth Rhapsody of Liszt, from the powerful and impulsive Carreno is a very different thing from the same work played by the exact and self contained Rive-King, but such details of difference are both logical and poetic, for it could not be said of either artist that she slights or alters the text materially. Those who justify slovenliness and absurd eccentricities, on the ground of inspiration and original conception, are unfortunately, too numerous, and against them is the present Philipic directed.

The name "Pianoforte" is significant; soft-loud, with the word "harp" understood, is the meaning of the term. It would not take great acuteness on the part of the student to suspect, therefore, that variations of intensity are easily made by this instrument, and are inherent in its very nature, since from that one peculiarity its name is derived. It has been said, with more wit than truth, that Rafael Joseffy is a piano-player but not a pianoforte player, because his pianissimo is so exquisite. The converse of this proposition would more often find justification, for in all American cities are to be found pianists who regularly "do up" all the grand compositions of the pianoforte literature every season, and, to use a metaphor of the prize ring, they literally "knock them out of time", and not seldom badly damage their shadings, their colorings and the temperament of the instrument as well. These gentlemen are *forte* players, not *pianoforte* players. You hear such "stalwarts" defend themselves for bethumping, bethwacking, bethrumming the keyboard on the ground that they "dislike tame playing." Every tasteful connoisseur dislikes "tame playing" also, but tameness does not arise from pianissimo; it arises from indistinctness of technique, from overlapping with the pedal, and above all from the universal disregard of accents. Every musician knows that the first beat of a measure is called the "ictus," "thesis," or "down beat", and that it should have a certain degree of stress; and yet how seldom do we hear a conscientious, intelligent performance, with the accents all in place. To recur once more to the illustration from the parallel art of elocution, how meaningless and forceless would be a reading of poetry, or any piece of resonant prose where the accents were feeble. In conclusion then let it be said that a pianist who does conscientiously the things prescribed for him upon the dead page, cannot wander far from the domain of high interpretative art. He has accomplished ninety-nine hundredths of his task, and that last grain of personality which he owes us, though it be precious as the musk which, mixed with the mortar, forever perfumes the air of the Mosque in Constantinople, is nevertheless but one percent of all that the player has to do.

Who that ever heard Rubinstein deliver the "Emperor" concerto of Beethoven can be unaware of the beauty of pianissimo, and of the marvellous delicacy residing in this divine instrument, so much and so unjustly taxed with "coldness" and "lack of heart."

JOHN S. VAN CLEVE.

PIANO TOUCH, AGAIN.

EDITOR MUSIC:

It seems to me that Mr. Webster's argument on this subject in the July number of MUSIC fails to hit the real point at issue. Mr. Webster says: "The quicker the motion of the hammer up, the quicker its rebound and the shorter the instant of its contact with the string; and inversely," and then proceeds to show, with Dr. Helmholtz's aid, that the length of this instant of contact has much to do with the quality of tone produced. But, in making the duration of this contact between hammer and string depend inversely on the velocity of the hammer, he seems to forget that the quantity (loudness) of tone produced depends directly on this very same factor. The quicker the hammer moves, the harder it will hit the string; the harder it hits the string, the louder will be the sound produced; and inversely.

Now, as far as I know, no one has ever claimed that variety of quality of tone, can not be produced by different methods of "striking, pressing upon or otherwise depressing" an individual key. What has been claimed, as I understand the question, is that no variation in quality of tone can be produced *without a variation in quantity of tone also.* And this claim is in no wise invalidated by Mr. Webster's arguments; for the only means he indicates by which a variation in quality of tone is to be secured is the very means which must necessarily secure a variation in quantity also.

WILLIAM F. APTHORP.

"Transcript," Boston.

BAYREUTH.

II.

THE visitors who streamed into Bayreuth on the morning of August 1st 1886 were greeted with anything but festal tidings. A few hours before, close upon midnight, Franz Liszt, the old friend of Wagner, the man whose living presence still seemed to link the dead master with the world of men, had breathed his last, in the arms of his daughter, Frau Cosima Wagner, and in that "Villa Wahnfried" where the closing years of Wagner's own life had sped their tranquil course. Liszt had come to Bayreuth for the festival, which opened with the performance of "Parsifal" on the 23rd of July. He had witnessed that performance, and also the succeeding one of "Tristan and Isolde," on the 25th, but was in so feeble a condition that it had been necessary to carry him into the theatre. Almost immediately after this second performance he had been stricken down by an attack of pneumonia, which did its fatal work in less than a week. So there was somewhat less of bustle than usual in the streets of Bayreuth on that warm summer day; the men and women who stood and walked about wore serious faces and lowered their voices as they spoke.

The traveler who is disposed to grumble at trifling annoyances, will find cause to exercise his faculty if he attempt to include a Bayreuth festival in his itinerary. The place is difficult to reach, and, when reached, is both insalubrious and uncomfortable. The American traveler whose experiences I am about to relate reckoned with these drawbacks, but was possessed by a great love of music, and this caused the balance to incline heavily upon the side of the pilgrimage. He found himself in Dresden late in the month of July, and, knowing Bayreuth to be only about a hundred miles away, supposed that he could start at almost any time and get there in three or four hours. But upon making closer inquiry he found the journey to be a matter of at least eight hours, and he had only the choice between taking a train at five in the morning to reach Bayreuth early in the afternoon and taking an afternoon train to reach his destination some time after midnight. After some hesitation he chose the latter alternative, and found himself seated at about four P. M., in one of the compartments of a railway carriage. Here he was fortunate enough to fall in with Dr. Cohn, the distinguished oculist of Breslau, who was traveling with the same object in view, and who, having been at Bayreuth for the great festival of 1876, as well as for the later ones, was a congenial traveling companion. As the train carried its passengers on past the manufacturing cities and through the comparatively monotonous scenery of Saxony, the disadvantages of reaching Bayreuth in the middle of the night impressed themselves more and more upon the travelers, and they determined to break their journey at Plauen, a Saxon city close to the Bavarian border. This determination they had no reason to regret, as they found a clean and well-kept hostlery in that city, disposed of an excellent supper, and obtained a refreshing night's sleep. The next morning they resumed the journey, taking a third musical pilgrim into their fellowship, and reaching Bayreuth not more than an hour or two later than the time when the train was due there. It must be remarked that Bavarian trains, as well as other affairs, make a specialty of being behind time. There is a current proverbial saying in Germany to the effect that Bavaria will be a good place to live in when the end of the world approaches, as the event will surely be fifty years later there than elsewhere. Naturally, Bayreuth cannot be expected to provide hotel accommodations for the influx of visitors incident upon these festival occasions. But, like most old European cities that have declined from their earlier splendor, it has abundance of houseroom of one kind or another, and nearly every householder has lodgings to place at the disposal of the travelers. A register of the accommodations to be had is kept by a "lodgings-committee," which has its office in the railway station, and to which newly arrived travelers are at once referred.

Our trio had now little time to loose, as it was already two o'clock, and the performance would begin promptly at four. So, while one of them went to secure a carriage, the others applied promptly to the "lodgings-committee" for rooms, not without being besieged on the way by a crowd of anything but attractive Bayreuth citizens of both sexes, who all had elegant appointments to offer the strangers. At the office of the committee an address was promptly given to our travelers, who forthwith set out to take possession. They were driven up a side street towards the country and deposited in front of a machine-factory. The rooms, which were evidently the living rooms of the machinist's family, were plainly furnished, but perfectly clean—something quite out of the common in Bavaria—and were consequently taken at once. Our American pilgrim found himself in temporary possession of a canary bird, a sewing-machine and a piano, besides the more necessary articles of furniture. A little girl of four, who was very appropriately named Elsa, greeted the strangers with the gravity of at least four times four years. After the performance of a hasty toilet, they found that there remained just time enough to walk leisurely up the hill to the theatre, and take lunch at one of the mammoth restaurants temporarily erected there. The walk to the theatre is from half a mile to a mile and a half, according to the end of the town from which the pedestrian sets out. The theatre, as has already been stated, is not architecturally beautiful, but its appearance, as it rises from its isolated and commanding site, is at least striking. It is built mostly of a light red brick with sufficient stone ornament to give a pleasing variety. As seen from below, the entrances and auditorium are in the foreground, while behind them rises the enormous stage, whose tasteful facade does something to harmonize the two portions of the edifice. A road bordered by linden trees leads up to the grounds about the building, which are laid out for the convenience of promenades during the long entr'actes. The view from these grounds is exquisitely beautiful. As the performance begins at four and lasts until ten, the two intermissions, which are each nearly an hour in length, fall at the hours best fitted for the enjoyment of the view. The first is the hour of sunset, and the second that of deepening twilight. At the foot of the hill lies the old city with its irregular streets and its tiled roofs. Through the valley in which it lies, flows the Main, here a mere thread, on its way to Frankfurt. In the near distance are the low hills which approach Bayreuth upon all sides, and, farther off, the dark green masses of the Fichtilgebirge are outlined against the sky. And the natural beauty of such a scene as this is beyond measure enhanced by the spiritual exaltation of the observer, for it is to be remembered that, as he gazes, the universal harmonies of the artist's creation linger in his ears, and that his memory is still haunted by the ideal shapes in whose joys and sorrows he has but just before had a share within those enchanted walls.

But I am anticipating a little. At four o'clock a few long-drawn notes of trombones and cornets give the signal for the spectators to take their seats. They stream quietly in, the number of entrances obviating any rush or confusion. The doors are all shut, not to be reopened until the close of the act. The gas-lights are extinguished, all but one row, from which a glimmer is barely perceptible. The theatre is all but absolutely dark, and no inspection of costumes or reading of texts and scores is possible. For a minute or two the most profound silence reigns. Then the first notes of the overture rises from the mysterious space between the two proscenia. Any ill-bred stranger who should so much as whisper after the first note of the overture was heard would soon learn that he was in a place where art has all the meaning and demands all the respect elsewhere accorded to religion. One by one the instruments of the orchestra mingle their tones with the volume of harmonious sound which pervades the vast space and and yet whose origin no one can discern. The leading motives so characteristic of the Wagnerian music appear one after another and are wrought into complex harmonies by the invisible orchestra, each member of which is an accomplished artist, and determined that the performance shall not fall short of ideal perfection through any fault of his. The overture at last comes to an end, the great curtains are drawn aside, and the scenic picture is disclosed. It would be impossible to speak with too much praise of the scenic presentation of these works. In this respect, as in so many others, Bayreuth is comparable only with itself. The great continental opera houses approach the perfection which exists here, but they do not equal it. A parallel to the Bayreuth stage when set, say, for the shipboard scene in "Tristan," or the temple of the Grail in "Parsifal," is simply not to be found elsewhere. In presence of such scenes as these, and in contemplation of the lofty conceptions of character and fate which poet and musician have combined to give shape, all sense of time is lost. The two intermissions, indeed, recall to the listener his temporal existence but, once over, he forgets the interruptions, and lives on again in the ideal world.

In the festival of 1886, each of the two works was given twice a week for the period of a month. The first day of each week brought a performance of "Tristan," followed on Monday by "Parsifal." Then, on Thursday and Friday, the works were repeated in the same order Many visitors remained one and two weeks, making use of the intervening days to become familiar with the streets and buildings of Bayreuth, or to explore the mountain districts of the Fichtilgebirge. Our traveler, who was hard pressed for time, had to content himself with a single hearing of the works of whose beauties he had so long dreamed. The few hours which left him to his own devices were anything but wearisome. First of all, there were the streets, with their unwonted crowds of strangers, conscious of the sympathetic bond between all visitors to Bayreuth. Then there was Angermann, when one was tired of walking about. Angermann, it must be be explained, is a very old and famous *Kneipe*. The rooms are low and dingy, the furniture is of the coarsest description, but the beer is the best that Bavaria can produce. At all hours of the day, and most of the night, this place is filled to its utmost capacity by a throng of men and women zealously engaged in celebrating the rites of good-fellowship. Bayreuth finds its artistic expression upon the hill; here it finds its social expression. Here there meet upon a common footing visitors of high and low degree, the *prime donne* sit side by side with the fiddlers and the chorus girls. It is just after the performance that the life at Angermann's is seen at its keen and most animated. Then the audience and the artists stream in one confused mass down the hill, along the principal street of the town, and then, off a few steps to the left into the hospitable recesses of the *Kneipe*. In a few minutes the rooms are filled to the last square foot of standing space. Kundry and Isolde, as the Hebes who minister to the wants of guests are jestingly called, are overwhelmed with requests for attendance, and for two or three hours to come, "Gemuthlichkeit" holds full sway.

Aside from the pleasure to be derived from the contemplation of the heightened life of Bayreuth during its festival season, there are other things appealing to the curiosity and to the sentiment. The machinery of the vast stage may be inspected by the visitor, and the intricacies of the theatre explored. Wahnfried, the home of Wagner for the last ten years of his life, and still the home of his family, is an object of interest. It is a stone villa, simply and tastefully built for him by the King of Bavaria, fronted by broad lawns and foliage-bordered walks. The facade is decorated with a large central fresco, and bears also the inscription: "Hier wo mein Wahnen Friedenfand, WAHNFRIED sei mir dies Haus genannt," "Let this house be called Wahnfried, for here my yearnings found peace." Just back of the house is the public park, with its thickly wooded walks, and here, in a quiet and secluded spot may be seen the grave of Wagner, marked by a simple stone, and covered with votive wreaths. One more spectacle, simpler and even more solemn than that of "Parsifal," our traveler was permitted to observe before his departure from Bayreuth. On Tuesday morning, the 3rd of August, the body of Liszt was borne to its final resting place. It was in accordance with his expressed wish that he was buried at Bayreuth, although both Pesth and Weimar put forward claims for the keeping of the sacred dust. The day before, all Bayreuth had been hung with bright flags in honor of the Crown Prince of Germany, come with his suite to witness the performance of "Parsifal." This morning all was changed. The shops were closed, black drapery took the place of the German and Bavarian emblems, and the whole city went into mourning. The funeral procession started from Villa Wahnfried, from which thirteen years before, another funeral procession had set forth with the remains of the master himself, and slowly filed through the town to the suburban cemetery. It was headed by two heralds of mourning, then came the ecclesiastical dignitaries, followed by bearers of the many orders that had been bestowed upon the composer during his long life. After these came horses laden with great masses of flowers and wreaths sent from all parts of Europe. Then followed the hearse accompanied by mourners with lighted torches, and by the four pall-bearers. After these came the carriages of the chief mourners, Frau Cosima Wagner and her son Siegfried, the principal artists of the festival performances, the representative of the Grand Duke of Weimar, and many others; last of all the long procession of those who walked behind to pay the last tribute of love to the dead composer. The ceremony at the grave was exceedingly simple. The usual prayers were offered, a few brief addresses were made, and then the participants slowly dispersed. Few men of genius have commanded as Liszt did the love as well as the admiration of all who knew him, and few have been followed to the grave with such sincerity of grief.

The two works presented at Bayreuth in 1886 are perhaps the most typical of Wagner's comprehensive genius. Viewing his entire work broadly, it falls into two main divisions, corresponding with two well marked periods in his creative career. The line of division should be drawn at about the year 1853, and will be found to separate "Rienzi," "Der Fliegende Hollander," "Tannhauser" and "Lohengrin"—the four masterpieces of the first period—from "Der Ring der Nibelungen," "Die Meistersinger von Nurnberg," "Tristan and Isolde" and "Parsifal"—the four masterpieces of the second period. The works of the second period are distinguished from those of the first by a complex system of "leading motives." This system, which is developed in the later works of Wagner to a point never dreamed of by any earlier composer, makes these works incomparable with anything else ever done in dramatic music. Some traces of a tendency to attach special musical characters and ideas may be observed in the earlier work, and notably in "Lohengrin," but the immense fruitfulness of the conception was not revealed to Wagner until later. He has told us how it came to him as an inspiration as he lay, one sleepless autumn night of 1853, in his room at an inn of La Spezzia, thinking of the "Seigfried" music with which his brain was teeming. Wagner was comparatively free from the erroneous notion that music is capable of expressing definite ideas, but he had a deep sense of the condition between those emotional states produced by ideas and those to which music gives rise. He had studied the profound observations of Schopenhauer concerning the nature of music, and he had found them to confirm his own instinctive feeling that his art was far more comprehensive than any merely verbal form of art could be, that its abstractions far exceeded those of philosophy, and penetrated closer to the nature of things. But at the same time he conceived the idea of a more intimate union between music and poetry than had ever before been attempted. He sought to first embody a dramatic conception in appropriate but elementary language, and then to associate with each dominant character or idea a musical phrase which should be the absolute emotional expression of that with which it was associated. By this means, dramatic music would gain something of the definiteness of language, and the combination of these phrases, or "leading motives," would really embody a dramatic situation.

This is the theory or the system suggested in "Lohengrin," and carried out in all the masterpieces of the composer's second period. But the mere application of a system is a matter of scientific skill, and far more than skill is requisite in the making of a masterpiece. It is only the man of supreme genius who can represent in tone, and with unerring insight, the emotional value of an idea; it is in the construction of these very "leading" motives that the artist appears. Such a phrase as the Siegfried motive, or the Grail motive of "Parsifal," would alone stamp its creator as one of the greatest of his kind. It has what Mr. Matthew Arnold, speaking of poetry, calls the "grand style." If all the poetry of Milton were lost but a single verse, and that verse "On evil days though fallen, and evil tongues," we should still know that he who wrote it was "like a star and dwelt apart" in thought from the ranks of mankind, and we should likewise know that Wagner dwelt in the world of harmony, apart from other composers, if nothing remained of all his work but the Grail motive from "Parsifal."

"Tristan and Isolde" is the greatest work of dramatic music, expressive of purely human emotion, that exists. The subject is indeed drawn from the storehouses of myth, but the supernatural element is eliminated, except in the one necessary instance of the love-philter, and the characters of the drama appear as loving and suffering types of humanity. In the choice of this, as of his other subjects, Wagner was led by a happy instinct. It was not his business to create characters, but to interpret such as he found created to his hand. And as his interpretation was to be made by means of the most universal of the arts, he recognized his most fitting types in those creatures of a racial rather than of an individual, imagination, which are found in the rich treasure-house of Aryan myth and folk lore. It would be difficult to estimate the breadth which was gained by his artistic endeavor in thus electing to work in the wide field of national and even of racial legendary lore. The immense difference between an "opera" and even the least of these great typical reproductions is in no other way made so impressive as when we contrast the heroic figure of a Tannhauser, a Lohengring, or a Tristan with the conventional heroes of Rossini and Meyerbeer.

The preparation of the text for "Tristan and Isolde" was no easy task. The Tristan myth as handed down from the middle ages is so fragmentary, and its different versions so contradictory, that Wagner was first compelled to construct, from the elements thus preserved, a coherent legend to rest at the basis of his work. It would be useless to embody in a poem intended only to be sung with accompanying music, all the verbal subtleties which independent poetry must have to be of the highest sort. But it is of the utmost importance that the poem upon which a work of dramatic music is to rest should clearly depict the fateful moments of the action, and the essential relations of the actors, leaving the music to do the rest. It is erroneous to attribute to Wagner the belief that the art which he sought to establish could combine all of music with all of poetry. There are enthusiastic Wagnerians who claim for his texts, considered as independent poetry, the highest excellence. While this, in spite of their marked poetic quality, cannot be allowed, it must be admitted, not only that they have an absolute value beyond the librettos of any of the earlier operas, but that they very nearly fulfill all the requirements of texts for the musical drama. A more extensive introduction of analysis and of figurative speech might add to the pleasure of reader, but it would not sensibly increase the pleasure of the listener, for whom the music supplies what is lacking in the words, and more, indeed than mere words could give. He must be dull of apprehension and sluggish of soul who can hear this glorious "Tristan" music, this intensest expression of love and death—of love supreme in triumph over death without perceiving its transcendant perfection, and without being moved to the utmost depths of his being. The marvelous closing symphony of the last act has the very breadth and majesty and tumultuous life of the sea, whose billows seem typified by these waves of passion that surge upon the sense and fill the "ear and heart with a rapture of dark delight." Fitting consummation of a work which is to so many the highest achievement of the master's creative career: one is almost tempted to say that anything greater or more sublime it never entered into the heart of man to conceive. A great English poet, who has himself been constrained to give artistic form to the Tristan myth, has subtly characterized this work of Wagner, with its tragic burden of inexorable fate, in simple and beautiful verse.

> Fate, out of the deep sea's gloom,
> When a man's heart's pride grows great,
> And nought seems now to foredoom
> Fate.
>
> Fate, laden with fears in wait,
> Draws close through the clouds that loom,
> Till the soul see, all too late,
>
> More dark than a dead world's tomb,
> More high than the sheer dawn's gate,
> More deep than the wide sea's womb,
> Fate."

Of "Parsifal" it is difficult to speak adequately without speaking at great length. The legendary material of the work is itself unfamiliar, and in the hands of Wagner it has been given an import far beyond what it has in the mediæval epics from which it is derived, and also beyond that even of the other works of the composer. Some account of the action must be given to make what is said of it intelligible, but the fullest account, even the text itself, seems bare and crude without its investiture of divinely harmonious sound. I will, then, make the attempt to indicate in a few words the dramatic content of this masterpiece of comprehensive symbolism.

The Grail—the sacred vessel which held the blood of Christ—and the holy knighthood vowed to its service, is the central theme of the work. The treasure is guarded in the temple of Monsalvat, a mountain in the north of Spain. Upon the southern slope of the mountain, the magician

Klingsor, typical of the heathen powers, has built his enchanted castle, and wages war against the power of the Grail. By the aid of beautiful women subject to his power, he seeks to seduce the knights from the purity of life enforced by their vow. Amfortas, the King of the Grail, has been led into sensual sin by the beauty of Kundry, one of the women in the power of Klingsor, a woman whose figure is represented as analogous to that of Ahasuerus, having mocked the agonies of the crucified Christ, and having been condemned by him to laugh ever after when she fain would weep, until she shall again find him and he remove the curse. In consequence of his sin, Amfortas has received a wound from the sacred spear of the Grail, which has fallen into the hands of Klingsor. This wound refuses to heal, and the King suffers from it for long years, for the touch of the weapon that caused it is alone potent to effect a cure, and this weapon has passed into the possession of the heathen magician. But one consolation remains to the suffering King; a mysterious prophecy has pointed out the final deliverance from his woes. This prophesy bids him await the coming of one described as the guileless fool, who shall attain to healing knowledge through compassion—"Durch Mitleid wissend, der reine Thor." The deliverer is Parsifal, and his fulfilment of the prophesy is the theme of the drama.

Parsifal is represented as a youth who has grown up in depths of the forest, in simple ignorance of the world of the men—an undeveloped nature to whom right and wrong, joy and sorrow, are alike unknown. Chance leads him, in his wanderings, within the sacred limits of the Grail country, and he first appears upon the scene at the moment when, by a thoughtless impulse, he has shot a wild swan with one of his arrows. Shocked at the wanton cruelty they have witnessed, the Knights of the Grail seize him, and one of them, Gurnemanz, questions him as to his origin and the motives which prompted him to such an act. His plastic nature is quickly wrought upon, and in the first impulse of remorse that he has ever felt, he throws his arrows in horror from him. Gurnemanz already conceives the hope that this youth may be the promised deliverer, and leads him to the temple of the Grail, where he stands an amazed but impassive spectator of the sufferings of the King, and of the ceremony of the unveiling of the Grail, once more invoked in vain by the stricken monarch.

In the second act Parsifal, having been spurned from the precincts of the Grail, the spectacle of suffering he has witnessed still unfruitful of compassion, strays towards the castle of Klingsor, whose magic art enables him to recognize the promised deliverer. The spells of the magician are at once invoked to seduce the simple youth and avert the impending disaster. A garden of wonderful beauty is created by enchantment, and Parsifal, straying into it, is surrounded by a throng of ravishingly beautiful maidens—each of whom represents a single huge flower—who entice him to yield to their charms. He is bewildered, but unmoved, as they dance and sing about him. At last Kundry herself appears, and seeks to accomplish her master's purpose. She calls him by his name—the name he has not heard since it fell from his mother's lips long before. In a wonder of confused recollection he allows her to come nearer and nearer; she bends over him—in this fateful moment, so large is the symbolism of the work, the fate of humanity itself is impending she impresses a kiss upon his lips, and then there rushes upon him like a flood the recollection of the scene in the temple of the Grail and the sufferings of Amfortas; he spurns her from him with the cry—"Away! away! forever!" The prophesy is fulfilled, he feels the divine emotion of compassion, and with the feeling comes knowledge, the knowledge of good and evil, of his moral nature and his high destiny. "Should I for one hour forget my mission in thy embrace we were both damned to all eternity!" In her baffled rage, the enchantress calls upon her master. Klingsor appears, armed with the spear of the Grail; he hurls it at Parsifal, who seizes it in mid-air, and waves it in the sign of the cross. The magician's power is broken, the enchanted castle sinks, the garden becomes a desert, and the flower-maidens fall as withered blossoms to the ground. Parsifal hastens from the scene of desolation, with a parting word for Kundry: "Thou knowest where only thou canst see me once more."

In the third act, Parsifal appears as the deliverer. For many years he has wandered about, armed with the sacred spear, seeking the temple of the Grail. At last, after a long and weary pilgrimage, one Good Friday morning, he draws near to his goal, and meets Gurnemanz, grown an old man, and the repentant Kundry, serving the holy man in his hermit life. For the knighthood of the Grail has suffered greatly since the sin of Amfortas; its power has become broken, and many of its members are scattered or dead. From this moment on, Parsifal, who has attained to entire self-knowledge, assumes the pontifical character; he is the long-sought Saviour, and the symbolism of the Christian faith is once more realized in his acts. As a first exercise of his priestly office, he baptises Kundry, who falls weeping at his feet, freed at last from the curse. Gurnemanz then leads him to the temple of the Grail, where again we behold Amfortas, driven to complete despair by his suffering. The Knights remaining demand the invocation of the Grail once more, but the king refuses, and, in desperation tears open his wound, calling upon them to end his wretched existence. At this moment, Parsifal slowly approaches, and, with the outstretched spear, touches the gaping wound, bidding Amfortas be healed. He then declares himself King, and bids the shrine of the Grail to be opened. He takes the sacred vessel in his hands, and falls on his knees in prayer. The Grail glows with rosy light and sheds its radiance over all. Kundry sinks to the earth and expires in an ecstasy of joy. Gurnemanz and Amfortas fall at the feet of Parsifal, while from on high a white dove descends and hovers motionless over his head, and the knights around, and the singers in the dome above, join in a chorus of praise and thanksgiving.

It is obvious, that "Parsifal" is intentionally and consciously the symbolized presentation, not merely of types of characters, but of periods of universal history, and of the fundamental elements of human nature.

"Parsifal" is in nothing so entirely ideal as in its expression of the religious emotions. "This is no theatre; it is a place of worship," said one of those who witnessed the first performance in 1882, and the saying has been echoed by many thousands since. There is much in the earlier work of Wagner to show how deeply religious sentiment, apart from dogma or idea, entered into his nature. The inspiration of "Tannhauser" is almost entirely religious; the most profound things in "Lohengrin" and "Der Ring der Nibelungen" are expressions of the religious emotions. But "Parsifal" appeals to these emotions far more powerfully than any of its predecessors; it is a sacred composition in the most exalted sense. We may, perhaps, find for it a new significance in the light of this passage from an eminent English critic. "The one cardinal service of the Christian doctrine * * * has been the contribution to the active intelligence of the West, of those moods of holiness, awe, reverence, and silent worship of an unseen not made with hands, which the Christianizing Jews first brought from the East. * * * The fact that these deeper moods are among the richest acquisitions of human nature, will not be denied either by those who think that Christianity associates them with objects destined permanently to awake them in their loftiest form, or by others who believe that the deepest moods, of which man is capable, must ultimately ally themselves with something still more purely spiritual than the anthropomorphized deities of the falling church." Those of us, at least, who are compelled to believe as these others do, may find no little consolation in the promise which "Parsifal" gives of the perpetuation, in ideal form, of those moods whose loss we cannot but feel would make humanity the poorer, and yet whose dogmatic basis, hitherto found serviceably steadfast, is now visibly crumbling away before the waves of the advancing tide of thought.

WILLIAM MORTON PAYNE.

EDITORIAL BRIC-A-BRAC.

There is room in Chicago for a new choral society, addressing itself to smaller works of superior quality, such as some of the church cantatas of Bach, and other similarly forgotten works of historical and individual importance. Such a society would necessarily be limited in members to those who could at least read music respectably and have real taste and desire of improvement in it. It would have to be led by an enthusiastic musician, of powers and influence adequate to command respect in an artistic enterprise so exacting. The support would have to come from a limited circle of society. If the concerts were not given upon the largest scale, and with local artists in the solo roles, (preferably by members of the society) and with a carefully selected small orchestra where orchestra is needed, the expense would not be very large, and a moderate associate membership would suffice to pay the bills. The appeal to membership would have to be addressed to that part of society which is inclined to support art. The number of singers need not exceed forty or fifty at most, and all should be solo singers of approved powers. Such a society, with picked and well trained voices, actuated by genuine social enthusiasm for the music and the work, would be capable of doing something extremely well worth hearing. The tender point, naturally, would be the leader—musicians capable of good vocal training and musicianly in the highest sense, at the same time, being very rare. It is possible that Mr. Thomas himself might be the best man for leader, though this is hardly likely. Not so much because he is not distinctively a vocal leader, as because he has so much to do, and is perhaps now past the time when his enthusiasm in the cause has this much of surplus to spare over and above the work he must do with the orchestra. It is known to many that he has cherished for several years a plan of this kind, but has forborne to undertake it in Chicago, in order not to appear to antagonize the Apollo Club. But the Apollo Club is an old and strongly established association, and the work of a choice and small society, of the kind here mentioned, would in no way conflict with its concerts. A society able to rehearse four hundred singers regularly, and to increase its chorus to a thousand upon occasion, has nothing to fear from any small body of forty or fifty singers, no matter how choice may be their personnel, nor how fine their work. The small society would appeal to the few; the large to the many.

* * *

And speaking of numbers of singers, it is open to question whether the Apollo Club itself would not be more enjoyable to the members and to the public if its membership were once more reduced to little more than half its present numbers. Two hundred and fifty singers, comprising all the really effective voices of the present society, would do better work and make better effect than the present body. This is especially the case in the part songs, and in new works, where latterly all have suffered from insufficient preparation—a fault due mainly to imperfect attendance at rehearsals.

At its best the Chicago Apollo Club affords a glorious illustration of choral singing, in which the vitality and spirit are so present as to impress the works upon the hearers in much the same manner as a first rate solo artist impresses upon the hearer whatever he may happen to sing. And the source of this vivid impression is the same in both cases, namely, a very vivid conception on the part of the artist, and a finished technic of realizing it. Only in the case of a society made up of an aggregate of personalities, many of which necessarily are somewhat conventional, not to say passive, the difficulty of realizing such a conception is naturally much greater, and dependent entirely upon the conductor—in this case one of the few men in America able to do such a task. The failures in the performance of new works, mentioned above, have resulted from the conception of the new work not being sufficiently grounded in the singers. It is impossible to have perfect unity in the singing of the club and at the same time leave the individual members in such a state of freedom that under the spur of excitement they can do better than their ordinary work in rehearsal. If the team is to be depended upon to run away when the road is unfamiliar, and the grade requires speed, it cannot at the same time be depended upon to do fine steering. This is a point which has not always been taken into consideration.

* * *

The plans of the Chicago Orchestra for the coming season are now complete, and concerts actually begun.

OCTOBER 19 AND 20. SYMPHONY PROGRAM.

Overture, "Sappho," new .... *Goldmark*
Symphony No. 7, A major .... *Beethoven*
Serenade No. 1, D major .... *Fuchs*
Vorspiel, "Meistersinger." .... *Wagner*

OCTOBER 26 AND 27. POPULAR PROGRAM.

First Suite, op. 43 .... *Tschaikowsky*
Mad Scene, "Hamlet" .... *Ambroise Thomas*

MME. BLAUVELT.

Overture "Des Francs Juges," op. 3 .... *Berlioz*
Vorspiel, Introduction to 3rd Act, "Lohengrin," .... *Wagner*
Songs.

MME. BLAUVELT

Carnival of Flanders (new) .... *Joh. Selmer*

NOV. 2 AND 3. SYMPHONY PROGRAM.

Overture, "Euryanthe." .... *Weber*
Symphony No. 5, E minor, "From the New World," new .... *Dvorak*
Overture, Entr'act, Invocation of the Alpenfay "Manfred" .... *Schumann*
Mephisto Waltz .... *Liszt*

* * *

Of the educational value of this remarkable series of concerts, there are no two opinions among musicians and musical people generally. There is not one dissenting voice. A body of players comprising some of the best artists upon their several instruments at present existing anywhere in the world, comes together for the whole season under the leading of a conductor who is one of the most celebrated masters of the present time, well known the whole world over for his unswerving allegiance to art, and at same time a practical drill master of the first order. Everybody knows that under his leading some of the very best playing ever heard in America has been done.

With this it is easy to understand the force of the appeal which the Trustees of the Orchestra are now making to the cities of the West. They say:

"The contracts which the Orchestral Association must make in order to secure the best players cover a period of seven months in every twelve. As only five months of concerts can be given in Chicago, there remains a period of eight weeks in which the orchestra and Mr. Thomas can be available outside of Chicago. It is necessary to the permanency of the orchestra that these eight weeks be remunerative. If they can be made remunerative up to the point of meeting fixed expenses, a long step is taken toward making the orchestra self-supporting. It seems, then, a fair appeal that the trustees make to representative western cities asking them to organize in their business, social and musical circles to receive the orchestra for one or more concerts each season. With the active co-operation of representative people of the cities of the West the orchestra could come every year into their musical and artistic life. Were the cities to do this they would at once put themselves upon a metropolitan plane. In the larger cities where choral societies already exist, some plan of co-operation could be arranged which would meet Mr. Thomas's approval, and with the co-operation of eminent soloists, such a series of concerts could be given, say in the spring months, as would not only enlist the enthusiastic support of all cultivated people, but would give the city undertaking it a prestige otherwise impossible. There can be no question as to the financial results of such a plan, if all will interest themselves in it.

Should this appeal be met in a proper spirit, we would have next spring a series of great musical festivals, occupying perhaps six weeks, one week in each city, in such metropolitan centers as Minneapolis, Kansas City, St. Louis, Salt

Lake City, Denver, San Francisco, Seattle, Omaha and the like. The local forces would be organized for the preparation of great choral works; there would be two or three symphony concerts, and in all ways the city would experience the benefit of co-operation in the higher forms of art. It would be much easier, and at the same time more advantageous, to undertake local co-operation upon a plan of this kind than merely for orchestral concerts alone. A very large sum of money for a grand thing is more easily provided, and more easily and surely realized, than a smaller sum for a purely specialized matter like orchestral concerts alone. But whatever form the co-operation may take, the opportunity is certainly too advantageous to be lost, and has in it too much promise for the future of western music. Nor is the proposal very hazardous. Thomas concerts have been given over and over again to remunerative business in at least twenty cities west of St. Louis. And this was twenty years ago.

* * *

Any reader, fond of musical suggestions of a humorous and occasionally sarcastic cut, will be amply repaid by sending a two-cent stamp to Mr. Emil Liebling, at Kimball Hall, and asking for a copy of his "As Others See Us"—an advertising pamphlet just issued. The book is printed in elegant style, and is dedicated to that modest but most efficient of men, Mr. Albert C. Cone, treasurer of the Kimball Company. The first twenty pages are occupied with what the author calls "Glittering Generalities"—which in fact they are. The Liebling pen is a sort of modern thousand-pointed machine gun, reaching objects at long range with the utmost directness, and covering the widest possible range of horizon with a rapidity truly startling. It abounds in pity apothegms, and many samples were marked for quotation here, but are unavoidably omitted at this moment for want of space.

Coming down to the general question, Mr. Liebling played last season fifty concerts or thereabouts, in many parts of the country; and covered a range of compositions, and in a manner, also, possible to none but pianists of the first rank. He plays the Kimball piano because it pleases him, and recommends it to his friends for the same reason, and in order that they also may share his blessedness. This fact is not concealed in the pamphlet in question. And for those who would like to employ a pianist-lecturer, this little brochure of Mr. Liebling's will demonstrate the location of one candidate, concerning the celerity and penetration of whose intellectual faculties there will be no question.

* * *

It is as if some one had said: "These are our goods, and we hope you like the style." And this the reader is pretty sure to do.

* * *

The Apollo Musical Club has made its announcement for the season. Four concerts are to be given, the first being the annual "Messiah" performance, Dec. 20; Bruch's "Arminius" will be given Feb 7; a program composed of Sullivan's "Golden Legend," a Selection of Handel's "Israel in Egypt," March 7; and the fourth concert, April 25th, will be devoted to part songs. It is proposed to enlarge the chorus to 1,000 voices for the "Israel in Egypt."

* * *

Last season when the question of the future of the Chicago Orchestra was up, a large number of the faculty of the Chicago University put themselves on record in an honorable way. They signed and circulated an appeal to the public, urging the maintenance of the orchestra upon public grounds, for its ministry to art. In this they not only showed their intelligence and public spirit, but distinguished themselves honorably from the old time philistine position of literary men toward music as an art.

* * *

We have in Chicago a large number of music schools, which as a rule are as good as the music schools anywhere which have to depend upon tuition fees for the maintenance of scholastic advantages. When Dr. Ziegfeld established the Chicago Musical College, he did so in the expectation that the fees paid by the pupils would not only pay the teachers, defray the cost of apartments, and provide accessory advantages for the pupils, but also leave him a handsome profit over and above his proper fees for his own teaching. It is generally understood that the phenomenal success of this institution (which is one of the largest in the world) has amply fulfilled this anticipation. When Mr. Samuel Kayzer established the Chicago Conservatory, he did so with the added difficulty of employing all his leading teachers, many of whom are of the highest class, and of paying, moreover, the rent and all the other expenses, and having a profit remaining over. So also it was in the case of the Gottschalk school, the American Conservatory and all the other schools that have name in our city. All depend entirely upon the tuition fees for resources to pay the teachers, rent and expenses, and to leave a margin for profit. Hence it happens in all our music schools that the greater part of the teaching is performed by teachers whose natural price would be somewhat lower than that charged for their work in the school; otherwise there would not be any room for the margins needed.

In other branches of education this is not the case. A student attending the Chicago University, for instance, pays a matter of one hundred dollars a year for tuition, and at the same time participates in the advantages of the school, to acquire which an endowment of about seven millions of dollars is already invested. Hence the pupil not only gets back teaching which costs the University all the $100 which he pays, but as a rule from twice to thrice as much more. In certain departments the disparity is much greater. For example, at the head of the biological department is Dr. Whitman, head of the Agassiz School at Woods Holl, Mass., his present salary being $7,500, it is said. Dr. Whitman is one of the first biological experts in the world. Now his work is mainly done with post graduates, and taking the department as it stands at present the class requiring his personal teaching rarely numbers more than ten. Thus we have the pupil paying his fee of $100 per year, and receiving teaching which costs the university about $750, besides other large expenses in rent and apparatus. The same takes place in all the other great departments. And this is the same abroad as here the fees of the student bearing but a small part of the expense.

* * *

In Germany the large conservatories are supported by municipal or national endowment, and the disproportion exists there, as in university cases here, between what the pupil pays and what he receives. In the Cincinnati College of Music there is an endowment which furnishes the buildings and provides for general running expenses. The trustees are now pursuing the policy of employing all the tuition fees in the educational provision, whereby the student receives back tuition which costs exactly what he pays, taking the school in the large, and something more in the way of elegant and convenient appointments, concerts and lectures. The same thing happens at Oberlin, where there is a partial endowment for the music school. Mr. Greene of the Metropolitan College of Music has long been endeavoring to secure an endowment for his school, in which, as our readers know, co-operate a round half dozen of the leading American musical educators,—but so far without success. The Thurber conservatory ostensibly gives the student more than he pays, but reliable information upon this point I have found it impossible to obtain. Private information from pupils, to whom have been awarded so-called free scholarships, leads me to suspect that all is not gold that glitters.

* * *

In all these American schools there is one very important difference between the manner of the relation of the head teachers to the average student, and that which subsists in a real university. In a university the great masters are saved for the class of pupils who are prepared to take their best instruction. That is, for post-graduates, matured by years of systematic, well directed and successful effort. This is the case everywhere outside of music. But in our conservatories anybody can have lessons of the head master who will pay the fees, exception being made to such obvious dunderheads that the master himself refuses to take them. In other words, the pocketbook of the student grades him, or at least grades the quality of the instruction he receives; while very talented pupils might be relegated to teachers of inferior grade. Of course I do not forget that the competition is so great between the different schools and the desire to have good players for the credit of the school, that very clear cases are liable to obtain a free scholarship, and occasionally the work of the head master himself, even when the pocket of the student may not be commensurate therewith. But in the long run the pocketbook is the main element in assigning students to the different teachers. This is in the nature of things, and holds of private teachers quite as much.

* * *

There is therefore a time to be looked forward to, when some university, like that of Chicago, will have a musical endowment of first class rank. A round half million of dollars, administered under conservative university auspices, for the good of the school, would make all the difference in the world with the future of our talented young students. It would also have in it much for the advantage of the public musical taste, and would be a leaven whose after growth no man can foretell.

* * *

One of the main disadvantages of acquiring all of one's education in America is that the great composers remain in part mere abstractions, or at least our ignorance of the geographical relations of Europe leaves their history a mere catalogue of names and dates, in which the works properly stand out as the main thing, as indeed they should, but the personality and environment of the composer are not felt at all. And so when the American teacher goes abroad one of the pleasures anticipated most agreeably is that of visiting the dwelling places of some of the great men of the musical pantheon. It is astonishing how much this does for the best of us. A work is one thing; the room where a great master has lived and labored is something which still has in it a personal suggestion which the work lacks. The writer experienced something of this kind in his own person lately. He had passed Bonn several times before without stopping—partly upon the ground that the Beethoven life here had been only that of his apprentice years, and his birth that of obscurity; while in Vienna his active life had been passed; and partly upon the ground that, after all, the real Beethoven is to be found in the works, and not in the merely material environment where he was born, moved, and did his work. Nevertheless, a few weeks ago upon coming down the Rhine we stopped at Bonn. Taking a carriage we were driven to the sights of the town, coming first to a house in which Beethoven lived one or two of the last years in Bonn, and then later to the Beethoven monument in the public square—that splendid bronze, with which Franz Liszt had so much to do; and at the inauguration of which he performed so splendidly—as chronicled by Berlioz. Then we drove to the churchyard and saw the lovely monument to Robert Schuman—for it was near Bonn that the beautiful spirit of Schumann left earth. Then last of all to the Beethoven House—where is now the Beethoven headquarters of the admirers of his spirit from all parts of the world. A plain house in a middle class street, the ring of the bell brings to the door a good-humored German, about thirty years old, one of those sincere men, simple and worshipful, such as America produces in small measure, but the great Fatherland turns out in such numbers. And so we entered, coming into a passage way which would be the carriage entrance to the courtyard, if the dwellers there had a carriage.

The house upon the lot is very deep, and the front and back portion evidently made two tenements. The rear portion is much older, and in the attic of this Ludwig von Beethoven was born. It is a small room, perhaps ten feet by twelve, with low roof (being what is called in some parts of America a "half-story"), the light coming in from a dormer window. A plain room where most likely the family lived in great plainness of appointment. The sitting-room was next, but either then or a little later the family occupied the story below as well, making an apartment of four or five rooms, rather small but not uncomfortable. In the rooms as they now stand are a few articles of furniture which either belonged to Beethoven, or are from the same time and of the same stratum of society.

Passing through into the front of the house we enter the Beethoven museum proper. Here are several of his MSS., a large collection of portraits, several of which I had never seen before, portraits of Beethoven's friends in Bonn, and of his Vienna friends, portraits of the officers of the Beethoven house, Joachim at the head; and several pianos and harpsichords which at one time or another he used or owned; his collection of two violins, a viola and and cello, in a case. It was upon these instruments that some years ago a festival performance of one of the greatest of Beethoven's string quartettes was given in his birth room, with Joachim at the head. And so, as we lingered over one treasure after another, the personality of the man Beethoven came nearer to us, and we passed a most delightful hour. The Beethoven House is maintained by a society, drawn from all parts of the world: and from the fees for showing the place, 25 cents each person. The guide, of whom I spoke above, was everything that could be desired in the way of politeness, sympathy and good will. He is most likely a student. There is a sort of reading-room there where a certain number of musical publications from all parts of the world are found on file. There are the usual vines covering the house and from these the ladies picked a few leaves for souvenirs.

* * *

In quite a similar strain a private letter just at hand from two American students on their way to Leipsic has the following:

"We left Cologne by steamer, and had a delightful day. We were on the Rhine until 10 o'clock at night before reaching Mayence, and saw the river by sunlight, twilight and moonlight. And, if we were going to spend one or two more days upon it, would perhaps think it quite equal in beauty to our own Hudson. After a night at the Holland house at Mayence, we took an early train for Frankfort. As soon as we had checked our luggage at the station we started out to see the Gœthe and Schiller monuments, and to find Mme. Clara Schumann. We found it no easy matter to make our wants known, as my German did not seem to go very well, and the French of my companion not at all. At last I found that that Mme. Schumann had met with an accident a few days previously, a carriage had run against her, and her physician had advised her going to Interlaken. There was a notice in one of the city papers to this effect. Ascertaining where her house was I determined to go there to make quite sure. So we went there only to find the blinds down and the gate locked. I picked an ivy leaf and a bit of arbor vitae and went away disappointed, but somewhat comforted to know that at least she had arrived at Interlaken after we had left there. We saw the Gœthe monument, the house where he was born and many other sights, including the art gallery in which there are a few very good pictures and quite a good many poor ones. Arriving at the station we found that a train would leave for Eisenach in two minutes. Not liking to hurry enough to catch this we waited for the next, which proved to be a very slow one. But it brought us all the same to Eisenach by 10 p. m., where we went to a Gaze hotel—which we did not at all like, and were glad to leave it the next morning. We took took a carriage to see the interesting old town. There was the Bach monument, the houses where he and Martin Luther were born, and the castle of the Wartburg.

* * *

The castle was intensely beautiful, though not so grand and beautiful as that at Heidelberg. We saw Luther's room and the place where it is said he threw the ink bottle at the devil. The stain has been cut out, but now that I have seen the place where it was I believe the story, of course. We went into the hall where the Meistersingers had their contest, and from the windows looked out upon the lovely Venus mountain referred to in "Tannhauser." In the hall was a very large picture of the Meistersingers, which was also interesting. Then we had a surprise. As we were turning a corner whom should we meet but one of my companion's teachers in the University of California, absent like her on a year's leave of absence, and (good luck) also going to be in Leipsic this winter.

At Eisenach we entered the house where Luther was born, but were told that tourists were not allowed to enter the house where Bach was born. I had an irresistible desire to go in, and thought there could be no harm in trying. A big fat old German, smoking a very long German pipe, came to the door. He did not know English. I asked, best I could, if he had any photos of the house. He said that there were none. I was not getting on very well, and thought I might as well know the worst at once, so I asked if I might not just step into the house where Bach was born. Then he was very lovely and made me feel quite welcome, called my attention to the old knocker on the door, to a big old oven in the hall way, to the heavy door that opened into a big old-fashioned garden, the little window under the roof, and an old grape vine that nearly covered the back of the house. He took me out into the garden, asked me if I was English, and when I said "No, American," it seemed to impress him greatly to think of my coming so far. I told him that I was passionately fond of music and a great lover of Bach. He took his pipe out of his mouth, stooped and picked a flower, passed it to me saying in German, "Here is a flower from the great Bach's garden for the dear American," patted me on the shoulder and shook my hand as if he were having an awfully good time. Afterward we drove through the town, saw the Goethe and Schiller mausoleums, their monuments, the houses where they lived, also the monuments of Herder and Wieland, but the greatest charm for me was the Franz Liszt house.

It was such a delightful surprise (you may know but I did not), to find that the house is left just as it was when he received his pupils there. The same old housekeeper, the same pianos, his books, music and everything were there but the dear old man, and it seemed as if he might step in at any moment. I was there about an hour. The housekeeper was very nice, called my attention to everything and explained in German that I could understand, and when we left she gave me some flowers from a vase standing before the bust of Liszt."

These adventures, it will be observed, were all comprised within two days time, thus suggesting the richness of certain parts of Germany in historical associations.

* * *

Some months ago mention was made of the remarkable and beautiful work called "Famous Composers and Works," published by the J. B. Millet Company, Boston. This magnificently gotten up affair is in thirty parts, at 50 cts. each; sold only by subscription. It contains about 900 small quarto pages of biographical and critical matter from some of the best musical writers in the world; and about 700 pages of music. The literary editorship was by Prof. John K. Paine of Harvard. The illustrations, which are numerous and valuable, have been edited by that most successful of photographers, the veteran Karl Klauser. And the musical selections were supervised by Mr. Theodore Thomas. No such popular book upon musical subjects has ever before been offered. I am informed from private sources that the sale of this great work has now reached more than 24,000 sets, despite the hard times.

The same house is now engaged upon another undertaking of a musical character, little if any less commanding. It is called "Half Hours with the Best Composers," and a large number of composers are represented by compositions, portraits and brief biographical sketches. As the work is edited by Mr. Klauser in the interests of the buyer, and of art in general, this bids fair to make a desirable companion to the other work. By writing to the publishers, a descriptive circular can be had. In the next issue of MUSIC a detailed notice will be made of the first ten parts.

W. S. B. M.

PUBLIC SCHOOL MUSIC: SUCCESS OR NON-SUCCESS.

THE CECILLIAN SERIES OF STUDY AND SONG. John W. Tufts. Boston, New York and Chicago, Silver, Burdett & Co.

Book I. For one voice.

Book II. For soprano and alto voices.

Book III. Unchanged voices. (Added notes for basses and tenors.)

Book IV. For mixed voices.

The public school and general evolutionary tendencies are at cross-roads with each other in several respects, but mainly in this; that in an age of specialties the education of children is still left to the handling of teachers who, as a rule, have no positive aptitude for or acquirement of knowledge in any special direction, and consequently fail of inciting in the pupils that living interest which adds zest and operative force to the hours of recitation, and has in it also the promise and potency of a future of scholarship. Or, to put the case differently, we might say that as yet the public school finds itself in bondage to the personal element in school management: esteeming personal intimacy with the pupils a better ground for the teacher than any kind of special knowledge unaccompanied by such personal relation to the individuals to be taught. Consequently, school life always struggles against a tendency to run in ruts and to communicate the words of knowledge rather than its substance. Music, however, like drawing and calesthenics, is itself so much a specialized form of activity that the specially gifted teacher still has more or less to do with its administration—although as a rule too little to impart to the study the vitality which it ought to have, in order to meet the demands of its own conscience as a department of art-science.

It is only in the lifetime of those now living that the first American attempts were made to introduce the systematic study of music into the common school course. This was the work of Dr. Lowell Mason in Boston, his efforts upheld and seconded by such broad-minded men as the late Samuel Elliott (father of the Harvard president), and others. It was in 1837 that he began the work, and his own connection with the Boston public schools ended in 1850. But so decided had been his success, and so unmistakable had been the value of the new exercise, that although the grand old teacher went out, the work went on. Previously, public school singing in America had been merely that of rote songs. Mason's idea was that every child ought to learn to read music as he would a book, and with this that he should acquire some measure of sensible use of his vocal organs, and perhaps above all be subjected to the incitation of patriotic and noble song. Hence, the study was defended upon one hand for the sake of its disciplinary value; and otherwise for the sake of its utilitarian value.

Times have greatly changed since Mason's day. Fifty years have pretty well settled it, in the minds of American educators, that singing in some form is indispensable to a happy school room. Opinions are divided as to what books should be bought, and as to the central motive which ought to rule the work; but singing in some form has come in the public school to stay. Undoubtedly there will still be now and then newspaper clatter that the state has no right to undertake to teach anything not indispensable for citizenship. And without waiting for the crank who is sure to arise, proposing to add the ability to sing songs of a certain texture as a test of voting qualification, many short-sighted folks would like to see singing debarred. These, however, do not count; for, as already said, singing has entered the school room to stay. Nevertheless, we are little nearer than before the full settlement of the question as to the most profitable use of music in the school-room, and the scientific method of applying its ministrations to the unfolding mind of the child. This is the question which the present paper undertakes briefly to consider.

Contrary to the popular impression, the scientific application of musical instruction in the common school-room does not mainly center at the ability "to read music," in the sense of being able to define the place of "do" in different signatures, and to call the key names of the tones irrespective of accumulations of flats or sharps. The real point lies deeper, the scientific value of the musical instruction centering in the cultivation of musical perceptions. Whole roomsfull of pupils able to call the key-names of tones in any designated signature might still fail totally when asked to write upon the board a melody from dictation, even although no transition into foreign keys might be found in it; while it is doubtful whether the choirs of our large cities contain as high an admixture as one per cent of singers able to correctly note down melodic passages from dictation, when they involve even quite ordinary transitions into foreign keys—such as almost every anthem or part song contains. The paid solo singers are but little more competent, the great majority of them ascertaining their melodies by picking the notes out on the keyboard of the pianoforte, or still better by having the organist play them for them—in which case they also acquire some sense of the musical meaning of the passages. These limitations are quite the same as saying that in teaching music the student is asked to read before he can talk. Signs are introduced and explained, while the concept which the sign represents is still unknown to the student. The justice of these strictures will be denied by many teachers of music in the schools, but it is believed that actual school-room tests will amply demonstrate their truth and moderation.

It is not denied that the majority of the pupils in any school-room, where singing is regularly taught, will be found able to sing the scale tones from any pitch assigned as tonic, and sing them approximately well. It is also admitted that the simple relations of rhythm will be recognized. In occasional instances a modulation might be correctly explained, and perhaps correctly sung without the aid of an instrument—though this latter point is very doubtful. But as soon as the pupil is thrown upon his inner conception of tone relations, as when he is asked to write a melody sung to him or played to him upon the instrument, he will fail not alone upon the first trial but upon repeated trials. Still more if he be asked to sing a soprano phrase while an alto is played to it, and then immediately write the alto which was played. This is rather a nice point, but it is by no means an advanced dictation. In fact, not to multiply instances, the general fault of the training is that the inner something upon which singing depends, musical perception and musical conception, are left half formed.

If it be asked why this defect should still remain in our common school instruction in music, there might be several reasons assigned, all of which have co-operated in the result. For one thing, we are still too much in bondage to our standard notation. The staff is almost an ideal notation for instrumentalists, but it is by no means equally definite for vocalists. The fundamental fact for the singers is the relation of tones in key; and this information the staff sometimes gives and sometimes fails to give. A transition into a foreign key may overload the notation with confusing accidentals where the actual relation is very simple; and, on the other hand, a transition may occur to quite a remote key, without the fact showing at all in certain of the voice parts. And in simple music, especially, the staff is very misleading. The simple diatonic relations, within which folk-song moves itself, are very few, and are exactly alike for all keys. They can be perfectly taught to pupils in the primary grades if attention is duly given; but when it is asked to represent them upon the staff, the entire apparatus of signatures and clefs might be needed. Thus the mind of the child is directed to the *sign*, the notation, instead of the *thing* itself, music.

Moreover, we have never yet had in this country a complete apparatus for teaching elementary music. The absurd bondage to the staff prevents our teachers from discovering the scientific value of a very remarkable teaching apparatus developed by a generation of workers in the Tonic Sol-fa, in England—an apparatus which has not only extended the range of fine chorus singing in England vastly beyond anything which we have ever dreamed in America, but has given a genuine development of musical taste, and a scientific precision, still more beyond anything which we have yet developed. In some of the manuals of public school singing an effort has been made to introduce certain of the features of this method. The so-called "modulator," or diagram of key relationships, is one of these;

the "time-names" are another, although the latter owe their first invention to M. Paris, a French teacher, where also a system similar to the Tonic Sol fa enables the teachers to dispense with difficult notations in the lower grades, and concentrate the attention upon the real thing in question—namely tonal effects and relations.

A foolish misconception has prevailed in this country that to employ the simpler notation was to render the instruction unscientific. The average instrumentalist believes this, not knowing that the Tonic Sol-fa notation, or the figure notation of the French Orpheonists, furnishes a generalized notation for all relations of tones in key, such as the staff utterly fails to provide, and for want of which almost all of our training of singers is defective in exactly this generalized view of tone-relations.

Music will be scientifically taught in the public schools only when the real thing, musical effect, is taught in such manner that any song proper to the grade can be written down from ear as certainly and as easily as a passage of prose or poetry is written from dictation. The teaching will have two sides, which will be equally developed. On the one hand the pupils will be able to reproduce with their voices, entirely independent of instrumental help, any musical passage or relation indicated by pointing upon the modulator or presented in notation; and on the other hand they will be equally ready to put into notation any effect proper to the grade, which may be produced in their hearing.

When this is done certain later consequences will follow, the most important being a foundation for sound musical taste, and so the development of a fondness for the greater composers, and a real perception of the superiority of their music over the ephemeral and transient jabber, such as prevails for instance in Sunday schools—where music touches its lowest depth. The reason why such results will follow a proper cultivation of music in the public schools is to be found in the fact that the entire basis of superiority in the music of the great composers over that of the cheap writers lies in the superior fineness of musical perception, and the accuracy with which they are able to touch the feelings through the employment of musical combinations properly related to feeling and inner moods of soul. And unless those who hear this music have already a certain aptitude in musical perception they will fail to enter into these less usual combinations, and therefore fail of being affected by them. Moreover, it is not a question alone of coming into the use of better vocal works; the entire musical cultivation is affected in the same measure, and the students later will show the same aptitude for fine combinations in instrumental music, and the taste in this apparently unrelated department be elevated in like degree.

Moreover, this method of using the musical instruction is thoroughly scientific, and consonant with the movement of the present times, when the cultivation of all the powers and aptitudes of the composite being is sought with so much diligence. To appreciate fine musical effects, to discriminate closely between them, and to have so perfect a concept of them as to be able to reproduce them at call, is to have acquired a refined and trained sense of hearing, which will have many relations to other departments of activity, besides tending to the development of greater brain power. In just the same way as the brain is developed by every added activity of sense perception.

From what has thus far been said it will be easily inferred that in the judgment of the writer our primary and lower grammar grades of musical instruction would be better if the staff were entirely dispensed with, and a simple notation like that of the Tonic Sol-fa substituted. But this is not to declare war upon existing systems or to proclaim that it is impossible to obtain results of scientific value under them. Everything depends upon how a book is used, given a certain minimum of technical material: and this comes back to the skill of the individual teachers—a large question into which no one could understandingly enter without a large observation in the school rooms.

Upon one point, at least, American educators may well pride themselves, namely, upon the production of a succession of collections of school songs of constantly advancing excellence. From the admirable "Song Gardens" of Lowell Mason down to the latest in the list, almost every important collection has shown an advance in one direction or another. Among the latest collections are those whose titles are given above. They are the work of an excellent musician, Mr. John W. Tufts, expert by practice and experience in recognizing the demands of school rooms. Of these the first volume, for a single voice, is perhaps least satisfactory, both in music and in text. The words and music at times disagree lamentably, one of the most glaring instances being in a song called "Spring," (79) where the lines "Everything now is bright and gay," "Why is the sun so bright, so bright," and "Why do the soft south breezes blow?" are set to a minor strain beginning with a diminished seventh and descending throughout the line to a cadence in the relative minor. Another point liable to question is as to the wisdom of employing nonsense jingles to solemn music.

The second volume for two voices, where there was more room to select from the lighter German writers, is better; and probably commendation may be given generally to volumes III and IV—the latter having been the first prepared and very successful. These volumes were intended to supplement the readers of the Normal Course in music of Messrs. John W. Tufts and H. E. Holt. The weakness of the series lies in the first volume, where there is a lack of healthy diatonic melody. The books are handsomely gotten up, but it is a question whether it would not be better for school room purposes to have them less expensive. This, however, is a point where publishers and buyers may properly disagree.

W. S. B. M.

REVIEWS AND NOTICES

Musical Education and Musical Art. By Edith V. Eastman, Boston, Damrell and Upham. 1893. 12mo. Pp. 170.

To quote from the preface, the present little work "consists chiefly of gleanings from various sources, collected and combined for the purpose of throwing light on the difficult subject of Musical Art: and of aiding, in however small a degree, in the discovery of a new and more living way of bringing music into the lives of the working classes, or of any others who are now outside its sphere of influence."

There are nine chapters altogether, the topics being these: "The Language of the Sense; The Uses of Science; Art in Education: Characteristics of Musical Art: From the Conservatory to the Kindergarten: The Eye versus the Ear: The Voice and the Ear: Fences and Gates; The New Education."

Two elements at least are to be praised unreservedly: they are the style of the book, and its general tone of helpfulness. And to take the modest proposition of the author, quoted from the preface above, it is certain that the little book will be well received by many and do good. It is less certain, however, whether more good might not have been done had the author been a trifle less self effacing, and have taken up her subjects and treated them from the ground up in her own way. Because as soon as important subjects are tackled in this way, something essentially new is apt to follow. It is not possible to think a subject through seriously from the foundation without arriving at something new, and something essentially authoritative. Whereas it is the great misfortune of the quasi "proof-text," which one collects from the poets and other good writers concerning music, that they generally come from persons outside music, who know it merely in its externals. There are evidences of this limitation in not a few of the passages quoted in Miss Eastman's work. On the other hand many of the observations of the writer herself are new and valuable. One of the most charming tells of what was probably her own experience with a class in a "mission" sewing school. Having a number of troublesome and rather untaught and unruly girls to form, she found herself at first almost dismayed at the strong language and rude instincts and habits. But after quite a long delay in beginning order, one day the teacher happened to see in the paper the verses of Susan Coolidge beginning:

"The red rose says 'be sweet,'
'The lily bids 'be pure,'
The hardy brave Chrysanthemum,
'Be patient and endure.'"

This was her cue. There were not flowers enough to assign one to each member of the class, but the ready teacher added other verses, and then she assigned one flower for each girl. Placing an ill natured, scowling girl first, she gave her the first line to commit: the second line to the next and so on—each girl standing for one flower. Then later whenever manners began to get "rocky," the teacher sweetly called for the verse—and in a short time that class was brought into a state of order previously unexpected.

A few of the opinions of the book should be taken with a grain of salt. For instance she speaks of Mendelssohn being called down from the first seat in the synagogue of his own day to a humbler position in later times, and adds that while he might very properly stand below his teachers, Beethoven and Mozart, he could not in honor take any place lower. The objection to this passage arises not so much from a desire to relegate the highly gifted Mendelssohn to a lower place, as the distinct voice it has of ranking him above several later masters who were his superiors in many respects, and most of all in the most vital points of the composer's art.

Again, on the relative color of different keys she is somewhat at fault. She says "supposing for instance that the distance from C to D is greater than from D to E, and if from E to F is not the same as from F to F sharp, it follows that different scales, and from them different keys, do actually have different qualities and effects." This passage, however, falls to the ground before the dilemma that if we are here speaking of perfect intonation, in which alone these differences would exist, then all keys would also be perfect, and consequently have precisely the same effect, save in one particular, to be hereafter noted. And, second, that if we have temperament, we have not a different distance between C and C sharp, C sharp and D, and so up the chromatic scale, but an entire octave divided into exactly twelve equal half steps and therefore no difference at all between one key and another—save the exception before noted, which is this: The effect of keys appears to depend upon the absolute pitch of the keynote, and consequently the entire range of pitch. This does not mean that one key contains different intervals from another, or that any inequality subsists between them: but simply that lying one higher and another lower in the musical scale, they are related differently to the psychological feeling for pitch and tension. The more you ascend in pitch, the farther you get away from the stronger and masculine element. The high soprano may be a very devil—but at all events she is a far more high-flying one than the low alto who joins with a bass Mephisto. Take a Schubert song written from the standpoint of soprano, and sing it in an alto register, and you will find that not alone does the song itself sound differently but still more does the accompaniment, and this will be more and more the case in proportion to the value of the accompaniment. For instance, take the lovely "To be Sung on the Waters," which is written in C flat. The alto will sing this in G flat, and the accompaniment will sound entirely different, and the song be far less inspiring.

In another place Miss Eastman regrets that while the new education enables a child to write, form things with his hands, and compose prose and poetry, it does not as yet do this for his music. Why should he not write music by ear, she asks, and why should he not even bring to his teacher little melodies which he himself has composed and written out correctly. The question is put, but it omits to recognize the fact that the Tonic Sol-fa system of elementary instruction does in fact give exactly this training of the ear, and this command of musical concepts from the inside, and the ability to perpetuate the little bits of musical fantasy which the child may have. Ordinary school music teaching does not do this, for many reasons, but first of all for the reason that owing to an absurd unwillingness to permit the child to adopt for his early musical exercises a notation which he could fully understand and use intelligently within the time of his early school grades, the entire teaching reduces itself either to mere rote singing, and a training of ear in musical feeling and expression; or else to the still more barren work of teaching staff notation—without in any real sense teaching the things for which staff notation stands. Elementary music teaching is bad enough, but as yet there does not seem much chance of greatly improving it in this country. Here we have to do with our prejudiced music-masters and our short-sighted boards—impartial because wholly unprejudiced.

Meanwhile Miss Eastman's book will reach many readers who will enjoy it, and by it be set upon trains of thought which very likely will later lead to something still deeper. This is one of the books which our library making friends should make a note of.

LESSONS IN AUDITION. To be used in Private or Class Instruction for the development of Musical Intelligence. Prepared by Helene M. Sparmann. Cincinnati, John Church Company. 1893. Large 8vo. Pp. 104. Bds. $1.50.

Many teachers will find this work of value, since it addresses itself to one of the most important problems in musical education, namely, ear-training. Miss Sparmann begins with exercises consisting of phrases and passages played for recognition of higher or lower pitch, individuality of tones, etc. In one instance she first plays the tones C, D and E, and then plays passages passing over these tones, the pupil being required to attend carefully in order to discover whether any other tones are included. Then comes the scale and exercises for recognizing scale tones. And so one way and another many points are covered, including measure, rest, and the notation belonging to them. There is no doubt that any teacher who will use the book according to directions will find it of benefit and of interest.

It is to be regretted that Miss Sparmann had not made a more careful study of the Tonic Sol-fa method of ear-training, as elaborated by Mr. Curwen. In many respects Mr. Curwen was in advance of the present work. The fundamental defect of Miss Sparrmann's work is that while there is in it a progress from easy to difficult, and many phases of the problem are well treated, it does not build upon ear-training scientifically—that is, according to the laws of tone-relation, in accordance with which music is made. Hence some things are left to the end which belong early as the triad, and the attendant chords of the keys, and some things occur early which properly belong later. In making these strictures, however, it is to be remembered that the problem of making a progressive primer of ear-training for the use of the piano pupils is by no means an easy one. A careful reader, of English preferences, would also have preferred "Ear-Training" to "Lessons in Audition" as a title of the work.

THE SYNTHETIC METHOD FOR THE PIANOFORTE. A SYSTEMATIC DEVELOPMENT OF NOTATION, RHYTHM, TOUCH, TECHNIC, MELODY, RHYTHM, HARMONY AND FORM. By Albert Ross Parsons, and Kate S. Chittenden. Part 1. The elements of Music and Piano-playing. Silver Burdette, & Co. 1891. New York, Boston, Chicago.

This work is a book for teaching children, in a method designed to awaken musical intelligence at an early stage in the studies, and lay the foundation for better work later. It follows similar principles to those illustrated in a number of elementary works produced within the last five or six years. The present book (probably the work of the junior editor) is original and interesting. The exercises for developing the tonic sense are particularly to be commended. In spite of the care taken to put "the thing before the sign," according to the principles of Pestalozzianism, quite a number of violations occur in this work. For example. "The difference between one letter and another is called an interval." "Between C and D is an interval of a second, *because there are two letters concerned.*" A statement of this kind is more honored in the breach than in the observance. An interval is difference in pitch between two scale-tones. Intervals are measured by the scale compass involved, and letters are applied to the pitches according to the same criterion. We know of no simplification that results from teaching a pupil the misleading and unscientific form of statement above mentioned.

So also, "A second lies between a line and a space." Here the fact called to the attention of the pupil is useful; but the form of the statement is unscientific and consequently less easily apprehended than the true statement, which is that intervals of a second are represented by adjacent staff degrees; a second from a line being a space, and vice versa, the second from a space being a line. So also "A third extends across two lines and a space, or two spaces and a line." The statement is true, except that a third being a musical phenomenon is heard and not seen; its representation is seen, extending as above.

Another statement to which exception may properly be taken is that "A sharp written before a note changes that note every time it occurs in the same measure." This statement is not only defective, but radically wrong and misleading. A sharp in no way affects a note. It affects a staff degree: the note remains a quarter, a half, a whole, as the case may be, entirely independent of accidental sharps or flats, and entirely independent of the staff degree upon which it is written. Staff degrees and chromatic signs represent pitches; notes represent utterance and tone-length.

Little defects of this kind are probably due to preoccupation on the part of the senior editor, who is eminently of a contemplative and scientific turn of mind, and philosophical in the matter of expression. They are merely blemishes upon a work which in its intention and execution is admirably adapted for primary work with small children.

ZWOLF CONCERT-ETUDEN FUR PIANOFORTE, VON E. KROEGER. OP. 30. Leipsic New York. Breitkopf and Haertel. 2 Books. Each 3 Marks.

The studies above mentioned are the work of a young American author, despite the elaboration of foreign particulars upon the title page. A rose spelled in German often smells more sweetly in music. The studies in question are all difficult, and upon unusual technical motives. 1. Octaves with a double finger touch alternated. 2. Extended position for left hand, all five fingers playing arpeggios covering intervals of a tenth or twelfth. 3. Running thirds for the right hand. 4. Extended positions for the right hand with rapid finger work. 5. Heavy chords, held while a long arpeggio is run by the two hands cooperatively, after which the melody is resumed. 6. Rapid octaves, at first for the right hand, then for the left. 7. Double touches in chords with each hand alternately. 8. Extended chords with firmly sustained melody. 9. Homesickness. 10. Unrest, chord and two-voice arpeggio movement with each hand, always upon extended positions, somewhat after the style of Henselt. 11. Romance, the melody coming out in different locations of chords taken simultaneously with it. 12. Storm, a study in interlocking triplets of hand touches. Musically the pieces are well handled, although it remains to ascertain by the test of time whether the substance is equal to the display here made of it. As indications of ambition on the part of the composer the work is to be commended. Of course it is well printed. All the pieces are difficult.

MADONNA BY BOUGUEREAU.

MUSIC

DECEMBER, 1894.

A REHEARSAL OF "THAIS." AN IRONICAL REMINISCENCE.

CENE: The Opera. A few jets of gas lighted; long rows of empty seats, among which here and there a few personages can be made out. In the foreground, seated before a little table, M. Bertrand, who with a weary air, takes notes. Near him M. Gallet, the author of the libretto trying to take something from something else. Around them other leading people, such as the chief costumer, the head shoemaker, the master of cordage, and others with names as sonorous as those of personages in "Salammbo." Upon the scene M. Gailhard conducts himself like a lovely southern Mephistopheles. And finally, far up among the flies, the premieres of the ballet, like the chief angels of paradise. M. Jules Massenet himself contemplates his work; visibly he is satisfied with it, as indeed he well may be, for M. Jules Massenet well knows when he has done a good thing. One sees at his side certain favorite pupils, among whom now and then the master's music arouses a fugitive smile; they have their heads uncovered, and are respectful, according to the usage established by M. Jules Massenet. From the place where we are, we see very well the author of "Thais." Head bald as a billiard ball, brow creased by five wrinkles, carrying a music roll, his locks falling upon the collar of his coat; air amiable, inquiet, feverish; little black eyes very lively and defiant; many gestures. At one moment he is enthusiastic, applauds, manifests an intense joy; at another he is desolate, pours out maledictions, collapses into the most profound discouragement. He descends then from his heaven, walks in the corridor; shakes his cane, reappears upon the stage, and, at last comes back again into the audience room where he beats his hands at each change of scene. The rehearsal begins.

M. GALLET, THE LIBRETTIST.

PRINCIPAL PERSONAGES:—The Electrician, Costumer, Chief of the Battery (gong, big drum, triangle, side drums, etc.), the Chief Machinist and the Stage Manager.

AUDIENCE.—Directors, Editors, Reporters, Musicians, Chiefs of Orchestra, Secretaries, Chiefs of Chorus, and other chiefs of little importance — Anatole France, himself.

All the actors are in costume except M. Delmas, Mlle Sanderson and the Monks. thing is more strange than to see Athanaël, dressed in a

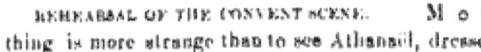

REHEARSAL OF THE CONVENT SCENE.

jacket, preach renunciation to Thais, dressed in street gown and a little hat.

Prelude by the orchestra; M. Jules Massenet remains indifferent. The first curtain parts, the second curtain rises, and at last the third curtain opens and permits us to see the desert of the Thiebaide. M. Jules Massenet awakens; the Monks are eating.

M. MASSENET Applauds.

MONKS.—"Behold honey; behold pure water."

M. JULES M.—interrupting—"There are not enough Solitaires."

THE ABBE ANTINOE.—"Two are sick, and one is tardy."

M. JULES M.—"This is not enough; it is too few; M. Bertrand, take a note (with authority). It is very strange that in a house where there are a hundred machinists they give me so few monks."

M. GAILHARD (in beautiful grave voice, from the fountain of the south).—"Fear nothing; you shall have them—your solitaires."

M. ANATOLE FRANCE.

M. JULES M. (in the most complete discouragement).—"When? When? the morning of the first performance? Is it so! If I do not have my numbers of Solitaires, we do not pass Wednesday, I promise you."

M. TAFFANEL (to the orchestra).—"From measure 37." (The solitaries begin to sing with mouths full.)

M. JULES M.—"Turn down the light when Mr. Delmas enters. The effect of night is very important. Light the torches, light the torches."

THE ABBE ANTINOE, to M. Delmas.—"My son, we do

not mix with the affairs of heaven." (M. Delmas lies down and sleeps; the scene lights up and we see Thais dancing before the people).

M. JULES MASSENET (delighted).—"Oh, but this *is* beautiful! What a marvel! But, sapristi! *more* light than that, so one can see well." (Singing Tra la la tra la la.) "More light; double the lights. There, well! It is truly delicious."

M. DELMAS, (exit towards the town).—"To lead her to God."

THE SOLITAIRES.—"Lord, shine upon him."

M. JULES M. (restless)—"The curtain; the curtain; why not the curtain? What is the matter with the curtain?"

M. GAILHARD.—"Have no fear; they will get it directly."

M. JULES M. (exasperated).—"Is this what you call being ready? I will come to the day of the performance without ever once seeing this curtain. (Mournfully) Misery of misery! I will *never* see this curtain."

M. Gailhard wrestles with the curtain. M. Bertrand takes notes.

"CURTAIN! CURTAIN! Where is that Curtain?"

M. JULES M. (In the Entr' Act.)—"It is delicious, this subject; the first act severe, the second vibrating with passion, abounding in love; a third act, infernal and tragic, This monk and this courtesan who meet each other" (referring no doubt to some of his previous works, such as for instance "Marie-Madeleine," "Herodiade," "Manon" and "Mage.") "Every time I have taken a monk and a courtesan, I have had a great effect. M. Gailhard, please increase the white light in the first scene; a torrid sun." (Second Act.) "What delicious decoration. From the second tier of boxes one can see birds fly, and the shops in the town. And how the white costume distinguishes itself from those of rose. For example, note the force of the white embroideries for Nicias. How? The handsome shoes of Athanaël have not yet arrived? Thunder! We are not ready, not ready, NOT READY!"

M. GAILHARD.—"We still have time."

M JULES M.—(Violently) "Today is the second, is it not? And here is M. Delmas with bare feet. It will be a delightful effect." "Always the same story. For months we have been studying this work, and here the shoes of Athanaël have not yet arrived. It is a shame." (At the entrance of the flute players he becomes composed again.) "Ah! This is entirely successful! I am content; the success of this *entrée* is sure, sure!"

CONVENT SCENE
At Performance.

MLLE SANDERSON. (Her arms concealed under her mantle, like works of art in books.)—"I will be no more to him than a name."

M. JULES M. —"The curtain, quick! Good, this time." (The scene changes.) "This decoration is exquisite, bravo, M. Carpezat! my compliments."

MLLE SANDERSON.—"Venus, will I be beautiful eternally, eternally, eternally?"

M. JULES M. (Singing)—"Eternally, eternally."

MLLE SANDERSON.—"Eternally, eternally."

ALL THE SOLITAIRES. (mumbling)—"Eternally, eternally.

M. DELMAS. (Unbuttoning his jacket)—"I am Athanaël, monk of Antioch." (Entr'Act: violin solo, the celebrated design for violincellos,' in which M. Massenet so much excels; other decorations.)

M. JULES M.—"Leave the lamp near the little statue of Love; it is very important."

MLLE SANDERSON. (Singing)—"Love is a virtue rare."

"M. JULES M.—"More passion, more passion!"

"M. GAILHARD—(at this moment it begins to be day). "Make the day faster, I pray you!"

MLLE SANDERSON (taking the little statuette of Amour). —"When Nicias loved me he gave me this image."

M. DELMAS (breaking the image)—"Nicias!"

M. JULES M.—"Hurry on the people. And the fire.

THE TEMPTATION SCENE.
Mlle Mauri and M. Delmas.

When are you going to decide to kindle that fire? Better than that! All red." (M. Bertrand takes notes. Change of scene. Again the Thebaide. The solitairies are bowed before the storm.) "That thunder then signifies nothing. Make the thunder again, and let there be something more than mere sparks. See?" (The storm redoubles.) "Very well."

M. DELMAS reclines and sleeps. (Second apparition of Thais.)

M. JULES M.—"The blue light. For God's sake the blue light. Stronger!" (Stroke of the tam-tam.) "M. Gailhard, have you no other tam-tam? This one has not resonance enough."

M. GAILHARD.—"We have only two tam-tams; I have given you the stronger one."

THE CHIEF MACHINIST—"Mister, it is an old side-drum."

MLLE SANDERSON.—Nicias has given it to me.
M. DELMAS.—Nicias!

M. JULES M. (angry)—"The public will not stand that. I desire a true tam-tam, cost what it may." (The Sabbath.) "Force the red light. Force it."

M. GAILHARD (to the Electrician.) "When Mme. Mauri holds herself so," (She holds herself in the pose of the Apollo Belvidere.) "inundate her with a ray." (Mlle. Mauri completes the seduction of M. Delmas. Sudden night. The storm redoubles. Voice of M. Jules Massenet from the darkness.) "The star. The star. Make the star descend. Where is that star caught? What a theatre! (Here one would swear that there were very few employés in Paradise.)"

THE ANGELS.—"The star! Enough of organ! The star!"

DIRECTORS AND MACHINISTS.—"Where is the star? Make the organ cease." (The organ consents to be silent, the star appears. Quiet again. The bacchanale resumes, fusées, Bengal lights, tam-tam, pyrotechnics, the Chatelet of the beautiful days of "Le Tour de la Monde." Third apparition of Thais.)

M. JULES M.—(At length again happy) "Lights, lights, and still more lights."

(Last scene: Thais dies in the abbey of the White Nuns.)

M. JULES M.—"This will go nicely with the costumes."

MLLE SANDERSON.—"Do you recall the conversations in which you showed me the way to heaven?"

AFTER THE REHEARSAL.

M. DELMAS—"I have deceived you."

M. JULES M.—"Here an electric light. M Taffanel, I have marked an electric light in the score; it is too late." (The light shines out glorifying Thais and Athanael.) "Perfect; after three rehearsals we will be ready.

(Audience retires to the exit.)

1st IMPARTIAL SPECTATOR. Have you noticed that M. Jules Massenet has not made a single observation to the orchestra, nor yet one to the singers?"

2nd IMPARTIAL SPECTATOR—"It appears to me that I have read a romance by M. Anatole France, entitled "Thais." I found there a saint upon a column; but if I remember rightly there were no red and blue lights, no tam-tams, no pretty little women in chemises, and no fires of Bengal lights. It is curious how different subjects modify themselves according to the temperament of artists treating them."

M. Jules Massenet.—(to the Directors.) "I have the

idea of taking another lyric comedy from the Apocalypse. I suppose the Magdalene amourous of John."

M. GALLET.—(Following the idea.) "In the third Act quadrille of the seven angels: seven entrees for the seven openings of the seals; mixed with thrones and dominions."

M. JULES M.—"I have already the motive of the spouse, sighed by the violincello, passion intense, mystical. Delmas will be magnificent in the role of John; splendid apotheosis."

M. GAILHARD.—"Fine idea. The tree of the Valkyrie will answer nicely."

M. GALLET (dreaming.)—"Rosita Mauri upon the pale horse."

(They lose themselves in the night.)

PIERRE VEBER.

———

A RAMBLE.

SUGGESTED BY GOTTSCHALK'S "NOTES OF A PIANIST."

THERE is at the present time more curiosity current to find out something about a famous man's personnel than about his works. We are anxious to know how he dined and wined, loved and was beloved; whether he broke his eggs at the big or the little end, and whether he really ate his pie with a knife or fork. The divinity which is said to hedge in monarchs, casts a halo around artists also, and even during their lifetime do the most extraordinary stories and rumors find ready believers: in fact, the more fabulous the story, the more apt the public to take full stock in it. The improbable character, too, of the anecdotes naturally increases in the same ratio as the number of years which have elapsed since the death of the subject under eventual discussion; those anecdotes especially which are marked "historical" are without exception infernal lies.

The public should be made to realize that an artist's private affairs are his own concern, and that a multiplicity of husbands, for instance, does by no means impair an artist's usefulness, indicating rather a very proper appreciation of the fact that there are as good fish left in the sea as were ever caught. When the audience has paid the customary obolus, shekel or whatever the current coin of the realm, and has therefore received its dues in the shape of the artist's talent, the contract has been fulfilled. Then let the artist alone; if he finds a necessary reaction over beer and head-cheese in the cloudy and tobacco-laden atmosphere of the beer hall, while you are still fondly lingering over the last strains of the Chopin Nocturne, do not make him responsible for your own shortcomings in that regard.

Much of this morbid appetite has been satisfied by the appearance of memoirs and conversations of great men;

they are almost without exception dreary reading, as those talks on everything under the sun with which Goethe regaled Eckermann; likewise the epistles which passed between the same great man and Schiller, and Schindler's reminiscences of Beethoven; it is hard to realize the fact that a great man can write a commonplace letter, and a commonplace person may produce a great epistolary effusion, under extraordinary provocation.

The subject under discussion has much to do with it. Of course there are exceptions, and we find the same delightful quintessence of quaint humor in Lamb's letters, which distinguishes all his works; and a collection of Thackeray's letters, published within late years in "Scribner's," shows the master in his most lovable moods; and yet one feels pained in seeing lines which were penned to give pleasure to one sympathetic soul scattered broadcast to gratify what is after all a more or less idle curiosity on the part of people, whose life and mode of thought are far removed from the feelings which dictated the original letters. Lord Byron's letters contain very little beyond constant appeals for money to his publisher, Murray; Berlioz, that brilliant firebrand, fights all his battles over again in his Memoirs; Mozart's letters are as bright and harmless as those of a school boy; never reflective, discoursive or descriptive, only giving a succession of trivial facts; Liszt who was eminently "all things to all men" (and women), presents a glittering kaleidoscope of every brilliant and noble emotional quality in his letters—but then, Liszt would have been a great man even if he had never seen a piano; he was cast in a great mould; many other celebrities have feet of clay, which sooner or later are discovered. Ehrlich's Memoirs, which have lately come out, show the anticipations of the youth, but lack the healthy realization of riper years and the subsequent happy resignation of old age. It seems difficult to understand why they were ever published, for surely the subject is not one of paramount interest to the musical world. A bitter tongue and pointed pen made Ehrlich a feared critic for many years; he was a brilliant writer, and the most influential German papers were glad to publish his articles; the Rosenthal imbroglio at last deposed him; the man is characterized by his futile claim to have written Liszt's Second Rhapsody; he might just as well have claimed the entire fifteen while he was about it.

I have found a plausible explanation and a "*raison d'être*" for the appearance of Ehrlich's Memoirs in the possible desire of the author, to emulate the example of Mephistopheles in "Faust," and make his exit, leaving a sulphurous smell behind him. It is the hardest thing for superannuated celebrities to appreciate the fact that they are back numbers, and not likely to be "called out" again.

Musical criticism in Europe is much on the same lines; the young and healthy blood which pulsates in this country is totally wanting there; the same lot of old fossils write for the papers of to-day in Berlin, who already performed similar service twenty-five and thirty years ago; men who have made a bed of Procrusteus on which the artist is laid: if he is too short to suit their preconceived notions he is stretched to fit the last, and if he is too long, his limbs are chopped off accordingly. To suit them a regulation program must be played in a regulation manner; what they call playing "in the spirit of the composer" is like the plaintive wail of the feeble-minded idiot, who continually drivels about the "good old times." They share, however, with many of our American critics the rare gift of second-sight—a kind of analogous prophecy, which enables them to simply look in at the door of a concert hall, so as to satisfy themselves that the concert is really taking place (thus avoiding a possible scoop), then leave, and yet write a complete and extensive critical review of the entire concert; the fact that an important program, carefully prepared and artistically performed imposes upon them a certain obligation, does not impress them at all; they are assigned perhaps three concerts on the same evening, and it is so much easier to reprint the ready-made notices sent in by music schools; for my part, I cheerfully resign all hope of publicity if procured in that way; a critic does me no favor by attending my concerts; if he cannot hear my programs which are always made up with a view to artistic unity in their entirety he is respectfully, politely and firmly invited and requested to remain away.

The best proof of my former assertion is found in the extreme paucity of the make-up of European programs; new works are but rarely heard, and there is more new music of value performed in America in one season than in Europe in five; the artist here finds encouragement from the public and critic.

There is an excuse for letters and reminiscences when they deal with actual events of importance, such as Captain Cook's letters and Chamisso's delightful record of his trip around the world at the beginning of this century on the Russian sailing vessel Rurik: in many other cases again one wishes that Cook's untimely fate had befallen the historian before he had time to jot down his alleged experiences. A melancholy interest attaches to some letters of Lenau, the Austrian poet, who also wrote the inevitable poem on Niagara Falls while in this country; but it is hard to see what purpose is served by the publication of the Wagner-Liszt letters, or the notoriously inaccurate book by Prager on "Wagner as I thought I knew him."

Mendelssohn's letters make perfectly safe literature for young ladies' seminaries; after reading a couple of them the average man feels like going out into the back yard and swearing a blue streak, just by way of contrast; they were evidently written for publication. Chopin's letters are singular exhibitions of a somewhat weak and vacillating character, and yet when the vital point, money, is reached, he is very positive and resorts to all sorts of subterfuges to sell his Tarantelle to that old Jew, Schlesinger (as he designates him), before the German edition by Whistling comes out and reaches France; the only genuinely felt letters are those to his teacher Elsner. Schumann's letters give very little idea of the man who could pen the Concerto in A minor and set to music Chamisso's Frauenliebe and Leben. A record of one's life must note some achievement, some positive attainment; it is not sufficient to, like the late Bettina Walker, dawdle around a man like Henselt and then write a book; such books and others of the same sort are misleading in their very title, and are invariably made up of silly gush, containing absolutely nothing of value to the student, for whose edification they claim to have been especially produced.

Eminently exceptional in character and importance are the collections of the letters of Moltke and Motley. The great warrior shows himself the tenderest of husbands and wisest of counsellors in his home communications, and Motley's letters furnish an epitome of contemporaneous inside history not accessible within official blue-books.

It is really doubtful whether anyone ever succeeds in really knowing anyone else; most everybody is a "poseur;" perchance the "valet de chambre" enjoys unusual advantages in getting nearer the real man, when this aforesaid man hunts for a lost collar button, or happens to bite his tongue; some people have even succeeded in cheating not only others, but also themselves, and live in an incense laden atmosphere of their own imagery, which is never dispelled by one healthy puff of wind from the outer world; it is, therefore of very doubtful value to read the letters and memoirs of the departed great, for you can never know whether you are really getting at the man you are after; and then as to letters, it used to be an event in former decades to either write or receive a letter; this was of course before the days of the penny-post and two cent letter postage; before the invention of the envelope or blotter; at that delightful rococo period a letter was very circumstantially composed and prepared; the address and title of the addressee and the humble subscription of the sender at the finish were matters of ceremony and great concern; the ink was dried with fine sand and the letter folded with mathematical correctness, to be finally entrusted to the mail coach. How different now, when between the "Dear Sir, Your favor of so-and-so duly rec'd." and the "Yrs. Truly" there is only the baldest business matter, laconically expressed;

with the invasion of the barbarous (but delightfully inexpensive) postal card the art of letter writing met a sudden and shocking death.

The most divergent opinions are expressed about the artistic standing of the late Mr. Gottschalk; his compositions present a curious mingling of bright ideas and crude, often even amateurish treatment; his playing undoubtedly created a furore; Mr. Duvivier is positive that not even Litolff approached Gottschalk's magnificent performance of Weber's Concertstueck; Mr. Chas. Kunkel assures me that Gottschalk had all the classics at his fingers ends, and simply did not play them because he did not choose to, and when I discuss the matter with Mr. W. S. B. Mathews and tell him that Gottschalk undoubtedly did play Beethoven and Weber in France successfully for years before he came to America, Mr. Mathews expresses views anything but optimistic in regard to the possible and probable Beethoven-playing in France at that remote period; now I repose a great deal of confidence in Kunkel's judgment pertaining to matters pianistic, and also respect Mathews' experienced views; hence my dilemma. Some time ago I borrowed from a friend Gottschalk's "Notes of a Pianist" compiled from his diaries by his sister and published after his untimely death in Rio in 1869; in accordance with the common usage and unwritten law which makes the return of an umbrella a criminal offense and forbids the return of borrowed books and music, either at all, or at least makes it incumbent to return them in as dilapidated and damaged condition as possible, I have so far appropriated it; perchance after the covers and half the leaves are gone my friend may see his book again; some people build up a valuable library in that way; impecunious pianists are fond of racing all over town trying to borrow the score and orchestra parts of concertos; there are enough different orchestra parts missing from my collection of concerto scores to make a new concerto; it is best to refer that gentry to the circulating library; rather a delicate point came up in our city some years ago, when a pianist played a concerto but refused to furnish score and orchestra parts; the impressario fumed and chafed and claimed that it was none of his business to furnish sheet music, but he finally gave in, ordered the parts from Schirmer and paid for them, thus establishing a new precedent.

A perusal of Mr. Gottschalk's book revealed much of interest. He was bright, witty and observing; evidently a man of the world and of affairs; well posted and of that sort of general cosmopolitan culture which only extensive travel can give; the notes are jotted down on the spur of the moment and without any pretentionsas to depth or literary finish, and hardly furnish a fair criterion of the man; yet they present interesting pen pictures of musical life in this country and South America at the period which preceded the present reign of the musical fad.

[TO BE CONTINUED.]

EMIL LIEBLING.

BEETHOVEN'S SPIRIT-BIRTH.

Beethoven in a letter to the Archduke Rudolph summed up his views of his art and what he hoped to accomplish thus: "There is nothing higher than to approach nearer to the Deity than other men, and from such proximity to spread the rays of the Deity among the human race."

Knell-like, the minster clock, with measured stroke,
  Tolled out its requiem in the pillared nave;
The wedded gloom and silence, startled, broke
  In echoes, as from sculptured lips, that gave
The quickened soul a spirit-hush profound.
  A yearning awe, yet shrinking sense of dread;
The vaulted roof grew vocal with a sound
  Divine, and voices, oft repeating, said:—
"Pray, pray!"

Bowed in the organ loft, with humbled pride
  The master prayed for grander, nobler art,
A power of song to lift man on the tide
  Of thought to God, a strain to soothe the heart
In grief and woe, a pæan glad with hope
  'Mid toil of strife, a cadence-help for will
To sift from deed its dross of wrong and cope
  With all that makes resolve the sport of ill.
He prayed:—

"Too long my hands, with erring touch, have strayed
  To call the ripple of a pleasing tune
From keys that, struck with apter skill, had made
  A harmony of soulful worth, a rune
Of mystery supreme, till then unknown;
  And I, who seek the true in tuneful sound,
Deaf to its latent power and noblest tone,
  Have ever waked a siren-song, but found,
No truth.

"Break, Heavenly Father, break the clogging ties
Of selfish aims and cares: in sympathy
I'd share earth's every smile and tear, and rise
Nearer than mortal e'er aspired to Thee;
To all, sink they in age or strive in youth,
I'd be song-herald of a faultless ken,
Make mine ear visual in perceiving truth,
And music but a prophet-voice to men,
Through me."

Mute now the suppliant lips: the minster bell
Again its message brought from heaven to earth,
Pealed joyous, as with welcome words to tell
Of hope for art: the moment marked the birth
Of praise sublime, whose measures thrilled the ear
With strains no master's mind had ever dreamed
Or hand had raised: the soul of song was near
The loft of prayer, and self-revealing seemed.
It said:

"Search thine own mind, and what thou findest best
Give to the list'ning world,—a hymn from God:
Probe thine own heart,— the sense-bound will be blessed,
Can they its fulness drink, as withered sod
Drinks nature's dew: thine ear attuned, to thee
Earth's meanest sound shall be a song, unheard
Of men: for all with God is harmony,
And thou, interpreting, shall speak His Word,—
In melody."

The founts of feeling broke, and, welling strong,
Flooded the night with music rich and pure,
And filled the gloom-wrapt church with waves of song
That might an erring heart to heaven allure.
Scarce on the keys the master's eyes were bent,
But, yielding to a passion's checkless sway,
The facile hands, with touch by instinct lent,
Gave thought to sound and soul to cadence' play,—
In praise.

The music flowed,—the language of a life
  That fought and fainted, suffered, sorrowed, strove,
Of fate complained, yet clung to pleasures rife
  With heart-aches and regrets, till trust and love
A better aim and ampler wisdom taught.
  Despair in broken notes wailed out its groan
Of pain, and pity sobbed in accents fraught
  With woe, till faith pealed forth its clarion tone,—
In hope.

From charms of sin to duty's staid delight,
  From human wishes to the infinite will,
From depths of sordid sense to sapient light,
  From bootless rage to reason's "Peace, be still,"
Grander and grander swept the anthem-peal,—
  The world a book and life an open scroll
For men to read in music's new ideal,
  Whose swelling chords were pulse-beats of the soul,—
With God.

Long rose the strains, now plaintive, now austere,
  In rhythmic flow—the tribute of a heart,
Incense at worship's shrine to heaven more dear
Than words of praise devoid of soulful art:
  The laden air was quick with holy thought,
And, born of sound, a sacred spirit crept
  To feeling's source and transformation wrought.
The master, song-rapt, bowed his head and wept,
Then spake:

"My first delight forgot,—a boyish dream
  To please the ear with cymbals' tinkling call,
Religion hence shall be my constant theme:
  My task, to strengthen, lift and chasten all.
O ye, who feel affliction's crushing might,
  Who sink, with faith renounced, 'neath sorrow's rod,
Who grope in prayer and blindly seek for light,
  To you I give my song, my word from God,
For evermore."

FREDERICK W. MORTON.

THE "OLD ITALIAN METHOD."

THE immediate reason for this article is a question propounded at the office of this magazine, in substance, this: "Was there an old Italian method of voice culture, a scientific system of teaching singers in Italy in the old days, administered with more knowledge of the subject than is possessed in our day?" Now, the card of every second singing teacher you meet bears the legend "Italian method;" or, as a higher recommendation, "Old Italian method;" or to put orthodoxy beyond all possible cavil, "Pure old Italian Method!" But it is remarkable that while so many are professing to teach the old Italian method there should be so much inquiry as to what this method is. The correspondent of this magazine puts it thus: "I have had a great many lessons in voice culture from a private teacher professedly in accordance with the old Italian method. I am now in a position where I think I can do some good in imparting this instruction to others, *but I know nothing of the principles of this method*, as such." (The italics are ours.)

Italian voice culture in the olden times,—the epoch which has been considered the golden age of song,—was something like the making of violins by the Cremona group of makers. It is not likely that the ancients had, for either violins or voices, any science reducible to figures or exact phraseology, which we do not possess to-day; but they had the right conditions under which to work, the right material and the knack of putting things together. The result therefore was something which plays about the imagination of our epoch, and leads many to feel as though voice culture, like violin making in these later days, were a lost art.

To use a homely illustration: We men of to-day, in certain unpardonable moods, are sometimes known to harass those angels of the household who make our homes for us, with dyspeptic comments upon their efforts to give us what we want to eat; and we say, "Now, mother used to do this a great deal better. I wish you could only make things taste as she used to!" Such comments are usually very unphilosophical. We fail to take into account a multitude of circumstances which make such comparisons odious and generally unjust. Without disparaging mother at all, her efforts to please us were at a time when we were much less difficult to please than at present. Very likely what is offered us to-day is put together with as much knowledge of the culinary art as mother had; but we do not bring to bear upon it the youthful zest, sharpened by the vigorous exercise of yore. But however this may be, every one knows that cookery is not a lost art. Some of the violins made to-day when they are as old as those of Stradivarius will probably be as good; and voice culture—well, let us see.

There are many reasons why the imagination lingers upon the olden times, and paints the achievements of the singers and teachers of a century or two ago, in more glowing colors than it is willing to devote to their successors of to-day. In the first place, distance lends enchantment. Whatever was excellent in the past suffers no diminution as years roll by. The age from which come such glowing accounts of vocal achievements,—the time of Farinelli, Caffarelli and Grizziello, was an impressionable one. Possibly the achievements of these artists if brought under the cold judgment of the 19th century would shrink somewhat, or, at least, would not seem evidence of extraordinary teaching.

In those old times there was no such eager and impatient throng of contestants for musical honors as there is to day. Decided talent was conspicuous; it readily found a patron in royalty, nobility or the church, and was enabled to pursue the paths of development without jostling or disturbance from a crowd of competitors of small possibilities. If there were fewer failures in those days than in ours, it was partly for the reason that fewer undertook to achieve distinction as singers, who through lack of natural gifts were foreordained to failure. They took it easy, and waited upon natural development without experimenting for means to accelerate it beyond what was reasonable. Many of the great singers of those days were designed for the profession of singing from childhood, and devoted their lives to it, achieving fame at middle age. How seldom can that be said to-day. Very many of our prominent singers have first attempted to follow other careers; but on finding that they had voices, and thinking there was "money in them," they put themselves under hot-house development and prepared for professional work, devoting to this preparation an amount of time which would have been considered entirely inadequate in those old days. The fact that these singers succeed as well as they do speaks well for modern methods.

The musical compositions and the ideals of the former epoch were very different, and much more favorable to voices than those of to-day. What those singers of old were set to practice was not impassioned declamation, intense climax, and such tones as are required by the highly wrought dramatic music of our day; but in place of this what was expected of them was lightness and agility in their work. Now, the person who practices exclusively scales, runs and trill, for eight or ten years, and who uses for this purpose mostly the high, light register, (for men used to employ the falsetto in those days almost as freely as a contralto does middle register), is sure not to strain the voice at any time, and is certain to develop it in a free, flexible, graceful form, which in time will give it every possible charm.

These old singers were at no time obliged to sing with an overpowering accompaniment. Even in the later days of old Italian song, the orchestras which accompanied it were of the kind contemptuously referred to by Wagner as "big guitars."

Let the reader therefore who would get a just view of this subject note the enormous difference in the circumstances surrounding the singers of old Italian times and our own. The ancients took time for development, and worked under conditions which allowed of no forcing of the voice; whereas the moderns, at least those who sing in what are called the highest styles of vocal music, cannot attain pre-eminence unless they can sing above the enormous modern orchestra, employed by later composers. Then, in spite of increased demands upon physical resource, they are restless during the period of training, and unwilling to give more than half the time which the ancients thought necessary. That we have any good singers to-day is, as was said above, an eloquent tribute to the excellence of modern singing methods. That we have many failures is due not so much to methods less scientific than those of the ancients, as to the modern conditions which surround our singers.

The first work on voice culture which is still extant was one by Pierfrancesco Tosi, which was published in the early part of the 18th century. It was written at the time when the Porpora school was at the zenith of its glory. The title of the book is "Observations upon Florid Song," the term florid song describing what all singing students aimed at in those days, in order to attain eminence as soloists. The great operatic artist of Porpora's day was one who could invent *fioriture* by the page, and who could improvise new trills, chirps, twitters, cadenzas and vocal gymnastics of every conceivable sort, both landish and outlandish, every time he sang his melodies before the public. This sort of thing crept even into church music. Even solemn old Bach who, like all the world of that day acknowledged the leadership of the Italians in the matter of vocal music, manages to put some runs and other vocal quirks into his cantatas, where in the opinion of some they sound awkward and out of place enough. Handel was more successful with this sort of thing, and paid his tribute to Italian supremacy and the florid mode of the day by inventing the "Handelian run", which is an absurd thing from the point of view of genuine expressiveness, but which we accept with pleasure as a convention. A modern composer who should employ the florid style in an oratorio would be laughed at. That part of the "old Italian method" is dead as a door nail. Singers who sing the old operas, however, must practice in this style, and may consider that for such part of their work they are using the "old Italian method." But pupils, who study for the later day concert, church and drawing room singing are not likely to have much to do with the elements which differentiate the old Italian school from the teaching of to-day, however much they may be assured of antique orthodoxy, by teachers who find "old Italian method" a good term to conjure with.

If there were any special science current in those times it certainly would have cropped out in Tosi's work: or, if not there, in the next important work on voice culture, that by Mancini, published fifty years later. But the most scientific thing in either work is of about this grade: "Let the pupil stand erect in any easy attitude; let the mouth be opened neither too widely nor too little; let the tone come freely out of the mouth."

The great thing in voice culture, the *messa di voce*, or the "placing of the voice," as the current term is among singers of to-day, was doubtless understood by a larger proportion of the teachers of antiquity than of the vocal professors to-day. But those who understand it to-day probably understand it fully as well as the best of the ancients. During the last fifty years the instrumentalists have held an ascendancy over the vocalists, exerting a preponderating influence in the musical domain. The result of this has been unfavorable to singers in several respects. Pitch was greatly raised that instruments might sound more brilliant, and this regardless of the fact that the human voice has limits. The orchestra has been greatly enlarged by composers like Wagner, who believe that finer artistic delineations are attainable with instruments than with voices, and who have no interest in the voice except as a machine for speaking words to interpret the efforts at expression confided principally to the orchestra. These composers offer no inducement to singers to cultivate anything but robustness, just audibility. Under these and other modern requirements for supernatural vocal attainments, everything has been ransacked that might give proficiency to voice culture. This has led to all sorts of scientific or pseudo scientific experiments, theories and discussions, which have distracted attention from the fundamental principle of *messa di voce*, and have led many modern teachers to wander in the wilderness. As an illustration of this point, the venerable Manuel Garcia, inventor of the laryngoscope, which gave such an impetus to these scientific discussions, now says that nothing of value to voice training has come from his invention. We have however at present arrived at an epoch where, theories and new fangled ideas having been pretty well exploded, there is a perceptible return to those simple fundamental principles of voice training, which might perhaps be called the old Italian method, if one preferred that term, but which the old Italians themselves considered such self evident matters that they made no claims concerning them. And should Porpora revisit the musical world to-day he would probably be very much surprised at hearing the principle of *messa di voce* referred to as an especial possession of his time. "Oh ye degenerate moderns" is one of Tosi's remarks to his contemporaries, in which he shows that they did not consider themselves to be the custodians of any great arcana of voice. *Messa di voce*, or in other words the placing of the voice, the resonating of the voice, finding the sounding board for the voice, holding the tone forward, bringing the tone to a focus, etc., although really a simple matter, is a subtle thing to grasp. The definition in the dictionaries, "the swelling of a tone," shows that it is not commonly understood. But when one has mastered this principle, he has nine-tenths of the whole subject of voice culture; and whether he call it "Italian method," or the "natural method" or "A's method," or whatever, it is like the spelling of Mr. Weller's name "according to the taste and fancy of the speller." Most of the best teachers of to-day make no use of the term "old Italian method." Their view of the subject would be expressed in the words of a professor in the Milan Conservatory, a lady who teaches in the apartment formerly occupied by Lamperti, and where as she says the traditions have been unbroken and unmodified for nearly a century: speaking of the method employed she said "it is very simple, *very* simple."

FREDERICK W. ROOT.

Chicago.

SHOULD THE FUGUE AND THE SONATA-FORM BE THE REQUIREMENT FOR ADMISSION TO THE COMPOSER'S CLASS OF A MANUSCRIPT SOCIETY?

THE object of a manuscript society is, in general terms, the advancement of musical composition *in all forms*. In order to accomplish any good work, such a society must exclude the musical rabble, those parasites whose inferior musicianship delays the advancement of music, and who resort to the most unprofessional tactics for the purpose of transferring the money of the musically ignorant to their own pockets. It is evident then that the standard of musicianship must be made high, particularly in the case of the composer's class. The question that presents itself is, how to preserve a high standard without becoming pedantic. The usual solution is to require the submission on the part of the candidate for admission to the composer's class (for it is of the composer's class that I shall speak in this article) of a composition in the form of a fugue or containing a fugue, or in the sonata-form, the acceptance of which entitles him to admission. In my opinion this solution fails to solve, because it is too narrow and restricting. The fugue, in the hands of the ordinarily gifted musician is a mere mass of technique, and the sonata a series of platitudes repeated through three or four movements. That these forms are most difficult to write in, is shown by the fact that only a few musicians, in all time, have succeeded in saying anything vital and original in them. And while the fugue seems to be outworn, the sonata remains as the form in which the most glorious instrumental music has been written. It is because the sonata form is so vast, that I would not have it tampered with. A bad song or a bad nocturne may be laughable, or even annoying; a bad sonata seems like a desecration. The acceptance of the fugue and sonata-form criterion would naturally result in the production of many bad, or at any rate unique sonatas, the only merit of which would be the negative one of being written in that broad, massive form.

A modern poet is not required to write in strict classic forms, in order to be recognized as a poet. If he is lyrical he is not expected to be dramatic, and if he is dramatic he is not forced to be lyrical. Like the rest of modern workers, the poet is apt to become a specialist, and to write in those forms for which his individuality is best suited. Let us imagine, nevertheless, a society of poets the condition of membership to which was the ability to write either a sonnet, or a tragedy in blank verse. A sonnet is a poem of fourteen lines, written in iambic pentameter. It is usually divided into two parts an octave (eight lines) and a sextette (six lines). The rhymes in the octave are two, one for the first, fourth, fifth and eighth lines, the other for the second, third, sixth and seventh lines. In the sextette the rhymes are three, the first for the ninth and twelfth, the second for the tenth and thirteenth, and the third for the eleventh and fourteenth lines. The poet who wishes to write a sonnet must, therefore, arrange words of different lengths (monosyllables, dissyllables, trisyllables, etc.,) so that each foot shall contain an unaccented syllable followed by an accented one, and so that his lines shall be five feet long; he must fulfill the prescribed form for rhyme; he must arrange the series of thoughts which he wishes to express, so that it may be contained in fourteen lines. "Here Shakespeare hung his verse Orlando-wise," and Wordsworth, Keats and even Heine the unaccountable, have written superb poems in this form. But woe to the wight who attempts by its aid to climb to the company of the great. They are masters of the form, he its slave.

The tragedy in blank verse is, perhaps, the broadest of poetic forms. To write in it a poet must not only possess great technique and knowledge, but he must also be thoroughly human. Life in its complexity, with its stirring events and its brilliant coloring, its passions and its miseries, is his theme. Jews, Christians, honest men, thieves, virtuous women, courtesans, heroes, cowards, drunkards, vagabonds, all sorts and conditions of men are at his disposal. He is no longer subjective; he is objective. His story unfolds itself before our very eyes, we see his men and women, we hear them talk, and we are convinced. But oh! how great an intellect he must possess to handle materials so vast; how human he must be to depict without exaggeration characters so different; how poetic he must be to select the useful from the useless, to weld all together, and to make of the whole an art-work. A society requiring of its members the ability to compose in one of these forms would surely be exclusive enough. Nor could we find fault with the standards adopted on the ground that they were not sufficiently high. The society would have many traditions and few members, and its influence would be (as a society) almost nothing. Or, if the ability to compose in one of these forms were sufficient, and the quality of the work not taken into consideration, the society would be composed of pedants not poets; literary schoolmasters who care more for the form than for the truth which it contains; fogies of classicism.

The fugue is incomparably more strict than the sonnet. One must write a stiff, unmelodious theme, (in the language of the text-books a theme capable of contrapuntal treatment) answer it in the fifth above or the fourth below, thump it out over a pedal point, jumble it up in the stretto, and all the rest of it. As exercises in counterpoint the thousand and one fugues written every year are admirable. As art works their value is very slight. Vocal fugues are usually more interesting than instrumental ones because the voices involuntarily lend them beauty and grace. But of all fugues (perhaps I should say all instrumental fugues) ever written, what remains to-day? The work of two Bachs, Handel, Mendelssohn, and a few others. And they remain, not because they are fugues, but because even into that form the composers have succeeded in instilling vitality, sincerity and vigor. Bach shows through them his simple, earnest, smiling face; Handel appears in his wig and court-clothes; and Mendelssohn's sensitiveness and unerring taste are again made present to us.

The principal difference between the American sonata and the American fugue is, (it might be cynically said) that the American fugue never tires the hearer for more than ten minutes at a stretch, while the American sonata being a more "sustained flight," is able to tire for forty-five minutes consecutively. To this sweeping statement there are shining exceptions, such as Gilchrist, Chadwick and Mac Dowell.

Any musician can write a sonata. All that is necessary is a little knowledge of counterpoint and form, a copy of Beethoven's sonatas, (Von Bulow edition) and pen, ink and paper. The recipe is simple. Model all the themes after Beethoven; when you come to the free fantasia part stick still to Beethoven; for the rest of the sonata stick closer than ever to Beethoven. The result will certainly be a sonata, the highest form of instrumental composition, a work admitting you to the composer's class of a manuscript society. But will it have either vitality or originality?

What, then, can be accepted as a standard of manuscript necessary for admission to the composer's class? Simply stated, the ability to compose in more than one form (either small or large according to the composer's talent) compositions which are not only correct harmonically and contrapuntally but which are original and meritorious. Is not a a good nocturne better than a bad sonata, and a clever song better than a poor fugue? Is there not more real musicianship shown in the composition of the former than in the construction of the latter? And while most musicians regard the sonata-form as the highest of instrumental forms, and desire to compose in it, there are some (particularly the younger men) who, from modesty, refrain from writing in it. They know that a composition in this form must stand comparison with the works of the greatest writers.

By what criterion can we separate that in music which

is deep, true and lasting, from that which is merely technical, fashionable, or academic? How find a measure by which to judge the merits of a composition, regardless of tradition and of school? By what course of reasoning do we accept Bach, Beethoven and Schumann as great, and reject the claims of Dussek, Kalkbrenner and Herz? These are questions which continually recur to the minds of thinking musicians. To answer them practically is their ceaseless endeavor. Music, as well as other strivings after the beautiful, must be in accordance with natural laws. Time, the great and just judge, rewards conformity to them with eternal life, punishes sins against them by oblivion. "The wages of sin," in music as well as in life, "is death." But, perhaps, of all men, who, looking backward into Time's face, have attempted to formulate these laws, John Addington Symonds has succeeded the best. He says, (and with his great words I shall end this article): "Our hope with regard to the unity of taste in the future then is, that all sentimental or academical seekings after the ideal having been abandoned, momentary theories founded upon idiosyncratic or temporary partialities exploded, and nothing accepted but what is solid and positive, the scientific spirit shall make men progressively more and more conscious of these *bleibende Verhältnisse*,* more and more capable of living in the whole; also, that in proportion as we gain a firmer hold upon our place in the world, we shall come to comprehend with more instinctive certitude what is simple, natural and honest, welcoming with gladness all artistic productions that exhibit these qualities. The perception of the enlightened man will then be the task of a healthy person who has made himself acquainted with the laws of evolution in art and in society, and is able to test the excellence of work in any stage from immaturity to decadence by discerning what there is of truth, sincerity and natural vigor in it."

*Almost untranslatable; perhaps "lasting fixed relations" comes nearest in English.

NICHOLAS DOUTY.

NOTES OF A SUMMER TOUR.

(CONCLUDED.)

OUR next undertaking was one of those which read so innocently in Baedecker, and you do not realize until afterwards what a deal of reading between the lines one ought to do in order to take it at its full value. It was nothing less than going to Aosta, and so up to Zermatt over the Theodule pass, between Monte Rosa and the Matterhorn. This is gently recorded in Baedecker as a matter of about five hours up and about the same down, and I had proposed to divide it by staying at the top over night. But things turned out differently, as will appear.

From Courmayer we took carriage to Aosta, down the beautiful valley of the same name. This was one of the most delightful drives of the trip. It was all the way down hill, the descent being two thousand feet in twenty-one miles. The road was excellent, and the team, for a wonder, was likewise, and we took the trip in a smart trot, with little interruption. Old castles, and queer old Italian villages were the features, with inspiring views of Mt. Blanc in the background, and other peaks in various directions made up a romantic landscape, or a series of them, all that bright summer afternoon. At Aosta we took train a few miles to Chatillon, where we stayed all night. This was our first point of departure for Zermatt. Chatillon lies (perhaps sits would be a better word) at an elevation of 1800 feet. From here by carriage to Val Tournache there is an ascent of three thousand feet, which means walk the horses all the way. But the valley is very romantic and grand, and the drive was memorable. At Val Tournache, pause for dinner. Here the guide engaged at Chatillon appears, with the two mules ordered for the ladies and the other baggages. Then an afternoon trip of three hours for

Breuil, where the walk over the Theodule properly begins.

was a most delightful if arduous walk up the valley. The scenery becomes grander and grander. Presently the Matterhorn appears towering before us, and remains our landmark all the way and all the next morning, as will appear. It was a succession of waterfalls, romantic gorges, and the like, and at length a desolate valley and the hotel of Breuil, situated at the base of the hill leading up to the Theodule. It is a good hotel, and we had a dinner and a comfortable night—what there was of it. For it was here that our trouble began. Upon asking the guide at what hour we ought to start, he sweetly remarked that we would be called at 3 A. M., have breakfast at 3.30 and set out at 4, meaning to get over the glacier before the sun had softened the snow. And this we did. The calling was trying; the breakfast was one of those things more honored in the breach than in the observance, and in the cold morning dusk, an hour or more before sunrise, we made our start.

Two of the ladies rode, the guide walking ahead with one of the packages. Two girls led the mules, which were to be left at the beginning of the glacier. There was also a porter to carry the baggage over the glacier and down to Zermatt. Thus with the two pedestrians there was quite a cavalcade, but there was nothing to see for an hour, nearly, and it took all the attention of the laboring pedestrians to get their breath and keep the path. Breuil is at an elevation of nearly seven thousand feet (6880) and we had in view the pass at an elevation of 10,900, the highest point we reached. It was a very difficult walk, but as soon as light began the view was most inspiring and repaying. Down the Italian side were the lower snow peaks of the Monte Rosa range; past the Matterhorn, and far away south were other notable peaks. Meanwhile in front of us, a little to the left was the great Matterhorn, which from this side appears very different from what it does at Zermatt, the whole lower part of it being visible as well as the conical peak. This also appears much larger from the Italian side, but the mountain seems equally inaccessible from this side. I could understand many things in Tyndall's account of his reconnoitering the mountain from this side, which before I had not realized at their full force. And so we toiled on. At length after about three hours and a half we reached the glacier, where the novel experience began. The promised overshoes of yarn were not forth-coming for rendering some of the passengers more sure footed upon the ice, and so we all went on as we were. The Theodule glacier of this side is very hard in the morning, there are few or no crevasses upon this side. But the hour and a half of crossing it involves also much going up hill, and this, with the elevation and the care needed for keeping footing upon the ice, made the passage trying.

At length we reached the dismal little hotel at the summit. Coming off the glacier there is nothing in sight but the pillar which marks the boundary between Italy and Switzerland, but around a little turn in the path we find a one story building of stones laid up closely without mortar, and in it a hotel which Baedeker credits with fourteen beds —though I do not see where they could be placed. It was very cold and dismal, and almost immediately there came up a storm from the Italian side, and a cold mist blew across the pass and made life miserable for everyone. The food obtainable here was very bad, but they built us a fire in the dining room—an attention which I appreciated the more from the fact that there is no way of getting wood here except by bringing it on men's shoulders across an hour and a half of ice, after it has come upon mules' shoulders some distance further. Fortunately the snow storm was short, and we were presently upon the road down.

This was a more serious matter. All the way up, and especially after we had found the glacier upon the Italian side so free from danger, we had imagined that the guide had been bluffing us by bringing a needless rope, as if we were going upon a serious glacier expedition. Nor was this suspicion diminished when he began solemnly to lay out his rope in the narrow passage way of the hotel at the pass, making a great loop once in every nine feet. The he placed us in an order pleasing to himself, the loop of the rope being drawn tightly around the waist of each passenger in succession, the rear being brought up a by new addition, a porter returning to Zermatt, from whom the guide had borrowed another rope, affording its owner the additional safety of its aid. But well roped together, eight of us in all, we made our way gingerly down the steep rocks to the Theodule glacier which comes down towards Zermatt. This was a very different matter. The hour was now about nine A. M. The snow upon the surface of the glacier was soft, and the crevasses were frequent and awkward. Hence long detours, and occasional jumping across ugly gaps, from which the rope would save the unfortunate who might miss his footing.

It was hard upon the shoes of the ladies, and we had more than an hour and a half of it. Then we emerged upon the lateral morraine, which here is composed of boulders of all sizes, with scarcely anything smaller than a paving stone among the mass. Hence very disagreeable walking for another hour. Then we came out upon ledges worn smooth by glaciers, and varied the proceeding by skipping across glacier torrents which now were at full head. Occasionally a bridge was missing or overflowed, and more wet feet were in point. Then at last the welcome pastures.

All this time the view had not been up to expectation. While the actual storm had passed away, there were still clouds which hung upon the mountains at an elevation of about 12,000 feet, cutting off all the higher peaks. Hence there was little of the Breithorn to be seen, and none at all of Monta Rosa. But down in the valley there was beautiful sunshine, and along both sides of it there were the splendid peaks which stand like great sentinels on either hand, the White horn being the main feature upon the left. It was a great view, especially in the matter of ice. The two glaciers which had cost us a good three hours merely to walk across were mere bagatelles beside the vast fields of ice and snow which fill up nearly all the immediate surrounding. The vast Gorner glacier, which takes all the snow drainage of Monta Rosa from this side, was of course the main feature, covering an area of more than twenty square miles.

And how Zermatt receded! The trip down, which I had expected to be able to do in three hours or such matter, lengthened to about five hours, and a more tired lot of passengers than those who straggled into the hotel Monta Rosa in Zermatt that afternoon, at about 1:40, I am sure rarely reaches that home of the ambitious and the expert. We had been upon the road since four A. M., and after the usual continental breakfast of bread and coffee, with merest pretense of a lunch at the top we had done about nine hours of as hard work as I ever did, or want to do. Restoratives were in order, and the ladies, all of whom had walked at least six hours of the way, and one all the way, were too tired to eat.

After the Theodule we rested. And we saw the sights of Zermatt, which were worth while. But a day later the fit took us to carry out our original intention of walking up to the Gorner Grat, a rocky ridge which rises to a height of 10,200 feet near Monta Rosa, about an hour and a half from the Riffle hotel. This is a very serious walk of four hours or so, involving about 4,000 feet vertical. The path is very good, and the view at the end one of the most characteristic in Switzerland, for directly in front of one is Monta Rosa, only the great Gorner glacier intervening, and stretching out towards the right hand are the peaks of the same chain, including the Theodule horn, the Breit horn, and upon the extreme right the Matterhorn, which from this point of view presents the familiar outlines so often seen in pictures. The entire foreground is filled with glacier. Not alone is the head of Zermatt valley thus occupied, but so deep is the valley that from this point one is not able to see it at all. Only the snow peaks and glaciers, which bound it on either hand, make up the landscape. The day was perfectly clear, and the view everything that fancy had painted it.

The hotels at the Riffle Alp had been enlarged very much

since I was here ten years ago, and upon this occasion we found a new hotel nearly finished at the Gorner Grat, and saw surveyors busily engaged in taking levels for a railway which will be built up the mountain next year. This will form another great mountain road, the like of which now almost every important scenic point in Switzerland is provided with.

From Zermatt we went out by rail, the road down the valley to Visp being upon the combined system, in which they use the ordinary method where the grade is not too steep, but at the other places have sections of ratchet work between the rails, which engage the teeth of a cog wheel

THE MATTERHORN, FROM ZERMATT.
The Theodule pass comes over the glacier behind the ridge in the center of the picture.

upon the shaft of the locomotive. The road to Visp descends about 3,000 feet in twenty three miles, and much of the way the valley is just wide enough for the brawling tempestuous torrent of the Visp, which tears wildly down the steep descent. The space for the road is blasted out of the mountain side, and the ride although in the cars is very interesting. It is a tribute to the enterprise of the Swiss that in spite of the difficulty of getting supplies to Zermatt, the hotels there and above at the Riffle are among the best we found anywhere in Switzerland.

Our present destination was Brigue, the starting point for the Simplon, as also for the Furka and the Rhone glacier. The latter was our destination, and up the valley of the Rhone we rather leisurely drove the next day. Wilder and wilder gets the scenery, until at last one comes to the end of the valley, where the great Rhone glacier breaks over a precipice, making an ice fall of a thousand feet or more in height. Directly in front of the valley is the slope down which the road comes from the Furka pass, in long windings. And at the side is a very steep incline over which the route to the Grimsel pass goes. At the open space between the hills stands the hotel of the Rhone glacier, a fine house kept by one of the Zermatt Seilers. We visited the ice grotto in the glacier, but we did not get a satisfactory view of the upper part of the vast glacier out of which the Rhone issues.

Next day we walked over the Grimsel pass. This is not a difficult walk, inasmuch as there is now a new carriage road nearly done all the way to Meiringen. This is one of those great enterprises which the little country of Switzerland undertakes and carries out in so thorough a manner that it does not need to be done again for a century. Of this sort is the Furka road, and many other roads in this country where nature is so grand, yet for purposes of communication so inconvenient. What is commonly called the Bernese Oberland consists of a great mountain chain extending from the Furka, or more properly from the lake of Lucern, to down near the head of lake Geneva, the valley of the Rhone bounding it upon the south. From the Grimsel there is no other practicable point where a road could be carried across until the Gemmi is reached, a distance or at least fifty miles, and beyond that again there is another reach of this great mountain wall. Hence the importance of this Grimsel road. The Grimsel road is fifteen feet wide, laid out as well as a rail road, and built of macadam, with retaining walls, etc, in the most solid and finished manner. All the way up the pass it is simply the

1,800 feet of mountain side with zig-zag road. The view is not much to speak of, since there are few or no salient points or celebrated peaks within range. About an hour beyond the top we come to the Grimsel Hospice, something on the order of the Grand St. Bernard, where travellers put much or little in the box, according as conscience is rampant or quiescent. After about three hours walk down we come to Handegg, where there is a magnificent fall, and here we take the diligence for Meiringen. All the way down, the valley is charming, and we have had no finer drive than this. Interlaken is reached at about nine P. M.

Our walking the next day was also of the Mark Twain order, a carriage for Grindelwald and Lauterbrunnen being the order of its going. This being the usual caper, it is not necessary to say much about it. Since I was last here (four years ago) the railway has been finished and opened not alone to Grindelwald and Lauterbrunnen, but also up over the Wengern Alp, one of those famous scenic walks, where four years ago I found 4,000 feet vertical to be overcome for the sake of the magnificent views of the Jungfrau to be had from the top. This time I went on the other side of the valley up the inclined railway to Murren. The ascending railway is a rope affair, ascending 2,000 feet in a very short distance. There is a single cable with a car at each end. The motive power is gravity, the descending car being weighted by running water into a tank underneath. There are powerful brakes, and it is not impossible that, should the single cable break, the cogs and the grip brake might hold the car; but I confess I would rather be somewhere else at the time. And on the whole I consider this the most hair-raising ride I ever undertook. Once at the top, we take the electric railway which runs around the side of the hill to Murren, all the way either on the very edge, or so near as to make it uncomfortable. I suppose that as matter of fact the road is nowhere very near the edge. But as from Lauterbrunnen one sees plainly that the valley wall consists first of a sheer precipice of more than a thousand feet height, while above that there is still from one to two thousand feet of extremely steep hill side, along which the pines and firs dizzily balance themselves, one feels nervous. It is a remarkable trip. All the time the Jungfrau was shining in all her glory—or would have been but for the clouds which now overcast the sky, followed by rain. Murren is one of the famous scenic points, and I fancy would be well worth staying in for some days.

From Inter-laken to Lucern over the Brunig pass, which is a very easy one, only some 1,200 feet ascent—all by rail.

Lucern is more like home than any other place we have found in the country. The mountains are still high enough to look imposing, but the highest of them are lower than many of the passes we have walked over. We walked up and down the Rigi, and when at the top were still four thousand feet lower than we had been at the Theodule pass, and nearly as much lower than we had been at the Gorner Grat.

Like all good tourists we took in the organ concert at Lucern and heard various and sundry selections, in the immediate foreground being Dudley Buck's "At Evening." The organist appeared to be a sound musician of the German school, but it was to much trouble to hunt him up. Here the rain and the cold together hindered our carrying out our intentions with regard to other ascents, and when coming down the Rigi it dawned upon me that I had had enough and that home would be a better place. So from here it is a question of Strassbourg, Heidelberg, Cologne, the Rhine, and Holland, all in time to catch the Parisian out of Liverpool September 20th. And so will end vacation.

W. S. B. M.

THE HARMONIC NATURE OF MUSICAL SCALES.

IV.

(CONCLUDED.)

THIS sub-conscious harmonic sense, then, cannot be proved to have asserted itself in any of these instances, but on the contrary is conclusively disproved by the very existence of tone systems which either embody intervals showing irreconcileable disparities from the constituents of the assumed generating chord tissue, or which exhibit an entire absence of some of the most essential components of the latter. What can actually be substantiated is only this, that the selection of the octave, fifth and to some extent the major third, which together form the tonic chord, has been governed by a principle which, taken in this limited sense, might be termed a harmonic principle.

It can not be denied that in the case of the trained musician, and perhaps in a much lesser degree in the untrained in music, there exists such a harmonic sense. But is this sense a natural instinct? or has it merely been acquired in consequence of constant and invariable impressions of harmonious combinations in hearing and performing modern music? Two things appear to favor the latter view. First, it is more than improbable that a harmonic sense which is based on a structure so artificial and embodying such incongruities as our modern tone system, should have been decreed by natural law, and as such connate with human nature. And second, the very fact that this harmonic feeling has not always been manifested, and that a definite period can be assigned when it has taken its rise, forces on us the conviction that there was a time when it was not active. And when we go back to its source, we shall soon be convinced that it is not inborn in human nature, and that it has not been created from within and by an internal necessity. The nature of this process can probably be most clearly perceived in those rudimentary harmonic attempts which are met with in primitive music; for there we have an opportunity to observe the human mind in its infancy when passing through its first stages, which to history are either entirely hidden or else much obscured. And the mental laws that govern primitive races now are those that governed our remote ancestors; and by studying the former, as manifested at present, we gain a retrospective view of the early history of our own race. To this purpose let us once more briefly revert to primitive music and endeavor to find in it the key to this harmonic sense.

It may appear strange to search for the origin of the harmonic principle in tone systems when we have proved its absence. But it must be borne in mind that we have not claimed its entire absence; and in its application in the now limited sense in which we have found it active we may find the clue for which we are in search. When stating that primitive music is monophonic, we have qualified this assertion, and we may now qualify it more definitely. Monophonic music strictly speaking means melody sung in unison. Generally, however, melodies sung in octaves also are included in the term; and singing in octaves is quite as frequently met as singing in unison. When, namely, two or more voices of different compass would sing a melody simultaneously, the difference of their compass would compel one or some of them to sing the melody higher or lower than the others; and the interval almost universally chosen as the most perfect consonance was the octave. Although all peoples may be said to sing thus in octaves, they not uniformly do so. By taking a melody an octave higher than sung by the lower voice, it might again pass beyond the compass of the voice and to prevent this an interval between the extremes of the octave was necessarily resorted to; and this interval was the fifth, the most perfect consonance after the octave. Other intervals, especially the fourth, third and sixth, have in rare cases been employed; but among peoples of a low degree of civilization singing in octaves and fifths is by far the most prevalent. This will be at once conceded in the case of the octave; but perhaps not so readily in that of the fifth. In modern music consecutive fifths are, after consecutive octaves, the most obnoxious transgressions of the laws of harmony. And to this fact probably more than to their inherent offensiveness must be attributed the horror in which musicians stand of successions of perfect fifths. We shall later on see that consecutive fifths have not always been regarded with such disfavor. Here it must suffice to state that among primitive peoples successions of fifths are, to judge from their frequent use, considered very well sounding. In India, for instance, some stringed instruments have two sets of strings, a principal set and either a sympathetic or else a secondary set; the sympathetic strings having their partials,—and mainly those which correspond with the octave and fifth of the tone sounded—evoked by the vibrations of the principal strings, while the secondary strings, which are sounded simultaneously, are tuned in octaves and fifths to the latter, both yielding an effect not unlike that produced by the mixture stops of a pipe organ. Successions of fifths play also a great part among the Indo-Chinese, the Malays of the Indian Archipelagos and the Polynesians, all of which have arrived at a stage of musical development considerably removed from what we commonly term primitive music. The following fragment of a "Hymn to the Ancestors," (p. 141) quoted from Rowbotham, History of Music, vol. i, chap. 8, where it is given in full score as performed by a native Chinese orchestra, is a fair specimen of this rudimentary harmonic treatment. The series of consecutive fifths is played simultaneously on both the Kin and the Ché, which are the national instruments of the Chinese and are, according to Auriol, invariably played in fifths.

Another mode of rudimentary harmony consists in an attempt to sing or play together two melodies, which in some instances differ only slightly from each other, in others

stand in a more or less easily perceptible relation of melody and accompaniment. As a rude effort at such a polyphonic structure I quote from Crotch, "Specimens of Melodies of different Nations" the following "Song of the Indians of Norfolk Sound," the upper part being sung in octaves by a chorus of men and women, the lower by the chief.

A more advanced stage meets us in the following polyphonic attempt from Polynesia, quoted by Rowbotham from F. Wilkes, United States Exploring Expedition, vol. iii.

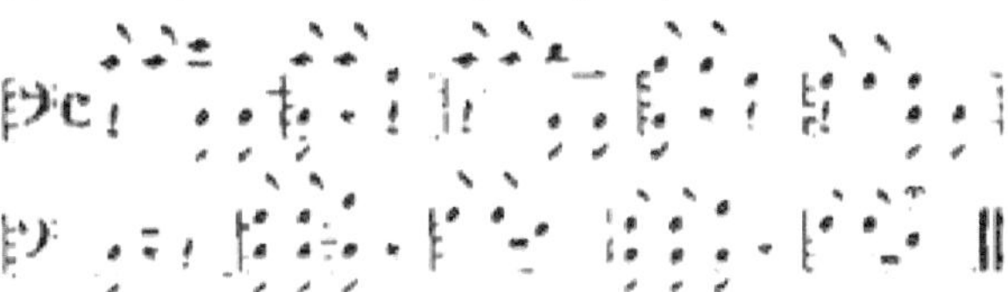

And now from these rude attempts of half-civilized peoples let us turn to the cradle of harmony in Europe. The time of its birth is the 10th century, and the following quoted from Hucbald's "Musical Enchiriadis" is the form in which we meet it.

We find here again the same mode of a harmonic accompaniment proceeding in fifths parallel with the melody. In other words, harmony in Europe commenced exactly where in Eastern Asia it left off. It was a succession of octaves, fifths and occasionally fourths (just as we find it today among some primitive races) that formed the germ from which subsequently sprung harmony.

The possibility of such an accompaniment in fifths and fourths has given rise to much contention for and against. The opponents of this theory have claimed its impossibility on the strength of the intrinsic offensiveness of consecutive perfect fifths and fourths. We have already intimated that the aversion felt towards such sequences is due less to their actual offensiveness to the ear, than to the fact that musical theory has always strictly prohibited them, not so much on account of their lack of euphony, however, as for the reason that they tend to obliterate the progression of independent parts. In other words, although a progression of fifths may be objectionable in the musical art work, yet apart from it, the sensation produced by such a succession is not accompanied by an actual feeling of pain, or even discomfort. Indeed, whoever had the opportunity to listen to such progressions must confess that they are productive merely of a sense of strangeness, owing entirely to the fact that they are heard only in exceptional cases. Yet, notwithstanding the dictates of theory, all the great masters have not hesitated to employ consecutive fifths whenever the natural flow of independent parts demanded such a progression. And it is by no means seldom to hear inexperienced singers intone a melody, which is played on an instrument, in fifths, without apparently experiencing the slightest compunction. And even singers of some experience find these progressions by no means so ugly as musicians are wont to consider them. At the Third International Concert during the Columbian Exposition I heard a chorus "l'Exile," sung by French mariners throughout in fifths, with an additional upper octave; and the effect was by no means unpleasant, and others whom I questioned found the performance strange, "but in no case, ugly." And the singers themselves must certainly have derived some gratification from it; otherwise they would not have subjected themselves to the training which the performance betrayed in other respects. Moreover, the frequent use of consecutive fifths in primitive music goes to prove that such progression must yield a certain amount of pleasure to minds which have not, like those of trained musicians, been biased by rules imposed by considerations of an entirely different nature.

Seeing therefore no reason to warrant the offensiveness of progressions in fifths, we can easily understand that these intervals should have been hit upon during the first stages of European music in precisely the same manner as that in which they found a place in primitive music, being chosen in preference to other intervals in conformity with the physical constitution of sound. And gradually we see later in Europe these series of consecutive perfect consonances pass into a series consisting of a succession of octaves, fifths and fourths in alternation; and still later we find occasionally thirds and sixths interspersed with the perfect consonances; and when these consonant intervals begin to be connected by passing notes, changing notes, etc., and thereby the parts become more independent and florid, the period of Discant and subsequently that of Polyphony are ushered in. But throughout this entire period, although we have sequences of simultaneous tones, and in this sense harmony, the character of music has remained true to its origin, the melodic motion now as before being the sole end in view. And essentially it retained this character up to the climax which polyphonic music reached in Bach; the harmonious sounding together of the voices was then not, as it is now, the end sought, but a mere by-product, or as it has aptly been stated, "consonance was not the object in view, but its opposite dissonance was avoided." Harmony, then, has been developed not for its own sake, but as an accessory attendant upon the acquirement of greater freedom of melodic motion. And from this we must infer that at a stage prior to the acquirement of this melodic freedom this so-called harmonic law was not active, and that the force which at present it asserts over the musically-trained is nothing but the force of long continued habit.

In the music of Mediæval Europe, then, as well as in

that of primitive races, we have found that the germs of harmony have not sprung into existence at the bidding of an internal harmonic sense, but conversely that they are the result of a necessity to adjust, when singing in chorus, the intonation of the melody to the compass of different voices. Harmony, therefore, owns its existence to no innate harmonic sense, and the existence of the latter is actually proven impossible by the very nature of the first harmonic efforts. For harmony first was exactly that which the theory of harmony in all its subsequent stages absolutely forbad, *e.g.* a sequence of perfect consonant intervals. And on these ground we are forced to the conclusion that the hypothesis assuming the universal presence of a subconscious harmonic principle in its wider meaning is lacking of evidence to support it, and is therefore untenable. The assumption of such a principle can only be explained as resulting from a tendency on the part of musicians to consider tone systems of other races in the light of our own, and capable of being expressed in terms of our own; and to explain deviations from it, no matter how striking, as merely a failure to intone correctly according to our notions, and that even in cases where theories, established for centuries before our own tone system had assumed its present form, give exact directions as to the precise mode of tuning scales, thereby proving beyond dispute, if such proof were needed, the existence of tone systems which resist all attempts to impose upon them even the simplest harmonic relations. All that can really be substantiated as having taken part in the selection of scale intervals is an approximately uniform and universal action of the three principles which we have distinguished, and which, co-ordinating in various modes among different races, have resulted in corresponding disparities in their tone systems; and any attempt to conceal these diversities by assuming one determinative principle to have conditioned all musical utterance, no matter how alluring in its simplicity, is useless as well as unscientifical.

JEAN MOOS.

Ripon, Wis.

A REPLY TO "A PLEA FOR CORRECT BREATHING IN SINGING."

IN the last issue of MUSIC Homer Moore fitly remarks: "It would do about as much good to turn a sick person loose in a drug store as to turn a pupil loose in a library of works on vocal culture, breathing and singing."

Unhappily, this is an incontrovertible truth. There is hardly a conceivable distortion of the respiratory organs that may not be made to look respectable to the amateur by the citation of pretty well known names. Many current writers miscall the tools they are plying. Cappiani repeated the mistake made by Haller just a century ago, in giving the diaphragm the office of compressing the lungs by its upward movement or contraction. Haller wrote that he actually saw it move up in disemboweled animals. Koffer declares that only the abdominal muscles should be contracted to support the voice, though their mightiest unaided effort can hardly support an audible whisper. Mandl argued famously from birds with no midriff to man with a powerful diaphragm; while Fournié reasoned from dogs and old horses to man, with equal acumen. A little later Merkel ridicules Mandl and displays his own pet errors. Then, still later, Duchenne accuses Galien, Vesale, Magendie and Beau and Maissait of failing to consider the state of the abdomen; while Monsieur Debrou, in the *Gazette Medicale* for 1843, declares that he performed similar experiments to those of Duchenne, with contrary results. Duchenne wrote that Beau and Maissiat did not acknowledge that the abdominal contents were the support for the contraction of the diaphragm, though no recognized authority would now dispute the fact.

We sadly see that the entire past century has been full of quarrels among the highest, or at least, the most celebrated authorities; and the inquiring pupil almost hope lessly asks, What is the safest course to pursue, the one which is the most likely to lead to knowledge of practical value?

Special authorities alone are valuable. Those who have studied this or any kindred subject will have noticed that a writer who has succeeded in one branch of science is exceedingly prone to throw out haphazard opinions on other subjects. The famous Dr. Delafield once remarked to me, as a fact of rather novel importance, that the voice was produced during expiration. Many of the physiologists who have made one branch a life-study, fail to employ the same caution in treating of other branches.

Observation of great artists is not conclusive. It might be supposed that the very highest practical artistic success would presuppose the correct, or nearly correct, employment of the respiratory agents. Have we any evidence of the mode of breathing used by the great artists of the so-called old Italian school of singers? Dr. Morell Mackenzie declares that they inflated the chest in inspiration. Where he learned this I cannot tell, for neither Tosi nor Mancini says one direct word about it. Mancini, indeed, cautions his readers against too long practice, "because it will weaken the chest," and this is pretty good circumstantial evidence. "Mit vollem Brust!" say nearly all the German masters.

But suppose we let the writers, past and present, alone for a while; what do we, of today, witness in opera or concert?

Without exception it may safely be asserted that not one of all the more prominent female vocalists fails to use the chest, and especially, as it appears, the upper chest in breath-taking. They allow both the shoulders and the clavicles to rise. I took great pains last winter to observe the four *prime donne*, Melba, Eames, Calvé and Nordica. The most prejudiced observer could not have willfully closed his eyes to the exceptionless rule of expanded chest and elevated shoulders and clavicles. My powerful field glasses could not have been mistaken. One of the artists might have been fairly criticised for raising the chest unnecessarily high, not having hit upon the knack so observably made use of by Patti, Sembrich, Moran-Olden, Materna, Marimon and Lehmann—a bending forward of the upper frame to favor the expansion of the back as well as the chest, without raising the latter quite so high. Indeed, Nillson was the only one of the splendid stars who failed to incline at least slightly forward at each inhalation. Humphrey, in his *Human Osteology*, calls especial attention to the fact that the lungs lie somewhat more in the back than in the chest.

Consider, then, a few of Mr. Rowley's errors in detail: "For this unnatural inflation of the upper portion of the lungs, to the exclusion of the lower, causes the cellular tissue of such lower portion to dry up and shrivel for want of use."

Personal experiment no. 1. Clasp the waist rather low, about half-way from the arm-pits to the hips, and take breath by trying to expand the upper chest, or even by determining to raise the clavicles, while you endeavor to check all expansion of the lower ribs. Notice that this is absolutely impossible; for the hands will instantly feel a corresponding expansion of the lower ribs. Indeed, the ribs which form the frame work of the chest, the trellis work, are so firmly bound together that it is simply impossible to move one section without moving the whole structure.

Does Mr. Rowley harbor the belief that the diaphragm alone can suffice for a full inhalation, such an one as the vocalist requires? I was greatly surprised to find that a single mouthful of breath, the cheeks being distended, would blow down perfectly flat the diaphragm of a child of about ten years. The left lung of a large man, when removed, was lengthened by extreme inflation from ten inches to eleven and one-half inches, a gain of only one and one half inches made by the extension both of its apex and its base.

But the grand mistake is to overlook the fact that in upper (and necessarily lower) rib-raising and spreading, the whole circumference of the diaphragm is raised as the ribs rise, so that it is not pushed up against the lungs, but is stretched out to afford them a wider and flatter floor. It follows that the persistent checking of that abdominal flattening, which is the only means of preserving the original diaphragmatic curve, also checks this favoring, ease-giving flattening of the floor of the lungs, as anyone may prove.

PERSONAL EXPERIMENT NO. 2. Again clasp the sides and endeavor to inhale breath by raising the upper chest and collar bones, while you keep the abdomen wholly unmoved. Notice the extreme effort required, and the feeble inspiration

Then, without thought of upper rib-raising or expanding, try to inhale breath by expanding the lower ribs and separating the clasping hands, but do not allow the abdomen to flatten. Notice the great strain and the small amount of inspired air.

Finally (and correctly), expand and raise the upper chest, and raise, of course, the collar-bones while you allow the abdomen to flatten, as it naturally will. Notice the infinitely greater ease, and the vastly larger volume of breath inspired. It will be well to sip in the breath, somewhat as in sipping hot tea or soup vulgarly, as the inflow of breath can thus be more accurately judged.

The clavicles, or collar-bones, cannot rise more or less than the upper rib and the breast-bone. To the latter, they are bound by four strong ligaments. There is no muscle which could raise the clavicles without raising the upper ribs. And this rib is the most movable one, as Magendie proved. Henle decided the question beyond doubt by sawing off all the ribs at some distance from the spine, and testing their rigidity. He declares, and is supported by Rosenthal, that the upper rib is, indeed, the most movable; and that this mobility decreases to the seventh rib.

We read: "It is quite a physical effort to hold the shoulders in such raised position any length of time." But no well-trained singer would ever dream of holding the shoulders elevated. "So the singer pumps them up and down rapidly, like the piston of a steam engine." On the contrary, the volume of air thus inspired is so much larger than in lower breathing that breath needs to be taken at longer intervals. Mr. Rowley is exactly in error.

Upon what does "the severe strain of holding the shoulders upraised" fall? Few bodily movements are easier than shrugging the shoulders; and no advocate of higher breathing pretends that the shoulders should be raised more than just enough to favor the expansion of the upper chest. Indeed, our author is wrong in making "clavicular" synonymous with shoulder raising, as he does, both at the beginning and the end of his paper. It is not disputed that the shoulders must rise with the rising of the clavicles, but properly they rise no more than the latter. Let every reader carefully watch all the singers of really high repute who will be heard during the coming season. Not one in ten will fail to raise the shoulders perceptibly.

And how can "This pumping process drive the air with terrific force against the vocal chords, and necessarily produce a loud noise? Try for yourself.

Personal Experiment No. 3: Expand the chest, and even raise the shoulders unnaturally, excessively, and so hold them for a moment. Then suddenly, at the instant of singing the vowel ah, let them drop with the most full and sudden collapse and fall, but avoid adding any other voluntary expiratory effort. Notice that the tone will be exceedingly weak and breathy.

Wonderful Harless more than 50 years ago declared that no voluntary collapse of the respiratory parts would be powerful enough to produce a natural speaking voice, much less a sonorous singing tone; that actual expiratory effort would be necessarily added. This experiment also discloses the fallacy of "reserving the breath," a mistaken notion fostered by many teachers and writers, whose watches should have shown them how many more seconds a loud tone can be prolonged with consciously applied expiratory effort, than a soft one with the breathing intentionally checked. This fact has been noticed and commented upon by Harless, Merkel, the elder Garcia and many others.

Precisely the opposite danger threatens: Instead of "terrific force of breath" should be read "terrific strain of vocal muscles," by simple reason of the weakness of breath-attack and pressure. For all special authorities agree in asserting that a soft musical tone requires more effort of the throat muscles than a loud one. The explanation of this apparent paradox is, that the breath-pressure itself raises the pitch of the voice, and so far relieves the chord-stretching throat muscles; Mueller says that this gain may be five notes, Bagniard di Latour says a full octave.

Soft singing is unsafe. At the World's Fair Musical Congress I gladly availed myself of an opportunity to warn teachers and students against this most perilous error. Nor is the warning out of place in a paper upon respiration; for the pernicious practice has always, at least in my own experience, been coupled with advice to reserve the breath by actual efforts, to prevent the sudden recoil of inflated respiratory parts. Especially in Chicago is this error rife, leading to disastrous results. The youthful throats, striving to keep the tone pure while checking the natural outright utterance, almost inevitably increase the efforts that can be most plainly felt, and these efforts are just those put forth by the tongue, palate and jaw, which soon become habits, making the fuller volume impossible, especially in the middle compass.

No one respiratory mode is advised The article now being discussed objects to the movement of the collar-bones and shoulders, but does not announce any particular mode to be adopted as the true one. If the author holds strictly to his text and debars all such clavicular movement, he confines himself to the contraction of the diaphragm, for the reader has already learned by private trial that the lower ribs can no more expand without the upper, than the upper without the lower.

And it is to me incomprehensible that any one with decisive trials so easily made upon his own person, can continue to defend diaphragmatic inspiration. Let a concluding and conclusive experiment be made.

Personal Experiment No. 4: Let the whole upper frame be entirely at rest while you clasp the waist about half way from the arm-pits to the hips. Now sip in breath as before, by pushing the abdomen forward, but surely check all expansion of the lower chest. Notice the great sense of straining and the feeling of helplessness and the small inspiration.

Then repeat, now holding one hand upon the upper chest, or on the collar-bones, and endeavor to expand the lower ribs as well as the abdomen. Notice that hardly an additional cubic inch of air can be added, though the strain is uncomfortably increased.

Let each reader make his own experiments, new ones as they occur to him. He will find himself absolutely forced to movements of both clavicles and collar-bones. There is otherwise no possibility of a full breath being taken. The higher breath is expressly termed "deep" breathing by Hutchinson, Rosenthal and Dr. Landois, though the adjective now-a-days is commonly applied as a misnomer to the lower mode of inhaling, hinted at, if not expressly described throughout the article in question.

Formidable, indeed, is the testimony of genuine specialists. It is true that the general physiologists, like Flint, Carpenter, Marshall and Foster, fail to recognize the opposition between the diaphragm and other inspiratory muscles, but those who have devoted years to the study of respiratory movements agree with each other, for the case is a plain one.

Hutchinson's experiments embraced about 5,000 individuals of both sexes and of all ages. He is quoted by nearly every one who unites upon the question. Briefly quoted, he says: "Extraordinary breathing in both sexes is symmetrical. The clavicles, shoulders, scapulæ and superior ribs rise, and the sternum (breast-bone) advances. The infra-clavicular region (below the collar-bones) swells remarkably upward and outward (especially in females), the whole apex of the thorax is rendered more obtuse, especially in the antero-posterior diameter. The lower ribs spread outward * * * . The abdominal space within the arch formed by the junction of the sixth to the tenth ribs, *sinks inward.*" [These are his only italicised words.] Therefore the breathing is costal, commencing with the superior ribs and terminating over the abdomen. In fact, when we inspire deeply, we feel as if we directed all our power to the four or five upper ribs, giving the greatest expansion to the very apex of the lungs.

"When we look at the thorax's cavity we see why this great power and mobility is given to the upper part of the chest. We see that the six upper ribs encompass more space than the six inferior ribs. So that where we command most movement, there is the greatest portion of lung to be expanded * * * . If this fine swelling movement is absent in deep breathing, disease is present."

Could Mr. Rowley's statements be more directly contradicted? The writer, as recorded in his "Physiology of Artistic Singing," repeated his measurements upon one female and three male subjects, and found their truth confirmed.

Acting upon the advice of Bishop, the indefatigable Sibson gave years to the study of vertebrate, or back-boned animals. Flint, in the last edition of his Physiology, declares that Sibson has undoubtedly given more study to the respiratory movements, than any one else. This special student concludes that the breathing of man is performed more largely by movements of the upper chest than that of any other animal. Dr. A. Ransome agrees with Hutchinson; so does Dr. Chas. Benson a special student.

In the last of the four editions of Dr. Landois' Physiology, a shining work, we read: "In extreme, or deep breathing the sexes inspire alike; the chest expands and the abdomen is drawn in."

A private letter from Mr. A. P. Barnes, of Boston, inventor of the dry spirometer, says:—"In breathing I consider it best to expand the chest only and to allow the abdomen to act involuntarily. In breathing through the nostrils in an erect posture, with the mouth closed, the abdomen contracts involuntarily, and that I consider the best and most natural way."

No single response from players of wind-instruments has failed to condemn abdominal expansion. "Stomach breathing," says an excellent cornetor, "has ruined many a young player." Arban in his Cornet School writes: "In taking breath expand the chest. Do not push forward the abdomen, but rather allow it to flatten as the chest dilates."

Similar evidence might be added multitudinously. For instance, I cannot recall a single physiologist who does not declare that, even for ordinary respiration, the female chest expands as well as the abdomen; and the male chest is said to expand also, though relatively not so much as the female. How unreasonable does it appear to state that for the extreme or deep breathing a movement should be checked which is functional for ordinary breathing! Again, no one could witness a demonstration of the chest and see that the lungs had fallen away from the upper ribs nearly two inches, from the lower barely one, without being convinced, even against his will, that the lungs were designed to expand more extensively where their cells were the most numerous, and that their surrounding trellis-work of ribs was made more yielding and movable for this very reason.

In conclusion, I would advise the earnest student to disregard the average book on voice, so far at least as respiration is concerned. All of them combined could not match the authoritative words of the special students just quoted. But without names or books the student has two sources of valuable aid. The one is the example of the great singers. The other is private trial of different possible modes. Let me close this argument by giving an exercise to be practised perhaps ten minutes a day for a week. It will lead to the inspiration most commonly adopted by the leading artists, aptly called clavicular, because it includes the two movements which have long been associated with the term;—the expansion and rising of the upper chest, and the sinking or flattening of the abdomen. Exercise: Sit with your back against the back of a chair. First, without regard to breath, bend the upper part of the upper frame forward without letting the middle back leave the chair-back, and at the instant of bending, flatten the abdomen loosely backward.

Having made these movements easy, repeat them while sipping in a copious amount of air. Notice that the back will be much expanded, and the chest swell forward with the sensation that its upper part is being filled out with the inhaled breath.

Finally, after several days of the above practice, repeat the movements with the back free from the chair, either sitting or standing. Notice that no thought will need to be given to the abdomen after a time, for it will flatten just enough without effort. Notice also that now the forward bending of the upper frame will be very slight.

(Expiration). To commence the tone, let the whole upper frame instantly relax and fall to its natural position, and the abdomen rebound forward, adding, of course, the voluntary expiratory effort with which, beyond this collapse, the present article has no concern.

JOHN HOWARD.

New York City, 137 East 53d St.

MASSENET'S "THAIS."

A LYRIC COMEDY IN THREE ACTS AND SEVEN TABLEAUX. Poem by Louis Gallet, after the romance of Anatole France. Music by Jules Massenet.

THE embarrassment of critics is extreme when they attempt to study in good conscience a lyric work by M Massenet. If analysis in general is incapable of explaining musical emotions and of bringing them out into clear light, its incapacity and inutility never appear in a more forcible light than when directed to the seductive, if somewhat fragile, works of our contemporary master.

Such a passage which charms us, such an effect which enchants us—and this occurs sufficiently often—afford very slight hold for reflections or comparisons. If so amiable a role would not have been written except for the profit of an interpreter in vogue—and this also happens—it may very well happen that its value will be more momentary than durable, and restricted above all to the vocal qualities of this interpreter, if not even to her plastic advantages.

The case of M. Massenet is so interesting, so complex, so exceptional, that it becomes to us, who would narrate and appreciate the work, particularly ungrateful. Behold a musician of temperament, I was going to say of birth, richly endowed, capable as no other, to whom his natural abundance constitutes a sort of genius; he knows and he feels; he excels in charming; he may even move us upon occasion; he produces quickly, well and much; his merit is immense, his happiness equal to his merit. When he is bad it is not by accident, but because he wished it to be so, and believed firmly that success was to be had at this price. And always, at the side of his feebleness, the vices of a grand seigneur who has broken bounds, he lets you see clearly what he is and where he might be. The irritation which you experience becomes appeased, and certain measures full of a penetrating musical voluptuousness compensate for long and tiresome wanderings.

So, when one would speak of Massenet, one hesitates, one dreads to take a false route, and to argue in the dark, for this artist is the most capricious of men, and his clever calculations often differ most agreeably from our own. Therefore when he gives a new work we essay in general, with the best faith in the world, to know what he has undertaken and what logic he has followed; it is a first fault, to which we have often added another, that we have to find out later what was really the chosen subject, and the realization which it contained. But why so long a prelude? Is it not essential for the musician to charm the ordinary public? Surely one hour of agreement has not become so despicable nor so common. It is a strange enterprise, this of seducing an audience of *blasé* hearers, and of making commonplace people laugh.

This, undoubtedly, is the reasoning of the composer; in any case his publishers would have made it for him. Shall we dare now to brave their arguments, entreaties and the light raillery, which they direct with right good will against critics capable of preferring a former work of M. Massenet to the one most recently put upon sale? We will try it.

II.

The poem of "Thaïs" has been taken by M. Louis Gallet, a capable librettist, from a very subtile philosophical story by M. Anatole France. And here one might object, may be, that the name of poem does not apply with perfect justice to a text from which rhyme is absent.

To this I reply that poetry is not synonymous with versification, and that a text in "blank" verse (as in the case of "Thaïs") might strongly merit the name of poem. The initiative which M. Gallet has had the hardihood to make and the chance of experimenting at the opera appears to me happy on principle, since many authors have thought the same this long time, and many celebrated musicians, to begin with Mozart, have signalled the frequent inutility of rhyme. The fact of having submitted to the public upon the scene of

... Thais,
to reign in
where Ath-
him before
ortance, be-
while the
is extended
indicate the
ascetic; but
little marked
amid the
possibly
to appear
later to the
syncopated,
theme eluci-
of the cour-
vapors of the
the theatre
beats its
and desire,
her glorious
of heaven; he
God sends
rhythm arises,
expressing the
effects ro-

sonorous intro-
of the violins,
wind instru
the Valkyries.
the house of
of Athanael,
contemplates the
in an effect-
redundant form
prelude. Nicias

the opera, a work of vast proportions, and of having proved to many hearers who had not noticed the fact, that rhyme is in no way necessary to lyric chant, is not less considerable, and it is proper to congratulate the author upon it.

Nevertheless, the question arises whether the role of rhythmic prose and its relation with music, such as M. Gallet on one part and M. Massenet upon the other have accomplished, are such as we have desired, and such as will exercise a large influence upon the national drama of France? I doubt a little. It appears to me that in the realization of "Thais," from this point of view, the arbitrary holds rather too much place; we do not perceive in the poetic rhythm of the discourse a necessity sufficiently imperious for necessarily determining the vocal forms employed, and to impress in significant fashion, by the mediation of these forms, the ensemble of the dramatic symphony. But whom should we accuse? And this which we might consider as too vague and too elastic in the poem of the librettist, is it not very much aggravated by the manner of the composer of the music? I cannot forget, for instance, that in "Werther" the prosodic accents of the romance "*Pourquoi me reveiller*" are less just with the French original text than with the German translation. One can easily imagine that the problem accomplished by M. Louis Gallet and his composer might be of redoubtable complexity, and that for defining its precise value I might await another day. The works of Wagner, so fruitful of suggestions of all sorts, throw in this direction the most vivid light; nothing is more instructive than to study deeply the relations, variable without ceasing, between the poetic text and the vocal melodic form, (examined in its accent, its intervals, its expression and its rhythm) in the "Ring of the Niebelungen," where rhyme is constantly absent, or in "Tristan" or "Parsifal," where the usage of rhyme alternates with other laws of versification—iambic meters, alliterations, assonances. Still, at a glance, the question is vast rather than difficult. It has happened to me from years of labor devoted to the new translations of the "Valkyrie" and the "Mastersingers," to arrive at precise opinions of the importance of certain of these aspects, but it is not in a few lines that it is possible to state my conclusions.

Let us come to the subject itself. In the narrative of M. Anatole France, inspired, we believe, by the "*Vie des Pères du Desert*," and by the religious theatre of "Hrowistha," without prejudice of souvenirs of Flaubert (*La Tentation de Saint Antoine*), and of Renan—Thais, the courtesan of Alexandria, is led to faith and virtue by the anchorite Paphnuce. But the latter did not with impunity arrest Thais out of her luxury; it seems that the sin, in abandoning the priestess of Venus, entered into the heart, into the body, of the saint. Desire and sensuality are awakened in Paphnuce, and his triumph over the infernal powers is rendered vain; and at length while the former prostitute is secluded in a nunnery among the elect virgins, ascending day by day in sanctification and grace, the solitary, beseiged with temptations and doubts, glides each day lower towards damnation. At last he dies in despair before he has been able to sieze and possess the one whom he had rescued from a life of shame; and she dies glorified in the ecstasy of the blessed.

M. Anatole France, in this strange story of exquisite art and suggestive thought, has not wished, it will be seen, to make the victory of grace total, and without shadow; nor has he suggested the consoling, piously optimistic issue, that the holy monks, converters of Hroswitha, Abraham or Paphnuce, their work accomplished, should return to the beatitude of their contemplation. Has he desired to persuade by this of the truth, well known to theologians, that pride of spirit and abuse of divine assistance are punished by the fall, even of the flesh? Or, which is more likely, has he been inspired by his personal skepticism, by his dilletantism of art and philosophy, showing that all absolute solutions are vain, that the beast takes his revenge upon the angel, and that concupiscence, overcome upon the field of battle, never ceases until it has triumphed over the other? Be this as it may, a psychological drama, a passionate drama appears clearly in his book; it is the double moral evolution of the courtesan and the anchorite, the ascension of the former and the fall of the latter.

Such a drama is touching in certain aspects, terrible in others. It is human in any case, simple and profound, by consequence musical. I regret to say that the great scenes where the moral convulsion ought to produce itself before us, have been merely sketched by the librettist; but here again I suspect that he has acceded, if not to the wishes of the musician, at least to his own knowledge of nature and taste.

And has not M. Massenet erred in not making music to *this* drama where the passionate action is so grave, and which expresses equally two fashions of comprehending life and human destiny? Has he had good reason to prefer a musical expression wholly superficial, wholly of agreement and accessory, an emotion merely of the surface, if I may say so, and to submit his particular art to that of the choreographer, the costumer, the decorator and the stage manager? Reply is dangerous. All that can be safely affirmed is that M. Massenet in adopting the second part has conformed himself, on the whole, to a rule which he has always observed, and which has never succeeded with him more than one time. Let us see, then, what results he has this time obtained.

III

The "lyric comedy" of MM. Gallet and Massenet has no overture. After certain measures of introduction a theme defines itself, repeats itself by successive imitations; it expresses the cenobitic life, the calm life of the solitary recluse; simple harmonies sustain it, and one observes, as it passes, reflections of ancient modes. This archaic melody, a bit oriental, does not lack of austerity; it is in the situation, and gives to this first tableau a unity sufficiently happy, but offsets with difficulty a certain inequality in the phrase of the old cenobite Palemon, *Chaque matin*, very much too modern in musical color. But now comes Athanaël (the Paphnuce of M. Anatole France); a slow motive, with trembling accompaniment, full of dolorous sadness, while a new rhythm emerging from the bass paints its growing march. He comes, he recounts the scandal which desolates him: Thais, the comedian, Thais, the courtesan, causes sin to reign in Alexandria. The phrase *Hélas enfant encore*, where Athanaël avows the trouble which Thais had given him before he had renounced the world, has a certain importance, because M. Massenet has assigned it to the orchestra, while the cenobites have regained their cells and Athanaël is extended upon his couch for slumber. It suffices to indicate the memory of Thais hovering in the sleep of the ascetic; but of itself this phrase is sufficiently empty and of little marked effect. Then come dreams; upon rapid arpeggios, amid the glancing of broken chords with augmented fifths, possibly of Wagnerian origin, a design in triplets begins to appear (observe that this ternary rhythm attaches itself later to the person of Thais); later the melody becomes more syncopated, and at the same time more chromatic, and the theme elucidates itself, which we may consider significant of the courtesan and her lascivious grace. Below, in the vapors of the night, a light arises; the dream of Athanaël recalls the theatre of Alexandria; upon the stage, while the crowd beats its hands, cries, reddens, intoxicated with admiration and desire, Thais opens her veil and reveals to every eye her glorious nudity. Athanaël arouses himself, as inspired of heaven; he calls the other cenobites, announces to them that God sends him to Thais in order to convert her. A new rhythm arises, whence come in the next act the motives expressing the apostolic zeal of Athanael. In the finale, certain effects recall a little the style of the "Magi."

The second act opens with a sufficiently sonorous introduction in E major, where the rapid trills of the violins, contrasting with the martial rhythms of the wind instruments, for an instant suggest the Ride of the Valkyries. The curtain opens, showing the terrace before the house of Nicias—a young sybarite, a former comrade of Athanaël, near the gates of Alexandria. Athanaël contemplates the wicked city; condemns it, invokes divine succor in an effective arioso, *Voila donc la terrible cité*, full of redundant formulas which accompany the symphony of the prelude. Nicias enters leaning negligently upon the shoulders of two beautiful slaves, Myrtale and Corbyle, whose joyous laughter sparkles in vocalises of thirds. In the conversation between Nicias and the cenobites we hear repeated, but in shortened form, the motive which in the first act signalizes the entrance of Athanaël; later a theme is brought out in the words of the monk, "*Je veux la remener a Dieu;*" it grows out of a design previously established, and upon the other side attaches itself to the rhythm of which we have spoken above. The scene where Corbyle and Myrtale respond to the demand of Athanaël, (not to frighten Thais at first by a too severe an exterior), to prepare for him sumptuous vestments, is musically feeble, and scientifically very artificial. The gaiety in it is false, constrained, and the situation becomes at the same time ridiculous and painful. Nothing need be said of the little quatuor which ends the scene, all this music is useless for the monks.

Then dance rhythms are heard; it is Thais who approaches, preceded by actors and comedians. This little instrumental entrée has color, a character oriental, always archaic, where the Massenet of "Erinnyes" reappears for an instant; this character appertains, in great part, to the melodic cadence which shapes the first design (second ascending) and to the succession of conjoined major thirds which one remarks in the second. A pretty page, if but little new (for it recalls strangely "Manon")—is the song of Thais to Nicias, a a phrase with difficulty sustained upon discreet harmonies; *C'est Thais l'idole fragile.* We note solely that the syllabic declamation by equal values, dear to M. Massenet, is there followed with a persistence which would be hardly supportable if the interpreter had not the license of holding the movement at his will, the orchestra obliging itself to follow with docility. Nevertheless Athanaël advances towards the courtesan. Thais regards him with astonishment, while the violincello develops a langourous motive, in ternary rhythm. To the rude apostrophe of the monk, Thais responds, according to the ordinary poetry of the opera, by an air of surprise: *Qui te fait si sevère*, of a melody extremely empty, which suggests certain remarks of prosodical complexion; (why, for instance, should the first syllable of the verb *dementir* fall upon the strong beat of the measure?) the motive of which we have just spoken is there transformed, becoming the figure of the accompaniment, that is to say, into a series of descending steps attacked upon a syncope, generally by a skip of an ascending sixth, where the flute plays the principal role. The vocal theme is taken up by the chorus, and directly the finale, a very short ensemble, traversed by the clamor of Athanael *J'irais dans ton palais te porter le salut.*

A symphonic interlude, a musical description of the pantomime of "The Loves of Aphrodite and Adonis," the triumph of Thais in the theatre of Alexandria, leads into the tableau which follows. This interlude reproduces in the development, and enriches by new motives, the vision of Athanael in the first act. The motive of the courtesan persists nearly alone, more or less altered in the form and in the harmonies which accompany it; Thais is upon her return to her palace, fatigued, inquiet at the coming of day. She consults her mirror and sings an air to the success of the piece, an air which recalls certain pages of "Manon" and "Esclarmonde," and in it the declamation in notes of equal value becomes irritating to a supreme degree. *Dis moi que je suis belle,* is a formula which is entirely too habitual to M. Massenet, one mark of workmanship which ends by becoming disagreeable. The sole sensation a trifle new which we find in this air is the little phrase of invocation to Venus, with the design of the flute answering to the psalmody of the voice. Athanael by this time has come in. The orchestra, under the words of welcome from Thais, takes again the figure of the accompaniment to the phrase *Qui te fait si severe,* sung in the preceding tableau. In the discourse of the ascetic to the pretty sinner, one rarely finds the just accent and expression of real moral conflict; it is necessary to note the harmonies which sustain the words *Je t'aime en esprit, je t'aime en vérité* which repeat themselves a little farther on. A great motive, sprung out of [illegible] imposes itself fortissimo in A [illegible] a proselyting enthusiasm: [illegible] This theme is also [illegible] of M. Massenet, and one can [illegible] earlier works of the young [illegible] to say that we love it, with its [illegible] sonority: one recalls with [illegible] muscles, the re-entrance of [illegible] again resound the motives of [illegible] interrupt the feeble supplica- [illegible] energetic and pounding theme re- [illegible] step higher than formerly, [illegible] but which never fail of a [illegible] the curtain has fallen it still [illegible] conclusion of this tableau.

[illegible] pages of the work. The [illegible] interruption; the motive of the [illegible] hearing, reappears and seems [illegible] a change of mode, in [illegible] violin solo, accompanied by [illegible] which M. Massenet calls a [illegible] has for its object to show [illegible] the ecstatic transfig- [illegible] Thais." This part has [illegible] certainly it is agreeable; we [illegible] where the author has been [illegible] does not lack charm, [illegible] fervent things, not alone by [illegible] meditations" and elevations" [illegible] the mode of the day; [illegible] of the reservations which [illegible] tranquilly, having a [illegible] so many little phrases [illegible] reading the score ren- [illegible] in the theatre. I [illegible] picturesque, which

[illegible] Athanael and speaks to

him, while from a distance resounds a dancing air, of an orientalism a trifle artificial, but characteristic nevertheless. The effect, recalling the scene of the Course de la Reine in "Manon," is not less happy; it is a moment when the decoration, the music, and the moral situation of the two personages, the language which they hold, concur neatly to make an impression upon the spectator, just and not banale. All this conversation is in a subdued color, down to the moment when Thais, as Athanael desires, resolves to destroy her wicked riches, but prays that a little statuette of Eros may be spared from the wreck, "in order to place it in some monastery." The short andante which tells the conversion is not ugly, but poorly acceptable, nevertheless; one finds there a slight reminiscence of the style of Gluck. Furor of Athanael, showing the inconsistent jealousy which chains him; arrival of Nicias and his friends, and the crowd; reproaches, injuries, fugitive reminiscences of the "Mastersingers," also short as textual (*Adieu Thaïs*, role of Nicias) and the fortissimo finale.

In the third act the first tableau shows us again the Thebaid, the cenobites, who are inquiet at the approach of a far-off storm, and one hears the initial motive of the first act. Athanael re-enters; he has conducted Thais to the monastery of White Nuns, where the pious Albine governs; but peace is not to come again into his heart. The beauty of the woman haunts him and tortures him; for the third time reappears the motive which accompanies the entrance of Athanael at the beginning of the work. After this scene the ballet follows, representing the dreams of Athanael and the temptations of the flesh. This ballet is something without musical interest, without choreographic interest, and the mystic episode, which occurs in it—the star of redemption illuminating for an instant Athanael and his seducers, who surround him—produces in the theatre a most shocking effect. I hear that this episode was suppressed after the second representation; let us hope that this news is true.

When the visions of the ballet dissipate themselves we find Athanael asleep. Thais appears to him, and (which we did not desire) the motive returns of the *Qui te fait si sevère*. A second dream succeed to this: Thais dying in the midst of the White Nuns. Athanael awakes, tears himself away in the direction of the monastery.

The first tableau, the death of Thais, is preceded by an instrumental passage where the religious "meditation" of the second act is revived, in the key of B major. The opening harmonies of the scene where the White Nuns pray for the soul of the dying, are of a character very appropriate to the situation. Pending the final duo of Thais, ecstatic, and Athanael, lost in despair and furious with desire, the orchestra takes up again the religious meditation, this time in the primitive key, D; a motive of apotheosis then disengages itself and gives the work its musical conclusion.

IV.

To resume; we find ourselves in the presence of a work where the passionate subject has been treated inadequately; where the composer, usually prodigal of his resources, shows a musical discretion almost parsimonious. "Thais," as we have seen, is traversed by leading motives, at least of motives which recall themselves, very ingeniously managed. But what, I ask in the name of goodness, are we to make of these motives pretending to occult meanings, yet so short, so poor that they can support neither interesting transformations nor symphonic development. Would it not be better to offer us instead the musical architecture of the old opera, with its noise and its convention, free at least and solid; in place of these hybrid works, which affect the free and continued forms of the new drama, and are nevertheless as conventional as possible. I neglect on purpose the subordinate means of an adventitious character through whose influence it is hoped to retain a hold upon the public; attractions of this kind, numberless in "Thais" have nothing in common with art, and it is not necessary to speak of them. We have spoken here only of the music, and admit that there is too little of it—entirely too little.

ALFRED ERNST.

(Translated for MUSIC from *La Revista Musicale*.)

INTERVIEW WITH SIEGFRIED WAGNER.

I WAS fortunate enough a little while ago, to have a most delightful and informal interview with young Siegfried Wagner, and I was perfectly charmed with his unaffected joviality and keen sense of humor. As we sat talking over our cigarettes and coffee on the terrace of one of the large Swiss hotels, many eyes turned curiously toward the talented conductor, whose likeness to his father is so strikingly unmistakeable. His command of both the English and French languages is remarkable, and, though we talked chiefly in German, he gave me numerous entertaining anecdotes in my native tongue. His conversation is now and then sprinkled with a delicate French humor, which he inherits directly from his mother and his grandmother, who was "Daniela Stern" the well known authoress.

After discussing the beauties of the scenery surrounding us, he amused me highly with an account of a trip around the world, which he had taken in company of a rich American friend.— "Of course my experiences were too numerous to relate" he said, "they would fill more than one large volume, should I attempt to write them, but of my night spent in Hong Kong I must tell you. We arrived, my friend and myself, just after the city gates had been closed for the night, and accordingly pitched our tent on a little elevation, just outside the walls. I was very tired, and so fell off into a deep sleep almost immediately, but my friend, poor fellow, did not fare so well. About five or six A. M., I was awakened by the most heartrending groans, and turning to see what had happened I found my companion was seized with a terrible attack of cholera, and would certainly die unless medical aid could be at once summoned.

Without even stopping to put my clothes on, I rushed out in my pajamas, and in a few minutes was running at full speed down the main street, pursued by the guard and a number of Chinamen, who, rather naturally I must own, thought that I was an escaped lunatic. Once or twice I tried to explain my errand, but quite uselessly, and they finally seized me and marched me, very fortunately, straight to the foreign office, where I was provided, firstly, with a coat of many colors, and secondly with the necessary medical help. For two or three days my friend lingered between life and death, but he finally recovered, and we were very glad indeed to shake off the Chinese soil and once more turn our steps toward dear old Europe, which at one time I feared I might never see again, as the plague was then raging in Hong Kong."

"So much for my travelling experiences, now I know you are wild to know about the performances at Bayreuth this summer, or does Switzerland prove so attractive, that music is no longer necessary food for your imagination?" I laughed and told him I was afraid that had been the case this time at any rate.— "Did you make much of a profit on the performances?" I asked, "I suppose you are aware that various rumors not to the contrary were circulated." "Well, all we did was to clear the expenses, and we do not always do that," he added with a smile, "just think of the expenses and outlays; why the new scenery for the Venus Berg, which was entirely my mother's own conception, cost alone about eight thousand marks."

"The critics were a little severe on you, were they not?" "O yes, but then we had especially critical audiences this summer. You see, the usual opera going people thought that Tannhaeuser and Lohengrin could be heard any where, and they did not find it worth while to go to Bayreuth to hear such well known operas, consequently it was mostly the real art connossieurs and appreciative musicians that assembled for this year's festival."

"The performances of "Tannhaeuser" and "Lohengrin" were superb, and unique, and the costumes were wonderfull, my mother and sisters having spent months in studying all points connected with the dress and habits of those days. It was Isolde who discovered that quaint braided coiffure which became Mme Nordica so well, in the second act of "Lohengrin." By the way, he added, what a voice she has, so clear and true, and she is such a lovely woman, how could her husband go off the way he did! She is "*Eine ideale Elsa*," and you are mighty lucky to be able to claim her as a compatriot. The best in both Music and Art is now to be found in America."

"When will you go to the New Continent?" I asked.

"I do not know," he said, "I have had several engagements offered me for a season in the States, but the terms have not been sufficiently tempting as yet. I am going to London to lead a series of Wagner concerts there, beginning the end of October. Next time you must come to Bayreuth, I shall probably conduct. "Will it be next year?" Hardly, as we hope to give the "Nibelungen Ring;"—"*Also aufwiedersehen uber nachstes jahr*"—A hearty shake hand, and his youthful figure vanished down the wooded path, and I was left alone, quite under Siegfried's charm.

EDGAR DENBY.

Paris, 6 Rue de Seine.

MUSICAL CENTERS OF CHICAGO.

VI.

THE AMERICAN CONSERVATORY.

MR. J. J. HATTSTAEDT.

FROM a very modest beginning a few years ago, the American Conservatory has quietly built up a business which places it among the largest and most competent music school in this country. Its director, Mr. J. J. Hattstaedt, was teacher of piano at the Chicago Musical College, from 1875 to 1886. Withdrawing from that institution he founded the American Conservatory, and has gone on in a quiet and capable way, gathering one eminent musician after another to his faculty, until at the present time there are about forty teachers connected with this school. First of all, as the one around whom all the wheels revolve, must be mentioned the director himself. Mr. Hattstaedt is an earnest musical scholar, a capable teacher, and a well informed musician of sincere and high aims. He not only devotes himself to teaching the piano, but also lectures upon musical history and the art of teaching and supervises the entire work of the school.

MR. HARRISON M. WILD.

Closely associated with him in the piano department are a number of well known musicians, at the head of the list being Mr. Harrison M. Wild, the distinguished concert-organist and organ virtuoso. Mr. Wild is almost as good a pianist as he is organist, which is saying about all that can well be said upon the subject. He is one of the most notable examples of the combined advantages of study abroad and at home, in his case long and arduous studies here in Chicago having been made after he had already been in Berlin for a year or more. Upon the piano his teacher was Mr. Emil Liebling, and I doubt whether I could find a better compliment to pay to that ready and eminent person than to credit him with having been chosen and adhered to by so intelligent and masterly a pupil as Mr. Wild. In my opinion we are likely to hear a great deal more of Mr. Wild as pianist than we have yet done. He has already given many recitals which have been largely attended. He has a great technic and a

MR. VICTOR GARWOOD.

MR. ALLEN H. SPENCER.

MRS. GERTRUDE HOGAN-MURDOUGH.

MR. NOYES B. MINER.

wide acquaintance with all schools of music. As a teacher he is one of the most careful.

Still this is not to diminish in any way from Mr. Wild's fame as organist. In this department he practically divides the organ teaching of Chicago with Clarence Eddy; and besides having given some hundreds of organ recitals here, which still continue, he plays many concerts in all parts of the country.

Another highly successful teacher is Mr. Victor Garwood, who in addition to native advantages has enjoyed the teaching of such masters as Theodore Kullak, Oscar Raif, Ferdinand Kiel and others. The faculty has lately received an important accession in the person of Mr. Allen H. Spencer, who is now attracting attention as a player, having given many recitals in connection with the conservatory. Mr. J Clark Williams is another of the piano teachers. Graduated from the American Conservatory, he afterwards studied in the Royal High School of Music, in Berlin, and has now returned to teach in his alma mater.

MME. RAGNA LINNE.

There are also a number of lady teachers, all earnest and capable musicians, and most of them graduates of the American Conservatory. One is Mrs. Gertrude Hogan-Murdough, who has been a pupil of Leschetitzky and Raif. She here devotes herself to teaching after the system of Raif.

Miss Florence Castle, an

MR. P. C. LUTKIN.

accomplished pianist, has also pursued a post-graduate course with Leschetitzky, and has greatly distinguished herself in the American Conservatory.

At the head of the department of singing is Mr. Noyes B. Miner, who for many years has occupied an honorable, useful and highly distinguished position among Chicago teachers. If I remember aright he made his first entrance into the musical activities of Chicago as teacher of the voice in the Chicago Musical College, but came out with Mr. Hattstaedt at the founding of the American Conservatory. Among his masters are to be mentioned such well-known names as those Vannuccini of Florence, Mme. Biscacciauti, Signor Rotoli and George Henschel. Mr. Miner excels in placing the voice and in securing agreeable and musical tone quality. He is also very successful in imparting the proper style for the French Chansons, and the songs of such writers as Massenet. This is equivalent to crediting him with no small degree of refinement and fastidious taste.

Another prominent teacher of voice in this institution is Mme Ragna Linne, born in Christiana, Norway. This brilliant lady represents the method of Mme. Marchesi, whose pupil she was for several years. She is a concert singer of exceptional merit.

MR. JOSEPH VILIM.

MR. FR. HESS.

Composition and theory are well handled at the American, I judge, for on the list of teachers I find the names of Messrs. Peter C. Lutkin, Hubbard William Harris and A. J. Goodrich. All of these gentlemen are so favorably known among musicians as to make it unnecessary to enlarge at this point upon their merits, except to mention the possibility that the usefulness of Mr. Lutkin in the conservatory will come to an end before long, if indeed it has not already reached that point, through the not uncomplimentary circumstance of his making an unprecedented success of the music department of the Northwestern University at Evanston, where after many years of bad handling music is once more looking up under Lutkin's intelligent direction. As in Evanston, being Professor in the University, he will naturally have opportunities which will occupy all his time, I fancy the conservatory will presently lose his services. But his membership is none the less complimentary to the management of the American Conservatory, since here he has worked during a number of years.

MR. ADOLPH WEIDIG.

Mr. A. J. Goodrich bears one of the names best known in musical theory, taking the country through. I have never had the pleasure of attending any of his lectures, but I should expect to find them full of information and well expressed. His "Analysis of Music" is used as text book in his department. Mr. Hubbard W. Harris is both teacher and composer.

The department of orchestral instruments is well represented at the American. At the head of this department is Mr. Josef Vilim, a good musician, a careful teacher and a fine player. Mr. Vilim was educated at the Prague conservatory, and has the rare ability of awakening interest in his pupils. Associated with him in this department is Mr. Adolf Weidling, one of the first violins of the Thomas Orchestra, a well-known player of chamber music and the like, and a composer of decided and uncommon ability. Another well-known musical figure in Chicago musical life is that of Mr. Frederick Hess, the cellist, also a member of the Chicago Orchestra. For some years past a string orchestra has been maintained composed of pupils.

MR. A. J. GOODRICH.

It is understood that the school keeps up the regular series of concerts, settling with the American composer by an annual "game dinner" of American compositions, giving a large amount of the very best music.

Its quarters are advantageously located in Weber Hall, at the corner of Jackson and Wabash Avenue. The rooms are commodious, comfortable and elegant, and the school counts and deserves to count as an important factor in Chicago music.

EGBERT SWAYNE.

MR HUBBARD WILLIAM HARRIS.

SHOULD A MUSICIAN THINK?

TO THE EDITOR:

I have been an interested and grateful reader of the discussions upon piano touch, recently published in "Music," and I am sure I voice a common wish when I express the hope that you will invite similar discussion upon other subjects of equal, or perhaps greater, importance to many of your readers.

A department permanently devoted to the publication of expert opinions upon subjects of interest not only to professional or even amateur musicians, but as well to that vast majority of cultured people who do not play or sing, but who desire to qualify themselves to listen intelligently—even critically—to the better class of musical works, would, I am sure, be welcomed with eager enthusiasm by many thousands, who have never been directly addressed, have never been efficiently subserved by any music journal. This would be thoroughly consistent with the policy of "Music," which from the beginning of its career has maintained a position of mingled neutrality and independence, being non-sectarian in art and biased by no creed of aesthetics, but lending aid to whatever tends to make music better understood, and more deeply and truly enjoyed.

Now, would it not be eminently appropriate and desirable, since you have published the views of so many distinguished authorities upon the purely technical requirements of the pianist, to invite the same earnest and free discussion upon the mental equipment of the musician and lover of music, upon the requirements of taste, using the word in its broadest sense as correspondent to the beautiful. It is generally admitted that too much attention is given to purely technical study, and far too little to acquiring that knowledge which taste requires for its enlightened exercise, and it is not irrational to presume that this tendency is due in a large measure to the absence of a correct and generally accepted theory of the value of such knowledge.

Every student who would pursue the study of his art beyond the narrow domain of the key-board, and every listener who aspires to more than the mere sensuous pleasures of music, needs as a motive and guide, not the bare statement that this and that class of information is valuable, but a simple and sufficient *reason* why the possession of such knowledge will reward the time and effort expended in its acquisition. My own study in the line of æsthetics has revealed to me a surprising void in our literature just where it seems to me information is most deeply needed. There are innumerable works upon musical history, biography, etc., but not one whose object is to explain, in a way that the average student may understand, *why* such knowledge should be sought, and *wherein* it directly contributes to the attainment of a desired end. In all other departments of art we find many works of this kind, but the writers uniformly betray their incompetency to extend their theories to music with any degree of definiteness and logical conclusiveness. Our American student is generally very practical. He wants to know the reason of things, and the friend of culture is equally exacting. Both insist upon knowing *why* they should expend valuable time in what to them appears a dry and profitless study. When we can prove to them that a certain class of knowledge directly subserves some worthy end—that a piece of music by Beethoven gains in expressiveness and beauty, and consequently affords greater pleasure when we are thoroughly familiar with the history of music, with the life and character of the composer, with the circumstances of his environment, with the conditions immediately attending the production of his work, and with what has been said of it by the best writers—then and not until then shall we have a right to blame our students and our listeners for neglecting to acquire such knowledge.

During the last few months I have addressed questions to hundreds of teachers, calculated to show how far they understood and sensibly appreciated the value of information which they are constantly and earnestly recommending to their pupils, and I can assure you that the result, were it fully stated, would appear most incredible to your readers.

I confidently believe that "Music" cannot better serve the public and the profession than by publishing from competent critics and writers such responses as may be elicited by the following questions:

1. Wherein consists the value of knowledge of the general history of music, as a direct aid to the student and listener?

2. Wherein consists the value of knowledge of the life, character and environment of the composer, as an aid to musical appreciation?

3. Wherein consists the value of analyses, technical, poetic etc., of the composer's works such as given by Ridley Prentice in "The Musician" and by Mr. E. B. Perry in his Lecture-Recitals?

4. Wherein consists the value of knowledge of the principles of æsthetics, as treated in such works as Dr. Edward Hanslick's "Beautiful in Music," Wilhelm A. Ambros' "Boundaries of Music and Poetry," Mathews' "How to Understand Music," and the like?

Very truly

824 Walnut St., Chicago. Wilber M. Derthick.

PIANO TOUCH ONCE MORE.

PERHAPS the readers of MUSIC may have already considered the subject of piano touch sufficiently. Nevertheless, it is a very important subject; and I believe nobody has yet given, in this magazine, the scientific reasons why the quality of tone of a piano is modified by the touch of the player.

We owe to that marvellous scientific genius, Helmholtz, the demonstration of the fact that tone-quality (*Klangfarbe*, timbre) depends on the number and the relative intensity of the overtones present in the complex tones which are always *produced* by a stretched string or other sounding body; and also of the conditions which determine what overtones shall be present and what their relative intensity shall be. Their conditions depend, in the case of the piano, in very large measure on the maker of the instrument, and not on the player. For example, the weight and tension of the strings; the weight and quality of the hammer, i. e., whether it shall be hard or soft, narrow or broad; and, finally, the place where the hammers strike the strings. A heavy, thick string will not divide up into so many small fractions as a light thin string, and, consequently, certain overtones cannot be produced from it, under any conditions. A hard, narrow hammer, with a sharp edge, will divide a string into smaller fractions than a broad, soft hammer. Finally, the place where the hammer strikes the string is the place where it has the greatest amplitude of vibration; so that all overtones produced by segments which have the middle point at the place where the hammer strikes are reinforced and made prominent; while all those which have a node at that point are either extinguished entirely or are so greatly weakened as to become nearly or quite imperceptible.

With all this, of course, the pianist has nothing to do, except in selecting his piano; but there are certain conditions affecting the relative prominence of the overtones which are directly dependent on his touch. These condition are *the relative force and suddenness of the blow of the hammer upon the string.* A sudden blow from a very soft hammer will divide the string into smaller vibrating segments than a gradual pressure from a very hard hammer; and the more powerful the sudden blow, the greater the number of small segments of the string set in vibration. A sudden, powerful blow from a hard hammer, especially if it be narrow-edged, will divide the string into many small segments, most of which produce dissonant overtones. These will soon disappear, if the damper is held from off the string; but while they continue, the tone is sure to be harsh and unpleasant. This is the secret of the bad tone produced by many players who keep the hand and wrist rigid; the touch made by a rigid hand has a stiff, unelastic character which makes the impact of the hammer on the string a sudden, violent one, even in soft playing, and produces invariably a bad, impure quality of tone. On the other hand, an elastic hand and wrist, caressing the keys with a pressure touch rather than striking them a blow, makes the impact of the hammer on the string a comparatively gradual one and produces a pure tone, provided the mechanism of the instrument is capable of it. Of course no touch will produce a fine tone from a badly constructed piano.

Of course, also, there are many grades of power and of suddenness in the impact of the hammer, even when it is effected by means of pressure touch. There are many degrees and kinds of touch, and each one of them produces a different quality of tone, even though the difference may often be very slight: because every shade of touch affects, in greater or less degree, the relative intensity of the over-tones.

To define, enumerate and classify all the varying kinds and shades of touch, each of which modifies, more or less perceptibly the quality of tone, would obviously be as impossible as to do the same for the infinitely subtle gradations of a fine human voice in speaking or singing. Where the hand and wrist are supple and elastic, and the player has real musical perception and feeling, the shades of tone-quality produced by his unconscious modifications of touch, induced by the musical ideal in his mind, are infinitely subtle and varied. Such playing, and such only, is genuinely musical and artistic. Imagination, musical perception and musical feeling are the fundamental requisites of artistic interpretation. But equally indispensable is such a condition of the hand, wrist and arm, and such control of the nervous and muscular apparatus, as makes all this mechanism the unconscious and automatic servant of the perceiving and feeling mind. The action of the piano, also, must be so finely balanced, and so perfectly constructed, that it is practically an extension of the nervous and muscular apparatus of the player; sympathetically responsive to the slightest shade of feeling, the most subtle modification of the musical conception.

But while an exhaustive enumeration and classification of the infinitely varied shades of touch and of tone quality would be impossible, while it is true that all the most subtle effects of the artistic pianist are produced unconsciously, in the effort to realize a purely musical ideal; nevertheless, there are certain broad distinctions to be made which sufficiently cover the ground, for all practical purposes of playing and teaching. These are not far to seek, and I have already touched upon them. Touch, in general, is of two kinds; that based upon the blow principle, and that based upon the principle of pressure. The former was the kind of touch formerly universally prevalent. It is exemplified in extreme degree in Plaidy's Technical Studies and in Lebbert and Stark. Unmodified by other ideals, it produces a hard, rigid, unelastic touch, and a corresponding dryness and monotony of tone quality, such as makes really expressive and artistic piano playing impossible. This is the reason why the Stuttgart conservatory, with its hundreds of pupils yearly, turns out no real artists. The pressure principle has found place in the playing of many artists, and in the teaching of many European pedagogues, without being adequately analyzed or explained. Julius Knorr and his pupils employed this kind of touch with beautiful effect; but if any of them ever so much as mentioned the distinction between blow and pressure, I have never been able to hear of it.

The two most valuable means of producing that condition of the nervous and muscular apparatus on which a sympathetic touch, based on the pressure principle, depends, are, so far as I am aware, the two finger exercise of Dr. Wm Mason, and the "up-arm" touch. This latter is very lightly touched upon in the first volume of Mason's "Touch and Technic"; but it is of enormous value, as I have had occasion to know in the experience of the last years; and vastly more can be done with it than most players and teachers are aware.

Lastly, he who would become a fine pianist, or would teach others to become such, must be satisfied with nothing short of the best makes of pianos. No piano action, which is not sympathetically responsive to the most subtle shades of touch, is adequate for the finest artistic purposes; and no piano not scientifically constructed can produce the best quality of tone, however fine the action, or whatever the touch of the artist.

JOHN COMFORT FILLMORE.

Milwaukee.

EDITORIAL BRIC-A-BRAC.

ONE of the encouraging signs of the times is the success of the lecture recital business. We have in the field a large number of gentlemen able to give acceptable performances of music, prefaced by comments both technical and aesthetic. To mention a few names, there are Sherwood, Liebling, Mr. Jaroslav de Zelinski, Constantine Sternberg, John S. Van Cleve, and last, but by no means least, that wonder of industry and success under difficulties, Mr. Edward Baxter Perry. Each one of the gentlemen mentioned has his own individuality, and to an extent his own characteristic repertory.

The lecture recital is a musical means of grace which is only beginning to obtain its just estimation in this country. A piano recital, pure and simple, no matter how much good matter it may offer, appeals to a public which is still limited—in spite of the vast amount of music study, such as one would suppose would make for this form of art a great and an appreciative public. The difficulty is that a program of great works, played one after another without comment, passes but half appreciated. The playing may astonish and delight; but the works fail of being duly enjoyed. In fact nothing is more common than to find hearers who do not even know where they are "at" in a program, if a sonata or suite with its several movements has intervened. This being the case it is apparent upon statement that considerations of style and poetry of the several selections cannot have had attention—for when the hearer is entirely at sea as to which one of the pieces upon the list is being played, how shall he be able to edify himself with appreciations of the style and subject-matter of an author?

Moreover the country contains some millions of people who as yet have never willingly and knowingly heard a sonata; and if they were to be told, after enjoying a piece of music played upon the piano, that it had been a sonata, they would still have only the most hazy consciousness concerning it, and perhaps feel much as if they had gotten nicely over an unexpected but mild attack of varioloid. Now of these many millions who have the musical cultivation still to get, (or else to die without the sight,) very many have aspirations, and if only they knew how to set about it might still fill out their remaining span of life with somewhat of the delight which music would give. All this part of the public has to learn to appreciate music without being able to compose it or even to play it. It is the same in other forms of art, where in order to appreciate and admire a splendid temple one needs not to be professionally educated as architect, stone-cutter, or carpenter— or in all of them, as the university idea would have it. One might carry a musical watch and be able to tell the time of day by it, without being able to repair it, or even to wind it up.

There is a great deal of wasted musical performance through faulty hearing. The hearers, with the best of intentions, do not know where they ought to pay their main attention. They neither know what they ought to listen for, nor what kind of an idea the piece is supposed to represent. Hence they remain under the denomination of that most stunting of musical delusions, the expectation of a "tune", or of something "pretty"—or even of "cute", as the American girl called Mt. Blanc.

Of course too much may be made of the adventitious aid of analysis. Analysis is just the same aid, sometimes, in music as it would be when applied to the girl one likes best. She has organization, parts, members, which bear certain relations of symmetry and of use. And her charm may in part depend upon incidents of this kind, which analysis might to a certain extent explain. But the minute you analyze the girl too much, her charm departs: not because anything has gone from her, but simply because you have placed yourself outside of its influence. A class once set upon hearing a fugue with attention, in order to report how many times the subject has appeared, is not a class in proper condition to appreciate the fugue as emotional-harmonic-melodic tone-poetry—which every fugue of Bach truly is. The exercise of listening for the number of times the theme occurs may be advisable, as a stage in training; but one has later to take the fugue in its entirety, like a story. One might as well count the paragraphs or chapters in a thrilling story, in order to come upon the source of its power. Analysis may be overdone.

But there is such an element in art-appreciation as "standpoint". Every work of art is created in order to represent something, to *tell* something. What is this something? This is the real question. From a technical standpoint one learns nothing from the fact of Chopin's having composed the twelfth study, of his opus 10, after hearing of the fall of Warsaw; but from a poetic and imaginative point of view, the fact explains the tone-poem. All the tumult is there, all the sorrow and all the despair. And this it will be seen, quite one side the question of motives, periods and counter-subjects. Now if a pianist introduces this piece in the midst of a recital, without explanation or comment, the untaught hearer observes merely that a very rapid, noisy and unpretty piece is being played. But the minute the noise, the hurry and the passion are explained by the incident which gave rise to the tone-poem, all these features fall into their proper order and place.

Moreover, there is a way of looking at a piece (looking with the hearing) which brings one to the heart of it, and it is not easy to say which is the best road for bringing the hearer to this manner. The nature of the listening I have in mind may be inferred from a little simile of Ruskin's, in the second volume of modern Painters, I think it is. Speaking of truth of water he refers to the little pond by the roadside after a shower. To the eye it appears simply a puddle of dirty water. But if you look deeply into it you will see mirrored there the waving grass upon its brink, the flowers, the more distant trees, and the clear blue sky and clouds of heaven; and at night the faraway planets and stars glisten back at you from the shallow and earth-stained puddle. This is not quite true in music, the puddle doing little or nothing in the way of reflecting the blue heavens of God, although the weeds about the margin get themselves into the picture well enough. But there *is* something in the figure. A piece which you hear for themes, periods, modulations and incidents of technical framing, without emotion and without response, may have in it, nevertheless, the bluest of heavens and the most beaming of heavenly bodies; it may mirror to us something better and more precious than either—the radiance of glorified spirit. But for this manner of hearing one needs to be upon quite a different key.

And here is where the lecture recital comes in. It is possible for the lecturer, if he be refined, poetic and sensitive, to put into his prefatory remarks exactly this suggestion of standpoint, looking from which with faraway vision we may respond to this inner voice of the tone-poet, which as Schuman says is "for him who listens intently, and with inner hearing." It is through the imagination that the transformation is effected between an untouched audience and one full of this inner sympathy and delight. Some men have a better faculty in this direction than others. Mr. Edward Baxter Perry is one whose late lecture recital before the Chicago Conservatory has led to these remarks. Mr. Perry is blind. An attack of scarlet fever, at the age of four left him within a few months totally without sight. With the gate of vision quite closed, he has had to attain his education, and to make up by superior retentiveness the disadvantage of total dependence upon the ministrations of a reader for all his knowledge of everything that is new, interesting and current in the world of mind and art. The route from beginning to completion is one of such arduousness that I am filled with wonder at the things which such men as John S. Van Cleve, Baxter Perry, and a friend of mine in Montreal, Mr. Septimus Fraser, have accomplished.

Perhaps even privation may have its ministry. Possibly the tonal sense may be more acute, and the inner world shut off from many disturbances of daily life, may have in it something sweeter than the older ones of us who can see retain into later life. However this may be, the recital-lecturer fills a place peculiarly his own. Mr. Perry, in particular, is to be praised not alone for the magnitude of the works which he presents, and the generally able manner in which he plays them, but still more for the moderate way and generally tasteful character of his introductory remarks. Possibly the pedigrees of some of his pieces are a trifle too long; one might not agree with his critical estimates of certain works, as for instance when he ranks the Chopin sonata in B flat minor above all other compositions for piano, by whomsoever. This may or may not be a just opinion. A "best" composition is like a best poem, or like the "best" of one's own wife. It is a matter of personal fitness and harmony. But in general his remarks are extremely well chosen, and, as they properly should be, addressed rather to the imagination and the poetic faculty than to the technical peculiarities of the works about to be offered. For, as already mentioned, what the hearer needs is not the information that Chopin is writing in such and such a key, with a motive so and so, and a modulation into so and so at the end of forty measures; but the story or general conception which Chopin might have had in mind. If possible, the story which he *did* have in mind, if indeed he had a story; and if not, a story which harmonizes with the tone-poem to which it serves as prelude. For in all these cases the first service to the untaught hearers is simply to awaken interest and admiration. Love is the beginning of better life, in music no less than in psychology. If an amateur can be brought to really love one single piece of serious music by a good composer, his musical salvation is possible. If he rests in the critical spirit, and finds everywhere only the tokens of inadequate treatment and old fashioned times, upon him has descended the curse of Mephisto:—"Every flower that he plucks shall wither."

Hence it is a great work for the public good that so

artist of serious intention and noble and poetic views of life takes upon himself, when he enters this lecture field, and one is glad to know that Mr. Baxter Perry is succeeding admirably in it. In the course of a season he gives some two hundred concerts or recitals, in all parts of the country, going mainly to boarding schools and to smaller places, where the usual means of musical culture need supplementing. He is a player of unusual powers, and as said, a lecturer of excellent good sense.

* * *

Upon the immediate occasion he played several pieces of his own. These were rather freely written for piano, the "Aeoline", "The Portent" and a ballade, "The Lost Island." The ideas in these works were pleasing and the treatment clever and interesting; they would make good studies for amateur pianists in general. It was of these that I thought when I said that perhaps the pedigrees of some of his pieces might be considered a trifle too long. For a large part of the history preceding these pieces was intended merely to lead to the main and central incident upon which the tone-poem had been founded. To a musician, the long story is unnecessary; to the unmusical, it sometimes takes the place of true musical appreciation. Nevertheless, all this is not to deny the fact that the pieces made much more effect under the inspiration of Mr. Perry's story than they would have made without this help—simply for the reason that the world still contains many millions of people who believe with Plato that it is not easy to make out what music signifies when words are not there to explain it. And it is perhaps true also that many, who ultimately arrive at musical and poetically musical feeling, do so by the way of poetic and imaginative aids, rather than through the direct and truly musical highway.

* * *

The question of the relation of a story to music, or rather of the place and importance of the representative element in music, comes up again apropos to the performance of selections from Schumann's music to Byron's "Manfred," in the symphony concert of November 3. The numbers given were the Overture, the Shepherd pipe, the Invocation of the Alpen fay and the apostrophe to Astarte. The overture, naturally, is devoted to the whole character of Manfred, who, as the reader will remember, was of a mysterious and complicated nature, such as later literature has made more familiar than when Byron wrote. The shepherd pipe is apropos to these lines:

"Hark, the note,
The natural music of the mountain reed—
For here the patriarchal days are not
A pastoral fable—pipes in the liberal air,
Mix'd with the sweet bells of the sauntering herd:
My soul would drink those echoes—Oh that I were
The viewless spirit of a lovely sound,
A living voice, a breathing harmony,
A bodiless enjoyment—born and dying
With the blest tone that made me."

The Invocation to the Alpen fay, to this passage:—

"Beautiful spirit, with thy hair of light,
And dazzling eyes of glory, in whose form
The charms of earth's least mortal daughters grow
Of purer elements; while the hues of youth—
Carnation'd like a sleeping infant's cheek,
Rock'd by the beatings of her mother's heart,
Or the rose tints, which summer twilight
Leaves upon the lofty glacier's virgin snow,
The blush of earth embracing with her heaven—
Tinge thy celestial aspect, and make tame
The beauties of the sunbow which bends o'er thee."

And the "Apostrophe to the lost Astarte was this:"—

"Hear me; hear me—
Astarte, my beloved; Speak to me:
I have so much endured—so much endure—
Look on me. The grave hath not changed thee more
Than I am changed for thee. Thou lovedst me
Too much, as I loved thee; we were not made
To torture thus each other; though it were
The deadliest sin to love as we have loved.
Say that thou lovd'st me not—that I do bear
This punishment for both—that thou wilt be
One of the blessed—and that I shall die:
For hitherto all hateful things conspire
To bind me in existence—in a life
Which makes me shrink from immortality—
A future like the past."

Concerning this music it is to be observed that it is not program music, properly so-called, in which music seeks to tell a story. The problem here is the exact opposite; the music seeks to interpret and intensify the attitude of the poem, and it was to be used in connection with the poem. That Schumann actually accomplished something better than the plan originally called for is now well known; but the poem is still in the foreground, and the music gains when we have Plato's suggestion of an explanation showing what it is all about.

* * *

To solve once for all the question whether music is better when it has an appreciable story, or when it is merely just "music," for itself and for what it has in it, is not for a passing occasion like the present. Time is long and art is eternal; there will be other days which perhaps will be more abundant than these in which we live. But if there is anywhere a piece of music which floats like a radiant cloud in the sunlight of the blest and the eternal, it surely is the Schubert symphony in C, which was given in the fourth symphony concert. From the heavenly beginning with that delicious melody for horns, through the driving Allegro, the leisurely and fascinating Andante, the irrepressible Scherzo with its mystical trio, clear through to the long Finale—this symphony is a piece of spontaneous melody, as free as the song of a bird. Nowhere from first to last is the note of passion and suffering touched. It sings and it soars from one idea to another, but never with morbid self consciousness, until at its close we seem to have been for a blessed hour in a higher world of melody. And then what delicious and characteristic instrumentation! How clearly Schubert must have heard these effects in order to write them with such masterly certainty. It was composed the year after Beethoven's death; yet there is not in it from first note to last a strain which recalls the ideas or the style of that great master, whom the young Schubert worshipped. What does it mean? What is its story for us who hear?

This is a question which may not be answered. The

symphony, like a beautiful landscape, is for what it is;.placed for the enjoyment of the beholder. A beautiful sunset needs no story. Nor are its beauty and impressiveness purely sensual or emotional—a trick of color and tint. The sun may shine after rain, but he who sees the shining may have slept during the rain which preceded it, and the shining as such may not have had a story within it. Is it therefore without a message? Surely, the radiance of the far-away gates of day may have in them something more than merely a beauty which the eye can see; in the clear light and immeasurable distance there is, as Max Mueller well suggests, a suggestion of the Infinite splendor, of which all earthly splendors and greatnesses are but remote and feeble types. And why not thus with a symphony like this?

* * *

What is it that one gets when through his spirit such a tone-poem has poured for a blissful hour? Is it merely something of emotional exultation? Nay, there is much more. It is not thought. For while Schubert is by no means to be spoken of in the patronizing terms of current English criticism, as a composer feeble in counterpoint (seeing that the thematic and contrapuntal work in this symphony are of a colossal order, yet always with the art which conceals art, and leaves the work as if it simply grew and grew and grew;)—it is not counterpoint which enthrals us,—nor are they ideas of power which we carry away with us from its hearing. It is rather a tone-poem, which for a time raises us out of the everyday world into the pure empyrean. Who knows but that the mere sounding within us of so many and so masterly chords of harmony may not have for our spirits something of the attuning power which Pythagoras believed music to contain?

It is curious also that the composer who in his multitudinous songs, covering almost every phase of poetic conception, has so widely illustrated the ability of music to harmonize with and explain a poem, should in this symphony and the unfinished, have written two works which do not admit of being saddled with a story; but which in spite of this fact have a coherence so peculiar, and a beauty and charm so commanding, that the world is content to admire and enjoy without endangering their charm by impertinent inquisitiveness.

* * *

Speaking of American composers and an American school of music, what is the matter with Mr. John Phillip Sousa? I went to hear his magnificent band at its four concerts in the Auditorium during the first part of November, and all my old admiration for this highly gifted artist revived and increased. Sousa's band is probably one of the two or three best in the world, and far the best that has ever been heard in this country. It is large and fully appointed, and its *personnel* is made up of masterly players, drilled into unity and sympathetic performance by Sousa himself, one of the best practical drill masters to be found anywhere. The range of their performances is something astonishing. Take, for instance, these two programs, of the last two concerts:—

I

Overture, "Raymond" .... *Thomas*
Plantation Dances .... *Maurice Arnold*
Excerpts from "Lohengrin." .... *Wagner*
Dance of the Bacchantes, from "Philemon et Baucis" *Gounod*
Douglas Club Two-Step (new) .... *Geo. Schleiffarth*

(Dedicated to the ladies of the Douglas Club, Chicago.)

Excerpts from "The Gotterdamerung." .... *Wagner*
Swedish Wedding March .... *Sodermann*
March, "Manhattan Beach." .... *Sousa*
Waltz, "Jolly Fellows." .... *Volstedt*
"Elizabeth's Prayer" (Tannhauser) .... *Wagner*

Mme. Francesca Guthrie-Moyer.

Fantasia, "Village Life in the Olden Time." .... *Le Thiere*
Overture, "1812" (The Holy War) .... *Tschaikowsky*
(A musical description of Napoleon's siege of and retreat from Moscow with cannon and bell effects, and occasional reminiscences of the Marseillaise and Russian Hymn.)
Excerpts from "Carmen" .... *Bizet*
Prelude, "Parsifal." .... *Wagner*
Sextette from "Lucia." .... *Donizetti*

Messrs. Bode, Griffen, Pryor, Lyons, Haase and Raffayolo.

"Ride of the Valkyries" and "Magic Fire" Scene .... *Wagner*

Minuet Antique. . . . . .Paderewski
March "The Directorate" (new). . . . . .Sousa
Prologue, "I Pagliacci". . . . . .Leoncavallo
Grande Waltz. . . . . .Venzano
Mme. Francesca Guthrie-Moyer.
Hungarian Rhapsody No. 14. . . . . .Liszt

From a high art point of view it is proper to mention particularly the performances of the selection from Wagner. These while written for orchestra, and therefore presenting peculiar difficulties when clarinets and oboes undertake the work of the violins, nevertheless have very strong claims of their own upon the attention of a band of this kind, since owing to the masterly effects assigned by Wagner to the brass and wood-wind, the characteristic coloring of the pieces in their original dress lies mainly in the very province in which this band is without a superior—namely in the horns, trumpets, trombones and reeds. In the "Ride of the Valkyries," for instance, the reeds and flutes have a very hard time of it in presenting the violin passages of the original, but the salient coloring of this strange work lies so much in the brass that the effect of the whole gives a very fair idea of the original, and it is unnecessary to add that the piece is telling. In the "Magic Fire" Scene, however, the band is not so satisfactory, the violin of the original passages being more important, and of a quality which no reed or flute can imitate successfully.

I confess, however, my admiration for Sousa rests quite as much upon his versions of popular songs as upon these great works. He is very liberal with encore numbers—sometimes I fancy almost too much so. When every important piece upon a program is responded to by one or two supplementary pieces of a popular character, it transforms the program as a whole in a little the same way as if in an elaborate banquet a few sandwiches of tongue, ham, or caviare, were passed around after every course. Gourmandism of this sort would very soon reach a natural limit, beyond which it would cease to be effective. But these intercalated numbers are often very clever as well as popular. For instance, at one of the concerts an old

resembling the well-
and the melody
and distant song-like
utmost delicacy. No
be nor how many com-
your mind, when you
glorified, like the familiar
ng or setting sun, and in
ts in the light of the eter-
"Marching thro' Geor-
enough to justify its intro-
d, and there is no musical

rank of his own. It seems
will lead to so many counts of
few months, but the cold fact is
Bell" and "Manhattan Beach"
months this year (closing Oct. 1st)
over six thousand dollars. The
will amount to about $15,000 for
Meanwhile another publisher is
of other pieces of his, with equal
benefit to Sousa, they having been
for a song, when as yet the name and
conductor were not recognized. This
means that these pieces have
originality, and that they please the
worth or more, upon a large scale, and
age, sex, or previous condition. It is
American music has to be taken because
the patent, or because the young composer
but simply because the music pleases.
to give Sousa credit for this. He is not
composition. He is simply a new kind of
song bird who sings because he feels good and
gift of melody. Heredity and environment have
much to do with the case. Italian upon his father's
German upon his mother's, he has been brought up to

manhood and professional success in the city of Washington, where a boy must be of poor nature indeed if he does not imbibe Americanism. Half way between north and south, in a sunny climate, amid surroundings imposing and suggestive of public festivals and emotions, and with his own way to make in the world, this young fellow had all the inspiration he needed.

I look for much greater things from him in the future. A great field is open to him, and I have no doubt that if he lives twenty years longer he will make himself a large name as composer. We live in a time when inspiration and impulse work off along the line of least resistance. This with Sousa as yet is through his band, and naturally in marches, the particular form of music which he oftenest needs for practical purposes. Later there will be higher demands, and the composer will meet them also. I understand that he has already written five operas. I hope they will be performed and succeed—as I am sure they ought. Then he will naturally write some more, and later tend more and more towards the type of grand opera, and so at length, twenty years from now, when we have found out the truth which all other nations have found out long and long ago, namely, that opera in a foreign tongue is merely a stage play with libretto accompaniment,—*then* we may have the real American opera, written by a master experienced, with light and firm touch; and with practiced ear, and not afraid of the deepest and most serious in music.

But speaking of credit, and of praise due, we ought not to forget that far-seeing and enterprising individual, Mr. David Blakely, without whose brain and management this band would not have materialized. Let us hope that the box office will duly remember to pay, day by day, the debt of a grateful country. As for glory, the press will take care of him, for no man has a larger or more advantageous journalistic acquaintance.

* * *

The excellent work of the Chicago Orchestra, under Mr. Thomas' direction awakens more and more admiration.

The program of the fourth concert was a very taking one. Here it is entire:—

Overture, "The Water-Carriers." Cherubini.

Concerto for solo violins, 'cello and strings, Handel.

Polonaise in A flat, opus 53. Chopin.

Instrumented for grand orchestra by Mr. Theodore Thomas

Symphony in C. Schubert.

The Cherubini work is Mozart-like in places; and pleasing. The Handel concerto, while now and then conventional, and recalling the cadences of the "Messiah", in other parts is very clever and fresh, and it made a very pleasing effect. The instrumentation of the Chopin polonaise is cleverly done, as one would expect, and the result is an interpretation of the polonaise beside which a piano performance sounds tame indeed, no matter who may do it. Mr. Thomas has had this piece in mind for many years, Rubinstein as long ago as 1874 suggesting to him that he ought to instrument it. It requires a very large orchestra.

* * *

At one of the recent symphony concerts Dvorak's fifth symphony was played, the one written since his living in New York, and called by him "From the New World." According to certain matter given out to the press, Dr. Dvorak has placed at the foundation of this work some "American" motives of negro origin. Passing the question whether the negroes are American in the strict sense of the word, and whether Indian would not have furnished at once stronger characteristics and more American ones, we come to the main questions, which in this case are two:—Has Dr. Dvorak here created, as his admirers claim, an "American" work? And, second, is the work itself great and beautiful. Taking the last point first, it may be said that the symphony is very lovely. The slow movement, which is founded upon a motive of almost prayer-meeting folk-tone, made a great success with the audience. The other movements are well done and pleasing, but in my opinion not so beautiful as those of the fourth symphony, played here under Dr. Dvorak's own conducting at the Fair. As to the first question, if there were more space available at this moment it would be interesting to go into it. Dr. Dvorak is a Bohemian, strongly national and racial in his individuality. He is one of the first masters of orchestral writing at present living. All his works show this; and all of them also show the unfavorable influence of an idea which the great master Haydn also had, that the *idea* in itself is nothing, but *treatment* everything. Many of the Dvorak motives are insignificant, and they do not lend themselves to the development of large ideas. In this respect it is only necessary to note the contrast between the ordinary motives of Dvorak and Tschaikowsky, the latter being longer, and capable of development from within—to climaxes far surpassing those of the Bohemian master. As to the American side of it, there is absolutely nothing in it. Fortunately for the national coloring, Dr. Dvorak has not retained very much of the negro motives, and in the form in which he uses them they would about as well pass for Bohemian. As to the workmanship, it is of course Bohemian, or rather German, with Bohemian rhythms and contrast.

This idea of bringing over a master of strongly marked racial and personal characteristics, already mature, and expecting him to produce for the first time a true "American" music, is worthy of expert admiration. It recalls the case of Mrs. Newrich, whose daughter lacking capacity, she proposed to buy her one. Residence of Dr. Dvorak in America is an excellent thing, for him; and not a bad thing for the country. It brings within reach of New York students the teaching of one of the first composers in the world. But that this excellent gentleman, speaking very little English, Bohemian and German to the core, will produce anything essentially different here from what he would while living in Prague, is out of the question, save in so far as the more liberal manner of living here, and the stimulus of new scenes and new friends may serve to give him a fresh incitation. The genial Mendelssohn was no more a Scotchman in writing the symphony bearing that designation than he was Italian when writing the next.

He was always of a Berlin Israelitish stock and a lovely personality, but never anything different from the station in which "it had pleased God to call him." This is the case with Dr. Dvorak. And while every new work from his pen will be received with pleasure and admiration, American composers and an American school are not to be imported at $15,000 a year, or any other sum, but must grow up here native to the soil.

* * *

I am exceedingly sorry to read in the *Music Review* for October notice that its publication will be suspended, for the present at least. The excuse assigned is that Mr. Cady requires all his literary time for working up his system of elementary music material, for which there is some demand. All the same I am sorry, for suspended animation is not always controllable at the will even of the suspender. The *Review* has been an interesting and capable periodical, and in conducting it too Mr. Cady has shown a journalistic ability of rare order. As a writer, readers of MUSIC know him to be thoughtful and idealistic to a degree, while as a practical musical educator he has ideas and methods which he has matured by years of active work and study. I have not learned what arrangement has been made regarding unexpired subscriptions.

* * *

Rubinstein is no more. He died of heart disease, at St. Petersburg, Nov. 20th, aged sixty-four. Thus departs one of the most conspicuous figures in the world of music. Incomparably great, at times, as a pianist, he aspired to be recognized as a still greater composer. In this he was not successful. While the many grand effects in his great works have been universally admired, the works as a whole contain many passages which are dreary in the extreme. Nevertheless he was a great and an imposing figure in the world of music. A Prince and a Ruler in Israel has fallen.

W. S. B. M.

REVIEWS AND NOTICES.

RICHARDSON'S NEW METHOD FOR PIANOFORTE. Revised by W. S. B. Mathews, with an appendix containing a Synopsis of the famous Pianoforte Technics of William Mason, Mus. Doc. Boston, O. Ditson Co., 1894.

Few of the American piano teachers now actively engaged in work can understand the influence which Nathan Richardson produced by the publication of his first work, "The Modern School" in 1852. That book practically consisted of the lessons which he himself had taken from the distinguished teacher, Alexander Dreyschock, with whom he studied for several years. Richardson had a hand which was utterly intractable for the pianoforte, and the fact that with all his ten hours a day practice he nevertheless could not play, was something which staggered Dreyschock immensely, for it had been one of his great principles that anybody could play who would practice. When Richardson came back to America and established himself in the music business in Boston, one of the first great enterprises was the publication of his work, and this was the first publication in this country of the Dreyschock-Tomaschek system of scales. The first work proved too difficult for use, and he soon set himself to make a simpler one, better suited to the popular demands. This work was "Richardson's New Method," which first saw the light in 1859, and, through the enterprise of the publishers, soon came in to a currency unexampled in the history of music publishing in America. Within a very few years the sales of this expensive book reached into the hundreds of thousands. From that time until the present the work has continued to enjoy a steady sale. The plates becoming worn, the publishers thought it a good time to make certain additions to it. Whence the present edition. All the matter in the original edition is here included, and a considerable number of new amusements are added, as well as important appendices, and a newly written system of the Elements of Music. In its present form it ought to prove even more popular than in its original guise. That it will not meet certain modern ideas of teaching is quite certain, for Richardson followed the German custom of his days and of the present no less, and made five finger exercises and the five finger touch the foundation of his system of technics. To all students or teachers, therefore, who hold to this method of building, the book makes a very strong appeal. The addition of the Mason principles of accentuation and the two-finger exercises will undoubtedly please many.

With reference to the general question of using or not using an instruction book in teaching, the determination is a matter of taste and convenience, which every teacher must settle for himself. There is this cast-iron feature about any instruction book, that an amusement which the pupil is quite ready to take up successfully may lie some pages in advance of the point which he has legitimately reached in his exercises. Moreover, the present writer thinks that there is a personal element in the Richardson Method, which has not been pointed out by any previous writer, namely, the early stage in the course at which his original work introduced the scales in double thirds and sixths. It would seem as if Dreyschock had introduced these heroic exercises in immediate connection with very easy pieces, such as the fourth Song Without Words, etc., in the hope of limbering up the rigidity of Richardson's hand. In the Modern School Richardson put these difficult exercises farther over in the book. But they still come in connection with a grade of easy pieces, such as would not agree with general usage. The copy at hand for the reviewer is in the so-called "American" fingering. It is a pity that this could not be abolished once for all, since its use only serves to confuse the student, who if he makes any considerable progress in playing is bound sooner or later to master the cosmopolitan system—the so-called "foreign," fingering, in which the thumb is called.

M.

CLASSICAL MUSIC. HOW TO UNDERSTAND IT. By Frank Parkinson, F. S. S., L. P. S. London. Printed by W. H. Whittingham & Co. 12 mo., pp. 105.

Presumably one is to take this well-intended little work in high seriousness. But in this case one must wonder at the public for which it has been prepared. To justify let us quote: "It is not necessary for listeners to sacred music to trouble their heads much to understand it, since it is invariably set to a form of words of which it is the choral counterpart. It is only in the preludes and interludes of dramatic oratorios that the sensibilities of hearers require to be somewhat on the alert respectively." (P. 15.)

A little later: "A short explanation of some high class work will now be given in elucidation of the foregoing remarks. Beethoven wrote the Moonlight Sonata upon a stone table by moonlight, under the leafy boughs of trees. (In Vienna it is referred to as the 'leafy sonata.') The Adagio sostenuto, which begins the work, breathes throughout the dejected calm of the complete despair of the occupant of a boat wandering by moonlight on the Lake of Lucerne. The short Minuet depicts an attempted kind of self-consolation, which should console the most disappointed lover. The Presto Agitato is full of impetuous tumult: and it is uttered in such a way as must move every suffering spirit for years and centuries to come."

"Weber's Sonata, Op. 39, in A flat major. This is essentially dramatic, and shows us the great dark forest with its muffled sounds, terrifying as if the moans of the condemned spirits are mingling with the blast of the wind, and sending a thrill of horror to the hearts of the young couple who are passing beneath the shadow of the trees."

THE EMBELLISHMENTS OF MUSIC. A Study of the entire range of Musical Ornaments from the time of John Sebastian Bach. By Louis Arthur Russel. Practically illustrated from the classics. Philadelphia, Theodore Presser. 1894. Cloth, 8vo., 60 pages.

In this somewhat extended treatise, profusely illustrated, Mr. Russel traces the history of all the musical ornaments, and shows the proper manner of performance. From a somewhat cursory examination it appears to be a well executed piece of work. It is published in good shape.

STUDIES IN SUSTAINED NOTES FOR QUICKLY ACQUIRING PROFICIENCY IN SEBASTIAN BACH'S METHOD OF PIANO-FORTE PLAYING. Composed with an explanatory History by Eduard Eggeling. Translated and edited by Albert Ross Parsons. Boston, New York, Chicago. Silver, Burdette & Company. 1894. Sheet music size pp. 51.

This work contains mainly five finger exercises of the old type, in which one or more fingers are held down throughout the exercise, while running passages are played by the other fingers. The present forms, have the great additional merit of being treated rhythmically, the movements progressing from quarters to eighths, and from eighths to sixteenths, sometimes twice or three times in the course of a page—the compass to which each exercise is carried. This type of exercise is of value for inducing a quiet position of hand, and if the fingers are not raised the tendency is towards a finer touch with the finger point than where the fingers are carried high and the hammer idea more rigidly carried out. They are, however, liable to one serious drawback, which the teacher must avoid by constant watchfulness: namely: the tendency to elevate the wrist and stiffen it. This is to be rectified by keeping the wrist invariably lower than the knuckle joints. The same end may also be accomplished by varying the elevation of the wrist, carrying it now high and now low—in order that the wrist may not fall into a set condition. A staccato touch, made by drawing towards the point of the finger, might advantageously be applied to the practice for a part of the time. These exercises are well adapted for use on the practice clavier, in which application the touch should be heavy a part of the time; and a part of the time very light, the up clicks alone in the latter case. While exercises of this kind cover but a small part of the whole field of technical development, they are useful at times, and indeed are hardly to be dispensed with. Applicable to a very limited extent in the second grade, a little more in the third, and still more in the fourth.

In the remarkably handsome November number of the Ladies' Home Journal there is a clever and interesting prize Christmas anthem, "While Shepherds watched their Flocks by Night," by Bruno Oscar Klein, of a character distinctly better than the generality of such compositions. There are in it, however, some rather queer cases of undesirable accentuation of the text, *e. g.*, at the word "Glad tidings of great joy," quite in the vein condemned by two writers in a former number of MUSIC. While Mr. Seidlinger is not right to the full extent in his position that the singer is to consider the text of an anthem as its only *raison d'être*, he is right to this extent, that unless the music intensifies the text, by making it sound more poetic, and imaginative and full of feeling, the music has no excuse. Moreover, the very first step towards this legitimate intensification of the text is to begin with the text itself, and deliver it better in the music than the elocutionist can do without the music. So is it in all the best cases of association of music and words.

HALF HOURS WITH THE BEST COMPOSERS. In 30 Parts, 50 cts each. Sold only by subscription. J. B. Millet & Co. Boston.

This intelligent work is published in uniform style with the "Famous Composers and their Works", noticed last month. Each number consists of forty-eight pages, quartos of which all but the first four are music. There is a portrait, a facsimile, and a very brief sketch of some one musician in each number, and in all that have thus far appeared the candidate is American. Thus we have here portraits of Karl Klauser, Reginald De Koven, Clayton Johns, Richard Hoffmann, Ethelbert Nevin, Emil Liebling, Arthur Bird, W. W. Gilchrist, Ad. M. Foerster, and Margaret Ruthven Lang. No. 10, for example, in which Miss Lang appears, has the following list of contents: "Twilight", and "Starlight", by Miss Lang; Romance sans Paroles, Camille Saint-Saens; "At the Fountain," Hermann Schultz; Mazurka, Leschetizky; Intermezzo, Jensen; May Song, Schumann; Andante Religioso, from 4th organ sonata, Mendelssohn; Impromptu, H. Kjerulf; Albumleaf, Grieg; Gavotte, from the opera "Roderigo," Handel. All pieces within the limits of the fifth grade. The two volumes when finished will form a handsome addition to the library.

THE MUSICAL YEAR BOOK OF THE UNITED STATES. Volume X. Season of 1892-1893. GEORGE H. WILSON AND CALVIN B. CADY, Editors. Chicago: published by Clayton F. Summy. Price $1, net. 32mo. Pp. 242.

This admirably made little book will be very valuable for libraries, and for statistical purposes, the more so because it not only gives a very large amount of particulars of the musical novelties brought out in various of the leading cities of this country, but contains a full list of the music of the World's Fair, from official sources. To the program maker, the connoisseur, and the musical statistician, it will be invaluable. Moreover there are brief reviews of the musical season in Boston, Mr. Philip Hale; New York, Mr. H. E. Krehbiel; and Chicago, Mr. Cady. The latter is extremely good.

SEVEN SONGS FOR MEZZO SOPRANO. The words collected from the poems of Alfred, Lord Tennyson. Music by Sydney Thompson. Four shillings. London, Novello, Ewer & Co.

Ask me not Why.
Tears, Idle Tears.
The Millers Daughter.
The Poet's Song.
As Thro' the Lands at Eve we Meet.
Now Sleeps the Crimson Petal.
Go not, Happy Day.

The harmonies of this collection of songs are modern, in the extreme. As an example mention may be made of the bass fifth, A—E bearing the triad of G in the next octave, which later resolves properly into the seventh of A. This a trifle reminds one of the story told of Whitney, the basso, in the older days, when Wagner was not so much an accomplished fact as at present. Some one asked him how he managed to find his proper note in such complicated selections as those from the "*Götterdämmerung*"; to which the basso replied, in that massive voice, which the world remembers with so much pleasure:—

"Perfectly easy my dear fellow. You see there are generally at least six notes of the scale sounding in any one of these chords; all you have to do is to notice which six these are, then taking the missing one, there you are."

The settings are musical, and occasionally strong.

WOMAN IN EPIGRAM. Flashes of wit, Wisdom, and Satire from the World's Literature. Compiled by Frederick W. Morton. 16mo, linen cloth, pp. 301. Chicago, A. C. McClurg & Co. 1894.

In this charmingly made little book Mr. Morton has accomplished something new. With ample skill he has caused two blades of grass to grow where there was but one before: he has written quite a number of new epigrams himself and he has brought together a collection of the most interesting blades, blades is the word, from the gardens of the world's literature. The result is something to be read for amusement and for fellow feeling. Even the gentle charmer herself will not find these exquisitely printed pages unenticing. This is merely another mirror held up for her—often one of those queer mirrors which with a surface of its own reflects back the image not in its just proportions, but distorted into something rich and strange. Women are fond of seeing themselves occasionally in mirrors of this sort, not taking the distorted outline to heart, as the honest opinion of the refracting glass, but as a joke, for right well every woman knows how she looks in a right-minded mirror. Therefore they may be expected to turn their attention to this new mirror of Mr. Morton's, in the which they will find such images as the following, culled at random:—

Proverb, "Second thoughts are best. God created man; woman was an afterthought."

Of quite opposite leaning is this from Alexander Dumas. "Woman they say was the last thing created, late Saturday afternoon. It shows fatigue." Or this from gentle William Shakespeare: "Two women placed together makes cold weather."

Honoré de Balzac:— "Woman is a creature between man and the angels."

Heinrich Heine:—"I do not know that she was virtuous: but she was ugly, and, with a woman, that is half the battle."

Antoine Pierre Berryer:—"There are no ugly women: there are only women who do not know how to look pretty."

Saint-Beuve:—"It is rare that after having given the key of her heart, a woman does not change the lock the day after."

Anonymous:—"The secret of youthful looks in an aged face is easy shoes, easy corsets, and an easy conscience."

Martin Luther:—"There is no gown or garment that worse becomes a woman than when she will be wise."

Frederick W. Morton:—"Psyche discovered her beauty in a quiet pool of water; and the first peep into Nature's mirror was the birth of vanity."

Frederick Sheldon:—"A woman's power lies in her petticoats, as Samson's lay in his hair; cut them off and you leave her at the mercy of every brutal Philistine, who now dares not be rude to her because she is sacred."

Chinese proverb: "Silence and blushing are the eloquence of women."

George Elliot:—"I dare say she's like the rest of the women,—thinks two and two'll come to make five, if she cries and bothers enough about it."

Wm. R. Alger: "There never were so many morally baffled, uneasy and complaining women on earth as now, because never before did the capacities of intelligence and affection so greatly exceed their gratification."

Jules Michelet: "Woman is a miracle of divine contradictions."

Latin Proverb:—"Trust not a woman, even when dead."

Italian Proverb. "Women, asses, and nuts require strong hand."

Frederick W. Morton:—"Faded beauties have this in common with time-stained abbey and other architectural ruins. They show to better advantage in moonlight effects."

Anonymous. "In this advanced century a girl of sixteen knows as much as her mother, and enjoys her knowledge much more."

Balzac:—"In love, a woman is like a lyre that surrenders its secrets only to that hand that learns how to touch its strings."

Frederic Shelton:—"Women are compounds of plain sewing and make-believe, daughters of Sham and Hem."

Barry Cornwall:—"The sweetest noise on earth, a woman's tongue; a string which hath no discord."

Anonymous:—Women are demons who make us enter hell through the doors of paradise."

Douglas Jerrold: "Virtue is a beautiful thing in women when they don't go about it like a child with a drum, making all sorts of noise with it."

Anonymous: "An opinion formed by a woman is inflexible; the fact is not half so stubborn."

Lemontey: "Of all heavy bodies, the heaviest is the woman we have ceased to love."

Marguerite of Valois:—"A woman of honor should never suspect another of things she would not do herself."

Julia Ward Howe:—"Man carves his destiny; woman is helped to hers."

George Brossin de Mere: "Beauty is the first gift nature gives to women, and the first she takes from her."

OTTO'S INSPIRATION. By Mary H. Ford. Chicago. S. C. Griggs & Co. 1891. Pp. 243. Linen cloth.

A very pretty story of the son of an eminent musician, left in poverty, but gifted with great talent. Tramping in rags and half-starved, playing his violin, his father's legacy, he comes at length to a farm house in New Hampshire, where somewhat grudgingly he finds harbor, and a sweet girl who later shares his lot. There are three motives in the book:—The musical heredity of the boy, and his habit of seeing invisible helpers, who teach him true musical expression, but not so obtrusively as to unfit him from learning from teachers; the socialistic discussion, tacitly in the history of the boy, and openly in the situation of Miss Herrick, the independent daughter of a wealthy New York financier, who herself breaks over the barriers which society and convention too often build around warm human hearts, to the studying of well meant human lives; and the narrow and grind-grind life philosophy of the farmers, Mr. and Mrs. Mayhew.

The book is worth buying as a pleasant and suggestive musical story; and it in no way distracts from its value that it also opens suggestions in many earnest directions.

NEW MUSIC.

(John Church Company.)

TARANTELLE. Opus 61, No. 3. $1.00. E minor. 7th grade. Xaver Scharwenka.

The celebrated composer, Mr. Xaver Scharwenka has here accomplished something which is not easy, namely to make a new tarantelle which is at the same time pleasing and original. The present work is clever, admirably adapted for teaching purposes, and equally grateful as a tone-poem for salon use. Modulations are fresh and pleasing, and the piece as a whole to be commended.

FOLK MUSIC OF THE OMAHA INDIANS. Collected and arranged for Young People, by John Comfort Fillmore, A. M. Director of the Milwaukee School of Music. Joseph Flanner, Milwaukee. 30 cts.

1. Call to the Feast.
2. Game Song.
3. Pae! G' Thun Song.

From an ethnological point of view, these melodies are interesting, and it remains to discover how interesting they will be to young people. They are easily arranged, falling within the third grade of difficulty. Aesthetically they belong to the primitive beginnings of melody, proceeding along harmonic lines.

"JOY TO THE WORLD." A Christmas Anthem. By Eduard Marks. Op. 40, low key, E flat. 75 cts.

A melodious anthem for single voice, with an effective climax. It is neither a declamation of the text, nor yet mainly a strophic song, but something between the two. The harmonies are modern, and the whole worth using.

"THAT LITTLE WIFE OF MINE." Song and dance. Music by Chas. H. Willis. For the popular ear.

"AWAKE AND HEAR MY VOW." Song for low voice. Music by Grace Allington Jones. 50 cts. Key of D major.

Effective for the voice, but evidently the work of an unaccustomed composer. On page 4 there is an atrocious open fifth between the soprano and bass, "craving now".

Piano Arrangement from "Madeleine, or the Magic Kiss." By Julian Edwards. $1.00.

Popular and pleasing, potpourri.

MENUETT. Op. 65, No. 1, G major. Middle piece in G minor. 5th grade. 50 cts. Xaver Scharwenka.

This composition has the merit of a decided rhythmic movement, which is more exactly that of the ancient minuet than one usually finds in modern pieces of this name. The motion is of eighths, in 3-4 measure, giving a six composed of three two's. From a popular standpoint its usefulness is a trifle impaired by the abundance of motion in the middle voices, which with changing harmonies give certain measures a bit of the character of organ music. But as a whole the piece is effective, and should meet with use.

BARCAROLLE. Op. 62, No. 2. Xaver Scharwenka.

An effective piece, but with a left hand part which will require a little practice to bring it into the necessary subjection to the melody, and up to the proper tempo. 8th grade.

TWENTY-ONE PROGRESSIVE OCTAVE STUDIES, for the piano by Carl Preyer. Book I. Easy.

This first book of octave studies, the only one which has reached the reviewer, is admirably adapted to the purpose for which it is intended. The seven studies it contains are not only moderately easy and progressive, but melodious and musical. Four of them have names appropriate to their contents: Melodie, Tarantella, Barcarolle and Gavotte. It will be of benefit to teachers and pupils to have their attention called to these excellent works. J. C. F.

ETUDE, Op. 25, No. 6, Chopin, arranged for the left hand by Leopold Godowsky. H. Kleber & Bro. L'td, Pittsburgh, Pa.

The original of this study is a very difficult and very productive one in double thirds, for the right hand. Mr. Godowsky has made a most admirable arrangement of it, giving the left hand the same practice in double thirds, which the original gives the right hand. He has done this with musician-like knowledge, good taste and discretion. The work is extremely difficult; but will prove of great value to accomplished pianists. J. C. F.

TWO SONGS: "Does the harp of Rosa Slumber?" and "'Twas Eve and May", Words by Lord Lytton; Music by Leopold Godowsky. H. Kleber & Bro., L'td, Pittsburgh, Pa.

These two belong to the better class of songs which aim at characteristic expression rather than at mere tunefulness; although the second is decidedly melodious. However, it is hardly fair to judge of the melodies by themselves, because they are so intimately bound up with the harmonies of the accompaniments, and grow out of them. These accompaniments are by no means easy to play, that is, for the ordinary run of pianists. They are well made and musician-like, and can be done well with a little practice. But both songs require a good singer and a good accompanist.

J. C. F.

LIEDER UND GESÄNGE, für eine Singstimme mit Pianoforte, componirt von Oliver H. P. Smith. Berlin, Ries & Erler.

Of these nine songs, six have texts by Heinrich Heine, including the well-known "Du bist wie eine Blume", one is by John Suckling, and the remaining two are by Mr. Smith, the composer of the music. The music shows that Mr. Smith's ideal is that of characteristic quality and expression rather than mere tunefulness; although the songs are by no means lacking in melodious quality. Character and expression are considered also in the harmony and modulations as well as in the motives, figures, and rhythms of the accompaniments. In No. 6, entitled "The Blacksmith," there is a predominance of 5-4 rhythm, which makes a very strong characteristic impression. In short, Mr. Smith is to be credited not only with a most sincere and earnest attempt at song-writing on the lines above suggested; but also with intelligence, no small degree of musical knowledge and technical skill, and an amount of poetical quality which awakens admiration and respect. Singers will do well to examine these songs thoroughly and carefully.

J. C. Fillmore.

WE also acknowledge the receipt of the following pieces:

A SERENADE: Four part song, by Frank E. Sawyer (White Smith Co., publishers.

This serenade is a very pretty good night song, most suitable to a male quartet, by that very gifted young composer, Frank E. Sawyer. The first tenor or soprano lies in the upper register entirely, and when well worked up is capable of some lovely effects.

THE ENCHANTED SPOT, and IN THE CLOISTERS are two songs out of a group of six, from the same composer, Frank E. Sawyer. (White Smith, pub.) The former is very beautiful, of a dreamy nature, for soprano, key of A. The beautiful words are from the "musicians' poet," Heine. The latter, In the Cloisters, is not as pleasing, being of a more sombre hue; still not bad.

From the same publishing house (White-Smith) come two little songs that are quaint and pretty. One, MY COMPLAINING IS BUT FEIGNING, is very dainty indeed, with a dash of coquetry in it, by F. A. Brown. The other, MAIDS ARE SIMPLE, is also by F. A. Brown. These two songs are suggested by, or revised from, old songs of the seventeenth century, which accounts for their quaintness.

DOES THE HARP OF ROSA SLUMBER? by Leopold Godowsky (Kleber and Bro.), is a song for high soprano, with an accompaniment to represent a harp. It is cleverly done, and of a pleasing character.

ELOISE, a song by T. Leslie Carpenter, is for a mezzo voice, pretty if with rather a common-place subject. It would be a good teaching piece, as it lies well for a mezzo voice, and is smooth and even.

AT DEWY MORN, H. Lane Wallace, is a very pretty duet for soprano and alto.

GRATITUDE, by C. F. Stayner, is a piece for piano, dedicated to Mr. Wm. H. Sherwood. One sometimes wonders why so fine player does not inspire more beautiful things. This GRATITUDE is a trifle prosy, about advanced third or beginning fourth grade. A good exercise for tied and slurred notes.

ESPANOLETTA MARCH, Harriet F. Jackson, is a pretty march for guitar, nicely marked as to fingering and phrasing.

THE SPINNE TANZ, Charles J. Wallace, is a bright piece, as its name implies, about fourth grade. It is a good exercise for accidentals, and chromatic scales.

FIRST VALSE LENTE, S. G. Cook, is a waltz in not a very marked degree, third grade.

THE PRACTICAL TEACHER.

"Will you please tell me how to get the benefit of Mason's Touch and Technic when I have but one hour a day to practice? I find the scales in Vol. 2 much easier than the two-finger exercises."

If the correspondent means that he has but one hour a day in all, for exercises, studies and pieces, not very much can be done. Naturally the two-finger exercises are more difficult, because they cover precisely that part of piano teaching which is neglected in all other systems, namely the manner of obtaining tone-quality. These forms are more productive for short time than either the scales or arpeggios. Therefore with only one hour in all, let at first twenty minutes per day be devoted to the two-finger exercises, working upon the first two pages for perhaps a month; then advance to the broken thirds, working at them about a fortnight; then to the other forms. After about two months of this leave the two-finger exercises for a while and work at scales. But in any case the time proposed is very short, and will lead to regular progress only in the case of very young pupils whose hands are flexible and who have everything to learn and not much reason to hurry. If one wanted to advance rapidly in technics, one would need twenty minutes a day for the two-finger exercise, and thirty or forty for the scales and arpeggios, with occasional changes off to the octave vol.

"Will you kindly inform me of a work on the "Forms" in Composition which would enable me to study the different forms without the aid of a teacher."

Probably the "Primer of Musical Form," by W. S. B. Mathews (A. P. Schmidt) will answer the purpose as well as anything, inasmuch as the teaching is clear, and the examples and analyses numerous.

SCHOOL RECITALS.

THE question that seems to bother the average teacher the most, and especially one connected with a school, is the question of a recital. "About once in so often," it really seems necessary to have one, for people seem to think that in no other way does a pupil show that she is advancing, while if the truth were known, the pupils never play so badly as at a recital.

A teacher thinks over the list of pupils, mentally takes account of how many are able to appear in public with any degree of success, or without making a total failure, and out of a class of 25 or 30, thinks himself lucky if he can get ten numbers.

Then after selecting the scholars, comes the extra practice, the partially laying aside of other things, in order to be able to play that one piece fairly well.

Of course it is never satisfactory, and the teacher groans inwardly and vows never to have another, while the pupil goes off and weeps and declares she will *never* play at another recital.

Having had a few such experiences, it was decided to vary the recital in a certain school, and call it "Literary Musicale." Several days before hand there was written on the blackboard a list of composers, at least as many composers as there were pupils.

Each one made her own selection, and as soon as she had selected one she went to the board and erased the name, so that the others would not take one already chosen. Each was required to to write a short sketch of that composer not less than 150 words, and not more than 500. All the essays had to be done by a certain time, that being obligatory; but of course the teachers stood ready to loan books with data, or give any suggestions that might be needed. When all was ready, on a Friday evening, they had the musicale. Each girl reading her own essay.

It seemed while being planned that it might be tedious, but it was a most interesting evening, all doing admirably well.

Now comes the question, what good did it do? And the counter question, what are you teaching for?

If you enjoy "Moonlight on the Hudson," "Old Black Joe" with variations, "Maidens Prayer," "Silvery Waves," and such pieces, then such an evening as described would do you no good, and one could just as well ask, "What are you teaching for?" If you have in mind merely the playing of a piece or the running of a scale clean and even, if, in fact you are working for outward show, you would not enjoy it. But if instead you try to let the scholars know that the names at the top of the sheet are the names of men who really lived, and some of them not so very long ago; if you can make them realize that those whose music has lasted the longest and is today as fresh as though just written, that those are the men whom we honor, if, I say, you can do ever so little towards this, then is your teaching not in vain, and you will see at once the value of such an evening. One pupil remarked she never had noticed who the composer was until she came to school; and while one might admit that her selections were not always according to her light, still she did notice, and it was a step in the right direction.

There is so much to learn in order to give even a half intelligent interpretation. The difficulties in the way do not sift themselves down to a Scylla and a Charybdis, for after you master the Scylla, right notes, and get around Charybdis, time, you still encounter the fingering, and after all these comes the pith of the whole thing, the expression. Of course all will admit that a knowledge of the man, the times he lived in, and his environment will help to a better understanding of the things he wrote. So try a Literary Musicale, if only to arouse in your pupils a spark of interest as to who wrote the piece, and who are the best composers, and so work on towards a *musical education* which is *not* a piano education only, but has to do with the head and heart. Try it and help on the cause.

E. C. M.

FRAU ROSA SUCHER
As Brünnhilde

MUSIC

JANUARY, 1895.

STUDIES IN SEMI-MUSICAL MYSTERIES.

NO Buttles to my knowledge, and certainly no Bobbs, (Mrs. Buttles was a Bobbs,) has ever showed a trace of musical ability, but as under the stiffest rules there are exceptions, our son Isaac Watts is developing a pretty talent for piano playing, which is at once my delighted wonder and my regret. I say regret because I had intended him for commerce. As our oldest son Jonathan Edwards is to be a preacher, I very naturally want some one to depend on in my old age, and I admit to sharing the current impression that musical gifts are not an unmixed benefit to a man. However Isaac Watts is here, and he has the divine something that sets the tone wizard apart from his kind, and there is no more use in hankering to have his powers exchanged for those that win in the Stock market than there is in wishing his red hair black, or his gray eyes brown. And as I listen to the sounds he evokes from his mother's jingling piano I find myself receiving three distinct pleasures. First comes my fatherly delight in his talents. Then comes the ear's pure enjoyment of the harmony or melody he is interpreting, and last but not least is the fascination of the ideas conjured up, the disclosure and even outpouring of what in articulate speech we attempt to qualify or gloss over, the pictures of human experience summoned before the mental eye. It is of this illusive third pleasure that I would write, yet as fancy is far more difficult than fact to enweb in words, and as my knowledge of the technic of the divine art is limited, I set forth my reflections with the "umbleness" of the immortal Mr. Heep. Perhaps they have naught to do with music and should be otherwise classified. When out of his pulpit, and down and out where he can be contradicted, a preacher is like a trout out of water, or a goose trying to perch on a tree, not quite at his best.

The mystery of time first claimed my attention. I noted it was a deeper matter than mere rapidity or slowness of execution, and is of the very essence of a composition. I doubt if Schumann himself could have explained why he wrote Grillen in 3-4 time, Ende vom Lied in 4-4 time, Warum in 2-4, and the exquisite Romance in F sharp in 6-8 time. Nor could Beethoven have told why he wrote the so called Moonlight sonata in 4-4, 3-4, and then in 4-4 time; and skipped around C in op. 27, No. 1, from 4-4 to 6-8 again to 4-4 then to 3-4, from which he went glibly, after going from gaiety to gravity, into 3-4. With these two as with the other masters all the answer to the questioner must have been, "They came so. No other time would have told the tales." Now it seems to me that each human being is set going in a certain measure, and after all what are we each one but a composition? Prof. Asa Popover is for instance a notable example of rapid 4-4 time, a sort of human gigue tripping about in the most industrious manner, and sure to close his life in just the phrases in which it began. Circumstances might have caused him to devote his days to Hebrew, or Latin, or the Hottentot dialects, if such there be, instead of to Greek archaeology; but no power on earth could change his pace or give him a glimpse of the far horizons commanded by his work. Not so Ezekiel Jubb, professor of Old Testament exegesis at Athensville. Nature started him off in the slowest variety of psalm time, and he has never indulged in accelerandos. But his is not a limited spirit. Every year he rises to a new height from which he sees fairer vistas, and only the brevity of life, and the slowness of his rate of speed will save him from the reprobation of those watchers on the out-posts of Zion, who keep their spy glasses trained for such as "abide not in the doctrine" as they understand it. Roger Harbottle is quite another sort of combination. I never know where he is. Sometimes he is in 2-4 time, and going at buzzsaw-like rate; sometimes he is in 4-2 time *adagissimo* at that. It is as if he were composed "quasi-fantasia," and I believe he is. Difference in ingrained time movement and musical feelings are just now fomenting a rumpus in Griggsville. The "casus belli" is in this locality as in others, both idiopathic and epidemic, as the doctors say. The young and middle-aged folk of quick tempo have some of them been dancing, and the slow coaches are after them with such speed and rancor as they can muster. The very slow people declare that it is pious to be slow. The allegretto and scherzo contingent protest it is pious to be joyful, and there is a great clatter of tongues on both sides of Turkey creek. Mr. Holler, the Methodist pastor, has come out strong and at both ends of the gamut, with all sorts of staccato and sforzando embellishments in denunciation of the practice, and I have brought down on my bald spot the wrath of the elect for failing to speak on the subject, and the vexation of the dancers for not taking their part.

"I," said old Dea. Bullhead who weighs two hundred and walks like a mud-turtle, "I think it's immoral. What do you think Dr. Buttles?" "Well I would not call it immoral exactly," I said slowly, and scanning my mental horizon for a convenient knot hole to slide into. "I sh-should rather call it, an unmoral mystery."

"Um!" said the Deacon who is very dense. "Well, perhaps it is."

"What's the harm of dancing?" demanded young Mrs. Dewberry last Sunday as we went down the meeting-house steps. "I wish you'd tell me Dr. Buttles what you think. Don't you think it's moral?"

Now as a 4-4 time man in very moderato movement, it is probable that under no circumstances would I have danced. And I am not only a preacher, but the son of a preacher. It is however the penalty of being "moderato," to feel both the secret of the allegrettos, and the andantinos. I fam-bled in my head for evasive phrases that would tell the truth, and not reveal all my thought, but I had to resort to my old answer. "I think," said I,—"that dancing is an unmoral mystery of ingrained time."

"Ah!" said Mrs Dewberry. "Ah."

After the subject of time comes the fact that one can start say on the key of C and unfold a tale of dissatisfaction, of baffled hope, of weariness, of rage, despair or grief; or by shifting a semi-tone tell something quite the opposite, nay give even a vision of that perfect happiness we call for lack of any other name, Heaven. And, as in the mystery of time I am reminded of human beings I have known, so does the mystery of mode again evoke a panorama. This afternoon I made ten difficult calls, and as usual I tackled the worst job first, and went to see old Zilm Pentlow. He has plenty of money for his wants, and is in very good health for his eighty-two years, but there is not for one good thing he has, or has had, a drop of gladness in him. All his long life he reviews every chance he gets with resentful bitterness, and while you listen to his ear-rasping you grow to feel responsible some how for his deep irritation. "I hed to be born in war time when victuals was high, an' comforts skurce," he recited when we were seated before his blazing grate. "I want nussed but brung up on a bottle, an' I'll bet th' milk was sour half the time, fur I remember well the kind o' pickle that Matilda was as hed keer o' me. I slept whur the snow drifted in nights, an' thur minute I could work I was set at it, fur our folks was a runnin over full o' childern. Nobody ever done nothin' fur me. 'Taint no wonder I've allus ben a kind o' a nubbin o' a man an' kind er shrunk up. I wonder I'm alive, I do." Try to run him off the track by praising the weather, and he will at once assure you it is the worst possible for his "nuralger." Mention somebody's troubles to take his mind from his own, and he will at once declare that the trials mentioned are mere flea bites to what he had to put up with way back in the thirties, and no end of times since. Speak of any one's good luck and he will at once tartly point out how little the blessing was deserved, and how much more be, Ziba, deserved such a fortune. Even when Peter Snell died after agonies of pain from cancer, Ziba would not abate one note from his symphony of miseries. "P'raps he did have to put up with a good deal," he snapped, "but what I've put up with, I haven't told. I don't tell all my feelings."

Next door to Ziba lives Jane Ann Todd. Her twin sister Miss Jemima Arabella lives this side of Turkey creek. Each one lives alone in a wee house, and each one has much ado to make, as Miss Jemima says, "buckle and strap meet." Miss Arabella was over to see her sister, and at sight of her Miss Jane Ann began to weep and Miss Arabella to smile. "So glad to see you," said the latter. "Dear me, isn't this splendid weather to be out."

"Yes so glad to see you once more," echoed Miss Jane Ann, her tears beginning to course down her cheeks. "Now days when I see anybody I say 'once more,' and ask myself will I live to ever again put eyes on 'em? We're poor frail worms Doctor, and fade as a leaf."

"Pshaw!" exclaimed Miss Jemima poking at her false front. "We're the children of God and made in his image. It says so in the Bible. And we'll live our 'pinted time."

"I don't feel sometimes as if I could live my 'pinted time," whimpered Miss Jane Ann, sniffing hysterically. "I aint like sister, Dr. Buttles. It aint in me to do as she did last summer, take about all she had in the world to go down into the bowels of the earth to see things that had better in my opinion be left covered, if they do call it the Mammoth cave. I feel that at seventy the place for me is home."

"But you like to stay home, Jane Ann," said Miss Jemima cheerfully and historically, "and you do like to cry."

"Well," sobbed Jane Ann giving way entirely, and putting up her handkerchief. "If I cry it's because it's all the comfort I have except going to the grave yard How can I do anything else a thinking of them that's gone."

Miss Jemima turned her sweet, keen, old face toward me and said softly as if in explanation, perhaps of the trip to the Mammoth cave, "it's because of those that are gone

I try to interest myself in things outside my home. And why shouldn't I? It is so pleasant to live." We went along together over the bridge and for the first time since I have known her, Miss Jemima spoke of their odd separation. "I can't stand Jane Ann's taking on," she said in her quiet way, "and I find my cheerfulness is actually wearing to her. Here we are 70, and we'll be 700 before we can live together I fancy."

"True, but how strange!" I told my myself. "Two lives start together and are born of one mother, but one is in E major, and one in E minor, and there is nothing to be done but to keep them apart and it is well that Turkey creek is wide."

I keyed myself up for the rest of the duties of the afternoon by dropping in to see the Widow Bassett. Long ago she lost husband and children. Then came money troubles and first one and then another incompetent relative saddled himself upon her patience. Just now she is burdened with her husband's niece, a lump of misfortune who has a dozen or more imaginary diseases, and would wear out an iron image. I found the little woman sewing buttons on a great pile of overalls and softly singing, "There is a land of pure delight." A bottle in which were a few white clovers was on the table beside her, and she greeted me as if hers were the finest house, and the happiest lot in Griggsville. Not until I was well under way toward the Bullhead homestead did I recollect that I had intended to give a glance at her wood pile, so completely had her self-forgetful cheer made me lose sight of the fact that she is old, and lone, and poor. And just here is another mystery. May not the most engaging major humor owe much to certain worries and perplexities kept out of sight, even as the high lights in a major composition owe much to the shadows etched in by minor dissonances? Just what we owe to our tribulations we can never know. Trial seems necessary to perfection in all grades of life, spiritual, mental, physical and even vegetable. Last spring I for the first time planted squash seeds in my garden. Naturally I watched them from the day I first found two fat cotyledons open and ready for business. But just as the golden blossoms began to enclose I went over to Pontiac, and when I returned a myriad ill-favored and ill-savored bugs were teetering up and down my vines. My wife claimed to know squashes, and she declared the bugs were essential, so to speak, to their salvation. I did not believe it, and arming myself with one of her long hat pins proceeded to pick off the enemy. Not one tendril or succulent twig was crushed in the process, but for secret and occult causes those vines wilted, blackened, died, and I have had to buy my Hubbards as usual; and it has been borne in upon me that the good old-fashioned doctrine that trouble is a means of grace has much to vindicate it. But secretly and always when I hear Isaac Watts doing something mournful and minor, I tell myself that too much has been made of the words of Eliphaz the Temanite, and that if "man is born unto trouble as the sparks fly upward," an occasional and not a continued state is indicated. Healthy human nature finds satisfactory expression only in the major music, and in this I find subtle suggestions that our true dower here is happiness, and a little later,—Heaven,—but this like all the rest is a great mystery.

URIAH XERXES BUTTLES, D. D.

ON THE CULTIVATION OF MUSICAL MEMORY.

IT should be stated at the outset that it is not the purpose of this essay to deal with the process of memorizing musical selections for reproduction, a subject which already receives, perhaps, more than its proper proportion of attention, on account of its utility for purpose of display; but to discuss only those less complete forms of memory which have to do with culture and mental development, and are, therefore, for the most part, entirely overlooked by teachers and pupils. I do not intend to disparage in the least the value of playing without notes, but when the immensity of the field of good music is borne in mind, it is difficult not to question the wisdom of devoting so much time to the exact memoriter study of the trifling handful of pieces that the pupil can learn, and leaving almost neglected, so far as scientific study goes, the broader and to my mind more valuable field of the partial memorizing of many great works.

It must be considered that what the ordinary student can learn for his own performance is but a mere handful of water dipped up by the shore. The great ocean of art lies outside. Suppose that he begins at the age of eight or ten with memorizing Kinderstucke and sonatinas for the piano. What he learns by heart keeps pace only with the growth of his finger technic, which is slow and painful, not with that of his mind, which may be swift and joyous. When his musical education is "completed" his memory may be well stored—with what? With those selections for the piano that lie within the scope of his fingers and which he has had time to memorize. He can perhaps sit down and play some hours at a stretch. When his repertory has been gone over he is like an automatic organ that has got to the end of its perforated strip, except—and this is a large exception—for such fragments of outside music as may have stuck to his untrained memory. It may be retentive, and then he seems to us a prodigy, so unaccustomed are we to storing away the treasures of the tone world systematically in our minds. But if his memory is naturally unreceptive his knowledge of music is likely to be of the parrot order. He will be a mere barrel organ to repeat the music he has learned.

Is this an exaggerated picture? How many teachers concern themselves with the musical memory of their pupils, except so far as it is concerned with "playing without notes?" How many pupils spend any time at all in the systematic training of their memory, or are devoting the precious years of their youth to fixing indelible impressions of great master works in their minds? And yet the best, the richest part of culture comes from that very thing, the quiet, unceasing storing away of piece after piece till the memory is a treasure house of good things. Here we need the assistance of a teacher of music to supplement the work of the teacher of the piano, or the violin, or the 'cello, or the voice. In the absence of such a teacher, either these specialized teachers of performance must lend their assistance, or the pupil must shift for himself, and in either case these hints may afford some help. They are deduced from my own experience as a critic, in the course of which I found that an additional training, not given in the music schools, was required. Instrumental work, harmony, musical history, were all very good, but none of them quite hit the right place.

The needs of the musical critic may seem a little outside of the regular field of musical study, and yet, when you stop to think of it, the requirements of his profession are only the requirements of complete artistic culture. He must know practically the whole field of the best music, so that he may never write a scathing review of a Gade symphony and find too late that one by Beethoven had been substituted, as befell a Zurich critic the other day. He must never speak of Gounod as the writer of the Manzoni Requiem, a disaster which once ruined the career of a Chicago critic. Could anything less be required of a cultured musician? He must have the background of a well-stored memory, which is the only standard by which the worth and originality of a new work can be determined. It may make all the difference in the world in the value of a new composition whether its best themes are original or borrowed from Wagner or Beethoven. The critic must *know*, or so far as that is concerned he is no critic. Would any educated musician be satisfied with less? Then why not make the years of musical education, when enthusiasm runs high, when the mind is quick and flexible and the memory retentive, bear upon this very thing, instead of leaving the student to pick up in a haphazard way what stray bits may happen to stick to him.

It has often struck me that a majority of the professional musicians of my acquaintance are surprisingly ignorant of the musical literature that lies outside of their special field. There are of course many distinguished exceptions, like Bülow and in our country Theodore Thomas, men who know everything; but as a rule a musician is not to be counted on outside of the special field in which he is himself interested. One will find great oratorio singers who could not for the life of them identify Beethoven's C minor quartet, or Schumann's "Etudes Symphoniques" or Chopin's E minor piano concerto, though they may know the whole oratorio repertory by heart, while it will often be the case that a pianist who has literally hundreds of great works, from Scarlatti to Schytte, at his finger tips, will be puzzled to place a Franz song or a Mozart quartet. If this is true of men whose whole lives are given up to music, a much stronger statement might be made of the musical amateurs whose memories are burdened to retain a scant half dozen selections at a time, and whose opportunities for hearing music have been comparatively limited. The cause of this weak development is not so much excessive attention to memorizing, although that may be carried to such an extent as to absorb an undue proportion of the pupil's time and energy, as to an unfortunate neglect of these lower, or rather less complete forms of memory which from their vast scope are infinitely more valuable for purposes of musical culture than the memorizing of the few study pieces that can be learned in the class room.

As no essay can make any pretentions to scientific weight nowadays, unless it starts off with a little psychology, it will be well to give an analysis of this inferior or imperfect memory which has generally been allowed to grow at its own sweet will. Stiedenroth in his "Psychologie" Berlin, 1824. p. 82, says: "Forgetting admits of several degrees or stadia," and these, ennumerated, are as follows:

1. Momentary displacement of an object which is certain to spring back as soon as the object displacing it is gone.

2. Withdrawal of the attention as when we seek to forget a painful object.

3. Slip of the memory so that an object does not present itself spontaneously, but must be thought of.

4. Slip of the memory so that we bethink ourselves in vain.

5. When the object has vanished for so long a time that we question whether we can by any effort bring it back.

6. When we conclude that we are absolutely certain that we cannot bring it back.

A captious critic might object that in spite of his system the learned German has omitted several "stadia," as for instance, when we know that we could think of something if the pianist in the next flat would stop practicing "After the Ball," but there is nevertheless practical utility if not scientific completeness in such an analysis, and I propose a corresponding series of stadia for musical remembering.

1. Complete—Power to reproduce the whole (memorizing).

2. Power to reproduce themes and harmony, and indicate form and order.

3. Power to reproduce leading melodies.

4. Power to recognize theme and form, and detect incorrectness in playing.

5. Power to identify some one theme when heard.

6. Power to identify the piece as a whole without specific recognition of theme.

Of these stadia the only one which is commonly recognized and systematically taught by most teachers is the first, and indeed the lower forms scarcely seem to be regarded as memory at all. One is reminded of the English boy who had much trouble in remembering dates, but none at all in giving the list of Derby winners. "That is not memory at all," he explained lucidly, "that is just knowledge." A psychological observation which is not without value for the teacher. It may be admitted that the first is the ideal form of memory. Just so, one might wish to have the whole range of literature committed to memory verbatim, but since that is impossible, it is much better to have a vivid impression of all the great masterpieces from Chaucer to Browning than to spend too large a share of the time devoted to literature in preparing pieces for recitation.

The second degree of memory is that which musicians commonly have of a piece which they have studied but have not memorized, and it is almost as useful for esthetic purposes, while involving for most persons only a tithe of the time required for memoriter study. This degree of familiarity is also attained by musicians and gifted amateurs through the simple hearing of a work one or more times according to the receptivity of the memory. And here I must say, though I may be treading on heretical ground, that the ability to reproduce large portions of a work from a single hearing is not necessarily a concomitant or a sign of musical ability, although they are often found together. To draw an illustration once more from a cognate art, it does not at all follow that a great poet or a gifted critic of letters can reproduce whole scenes from a new drama he has heard once, nor does the ability to do so constitute one a litterateur. It is, however, true that such a memory for musical themes is commonly a sign of a musical physical organization and that the ease with which it enables one to store away materials for comparison and analysis is an immense help in study, though it by no means necessarily gives critical acumen.

The third degree, the power to reproduce at will leading melodies, is that commonly possessed by musicians in regard to pieces that they have heard but have not studied, and by amateurs in regard to pieces in which they are specially interested. After an opera persons with good memories may be heard humming or whistling snatches of favorite airs which are usually soon forgotten as some new favorite takes their place. When systematically remembered these partial impressions may be made the basis for a development to the next higher stadium.

So far, all these forms of memory involve the power of reproduction at will, which is, as everyone knows, much more difficult than the recognition of music when called to mind from outside. This, in its most perfect form, is the fourth stadium, the power to recognize themes and form and detect incorrectness in playing. It may seem surprising that such intimate knowledge should exist, but everyone can think of many selections which he could not recall for the life of him, but which he would yet know intimately as soon as he heard them. This is especially the case with pieces which musicians have studied thoroughly and then outgrown and forgotten, school room studies, etc., and also of selections which have been heard many times in an absent-minded way without any sharp effort of the attention. The problem here is to convert this passive knowledge into prompt and spontaneous knowledge, and it is often surprising how little effort is required to develop a selection from this to the second stadium.

The fifth stage, the power to identify the leading theme when heard, is perhaps as elementary as will allow any one to claim any knowledge of a selection at all. Yet it is not without value, for the reason that it gives a nucleus about which a more intimate acquaintance may grow. For purposes of musical scholarship it is also worth while to know many pieces in this way which perhaps need never take a more intimate place in the contents of our minds, just as a student of letters, again, must be able to "place" many out of the way pieces and essays in which we have no special interest. It is necessary for the music critic, in particular, to know hundreds if not thousands of lesser selections in this way, although he may not care to burden his mind with any special study of them. Among these are to be reckoned the countless operatic arias of the schools which are now rapidly fading, but which still hold a place for display purposes on the stage. It should be a constant effort, of course, to rais the worthier of the selections which are known in this way to a sharper and more definite form, such as the third stadium.

The sixth and lowest stadium is but the shapeless protoplasm out of which more definite memory may be created. It is the memory which an untrained person has of a work which he has heard recently, unless some striking theme has implanted itself upon his mind, or which a person with specially good musical memory has of a work which he has heard in the remote past, without any effort to renew his impressions. To the music critic it is not without value, because it may protect him from blunder in the event of a change in the program, and it is doubtless necessary for everyone to keep a large proportion of the selections that he has heard in this limbo of outer darkness, halfway between remembering and complete forgetting. It is possible to have a good deal of knowledge of a piece stored away in this rather nebulous form, so that much less attention is required to attain a good memory of it than would be the case with an entirely new piece of music. It is a good deal as it is with the houses on the street which you have walked past so frequently that you never think of noticing, and which you would have difficulty in describing, although a few minutes of close attention would reveal to you how much you had really known, almost unconsciously.

The advantage of such an analysis of the contents of the memory, is that it enables one to classify selections in a rough way and check them off as they are advanced from one stadium to the next. The advantage of a little system in this respect hardly needs to be pointed out. It is not a bad idea for the student to sit down with a few sheets of blank paper before him and try writing down the names of the works which fall into each division of his memory. For most pupils probably a sheet or two will serve for the first stadium, and the space required will increase as the lower forms are reached, till in the fifth and sixth classes it will be necessary to make a selection, writing down only the things that one ought to know better. Some years ago I found myself with plenty of leisure in a rather broken form, and as reading tired my eyes while traveling I set to work to exercise my memory on English poetry, and by systematically applying the method here described to verse, I soon found myself with a choice corpus of over 200 poems, acquired without the slightest trouble, and retained in memory by the minimum of exercise. The plan which I used for keeping track of my work was to write the title of each poem on a visiting card or pasteboard of that size, and arrange them according to the stadium which they had reached. When a piece was better learned it was advanced to the next stage, when it showed signs of slipping it was put back a stage, and by running over a few each day, the whole body, which it would require days to go through entire, was easily kept in memory. The same method will be found equally applicable to music.

It should be remarked as a caution that while it is desirable to guide the work of the memory so as to secure as complete a body of the greatest music as possible, it is better to follow the natural lines of interest and opportunity, leaving the gaps to be filled up as one is able, rather than to set out to learn everything by main force. Utilize rather the existing contents of your mind. If you have the unfinished symphony in the third stadium get a score and bang away at it until you get it to the second. If you know nearly all of "Elijah," look out for the omitted portions and work them into your scheme by degrees. When you are all warmed up on a new work keep up the interest till you have indelibly stamped it upon your mind, and at every new hearing add a little increment to the existing nucleus. Much greater results can be obtained in this way than by setting out in cold blood to fill out your collection, and in the course of years the repertory of your memory will become rounded out and complete if attention is paid to a careful selection. Almost every concert may be made the means of advancing some great work from an imperfect stage of memory to the next higher.

Every one has his own method of remembering, and it is of little use to borrow that of another person, but it is possible that a few hints may not come amiss to those whose memories are treacherous. The one great secret is concentration of attention and the one great difficulty in securing that at a concert is the quantity of matter that is given. For the beginner it is like pouring a gallon of water into a pint cup. When his memory is full, his attention becomes distracted, and in this way there is a danger of forming a habit of mind-wandering which is fatal to musical success. Too many students listen to music only as a succession of sweet sounds: it comes in at one ear and goes out at the other, and it leaves no more effect than running water. It is by no means true that it is always wrong to give oneself up to the emotional enjoyment of music, and to indulge in revery as we would in the presence of a gorgeous sunset, without any critical study of form, or effort to fasten the contents in the memory. But if this is allowed to become a habit, the effect is ruinous.

The student who is not unusually favored in his surroundings will be more or less hampered for lack of opportunity to learn music which he does not himself perform. For many the only resource is concert going, which is a poor enough makeshift for studying music, compared with the inestimable advantage of being able to hear a thing over and over again, to go back and observe, to repeat portions ad libitum. The piano student has a great advantage over other musicians here, in his power of not only reading but playing scores, an accomplishment which should be strenuously cultivated. An hour or two of diligent practice at the key board *before* a concert will add many fold to its value. With the motifs and general treatment committed to memory, the mind can be left quite free for the study of the ensemble, instead of being so engrossed with the scale relation of a few tones that little power of attention is left for the orchestration, the execution, or the inner meaning of the work. The score is the medium from which the greater part of one's musical education must be drawn, and skill in its use cannot be too assiduously cultivated. And here I am tempted to put in a word of defense for those automatic devices so much scorned of musicians. That they are a wretched substitute for the spontaneous living music of an artist, goes without saying, but that is hardly the point just at present. There are several automatic arrangements that will play overtures, sonatas and symphonies with accuracy, and for which a large repertory of the best music may now be had. There is to my mind no doubt whatever that the violin or voice pupil who is unable to play the piano, and has no friend who is willing to oblige him at the cost of considerable trouble, can hardly do better than set up an automatic organ or piano in his room, and diligently exercise himself in feeding the stripe of perforated paper through the mechanism. The results will, of course, be atrocious, but he can neglect everything but the harmony, and the machine has at least the merit of being patient. It will go back as many times as is desired, and repeat one theme till all the neighbors in the block are crazy. I do not love automatism in music, but the one thing needful is this patient exercise of the ear over passages of harmony repeated again and again. Every music student should learn the piano if he can, but if this is impossible he must fall back on the next best thing.

Much may be done toward the cultivation and storing of the memory, however, simply from attending concerts, by one who will take the pains. The great thing is to prevent mind-wandering. This is a suggestion more easily made than carried out, for an untrained mind is simply incapable of listening with undivided attention to a concert two hours or more in length. It is bad psychology to attempt any such thing at first. It results in an over-straining of the attention and a state of hypnotized stupor from which the memory carries absolutely nothing away. Much better for the untrained mind is it to pick out one or two selections, preferably those at the beginning of the program and to listen with the keenest, most absorbed attention to every note of the music, striving to implant it in the memory. If one could leave then it would be well, but the time spent if one remains need not be wasted. The varying orchestral effects can be noted, and specific things can be looked for, even though the mind is no longer capable of its first fierce vigor of application. Little and often is the motto for genuine artistic growth, and it is the reversal of this principle which makes the music festivals of our smaller cities so comparatively ineffective for culture. Half an hour a day or fifteen minutes twice a day of close listening is infinitely better than six hours of somnolent listening once a week. I should like to see a conservatory of music establish a course of daily recitals just twenty minutes in length, with a special premium to students for the amount which they were able to remember. I think that the graduates of that school would carry a good deal more away with them than they do at present.

I feel some diffidence in presenting a trifling device of my own for remembering rebellious melodies, but I have found it so helpful myself that I am encouraged to believe that others will find it of utility. It is possible that many have hit on the same scheme, but I have never seen it described in print. It consists simply in sketching the general outline of the melody in light dots, the duration of the notes being roughly shown by the size of the dot, and the pitch by the distance above a real or imaginary line takes as the key note. No staves are used, and no special effort is made to make distance accurate, the only idea being to afford a starting point for the memory when it is overwearied with many selections. It is astonishing how frail a peg will serve to hang a complete recollection upon. For instance the leading melody of Chopin's G major nocturne, op. 37, No. 2, I would sketch roughly thus:

the first four bars of the Schubert "Serenade":—

Unusually prolonged notes may be indicated by drawing the hand along slowly at a uniform rate while the note is held, and as every motion is to be made exactly as the corresponding tone is played, the relative lengths will be found a close guide.

For years I have been accustomed to cover the margins of my programs with these jottings, and find myself able to recall a dozen themes where it would be difficult to remember three without such help. At the same time it is free from the objection of enervating the memory, for the reason that it is so elementary, so fragmentary, so sketchy. It gives merely a salient outline or two, only a point of departure for the memory. It is of course open to the objection of substituting a visual for an auditory form, a substitution which has always impaired our musical education, but it is less open to to this criticism than the consulting of a score, because the bulk of the work is left to the purely musical memory. If a system of recording notes without such a symbolism in terms of space could be invented it would be preferable, but I myself know of none but the phonograph, and that is hardly available yet for use in concert halls.

It might be observed in this connection that one of the great difficulties in remembering music lies in the isolated character of its phenomena. With objects that lie in the material world one sense helps another. The impressions of sight rest on those of touch, and in both the relations of proportion, direction and form are the same. But in music proportion and form are blank mathematical abstractions, which can only be compared to objects in the visual world by a forced analogy. There is not even such a thing as direction in music except by an arbitrary convention. There is no real reason why the left end of a key board should be called the lower end, nor why we should speak of the soprano notes as high or the bass notes as low. When we speak of singing up and down a scale we do not mean that one note is really above the other, but our minds are so enslaved to the forms of space that we can hardly conceive of tonal difference in any other term. This is undoubtedly one of the things that makes the musical memory so treacherous. The ordinary laws of association go by the board. Not even names are so slippery as airs and harmonies can be at times. Who is there who has not been in the state of the grave-diggers in Hamlet?

2nd Clown: Marry, now I can tell.

1st Clown: To 't.

2nd Clown: Mass, I cannot tell.

To hold an air thus in the dim limbo of the mind, neither forgetting nor remembering it is a real torture, and when the unwilling melody finally responds to the memory there is a joy such as follows a painfully deferred sneeze. When the notes have slipped the mind there is no use in trying to pounce upon them, they are too cunning and elusive. Nor can one stalk them under the shelter of shrewdly devised parallel approaches of associated ideas. The best that can be done is to outdo them in cunning, to pretend to have forgotten their existence and engross the mind in something else. Then the coy tune stealthily approaches and if one has luck it can be captured before it can escape. It is a curious phenomenon that the themes of a newly heard work often vanish entirely from the memory for the time being, and reappear in the most unexpected manner, days or it may be weeks afterwards.

This unique character of the musical memory makes any system of mnemonics of little avail, and indeed such systems are generally of but little utility in any field and are likely to injure the memory by allowing it to lean too much on crutches. A few years ago a notorious character who had pilfered and put together a system of "Physiological Memory" took many thousands of dollars out of the pockets of college students and professors for his secret. Among his victims were many music pupils, but the sole consolation that they found was in the following paragraph in the lessons:

"Another result of this genuine memory training is that my pupils can hereafter learn to play or sing or speak without notes, and this is done without any resort to devices, but solely from the new memory power. Musical notation, as in a tune to be remembered, is a series of complex symbols; and to resort to any device to enable you to remember that series, would be only imposing another burden on the memory."

That is to say, he gives musical mnemonics up as a bad job, and he is quite right. The only pity is that he was not equally sensible about other things. Nevertheless some pupils seem to think that there is such a system by which they can learn to remember with less labor. The sooner they cease to entertain that delusion the better. It is based upon a mistaken idea as to what is remembered, which also crops out in the paragraph quoted above. In exceptional cases, as with the blind who have the score read to them note by note, the symbol may come to be the thing that is remembered, but the normal method has nothing to do with symbols. The tones themselves should be remembered, and as directly as possible, with no lame reference to a staff, or a keyboard, or a finger board. It is likely that the blind and others who memorize symbols usually retain these only long enough to transfer the purely musical impressions to their minds and then make the latter the basis of their memory, and a symposium on this question among those accustomed to learning music in this way would be of interest. But while mnemonics are of no avail, the system of sketching indicated above will serve to give that typographical assistance which one relies upon in remembering objects in the outside world, and the lack of which constitutes a great difficulty in musical memory. It is astonishing how much the merest hint will do in recalling a half forgotten air.

A method which hardly comes within the field of legitimate music study, and which is yet at times surprisingly helpful, is that of associating words with instrumental themes. It is a matter of common experience that songs are much better remembered than music without words. The association of poetry and music undoubtedly helps the mind to retain both. It is hard for one who has been thrilled with the magnificent soar and sweep of Gounod's melody to forget "Plus grand dans son obscurité," from "La Reine de Saba," and scores of the exquisite lyrics of Schubert and Schumann are held in memory when as instrumental airs they would perhaps escape. To hear "He, the best of all, the noblest," or "Hark, hark, the lark," is to remember it once for all. That there is convenience, then, in applying the same principle to instrumental music can hardly be denied. How far it can be legitimately carried is another matter. To take an illustration, the opening bars of Beethoven's beautiful sonata, op. 31, No. 3, have been ingeniously coupled (perhaps by the editor of MUSIC himself, for I first heard it in an uncommonly interesting lecture by him a dozen years ago) with the words "Liebst du mich?" "Nein, nein, nein, *nein!*" an association which is not only irresistibly funny, but holds that melody in the mind as though it were glued there. Yet, the effect is a little shocking, and one needs to be very careful before admitting any such associations to the mind, for once in, they stick like burrs, and to one's dying day they cannot be forgotten. Has not the exquisite trio of Chopin's "Funeral March" been ruined for many a gentle soul because some miscreant who has never got his reward in this world but will in the next, deliberately set it to—*horresco referens*—"Somebody's coming for a twilight call." A dirge that might serve as the requiem of a universe, and this paltry knave could see nothing in it but "Somebody's coming for a twilight call." It was for such people that Judge Lynch invented his celebrated code of criminal procedure. So it is well to be cautious how we couple fine themes with any words whatever, but if an air is not especially endeared to us this is a convenient way of engraving it upon the tablet of our of our memory. Take the well known theme from "Rigoletto" sometimes set harmoniously to "You will hardly ever hit it, ever hit it if you try," and see if you can ever forget the combination.

A matter upon which it is impossible to lay too much stress is accuracy. One who has known by experience what subtle changes creep into even a carefully memorized work by frequent repetition without consulting the score can best appreciate how a partly memorized selection is likely to become altered. It is not sufficient to think a work over at intervals; it must be carefully compared with the original, either in the score or at a performance, or grotesque variations are likely to creep in. Groups of eighths and sixteenths get smoothed out to triplets, dots are interpolated where they have no business, wrong notes somehow get to seeming right, and in the course of a few years that air is altered so that the author himself would hardly recognize it. Then the student is struck with wonder some day at a fine original air floating in his mind, and puts it in a composition of his own, and is very indignant when critics point out resemblance to Beethoven or Schubert or Wagner. This is the natural history of nine-tenths of the cases of plagiarism that occur. They are simply instances of faulty memory. The best memory is a careful cultivation of the faculty of accurate remembrance, on the lines here suggested.

What, now, is it possible for the teacher to do to assist the pupil? Much. In the first place, by teaching him harmony and musical form as early as possible he can equip the memory for more than the bare melody. After a concert or recital he can examine the pupil as to what he remembers of the most notable pieces, and by a few helpful suggestions show him how to retain the leading ideas in mind. He can stimulate the interest of the pupil in great works and in every way inculcate the desirability of knowing them. When an air from an opera or oratorio is studied he can explain how much better it is to have the context, to read over the rest of the work, instead of trying to simulate an emotion in regard to something which is not at all understood. Mr. Leland in his entertaining memories tells of a great actress who had taken the part of Ophelia for many years in the most brilliant way, and one day while talking with a friend asked innocently enough, "By the way, how does it come out?" She had never read over the rest of "Hamlet" after the death of Ophelia. Too many vocal pupils sing their detached airs in quite as blind a fashion. The teacher can also do much to aid the memory by stimulating interest beforehand in works that are to be heard in concerts. When a pupil knows what the pilgrim's chorus and the Venus music stand for, and has been shown how they cross each other in "Tannhauser" overture, he will remember more of that overture with one hearing than he would with half a dozen without such a stimulus of the attention. Still more is this true with such explicit program music as

St. Saëns "Danse Macabre," "Rouet d' Omphale," and "Phaeton," where a little personal interest will do more than the learned exegesis of the program book, which too often takes the selection on the program only as the point of departure for a profound essay on Greek mythology. Often the teacher can profitably reinforce the educational value of a concert by playing a selection over again and again, telling the pupil to listen now to this and now to that till it obtains a permanent lodging in his mind. He can do the pupil a real service, too, by insisting upon an exact bibliographic knowledge, the precise opus number of a work, the correct key, the spelling and correct pronunciation of titles, and the names of composers, a minor but important field of culture which is now all too neglected. It is by thus departing from the narrow routine of technical instruction and supervising the intellectual growth, that the teacher can help to make not merely a performer but a musician; and every scheme of education should provide for enough time in the class room to give leisure for this very thing. Not the least of the advantages of study in a conservatory, is the opportunity which it gives for concentrating many lines of work. The unification of studies is the greatest advance in common school education which this century has seen, and a few cities in this country have already realized the fact, but in musical education the problem has hardly been touched.

To summarize, then, the conclusions that have been reached in a rather discursive way.

1. Too much time is spent by some teachers on playing without notes.

2. Not enough time is devoted by most teachers to the partial memorizing of many works.

3. A well stored memory is one of the most efficient means of musical culture.

4. Selections should be classified according to the completeness with which they are remembered, and advanced from one stage to the next as they are better learned.

5. All the selections on the list should be reviewed as frequently as possible, and corrected by the score to insure accuracy.

6. No system of mnemonics is of any avail, and the correlation of words with instrumental themes is dangerous.

7. Teachers should extend the scope of their work so as to teach music as well as one special kind of performance.

8. The one great secret of memory is the power of intense application of the attention.

Springfield, Mass. FRANCIS E. REGAL.

CHOPIN.

Out from the ocean's heart a deep lament,
Out from his bosom sob and sob are sent.
What other ear than this has heard his grief?
What other voice has phrased its hid intent?

PHILIP BECKER GOETZ.

MUSICAL POSSIBILITIES OF POE'S POEMS.

WHENEVER a poem illustrative of American life and sentiment receives an adequate musical setting from a composer whose education and experience have been American, an interesting answer is given to the question whether there can be a national American music. The poems of Longfellow, Taylor, and writers still living have inspired our composers to produce songs which are in the broadest sense national. Yet the poet whose genius was of the highest quality our country has produced, whose writings have had the deepest influence along certain lines upon our literature, who is recognized as wholly unique and peculiar to America, this poet, Edgar Allan Poe, has been quite overlooked by American musicians. The general reader knows Poe by "The Raven," "The Bells," "Ulalume," and a few prose tales. In these, it is true, he is most original and striking. His power of presenting the weird and horrible is so great that it satisfies us, and disinclines us to look for other perhaps more elusive qualities of his style. Yet he who is most in sympathy with Poe values more highly his expression of the beautiful, not merely knowing but loving him for "Lenore," "Annabel Lee," "Israfel," and several exquisite short lyrics.

A composer seeks in a poem certain qualities: euphony, forcible diction, rhythmic flow, intelligibility, and, above all, the lyrical or dramatic spirit. Lacking some of these qualities many poems, like those of Browning, are unsuited to music. The poems of Poe are a fresh, untrodden field of lyrical beauty. In respect of euphony, Poe, like a master musician before an organ, has drawn from the English language tones which equal the softness and richness of the Italian. What musician would not love such phrases as "crystal, wandering water," "From grief and groan to a golden throne," "with love in her luminous eyes." Seldom does our speech offer to music such richness of sound effect. Poe's diction is always elegant and suited to the prevailing mood; beguiled by its charm one is sometimes in danger of overlooking the poet's meaning. In rhythm perhaps, even more than in euphony and diction, is Poe's original power displayed. Consider the military precision and stately sweep of the first verse of "Eldorado:"

> Gaily bedight,
> A gallant knight,
> In sunshine and in shadow,
> Had journeyed long
> Singing a song,
> In search of Eldorado.

or the sombre, mysterious roll of "Dreamland:"

> By a route obscure and lonely,
> Haunted by ill angels only,
> Where an Eidolon named NIGHT,
> On a black throne reigns upright,
> I have reached these lands but newly
> From an ultimate dim Thule—

with the bewildering, surging rush of the following lines:

> Bottomless vales and boundless floods,
> And chasms, and caves, and Titan woods,
> With forms that no man can discover
> For the dews that drip all over.

the impassioned movement of "Lenore" the delicate, tripping grace of "Fairyland"—all these rhythms are suggestive to the composer. Poe is usually intelligible, and always lyrical or dramatic. It would be difficult to find in his poems, with the exception of those which are definitely personal, a line that would be unsuited to music. To the composer of ballads four striking poems especially appeal. "Eldorado" is a picture of strong, unswerving purpose, carried out in spite of failing strength, and finally justified by a spiritual interpretation. One can imagine how the music, at first bold and strong, would gradually grow weaker, sinking to the last verse, when it would rise again and make a glorious close. Or in the pathetic "Bridal Ballad" the first verse could be dreamy, happy recitative, followed by a simple narrative melody for the two verses containing the bride's retrospect. Then again recitative, this time troubled, discordant, leading abruptly to a passionate climax, and dying away interrogatively with the words:

> Lest the dead who is forsaken
> May not be happy now.

"Dreamland" and "Fairyland" with their wealth of scenery might become as good ballads as the famous "Kleiner Haushalt" of Löwe. But when our American Löwe is in a purely lyrical mood, what could suit him better than the lines beginning.

> "Fair river in thy bright, clear flow
> Of crystal, wandering water—"

Other lyrics in different veins are "Spirits of the Dead," "The Evening Star," "A Dream Within a Dream," the "Hymn," "To One in Paradise." Three longer poems which offer our composers full scope for display of their powers, are "The Haunted Palace," "The Conqueror Worm," and "Israfel." A great musician might make these songs worthy of a place beside the "Erl King." Three of Poe's greatest poems, "The Bells," "The Raven," and "Ulalume," occur to the amateur in this connection, but professional experience leads us to set them aside. "The Bells" depends for its effect upon its imitation of sound, and would only lose its charm in the presence of actual music. "Ulalume" and "The Raven" are too long for songs, and too vivid personal experiences for longer vocal works. But a composer might study the changing moods of "The Raven," and if he could express them in orchestral music, he might create a magnificent Symphonic Poem. "Annabel Lee" and "Lenore," in which there is only pure, ennobling sentiment, also transcend the limits of a song, but are admirably suited to a broader style of composition. They should receive a setting for chorus and orchestra. More than any other of Poe's poems, "Lenore" excites the composer's imagination. The situation is dramatic. A lover and false friends stand over the bier of the departed maiden. The friends lament her death in conventional phrases, and gently chide the lover for showing no signs of grief. This leads him to denounce them as the real cause of her decline. They seek to avert his wrath by a soft invitation to join in a common lament, but he turns away and expresses his belief in immortality as a blessed state to be viewed with joy and not with grief. The orchestra might begin with a picture of the lover's deep, strong emotion, dying away and giving place to the solemn, march-like strains of the chorus:

> "Ah! broken is the golden bowl, the spirit flown forever.
> Let the bell toll, a saintly soul floats on the Stygian River."

When this passage has grown intenser and reached a climax, a solo quartet might sing in different style, to the lover.

> "And Guy de Vere, hast thou no tear? Weep now or nevermore:
> For on yon drear and rigid bier low lies thy love Lenore."

The chorus taking up the closing words could lead back to the opening strain with more intensity and grandeur. And then with what fierceness the lover would break forth:

> "Wretches, ye loved her for her wealth, and hated her for her pride"

adding with poignant grief:

> "And when she fell in feeble health ye blessed her—that she died."

Then an almost frenzied outburst:

> "How shall the ritual then be read, the requiem how be sung
> By you—by yours, the evil eye,—by yours, the slanderous tongue,
> That did to death the innocence that died, and died so young."

For a moment the orchestra should play alone, while this passion subsides, then the chorus gently, persuasively mingle their voices:

> "*Peccavimus;* but rave not thus! and let a Sabbath song
> Go up to God so solemnly the dead may feel no wrong."

The whole verse should be gentle, sweet, consoling, and of rare beauty. Then the lover rouses himself, a man who has found comfort in his own soul, and sings in vigorous, inspiring melody:

> "Avaunt! tonight my heart is light, no dirge will I upraise,
> But waft the angel on her flight with a pæan of old days."

Such are the possibilities for music which lie hidden in the works of Edgar Allan Poe. Have we no composer who will undertake to realize them?

CHARLES SANFORD SKILTON.

THE STORY OF BRASS-WIND INSTRUMENTS.

A Study in the Evolution of the Orchestra.

LITERATURE and sculpture alike prove that the Romans were acquainted with two varieties of trumpets. The *lituus*, which Forcellini derives from the Greek *litus*, *tenuis*, was a small-bored cylindrical trumpet, the progenitor of the modern trumpet-trombone family. From the *tuba* with its large-bored conical tube is derived the family of bugles, horns, cornets-à-piston, bombardons and ophicleides. From these types two distinct tone qualities were produced, the large cone and bell favoring the production of the fundamental tone and lower harmonies, the long contracted pipe speaking freely in its upper octaves.

The natural resonance of the harmonic divisions of the tube in both instruments, permitted the production by the lips and breath alone of a harmonic scale, which commencing with C of the second line below the bass staff goes on with C octave then ascending G, C, E, G, Bb, C, D, E, F sharp, etc.

A means of supplying the harmonic gaps was early found in the application of the slide principle to the trombone. Indeed as early as 1520 Hans Menschel made trombones as good if not better than those now in use. By successive elongations of the tube, seven "positions" were obtained, each of which was provided with the harmonic scale given above. From a suitable combination of the different positions a complete chromatic scale was obtained.

The application of this principle to the trumpet did not follow until much later, because in its upper part the harmonic series closes in on itself, and the notes become almost consecutive. The few missing notes can be supplied and a diatonic scale formed by a good lip, without the aid of mechanism.

Little complete music has survived from a period as

late as the XVI century, for there were no partiturs and the preservation of the numerous part books was impossible to expect. But the general character of the music was the reduplication of polyphonic voice parts by various timbres, the whole having little cohesion, because the harmony was without a firm foundation.

The creation of true chamber music at this time assisted materially the advance of instrumentation, but brass was only included in dance orchestras. We know the constitution of several bands of this period, from the account books of Edward IV, Henry VIII and Elizabeth. Henry's included fourteen trumpets, ten trombones, four drums and three tambourines, against a total of only nine stringed instruments. Similar organizations were supported by the Dukes of Ferrara and Tuscany, and other European princes. It would be difficult to understand how these instruments could be employed together, if we did not know that the custom of writing in the form of a dialogue was already common.

The next great step was the invention of the basso continuo, which provided a firm foundation for a complete harmonic structure and the union of diverse timbres. To Louis Viadana, a monk of the Observance, was due this great advance, which as he states in the preface to a volume of his motets, published 1603, occurred to him in Rome six years before. To prove that an increased number of parts only made his invention more valuable, he added in the later pieces some instrumental parts, including trumpets and trombones, the latter reinforcing the organ and bassoons on the basso continuo. The system quickly spread throughout Europe, being introduced into Germany by Stadelmayer 1611, into Holland by the Englishman Richard Deering 1597, and into France by Henri Dumont 1652.

To this period belongs the origin of the Italian and German instrumental schools; from the former has sprung the dramatic, the latter, the symphonic orchestra. "In Italy the human voice was sovereign, in Germany the first of instruments, *primus inter pares*."

In Germany the orchestra developed without losing any

of the resources which it had in the XVI century, but in Italy the string quartet was formed only by a sacrifice of all the brass and, in some cases, wood wind. In the *San Alessio* of Landi (1634) all wind both wood and brass are banished.

The constant doubling of the vocal parts, which naturally resulted, was found to be very monotonous. Scarlatti (1649-1725) remedied this by introducing the recitative obligato, in which the orchestra was given a free part.

In the operas between 1640 and 1700 we still find a sparing use of the brass. In *Ercole in Tebe* (1651) by Jacopo Melani, a chorus of demons is supported by cornets and trombones. The *Partenope* (1699) of Mangi has a soprano aria in which trumpets are introduced together with wood wind and strings.

In the chamber music of the period we find trombones introduced often in curious combinations. As in the Symphony of Bartolomeo Montalbano of Bologna, for first and second violins, four viols, organ and trombones, and the Sonata of Neri written in twelve parts for two cornets, four trombones, a bassoon, two violins, two viols and a theorbo.

It was about 1660 that trumpets and trombones finally gave place in Italian music to violins.

The Italian orchestra was introduced into France by Cambert at the request of Cardinal Mazarin. This event owes its importance to the fact that it paved the way for Lulli.

The chief innovations of Lulli were the restoration of trumpets and timpani in *Cadmus and Hermione* (1673) and the introduction of a complete quintet of hunting horns in the first intermezzo of the *Princesse d' Elide*. These had made their first timid appearance in an aria with obligato parts for two horns and two clarinets by Gossec in 1757. The horn differs from other members of the lituus family in the considerably greater length of tube (16-17 feet), wider expansion of the bell, spiral form of the convolutions, softer quality of tone and greater compass. As the fundamental tone of so long a tube is very deep, the harmonics in the middle of the scale lie close together and produce many consecutive notes.

Lulli beside using the trumpets with the violin in tuttis, wrote for them alone in three or even five parts with a characteristic bass on the timpani tuned in the tonic and dominant.

Among the Germans Heinrich Schutz (1585-1672) was the first to practice a complete system of instrumentation. He had studied in Italy in 1620 under Gabrieli, and introduced into Germany the lyric drama created by the Italians. In his opera, based on Rinuccini's *Dafne*, he followed the tradions of Peri and Monteverde. The fragments of his work preserved by Winterfield show us such combinations as a bass solo accompanied by a quartet of trombones and organ, and a cornet, trumpet and bassoon accompanying two tenors and a bass.

Prominent among his contemporaries was Johann Stadelmayer (1560). We have no proof of his having visited Italy, but his works show unmistakeably the influence of that school. Like Schutz he used the brass more liberally than his Italian contemporaries. In the *Missae Concertatae* 1642 we find alto, tenor and bass voices doubled by trombones.

The successors of these masters contributed to the development of German instrumentation by enlarging the scale of the motet to include instruments.

Among the most curious of their works is one that proves that history was merely repeating itself in the Peace Jubilee band of anvils and cannons. This is the *Currus Triumphalis* of Andrea Rauch, printed 1648 and dedicated to the Roman Emperors. Beside sustaining the voices with violins, cornets, trumpets and trombones, he used "noisy engines of war." He has not used all the resources of his orchestra together. The second piece, for four choruses, is accompanied by two trombones, two violins and basso continuo. In the sixth for twelve voices we hear, for the first time, the timpani and cannons. In the tenth, the brass receives brilliant treatment, and includes two soprano, alto, tenor and bass trumpets and four trombones.

Of that polyodic style which replaced in Germany the true polyphony or strict contrapuntal writing of the XVI century, Johann Sebastian Bach was the greatest master and exemplar. No one understood better than he the proper orchestral support of the vocal parts. Thoroughly recognizing the necessity of using the stringed band as the basis of the whole, he preferred to employ wind instruments for the purpose of enlarging the original design, rather than that of strengthening or decorating it.

His use of the trumpets is notable for its brilliancy and difficulty of execution. Indeed, with the mouth pieces now in use, they would be quite impracticable, even if the art of playing on the old fashioned trumpet were not entirely lost. Bach often uses three, at times calling for three *trombe*, again distinguishing them by the names of *clarino* and *principale*. The former, a small-bored instrument, was given florid passages principally in the octave above the principale, which was apparently of a larger bore, with a bold eight foot tone, resembling our modern trumpet. We find four in the second cantata *Feria I Nativitatis*, No. 63 and *Bei der Rathswahl zu Leipzig* 1723, No. 119.

Sometimes these instruments enter in the tuttis, as in *Wo soll ich fliehen hin*, sometimes as in the motets of the XVII century, they interrupt the violins and voices with brilliant ritornelles. Again three with a timpani bass constitute the entire orchestra of accompaniment.

A species of chromatic trumpet, called *tromba da tirarsi* from its sliding grooves, is not uncommon. On the other hand I have been able to find but one instance of the use of the name *lituus*. In the cantata *O Jesu Christ mein Leben's Licht*, No 118, two were combined with a cornet and three trombones.

In his use of the horns we find a striking contrast to modern usage. Instead of completing the wood wind choir, they are united to the brass, even replacing trumpets. Sometimes the horn has an important part in the choral of a Cantata, as in the *Festo Annunciationis Mariæ* No 1, where the second horn varies the theme while the other instruments double the voices. Still the horn is by no means recognized at its true value, for it was not until about 1753 that Hampl, the court horn player at Dresden, discovered that by placing his hand in the bell of the instrument he could lower the pitch a semitone and thus complete the natural scale.

Again, when we turn to the trombones we find their true character but little apprehended, for instead of the dramatic place they occupy in later writers we find Bach content to leave them "chained to the voices." It is his common practice to double each voice in a choral with a trombone, but sometimes the first trombone is replaced by a cornet.

Handel used a larger orchestra than Bach and gave it very different treatment. Instead of writing in many real parts, he preferred to subordinate the instrumental parts to the vocal. But his great advance in orchestration was his treatment of the orchestra as a body composed of two choirs, each complete in itself and contrasting with the other. This was an important step toward our modern conception of the triune orchestra, composed of string, wood and brass choirs.

Handel's use of the trumpets does not differ greatly from that of Bach. We find the same brilliant effects from the first trumpet, "vying in virtuosity with an Italian castrato!"

He wrote important trumpet obligatos to "Thou art the King" in the *Dettingen Te Deum*, "Let the bright Seraphim" in *Samson* and "The trumpet shall sound" in the *Messiah*.

Grove relates that this latter obligato was formerly played on a small alto trombone, the German title being "Sie töul die Posaune."

In the various oratorios and operas we find the number of trumpets ranges from two to four, the timpani supplying their characteristic bass.

In his second period he wrote important parts for the horns, usually employing two as in *Samson*, *Concerto*, for orchestra, and the *Water Music* p. 26, where they alternate with oboes, bassoons and strings in the presentation of a characteristic theme.

Again he calls for three as in the *Fireworks music*

p 100 or even four as in *Julius Cæsar*. It was not until 1720 in the *Rhadamisto* that he used them in his English and Italian operas.

The trombones play an important part in the orchestra of Handel giving both vigor and brilliancy to the ensemble. He writes for them in C, D and G and employs their difficult third octave fearlessly and with fine effect.

Fine examples for three trombones may be found in *Israel in Egypt* and in *Saul*.

A marked reduction in the use of the third group is characteristic of the classic masters of the Symphony. Haydn and Mozart have entirely abstained from its use in some of their masterpieces, for example the G minor Symphony of Mozart. When it does appear it is reduced to two trumpets and timpani, the two horns being joined to the wood wind.

Since the piercing timbre of the trumpets excludes them from use in conjunction with the wood wind in polyphonic development, the usual role of the group, as Gevaert remarks, is analogous to the mixture stops of an organ.

The sonority of the trumpets and timpani enriches the harmony of tuttis. The ordinary methods of employment are interior pedal points in octaves reinforced by timpani, and short rhythmic groups interrupted by rests, against sustained chords of the second group. Though the trombone is not found in Haydn's symphonies we find three in the *Creation*.

That Mozart paid careful attention to the treatment of the horns is shown by an anecdote related by Jahn. His symphony K No. 16, was written during an illness in London. As he was at work, he turned to his sister who was sitting near him copying, and said, "Erinnere mich, dass ich dem Waldhorn was Rechtes zu thun gebe." He increased their number to four not infrequently, as in the *Divertimento* K 131, symphony in E♭, K 132, and symphony K 138, in the form of an overture, which is apparently the introduction to some dramatic work, possibly *King Thamos*, K 345.

is masses he regularly uses three trombones and four

trumpets and in the *Zehn Stucke* for military marches, we find five trumpets (three in C, two in D) and four timpani (C G D A).

Beethoven does not differ materially from Mozart in his treatment of the third group up to *Die Schlacht bei Vittoria.* But this work may be said to have been composed especially to exhibit the trumpet. The melodies or rather rhythms of the fanfares of the hostile French and English troops are the principal subjects of thematic treatment until the victory is gained and all is merged in *God save the Queen.* The trumpet also plays an important part in his symphonies, especially the seventh.

Beethoven was lavish in his use of the horn and exacting in his demands on the player. He was the first to make any extensive use of the stopped notes discovered by Hampl, his predecessor having confined themselves to a single note F natural (the eleventh harmonic lowered half a tone), which they used with the freedom of an open tone.

Even if we exclude the Sonata in F for horn and piano, the Sextet for strings and two horns, which is so difficult as never to be played, and the Septet, which contains a very trying passage in triplets for the E♭ horn, we still find a prominent and often difficult role confided to it in his other works. Some of the more important examples of his treatment are the trio of the *Heroica* scored for three horns in E♭ playing largely on stopped notes, a difficult passage in thirds for two horns in the low movement of the *Pastoral*, a long and important duet for two horns over a cello solo in the minuet of the *Eighth* and the famous fourth horn part in the *Choral*, which is so difficult as hardly to be playable on an E♭ horn without valves, for which it was written. The horn is often called on to take the initiative, preparing in advance and often without complete regard for the rules of tonality, the entry of a theme. In the last movement of the *Pastoral* a resolute C is given by the horns against the chord of F held by celli and violins; and in the first movement of the *Heroica*, the horns, apparently entering four bars too soon, give the first part of the principal theme wholely on the notes E, G, E, B, while the violins hold a tremolo on B♭ and A♭, fragments of the seventh chord on E♭.

With the great symphony No. 5, the trombones take their place definitely in the symphonic orchestra. In the musical drama they had been used since Gluck, with tragic expression, but in Beethoven their role seems merely decorative. Though by nature allied to the trumpets he prefers to treat them as a seperate body, of which the lower voice joins in the bass of the ensemble.

The use of two trombones in the storm scene of the *Pastoral* seems peculiar to Beethoven. An interesting reminiscence of Bach's treatment of the choral is found in the Ninth symphony, at the chorus *Seid umschlungen Millionen*, where three trombones move with the tenor, bass and alto voices, while the sopranos are supported by the upper wood wind. An exact parallel may be found in the cantata *Feria Paschales*, where the trombones accompany the lower voices and the soprano is reinforced by the cornet. While at Linz in 1812 he wrote three *Equali* for four trombones, two of which were adapted to words from the Miserere by Seyfried and performed at Beethoven's own funeral.

[TO BE CONTINUED]

ERNEST OSGOOD HEYLER.

A MUSIC STUDENT'S LETTERS.

VI.

March 31.

MRS. Klindworth had her Thursday "At Home" as usual and as it was the last for the season, the rooms were quite crowded. In the evening, P. and I went to hear Consolo, the Italian pianist, who is staying in the house. He did some splendid playing, but in about the middle of his programme, he hurt his finger somehow (the usual unintelligible announcement was made) and couldn't finish. We bought tickets some days ago for the Mozart Requiem, to be given next Thursday, and just heard today that Rubinstein will conduct his own symphony. There will be a great rush for tickets tomorrow morning, as it was only posted up today that he was to appear. I am glad we have ours, as they are for very good seats, which would now be hard to get.

We heard the boy-prodigy again, and his performance this time was about as near to being a bore as anything I have experienced in this beautiful city of music, soldiers and beer. In the first place, we walked slowly and calmly over to the Sing-Akademie, which is about a mile from the house, and is the hall where he played before. When we reached it and found it deserted, we proceeded to look at our tickets (which would have been quite a praiseworthy act had it been performed about one hour earlier), and to our intense disgust, discovered that he was to play in Philharmonie Hall, which is almost as far in one direction from our house as the Sing-Akademie is in the other. We hesitated for a moment; then we rushed to the nearest droschke and the *Kutscher* very obligingly stirred up the bag of bones which he respectfully referred to as "my horse", and to such good effect that we were not late after all our excitement. The programme was somewhat lighter than his first one, but I shall copy it for you; you may be interested in it, as you know his age and have seen his picture.

1. Mozart, Fantaisie D minor.
   Beethoven, 1st movement Sonate, op. 27, No. 2.
   Schubert, Menuett, H moll.
2. Chopin, { Prelude. Mazurka. Valse.

Here he was encored and played the Chopin D flat Waltz.

3. Rubinstein, Romance, op. 44, No. 1.
   Moszkowski, Gondoliera.
   Godard, Mazurka, B major.
4. Raoul Koczalski, { Gavotte. Valse.
   Liszt, Rhapsodie, No. 13.

At the end, he played two small encore numbers which I didn't recognize.

BOY PRODIGY

I would advise anyone to go *once* to hear him, but not twice. I fancied it would be so, and his light has already failed here, as there was not half an audience and no enthusiasm whatever; his reception was really quite painful. Poor baby! I find myself feeling quite sorry for him, although I know nothing about his private life, and he seems fat and healthy enough and doesn't look in the least as though he overworked.

Night before last we went to "Fidelio", and as the Z's

Mr. E. and we three had a *loge* together, we had a great deal of fun between times, and enjoyed the opera immensely. The night before that, the same crowd, with two other Americans from the house, went to the Tisch concert. Last night was the Mozart requiem and Rubinstein conducted his F major symphony and a movement from a violin concerto of his own, which Fritz Struss played. Rubinstein has a very *strong*, but to me disagreeable, face. His picture gives you a pretty good idea, except that it doesn't show how very much wrinkled he is. His manner is very quiet and unassuming, and he beats time continually with his left foot while conducting. He stands quite straight, but seems either to be very feeble or not to see well, as he faltered and went very slowly up the steps and down.

Miss Z. and I had a wager as to what Mr. E. would do last night: the dilemma being this: we were one horn of it and some other American girls whom Mr. E. knows, and who sat in a *loge* a little farther over, were the other. He was between the two horns in this way: he *always* comes over to call on us in the Pauses, as they call them, and last night there was only one Pause, so we wondered how he would manage to be diplomatic. He sat perfectly still all through the Pause! And we decided that he is not so young as we thought him. I shall copy the programme of the last Tisch Concert just to show you the average grade of the ten-cents-a-ticket concerts we get here.

FIRST PART.

1. Overture to the Water-Carriers....................Cherubini.
2. Adagio from the Clarinet Quintett ....Mozart.
3. Introduction to the Third Act: Dance of the Apprentices, and Greeting to Hans Sachs, from the Mastersingers ....Wagner.

SECOND PART.

4. Symphony, No. 3, F. major ....Joh. Brahms.
   1. Allegro.
   2. Andante.
   3. Poco Allegretto.
   4. Allegro.

THIRD PART.

5. Overture to the Vaudeville. "The Return from a a Foreign Land." ....Mendelssohn.
6. Concerto for Violin and Orchestra ....H. Wieniawski.
7. Rhapsodie, No. 6, ...Liszt.

April 4.

Last week we were out every night but one, but it was a rather quiet week in a good many ways. The Germans make Good Friday the most solemn day of the year; much more so than Sunday, as the opera and theatres are closed, which they never are on Sundays. As Frau Dr. K. said, "When we Germans close our theatres, it's something pretty serious." On Friday night there was absolutely no entertainment of any sort in the city, except the Bach Passion music, and nine-tenths of the audience there were dressed in black. And at the Ninth Symphony the next night, the dressing was noticeably more subdued than usual. Of course the opera house was crowded, as it was given this time by request. I have heard it four times now, and each time it is more splendid than the last. The rest of the programme was the Overture to "Parsifal" and the Unfinished Symphony,—and it was a perfect programme.

Sunday morning, I heard three sermons, which is what Miss Z. says she would call religious dissipation. I had never been in a German church before and the one we went to was extremely interesting. The building is round and has two galleries running all the way around. The pulpit is quite beautifully carved, and is one of the hanging ones like those in the Cathedral. It is on a level with the first gallery and is draped and canopied like a throne; directly below is the desk where the first part of the service is read, and when the preacher goes up to the little pulpit, a man goes with him and locks him in. It is a Lutheran church and the service is a good deal like that of the English Church. There were two little sermons; when the preacher had finished one, he made a short prayer and then preached another one. He speaks very distinctly and is astonishingly easy to understand. They have some most beautiful memorial windows, and all the glass is draped with a very thin, soft, buff-coloured material which makes the colour more beautiful and gives a more unreal effect, when the sun shines on it, than anything of the sort I ever saw. The music, which was what we really went for, was indeed *church* music—smooth, a beautiful quality, and perfectly appropriate to the service. There is a trained choir of fifty or sixty boys and ten or twelve men, and the hymns, which are sung (and sung well) by the congregation, are led by a precentor and four brass wind instruments. This was another of my new experiences, and one of the most pleasing of them all. German church is quite early, so after it was over we went, as usual, to the American Chapel, where service doesn't begin till half after eleven.

We are in doubt whether to go tomorrow night to hear one of Frau Dr. Hempel's lectures on Faust; to hear "Don Juan" at the opera house; or to the Tisch Concert, where there is to be a special programme. There is never any difficulty here about having something to go to; the only trouble is that you want so much to go to all there is that it makes it very difficult to choose. There is *always* more than one thing in an evening which you *particularly* want to hear.

ELIZABETH WORTHINGTON.

MUSIC FOR THE SICK.

THE appreciation of music as a medicine for the sick, invalids, convalescents, sufferers from all kinds of nervous diseases, especially insanity, has decidedly increased within the last few years. Allow me to add my testimony to this fact by describing the result of my efforts, in this direction. Thanks to Mr. Mathews' valuable letter of introduction and recommendation, I was, as he knows, enabled to thoroughly test the influence of music on the sick at one of Chicago's private sanitariums. The engagement was for one month as a trial, but I was almost immediately informed by the physician in charge that it was a success, and consequently I remained in the institution five months, which afforded me ample opportunity to satisfy myself that superior music artistically rendered, and carefully selected as to key and character, is a wonderful aid to medicine. My experience covered a great variety of cases, and the results were unmistakably beneficial to many patients. As an illustration of the power of music I cite the sad case of a young lady who had become mentally deranged from over-study. When I entered the institution, she would, when taken to the piano, sit down and play a single little tune of a few measures over and over again until stopped (I think she would have played it all day if allowed to). Her eyes were constantly cast down and closed tightly whenever an attempt was made to have her raise them. She had been in this condition for a number of years. My first attempt was to lead her fingers to different keys. She, by the way, used white keys exclusively. I taught her a few bars of a cradle song leading her fingers of the right hand, while I played the left hand part. To this beginning I added daily, patiently watching for results, and I was soon rewarded by seeing her show signs of interest. I tried the effect of all styles by playing for her; the first thing to rouse her being a Tarantelle Burlesque; she opened her eyes wide and became quite hilarious. Day by day, her nurse took her to the parlor for music, and I could notice constant improvement—she had been a good player before her trouble commenced—snatches of pieces came back to her memory and I concluded to send home for her music. It came, and I tried different selections with very gratifying results. In a comparatively short time she became interested enough to raise her eyes and look at the notes, then watch my fingers and face as I played, and finally read and played by note herself. She would play, for instance, one hand of a Mendelssohn song without words and I the other; after a while, she could read and play both hands with my help at keeping the place—then we tried a few little simple duets with success. I had a piano in my room, also a couch, the poor girl seemed to love to lie and listen to my playing and was very affectionate at times, but talked very little, in fact hardly at all, except when we were all alone; it was then that she played her best, very expressive at times. A hymn finally brought tears; she playing it from memory while the tears streamed down her cheeks falling on hands and keys. Her case having been of quite long standing, five or six years I think, I am sorry at not being able to record her complete recovery, but with my five months experience can safely say that if anything will accomplish it in the end, music and kind, interested treatment, together with skilled medical attendance will do it. Another young lady who was seemingly idiotic, and would not play at all, became interested enough to play such things as the Gavotte Stephanie, by note. Leaving such cases however, entirely out of the question, I now invite attention to the effect of music on persons afflicted with nervous disorders.

Although I had great faith in music's power, I was hardly prepared to meet with such an enthusiastic reception as was accorded me by the patients of the Sanitarium, the first day of my arrival, and the continued appreciation of my efforts in their behalf.

A lady whose room was across the hall from the parlor, at one time sent a request for me to play for her during the time that her husband underwent an operation in the next room.

She was ill and unable to leave her bed, but wanted something to keep up her spirits. Many a time requests for certain pieces came from patients on the 4th and 5th floors, the sound being conveyed through the elevator shaft. I usually played two hours in the morning and used music of all styles, playing according to requests, which were constantly received. Beethoven, Schumann, Chopin, and Mendelssohn were favorites, but my repertoire included compositions by Bach, Hiller, Weber, Liszt, Schubert, Grieg, Schytte, Wieniawski and many minor composers of light and popular music. One would hardly expect that Beethoven's Grand Sonata Appassionata, Moonlight Sonata and Sonata Pathetique would be favorites, but they were. At first I thought that Songs without Words, Romances, Reveries and the like would be most suitable, but I came to the conclusion that sometimes a brisk march, opera selections, as for instance "Il Trovatore" arranged by Melnotte, or Polka de la Reine by Raff, also Ballade and Polonaise by Vieuxtemps Rivé-King, Wieniawski's Kuyiawiak, the Schubert-Liszt Erl-King, etc, were undoubtedly extremely suitable for cases that needed stimulating. It brought life and cheerfulness to many a patient otherwise gloomy and homesick. Chopin's nocturnes and many minor little gems proved of lasting benefit and were constantly asked for. The day I left the institution a request came from a patient whose recovery a few days before had been very doubtful, to please have my own piano moved into the hall (4th floor) near to her room and for me to play Schumann's Traumerei for her. The request was granted as a matter of course, and was highly appreciated.

One of the patients used to sit on a trunk outside my room by the hour, listening to my practicing, until discovered and invited to a more comfortable seat within.

At an evening concert, arranged for the benefit of the patients, the large dining hall was completely filled. I was assisted by a first class violinist and violoncellist, and our program included a part of a Beethoven trio and some lighter ones besides solo numbers on all instruments. Our reception by the audience was most enthusiastic and the applause spontaneous. Lyon & Potter kindly loaned the use of a fine Steinway Grand for the occasion, which added materially to the success of the entertainment.

The rendition of light, popular music sometimes added no little to the general good humor of the sick—as for instance, an excellent imitation of the banjo played during mealtime, the twang of the banjo being imitated by covering the strings of the piano with paper. This, as a surprise, was heartily enjoyed by all except the head waiter, who greatly feared the destruction of dishes and victuals by the darkey waiters, whose feet would keep time to the music.

Before coming to Chicago, I had occasion to test the effect of music on restless infants with surprising success, a mere babe being so influenced as to be kept quiet an entire afternoon with soft, sweet music, when everything else failed. I can also record calls to private homes where music brought rest and comfort to convalescents, both ladies and gentlemen.

Any young pianists who might wish to try the effect of music on the sick for themselves, should invariably remember that the secret of success lies in the pianist's touch. The playing can be crisp, brilliant, even fortissimo as the music selected may require, but it must *never be harsh*. Better none at all. Any person of ordinary intelligence can play with a brilliant technic, but it takes an artist to interpret simple pieces poetically in such a manner as to benefit the sick. True music stirs up the finer emotions and thereby appeals to feeling. It is also essential that there be sympathy between player and listener in order to meet with the best results; and the selection of certain keys for certain persons must be attended to with care.

ALICE E. GETHER

A WAGNER DEVOTEE.

WHILE sojourning in lovely San Diego I made the happy acquaintance of Paul Colberg of Vienna. While enjoying my after-breakfast bout with the key-board I was interrupted by vigorous knocking, and opened the door. There stood a curious looking individual, with a dome like head, and an indescribably merry expression.

"That is sehr *schlecht*! That cannot be! It must go so! so!," said my visitor, placing on the keys fingers badly eaten by eczema.

"That," said I, "is by Rubenstein." To my astonishment, he did not appear to notice the name but stoutly stuck to his opinion.

Well, I soon learned that my eccentric caller was an undoubted genius, a mathematician of great profundity and a composer so superior, so learned in forms yet so spontaneous in melody, that I was never tired of listening to him. His violin and piano sonata ought to displace many of the hackneyed compositions of which we are already tired. He was the personal friend and companion of Goldmark, and author of "The Queen of Sheba" and "Merlin;" and of Franchetti, who wrote "Azrael." The last named composer was just at that time staying at the house of Colberg's father in Vienna. It was news to me that Franchetti was one of the Rothschild family and was, according to my friend, the richest single man in the whole world, possessing no less than 600,000,000 francs, or $125,000,000. The American composer with as many thousand is yet to be ashamed.

Well! we soon became inseparable companions. His *gushing* overflow of animal spirits kept every one about him alert and interested. With all his undubitable genius he was childish in the extreme.

As I was about to part with him one night I happened to mention Wagner. He shook his head sorrowfully and said. "Ah, I could tell you something very sad about him but it makes me feel so bad."

After a little urging I was rewarded by the following account.

"Wagner was coming to Dresden and I with a friend and about two hundred others went to the station to see him arrive. We were so lucky as to happen to stand directly in front of the platform from which he alighted. He turned to my friend and, mistaking him for some one else said: "Your uncle left his spectacles on the window sill; if you will call tomorrow I will give them to you."

My friend consented to take me with him. We were shown into a room where Wagner was eating a late breakfast. He got up, and Oh! he was *such* a little man; no bigher than this. (Here Colberg, himself rather short, touched his shoulder.) He came to my friend, inquired about his uncle, then turned to me, shook hands and asked; "And what is your name?" I looked at him, then at the wall, then at the ceiling, put my hands over my eyes and sank into a chair saying, "I have forgotten!"

Wagner looked at me so kindly, *just like a cow*, and gave us the glasses; but how I got out of that room I dont know!

"But what," said I, with practical curiosity, "became of those glasses?" "We broke them in two; I have half in Los Angeles and my friend has the other half in Dresden."

JOHN HOWARD.

JUNE.

Words by JOHN KENDRICK BANGS

JULIA LOIS CARUTHERS.

Vivace.

What doth the bee in the clo - ver

Dotting the meadow-land o - ver

So soft-ly croon?

Love is the word

Ev-'ry-where heard in June, June, June.

What is the butter-fly sing - ing

Ev-'ry-where heard in June, June, June.
What say the lads to the lass-ies
When it is noon?
Love is the word
Ev-'ry-where heard in June, June, June.

A VISIT TO CHOPIN, AND HIS LAST CONCERT.

PERIGNON came to put the finishing touches to the portrait so characteristic, which he had been painting of my father. He had married his model and had brought his wife to our house; several times we had kept them both to dinner, quite without ceremony.

One day they wished to carry me off with them upon the spur of the moment, to dine at their house; and as I made some objections, Pérignon said to me with an air of burlesque gayety:

"Madam Berton, you absolutely must come; we have designs upon you."

To which I replied, "What is then the great mystery!" This was a phrase in vogue at the time, and which had its origin in the mysteries, unexplained and unexplainable, with which certain writers of romance were wont to fill their pages.

Two hours later, in a house in the Rue La Bruyère, where Monsieur and Madame Pérignon occupied a small and modest apartment in the first story, and where there was a large and beautiful studio on the ground floor, I dined festively with them. They talked of everything and of nothing, but not a word was said about the mystery.

I had then completely forgotten the designs which they said they had formed concerning me, when after dinner we adjourned to a little salon where there was a piano. Pérignon opened it and, turning to me with the most charming manner in the world, said:

"I adore music; several people have told me that you have great talent for the piano. Will you not be so kind as to let us hear something?"

I bow, rise from the chair in which I have been seated I draw off my gloves, and I play from memory a brilliant piece, a difficult piece, a piece long practised, a piece then in fashion, a noisy piece, a piece which—a piece that—in fine, a piece!

I will do myself the justice to say that I did not strike a single false note and that I threw into it an energy—O, what an energy!

At the first few chords, Madam Pérignon, who could have been nothing of a musician, withdrew to a distance; our sex is timid.

Pérignon, like a man who is afraid of nothing and is conscious moreover that he alone precipitated the danger, established himself at my right.

His wife—I recall it distinctly, for I could see her perfectly in the mirror which hung facing me, above the piano—his wife wore an expression of profound melancholy, which I could not then explain to myself and of which I comprehended the meaning later. Inclined by nature to economy, she without doubt feared that it would be necessary to summon the tuner on the morrow.

As for me, serene and confident, having studied from the age of six years, the pupil of a leading professor, carrying off the first prize at the Conservatory, myself a teacher of several years experience, and now arrived at the age of twenty-five, during which time I had continually heard it said of myself,—"What fingers of steel! What a memory!" I now gave conscientiously one more proof of my memory and of my fingers of steel.

The thing came to an end, as everything does in this world—even grand *morceaux de piano*; I waited with impatience, but with absolute confidence the usual compliments; and while awaiting them, I put on my gloves. Pérignon did not keep me long in suspense, but uttered at once these memorable words:

"Ah! well. They have told me that you have talent: I fail to find it."

Immediately, my memory which was, at home, much more concerned with literary than with musical matters, recalled the scene of the sonnet in the *Misanthrope*. I thought that if Pérignon should assume for himself the role of Alcestis, I should not wish myself to play that of Orontes, and I said to him something like this:—

"Pray, Monsieur Pérignon, since my effort has displeased you, explain to me the reason. It is with me something besides a mere question of vanity, since I give lessons on the piano; and if I have until now taken the wrong road, I am still young enough to redeem the lost time."

Pérignon replied, "What do you wish me to tell you Madame? I am a painter, not a musician; I only feel that *this is not the thing*; I feel so, because I have listened to good music. What you have played, is music at *three sous the lot*. Let us see, have they ever made you play Beethoven?"

"Never."

"Or Mozart?"

"Never."

"Well, have you heard Chopin play?"

"Never."

"Ah, well; I think, myself, that these three things are what you need; and that if your taste is ever changed it will only be Chopin who will bring it about."

* * *

On the morrow, a beautiful day in autumn, I went to the house of Chopin, taking with me my little son. It occured to me that the sight of him might inspire the master with greater interest in myself. Children are the coquetteries of young mothers, and since mine bore the name of his father, a comedian of the first rank, the name of his deceased grandfather, Henri Berton, member of the Institute, the rival of Cherubini, author of *Montano and Stephanie* and of some other operas which enjoyed a deserved popularity at the time when melody held the place in music which harmony holds at the present day, I was sure that Chopin must have too wide a musical knowledge to be ignorant of the name of Berton; and thus it was, chiefly under the aegis of my little one, that I presented myself. It was an assurance and a support—the company of this diminutive cavalier with his Scotch blouse, his toque of blue velvet and his long fair hair. He too was a musician, but much more of a musician than I,—a musician by birth, as all the Bertons had been for five generations; and he already sang little airs of his own which he improvised as children do, as the birds do.

* * *

Chopin was then living where he had been, for a long time the neighbor of George Sand. He continued to live here in spite of their rupture. I had already heard vague rumors of the deep attachment which had sprung up between them, then of the painful separation and of the extreme delicacy of the health of Chopin who, they said, was destined to die young.

Arrived in the square of the Rue Saint-Lazare, the concierge conducted me to the door of the great artist, rang for me, and disappeared. My heart beat violently. I heard the tones of a piano; then they ceased; some one is coming to open the door. It is Chopin himself. Chopin slender, fragile, his face emaciated and pale, and with that delicate violet tint which the magic brush of Delacroix has portrayed for us in his sublime sketch.

With the aristocratic grace and courtesy which characterized him, he made me sit down in a large arm chair placed in front of a wide fire-place in which blazed a bright fire; then in disposing himself to listen to me, he seated himself opposite. My son remained motionless, holding fast to my dress with sedate gravity.

At one end of the apartment, which was of immense size, with a lofty ceiling and lighted by a large French window, opening upon a garden, a young girl or young woman with pale blond hair was seated at a grand piano. I perceived that my coming had interrupted a lesson; and excusing myself, not without some embarassment, I hastened to explain in few words the purpose of my visit. Then I finished my little speech by presenting to him at the same time my visiting card and my son.

Chopin took the one and embraced the other.

"I have promised myself," said he "to take no more pupils; but you bring me two names to which I can refuse nothing. I will enroll you upon my list and will write you directly to inform you of the day and hour which I find at my disposal."

Then, rising, he broke off a rose which was growing in a jardiniere, dropped on one knee before my boy, and in that attitude said to me—"Madame, we will make a great composer of him."

I was delighted with such a charming reception, yet nevertheless, was preparing to depart when the young blonde pupil, who was doubtless growing impatient although all this had occupied scarcely more than ten minutes, began to thrum a few notes on the piano—probably with the intention of recalling to herself the attention of her illustrious professor.

Then I had occasion to observe the extreme mobility of Chopin's countenance: I saw pass over it an expression of lively repugnance, and his look said plainly, "You see, my time is paid for; she fears that I shall forget it, and would put me in mind of the fact." Then I arose decidedly to take leave; but he made me sit down again and uttered in a voice rather stronger, although very feeble still, this sentence, which surprised me strangely:

"I have had the pleasure of meeting your father several times at the house of Madame Sand."

I knew perfectly well that at that period my father had known Madame Sand only through her writings; nevertheless, I refrained from contradicting Chopin, and replied, "So my father has told me, Monsieur."

He cast upon me a look full of recognition and sweetness, while I expressed my admiration for the genius of her whom he would never see more, and whom he would never cease to love. But then he was seized with coughing, and I saw upon the fine lawn handkerchief, which he carried to his lips, a trace of blood. It lasted only an instant: he made no complaint; only a smile of mingled pain and bitterness lighted up his pale face. Then, as if nothing had happened, he assigned me as a study, a selection from the preludes and fugues of Sebastian Bach. At last I withdrew, at once enchanted with his reception of me and saddened by the evidences of his enfeebled health.

When he had closed the door upon me and my little Pierre, I said to the child, "Don't make a noise, let me listen a little and hear how the gentleman who has given you a rose, gives his lesson."

The sound of the piano recommenced. The blonde pupil played very correctly but coldly, without shading and phrase by phrase; Chopin made her begin over again; perhaps at that very moment he was again raising his handkerchief to his lips to stanch those fatal drops of blood.

I returned home, profoundly touched; and when I recounted to my father that Chopin had said he had met him at the house of Madame Sand, the reply of my father was: "That is all as it should be; he probably felt the need of speaking of her. Poor Chopin!"

II.

Several weeks passed. One day I learned that Chopin was about to give a concert at the Salle Pleyel. The tickets were placed at twenty francs, and there were not enough to meet the demand; I was able to obtain only one. The hall was crowded; and the street was thronged with the most brilliant equipages. French aristocracy and cosmopolitan aristocracy, both represented mainly by their ladies, were met there. All were aware of the precarious state of the Master's health, and said sadly one to another: "Perhaps we are hearing him for the last time." The toilets were dazzling, diamonds flashed, and flowers exhaled their perfume. We had come to hear once more the poet of the piano; but it was the dying poet. Scarce a smile was seen upon the faces of the beauties who were professedly devoted to the music of Chopin. There were a great number of the *grandes dames* of Poland, proud of their fellow countryman.

Chopin felt himself at home in the salons of Pleyel. He had a particular fondness for those pianos with whose action he was familiar, and whose velvety tones were capable of infinite modifications and of an inconceivable delicacy of shading. The attention of all was concentrated entirely upon the master, despite the efforts of the renowned artists who essayed to make themselves heard beside him.

As for me, seated in such a position that I could see him perfectly, and endowed with excellent vision, I yet did not see him; I did not seem to hear him, and yet I heard him so well that I fancy I hear him still as I write these lines. I can scarcely refrain from irrepressible emotion at the mere remembrance.

He did not attack the note, he subdued it, he magnetized it, he made it speak, wail, sing, unroll itself in fantastic arabesques. The modulations, frequent and bizarre, with which his music abounds, rhythm, the most odd and unexpected, now the sound of a muffled drum, anon the tolling of funeral bells, the soft whisper of a breeze among foliage, the rocking of a gondola upon a calm sea: he portrayed all that. Then again it was some religious chant, the powerful tones of the organ, the deep passionate voice of the violoncello, the strings of a harp vibrating with celestial melody; again it was the human voice, and nearly always this voice flung out an appeal, despairing, beseeching, full of youthful ardor and fire. One heard fantastic waltzes written in triple time upon paper but played in *tempo rubato*, because these waltzes should only be danced by sylphs.

With the piano, one of the greatest difficulties is, that one cannot prolong its tones, except by the use of the pedal, and the pedal is liable to cause confusion and impair the clearness of the playing. Chopin not only used the pedal with a marvelous skill which few artists of the present day possess; but at that epoch he was the only one, and possibly is still today, who appreciated the strength and the weakness of the piano, and who wrote in such a style as to disclose the beauties and conceal the defects of this instrument-orchestra. Chopin's ten fingers were alert musicians, inspired withal, who sang in the notes wherever the piano suggests by its tones the human voice, while the accompaniment to those melodious songs was executed with bewildering rapidity; but always exquisitely shaded, and produced the effect of several violins playing in the distance, with a marvelous ensemble. The frequent and intentional dissonances, which made his music bristle with difficulties, were rendered by him with such lightness, such a virtuosity that they caressed the ear and threw the soul into that state of disturbed revelry in which one longs for what one has not, without knowing in the least what it is that one longs for;

when the sob is almost a smile; when the feeling for that which is beyond, hovers about us, and enfolds us.

The music of Chopin, executed by himself, was indeed that of an exile, devoted and dying, who still has not lost his faith; and with that faith he has written the music in Polish from beginning to end. The first time (it was years after this last recital,) that I heard Polish spoken, I recognized the music of Chopin. Chopin had studied with Moscheles; Chopin interpreted in an incomparable manner the grand and beautiful music of the Germans, but Chopin ever remained a Pole.

I once had related to me this typical saying of an Englishman, who was not fond of the music of Chopin: "Do you think it bad?" some one said. "No, but he was ill and I am in good health."

This remark confirms Michelet, who, while placing woman upon a pedestal, says, in his book on Love, that woman is an invalid. Ah well, it is women everywhere who delight to hear such music when, by a fortunate exception, it is well played. It is a disturbing music in which the feeling for the ideal forever dominates primitive sensation. In listening to it that evening we were all hypnotized, and hypnotism did not then exist. As for him, perfumed, elegant and enthusiastic as his audience evidently was, he did not think of it one instant, I am sure.

He was plunged deep in those dreams which had haunted him when he composed his music, and he had the air of improvising and of telling us without the consciousness that he did so, all that he had hoped, all that he had suffered, all that he regretted.

The work of Chopin is like the Divine Comedy of Dante; he has put into it his God, his country and his love.

Ah well. Would you believe it? There was that evening, something more beautiful still; it was Chopin playing Mozart. How, as he played on, with all the classical refinement, the sustained moderation which tradition requires, did the great artist seem to delight in this expression of a genius and a country, both so widely differen his own!

Mozart, the Austrian, born at Salzburg, between German and Italy, at a period when sorrow was not indeed unknown, but when it had not yet been made a sort of *cult* pursued even to desperation; Mozart who made us hear the songs of the birds, the voices of children and the young maiden; expressing a deep tenderness and disclosing an inexhaustible fountain of melody, which develops with a tranquil clearness at times bordering on the sublime; Mozart himself could not have rendered them better than did Chopin.

No, never has an artist attained a greater height, either in the interpretation of the work of another or in the delivery of his own; never has Chopin played better.

* * *

Upon reaching home I sank into an easy chair, without the strength to disrobe, and I remained there plunged in a sort of stupor until well on in the night. I revolved in my mind all that I had heard, that I might never forget it.

A short time after, I received a letter which announced the death of Chopin.

MADAME BERTON
(*nee* SAMSON.)

Translated from the French by Francis A. Van Santford.

THE ENGLISH LANGUAGE IN SINGING.

ANOTHER thing about which there is a great deal of foolish and harmful talk is the English language in singing. It seems to be considered a mark of artistic education among a certain class of people to decry our language as unvocal, hard, unsympathetic, the language of business, etc.— *ad nauseum*. This attitude is wrong from beginning to end. To speak thus of the tongue in which the poets from Chaucer, Spencer, and Shakespeare to our Whitman, Longfellow, and Whittier have given to the world the boundless wealth of their genius, would seem to be excusable on one ground only:—absolute ignorance of the writings of all those men. We point with proper pride to our literature as ranking with any of the ancient or modern world. It seems like an absurdity to speak of it at all. But leaving out the greatest names, to what language shall we turn for more exquisite lyrics, more sparkling ballads, more delicate sonnets than may be found in ours? And they try to tell us that this countless number of "gems of purest ray serene" are "unsingable!" Were it not that this misapprehension is so wide spread that we notice everywhere its baleful effects, it would seem incredible. But like other misshapen monsters that have forced their way in upon us, here it is and we must fight it. It is the older generation of singers and teachers who are responsible. It is a relic of that time when the voice was treated merely as an instrument for the production of beautiful tones. When not dramatic truth nor lyric beauty was what was in the composers mind, but how to show the tone color and mechanical perfection of the voice to its fullest capacity. The master of masters of those times was Rossini, and he it was who said when at the zenith of his fame, that he could write a grand opera with only the advertisements on the back page of a newspaper for a libretto, meaning that so long as the music was beautiful and well given it made no difference what the words were. That developed a race of singers whose technical powers seem to us now almost beyond belief. But for good or bad those days are gone. The Rossini singers are no more. The wheel has turned and art now demands that the instrument shall be beautiful, not for itself alone but that it may adequately interpret some beautiful thought. All other musicians thoroughly understand this great step that has been taken; only singers and singing teachers seem to be hoplessly in the rear of the procession.

What is the purpose of studying the voice? To become an artist. And what is an artist? One who knows how to speak the thought that was in the composer's mind. It is not necessarily the man who can sing the highest, nor the loudest, nor the longest. That has nothing to do with it. But he must be one who can so enter into the spirit of the writer that it becomes a part of himself, and who has his instrument so at command that he can make his hearers feel the music as he does. The artist is not he who stands on the stage to display his technical skill as Sandow shows the power of his muscles. He should be something more than a fine vocal athlete, he should be a man. A great piece of music well executed is in some sort a creation. The notes sound cold enough until one comes who can make the burning thoughts of the composer rise again.

Meanwhile what are our students of singing, our future artists, being told in the studio? Too often that such a vowel is unvocal, that such a word has a disagreeable sound, and that altogether our language is very ungrateful for the singer, with many more infinitely petty trifles. Then they are usually set to work on Italian, "the language of song." Now if these students only knew it, they may perhaps have crowded up out of the fire but they are still in the frying pan. At the hands of a poor singer that tongue can be made as unmusical as the crudest New England dialect. Still they go floundering on, singing they know not what, blundering over words and vowels until the whole thing is ridiculous, and then come to you with that rigmarole about its being so much easier to sing in Italian than in English.

There are delicate gradations of tone color in the Italian language which make it practically impossible for the foreigner to sing it correctly, and the student's Italian sounds to an Italian's ears a good deal as the turkey carved in German fashion looked to Mark Twain; he said that they used a club and avoided the joints.

Changing from one language to another shifts the difficulty without helping it a particle. The voice that is not well enough trained to sing "*I love you*"—with a beautiful tone, will hardly sing "*yo t'amo*" or "*Ich liebe dich*" any better. But were it done in English every hearer would understand for himself how poorly the tone expressed the sentiment, while if the singer confines himself to a language neither he nor any one else present understands, then no one knows whether it was well or badly done. We all have heard girls sing that great aria in the first act of *La Traviata*,—which vibrates with the passionate yearning of a soul that has strayed, for the pure joy of a holy love, the doubt, the hope, the despair, and the wild rush to drown such folly in any desperate madness,—with a simpering smirk which said that not the faintest notion of what it was all about had ever percolated into their minds. What could possibly be worse for anything like a healthy appreciation of art?

Leaving out of the question the Italian language, which has so small a part in the song literature of today, let us take the German. For singing in what respect is it superior to our own? Is its literature so far beyond that we may not compare ours with it? Do Goethe, Schiller, Lessing, and Heine so tower above Shakespeare, Milton, Dryden, Pope, Burns, and Byron that we may not match our names with theirs? Does it roll so trippingly from the tongue that ours may not compare with it for ease and grace? Is the beauty of the sound such that ours cannot approach it? Is "*Ich liebe dich mein Schatz*" so much more tender and delicately expressive than, "I love thee, my darling?"

Then why is it that all those who have any claims to "artistic" appreciation set up such a howl whenever any one of the "classics" is desecrated by being sung in English! There is one thing only to be said and that is that the music was written for one certain position of the words, and that a translation inevitably destroys the accent and the rhythm. There is a great deal of force in this and it has been a stumbling block to many who have felt that both by the laws of art and common sense, music should be sung in the language of the people. But I believe that vastly more pleasure to the hearers and benefit to music is lost by sticking to a foreign tongue and keeping the audience in ignorance of what it is all about, than injury is done any song by singing it in translation. This was painfully evident during our last season of opera, when some of the most dramatic singing that may be heard in all the wide world today, went for naught simply because the audience could not understand what the words meant as they were sung. And after a climax of unspeakable grandeur some one pipes up with, "but the tones were not sweet," which one with the feeling of a log could not have said had he been able to understand the words. To say that music is a universal language and that the words mean nothing at all is now, thank Heaven, recognized as folly. If the words mean nothing why do not composers write operas and songs with *la la* for a libretto? It would save them a great deal of work.

But the decree has gone forth. Music shall be sung in the original language. This is a canon of art which to disobey, is to be cast into outer darkness.

A minor consideration is the excessive badness of many of the translations. Indeed at times it seems as though this were far other than a "minor consideration." But there are songs where the words have been translated into exquisite little English poems, every whit as good as the originals. Only let the leaders of thought, and the followers too, demand music sung in the vernacular, and a race of fine translators will grow up quickly enough.

In this respect we are not so much worse off than other people. With what language do you associate "Faust" and "Carmen?" With Italian, I think. Yet both are French operas, and Gounod at least felt that his text suffered very much in translation. The standard translation of Carmen into Italian is so bad that it is always changed in a number of places, and as my old master said in speaking of one place in particular, "It makes the most perfect nonsense that it is possible to imagine." Now by what principle of art or common sense is a French opera sung in bad Italian better than the same opera sung in good English? Opera in America will never be other than a feeble, expensive exotic, until our people rise up and demand to hear it in a language they can understand.

Coming back to German again, the great German song writers have drawn many of their most beautiful inspirations from our poets. What songs are more perfect than Schubert's "Who is Sylvia," and "Hark! Hark! the Lark!" Yet there are Americans who commit the atrocity of singing them in their German translations. Schumann too has turned to Burns and Byron. Imagine, "My love is like a red, red rose," in German! There is another ludicrous disregard of logic by these same people, in cases like the songs of Grieg, Dvorak, and Chopin, which were written to Norwegian, Hungarian, and Polish words. They are usually sung in German. Now if they are to break their fundamental law that a song shall be sung in its original language by what right do they translate it from one foreign language into another, and then sing it to us Americans?

Our leaders in all art matters, the Germans, entirely disagree with this dictum. Enter any opera house in Germany and you will hear "Guglielmo Tell," "Il Trovatore," "Rigoletto," "Carmen," "Faust," "La Cavalleria Rusticana," and a host of others written in various languages, all sung in German. There is no doubt but that they lose something. I went from Florence just after hearing the creators of "La Cavalleria Rusticana," and heard the same opera in Munich. The change was very marked. A great deal of the color and fire were missing, yet who could but most heartily applaud the spirit of the Germans in demanding to hear opera sung in their own language!

The disciples of Wagner in particular are paying but scant respect to his theories of art in decrying the English language in singing, for one of the fundamental principles on which he based his life work was a national opera sung in the language of the country. Are his principles to hold good for Germany alone? Certainly when he began writing, Germany was not so thoroughly in subjection to the "barbarian foreigner" as is our own country today.

It is not to be expected that this great reform may be accomplished in a day, but the leading spirits among our musicians and critics feel that the theory is right, and the new thought is already leavening the mass. It does not mean that we discard on the instant all the music to which we are so deeply attached in its foreign setting, and sing it in any translation that may be found, no matter how bad it may be. But it is right that we hear the great works in a language that permits us to enjoy them to the full. If Berlioz's *Faust* may be sung time again from one end of our country to the other in English, why may not Gounod's? If a great play be written in France or Germany, in no time at all it is given here in English, and we all judge of its merits from a clear understanding of what the writer has actually said.

The present generation that has become accustomed to hearing music in the original German, French, or Italian, will miss a great deal, but more from sentiment and association, than from any real loss the music has sustained. But the rising generation that has its taste still unformed, if it learns to associate these same works with fine English translations, so far from missing any of the beauty, will wonder that their fathers so long denied themselves their full portion of the feast. We applaud Wagner for demanding German for the Germans. France demands French for her children, Italy, Italian for hers. But we, we young giants of the New World that are destined one day to be the law givers of the Nations, we must humbly accept whatever polyglot performance that lord of creation the Manager sees fit to give us, and never rebel unless by chance among the babel of tongues, some unfortunate should sing in English:—that cannot be tolerated!

KARLETON HACKETT.

A RAMBLE.

II.

BORN in 1829, Gottschalk was sent to Paris at an early age; after studying with Hallé he was placed under the care of Stamaty, who may be considered his real teacher. The gifted boy very soon courted publicity and appeared at the Salle Pleyel in concert, Chopin being present; the inevitable prediction as to the boy's future success was made by the older master, and happily fulfilled in this case; shortly after he gave a pay concert at Salon with fair success. It is interesting to note that up to this time he had only played compositions of Beethoven, Mendelssohn, Liszt, Thalberg and Chopin, but in 1846 he wrote his Danse Ossianique, quickly followed by a number of bright and showy salon pieces. He found that a great success was easily produced by a finished interpretation of these melodious trifles, and began to develope specialties in composition and piano playing, which in due time made him famous. After gaining the prestige of Parisian success, he went to Spain in 1850, enjoying the most distinguished attentions everywhere; the public, the nobility and even royalty were equally demonstrative in their approval of this young man, who instead of playing the classics dazzled them with the brilliant rhythms of the tropics, and reproduced national airs, transcribed with grace and skill.

Gottschalk's return to New York in 1853 elicited an offer from Barnum, which was refused on artistic grounds. As a financial venture his concerts proved a failure, although he easily took first rank among pianists, besides gaining many friends by his charming personality.

We have no record of his teaching; presumably he may occasionally have interested himself for brief periods in some talented person; he of course had many imitators, but no competitors. During the years 1855 and '56 he gave in

New York City eighty concerts, consisting almost entirely of his own works, and including the Last Hope, which has sold into the million copies. He received from the publisher fifty dollars for the composition.

Then followed a delightful trip to the Antilles, accompanied by Adelina Patti; his success was enormous and much money was made, besides some music. On his return to the States Max Strakosch offered him an advantageous contract, and under his management Gottschalk gave that memorable series of eleven hundred concerts, which brought him in actual touch with the musical life of this country at a time when benighted pianists only recognized three modes of touch, legato, non legato and staccato. Finishing his tour at San Francisco he then sailed for South America, repeating his success at Buenos Ayres, Montevideo, and Rio Janeiro, and here he was destined to die in the very midst of his triumphs.

If temporal success be a fair equivalent for individual effort, Gottschalk must have been satisfied, for excepting a short period of depression during his first stay in New York he enjoyed unequalled success everywhere, personally, artistically and financially. One cannot but realize, however, that this success was largely due to qualities which were entirely individual. You take a good-looking, well-groomed fellow, with or without long hair (the latter preferred) possessing personal magnetism to a large degree, and let him perform a number of popular pieces in brilliant style in public, and his success is assured.

In looking over his programs, one wonders if at the present day an artist could produce them and succeed; I doubt it. Even the most finished performance cannot evoke more than a passing interest in the March du Nuit, Last Hope, or Dernier Amour; the Tremolo amounts to a slugging match, and such compositions as the Bamboula, Banjo and March des Gibarros are too local in color to interest the audience at large, and yet who can but say that the same audiences who are visibly bored by the regulation program of the present day might not enjoy the very class of music which the classicists affect to disdain. Is the public really more educated than formerly? If so, how can we account for the sometimes sudden and often lasting popularity of some cheap, unmeaning musical jingle.

Here is a case in point. When D'Albert gave his recital in Chicago he played his own transcription of Bach's Passacaglia and the Sonata Appassionata for the opening number; without stopping to remove the dead and wounded from the hall, he followed with Mendelssohn's Variations Serieuses. By that time people had begun to leave and when he commenced playing pieces which might have produced enjoyment, hardly anyone was left to listen. Now who was the gainer? Nobody. Certainly not the artist, who had totally failed in his object, if he had one; neither the manager, nor the public. Possibly the looks of a big program may tickle the artist's vanity, but the outcome is almost always unfortunate. In the case of a reproductive genius like Rubinstein, where the personality was more intensely pronounced, the result was different. At his first concert in Chicago he opened with a piano arrangement of Beethoven's Egmont Overture, followed by the Sonata opus 53 and Schumann's Symphonic Etudes — surely a heroic dose; but the people seemed to like it; of course his specialties, like the Erl King and Turkish March, created a perfect frenzy; and yet Wieniawski's Carnival of Venice pleased more people than all of the great pianist's performances did.

Rubinstein's death brought out the usual number of silly interviews and reminiscences, more or less spurious like many posthumous publications. I have always considered the set of twelve books of Liszt's finger exercises published after his death a swindle. Some American publishers do not hesitate to use Buelow's name in the most unwarranted manner as coeditor of their publications. One fair correspondent brings the surprising information that Rubinstein was never fully satisfied with his own performance of the C major scale, and from an interview we learn that he had a peculiar way of playing scales. His Jewish origin gave such rabid anti-semitic papers as the Leipsic *Musikalisch. Wochenblatt* an opportunity to vent their spleen, and they took full advantage of it. Decades ago Wagner gave the cue, and a certain set of bigoted idiots have followed it up and are seeking revenge by turning the tables on the Jews and crucifying all they can lay their hands on. Buelow likewise has suffered at the hands of the posthumous editors, who would have done the great departed a signal service by omitting from a collection of Buelow letters a number of brutal and obscene allusions to Hiller and other Jews, which throw a peculiar light on the mental organism of a great man like Buelow, supposed to be above such relics of darker ages. In this connection it may be of interest to note, that during the present embargo which Germany has put on our pork, we are revenging ourselves by sending abroad successful pianists right along, who are forbidden the use of that succulent article.

It is high time that all this drivel about the alleged sayings and doings of artists should stop. What is the use in telling us that Pachmann, for instance, practiced the D major scale for a whole year; of course he never did, but I read the statement in a Vienna paper only a short time ago, and in the same article he was literally roasted for his Chopin playing; which goes to show that either we do not know anything about it in America, or that they are dead wrong in Vienna.

Artists are only a job lot at their best; let them alone; thank Heaven that they give us by their performances a demonstration of higher possibilities than is given to most of us to attain, and do not blame them for short comings which are credited to, but not missed by them.

EMIL LIEBLING.

WHAT IS CLASSIC MUSIC.

NOTE: Dr. Geo. F. Root, having been written to for a definition of classical music, called at the office of MUSIC to talk it over. When he had written his answer it was selected for these columns, because in a general way he covers the question so clearly and simply. ED. MUSIC.

OF all the music composed perhaps one number in a hundred lives more than a generation. Of these long lived compositions, only those that are considered best by all musicians are stamped with the word classic. Those which have only a local celebrity, or that have any defect or infelicity of form or harmony, (and there are such which have a good deal of vitality) are not admitted to the distinction of being classic. A composition to be classic, as that word is now understood by musicians, must first be a model of excellence in form and harmony; second, it must possess that mysterious vitality which makes it outlive its companions. And, third, it must be accepted by the common consensus of musical opinion as belonging to the first rank. Classic music is not a question of simplicity or difficulty. There are beautiful and living forms at every grade, from what are now regarded as the simple melodies of Mozart's, Haydn's and even Beethoven's compositions, all the way to the highest works of these and other great masters. A short definition of classic music might be "that music which for more than a generation has been considered by all musicians as the best."

GEO. F. ROOT.

REMENYI AS SEEN BY LISZT.

IN the letters of Liszt there are several very complimentary allusions to that veteran and experienced artist, Reményi the violinist. As this genial personality is widely known in America, and inasmuch as he has lately taken up his abode in this country, they may be perhaps found interesting to readers of MUSIC.

From Weimar Liszt writes to Carl Klindworth, July 2nd, 1854, "......Your *Murl*-connection, and *Murl*-wanderings with Reményi are an excellent dispensation of fate, and on July 6th, the day of your concert at Leicester, the Weimar Murls shall be invited to supper at the Altenburg, and Reményi and Klindworth shall be toasted '*for ever!*' —:" (The society of "Murls", Moors, Devil-boys—that is to say, Anti Philistines — was started at that time in Weimar. Liszt was Padischah *i. e.* King or President); his pupils and adherents, Bulow, Cornelius, Pruckner, Reményi, Laub, Cossmann, etc., were Murls.

From Rome, May 26th, 1864, he writes to Dr. Franz Brendel, "....Reményi, who has played here some half-dozen times in the Teatro Argentina, with *extraordinary* success, has a decided inclination to appear at the Musical Festival; I told him, however, that Concert-meister Singer had probably already been engaged. Should Singer not be able to come, I would recommend Reményi with absolute confidence. Of all the violinists I know, I could scarcely name three who could equal him as regards effect. Tell Bulow of Reményi's friendly offer, and let me know at your convenience whether it is accepted." Two weeks later writing to the same gentleman he says, "If a place is to be retained for Reményi he will fill it brilliantly. For both as a soloist and as a quartet player his accomplishments are extraordinary."

June 22nd, 1864, he writes to Eduard Liszt, "Reményi will come and see you shortly. He has spent nearly two months here, and has been heard here often at the Argentina Theatre with extraordinary success. I have invited him to come to Carlsruhe, as I am persuaded that he will succeed no less well there than in Rome. Meanwhile I beg you to give him a cordial reception."

From Weimar, September 7th, 1864, he writes to Eduard Liszt, referring to the *Tonkünstler-Versammlung* in Carlsruhe, "...Remenyi played magnificently, and Fraulein Topp is a marvel."

To Dr. Brendel he writes from the Vatican, September 28th, 1865. "....By the way, Kahnt would be doing me a favor by presenting *Reményi*, through Rozsavölgyi (Pest), with a copy of Pflughaupt's arrangement for pianoforte and violin of my "Cantique d'amour" and "Ave Maria"—and by granting my humble self a copy also, at his convenience. Reményi will be glad to play the pieces with Plotenyi and thus make them known, and I would get Sgambati and Pinelli to do the same here."

From Weimar, January 27, 1869, he writes to Johann von Herbeck. "....Friend Reményi whom I do not now need to introduce to you, will be the bearer of these lines to you. He has delighted and captivated everyone here, the Court as well as the public, and this is verily no small matter, for in Weimar we are accustomed to the most distinguished violin-virtuosos. I requested him to tell you how grateful I feel to you for your idea of a concert of Liszt's compositions."

EDITORIAL BRIC-A-BRAC.

DURING the past month there has been a large amount of chamber music played in Chicago, by the quartet parties, the schools, and the like, but much of it has failed of accomplishing the purpose which ought to have actuated its presentation. This purpose, need it be said? is to make the hearers more appreciative of quartette music and better acquainted with individual specimens. Already in this statement we are come to a fork of the roads, for it is one thing to present some great work in a manner that makes the hearer's spine thrill with aesthetic delight, and quite another to make up a series of programs illustrating a literature—or a province of literature.

When a school (for it is the schools that give most of the chamber concerts) offers a program, it is in a serious dilemma, or rather in a series of dilemmas. First, there is the question of the ability of the artists, who are all teachers actively engaged in giving lessons. Obviously they have little time to study new works, and little time to master new points of technic. This restricts them to such works as lie nearest, or to such as they have played in their student days. Then there is the question of attracting attention in the newspapers, for virtue is not its own reward in this field of concert giving. And to interest the newspaper critic to such a degree that he will actually come to the concert and sit it through—is a very difficult task. The chances are that if Liszt himself had come here to play, at least half the newspaper critics would have run in at some part of the program and perhaps have stayed through two or three pieces, but of the concert as a whole would have gone home in blissful ignorance. It is a great gain when the newspaper man has been interested to the point where he will so much as mention that such a concert was given, with such and such works. Hence a struggle to offer something which will look new, and hence one source of a great deal of bad and useless playing.

The school concerts, whether pupil or faculty, are too generally amateur in character. That is to say, the works presented stop short of the intensity of interpretation which interests and impresses the listener. If a student brings with him a copy of the work and follows it through, he will generally get a better idea of it than if he were to study it at home. But if bringing with him only his ears and a sensitive musical nature, he waits to experience some new rapture and beauty, the chances are that he will go home as empty as he came—or rather that a sense of having been bored will fill him with a dull impression that some one has been injured. And he is farther away from musical cultivation than if he had not come at all. Every great chamber composition offers difficulties of one kind or another. And it is no more discourtesy to say of an offhand performance of a Beethoven quartette that it failed of reaching the hearer, than to say of some college professor's Hamlet that it was amateurish. Of course it would be. We all know this; and yet there might be a case where just such a Hamlet would be a great deal better for the student than no Hamlet at all, or only such a one as he could create for himself by reading the book.

* * *

The fact is there are two kinds of concerts, and many of ours are neither one kind nor the other. There are concerts by artists, in which great works are presented with convincing charm, and every hearer feels upon going home that he has experienced a red-letter delight. These are very rare. Boston experiences something of this kind from the Kneisel quartette, and perhaps from some of its other admirable chamber organizations. We have nothing of this kind here, as yet. A quartette is never played in our concert rooms in a whole season in such a manner as to make you feel not alone that the players have thoroughly mastered it, but also have become full of its import and spirit, and feel it so deeply that their playing brings this feeling over to the hearer. What is the use of paying for tragedy which is not tragic? or for comedy which does not make you merry?

The other kind of concerts, which perhaps some of ours flatter themselves they are (but are not) is that in which the problem is to add something to the hearer's acquaintance with musical literature. It is a question of knowing the Beethoven works as a whole; or of knowing a series of works as a whole, and in their relations. The veteran Carl Wolfsohn gave such concerts for several seasons, playing the entire Beethoven sonatas, the entire works of Schumann, those of Chopin, and the chamber works of most of the classical composers. Very likely some of these performances were not quite up to the standard of the present day; but then with all our high standard we have no place now where a student can go through a great chapter of literature in this spirit. So there we are. And while it is true that our more finely educated students may be able to sit down at a practice clavier with a score before them and work out a concert with its orchestral accompaniment—upon the "absent treatment" plan—after all this brings us back to the point where many difficulties would be solved and great expense saved by taking all our concerts in the same manner. And to carry the principle further, if our food-taking and our love-making could be ministered in the same Platonic and idealistic manner, not alone would time be saved to the second individual, but many moral evils which now afflict society might be extirpated entirely. This, however, takes us too far. For the present, hearing music is as necessary as seeing pictures. To think about pictures is one thing; to see them is quite another. And while the vivid thinking which Raphael and Michael Angelo did would no doubt be far better worth having than the feeble seeing that most of us do with our own bodily eyes, it still remains true that after all the eyes are our main dependence, and the inner light comes to us later, through the ministry of these useful organs. And so it is with music. It is a swelling and sinking of the marshalled sounds, the delicate crystalization of motives, phrases, and imitations, the evanescent changes of color in the rich sunset glow of the symphony, which bring us the inflow of inspiration—the message which the seer, Beethoven or Schumann or Brahms, felt within himself, and received prophet-like in the vision of tones.

* * *

It is not to be expected that school concerts will reach this high level. Artists like Mr. Liebling, Mr. Sherwood, Mr. Seeboeck, men of vivid personality and the habit of public appeal, are artists of independent standing, whether the evening bear the label of a school or not. But the great rank and file of teachers, even many eminent ones, can never expect to attain to corresponding heights. It is a question of personal gifts and attainments, and of a habit of mind. When one has it, it costs him no more to play with the simple magic which Seeboeck displayed in the recent concert of the Columbian Conservatory than it costs some other to give a perfectly colorless and unmeaning interpretation of some great work.

And when it is a question of pleasing the hearer, unfortunately the musical gods are not, as Napoleon expressed it, "on the side of the heaviest battalions." It is not in the great works, but in the small ones, delicately done, that the largest pleasure comes to the average hearer. Put Seeboeck down anywhere in the world, with a good piano, and let him play his Menuet Antique or any other of a dozen of his dainty little things, and there you are The audience is captured, and nobody has any more to say against the program, the playing, or anything else. True, this is not great art, in the sense of reaching far inward to the deeper springs of soul; but then not every hearer has these deeper springs of soul (whatever they may actually be); but they all do have this capacity for a delight which lies near the surface, and which is true in its way, bearing after it no counter-charm of disgust at having been too easily or too unworthily moved.

There was something of this sort in Mr. Liebling's playing of his own dainty and clever little pieces, at his own recital and at the concert of Mr. Karleton Hackett. But here we are again at the pertinent question, what are our artists giving us! When Mr. Liebling, for instance, plays us one of Beethoven's sonatas, after years of study and many many times teaching it in detail to generations of fine players, he puts into his own interpretation about a tenth of the many small points which he has found there (not having had time ever to work them all into a single performance, if indeed they could be without contradicting each other); but this total may after all not be the total of that which Beethoven had in mind—nor yet equal to the measure of some smaller total which a hearer may have in mind as belonging to Beethoven. And here, moreover, we are on dangerous ground. The late delightful Autocrat of the Breakfast Table somewhere speaks of the minister's difficulty in the polarization which the words of the creed obtain by lying so long in one position, whereby there comes a time when to move one of the verbal landmarks out of its place is more dangerous than to trifle with the sacred ark itself; and we are not without something of this sort in the case of extremely fine compositions; compositions bearing evidently some kind of soul message, like these sonatas of Beethoven. The chords have lain a long time in such and such positions, and they have attained a polarization which the interpretative artist has to encounter.

When Mr. Liebling plays us one of his own charming things he is still not altogether out of the woods. For while he has many times assured us in print, and often again in private does he assure his pupils, that in writing these pieces he was not writing for posterity, nor yet for the Great Everlasting Over Soul, but simply composing convenient pieces for the pianoforte of today—even after all this education, some sweet soul rushes up to him and gushes of the hidden beauties and suggestions of his delightful tone poetry. In cases of this kind the Augurs go behind the altar and wink the other eye. Still upon mathematical principles it might be supposed that when Mr. Liebling plays us one of these things we are sure that the interpretation brings us all that there is in it and all that there ought to be in it. Why not? Did not this particular potter form and shape the clay? And had he not the power and the *savoir faire* to form it to honor or to dishonor? And note how delicately, and with what inner certainty of poetry, an artist plays his own things. Here is where you come upon the full piety of art. When he plays Beethoven, he may be praying in the temple; or he may be playing behind the altar—as sometimes happens. But when he worships at his own shrine, the artist is always sincere. Then we have him at his best.

* * *

Some years ago a young composer called upon me to play some of his compositions. Without being addicted to veal I can partake of it in small portions at seldom intervals. He began with a great deal about Chopin, and played among other things the Scherzo in D flat minor, opus 31. He had a great theory of this work. The middle part reminded him of a doomed city. (I felt like a doomed city, myself, when I began to realize where this interview was liable to take us.) But some time later a fortunate interruption took me out of the room, and the composer fell into one of his own pieces. They were common to a degree, platitudes, of a semi-sentimental kind, such as indiscreet girls confide to the piano at twilight. But oh the fineness of the interpretation, the deep inner feeling of it, the seer-like rapture! Here, evidently, we had the sincere milk of the word.

If ever an artist plays with a good touch it is in his own works. And here upon the question of touch we come to another element in interpreting classical music. Whenever a sonata is played with feeling (I say nothing of technic, because it is almost always fairly sufficient nowadays) and with musical tone, every listener gets something out of it. There is a quality of touch which makes every tone of the piano a pleasure to the hearer—like the mellifluous "Mesopotamia" of the celebrated preacher. Too few of our players have such a quality. The artists I have mentioned all have it at times, but they do not always bring their best resources to the clinging legato of sustained cantabile melody, and hence their adagios sometimes fail of producing the effect which a little more appealing quality in the tone would bring out. As for any particular mechanism upon the keys for securing such a quality—I am past it. There are fifty ways of making practically the same effect, and it is merely a question of the surest, the most convenient and the best looking, which is to be determined in each case for itself. But poor tone-quality ruins many otherwise commendable performances.

* * *

Speaking of school concerts, too great length is one bad quality. A notable example was afforded by the concert of Mme. Chatterton's Harp College, lately. Mme. Chatterton is a daughter of one of the most celebrated harpists of the century, and she has learned the instrument from childhood. Her technic is very large and her performance highly esteemed. In a concert of her school the hearers naturally desired much of her specialty. But in place thereof we had first a trio of Rubinstein, long and not over well done; and then a piano number by Mr. Nast, an artist unfamiliar to our stage. He played four pieces in one number: Chopin's Polonaise in A flat, the Funeral March (why at this particular juncture?) Schumann's Romanze in F sharp, and Liszt's 12th Rhapsody. Here was about forty minutes at a stretch. Now the playing was mixed, having in it both good and evil, but the evil unfortunately, like the tares in the field, a little ahead. The polonaise was taken very fast, and very heavy; this as every artist knows complicates its difficulty to a degree, although at its best it is far from a convenient piece. The consequence was that with false notes, pedal and pounding, the polonaise was honored in the breach rather than in the observance. If only the artist had gone a bit slower, and permitted his head to keep up with him, how delightful it might have been. The funeral march was much better, and as the occasion showed not unsuitable. The Schumann romance was done very badly, having about every fault that so easy a piece could have in an interpretation. Too heavy accompaniment, too much rubato and in the wrong places, and general short-comings of various kinds. Then the Rhapsody, again, was better, because it does not call for so much artistic quality. Still this also was sufferer from false notes, pounding and brutal tone quality. Which was a pity, for it was in Lyon & Potter hall, and the pianoforte, by Steinway, would have given an artist a great opportunity.

Mme. Chatterton herself was not quite at her best. Many things had gone wrong in the preparations, and she had been drawn upon in multifarious directions, to the thorough disturbance of an artistic mood; but her number was an interesting harp sonata by Naderman, which brought the instrument into a light not so common. Still the harp can never hope to contest the palm with such an instrument as the piano in thematic treatment or in sustained melody, and in a sonata we must have both. The harp is a most interesting instrument, and capable of much tone color—which under all circumstances has in it a personal element which is too often wanting from the piano. On the harp it is the player who actually plucks the strings with his fingers, and whatever you hear comes to you direct from the player. This is also the same with a good artist upon the piano; but also it is possible to do upon the piano what it is not possible to do upon the harp, "you touch the button, we do the rest." When a pianist has fired off a hammer they say in Boston he has lost control of it, and it is through second causes that an appearance of personal feeling comes into the tone. But upon the harp you actually make the tone, and make it louder or softer, thinner or fuller, musical or twangy by your own inflection in the touch.

* * *

The Chicago orchestra has been doing some magnificent playing lately. Beginning at the latest point covered by the present notice, there was a strong program December 14 and 15.

Overture to "Fidelio" .... Beethoven.
Heroic Symphony, No. 3, in E flat .... Beethoven.
Prelude and closing scene from "Tristan and Isolde." Wagner.
Bacchanale from "Tannhaeuser" .... Wagner.
Kaiser March .... Wagner.

The entire first part of this magnificent chapter of immortal tone-poetry, was rendered most delightfully, not alone with fine shading and delicate tonal valuations, as well as with the sweep which so grand works require, but also with that element of personal enthusiasm, which Mr. Thomas more and more reserves for a few things of Wagner, all of Beethoven, and important novelties of masterly construction or real genius. When moments of this kind are possible our great conductor is at his best. And after a really successful performance he is as delighted as any one in the audience—more so in fact, for he knows better what such an interpretation means.

6

At the rehearsal on Friday it was not altogether quite so smooth as on Saturday evening, but even that so filled me with a sense of having been moved, that I allowed my enthusiasm to bubble over in a presence where such enthusiasm has long ago ceased to flourish—namely before a celebrated musician. Who proceeded to cool me down with the query whether I did not think that it was about time that the Beethoven symphonies were shelved! Passing over the obvious claims of posterity to a share in works so well advertised as these of Beethoven, I was obliged to own up that I for one would be very sorry to have life made so much poorer as it would be by taking these and a few other musical works out of it. For since we are speaking of Beethoven, the reader may as well learn now as later that a well-known Chicago musician once entertained the project of re-writing the Beethoven sonatas for pianoforte, in order to adapt them better to Beethoven's ideas. This gentleman took a room with a teacher in one of the ward schools, who had a similar project in regard to the plays of Shakespeare and the poetry of all the older poets. Strange as it may seem, these two congenial spirits could not agree, the musician thinking that the poems were well enough as they were, and that it would be sacrilege to meddle with them; while the poet advanced precisely the same arguments with regard to to the great master works in music. The arguments becoming heated, both gentlemen were disabled physically, and were never afterwards possessed of enough vitality to rehabilitate a canary bird. Beethoven and Shakespeare escaped for that time. But perhaps next time they may not be so fortunate.

As for the Heroic symphony of Beethoven, it will be a very long time before I shall desire any improvement in it, any more than in those heavenly ones of Schubert. For Beethoven was not only a great poet, a seer, with a message which the world has gladly heard, and longs to hear, but also a great colorist, dealing with tonal hues as delicately as ever Raphael or Titian with tints; and showing in every least touch the trained sense and deep inner intuition of the poetry of color and its relation to the soul itself.

Blasé musicians may prate of the barrenness of the common chord as long as they like, and as loud; to my mind there is no product of the creative imagination so exquisite, so much like the doings of the gods themselves, as the great master-works of music. And I do not ever expect to hear (in this life or another) of a race so advanced and so noble, and so lofty, that the ideas of Beethoven seem to them puny and kindergarten in their caliber. Why should we look for something of this sort? Are we to expect a race of intellects so high that English speech will not carry their blooming greatness? And of such depth that no verb can agree with its nominative case and say it? Nay, verily, Those great men will cincture their massive brows with a golden band, lest thought should burst their aweary brains; and mate with the sundown and the horizon line, in their search for fitting progeny. But the affairs of the world will go on all the same, to the tune of human heart-throbs and aspirations just the same in nature as our own, though mayhap nobler. And as sunsets and the glorious openings of the gates of day will still have to answer as suggestions of divine splendor, so also will these great tone poems still stand sublime and commanding, no matter how far the progress of complication may go.

For consider how little there is in complication as a means of delight and power in art. Take Wagner himself. Here were the three striking and powerful selections from operatic scores, and the Kaiser march, of which it can at least be praised that it is not so deadly bad as that which he wrote for the American Centennial,—and the paralyzing fee; and what a striving, and a trying to soar; like a great clock bent upon striking twelve each hour of the solemn night. How tiresome it gets. Nothing saves it but the splendid sonority, and the impression it makes of some great soul trying extremely to think a great thought, and to say a great say. And at times Wagner does it; as in the *Isolde's Liebestod*; but at any other times he is merely laborious and masterly, without ever carrying us whither he would desire. The way of art does not lie there. Wagner himself tells us as much.

And as for a future relegation of these great works of Beethoven to the lumber room, about how soon are we to look for it? Bach lived and worked almost two hundred years ago, yet the musicians who know most of art still revere his mighty genius, and find in a large part of his music even more pleasure and higher culture than those of Bach's own day or the generation after him. Nor has yet the march of complication left these works behind. Rhythm and Harmony are as well at their best in Bach as in any musician since; and where would be our musical education were we to relegate his works to the musical lumber room? Or take it in poetry; have our modern and high-strung poets gotten beyond the simple and moving majesty of the later Isaiah? Man will doubtless improve somewhat—at least it is to be hoped so now that lovely woman is so well in advance; but the rate will be a stable one, akin to the great mountain-wearing forces of nature, which take periods of thousands of years to make ever so slight a modification in the figures of a chain of peaks. Or like the slow progress of average human weight, stature, or life-span.

* * *

Among the novelties of the symphony programs has been the Prelude to Humperdink's new opera of "Hensel und Grettel," and very pleasing music it was, and well played. Mr. Robert Goldbeck is in Chicago once more, after almost a generation of wanderings, and at the concert of Dec. 7th three of his pieces were played by the orchestra under the direction of the composer. Two were Mexican dances, concerning which the composer takes care to inform us that even the themes are not taken from Mexican folk songs but made up by the composer himself, and thoroughly characteristic of Mexican style. As for the music, it is rather common. The most meritorious of all was the cello concerto of Mr. Arthur Foote, played by Mr. Bruno Steindel. Although not gratefully written for the instrument, it contains much enjoyable music, and is treated admirably for orchestra. It is a serious and an important work.

W. S. B. M.

THE PRACTICAL TEACHER.

QUESTIONS ON MUSICAL MEMORY.

PRELIMINARIES.

A.—Musical Aptitude.

1. Have you a correct ear, a correct voice? What is the register of your voice?

2. *Precocity.*—At what age did you manifest an aptitude for playing an instrument, for singing, for composing? In what manner did your talent declare itself?

3. *Heredity.*—Have different members of your family remarkable musical talent? Have they ever had? What is their degree of parentage, paternal or maternal? (Give the exact details upon these principal points: correct ear, correct voice, musical sentiment, singing, playing instruments, composition).

4. State also the negative cases. Are there among your ancesters persons with very false voice or ear, and who detest, or have detested, music?

B.—Musical Culture.

5. Have you studied sol-fa, harmony, composition? What is your musical education? What have you played, sung, heard or read?

6. *Musical Preferences.*—What styles do you prefer? (Symphony, chamber music, opera, ballet, operetta, dance music, etc.)

7. What are your other preferences?

C.—General Qualities of Memory.

8. Have you good memory for words—for figures—for lines and colors, for countries, for faces, etc.—for muscular sensations, sensations of touch, taste, smell, for sensations of grief—for movements, etc.?

D.—Technical Memory of Music.

9. Have you a good memory for intonation—for absolute pitch of sound, for intervals, for tonalities—for the timbre of instruments and voices—of the relation of timbres.

10. Do you remember rhythms exactly?

E.—The Auditory Image.

11. Do the auditory images present to your memory the same characters as the corresponding external sensations?

a) Are the pitches of the same nature? Have they more clearness?

b) Is the intensity of these images comparable to that of the sensations? Is it weaker?

c) What is the timbre of them? (Certain persons say that their musical memories do not recall any real timbre.)

12. When you remember a chord, do you hear it as a single sound, or as a collection of notes?

III.—*Melody and Rhythm.*

13. Do you sometimes recall the rhythm separate from the melody? If so, in what manner?

14. When you make an effort to remember, is it the rhythm or the melody that you recall first?

15. When your memory fades, is it the rhythm or the melody that you recall last?

IV.—*Memory of Musical Works.*

16. Do you remember a work as it is written or executed—the melodic suites, the tonality, the harmony—the movements and the shading, the measure and the rhythms, etc.?

17. Or do you transpose it to the register of your voice? Do you alter the motives? Do you modify the measure, the movements, the rhythms?

18. Do you hear it in memory with the timbre of the voices which sang or the instrument which executed it?

19. Do you hear it with the timbre of your own voice, of the instruments with which you are familiar, or with a timbre ill defined, neutral, so to speak?

20. What is the intensity of your mental hearing, compared with your real hearing?

21. Do you remember the details of the execution of the whole of a symphony, the parts of the divers instruments?

22. As you read pages of music, do you hear clearly the sounds of the melody, of the accompaniment, of the orchestration?

V.—*Manner of Memory.*

23. *Localization.*—Is it in yourself that you hear music reborn, or does it appear to come through your ear from without? (Direction, distance, etc.)

24. Do you observe a difference in the precision or the intensity of your memories, according as they present themselves or you provoke them?

25. Do you hear them passively, or have you the feeling of producing and directing them?

VI.—*Conditions and Circumstances Favorable to the Auditory Memory.*

26. Can you determine the musical reasons that render more easy or more difficult the memory of a work?

27. Does not the knowledge of the rules of harmony and composition aid in reviving your memories, and in rendering them precise?

28. What are the exterior circumstances that favor the clearness of your auditory images (noise, silence, marching, etc.)?

VII.—*Verbal Memory.*

29. Do you pronounce mentally the names of the notes in recalling a musical fragment? Do the words of a song, the verbal designation of the tonality of a composition, etc., serve to awaken your musical memories, or to render them exact?

VIII.—*Visual Memory.*

30. Are your auditory images accompanied with the mental vision of the musical text?

31. Do you see the text before you hear it? Is it because you see it mentally that your auditory memories are aroused?

32. Conversely, is your mental hearing immediately followed by the visual image of the written or printed music?

33. Are visual memories of this nature continually associated with your auditory memories?

34. Describe these visual images of the music. Do you see all the notes with their position on the staff, and their value? Do you see the clefs, the bars, the divers signs, etc.—the written words if it is a song that you are recalling?

35. Could you write a composition that you thus recall?

36. Do your memories of a symphony, or an opera, evoke the mental vision of the orchestra, the theatrical scene, the artists with their costumes, etc.?

IX.—*Motor Memory.*

37. When you recall a melody, do you notice a change in your breathing? Do your lips and your larynx move as if you were singing? Is it necessary for you to murmur the sounds to represent them exactly?

38. While hearing music, do you feel a sensation of tension of the vocal organs, analogous to that of singing?

39. Is it difficult for you to represent very high and very low sounds, the reproduction of which is beyond the compass of your own voice?

40. To represent the tonality of a composition, or the absolute pitch of a note, have you recourse to the effort which you would have to make to intone it?

41. Do you revert to the memory of the movements necessary to the singing or the execution, to recall the melody? Is it these motor memories that arouse your auditory images?

42. Conversely, does the mental hearing arouse in you a sensation of the effort which you would have to make to sing or execute the remembered airs? Do you murmur them involuntarily?

43. Does the memory of the muscular sensations associated with the singing or execution of a work sometimes persist when the memory of the sound is effaced?

44. M. Stricker declares that one cannot represent sounds except through the intermediation of the muscular sensations of the vocal organs or of the ear. He adds that one can represent sounds under the form of muscular sensations, "*without* auditory images." Do you consider these muscular sensations to be the true equivalent, the possible substitute of the auditory musical images?

X.—*Memory of Emotions.*

45. Is the memory of emotions caused by music sometimes recalled to you in a very vivid and exact manner, in the absence of all auditory memory? Is this emotional memory for you a substitute for the absent musical images?

XI.—*Ease, Duration, Quantity of Musical Memory.*

46. After several lectures, hearings or executions, do you recall easily the melodies, the harmony, the orchestration of a work?

47. Are your memories lasting? Do you have to assist your memory by reviewing periodically what you have learned?

48. Enumerate the works of which you have actually exact memories.

XII.—*Divers Questions.*

49. Do musical recollections determine for you movements of expression? (Faces, attitudes, gestures.)

50. *Colored Hearing.*—Is your mental hearing of sound accompanied with the internal vision of a color, which varies with the sounds heard?

51. *Mnemotechnic.*—What means do you use for fixing or reviving your memory of music? (Do you voluntarily associate, for example, verbal, visual or motor, images with the auditory images? Do you use any means to strengthen your musical memory?

52. Have you schemes relative to music?

JULES COURTIER.

Note.—Mr. Jules Courtier, chief assistant at the Laboratory of Physiologic Psychology, at the Sorbonne, (Paris) requests those that read these questions, kindly to send their replies to him.

AN AMERICAN STUDENT AT LEIPSIC.

An American teacher of music, of some years experience, who has always cherished the idea of spending a year in study at Leipsic, found herself this season able to carry out the plan, and in the following extract from a private letter gives an account of her beginning.—Ed. Music.

AT the time of my last letter I had only been to the conservatory to see where it was, and to express my intention of entering for the coming year. And I had been directed by the Secretary to come on the following Tuesday for an appointment, and on Wednesday for an examination and to be classed. That was all right, but I know enough about conservatories to know how they are usually managed, and decided to prove my Yankee by trying to run this one to suit myself. I found out that Herr Johannes Weidenbach was considered by most unprejudiced persons the best teacher of piano in the conservatory, and he and Krause the two best in the city. I was also told that it was difficult to get into his classes unless one was already a fine performer, or had special ability, and intended to study for a long time to become a concert artist. Discouraging enough for me, to be sure, and true enough, no doubt, had I expressed my desires and gone to the management at the time appointed. But I did not. I decided to beard the lion in his den, the sooner the better, I thought, and Frau Dr. Niedermuller would go with me as he does not speak English, and I ought to add pretends not to understand the simplest sentence, and has a way of making you feel that he thinks you a subject of pity or contempt if you do not know the divine German. He received us pleasantly, and after Frau Dr., had told him that I was an American, expected to study in the conservatory for a year, and very anxious to be placed in one of his classes, he said what I half expected he would, that he would hear me play.

As you know, I had hardly touched a piano for months, until that very day, when I had worked on Frau Dr.'s piano for two hours, and got one little piece back into my head and fingers, thinking that one would be enough. I played it for him and got through very well, when, horrors! he asked me to play something else. I started a study and got half through when he said that would do, and would not I play something of Chopin or Schumann! He would pass me the notes if I did not remember, and would I tell him what I would play of Chopin? No! I would play the "Entrance" to the "Forest Scenes," and he listened to the end, then asked me for a lot of scales and chords, and after all that fuss made me happy by saying that I might enter one of his classes, and if I would come to him during the vacation week for one or two private lessons he could class me to better advantage, and I need not go to the conservatory for further examinations.

I went to him, and the Frau Dr. was kind enough to accompany me, so that I could get the full benefit of his German explanations. He had me bring Julius Knorr's System of Technics, and the first lesson was devoted to teaching me how to hold my hands and play the five finger scales and chords after his fashion. The next lesson I was to bring Döring, opus 38, Books I and II, and play for him the first four studies in Book I. I did not get on very well, of course, and ventured to say that I had been taught very differently, and was too stupid to change quickly, when he said with a great deal of energy, "There is but *one* right method: every other way is humbug, and the world is full of humbugs." He said that most of the Americans who came to him played as I do, and when their hands were large and their fingers long, he could think of nothing but big spiders going over the keys.

You very likely know what he wished me to do, keep the hand still, press the knuckles in, curve the fingers very much, and play everything very strong and loud: but the worst thing I have to contend with in pleasing him is in scale playing, the passing the thumb under the fourth finger. Instead of turning the wrist out the very least, or pivoting on the fourth finger, in order to get into the new position smoothly, I must move the entire hand suddenly to the right or left, keeping the wrist and arm quite still. Do you see? I cannot explain it, but could show you in a second what he wishes, if I cannot do it.

Besides the Döring op. 38, I have the opus 8, Book I, and the first book of the Loeschhorn opus 66. Some of the etudes I know by heart, but he usually says the same things:—"You must learn them better. *Sie müssen schneller spielen, und stärker.*" So I suppose when I get muscle enough to make a good prize fighter, I will be on the road to pleasing him.

My harmony with Herr Paul Quasdorf is a great pleasure. I

had supposed that I had forgotten all that I had ever known, and had myself placed in a beginners class, but at the second lesson he asked me to come next time an hour earlier and see if I could not do the work with a class that had been studying a year, and were now doing exercises in *canon forms*. My work satisfied him, I think, as he has kept me on in that class, and I notice that I get no more red marks than the other young ladies. I have also done ten chapters review work in Jadassohn's book, and shall keep on until I do twenty, which will bring me to the place where this class began.

Then the concerts, I am getting no end of pleasure out of. First I mention the pupil's recitals of the conservatory, every Friday night from six to eight o'clock, and sometimes Tuesday. There are about six hundred and fifty pupils to select from and many of them are very gifted, so you see the concerts are very good, and one can judge a great deal of a teacher by the pupils. One young lady played Schumann's A minor concerto; the next week it was played by a young Russian lady, a pupil of Rubinstein, at the the Gewandhaus, and last Friday it was again played at the conservatory by another young lady. One can learn a thing when it is heard so many times and so often, and this is one advantage of being here. Also last Friday was played Bach's Italian concerto, by a little fellow, William Bachhaus, hardly ten years of age, and he did it very well.

The Gewandhaus concerts are the best, of course. The pupils all have free admission to the rehearsals, take off their hats and coats, and go as if they intended to stay and enjoy it, and at the end of the rehearsal it is generally understood that they crowd to the front and applaud until the artist comes back and plays or sings specially to them. The hall is very beautiful, the orchestra fine, but I have not yet gotten used to listening to it. It is not arranged like the Boston symphony orchestra. Besides the different placing of the instruments, another thing I like very much—all the men who can play standing, stand during the entire rehearsals. There are to be twenty-two Gewandhaus concerts, and I also have tickets for six Liszt-Verein, and six concerts of the Akademic orchestra. At the first Liszt concert, Frederic Lamond, a young man from Frankfort, played Tschaikowsky's concerto in B minor, in a wonderful manner, as regards technic. Jadassohn said the next day that he had heard no one play octaves so well since Tausig, but I would say that the praises he won by his octaves were to a certain degree offset by his lack of *cantabile* in the beautiful slow movement the concerto, and in the Liebestraum.

Lillian Sanderson sang a lot of lovely songs in a lovely manner, and Lillian Nordica has also been here twice in opera, and is coming in the Gewandhaus concerts this week. I am enthusiastic over her, very; more from a patriotic principle than from an artistic standpoint, perhaps. I never cared so much for her before. She may have improved. She certainly is a great artist and is winning great praise. Krause said some hateful things about her, which created quite a war of words. I will get the notices and send them to you, which will be better than telling you about it.

I have dissipated to quite an extent during the month, in the way of opera, and intend to still more later on. First I heard Lortzing's "Undine," then the "Meistersinger," "Tristan und Isolde," "Lohengrin," "Fidelio," "La Traviata," and "Hansel und Gretel," a new opera by Engelbert Humperdinck. It was suggested by the old German fairy story of the same name, and the music is as bright and pretty as the story itself. Most of the conservatory pupils hear the operas in the third or fourth gallery and the tickets cost from fifty pfennige to one mark fifty (12½ cts to 37½ cts.) Think of hearing such an opera as "Fidelio" well given for 18¾ cts., and this is what I did, and it was a respectable thing to do. It seemed very strange to me at first, but I am getting used to it, and will hate to go home and pay two or three dollars for a similar affair. Another thing is strange, but I like it: it is to go at 6:30 and be home and in bed at 11 P. M. if one wishes; and Sunday night is as good an opera night as any other. It was Sunday night that we heard the "Meistersinger." And that reminds me, Shelper, who sings the part of Hans Sachs here, is said to be the best Hans Sachs in the world. The Leipsic people are very proud of him, and gratified that he will not accept offers to sing in other places, although he has had many valuable ones. Fraulein Ileur also has a strong, beautiful voice under good control, which as Ortrud made Nordica's Elsa seem weak at times. But Nordica was so artistic and her voice so intensely musical in the pianissimo passages, that I think a little weakness of the kind before mentioned can be forgiven. Herr Merkel, who does many of the leading tenor rôles, has not a specially good voice, but his acting is not so bad. Altogether the opera here is given much better than I had been led to believe, and the orchestra is so very good, made up for the most part of the Gewandhaus symphony men, that it is a pleasure you are quite sure of to hear them, no matter how the rest of the work may go.

There have been ninety different teachers connected with the conservatory since it was organized, and I amused myself the other day by copying the list. I found that Weidenbach has been here since 1873. Think what a number of pupils he must have bothered in all that time, just as he is bothering me. There were nearly 150 new pupils entered this last term, ever so many English and American.

As to operas I have heard since I wrote you "Mignon," "Falstaff," "Carmen," "Figaro," "Tannhäuser," "Genoveva" and "William Tell." We intended to hear "Preciosa" tonight but finally gave it up. I was very glad to have a chance to hear Schumann's opera and will say that the music struck me as being intensely beautiful although there is little else to greatly admire. As regards "Tannhäuser," I was pleasantly disappointed. The theatre here is small and the leading singers not so great as I have heard in America, but the work as a whole gave me far more pleasure, and I am quite certain that my criticisms are not influenced by the fact that I know the music better and have so recently been at the beautiful Wartburg. The Gewandhaus Symphony concerts I generally enjoy more than any of the others. The IV was the most attractive. The house was packed, Dvorak's Symphony "Aus der neuen Welt" and Nordica. Every one was wild over Nordica, and I think she did do herself proud; made me more than ever proud to think that I also was an American. The next day I was standing with one of the best lady pianists here, who is also a teacher of vocal music, and she could not say enough in praise of Nordica. I said, "But the Symphony! why do you not mention that, was it not beautiful?" She shrugged her shoulders and said, "ah, it was too long, it occupied fully forty-five minutes, but then it *amused* us very much, such funny ideas as he worked into it, so strange we never heard anything like it." She said that in that sweeping way as if the entire musical portion of Leipsic agreed with her. I think many of them did—others seemed to think Dvorak's working out, far better than his ideas, and that Brahms could have done the whole thing much better. From the half dozen programs I have heard I think the management a trifle old fogy, and when they get in the habit of giving new works more often to the public, the public will get in a better condition to judge of them. At the V Gewandhaus, I heard the beautiful C dur Symphony of Schubert and Sliott, a pianist from Paris, who played Chopin's lovely concerto in E major as badly as I ever heard it, and the people seemed to think he was great. They should hear Paderewski, de Pachmann, or even Aus der Ohe. Sliott played as if he was doing a Czerny Etude. Perhaps you will think I have been doing Etudes until I do not know anything else when I hear it. But let me tell you right here that after two months of Doring, Loeschhorn, etc., last week I got a Clementi Sonata to play, op. 20 No. 3. Some people have to work three months before they get one.

The second Liszt-Verein concert was as much of a Liszt program as the first, there was the Faust Symphony and piano concerto no. 2 of Liszt played by a pianist from Berlin, Mr. Ferruccio Busoni. I think at one time he taught in Boston. At any rate he was very good and when called back gave Liszt's "La Campanella" in a beautiful manner. As a whole the Liszt-Verein concerts are not as interesting to me as the Akademisches orchestra concerts. The first program was made up from Handel, Bach, Rameau, Gluck, Mozart and Haydn. The violin concerto in A moll of Bach played by Herr Prof. Brodsky was something to be especially mentioned and long remembered. The second program was wholly Beethoven. The Symphony No. 3 heroica, "Lenora" overture No. 2, and piano concerto No. 3, played by Marie Krebs. I was very glad of the chance to hear her and at the same time disappointed in not hearing Teresa Carreno. The management wanted Carreno for the Beethoven night, but owing to, or on account of a baby Carreno D'Albert, she could not come. I sincerely hope that she will be able to come later, and if she does I have not forgotten my promise to present her your compliments. I have not mentioned the chamber concerts of which I have heard three since I wrote you. At the last one I heard three Quartets, one of Rubinstein, Beethoven and Schumann. The Schumann op. 41 no. 1 was beautiful beyond description. These concerts seem to me like a very rare and valuable edition of something very difficult for the common person to obtain, and yet they come to me by way of my conservatory membership tickets. I suppose the reason I enjoy and value them so much is on account of the few chances I have had to hear that form of music at home. In addition to the operas before mentioned we have during the week heard "Der Freyschütz" and "Oberon" and I have said nothing of the church music, and evenings one or two a week at the conservatory. Last Friday night one of the young lady pupils played the same Chopin Concerto that Siloti played at the Gewandhaus, another played the Mendelssohn Capriccio op. 22, and another the 1st movement of a Dussek concerto, all with orchestra accompaniment. There were also an organ piece, three or four songs and a string quartet of Beethoven. I mention all this that you may have an idea of the pupils and program.

CARRIE BELLE HOSMER.

MR. REGAL ON MUSICAL MEMORIZING.

The subject which Mr. Francis E. Regal so ably presents in an earlier part of this issue, upon the "Cultivation of Musical Memory," is one of the most important in its practical bearings of any that have been presented during the entire history of this magazine. With his positions and suggestions I am for the most part in complete accord, but there are a few minor points where he is not clear—or was under a misapprehension. On page 218, he says: "I do not intend in the least to disparage the value of playing without notes, but when the immensity of the field of good music is borne in mind, it is difficult not to question the wisdom of devoting so much time to the exact memoriter study of the trifling handful of pieces that the pupil can learn, and leaving almost neglected so far as scientific study goes, the broader and to my mind more valuable field of the partial memorizing of many great works." This important sentence contains two implications which are liable to be misunderstood and do harm, while its general purport is admirable in every way.

First, as to the object for which memorizing is used in teaching pianoforte. Inasmuch as I was myself one of the first in this country to advocate publicly and upon a wide scale the practice of piano pupils memorizing a large proportion of the lessons they recite, I may be allowed to explain why I then did twenty-four years ago and do now, advocate the practice, and make it largely the rule in my own teaching.

One of the first steps which has to be taken in trying to modify the playing of a pupil is that of improving his method of study, in order to render it more accurate and retentive. This one modification of his mode of acquiring has in it the promise and potency of every thing else. The amateur plays you something which you hear indifferently. An artist plays the same thing and you attend with earnestness from the first note to the last. There is no way that I know of so effectual for doing this as to require memorizing. The best pupil no less than the worst will bring you something very different in the two parts of the same lesson, when one part has been learned by heart and the other is played by note. In the former the actual music has been scanned with a clearness and accuracy which in the second example is often very largely wanting. The details of the musical thought, and its implications of feeling are much more clearly brought out when the pupil has made it his business to know exactly *what* is said at every step of the discourse, and when the discourse as a whole is present in his mind from the first note, as when one has in mind not alone the close of the sentence one is speaking but the substance of several sentences ahead, which will be needed for completing the thought.

Moreover, memorizing has a very important influence upon the technic, in that it leads to ascertaining more and more perfectly the precise points of difficulty which hinder the easy performance of a given passage. Difficulties are very often entirely vanquished by memorizing the passage in which they occur; and in all cases they are very much diminished. This is to say that a large part of the faulty playing that we hear is mental in its source, and not muscular. When the mind knows clearly and certainly where it desires to carry the musical thought, the fingers manage to perform their part. Of course I do not mean to carry this principle to the extent which I understand Mr. Cady to do, when he says that there is no such thing as piano technic but that musical thought is everything, and when the is thought clear no excuse or special training are necessary for the fingers. (I do not intentionally misrepresent Mr Cady, for whom I have both the highest personal regard and a profound professional respect: but this is what I understand him to say privately as well as publicly. On the contrary, the fingers were not originally intended for playing the piano. And it comes to about the same thing whether we assume that they *were* primarily intended for playing the piano, and that other uses are accessory; because even in this case the intervening heredity of some thousands of years when there were no pianos to play must necessarily have retarded the maturity of an aptitude originally foreseen and provided in the creation. Or, we may take the opposite view, which is mine, that man has come up from tree climbing ancestors, (who may or may not have had tails,) in which state he had great aptitude in grasping and picking, but little manual talent of a literary sort. In this case man has in his civilized condition to acquire these new arts, such as spelling the English language, writing with a pen, running a writing machine, and playing the piano—which processes in many cases can be facilitated by exercise upon certain typical difficulties of muscular successions. But when technic has done its best, it has provided only a small part of the playing ability, and exact and clear musical thought, reaching inwards to the deepest feelings, are the conditions without which good playing is impossible. Therefore I require more or less memorizing at every lesson: and I always diversify the subject-matter of memorizing, having something of Bach or Handel, something of Chopin, Schumann or Liszt, and if we are at work on Beethoven, then we always memorize this. Also in the early grades I require the studies to be memorized, and especially the musical ones, like many of those in the Standard Grades. I do this because I wish the pupil to form a habit of paying close attention, and because I find that the technic gets along more rapidly and the playing is better. In the higher grades, in all the earlier stages of coming on, memorizing prevails. A Bach fugue cannot possibly be well played without memorizing until after the pupil has acquired a great deal of experience in this class of music; and even then the performance of any fugue will be very greatly improved by memorizing. It will not be necessary to do much criticism, if the piece is studied by a fairly competent pupil; merely memorizing and the influence of the music itself will transform the playing and render it definite and effective. Such style-forming pieces as the Chopin Etudes—must also be memorized, if we want their full effect. Pleasing pieces at all stages of the progress are memorized, for the convenience of having them handy when one wants to play them: and for the additional reason that this is part of the process of completely learning them.

The second misapprehension which Mr. Regal manifests is that this process of memorizing as an incident of study involves delay, and affords the pupil less material to work with than if the lessons were played from notes. This does not agree with my experience, although it no doubt does with the experience of those who use the ordinary system of technics, and perform most of their teaching upon Etudes played from notes, with only an occasional piece—which now and then they attempt to have memorized. The art of paying attention, and especially the art of analyzing musical thoughts and sequences, is no more difficult to the pupil than the ordinary class exercises of the school room. Any girl able to maintain standing in the high school or even in the upper grammar grades, is able to do similar work in her music, when she once finds out that it has to be done. Generally the girl of high standing in her school grades stands equally well in her music, a good mind being better to be chosen for musical purposes than great riches—though occasionally they go together. The kind of exercises practiced has a great deal to do with easy memorizing. Mason's treatment of the diminished chord arpeggios, and the rhythmic handling of them, opens the pupils' eyes to many things in passage work which they do not ordinarily notice. They know exactly what metrical treatment does to a motive or musical figure, and they are habituated to noticing slight shades in harmonic relations. This they get at first mechanically, by changing from one derivative to another; and later with the musical feeling of harmonic progression. Even if the Mason book of Arpeggios were only half as productive as it is from a finger standpoint and for the

PIANO TOUCH, AGAIN.

attainment of velocity early in the game, it would still pay to use it merely for the mental effect. It is my experience that a student practicing as I have indicated, making memorizing the rule of practice in every serious task from the earliest lessons (where playing by heart cuts even a greater figure) up to the most advanced, will find the following to be true:—(1.) At any given stage of progress, she will have more pieces which she can play creditably: (2.) She will understand all her pieces better. (3.) Here is what Mr. Regal did not understand, she will have acquaintance with a larger range of good music, and, (4.) will know it better and more productively. I will not tarry to enlarge upon the positions above. They are a summary of teaching experiences extending over more than thirty-five years, and covering the cases of individuals who before leaving study had reached a point where at the moment or after a very slight effort at recalling them, they could play some scores of the best illustrations of the pianoforte written of all the leading composers. In one case the total of pieces in the repertory reached above two hundred, including five or six concertos, a dozen of the best sonatas of Beethoven, large excerpts from Schumann and Chopin, and at least a dozen concert pieces of Liszt.

The difficulty is not that time is taken for memorizing which could be more profitably bestowed, but that the memorizing itself is not done economically. The time to memorize a piece is at the first study. Then the attention is fresh and the piece new; a small effort will put it in the memory before the fingers have learned their part. But if the memorizing be left until the piece has been thoroughly practiced the attention flags, and the playing already becomes half automatic, and it will require a much greater exertion to thoroughly possess the subject matter of the discourse. This is true in all grades—from the beginning to the ending. The only objection is that advanced pupils sometimes memorize wrong impressions of important concert pieces, which it will take them a very great trouble to set right again. This is obviated by educating a quality of study which does not take in falsities. In the case of pupils brought up from lower grades the good teacher has no difficulty; they master this point themselves and out of motives of economy. Those who come under good instruction at a point later, where they have great "execution" (it is a blessed word!) and poor attention, will have to learn in that school which is so expensive but so thorough and inexorable,—"experience." There is no royal road.

With Mr. Regal's proposed exercises for enlarging the student's half knowledge of musical literature; I am in hearty sympathy. I have myself long desired to find an opportunity where I could give a course of lectures, for instance, upon the Beethoven sonatas as a whole, the Schumann and Chopin works, etc., but there does not seem to be any satisfactory place where a class of students can be brought together for this kind of study.

W. S. B. M.

PIANO TOUCH, AGAIN.

Every subject proposed for scientific discussion may be approached from so many points, and treated in so many ways, that some limitation of the treatment and some definition of the point of approach is vital to effective discussion and productive deduction.

That limitation to the form of the discussion of piano touch in MUSIC was supplied by the original letter of its editor to the Symposium of writers who contributed thereto. My own contribution to the July number did not present the subject as I might have preferred to do it, but carefully confined its arguments to the particular phase of the subject proposed by MUSIC, which was suggested by a lecture by Mr. B. J. Lang. That phase is defined in this sentence from the letter from MUSIC: "Mr. Lang took the ground that the player has no control over the hammers other than to give them a greater or less degree of force, and that all so-called tone shading by means of touch is illusory." This was the question and this only. So rigidly did I confine myself to just this phase of the question that I entered a slight protest against Mr. Foote's introduction of the pedal element, although accepting his view.

Upon the same ground I must enter a most decided protest against Mr. W. F. Apthorp's reference, in the November MUSIC, to my article. Mr. Apthorp there undertakes not only to introduce a variation of the original question but asserts that "no one" ever made the statement quoted in MUSIC from Mr. Lang and refuted in my article!

Is it at all possible that Mr. Apthorp has not *read* the original proposition of the subject in the May MUSIC?

Mr. Apthorp seems to have always accepted his own statement of the question as the one under discussion, for he makes a similar statement of it in the *Musical Courier* of August 1, in a "Query to Mr. Lang" although in the same communication he quotes Mr. Lang, and himself italicises the words as follows: "*By pressing an individual key one can get only variety in quantity of tone, but never variety in quality.*"

Will Mr. Apthorp show that I did not treat that proposition or will he still prefer to maintain that "no one" ever made it?

The variation of the question which is introduced by Mr. Apthorp is, as I should prefer to state it, that a piano tone cannot be successively produced by finger contact alone so as to alter the quality without altering the quantity of that tone.

If Mr. Apthorp will father such a statement as that which is the one implied in his last article, it will give me great pleasure to show him how erroneous and unscientific it is "by the aid of Dr. Helmholtz" and of other accepted authorities for my acoustics, of the unabridged Webster for my vocabulary, of the rhetoric for my style, the grammar for my form and the Complete Letter Writer for my manners

HEZEKIAH WEBSTER.

PIANO TOUCH AND MUSICAL FEELING.

I have read with a great deal of interest the discussions of piano touch which different writers have contributed to these columns, but I am free to say at the end of it that I am not sure whether all or any of them understand exactly wherein the manner of attacking the keys has to be modified in order to color a tone so and so. All that I am sure of is this, namely which I commend to the attention of the reader, especially those who have the good luck to possess responsive instruments of fine tone. In so far as regards the manner of attacking the keys, I doubt whether anything is really to be added to the directions which are to be found in the first volume of Mason's "Touch and Technic," if one attends carefully to them. The working diagrams are not in all respects quite what I could desire. The first diagram, for instance, representing the positions at beginning and at ending the "down arm" touch fail at two places:—the hand in the first is not perfectly limp at the wrist, if it were it would depend a little more and not stand out quite so nearly in a line with the arm. Then, in the second position, the fingers are none of them upon the keys except the one which has played. In actual practice, where this touch is to be followed by the up touch, the finger designing to play that would also be upon the keys. Hence the proper position for ending the down touch, when it has to be followed by the up touch, is that of the lower position in the second figure. The figure of the second diagram is pretty satisfactory, and if the first position be taken a little higher, so that the point of the finger is about an inch above the keys, this diagram will afford a good working figure for beginning the down touch.

Another point where I think the directions of the book might be supplemented to advantage, is in regard to the fast forms of the two-finger exercises. I believe that in all the early practice, and most likely in nearly all, the forms which go fast are played with an exceedingly light and limp condition of wrist, approaching the devitalized as nearly as consistent with obtaining tone. Speed and limpness are the qualities first to be sought, and tone only in a very secondary degree. The whole force of this exercise is to contradict the over-vitalized condition of the playing apparatus which the severe forms engender, and which are the necessary concomitants of their effectiveness in developing finger power and command of tone. The heavy arm touches, both down and up-arm, are useful in two entirely different ways; first, for the sake of the broad tone which they give, and second for the sake of the control of wrist condition afforded by the loose condition at beginning and ending, and the extreme movement of wrist by which the playing is done. Even if these forms were not of any use in affording the player command of tone, they would be very valuable for wrist control, to such a degree that they form one of the best possible introductions to the octave school, in the fourth volume.

These directions and forms of exercise, however are the radical and typical forms only, and are here introduced mainly from a muscular standpoint; but they must be supplemented by other forms of practice in which tone quality as such is the main question. Mind, I do not mean to say that I do not have tone quality in direct observation while practicing these forms. I do. In the slow form a broad, deep and full tone is demanded, and forms the guide to the success of the exercise. But the finer modifications of tone are effected not by these simple touches but by combinations, in which finger, hand and arm all enter in different degrees. Hence when the student has learned to perform these exercises properly, and makes them a part of his daily practice, (there are no others which are so indispensable), he is still just at the beginning. His further progress will depend upon his studying tone in every piece that he plays. That is to say, there is always a certain quality, it may be appealing, it may be commanding, singing, sharply broken off and playful, or what not; but in every piece a kind of tone which is best for the melody of that piece, or for that part of a piece. Having formed an ideal of such a tone, it is entirely with the pupil whether he gets it. It is merely a matter of wanting it badly enough. When one desires a certain tone quality, it is a question of asking the piano for it, and of continuing to ask in a variety of ways until at last one gets it.

Nor is this a mere blind search. When one plays the exercises upon a really responsive instrument he will soon observe that each type of touch tends toward a particular kind of effect. Then when one wants an effect it is a question of the type of effect it radically belongs to, and of the modification to be made by combining some other touch with it.

Much of the earlier part of this work needs to be done intelligently; but there comes a time later when intelligence cuts no figure as such, but the modifications desired will come more easily and more certainly, as well as more delicately through the unconscious modification of muscular conditions by the musical sense. I mean that when the player is fully possessed by a musical ideal, his fingers will obtain results from the piano which many times he cannot duplicate even by concentrating all his attention. It is a question of desiring, of trying, and of listening. It is a question of being full of musical matter, and of earnestly seeking to express it fully. Under this need tonal results will always follow. But not when the general touch rests upon the misapprehension that the piano is mostly played with a stationary hand and moving fingers which are merely hammers. Whenever you feel in playing that you are really *singing* through your fingers, the kingdom of music begins to come within you. This is the whole story, and to a great extent it is open to a student living remote in the country and working by his own unaided exertions as it is to the student taking lessons of some celebrated city teacher at a fabulous number of dollars per hour. In a majority of cases these finer modifications of touch are ignored, by the city teacher, or if not ignored, worked with the most advanced pupils only.

And frankly I confess that I do not know which one of my contributors is right; Prof. Fillmore, Mr Webster, or any of the others. All that I do know is that direct intellectual effort will go only a very little way in this direction, but musical feeling will go a long ways, when once the elementary typical forms of touching the keys have been mastered. Without this preparatory practice of Mason the musical modification will not be so easily effected, though musical feeling has a genuine Christian science power over the technic. This I am sure of.

W. S. B. M.

The conservatories do not have altogether so easy a task in bringing their pupils to the study of musical literature, or rather to the study of music as a literature, no matter how sincere nor how well prepared they may be to confer such instruction. The practical difficulty is that some of the pupils live out of town, and it is not convenient for them to make an extra visit to the school. The same holds with a large part of the students living in the city itself. Many of them reside at a distance of half an hour to an hour from the school. This makes a trip there and back consume at least a full half day, and occasionally more. When they have come twice a week for lessons they generally feel that they have done all that they can afford. The situation is different with students in European conservatories, though the instruction there also generally restricts itself to theory and practice, and perhaps in no European conservatory is there a class where they study the works of Beethoven, Schumann and other masters in the same spirit as that in which the poetry of Browning, the plays of Shakespeare, and fiction and essays of the best prose writers are studied in the literature classes of good schools. Music is a very personal matter, and what the students really desire is first of all to learn to play, and second to learn to enjoy their own playing. But culture, as such, is not upon the bills, as they understand it.

REVIEWS AND NOTICES.

The Two and Three Part Inventions of Bach, Edited, Revised and Fingered by Dr. William Mason. New York. G. Schirmer, 60 cts. Pp 63.

Bach Two-Part Inventions for Pianoforte. Edited by F. B. Busoni, Leipzig, Breitkopf and Haertel, 31 Pp. $1.50.

The two titles above given are those of two of the most prominent editions of the Inventions of Bach, and the prices attached fairly indicate the public value of Mr. Schirmer's work in offering American students authoritative editions at a minimum price. It is not likely that the careful student will ever encounter an edition of his favorite works of Bach which will fully satisfy him. One will be strong in one direction, and another in some other. This one of Dr. Mason has the merit of careful fingering, complete writing out of the embellishments, and generally judicious phrasing, which however, is not always consistent with itself. Take for instance the first of the two part inventions. The first question which a student encounters is the extent of the opening phrase. This, Dr. Mason, Busoni, and Riemann make eight notes, the last G, being played with the fifth finger, requiring the hand to be moved before going on with the next four notes. The Peters edition, on the contrary, carries the first phrase without break up to and including the first tone in the second measure. Bach marked no phrasing, and the question is therefore, which author is right? Upon this point something can be said on both sides. The present writer prefers the Peters version, because while the first twelve notes of the invention are legitimately devisable into two phrases, they are also legitimately capable of being understood as making one single phrase, and the latter view of it seems to be preferable. That Bach often uses these two phraselets apart does not prove that he wished them to be made two in this instance and in the others following where the real first subject of the invention is used in its entirety. This is one of the points. Now for another. At the beginning of the second note of the third measure a figure in sixteenth notes begins and extends thirty-two notes. It consists of a sequence of eight notes, repeated four times upon successive degrees descending. Now Dr. Mason does neither one thing nor another in marking this passage. It can be understood and phrased in its grouping of eight notes at each repetition, the phrase closing in each instance with an accent. Busoni has so marked it, but has also drawn a larger slur over the whole, indicating that in his opinion while the player ought to be conscious of the construction of the passage and deliver it according to its meaning, he ought not nevertheless to divide it into its separate groups. Dr. Mason, however, begins his first slur with the first note of the passage, but it ends not on the close of the figure, nor yet upon the close of the second figure, or step in the sequence, but upon the last note of the measure, exactly one note out of the way of any possible construction to be put upon the proper delivery of the passage in question. The second slur begins with the first note of the fourth measure (which properly concludes the second step in the sequence) and ends with the measure, just one note before the close of the sequence. The probability is that this marking was done under the general conception that the legato mark indicates simply that the notes under it are to be played legato, but without implication of separating from that which follows or precedes. This principle, which undoubtedly underlies much of the marking found in music, is not entirely sound, and if carried out would render all attempts to indicate the proper delivery of a passage nugatory and contradictory. Busoni's marking is much safer for the student, at this point.

The Busoni editing is queer at another point, namely, the introduction of double bars at impossible points. The double bar if applicable at all in piano music, belongs at the close of parts, only, or at the limit of a repeated part. Busoni however, in the charming 8th Invention, puts a double bar at the end of the 11th measure, and another at the end of the 25th—in both cases one note before the end of the idea. If there is any reasonable justification, or any good end to be subserved by this placing, the present writer would be glad to be duly informed of it. It appears to him simply impertinent and misleading. The same thing occurs in several other places.

To return to Dr. Mason's application of the legato mark, it is likely that he did not take into account the reverence which thousands of sincere students in all parts of the country are disposed to render to any appearance of intelligence in an edition. They know nothing of the music but have procured these copies in order that they may be able to understand it for themselves. In many cases, it is agreeable to note, the legato marking is done very neatly by Dr. Mason. And in general the Mason edition may be accepted as the result of careful and painstaking work by the best authority we have in this country, and as good as we have anywhere. The print and style are excellent.

AESTHETICAL EDUCATION. The End to be Attained, and a Method of Accomplishing It. By Wilber M. Derthick. Chicago, 1891. 32 mo, Pp. [illegible]. Advance sheets.

Advance sheets of an ambitious essay by Mr. Wilber M. Derthick have been laid upon the table of MUSIC, and have been read with the care which the subject and its treatment deserve. The portion here exhibited gives the grounds of the argument, but does not reach the conclusion. We are promised articles upon several of the subordinate topics for these columns, in successive numbers of MUSIC, wherefore no attempt will be made to summarize the argument at this time. The literary handling is admirable, and the argument takes a wide range supporting itself by authorities and by much original work. It is sure to reach a wide acceptance with the literary-musical public (not so large a quantity as it ought to be) and cannot but add very much to the literary reputation of the talented and earnest author.

STANDARD GRADED COURSE OF STUDIES FOR THE PIANOFORTE. In Ten Grades. By W. S. B. Mathews. Ninth Grade. Large sheet music size, 23 pages. 1898. Theodore Presser. $1.00.

This series of graded studies, begun in 1891 has now reached the 9th grade, and the 10th is in press. In general this selection follows the lines generally observed by editors, but it works under the disadvantage of too limited space, when the studies required for the grade are so long individually as most studies of this difficulty are, and have to be. The scope of the present volume will be seen from the contents. Bravoura study, (thirds) Isadore Seiss. Henselt's "Ave Maria." "Romance and Choral refrain," and "Orage;" Hans Seeling, Study in Extended chords. Bach Fugue in C minor, from Clavier; Liszt "The Nightingale," and the Clementi study in triplets, in B major. Now while this is an exceedingly valuable lot of material, and furnished in this form at a price much lower than the usual cost to students, it cannot by any possibility be regarded as sufficient for the required work of the ninth grade. It would need several other studies of Clementi, and perhaps a few by other authors, making a whole about twice as large as this number. In other respects the different styles will be found balanced against each other in a manner fairly satisfactory.

(O. Ditson Company.)

Second grade. Instrumental. Pianoforte.

Fairies Mayday Parade. March, Harold Leston.

Fairies Flirtation. Scherzo.

Fairies Midnight Revel. Quickstep movement.

Fairies Swing Song.

All pleasingly written and available.

Four little Pieces by Anton Strelezki.

Rondino. A minor.

Paquita. Spanish waltz.

A La Polka.

Very simple teaching pieces. First part of second grade;

Dance Elegante. By John T. Clark.

Latter part of second grade or first of third.

Third Grade.

Le Sauteur. Intermezzo. John T. Clark. Study in staccato and light phrasing.

Bells at Eventide. Harold Leston.

A Mazurka in the style of Leybach, purely diatonic. Pleasing;

Petite Mazurka. W. Sapellnikoff. Op. 2.

Bells at Daybreak. François Behr.

Album Leaf. Heinrich Stiehl.

All rather commonplace compositions, but intended to appeal to average tastes. From this standpoint not badly done. All printed with a minimum of phrase marks, and with no finger marks at all, in order to so avoid offending the still remaining residuum of teachers using the so-called American fingering.

Fourth Grade, also rather common.

Loritta Waltz. Eduard Holst.

Song of the Night-Winds. Leybach.

Valse in D flat. C. Palumbo. (Slightly more modern than the preceding.)

La Lisonjera. Chaminade. More pretentious.

Church.

Trois Mazurkas, pour Piano, par Allessandro Longo.

1. B flat.
2. C minor.
3. E flat. 75 cts each.

These handsomely printed productions belong to about the fourth or fifth grade of difficulty, and are of the modern style of salon music. They are musicianly, and modern without being labored or displeasing. Those who are especially fond of good straight melody, of the olden folks song type, or even of such melodies and tonalities as one finds in the mazurkas of Chopin, will not be altogether satisfied with these. They are more modern, but by no means beyond the pale of amateur enjoyment. In fact they belong to the better class of new music for amateurs.

Mi Vida. (My Sweetheart.) Ball room scene. August Wm. Hoffmann. Key of F. 4th grade.

A pleasing motion, somewhat resembling the gavotte, popular style with a little something better in it. Pleasing.

Spanish Serenade. (Spanisches Ständchen. By Xaver Scharwenka. Opus 63, No. 1.

Key of A minor. An excellent study in staccato passages, played by the two hands interlocking. There is also a pleasing melody part of the time. Effective teaching piece, advanced fourth grade.

(Church.)

"A Song of Love."

"The Spectre of a Rose." Frank E. Sawyer.

Nothing gives more promise for the future of music in America than the progress we are making in songs. Our publishers are bringing out continually novelties in this department, upon good lyrical texts, treated in a manner at once rational, musical and impassioned. These two songs by Mr. Sawyer belong to the best category. They are thoroughly modern in musical handling, showing more than a trace of French training, but the final result is heartfelt and satisfactory to a degree. The text of the last is from Gautier.

ANTOINE RUBINSTEIN

MUSIC.

FEBRUARY, 1895.

MUSIC IN COURT.

I HAVE before me thirty odd cases decided by the several upper courts of Great Britain and our own federal courts, in all of which musical compositions were involved in some way or other. In the old world the musicians have long enjoyed the unenviable reputation of a "quarrelsome race," yet they have seldom appeared in court. It is the same in England and America. Music is not brought into court by the composer himself, but by the publisher—not the legitimate publisher, but by the pirate. A greater portion of this litigation is due to the uncertainty of the law and might have been easily prevented by the legislators.

In England the first act of parliament, defining and protecting literary rights, was passed in the eighth year of Queen Anne's reign (1709)—nearly two hundred years ago. It protected "books" but made no mention of musical compositions, either because there was little art in English music at that day, or (what is more probable) because no man with a sense for music had been elected to parliament. But the judges (notably Lords Mansfield and Ellenborough) had a keener sense of justice than the law-givers themselves, and by a somewhat strained process of reasoning arrived at the conclusion that the "book," originally meaning, in old Saxon, a sheet of bark employed as writing material, was to be construed as meaning any literary production, whether on a single sheet of paper or bound in a volume; and thus they succeeded in protecting sheet music under the broad construction of the statutory term "book," although music had not been specifically mentioned. Since 8 Anne down to 5 and 6 Victoria the English statutes had gone through a regular process of evolution, and in the course of time, musical compositions came to be expressly included among the subjects of copyright. The same process has been repeated in our country; it was not until 1831 that our national lawmakers deemed it proper to extend the temporary protection of the copyright law to musical compositions, granting to the composer the exclusive privilege of printing and selling his works for twenty-eight years (in case of a renewal, forty-two years) after publication.

The cases in which the right to print musical compositions has been called in question, may be divided into two classes: first, where the infringing work seemed to be an imitation of an older one, and second, cases of evident piracy where the pirate tried to defeat his opponent's rights through technical defects. In regard to the first class of cases I must say that, in the court-room the adjective "original" has always borne a meaning wholly different from what it has in the standard dictionaries. In *Reed vs. Carusi* (1845) the question of originality and authorship was left to the jury to be determined upon all the evidence. "If the composition be borrowed entirely from a former one," says the court, "or composed of different parts copied from older musical composition without any material alteration, and put together into one tune, only with slight changes and additions, then the composer is not an author within the meaning of the act of Congress. But the fact that the composition corresponds with old compositions does not prove piracy when the air in question is, in the main design and its material and important parts, an effort of the composer's own mind." Similarly in *Leader vs. Purday* it was held that an old air for which a new song and accompaniment had been composed, could be copyrighted as a new work. The same principle has been upheld in *Schuberth vs. Shaw* where a new and substantial adaptation of an old piece of music was held to be a valid subject of copyright.

Balfe's "Bohemian Girl" figured in the case of *Atwill*

vs. Ferret, 2 Blatchford 39 (1848.) The case shows one way to evade a law honestly. Music for this opera had been composed as the court says, "by one Balfe, in Europe." Being a foreigner, Balfe could not, under our laws, obtain copyright in the United States, but the prudent Mr. Atwill found a way out of the difficulty. In his own words, he made "many alterations of and additions to the said music, added new matter of his own not in the original opera and arranged and adapted the several pieces for publication." In the opinion of the court, this was sufficient proof that Mr. Atwill was the true author of Balfe's opera! The court looked upon Balfe as an employe furnishing materials to his employer Atwill who by the application of his skill created a new work. In respect to like cases of employment the court says: "to constitute one an author, he must, by his own intellectual labor applied to the materials of his composition, produce an arrangement or compilation new in itself." This is a definition which, it is admitted, would not do in a book on aesthetics, but which has been recognized by the courts. *D'Almaine vs. Boosey*, 1 Younge and Collyer, 288, proposes to test such adaptions by the ear. If the ear recognizes the original air, it is a case of piracy although it may have been arranged for a different instrument or as dance music. The fact that the air is somewhat changed is immaterial, if the change require little or no skill.

A similar point was raised in *Jollie vs. Jacques*, 1 Blatchford, 618, Oct. 1850. "The Serious Family Polka" had been copyrighted and copied, and a bill filed to prevent the infringement. The court, however, declined to protect a composition which, in fact, was neither new nor original, but a mere copy of another work already produced, with some additions and variations, it is true, but the changes being merely such as any musical writer of ordinary skill and experience might readily make. The court intimates that each particular case ought to be decided by experts, and if they should detect the old air, the composition should be declared to be an imitation. However, if I compose an original work and some one steals that which is its very essence and by skillful manipulation produces a new piece, I am entitled to the protection of the law, no matter how small the extent of the direct imitation may be. The question of piracy does not depend upon quantity—is the decision in *Bramwell vs. Halcomb*, 3 Mylne & Craig 737. The question of similarity is oftentimes quite difficult to decide, as it was in the case of *Blume vs. Spear*.

Miss Fannie Beane (afterwards Mrs. F. B. Gilday) was a youthful maiden when the music of a song which she christened "My Own Sweet Darling, Colleen Dhas Machree," was formed in her mind. When she was old enough, she had the song written out and sold the copyright to Mr. Frederic Blume, who published it under its mammoth title. The song achieved some popularity. Shortly after a certain Mr. Spear brought forth another song, entitled "Call me back again" which, as Mr. Blume claimed, was merely a colorable imitation of his own song. The court sustained his claim. It seems that the judge was a musician (our judges are supposed to understand everything, from the primitive miracles of the bible up to the most sublime mysteries of nature) for he gives musical reasons for his decision. "The melody is substantially the same," he says, "the measure is the same.... When played by a competent musician, they (the two pieces) appear to be really the same. There are variations, but they are so placed as to indicate that the copyrighted piece was taken deliberately rather than that the infringing one was a new piece." Mr. Spear tried to defeat Mr. Blume by showing that Miss Beane really was not the author of the song in question, but had borrowed its music from a prior composition. He produced a song entitled "Sweet Spirit, Hear My Prayer" as the alleged source of Miss Beane's inspiration, but the court did not find sufficient similarity between the two to declare that Miss Beane's composition was not original. "There are some short parts of them which appear to be alike," says the court, "but these parts are not continuous enough, nor sufficiently extended, to indicate with any degree of certainty that the author of the latter (Miss Beane) was guided or aided by the former." That is a sound ruling. Though the realms of music be boundless, yet it happens now and then that two composers strike the same or a similar tune without knowing of each other. It was only just that the case of *Blume vs. Spear*, 30 Federal Reporter, 629, A. D. 1887, should have ended with a victory of the complainant.

If only a part of a copyright work be pirated the rest being original, the court will enjoin only the infringing parts; in *Goldmark vs Kreling*, 35 Federal Rep., 629 (1887) the plaintiffs were exclusive owners of a MS. operetta "Nanon." The defendants were producing a play entitled "Genee's Nanon, the reigning Oriental and European sensation" which they claimed had been translated and adapted from an old French story, Nanon. The plays had many characters in common, not found in the French story, the scenes and situations in each were alike, etc. The court held that the infringing work was substantially the same with colorable changes only, and accordingly enjoined its performance with the exception of the orchestration which was Kreling's own.

In *Lover vs. Davidson* (1856) the plaintif had merely taken the air of an old song named "The Jolly Plowboy," added a prelude, words and accompaniment, and copyrighted it as "The Low Back'd Car." The court sustained his claim as "proprietor" of the new composition.

By the statute of Anne the author of a dramatic piece or musical composition was merely enabled to prevent any other persons from reprinting and selling copies of his production; but still everybody was at liberty to perform the play in public. This was remedied by Sir Bulwer Lytton's Act, 3 and 4 William IV. chapter 15, which gave a dramatic writer the exclusive privilege of both printing and performance, and Talfourd's Act, 5 and 6 Victoria, extended the privilege to musical compositions which, if copyrighted, may not be printed or performed without the owner's consent. Such is the law both in England and the United States. It was upheld in *Chappell vs Boosey*, Law Rep. 21 Chy D. 232, 1882, where an unauthorized representation of "The Bellringer" at a concert was enjoined although the song had been already printed.

However the author or composer who seeks the assistance

of the law, must comply with its requirements and provisions, and secure a copyright in the usual way. If he publishes his work without copyrighting the same, he is supposed to dedicate it to the public, and any one may reprint or perform it. Such a dedication does not, however, dedicate what it does not contain, and if I publish an uncopyrighted composition for pianoforte but keep the same as set for orchestra in manuscript, no one may make use of my orchestration. Such is the law of *Thomas vs Lennon*, 14 Fed. Rep. 849, 1883.

Our lawgivers have not been very generous toward our own composers, and they have been much less so toward foreigners. Indeed, until 1891 a foreign author or composer could not secure any rights in this country unless he were a *bona fide* resident or sold the MS. of his work to an American citizen.

The opera of "Iolanthe" was before the court in *Carte vs. Ford*, 15 Fed. Rep. 439, 1883. The authors were non-resident aliens. They sanctioned publication in the United States of the libretto and vocal score with piano accompaniment but retained the orchestration in manuscript. The defendant arranged a new orchestration but used the authors' libretto, vocal scores etc., and the court decided he was at liberty to do so. Similarly it was held (*Carte vs. Duff*, 25 Fed. Rep. 183, 1885) the publication of the libretto and vocal score of "The Mikado" was a dedication of the work to the public, and any one in America might reproduce the same. Again, in 1886, that self-same Mr. Carte was to learn, in *Carte vs. Evans*, 27 Fed. Rep. 867, that a non resident foreigner was not within the copyright law of our country. A like view prevailed in old England. Even there the foreigner was very little respected, though, in some curious cases, he occasionally managed to outwit the law. Thus a Bohemian composer's work was involved in a curious case, the case of *Cocks vs. Purday*, (1846-1848). The composition in question was a waltz entitled "Die Elfen" (The Fairies). The author, Mr. Joseph Labitzky, a citizen of Prague, sold his work to Mr. Cocks, who had it registered on the first day of September, 1842, the day of its publication in England. There was, however, a contemporaneous publication of the work at Prague, the capital of Bohemia. Mr. Purday issued a pirated edition and Mr. Cocks sued for damages. The main question before the court was whether a foreigner resident abroad could acquire any copyright in England — inasmuch as the English kept all "rights" for themselves and treated foreign authors and composers with very little generosity. The English statute required the first publication in England; accordingly the court left the decision to the jurors: if they believed the publication in both countries (Bohemia and England) to have been simultaneous, then Cocks should have judgement. The jury, it seems, had more sense for justice than the law itself, they found the publication in the two countries to have been simultaneous (which, in the natural course of things, is absolutely impossible) and awarded the plaintiff forty shillings damages.

Taking our own and the foreign laws of copyright into consideration, I may say that the foreigners are much more liberal than ourselves. We even hesitate to admit a foreign orchestra if its members may, under the law, be classed as "contract laborers."

J. J. Kral.

WOMAN BEFORE THE MUSICAL TRIBUNAL.

ONCE more woman is arraigned, not as on previous occasions for the entire absence of creative faculty, but for deficiencies in the higher fields of music and in the emotional force requisite for production, also for her incapacity to soar into the abstract, and her infirm hold upon the ideal.

At the outset it must be conceded that so far as music is concerned woman is a failure. That she should have given so little evidence of creative power in this, the newest of the arts, is incomprehensible. To whatever cause the lack of success may be due, in default of a final explanation, we may believe that in a general way the same conditions of life which have prevented the intellectual development of women in other directions have operated here.

Leaving out of consideration the special questions of music there are some reflections which naturally arise in connection with the kindred subjects of the imaginative or creative faculty. If, as we are told ("Is the Musical Idea Masculine," *Atlantic Monthly*, March 1894) the want of success on the part of women, even in the more practical things of life, is due to the lack of imagination, we can only say that like every other human impulse this requires encouragement; that it is apt to be exercised in proportion to the ability to realize its promptings. It is especially stimulated by confidence in one's power to surmount obstacles and dominate people and things. In other words one must carry victory in the heart. There can be no doubt that opportunity furnishes a tremendous whip to the imagination. This was never better illustrated, so far as business is concerned, than by the speculative spirit which showed itself in Germany after the Franco German war. The poverty of the people and their limited opportunities for acquiring wealth had previously held in check the exercise of the imagination in that particular direction, but so soon as the war indemnity was paid and new possibilities had revealed themselves, the German people, in their greed for gain, invented manifold schemes for securing it, and quite rivaled the American in his dreams of wealth during the days when the gold fever mounted to his brain.

Now with women, suppression and poverty of opportunity, as we shall show, have hitherto been the rule of life, and it is easy to conceive that the kind of imagination which has proven unproductive would naturally die of inanition. Although the imagination with them has found scant nourishment in certain directions, it has been stimulated at least so far as the ideals of love are concerned, and many of the great masters, Shakespeare among others, ascribe to women not only great emotional energy but the added disinterestedness of the highest forms of affection; and as for the expression of erotic emotion surely Miss Brower will admit that Sappho was not deficient in fervor. It is nevertheless true that civilization and especially the teachings of the Church have tended to foster modesty on the part of women and suppress the expression of passion.

It is admitted in the article to which we have referred that a maiden has her ideal as well as a youth; but it is also affirmed that she does not hold to it so tenaciously. Now, on the other hand if men were largely dominated by the ideal, since they have the privilege of chosing, they would scarcely make the marriages they do. In the selection of his wife, a man under the influence of exalted ideals would not be willing, as is too often the case, to content himself with the commonplace when he might have the uncommon, with the homely woman when he might possess himself of the beautiful, nor is there any reason for supposing that his imagination necessarily endows the one who is chosen with all the attributes of the Graces.

So far as marriage is concerned a woman does not choose in the largest sense of the word. She accepts for her husband the one who suits her best from among the men who show a preference for her, and for this reason, though she may sometimes attain to her heart's desire, she is often compelled to reconcile her ideal with the actual, but this does not necessarily prove that she is unhaunted by the idea of perfection. Indeed the one hopeful sign in the terrible frequency of divorce is the unwillingness on the part of women to put up with the conditions which fall so far short of the ideal. There was a time when men only, in the marriage relations, could be sinned against; but, with the fuller recognition of her spiritual claims, woman now seeks relief from wrongs which under the old system had no legal redress, and were therefore endured.

In answer to the various criticisms that have been made with reference to her imaginative and emotional qualities—both of which are so largely involved in the creative power—it may be conceded without fear of contradiction that women have not hitherto been the source of illumination in the intellectual world; but when it is asserted, as is sometimes the case, that genius, or in other words the creative faculty, has been denied the feminine sex, we cannot help thinking that injustice has been done its past history, and that so sweeping a denial transcends the power of prophecy in the implied limitation. Indeed a question such as the one under discussion cannot be fairly dealt with without taking into consideration the social conditions which hitherto have served to foster or retard intellectual advancement of women.

Daily experience should warn the most facile generalizer of the danger of pronouncing final judgement even in the case of a single individual; for unsuspected capabilities often lie dormant, awaiting the magic wand of opportunity or necessity to stimulate them into activity.

If it is difficult to predict the future possibilities of any one man, how much more so in the case of an entire sex or nation. There has been even less in the past history of the isolated Russian people than in the history of women to foreshadow the literary ability with which we have become acquainted in the intellectual outburst that of late has astonished the world and shown that power, with them, was only latent and not non existent.

The creative power has been conceded somewhat grudgingly to a few women at different periods of the world's history. Among these Sappho, Jane Austin and George Eliot have, perhaps, been most freely commended, but even these have their detractors among the critics. Under the circumstances, however, we are disposed to claim all that we can and even admitting that the women to whom the meed of praise has been most generously given are not to be placed among the immortals of the first magnitude, it cannot be denied that they at least have had intimations of immortality; and this is sufficient for our present purposes, for we would feign construe this intimation into a kind of promise and guarantee of the future full blown genius of the feminine sex.

The question has more than once been asked, "If men and women were created equal, when did the differentiation take place." When such differences exist the question of equality is relative and cannot be properly dealt with at all. Had Wagner and Leonardo de Vinci been contemporaneous, one might as well ask if the musician and painter were created equal, when did they begin to differentiate; or if Wilberforce and Catherine of Russia originally possessed equal powers, when did they take on their respective characteristics.

When we come to historic man, the ascendency of brute force is apparent all through the different stages of his progress. It can scarcely be said that the intellectual, pure and simple, originally had any value at all. It was only as it served to guide advantageously the savage instincts in maintaining ascendency by means of physical force, that the mind gained an indirect and almost unconscious recognition. In the exigencies of civilization, which from its very dawn has in the main been dominated by brute force, women necessarily have been pushed to the wall, and the estimate of her mental powers measured by the standards of war has sunk in proportion to her unfitness for that field of activity. Furthermore, in the division of labor which accompanies all social progress, the duties which fell to her share, not being of the militant kind, were naturally despised. Despised though they have been, "the deeds which unheeded die" were necessary and absorbing in their nature; they consumed both mental and physical force, and the mind was neither stimulated nor solaced by the reflection that such undertakings were noble or of any particular worth.

The diversity of occupation and interest led to still further separation in the mental habits of men and women. The exaltation of the one side of life and the depression of the other precipitated the differentiation of the sexes, which although one of the attendants of advance has been pushed to an extreme and injurious limit. The various theories as to what was feminine, and what was not, together with an enervating mode of life, have had the effect of rendering women physically and mentally weaker than we have any reason to suppose was their original birthright. Sexual selection has also played its part in developing certain qualities at the expense of others. Modifications of this nature are frequently to be found among domesticated animals.

The arrest of the development of women has very naturally awakened contempt for the weak body and the unused mind. In other words owing to the docility of their nature and the high estimate which has been placed upon military services and upon intellectual capacity of a certain order, women were readily enslaved and accepted the opinion which from their point of view men, in a measure, were forced to entertain of their abilities.

Nothing is easier than by denunciation and denial of excellence to lower the self respect and confidence either of a class or of an individual. If Shakespeare himself had happened to have lived among the ancient schoolmen, he might have lacked the sympathetic encouragement necessary for the development of his genius. It is not likely that Duns Scotus or Albertus Magnus, with their hundred arguments for or against a given hypothesis, would have found his highest strains of poetry at all comparable to a well framed syllogism. It is therefore conceivable that even this giant in an atmosphere of dry as dust contention would have felt himself dwarfed in his own estimate and paralyzed in the free exercise of his powers. Indeed, such is the influence of environment, it has been asserted that had the bard of Avon lived fifty years later than he did, like Milton he would have been obliged, according to the custom of the times, "to water his poetic wine with doctrinal eloquence."

The very fact of abating expectations in any form of

human excellence is in a certain degree to forbid its attainment. Women have accepted with slight protest the uncomplimentary estimate of their mental powers, and in consequence have sunk into a state of intellectual apathy; since nothing was expected of them in this one direction, it was but natural that they should become mentally lazy and unexacting of themselves. This all along has been the worst evil of the belief in the fatalistic limitations of nature, and it will take a great while even with the present stimulus to exertion to overcome the cumulative effect of long indulged intellectual indolence.

It may be said that the passive acceptance of prescribed limitations is in itself an evidence of inherent weakness, but such acceptance has not been confined to women alone. So great a people as the Italians, to say nothing of other instances, at one time completely succumbed to the dictates of the priest and the tyrant; they readily listened to the suggestion that Italian men at large were incapable of thinking for themselves and if they knew what was good for them they would stifle intellectual inquiry, and in all the higher concerns of life be guided by their self constituted leaders. Whole nations have been cowed by standing armies, and even at the present time men of the highest moral and intellectual aims are thwarted by the organized despotism of majorities. We infer from these instances that submission, or rather helpless acquiescence, in the presence of either moral or physical domination, is not peculiar to women alone.

There is another phase of life which has counted immensely against the intellectual advancement of women, and that is the comparative isolation of their lives. Owing to the similarity of their pursuits within circumscribed limits it has been impossible for them to gain much in the way of mental stimulus and refreshment from each others' society, and to a great extent they have been cut off, except through reading, from the larger interests of men. It would be difficult to find a single instance of a genius having lived separated from the various interests of the world, or of one who has not sought the companionship of other intellectual men engaged in similar as well as divergent pursuits.

The stimulating effect of mind acting upon mind cannot be overestimated. A boy destined for an intellectual career from his earliest youth has this sort of contact. Ever since the twelfth century, and even prior to that time, the Universities have been crowded with young men seeking the momentary stimulus of *viva voce* criticism, and gaining in addition to this, what is quite as important, the informing and often unerring judgment of their fellow men as to character and capacity. Think of the possibilities which lay in the assembly of thirty thousand men in the sixteenth century, at the University of Paris, and in our own times of the thousands who annually flock to learned institutions for the deliberate purpose of perfecting their powers, not only by the acquisition of academic lore, but by the enlargement of experience derived from measuring intellectual strength, one with the other, or with the great masters who teach them.

If only at long intervals we hear of a man who is preeminent among the hosts that are striving for distinction in the various fields of intellectual labor, it is scarcely to be expected that women will make any showing at all. To say nothing of remote periods when the number of competitors was too insignificant to be estimated, it may safely be asserted that within the past two hundred years there have been among the candidates for intellectual honors about one woman to every three or four thousand men. That the number of those who succeed is in proportion to those who enter the lists is shown by the fact that in the field of fiction where women have entered most freely, they have won greatest renown.

Notwithstanding the general impression to the contrary, even the success of the genius is not so entirely independent of circumstances as it is sometimes supposed. There is much in the past history of the mind to give one great respect for propitious moments and stimulating environment. It is noteworthy that great literary men generally appear in groups, Chaucer and Dante being the most conspicuous instances among "the fixed stars" in literature, who have come unattended by their satellites. Nearly all of the foremost men, or geniuses, have been scholars who have derived infinite profit from their predecessors; neither Chaucer nor Shakespeare invented anything worth speaking of, and this fact, as Mr. Lowell suggests, diminishes the value of mere invention. Chaucer began his literary career by imitating the works of others, and derived poetical suggestions from diverse sources. It is true he paid that "usurous interest" which genius, as Coleridge says, always pays in borrowing. Emerson has also said "that the greatest genius is the most indebted man." Furthermore, Chaucer had the amplest and most fruitful education, he was a scholar, a courtier, a soldier and an ambassador, therefore his criticism of life was characterized by energy of conviction derived from breadth of observation. Spencer was a scholar who learned much from the Italians, and imparted more to Milton, and something even to Shakespeare, as did the classic authors, whom the latter read in translations. Some of his commentators warmly resent the insinuation that he, who was everything else, was not a deliberate artist, one who familiarized himself with the accepted theories of the poetic art, such as were doubtless daily discussed by the men with whom he associated. Ben Jonson was a scholar, Beaumont and Fletcher university bred, Dryden, Milton and a host of English poets as well as Goethe and Schiller were learned men, all of whom travelled far in the world of letters, and most of them were enabled from personal contact with their compeers "to gather the rich harvest of the ear."

Furthermore these men were possessed by the conquering spirit derived from a wide horizon of possibilities, also by the consciousness of individual power reinforced by the prestige of their sex. It has not been said of men, thus far shalt thou go and no farther, nor have they, like women, been intimidated by traditional prejudice. "He must be well mounted" says Thomas Fuller "who is for leaping the hedges of custom." It is difficult to realize at the present time the load of discouragement under which the feminine intellect has staggered, or how difficult it has been to rise superior to the stigma of belonging to the inferior part of humanity. However much we may differ from the ultimate aims of Mrs. Lucy Stone Blackwell and many of her contemporaries, one has but to read the pathetic accounts of their efforts to secure a liberal education, to realize what a blight and menace to all mental development lay in the foregone conclusion that women were incapable of receiving light from the exercise of the judgement or from any other source than unreasoning intuition.

Now as we have said before, women as a rule have lived in a state of intellectual isolation, no university has set the standard of scholarship for them or provided the means for them or provided the means for attaining that which was considered essential for the training of men. What little learning they have hitherto possessed has been fragmentary and picked up in an unsystematic fashion. No Mermaid Tavern has brought together the bel-esprit and by comparison and good natural criticism, quickened the thought that was in them and rendered the spoken word nimble and "full of subtle flame."

Now George Eliot, the most scholarly woman of modern times, acquired her education alone, and not without the disturbances of household cares. Late in life she not infrequently called attention to the differences in the size of her hands, the right hand having greatly outgrown the other in the labor of making butter. Very few women in the pursuit of letters have been able to show exclusive devotion; the work in this line has been, in the main, a side issue and not the central motive of their lives.

In addition to the disadvantages we have already mentioned in connection with the mental development of women, there have been other obstacles even more powerful: viz., the subordinate and transitory character of all occupations not immediately connected with the rearing of children and the conduct of the home; important as this work may be, in which the chief glory of women will always be found, nevertheless in the routine of the household there is a wearisome repetition of work destined but for the hour and day, which makes of life a thing of shreds and patches. It is necessary to view these multitudinous cares at long range in order to lose their vexatious diminutiveness in the whole scheme of harmonious living. In contact with this side of life it is easy to see that it is one thing to be inspired by your occupation and another thing to be enslaved by it.

The effect of woman's occupation may be compared to that of the common soldier and the tradesman, whose intellectual force is dissipated in a variety of petty cares, which break up the continuity of thought and interrupt that brooding habit which is necessary for the holding of new ideas. No one has ever heard of a tradesman looming forth as a man of genius. The narrowing effect of trade and its apparent incompatibility with the highest flights of the intellect justifies, perhaps, the contempt with which it is sometimes regarded. On the other hand, however, it would be unreasonable to deny the existence of mental power in the case of tradesmen, for they frequently have been the fathers of men whose rare capacity has been recognized in other fields of labor.

So far from men being generally endowed with creative ability, there are whole classes who have never given the slightest evidence of that faculty. Take the common soldier, for instance, "whose duty it is to do and die and not to question why." The daily routine of drilling and the ordinary duties of his calling so completely use up his force that there is no chance for the spontaneous mental activity which is a *sine qua non* with the genius. Absorbed in the exacting details of his life, the soldier's mind does not soar into the abstract, and he is held fast in the bonds of conservative tradition, of submission and regulated activity. Although he must daily feel the need of improvement in many of the conditions of his life, there is no instance of any great revolution in arms or accoutrements due to the invention of the man in the ranks. In spite of the fact that the victory is usually won on the parade ground and in the housekeeping department of the army long before the battle is fought, the world is apt to ascribe the success to the general alone whose brilliant tactics would nevertheless count for little without the aid of his uninventive subordinates.

Women have been criticised for not having contributed to the store of the world's inventions, but if we are not mistaken the inventor of mechanical contrivances is one who has generally passed his life in a work shop; he has lived in the hum of machinery and watched with intense interest the delicate adjustment of a machine whose component parts have been gathered together from many sources. The successful machine is seldom an instantaneous creation, more frequently it is a compilation owing its perfection not to one mind, but to many. A book might be written on the progressive evolution of the telephone. In its rudimentary form it was used in the early temples of India. It was re-invented in modern times and as a toy it amused long before it became the perfected electrical instrument of every day use.

Of all men we should think the inventor was the one most dependent upon his environment. If this be so, it is not surprising that the sewing machine was not the work either of a seamstress or a tailor; their preoccupations preclude the form of mental activity peculiar to the inventor.

It cannot be denied that women have shown capacity for dealing with the abstract by meeting the test of the English mathematical tripos. To pass this examination is a *tour de force* of which very few men are capable, owing to the general inability of the average mortal to take in abstract conceptions. The Senior Wrangler who stands at the head of the first forty men who constitute the honor list is, according to careful computation, about thirty two times superior in the power and control of his mental faculties to the lowest man on that list. For a young woman to grapple successfully with problems which for a long time have taxed the intellect of a picked lot of men drawn from thousands of students, affords encouragement of a kind which hitherto has been sadly needed; success in this direction gives confidence to a large number of women who are now justified in indulging intellectual aspirations which to have entertained a few years ago would have seemed like the height of presumption.

If the success of women students at the higher seats of learning has not as yet produced any creative results, it has at least removed the distrust bred of ages of contemptuous criticism.

So greatly has this mistrust of herself weakened the power of woman for sustained and energetic mental endeavor that her most serious undertakings have generally seemed even to her illusory and fantastic.

There has been nothing more remarkable in this latter half of the nineteenth century than the way in which women have responded to the enlarged opportunities for development which they have slowly won for themselves. It has been asserted by an eminent political economist that the greatest advance which humanity has made within the past twenty-five years has been made on the part of that portion of it which hitherto has been denied capabilities for any other than emotional expansion.

It is a cause for congratulation that so far the generous confidence of the public has not been misplaced, and that there is good basis for the belief "that all its praises are but prophecies." Let us hope that the future call of genius will include in its ranks some woman whose presence will be a gracious justification of the faith of their brothers. Any undue exultation which this thought might induce is, however, apt to be tempered by the well recognized invincible and incorrigible personality of the acknowledged genius, which often renders him anything but a comfortable housemate. The dominating qualities which seem to accompany the cerebral excitation of great wits makes it easy to understand why the Buonarotti family was so much alarmed lest one of its members, Michael Angelo, should develope into a genius.

It scarcely seems worth while, however, at this stage of the world's history when, as has been well said, "the opportunities and privileges of the first comers have so greatly diminished," to quarrel about the distribution of the creative power. In truth it does not seem to matter very much where the power lies, either in music or in the other arts, so long as men and women work together for the harmonious development of both sexes and all classes.

CATHERINE SELDEN.

THE STORY OF A GENIUS.

I.

"MONSIEUR Alphonse de Sterny will come to Brussels in November, in order to direct his oratorio "Satan" in person." This short notice in the "Independent Belgian" created universal remark in Brussels.

The musicians shrugged their shoulders, and made scornful remarks about Alphonse de Sterny's art, and about the traditional injustice of the public toward home talent; the great world of Brussels—between ourselves, the most unmusical "world" in the universe—did what formerly it had never done for an artist, almost forgot its distinguished phlegm, spoke for quite a week—there is little to talk about in autumn—of nothing but "de Sterny" and really very much of his love affairs and very little of his octave technique.

Alphonse de Sterny was not only a great virtuoso of his time, but also had been a lion of society; the most distinguished ladies had sued for his favor, George Sand had written a romance about him—which romance this was, one really did not know—and the beautiful Princess G. had poisoned herself with sulphuric acid on his account.

But five years before he had suddenly withdrawn from the world, and during this time he had given no concerts, no more piano pieces of his, no paraphrases on favorite themes had been published. His name now appeared again for the first time and in connection with an oratorio! De Sterny and an oratorio! The world found that odd; artists found it droll.

II.

It is the fifth of November, the day on which the first rehearsal of "Satan," under the direction of the composer, is to take place. In the Grand Harmony concert hall the performers have already assembled. Although, in honor of the illustrious guests, a half dozen more gas jets are lighted, as is usual at rehearsals, the large hall with its gloomy auditorium, its sparingly lighted stage, makes a desolate, ghostly impression. A smell of gas, dust and damp cloth pervades the atmosphere. A gray mist which soon changes into a wet shine, is on the clothes of the last to enter. One notices, in the hall, how bad the weather must be without. The gay chorus singers with their broad, pear-shaped Flemish faces, their picturesque brownish linen, and their luxuriant growth of hair, beat the mud from their boots, and draw down their rolled up trousers; the women, whose tumbled hair is loosened about their shoulders, complain of indispositions and hand each other their wonder-working pastilles. The members of the orchestra are vexedly working with their instruments. In the midst of the dissonances caused by all the violins screaming at once, is heard the occasional shrill noise of a breaking string.

Two dilletantis have crept in—a young piano teacher of German origin, who is enthusiastic for the music of the future, and an amateur who is known in Brussels society by the nickname of "The friend of Rossini."

The instruments are tuned, here and there a violinist tries a run. The gas jets sing softly, the choristers stamp their feet to warm themselves, and rub the red knuckles of their hands together. De Sterny keeps them waiting.

The "friend of Rossini" has approached the solo singers. "I pity you, Madame," he says to the alto, an old acquaintance whose engagement he has been the means of. "I pity you truly. De Sterny is a representative of the music of the future. His compositions belong to the most unsympathetic tasks which one has ever given to the human throat. One need only sing his arias in order to atone for all past musical enjoyments."

"Your judgement is too hard!" replied the alto, "Really too hard, sir. One should, of course, not find fault with the hatred of a friend of Rossini for the music of the future. Besides, I grant that several numbers of the oratorio are really wearying, but with some others on the contrary you will declare yourself pleased."

"I will never declare myself pleased with the music of

the future," grumbled the fanatical friend of Rossini.

"Well, well, to a certain point I am fully of your opinion," said the alto flatteringly, "but you must admit that Wagner and Berlioz are genial musicians and that the music of the future has opened new regions in harmony."

"What has it opened? An arena for pretentious lack of talent. Now, Wagner and Berlioz I will let pass. They were at least genial evil doers! If they only had not founded schools. But that is such a new invention, that which they call 'descriptive music.' I beg you, what is it? A revolution of violins outscreaming each other, and the whole is called 'Cæsar's Death' or 'The fight of the Horatii and the Curiatii' or—or 'The Eruption of Vesuvius' in order that the audience may at least think of something during the strange performance—because they can feel absolutely nothing but—headache!"

Rossini's friend laughed heartily at his wit. "Hm, hm, and this beautiful work of Sterny's really contains the most masterly and brilliant paraphrases on the—poverty of thought!"

"'Satan' contains gems which will charm you," asserted the alto, and which the 'Swan of Pesaro' but, hark! Sterny is coming. I call your attention to the duet of the banished ones, the last, do you hear?"

Followed by the Capellmeister and a little group of intimate adorers, Alphonse de Sterny meanwhile stepped upon the stage. The German pianist rested a pair of eyes staring with delight upon him. De Sterny, who is accustomed to cause such excitement, smiles slightly, gives the enthusiast an encouraging glance, and nodding to the bowing orchestra steps in front of the director's desk. Then his falcon eyes wander over the ranks of his musicians. There is an irregularity in the place of the violinists. "Who is missing there?" he asks.

The violinists look at each other, murmur an indistinguishable name and add: "He is still ill, he has excused himself."

"He has only recently come from the hospital," explains the Capellmeister, "he is often irregular at rehearsals."

"And you permit that?" asks Sterny with his superior smile.

"He,—he never spoils anything at the representation and I am tolerant to him because—because," stammers the ashamed violinist—"but it, it is really an irregularity, an inexcusable irregularity which should be punished."

De Sterny shrugs his shoulders. "Do not vex yourself further," says he "only I hope the next time to find my musical troupe complete.

He knocks on the desk.

His manner of conducting has something quite peculiar and reminds one neither of the fiery contortions of Verdi, nor of the demoniac energy of Hector Berlioz. His motions at first are calm, almost weary; his face wears an expression of strong concentration; suddenly his eyes sparkle, his lips twitch, his breast heaves, at an especially striking musical culmination he raises his arms higher and higher, like wings with which he would free himself from the earth, and then suddenly lets them sink, with an expression of sad exhaustion.

"He will kill himself!" sighs the piano teacher in enthusiastic pity. Rossini's friend on the contrary says vexedly: "He is an embodied phrase, as thin as his music and just as full of grimaces!"

The opening fugue has only strengthened his prejudice against de Sterny: "A pretentious spectacle," he murmurs angrily while the enthusiastic pianist, her hand on her heart, asserts that she has heard the plunging of avalanches, and cold shivers have run down her back.

The fugue was repeated, the amateurs made some cutting remark; at length the perfecting of this master piece was put off until later, the alto laid aside her furs, rose, gave a glance at Rossini's friend, drew her mouth into the recognized oratorio smile, and began. After a somewhat dramatic recitation, followed a meltingly sweet, indescribably sad melody. Yes, really a melody, as tender and simple as the melodies of Mozart, but salted by a couple of dry melancholy, modulations to the needs of our modern ears, thirsting for pain—Rossini's friend scarcely believes his senses.

With every number—several bombastic intermezzi excepted—the beauties of "Satan" increase, until at last, in the duet of the banished ones, the duet in which all humanity weeps over the loss of Heaven, the orchestra rises and breaks out in enthusiastic applause. De Sterny sheds tears, assures them that this is the happiest moment of his life, that the achievements of the orchestra surpass all his expectations; the pianist goes into convulsions, and Rossini's friend grumbles, moving his hand in mechanical applause: "But where did he get that—a plagiarist—an immoderate plagiarist—but from whom?"

After the duet follows a very ugly finale, which the most unwilling musicians pardoned to the oratorio on account of the unusual beauties of the rest. The artists put their envy in their pockets, do not understand, and as if tamed, bow before a great wonder.

De Sterny in the Countess's coupe drives up the steep street of Montague de la Cour, to an exquisite breakfast, served by liveried servants, and lets gentle aristocratic voices surround him with their sense-bewildering flatteries. Suddenly he sees something that interests him, that frightens him.

Before a large red bill-board, which announces to the world the approaching representation of "Satan," stands a broad shouldered man, with down trodden boots, shabby clothes, and a soft hat drawn down over his ears.

The coupe had to stop on account of a carriage blockade. Once more the virtuoso sees the prolitary, this time in profile. Strange! The virtuoso becomes as pale as a corpse, and leans back shuddering upon the bottle green silk cushions of the carriage.

Does he perhaps know the prolitary, or has he known him before the brutalizing stamp of drink disfigured his face? Who knows? The appearance of the stranger is besides peculiar enough to call forth a glance, a shudder from every passer by. Stooping shoulders, a loose carriage, a shuffling gait—and still, in the whole personality an expression of crushed life, extinguished fire—a fine face, with a somewhat too bright red lips, strong nose, broad forehead, and eyes which half shut looked before him like like those of a bird of prey, dreading the light, or like those of a man who wishes to see nothing but the narrow path along which he is sentenced to wander through life, perhaps along which he has sentenced himself to wander, in the whole face a trace of an old pain and—of a new burden. Meanwhile the blockade is removed, and while the dun colored horses of the Countess C. move rapidly on to make up for lost time, to bring the great man to the Count's palace, the prolitary enters one of those butter shops behind which a brandy shop usually lies, and desires a glass of gin.

III.

The history of the violinist. Who was he? What was he?

One of those riddles which from time to time Heaven sends down to the earth, in order that she may solve it. But the earth sometimes finds the task too hard and buries the riddle unsolved in her lap.

He was born in Brussels the son of a chorus singer in a theater and of one of those Hungarian gypsy virtuosi who always in groups, like a swarm of musical will o' the wisps, appear, now here, now there, in the large and small cities of Europe and pursue their fantastic musical career. The mother—Margaretha von Zuylen was her name—gave the boy the baptismal name of his Hungarian father, who had disappeared before his child saw the light of the world. The son of the Flemish woman was named Gesa, Gesa von Zuylen. He had dark eyes, a face framed in black hair, but something rounded and heavy about his build reminded one of the sons of her flat canal-furrowed fatherland. His being was a strange mixture of dreamy phlegm and erratic warmth.

The alley in which he grew up was called Rue Ravenstein, and rough and crooked, dirty and forgotten of the world extended from the Rue Montague de la Cour towards St. Gudule.

That part of the city, very near its brilliant centre, is of ill renown, picturesque and wholly unknown to the good society of Brussels. No carriage can pass here partly because the alleys are too narrow, partly because their natural unevenness—no country in the world has a more hilly capital than flat Belgium—now here, now there is increased by a couple of wooden steps. In consequence of which the residents extend their dwelling places out in the open air.

The customs and the uncleanliness remind one of the southern cities. Foul remnants of vegetables, rabbit skins, paper flowers, and old ball gloves, ashes and other rubbish rest conveniently on the large irregular stone pavement, through the midst of which the water of the gutter slowly flows along.

Long legged hyena-like dogs, with crooked backs, and dirty coats, dogs like those of Constantinople, and which belong to no one, snuff around for food among the refuse. Knife grinders and other roofless vagabonds lie, according to the time of the year, in shadow or in the sun; untidy women in dirty night sacques, with carelessly arranged hair, bend out of the windows and hold endless conversations with each other; others, a red, swollen fist on each hip, stand in the doorways and blinking, watch—how time creeps on. The houses are unlike, some warmer and high, others broad and low, as if pressed down to earth by huge reddish green roofs. In some windows stand pots of flowers, others have thick curtains. Little, not particularly inviting, wine shops with dark wooden signs on which stands written in white letters "Hier reskoopt men Drank" frequently interrupted the rows of dwelling houses. All the alleys of this part of the city were, in Gesa's youth, similar in confusion, only the Rue Ravestein was perhaps somewhat more picturesque and of worse repute than her sisters. In the buzz of its idle life mingled the hard hammering of a coffin maker and the sharp blows of a stone cutters mallet. Against the rear wall of an old church, gray with age, leaned a huge cross, and under his time blackened halo, the Saviour looked sadly down upon the misery and crime which he could not banish from the world. Two very small church windows of stained glass mirrored themselves in the gutter—on those days when the gutter was clear enough.

In these surroundings Gesa grew up. His mother was

one of the women who stood in the house door and watched —how the time crept on. She was the type of a beautiful Flemish woman, large, somewhat heavy, with strong, large limbs, and a white and red face. Her red lips parted indolently over very white teeth, around her nostrils was a red tinge. She had protruding eyes, and that rich, waving lion-yellow hair, with which Rubens loved to adorn his Magdalenes. When she was not busy on the stage and was standing in the house door, she crouched on a sack of straw in her attic and read incessantly robber stories from old books which, bought from an antiquary, passed from one to the other of the good women of the Rue Ravestein.

Lazy to sleepiness, good natured to weakness, she had always a caress for Gesa, and a gay teasing remark for the fat gray cat who had run up after her. She lived only in the moment. In the beginning of the month she fed the child with dainties, toward the end of the month she contracted debt.

Gesa from his earliest youth was musical. Before he could speak, he looked upon his mother with delight shining in his large dark eyes, when cradling him in her arms, she sang a lullaby. A friend of Margaretha taught the child to play the violin. Gesa learned wonderfully quickly. The chorus singer's financial condition ever becoming worse, she was obliged to make use of her son's capabilities pecuniarily, and when he was scarcely nine years old she procured him an engagement in the orchestra of a circus which had pitched its temporary tent on the "*Grand Sablon*" and whose personal consisted of one acrobat of wonderful beauty, one rarely disagreeable dwarf whose name was Mosaro, of four monkeys, and a pony whose art culminated in walking on three legs, which was perhaps no art but an infirmity.

Gesa's orchestral duties consisted in accompanying with an old fiddle the unmusical performance of a narrow chested, long-haired young man, who hammered out waltzes and polkas on an old spinet, while, as he sighingly told little Gesa, he had all his life longed in vain to be permitted to perform a funeral march.

The circus gave its performances from two to four in the

afternoon and was always empty. While on the orchestral stage Gesa fiddled his simple part, his child-like eyes looked down on the circus. He saw the acrobat, decorated, painted and spangled, tricked out in a pink doublet and green silk tights, a gold crown about his head, turn somersaults or bend his supple body over a trapeze. He saw the dwarf with his great, rough, red head and his costume made of a blue half and a yellow half, forming a most repulsive contrast.

The dwarf was always applauded. The monkeys tremblingly performed their artistic tricks. The smell of sawdust, gas, orange skins and monkeys crept up to the little violinist's nose. He sneezed. Then he became sleepy. His bow wavered. "*Allons donc!*" panted the pianist, stamping his foot. He opened his eyes. His glance met his mother's who, blond and phlegmatic, sat on the edge of the ring below and smilingly nodded to him. He fiddled on. If the chorus singers were not detained by the rehearsals at the theatre, she missed no performance at the circus. Gesa imagined she came to hear him play.

But one fine day Gesa was rude to the dwarf Mosaro, and in consequence lost his position as member of the orchestra. Margaretha still remained the regular visitor of the circus.

And then came an April afternoon with cold showers and violently beating storm. Winter and spring fought outside. Gesa, who since he no longer had a regular occupation, incessantly read the old knightly romances of his mother was absorbed in a horribly startling story; both elbows rested on the top of a tottering little table, his thumbs in his ears, he bent over the yellow leaves of a very torn paper. Then Margaretha came up to him and remarked hesitatingly "Your supper is already prepared and in the cupboard, you need not wait for me—I shall come home late to-day. Good-by, my treasure!

"Good-by, Mamma," said he indifferently. He was accustomed to her coming home late and scarcely looked up from his reading. She went. After perhaps five minutes she came back again.

"Have you forgotten anything, mother?" asked Gesa.

"Yes," murmured she. Her face was very red, she touched now this, now that. At last she bent over the boy, kissed him once, twice, thrice while she pressed his head against her breast, murmured, "God protect you," and went. Gesa read on. Soon after he wished to rub away something shining which obscured the print of the paper, illegible without that. It was a tear from his mother's eye.

Gesa, as usual when Margaretha was busied at the theatre, went to bed without locking the doors, but when he awoke the next morning he found his mother's bed empty. "Mother" called he frightened, "Mother!"

He knew that she could not hear him, but he called the word to relieve his oppressed heart. He slipped into his clothes and hurried down to the street.

It was a cold morning. The gutters swollen with melted snow rippled in the morning wind. Slanting red sunbeams shimmered in the church windows. A few sad organ tones sounded through the gray church walls into the desolate street. Gesa wept bitterly. He cried ever louder, more pitifully, "Mother, Mother!" She had always been good to him.

He looked now here, now there; the whole world had become empty for him. He understood that his mother had left him. Children in the Rue Ravestein understand so quickly.

Then a long thin hand was laid on his shoulders; he looked up; near him stood a man he knew. He lived in the first story of the house in which Margaretha had a little attic room. He was deathly pale and looked very sad. "Poor boy!" he murmured, "she has left you." Gesa bit his teeth into his lower lip, became very red and shook off the stranger's hand. He was ashamed; he felt for the first time that compassion was humiliating. But the stranger stroked his hair softly and said again: "Poor boy, you must not take it amiss in her. Love is so—"

"What is love?" asked Gesa, staring at him.

The stranger coughed: "A sickness—a fever," he said

hastily. "A fever in which one dreams beautiful things—and does very horrible things."

IV.

M. Gaston Delileo, that was the stranger's name, but in the Rue Ravestein they called him nothing but the sad man, the melancholy man. He might perhaps be between forty and fifty years old, had a yellow face reminding one of carved ivory, wore a full beard and his long stiff black hair cut over his forehead. Out doors, in the hottest summer months, he never went on the street except wrapped in a dark blue, red lined *carbonari*.

Seven months before he had moved into the Rue Ravestein, petted the children, greeted the women in passing, was universally beloved and associated with no one.

Margaretha before her flight had secretly dropped a note in the formerly ever empty letter box before his door, with the request that he would take the boy, and had shown great knowledge of mankind when she counted on his pity. His wife was dead, his only daughter, at that time scarcely seven years old, was brought up by relatives in France as it would have been difficult for him in his bachelor establishment to give the child suitable care.

So widowed and solitary, burdened with a great heart thirsting for love, which in his life had never been satisfied, he took the boy to himself without any prudential consideration. "Come to breakfast," said he simply, took the orphans hand and led him in his house.

After the meal was over, and while M. Delileo with that rage for systematising which clings to all, especially impractical people, bent over his writing desk, formed a plan of education, a division of hours, and finally a long list of all those things which Gesa would need now and possibly in the course of the next ten years, the boy crept curiously around in the little room furnished with arsenic green tapestries and looked attentively at all the furniture, an antiquated and worm eaten mixture of stiff military Empire and pretentious crooked Louis Phillippe furniture.

On the walls hung a pair of sketches of a formerly celebrated master with dedications, "*A mon cher ami, etc,*" several poet's autographs in black frames, and besides those the quickly sketched portrait of a very beautiful woman in a white satin dress with many strings of pearls around the neck, and a little crown on her head. "Is that the queen?" asked Gesa of his new protector.

Whereupon this one, rising from his occupation answered not without a certain solemnity: "That my child, that was The Gualtieri!"

"Oh!" said Gesa and was just as wise as before. How should he know that "The Gualtieri" had been in her time the most celebrated and, alas, also the most disreputable artist in the world.

"She was also a queen—a queen of song," added Delileo in explanation after a little pause.

"And did you know her?" asked Gesa, still absorbed in the view of the romantically attired lady.

"She was my wife," said Delileo slowly, and with emphasis, while he made a speaker's gesture.

"Ah! then she certainly loved you very much!" remarked Gesa earnestly, only in order to say something pleasant.

But Delileo shivered and turned his head away.

Under the portrait stood day in and day out on a poor black marble round table, in a half broken blue delft picture a fresh bouquet of flowers.

V.

From the beginning of their life together, Delileo had rightly valued the musical gifts of his protegé, and, thanks to some artistic connections which still remained to him, had obtained for the boy musical instruction from a violin virtuoso at the Brussels conservatory. The rest of Gesa's education he cared for. Truly a peculiar education! "Careful orthography and extensive knowledge of literature are the two necessities of an excellent cultivation," asserted Delileo. "Further one needs nothing."

Gesa's orthography, in spite of the deserving exertions of Delileo, always remained somewhat uncertain; his knowledge of literature on the contrary rapidly made the most astonishing progress. It soon reached from the "Essais de Montaigne," the first hobby of Delileo, to his own romance, his second hobby.

The romance, which was called "Prometheus" and for ten years had waited for a publisher, formed an excellent pendant to Delileo's *Carbonari*. Like this romantic piece of clothing it smelled of mould, and was penetrated by a breath of out-of-date theories for the happiness of the world. It began with a fairy tale and ended with an ode. The old man passed many evenings in reading this aloud to the boy. Gesa always listened with the solemn attention which credulous minds bring to mysteries of which they understand not a word.

They formed a strange pair, the broken man with his nervous restlessness, the restlessness of those who have attained nothing and see the grave before them, and the merry boy with his healthy idleness, the arrogant idleness of those who feel a great talent within them and to whom life still seems unending. The weary mind of one incessantly wandered from the inconsolable soberness of the present to the Utopia of the year thirty; the strength of imagination of the other, restrained by no experience, galopped with a pair of unwearied chimeras, certain of victory, into the future. Both were enthusiasts—only Delileo by far the less practical of the two.

Poor Gaston Delileo! He belonged in the category of universal geniuses whose condition is measured by the fact that they have brought absolutely nothing into the universe. Music, painting, literature, national economy,—he had pursued all these with the greatest zeal, one after the other or even at the same time, had believed with the truest idealism in the capability of improvement in the social condition, in the theories of the St. Simonites, and had worn with enthusiasm the vest of the brotherhood as well as a frontlet adorned with its name.

The story went that the St. Simon society, with their practical division of work had at first limited his activity to giving out money and polishing boots, the only two things for which they could make use of him. Later they had initiated him into the batallion of that memorable "three hundred" who were selected to seek in foreign lands the mother of the sect, after Madame de Staël had declined this post of honor.

He had spent his money, his illusions had changed into spleen. Become melancholy, he had retired from the world, in order to hide himself and his disappointments. He wished nothing more than to forget and be forgotten, at least for the present;—for the future, a distant, misty future, he still hoped something—for his romance.

Meanwhile he passed his life in writing notes—like Rousseau.

* * *

Two, three years passed; Gesa became a youth, handsome as a picture. With Delileo he must gain cultivation of heart and mind, but he remained perfectly free from any characteristic of the eccentric St. Simonite. Ever more his being took on a stamp of dreamy distraction, which to a person with much knowledge of human nature foreboded nothing good for his future. He could never preserve the medium between sleepy illness and wearying zeal; he was completely lacking in capability for continuous hard work: what did not come to him by inspiration he made his own with more difficulty than the least talented conservatorist.

But his violin professor gave no thought to all this. He only remarked the gigantic progress of the boy, was proud of his scholar, and presented him before now this, now that amateur.

Gesa not only played the violin with unheard of virtuosity for his age, but he also improvised and really like no one else, so at least asserted his professor.

The phlegmatic Belgians were charmed with his musical eccentricities: also that his name was Gesa, that he had such a handsome dark face, and descended from a Hungarian gypsy. Their enthusiasm over his accomplishments always culminated in the same words: "*Comme c'est tzigane!*"

Then came a day on which Gesa for the first time was to play in public, to take part in a concert. With the colossal confidence of youth he rejoiced at his début; the discouraged Gaston Delileo on the contrary lost appetite and sleep. Anxiously expecting the boy's disappointment, he passed his time in lecturing him to make light of the fiasco.

Gesa did not take this lecture well; he ran away from the old man. Then, with his hat pressed adventurously on his forehead, his hands in his pockets, he stamped up and down in the Rue Havestein, and the old man crept up and down in his little room and feared.

On the evening of the concert the old man was not to be induced to enter the music hall. Breathless, panting, he stood before the artist's entrance and stopped his ear.

Suddenly, in spite of all his earnest efforts to exclude every sound he heard a strange noise. He let his hands sink. Was that a fire alarm?—No—it was the clapping of hundreds of hands, a bravo from hundreds of throats!—The next moment, bursting into the green room, he held his *protégé* in his arms!

All his fellow performers pressed the boy's hands, praised him, promised him a brilliant future. He took this allegiance as a tribute due him, with that naive conceit which one so easily pardons in young gods,—even if with a truly unpassionate smile; but even he, in spite of his uninjured self consciousness was startled at the extent of his victory when the door opened, and, stretching out both hands to him, an elegant young man entered—Alphonse de Sterny.

"My darling young friend," he cried, "I could not let the evening pass without learning to know you, without congratulating you."

[TO BE CONTINUED]

From the German of Ossip Schubin.

Translated by E. L. Lathrop.

THE STORY OF BRASS-WIND INSTRUMENTS.

A Study in the Evolution of the Orchestra.

II.

FOR the most part the masters of the classic period did not make important distinctions in their treatment of the orchestra for the symphony and the drama. But certain exceptions are so important that we must retrace our steps a little and carry our investigations of the dramatic school to France of the year 1767.

Gluck in his *Alceste* finally incorporates in the dramatic orchestra of France, the trombone which had, it is true, made an earlier appearance in the *Isminor* of Rodolphe. In *Alceste*, the trombones are intimately connected with the character of the god Apollo and "annonce du Dieu la puissance suprême." When the Greeks, overcome with terror, hear the voice of Apollo declaring his will, the majestic power of four trombones support the tones. But in the aria "Divinites du Styx," they represent the savage cries of the infernal gods. When the trombones are not used with especial dramatic intent, they double the voices in the traditional manner of the German school.

Mozart first shows the influence of Gluck in the passage for three trombones and two horns behind the scenes in *Idomeneo*. Only once does he revert to the method of Bach and then it is the invocations of the *Magic Flute*, where he desires to give especial dignity to the chorus. M. Lavoix has pointed out the striking resemblance between the aria of Apollo in *Alceste* and the recitative of the Comandant in *Don Giovanni*, which extends even to the harmonics employed.

Von Weber's most notable advance was in his treatment of the horn. By means of crooks, the scale of the natural horn may be transposed to any degree of the chromatic scale. In the overture to *Der Freischütz*, Weber, by ingenious combination of harmonic scales of four horns, in different keys, has been able to produce the charming effect of a hymn in four part harmony.

Beginning with 1830 the separation of the symphonic and dramatic orchestras becomes marked. The former, except in the hands of the neo-romantic school, remains contented with the resources of Beethoven. The latter, by the addition of recently invented brass instruments provided with complete chromatic scales, has been able to produce effects of timbre hitherto undreamed of.

This movement was begun in France by Meyerbeer and Berlioz, in Germany by Richard Wagner. The chief innovations of the leaders of the French school, was in giving to the third group, hitherto only an accessory, a part as essential to the organic whole as either of the other groups.

By the addition of two cornets-à-piston, soprano voices of the *tuba* type provided with complete chromatic scales, and reinforcing the bass with the powerful if harsh ophicleide, they obtained a choir well able to stand by itself. Still they ordinarily doubled the ophicleide with bassoons and filled in the middle range with the horns, thus impairing the general effect which is best when produced by a single variety of timbre.

With Meyerbeer the third group not only plays an important part in adding color to the ensemble but is entrusted with the highest dramatic expression.

In *Robert the Devil*, he identifies with Bertram the evil genius, all the harsh and sombre timbres at his disposal. In the invocation, his voice is supported by trombones, horns and trumpets; in the duo with Robert by bassoons, four trumpets and an ophicleide. The famous phrase, "Il est sur le tombeau," receives cavernous color from the eccentric group of bassoons, bass trombone, ophicleide and pizzicato basses. Again in the final trio, when he repeats after Alice the words of the oath, the feminine character of the melody as supported by flutes and clarinets is completely changed by the diabolical tones of the horns and trumpets.

In the chorus of Murderers, fifth act of the *Huguenots*,

he has used with striking effect the brutal color of the defective note of the trumpet.

Berlioz also understood well how to produce the most sonorous effects from the orchestral material at his command. In the *Dumrémont Requiem*, he calls for an orchestra of brass, which in mere point of size has not yet been surpassed or even equalled. In the *Tuba Mirum* of that mass, besides twelve horns playing with the second group, he prescribes four small bands of brass to be placed at the four corners of the great choral and instrumental body.

The first of these includes four cornets-à-piston in B♭, four tenor trombones and two bombardones; the second, two trumpets in F, two in E♭ and four tenor trombones, the third, four trumpets in E♭ and four tenor trombones; the fourth, four trumpets in B♭, four tenor trombones, two ophicleides in C and two in B♭. Besides this array of brass, sixteen timpani and two long drums are used in addition to the percution.

In his later works, *Faust* and the *Fantastic Symphony*, he allows the alternative use of the bass tuba in place of the ophicleide, but never I believe, prescribes it.

But his most important contribution to our knowledge of orchestral treatment was when, in his Instrumentation, he directed attention to the magnificent effects that might be obtained from trumpets and trombones, played piano or even pianissimo.

Richard Wagner, even in his earlier works constituted his third group much more logically than his French contemporaries.

French school.	Wagner.
2 valve trumpets.	3 valve trumpets
2 cornets-à-piston	
3 trombones	3 trombones.
ophicleide.	Tuba.

He replaced the cornets-à-piston, with their weak four foot tone and tuba timbre, by the sonorous eight foot trumpet, provided with cylinders which give it a complete chromatic scale. The tuba with its more musical tone is a decided improvement over "the chromatic bullock." The three upper voices balance the lower masculine voices, and each of the parts has sufficient space to move in.

The substitution, at first but partial it is true, of the valve horn with its complete scale, for the natural horn, made the laborious combinations of horns with different crooks unnecessary.

For special effects he sometimes augmented the number of brass. In the last act of *Tannhaüser* we find twelve horns playing in three real parts, and in the march a fanfare of twelve trumpets.

In the third act of *Lohengrin*, scene three, a wholly novel effect is produced on the stage by twelve trumpets, in five different keys. The scene portrays the assembling of the nobility.

Trumpets in *Eb* are heard on the right approaching from a distance, then a Graf enters. While a second Graf, heralded by trumpets in D, enters, we hear the approaching trumpets in F of a third. Trumpets in E are heard coming nearer and nearer. Then as the fourth Graf enters, four trumpets in C celebrate the approach of the king.

As he enters all the trumpets unite in a noble fanfare.

With the *Niebelungen Ring* which marks Wagner's later period, we find most important additions to the brass choir, which now consists of:—

3 valve trumpets.	2 tubas alto-tenor
1 bass trumpet.	2 tubas baryton-bass.
3 trombones.	1 tuba contra bass.

The old trumpet-trombone family is considerably augmented and includes eight individuals; three soprano and a bass trumpet, which is really an alto tenor trombone with pistons, three ordinary trombones and a contra bass.

Then we have a perfect group of instruments of the *Lituus* type, with uniform cylindrical bore, producing a chromatic scale ranging from *EE* to twice-marked *a*, which united will produce a homogenious sonority.

Turning to the *tuba* type, we find another group, comprising only masculine voices, but within its range from *EE* to twice-marked *f*, producing a chromatic scale of a timbre that is perfectly homogenious but differs widely from that of the trumpet-trombone group.

The tuba group consists of four tubas; alto, tenor, baryton and bass, which have received the name of "Bayreuth tubas,"* from the fact that the first examples were made under Wagner's direction, for the festival production of the "Ring" at Bayreuth. To these is added the contra bass tuba, which we have seen struggling to supersede the crude ophicleide in the orchestra of Berlioz.

This group plays an important part throughout the Tetralogy but especially in *Siegfried*, where they are identified with the character of the dragon Fafner. In the combat between Siegfried and the dragon, the bass tuba doubled in the octave by the contra bass tuba, follow all the movements of the monster, sinking into silence as he is slain.

However these groups are by no means rigidly adhered to, and we see instruments from both groups happily combined. Both in *Das Rheingold* and *Die Walküre*, the tuba is joined to the trumpets and in the brass orchestra which accompanies the song of Mimi in *Siegfried* the tuba plays an important part.

The horns to the number of eight have a definite place in the second group of the orchestra of the trilology. In the prelude to *Das Rheingold* the quiet flow of the river Rhine is wonderfully connoted by a waving mass of horn tone, produced by eight horns entering at half bar intervals, with the same ascending arpeggio on the chord of E*b*.

Finally if we stand and look back over the road we have travelled, we see a gradual but complete revolution both in the constitution and treatment of the brass choir.

We see its timid beginnings in the trombones and imperfect trumpets of the dance orchestra of the XVI Century; the addition of the hunting horn, with the subsequent discovery of stopped notes and the use of crooks, then the gradual application of the valve or piston principle and the final completion of the choir by Wagner.

Hand in hand with the introductions of new and improved instruments, we have seen the growth of better methods of treatment, until now by the richness and beauty of the brass sonority, we can express, without effort, the most profound and dramatic ideas.

"By using three metallic timbres of diverse color, the master has been able to translate into striking language the situations and characters of his epic drama. While the clear upper voices transport the spirit into a world of light, of ideal grandeur, among gods and heroes, the deep and sombre voices evoke the ideas of material force, of human sufferings, of fate; and the poetic voices of the horns arouse in our imaginations distant visions, recollections buried in the depths of the heart."

ERNEST OSGOOD HILER.

SOME ARMENIAN MELODIES.

A LONELY and exiled man, detained for six years in the horror of an Egyptian prison, wandering for twelve years longer through the alien countries of Europe, finding his way at last to Paris, the City of Happiness, only to die there broken-hearted;—these were the closing scenes in the life of Leon VI, the last King of Armenia.

Since then, the Armenians, once the most warlike of people, have been forced to submit to foreign invasion and rule. For six hundred years they have endured constant persecution from the Kurds, Persians, and Turks, who have ravaged the country with wars and laid waste her resources.

Sorrow has become to the people a strong bond of union, and instead of permitting themselves to be assimilated by their enemies they have held their tradition and their nation intact.

In no way, perhaps, has their suffering found more complete expression than in their national melodies. While pathos predominates in almost all these songs, others show touches of happiness which seem to prove that even an Armenian may have his joyful moments.

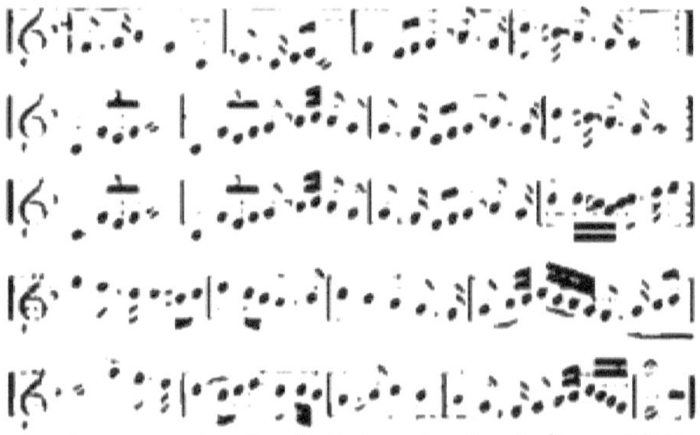

These melodies are unwritten, are of the purest lyric

form, and have most unique characteristics. The first example is a song in praise of the Armenian language.

Here is at once discovered the peculiar phrasing which is a very great charm in most of the songs. In a very beautiful and varied melody which is much too long to be reproduced here, occurs this passage.

During the song there appears an exquisite solo, beginning in this way.

At the end of the solo the chorus breaks out in a spirited response, quite military in style.

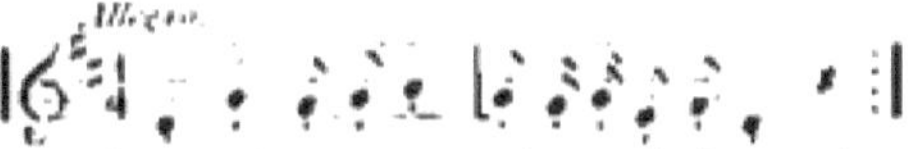

The whole tune bears a very close relation to the words, which constitute "A Song of Freedom," and part of which may be freely translated as follows:

> "Behold the dove of Noah's Ark,
> As it flies from the misty summits of Ararat,
> Proclaiming Freedom to the Armenian Cities,
> To the Armenians who are wandering here and there,
> It brings tidings of new glories,
> Saying, 'Enough, so many hundred years of tribulation,'
> Hear, because it is a divine message,
> Awake, now! ye Armenian sojourners,
> The days of your slavery are passing,
> The birds of your spring, with their beautiful warbling, sing to
> you of hope, and of love.
> On! now, ye sons of heroes!
> Leave behind cowardly hearts,
> Jealously lets leave behind,
> We are all equal, Armenian brothers,
> Our nationality is one, our language is one,
> Our faith is one, our ancestry is one,
> Our country is one, our glory is one,
> Why should not our hearts be one?"

In the early part of the 5th century Armenia, as a nation accepted Christianity; and although surrounding paganism has greatly lowered the intellectual and social conditions of the people, the church has been most miraculously preserved from the corrupting influence.

A pure and fervent Christian spirit is expressed in the following "Morning Invocation," only a few verses of which can be given here.

> "O Thou Morn of Light, Thou Sun of Righteousness, send out light to me.
>
> Awake, Lord, to help; waken the sleeping to be like the angels.*
>
> I invoke with my voice, implore with my hands, grant me thy blessing.
>
> Love, name of Jesus, with thy love melt my stony heart.
>
> For Thy mercy's sake raise me up.
>
> Let the dew of Thy blood fall on my soul, my spirit shall rejoice.
>
> Thou Heavenly Teacher, teach us, the disciples in the school of heavenly ones.
>
> Thou Expiator of Sin, redeem us, the thanksgivers, that we may sing praises unto Thee.
>
> When Thou comest in glory, in that awful day, remember me, O Christ."

This song is one of the very earliest, and belongs to what is called the "Golden Age," of Armenian literature. The tune is of special interest on account of the very unique ending, which is common to many Armenian melodies.

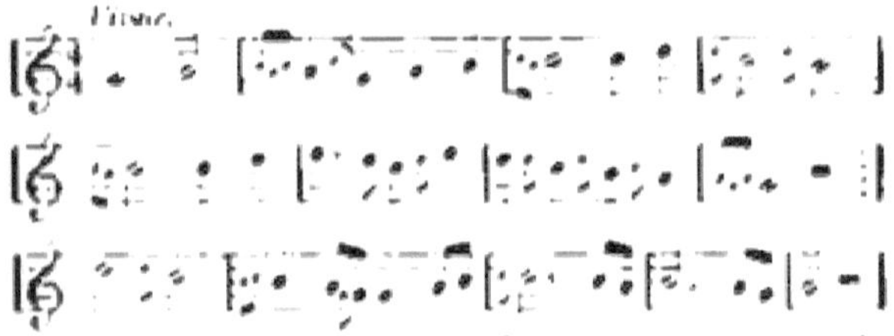

The small notes are given in order to represent, as nearly as possible, the "trill" made in singing these melodies, and should represent tones only one-third of a major second apart, not a full half tone, as written.

In America, the nearest approach to this "trill" is found in the pure negro melodies, as they were sung in *ante bellum* times, and even then there is a great difference.

The Armenians have not much idea of harmony, but

*The Armenian word for Angel means "One who is always awake." The beauty of the original is here entirely lost by translation.

sing and play as the church-choirs sang in the days before Palestrina, "in octaves and unison." The instruments of a large band will all play the melody alone, and the effect is tremendous.

However, upon one little instrument something like a mandolin, called the *tamboora*, an approach is made to a harmonic chord. It has four strings, three of which are tuned in unison, (and upon *two* of which the air is played,) while the fourth string is tuned a perfect fourth below for minor airs, and a perfect fifth below for major tunes, which last are very seldom met with, however.

This instrument is played with a thin strip of horn held between thumb and finger, in perfect time, but with a very rapid and peculiar rhythm.

To one hearing it for the first time this rhythm is most baffling to analyze, because of its frequent changes.

With the last example, "A Patriotic Song," is given a partial illustration of this unique accompaniment. This melody is much more modern than the preceding, and already shows the influence of foreign music.

Since the great American symphony, we have begun to realize more than ever before how perfectly the life of a nation is expressed in its people's songs. Though in all other things we may be widely separated from our Armenian cousins, the inner life is common to us all; and through music, its language universal, we may learn to sympathize with one another.

We have but called attention to the beauty and novelty of the Armenian folk-songs. Further investigation must discover much that is of interest and desirable, while the composer may here find a wide field for the exercise of his talent, — one in which he may revel to his heart's content.

MARY GRACE REED.

THE ARIA-GIVING METHOD OF TEACHING OF THE VOICE.

IT may seem like thrashing old straw, this time honored subject, but I am not addressing those who have heard it harped on until it has been worn threadbare. There is a class of students which has not as yet learned everything that the wisdom of the centuries has to teach, and it is with them that I wish to talk. As for the voice teachers themselves, I would never dream of speaking to them, for each one is as hopelessly convinced of the absolute correctness of his "method" as I am of mine, so there would only be confusion worse confounded. Then too, someone might feel that there was a personal point to my remarks, and might even lose his temper, which in a brotherhood so bound together by the bands of friendship and mutual esteem as are we teachers of the divine art of song would be truly a calamity. No indeed. On behalf of this magazine I now extend to all my co-laborers "tokens of our most distinguished consideration." I believe that is the formula. The only man to whom I take exceptions has an entirely different name, and lives many, many miles from here. Not one of you know him.

As I said before I wish to talk with the young students, those who do not already know it all, but are open to argument. Into their minds I should like to instil a "holy discontent" with some of the cut and dried "methods." The one which is most thoroughly wrong and to be fought on all occasions is what may be called the *aria-giving* method. It occupies a conspicuous place, its exponent is very popular and his following large. It may well seem fool-hardy to attack him in his very lair, but it must be done. It is an important fact that he always teaches the "old Italian method," or the "original Italian method," or he studied with so and so who was a pupil of Maestro Blank the very last master of the "true Italian method." By these "methods" I have known pupils in the second and third quarters to be put to work on arias that tax to the utmost the mature powers of the world's greatest artists. In no other branch of art is such utter folly attempted, to say nothing of its being insisted on by the teacher. We cannot imagine a raw piano student being told to prepare a Beethoven sonata. There are certain grades of technical difficulties in piano music that serve in some rough way to keep students in their proper place. If they take anything very much beyond them the mere fact of their complete inability to even "hit the notes," compels them to drop back where they belong, with no particular harm done and a very useful lesson learned. But when we come to the student of singing the same rule does not hold good at all. An aria is given just as far beyond the power of the student as the Beethoven sonata, but here the technical difficulties and simplest dictates of common sense are of no account. If by hook or by crook the pupil can yell his or her way through to the end—that is enough. They may sing the runs as I remember once to have fallen down stairs, bumpety bump, and head over heels; they may sing the sustained phrases as the Irishman played the bull fiddle, by main strength; but never mind, Miss —— runs home with the news at which there is a general family rejoicing, mutual congratulations over the daughter's great talent, and their good fortune in finding a teacher of such perspicacity and who wastes no time. Paterfamilias has a sort of undefined notion that he would have made a good business man, mamma sets a date when he really must come to dinner, and the poor girl with swimming head goes to bed, her slumbers sweetened by the thought of her dearest friend who is studying with that "old slow poke" and has only had one little song, that anybody could sing, and in English too. And alas for the fact, wherever the carnage is the thickest there waves the banner of "the something or other Italian method." Oh Italy! What dire crimes are committed in thy name!

No man believes more thoroughly than I in the Italian school for training the voice. I chose it for myself out of all Europe and spent the best years of my student life there. Then too, it has produced the overwhelming majority of the world's great singers, and this fact it is that has made it a safe cloak for ignorance. But let a man write "Italian" on his card and the pupils flock to him while he sits secure from every criticism. It has been the "Open Sesame" and "Pax Vobiscum" for the voice teacher. But there is always a penalty to be paid some day. Such disaster has come from many a studio that was a fountain head of "Italian Methods," that the thinking part of the musical community is beginning to inquire into the subject. When they hear the magic word instead of taking everything for granted, they wish to know what "Italian method" may mean; even they are are beginning to look askance. The first is wise, the second goes too far as reaction always does. Now a man may claim to teach the "Italian method" with no better foundation for his claim than his own assertion. I think that fact will be admitted. Now if he teaches this method he must have learned it somewhere, and from the place and teacher with whom he studied a fair estimate can be made of the truth of his claim. If students would use the same care in selecting a teacher that they would in buying a bicycle his fraud would seem to be so patent that no one would be deceived, yet he flourishes like the green bay tree, and "has lots to do." He cannot be classed among the well meaning but incapable; he belongs in another category. Then a man may have gone to the very seat of knowledge, but if he does not carry brains with him his opportunities will avail him nothing. Such a man must be recognized as he would be in any other walk of life, by his deeds.

As things stand today it is absolutely nothing in a man's favor that he claims to teach "the Italian method." There are so many doing that that things have gone back to first principles and a man must be judged by his individual worth and knowledge and stand or fall by what he can do. That word "method" that I have been obliged to use so many times, reminds me of another thing. Beware of "methods" and of the man with a "method." One of the distinguishing characteristics of the voice is that each individual has a voice that is different from every other one. The man who attempts to train all voices according to one cast iron set of rules, according to a "method" reminds me of poor Bob Allen who thought he might as well shut up his shop and go skylarking with Mr. Pickwick, because, as he said, his stock of drugs was so depleted that he had nothing left to dispense to his patients but calomel, and that would be sure to disagree with some of them.

The great teachers of all time have been those who understood this fundamental fact, and who by experience and that something that may be called the teacher's instinct, have been able to discover the needs of each particular voice and supply them. I remember last winter reading a ludicrously mistaken article wherein the writer set laboriously to work to prove that the elder Lamperti had no "method" because each one of his famous pupils, many of whom were mentioned by name, sang differently the one from the other. Had the writer known more of the voice he would have realized that each word he wrote was in the highest praise of the master's "method," for he was conclusively proving that Lamperti knew how to understand and develop to its fullest capacity each individual voice. What is the object of teaching? To produce an artist who shall have his instrument so well in hand that it will serve him as he wishes? Then do you imagine that these voices which are one day to express all the artistic feeling and experience of a grown man can be run off into the mould of a "method" and come out as like as a set of tin soldiers?

I have strayed some distance from my aria-giving teacher but I have not forgotten him. When I was studying with Vannini it was a year and a half before I had an aria, and I was not a beginner either. But I know many young girls here who can scarcely get the letters of the musical alphabet in their proper places, who can nevertheless talk glibly of the Jewel Song and the aria from "La Traviata." There is usually a little sequel in the yearly crop of strained voices that some teacher has to labor over for months of slow toil to put the voice back where it was in the beginning. But supposing the voice is tough and can stand the strain

Where is such study pointed? If a child has not learned to walk do we teach him by putting him on a bicycle and setting him flying down hill?

Listen to me a moment, you voice students, and realize that though I may be a little older I am still one of you and have passed through all the doubts and struggles that you are now fighting with. What are you studying for? What is your goal? To be singers? Not people who flounder about in the dark, but who have worked themselves out into daylight? Not people who sing at music, but sing it? You are giving your most earnest thought and doing all that in you lies; of that I feel sure. But you who are singing arias, answer me honestly, why are you doing so? Is your voice well poised so that you can sing from one end of it to the other with something like ease? When you vocalize a tone do you have a clear idea of how you wish to do it, and does the tone respond round, full and free? Have you reached a point where songs and ballads no longer have any difficulties for you, and you must turn to the aria to find a foeman worthy of your steel? When you are singing the aria do you feel such mastery over it that you revel in it and wish it were even longer and harder? Or do you thank your lucky stars if you get through without breaking down? If you can answer all these questions but the last with a square "Yes" then I have not a word to say. Go on and conquer. But if the "Yes" comes falteringly, then it is high time for you to stop and think. Look back over the past year and call to mind all the times you have heard some fellow student wrestling with "O Mio Fernando" when you know, and said so too, that she could not even sing a ballad, and you should think she would know better than make such a spectacle of herself. Now between you and me what do you think she said when you sang your aria? Well, that's honest. Do you think that was entirely due to jealousy or that she was right and you were right and neither of you had any business singing arias? Do you remember the girl that sang that dainty song that was not half so hard as your aria, or anyone's else aria, and yet for some reason everybody seemed to like it the best of any? Has it ever occurred to you to reason it out? Do you suppose it could have been because she could sing her number while it was quite evident that you could not sing yours? Well, you think it over.

What does all this mean? It means that in teaching the voice, common sense should be used as well as anywhere else, and that where a teacher violates its simplest laws you should beware of him,—not blindly chase the *ignis fatuus* of a name, and be left floundering in a swamp. Voice teaching goes by law as much as geometry, so bring your mind to bear on it. It may be summed up in the word *think*. Don't take everything that is given you for granted, nor expect to hire others to think for you. Begin to study out these problems for yourself. Remember that the only things you ever really know you must learn by your own thought and work.

KARLETON HACKETT.

A CONCERT DURING THE PARIS COMMUNE.

DURING the late visit of Grieg to Paris, he was given a reception by the artist Rafaëlli, at which his C minor piano-violin Sonata was played by two of the leading musicians of Paris, Pugno the late organist of St. Eustache, and Marsick, the celebrated violinist. The famous Norwegian composer also played some of his four-hand compositions with the latter, and a few days later was an appreciative listener at a concert in the Theatre D'Application, where exclusively works of Pugno were performed. I had not heard the name for a long time, and now that I suddenly saw it in the Paris correspondence of a musical contemporary, it called forth a host of reminiscences of revolutionary scenes, which were described to me by an eye-witness now eighteen years ago.

It was an evening in the latter part of March, 1871. The government of the Commune had been organized. Elections had taken place, new men were appointed to the public offices, new departments were created. The spirit of reform was reigning all over. In the brilliantly lighted *salons* of the *Préfecture de Police*, where the dignitaries of the Second Empire had celebrated many of their orgies, was assembled a company of elegant and refined looking men and women. At the magnificent Erard piano presided a dark eyed, dark-haired youth of Italian type, not more than nineteen years of age: Raoul Pugno, then assistant professor of piano at the Conservatory. There was Regnard, a doctor of medicine who had been elected General Secretary of the *Comité de Sureté Générale*. There was Edmond Levraud, chief of the first division of the *Préfecture de Police*, in the house of whose mother every Friday a select gathering of artists and musicians took place, at which occasion the chief works of modern chamber music were performed, Edmond playing second violin, Leonce, his brother, viola. There was Johan Selmer, a young Norwegian musician with an indefinably aristocratic air, and his friend, a tall slender German nobleman, musician and journalist, for many years the Paris correspondent of various German magazines. There were also Raoul Rignul, one of the most prominent members of the Commune; Vaillant, a delegate to the department of Public Instruction; the military form of General Endes—and among them all moved Louise, the beautiful young wife of the latter with her exquisite soft brown eyes, a woman of refined taste and highly cultivated mind. Who would have thought, as she stood there in her pale blue satin and white lace, that but a short time ago she had fought at the side of her husband against the Germans and the Versaillais! Pugno had played for the audience his latest composition, a "Hymne aux Immortels," by Victor Hugo; Selmer his "Scène funèbre," a powerful work in which was interwoven a highly original setting of the Marseillaise. Modern art, particularly modern music, became the topic of the conversation. Some one produced the Manifesto of Courbet, the printer who was delegate to the Department of Fine Arts, and read it:

"We want the free development of art, free from every guardianship on the part of the Government, free from every privilege; the equality of rights among all members of the federation; the protection of the independence and dignity of every artist by a committee, elected by the general vote of all artists."

Vaillant suggested a reorganization of the official musical department, especially the Conservatory and the Grand Opera. They were to be directed henceforth by musicians and not by politicians. Thus the intense political excitement of the period transformed a musical soirée into something like a legislative body. Mme Eudes thought it was not too late to have a musical season. A great concert to be given at the Grand Opera was proposed, and the idea enthusiastically hailed by all present, particularly by Mme Eudes, who saw in it an occasion to bring forward her talented protegé—Pugno. But there were more serious reasons than this for giving a concert. A fund had to be raised for the sick and wounded; the musicians of Paris so long without employment were to be given an opportunity to earn something; and last, not least, the adherents of the modern school of music sought an opportunity to press their claims. For at that time the library of the Grand Opera did not yet possess a single score by Berlioz and the general state of music in France was really deplorable. Thus the proposed concert was to serve two benevolent purposes, and a highly ideal one. It was to inaugurate a new era of music in France. Pugno was appointed its artistic manager, and was authorized to confer with Perrin, the director of the Grand Opera.

It is but natural that this man, who had so long wielded the scepter there, was reluctant to help an enterprise which was about to bring other men to the foreground. He created difficulty after difficulty; but the enthusiasm once roused was not to be silenced. Pugno and Selmer would not allow the opportunity to slip by, to have their works performed by such forces as the Grand Opera had at its disposal. In the meantime Mme Ugalde, directress of the Bouffes Parisiennes, a woman with magnificent voice, but considerably *passé*, had heard of the proposed concert, and decided to turn it to her advantage. There was a chance for her to appear once more before a large audience; there was also an occasion to instal a cousin, Eugene Garnier, in an influential position. She wrote to Cournet, the successor of Raoul Rigaul, proposing a reorganization of the Grand Opera, and the appointment of Garnier as director, and offered not only her own services to Pugno, but also the financial support of a banker friend, Monsieur Destables. The latter was something not to be discarded; under such circumstances the vocal ruin of Madame could be accepted in the bargain,—and as to Garnier, should he obtain Perrin's place, after the concert he would be disposed of. A meeting took place between Mme Ugalde, Garnier, Destables, Regnard, Levraud and Pugno at the residence of the former in the Chaussée d'Antin. There the programme was decided upon and a resolution was taken to push the scheme of the concert by applying to those connected with the government. The result of this movement became apparent in an announcement which was published May 9, in the *Journal Officiel*. It read as follows:

"The undersigned member of the Commune, delegate to the *Comité de Sûreté Général* and department of the Interior, declares:—

Whereas notwithstanding the present crisis art and artists must not suffer in Paris,

Whereas Citizen Perrin, director of the Opera, has not only done nothing to alleviate the trouble, but has beset with obstacles the plan of a grand national enterprise, a concert for the benefit of the musicians of Paris and the victims of the war, Be it herewith resolved:

1. That Citizen Perrin be dismissed.

2. That Citizen Eugene Garnier be appointed in his place, to act provisorily as director of the national theatre and opera.

3. That a committee be appointed to watch over the interests of music and musicians, consisting of citizens Cournet, Regnard, Lefébvre-Roncier, Raoul Pugno, Edmond Levraud and J. Selmer.

The delegate, etc., Cournet.

When Monsieur Perrin heard of his dismissal he thought he was to be arrested for mismanagement, and pretending to have gone travelling he hid in his residence. Soon however he learned that nothing was asked of him but to vacate the sumptuous apartments he occupied in the Grand Opera, and it must have been an intensely comic scene when the lank, cross-eyed man, who would have made a *distingué* impression had he not used so much perfume, came out of his hiding place to receive his successor, the dudish Eugene Garnier, type of the Paris *boulevardier*, who with great dignity took possession of his new office. Pugno and Selmer were thus relieved of a great many irksome duties, which must have been particularly distasteful to Pugno, who, it was rumored, spent his leisure in a distant *hotel garni* of the Rue La Roquette, where Mme Eudes received him.

The date of the concert approached. It was to take place Monday, the 22nd of May. The programme read as follows:

Overture: Carnival of Rome.................Berlioz.
Hymne aux Immortels, d'après V. Hugo.... Pugno.
2nd act from La Juive. ... Halevy.
Scène funèbre.. .... Selmer.
Patria. ... Beethoven.
Scène... Litolff.

2nd act from Don Juan......................Mozart.
Vive la liberté..............................Gossec.

George Hainl, the orchestra conductor of the Grand Opera, was summoned from his country retreat and arrived in Paris, May 16. Duvivier took charge of the chorus. Richard, a promising young tenor, had presented himself. The scenery was ready. When the rehearsals began, the difficulty of some of the selections necessitated some changes in the programme, but as this was to be only the first in a series of concerts, it did not discourage our optimistic young musicians. The last rehearsal was fixed upon Sunday, May 21. Intense was the excitement of the artists and their friends. Saturday, rose-red bills of gigantic size were posted at all available places in Paris. The rehearsal went on to general satisfaction in the presence of a number of prominent members of the Commune. All were in high spirits.

In the meantime another concert was preparing within the walls of Paris. From three sides the Versaillais had entered the city. The next day, by the time the orchestra was to strike the opening chords of Berlioz' work, the participants in the great musical enterprise were dispersed in all directions. The concert never took place. Paris resounded with the roar of cannon and the crash of bomb-shells. Early on Tuesday morning, Mme Eudes rushed into Selmer's room and implored Raoul Pugno to flee with her. He refused—to regret in a little while after she had disappeared. The Paris papers brought the news that the beautiful heroine of the Commune was killed on the barricades, musket in hand—but the statement was never verified. Raoul Rigault's life also ended that day. Regnard and Levraud fled from the fury of the Versaillais. Pugno, Selmer and their German friend remained in Paris at the peril of their lives. The latter went to America a year later and died there. Selmer has since resided alternately in Germany and Norway, and has earned a reputation as composer. I have had many an interesting letter from him on musical topics. Pugno I had not heard of until now.

A. Von Ende.

BEETHOVEN'S NOTE-BOOK OF 1803.

IN the Royal Library in Berlin is a sketch-book which lays claim in a more than ordinary degree, to the attention of the interested. It belongs to the days when a change took place in Beethoven's style, and contains the sketches, nearly complete, of a work, which, as the most important of that time, is especially fitted to illustrate the complete transition from one musical epoch to another, and to furnish material for the study of the transition. From the phenomena which this sketch book offers, deductions may be drawn of great importance in the histories of Beethoven's style and of his ways of working. The value which attaches to this sketch-book is also a demand that the following Exposition may be as thorough as possible. Brief extracts would avail but little. In order to observe the development, the genesis, the growth, the taking-on of form, of the work in question, it has been found necessary to present the needful sketches as completely as possible. Not only the beginning and the end of the creative process must be shown, but also those successive stages through which the work actually passed. The extracts must suffice, by fullness, to convince the reader. On later pages will be given the conclusions that may be drawn from this sketch-book.

The book in question is an oblong folio, consists of 182 pages, partly with 16, partly with 18 staves on the page, was bound properly by a bookbinder, has a stiff pasteboard cover, and was in this condition when Beethoven began to write in it. With the exception of six or seven blank pages and one page written upon with a lead pencil, the pages are all written in ink. Consequently Beethoven must have used it altogether indoors. Apart from five pages which have been torn out, it is today as perfect as when Beethoven ceased to use it. Before page 1, and between pages 2 and 3, four leaves are missing. But from page 3 onward, no interruption of the sketches occurs.

From the dates which one may attach to certain compositions in this sketch-book, it appears that this book was written in, if not wholly, at least in the greater part, during the year 1803. In attempting to fix the dates more closely one meets, however, with difficulties. The majority of the dates which have been handed down to us, are too late; they refer either to the time when a clean-copy was made, or to the appearance of the work itself, or they are in part too inadequately supported by proof to serve as a sure basis for argument. One hesitates between probability and presumability. Taking into account all the facts in the case, and with the qualification that at least nine months must have elapsed before the pages first to last were covered, we may say that this sketch-book was used by Beethoven between October 1802 and April 1804.

It is not necessary to discuss the peculiar phenomena which Beethoven's sketch-books in general present, nor his ways of working. Sufficient has been said on this point elsewhere. (Translator's Note; from *A Sketch-Book by Beethoven;* G. Nottebohm, Breitkopf and Haertel, 1865: "The sketches in a Beethoven sketch-book are mostly written on one line, that is on one staff, rarely on two or more. We observe in general, that Beethoven went to work in the most diverse ways, often in ways diametrically opposite, one to the other. Such differences become evident to one on studying the sketches of several movements based on the same form, and on comparing them. In one set of sketches the thematic procedure rules; the first sketch breaks off with the leading subject, and there follows transformation after transformation of this thematic germ, until it seems ready for development. Then the same thing is done with the middle measures. At every hand we find only beginnings, never a whole. The whole we find in the printed composition. There the parts which in the sketch-book were in scattered fragments, appear as collective entities. In the other set of sketches, thematic and mosaic work is excluded. Every sketch gives an entity. The first sketch contains a perfect and self-existant whole; the following are complete re-writings of this whole, or versions, having modifications of the total character; or a development of the middle subject. These two ways are the most unlike possible. It is natural that the majority of the sketches do not belong to either manner, exclusively, but approach one another.") One thing must however be considered. There is no doubt that the compositions in a Beethoven sketch-book were begun in the order of their occurrence in the book itself. But the pages were not written upon in their numerical order. Beethoven had the habit when he began a new piece, of starting on a new page and of leaving a number of the foregoing pages blank, for the continuation or completion of the foregoing piece. When, in working simultaneously or alternately at two compositions, the pages of the latter piece became all written upon, it often happened that recourse was had to foregoing blank pages, so that at last the sketches of several compositions became mixed, one with the other. But this crossing of the groups of sketches does not always justify the conclusion that the sketches appearing first in the numerical order of pages, were the first sketches written. A case of this sort occurs in the beginning of this sketch-book.

Whenever variants—differing versions—of the same sketch appear, the variants are indicated by being added, in part over the places where they belong, or, in part, by being brought-in later, the divided syllables of the word *Vi-de*, or the words *or*, *or* showing the points of connection. Whenever the word *etc.* appears after an extract, it comes from Beethoven's own manuscript. Sketches given by us only in part, bear the words—*and so forth*. Those of doubtful orthography, are marked with an interrogation point. Many notes in the original are without the proper chromatic signs; the reader may supply these himself. In the *Remarks* which close this work, material, chronologic and biographic, is to be found. Here it is that the reader may acquaint himself with a chronologic fact which we owe to this sketch-book, despite the other chronologic uncertainties of the book itself. Furthermore, it must be said that when in the exposition of the sketches it becomes necessary to show the end Beethoven had, or may have had, in his mind's eye, recourse must be had to the printed work itself. For we should often find the path of abstraction too unsafe if it were followed, and the printed copy permits not even a shadow of doubt.

We now begin with the sketch book itself.

On the first page we find sketches of unknown works

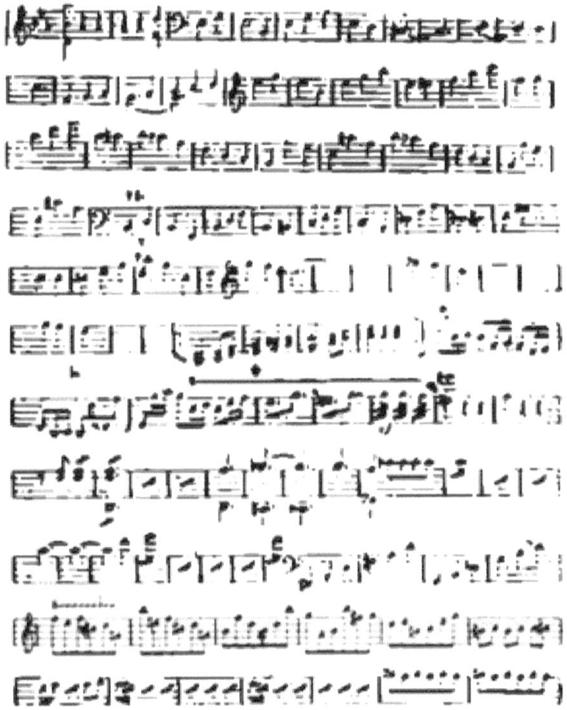

FIGURE 1

among them the beginning of a song—"*Zur Erde sank die Ruh'*" vom Himmel nieder—and (pp. 2, 3, 5) sketches for the variations for pianoforte on the theme—"Rule

Britannia." The latter resemble the sketches of similar variations by Beethoven. At first a number of different motives are written-down as the basis of the variations, in most cases the opening measures; later-on, some of these motives are worked out. (Remarks, 1.)

Between and directly after these sketches appear (pp. 3 to 10) short disconnected sketches for the first, second, and fourth movements of the Heroic Symphony, which however were penned later than the sketches which immediately follow them. To these we will refer on a later page.

The sketches which now follow (pp. 10 to 41) belong almost exclusively to the first movement of the Third Symphony. No single sketch, giving the complete first movement is to be found. The longest sketches that occur, refer only to a part of the movement. Four greater sketches, each with its own variants, and a large number of smaller sketches, are those which deal with the first part.

The first of these greater sketches (p. 11.) (Figure 1.) which breaks off abruptly shortly before the end of the part to which it belongs, is the best fitted, of all the sketches in hand, to illustrate the point at which the work stood when Beethoven began to write in this book. It shows that the work was already partly advanced. Consequently the beginning must have been made elsewhere. Indeed, it is possible that we have here before us the first connected extended sketch of the first part of this movement, in which are combined the short sketches of some previous sketch-book. In the first half of the sketch the more important themes and motives are indicated more or less clearly. The closest agreement with the final, that is the printed form, is shown (mar. 3) in the beginning of the leading

FIGURE 2.

subject, and (mar. 55) in the melody of the first subordinate subject. On the other hand, with the exceptions of a few motives, the second part is still in the faraway. The modulatory plan is in general established and the succession of themes and passages is on the whole settled upon, although they by no means have taken their final form. Let us now follow the changes which the separate parts and their constituents were destined to go through.

The first two measures (Figure 2) were later on changed by Beethoven. In all the following sketches which deal with the beginning of this first part, these two measures appear neither in their original nor in their altered form; nor do the two introductory chords

Figure 3.

which one finds in the score occur anywhere. So it seems that the latter were added after the movement had been finished in the sketches.

If, in regard to the way the leading subject was handled, we compare this sketch with the score, we observe amongst other things that in the sketch the leading subject is given the third time in B flat major, while in the score it stands in E flat major. An agreement with the printed reading is shown in a variant of this sketch (p. 10), (Figure 3) and also in the second greater sketch (p. 12), (Figure 4) But Beethoven did not follow the way opened by these sketches. In two sketches, to be given later, (pp. 14 and 20) the leading subject is brought in four times, and the fourth time in B flat major again. It seems easy to find a reason why Beethoven at last abandoned this frequent repetition of the theme and its use in B flat major. Three presentations of the theme sufficed to impress it upon the memory, and the anticipation of the B flat tonality would have weakened the following entrance of the subordinate

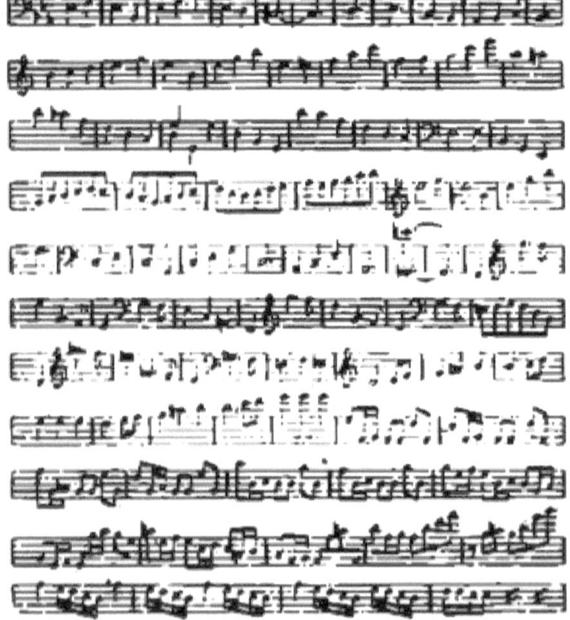

FIGURE 4

part in the same key.

In the first four measures of the variant just given, a motive may be seen which (by the prolongation of its tenth note) was destined to find employment in the second part of the movement in question, and which of itself formed an element of contrast to the repose of the leading subject. In the third greater sketch (p. 15 onward), (Figure 5) the motive has undergone a change; but the 2-4 measure rhythm is adhered to, and in the fourth greater sketch (p. 20 onward), (Figure 6) the so effective syncopations have also made an appearance. Herewith the leading subject, in all its essentials, can be considered as finished. The sketch-book contains no more sketches which can be referred to this part of the composition.

The transition from the leading subject to the first

subordinate subject,—which in the first greater sketch (meas. 43 to 54), and in its variant, may be found to be imperfect and to consist of a motive made-up mostly of quarter notes,—was given in the second greater sketch the rhythmic motive on which it is now based. Beethoven may have considered the motive in its earlier form as inappropriate, because its even quarter notes unfitted it for separating the themes of the leading and first subordinate

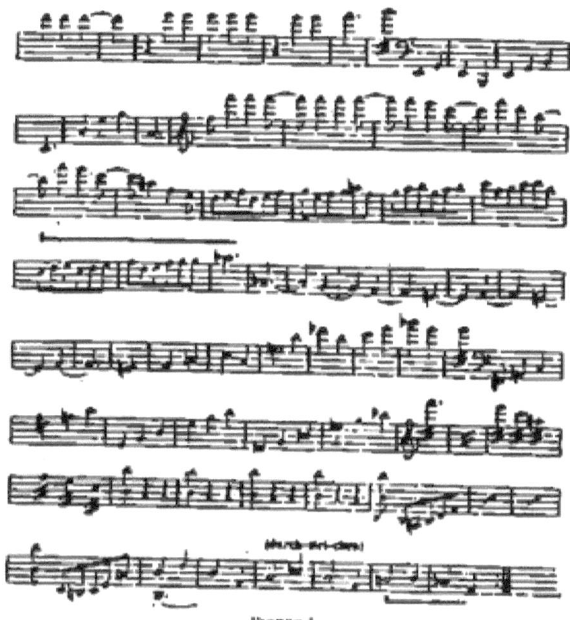

Figure 5.

subjects, both of which contained quarter notes themselves. In the third and fourth greater sketches, by leading the motive differently, the final form was at last approached and then essentially arrived at.

As the last sketches go to show, the melody of the first subordinate subject needed but few changes to bring it into its final form. On the other hand, the passage which connects it with the second subordinate subject required much time before Beethoven found that curved outline, and that extension by which we recognize it. As it appeared in the first greater sketch (mrs. 59 onward) there was much to be done with it. It is noticeable that in nearly all the sketches devoted to the working out of this place, however they may differ from the first sketch, there still remains the rhythmic motive of this same first sketch. In the second greater sketch, the treatment of the motive

FIGURE 6.

differs from that of the first greater sketch. Nevertheless the passage moves by hitches. This and other faults affect a few lesser sketches, which we pass over. The passage appears nearest the printed form in the third and fourth greater sketches. But in the former the ending was unsatisfactory, and in the latter that onward impulse from the beginning which belongs to the nature of the passage, as a passage, is retarded in the middle by the repetition of a measure.

[TO BE CONTINUED.]

From the German of Gustav Nottebohm.

Translated by BENJAMIN CUTLER.

ANTOINE RUBINSTEIN.

Seeking the perfect of his soul, that Love
  From which it sprung, he journeyed Heaven-ward,
Sending to us in music what he heard,
  The awe-compelling message from above.

And Sinai climbing, prophet-like, to learn
  The beauties of the Everlasting Word,
Sent back to earth a wonder-tale that stirred
  Us each to hasten upward in his turn.

With giant strides he climbed, and roughly hewed
  A Titan stairway to the grand Ideal,
Up which we struggled slowly but to feel
  A tithe the passion that his soul imbued.

But lo, when we had almost seemed to hear
  The voice that told such raptures, far on high
A cloud has gathered over all the sky,
  Obscured the upward path, and hid the seer.

JOHN L. MATHEWS.

ANTOINE RUBINSTEIN.

WHEN the great heart of Rubinstein ceased to beat, November 20, 1894, the last of the virtuosi of the fathers was lost to earth. An interesting and a picturesque character, was this great Russian, full of virtues and noble qualities, gifted as few men in any generation ever are, he died nevertheless a saddened, a disappointed man. It was another case of the contradiction of fate. A whole world bowed down in homage to the interpreter and the virtuoso, while at the same time refusing to grant the far more prized homage to creative talents of a very high order, if not even of genius of the first order. It was the lot of this great man to live in a wrong time. His was the distinction of the pioneer, who aided in developing the latent talents of his loved country, but not his to create a music accepted as national in the strict sense, still less his to create a music accepted by the great world of humanity as expressing its hearts, or any great part thereof. Nor yet was it smooth sailing for the great master even in his own country, where at first sight honors appeared to be showered upon him thick and fast. For Rubinstein was only partly a Russian. His Hebrew lineage and heredity allied him to that remarkable portion of mankind which, having in every generation exercised a controlling influence in the world's affairs entirely disproportioned to their relative numbers, has had to accept substantial regards in basket and store along with contumely and misrepresentation and ostracism to a degree. This was what befell Rubinstein in that Jew hating land, bigoted and ignorant Russia.

Yet it would be a great mistake to accept Rubinstein as a representative of advanced ideas in music. On the contrary, in the honor of the classical he went out to gain a meed of honor in a century of the sensational and the exaggerated. Wagner he hated as heartily as Wagner hated the Jews. And while ostensibly governed by the principles of classic composition, he nevertheless attempted the impossible in developing themes according to ideas not consistent with the older or the more recent school. The pianoforte dominated everything which Rubinstein composed. It was a pianoforte of limited thematic capacity, massive chords, dreary working out, and episodes which led nowhere. Among the long list of his compositions in classical form, consisting of trios, quartettes, concertos, symphonies, overtures, and operas, there is not one which is wholly satisfactory; nor yet is there one which does not show trace of a highly musical nature, and of creative gifts far above mediocrity. The man was rugged and self determined in everything that he undertook, and it was not his to sing with Schubert, or even to bring out the inner things of this world of sound with Beethoven or Schumann. Even in the instrument which he knew best of all, the pianoforte, he is rarely at peace with himself. Such a sympathetic working out of a theme as we find again and again in the works of Schumann or Chopin, it is impossible to find in the compositions of Rubinstein. They are deserts of tones. Beautiful oases there are, richly foliaged and shining like eyes of immortality, but they are only oases, and their surroundings are arid in the extreme. It is curious also that notwithstanding the fact of his mastery of the pianoforte, in which he stood above any man living ten years ago, he nowhere in his works produces a single composition of such fortunate character and of such inherent suitability to the genius of the instrument as to render it indispensible to the student. Neither as technical exercises nor as tone poetry are Rubinstein's pianoforte compositions to be placed above thousands of others, by masters far less highly gifted. Was this by reason of his head, or of his heart? Was it that the mixed heredity and contradictory nationality of his origin stood in his way, and never permitted him to arrive at free and reposeful self-consciousness? Why should Rubinstein with his mighty gifts and his opportunities attain a lower place in Russian music than his contemporary Glinka, or the younger master, his own pupil, Tschaikowsky? These are questions which it is easier to ask than to answer.

The salient facts of his career are briefly recounted. Born in 1829, Nov. 30th (new style) in an obscure village on the boundaries of Russia, his family removed to Moscow when the child was an infant. To this circumstance, apparently, the world owes its possession of this great genius. Taught early by his mother, and by an intelligent teacher named Villoing, the boy developed so rapidly that in 1839 he appeared as wonder-child, playing pieces by Hummel, Thalberg, Liszt, Field and Henselt. He was warmly applauded and the local papers spoke of his clear tone. When his talent had become thus unmistakable, his mother desired to send him to Paris to the conservatory, but there he was refused admission, just as Liszt had been seventeen years earlier, and as the American Gottschalk was a few years later. After a year in Paris, still under the instruction of Villoing, but hearing Chopin and Liszt, he spent a year or two in concert tours, and was well received in England and elsewhere. Enough money was made to help his father, and in 1844 the family reached Berlin, in order that Antoine, and his younger brother Nicholas, should have the advantage of instruction in composition. At the age of sixteen the boy was turned loose upon the world to carve his fortune, and right tough was the carving for quite a long time. In 1847 he started with the flutist Heindl to emigrate to America, and got as far as Berlin where his former teacher of composition, the theorist Dehn, dissuaded him, and the young man resolved to remain in Berlin. But the revolution of 1848 was impending and absolute want of business drove Rubinstein back again to St. Petersburg. It is whimsically told of his business there that he adapted his price of lessons to the pockets of the pupils, whereby some had the lessons at a rouble an hour, while others paid him as high as twenty-five. Of his operas composed during these years, several being brought out in St. Petersburg. Rubinstein always considered that their non-success was determined by the execrable quality of the singing which was done in them. One of them, "The Demon," made a great success later, and has just reached its two-hundredth performance in St. Petersburg.

In 1854 he spent some months at Weimar with Liszt, and his distinguished successes as concert pianist should be dated from about 1857. His American tour took place in 1872 and '73. The 215 concerts brought him in the then unprecedented sum of about $44,000. A considerable part of this work was done in connection with Mr. Theodore Thomas. His first recitals in Chicago were given early in 1873 in the theater which then stood on Wabash avenue, near the present site of the Auditorium. Later in the season he played with Mr. Thomas in concerts given farther from the heart of the city (the rebuilding after the great fire having not yet rehabilitated the central district) and in the Union Park Congregational church he played the Beethoven fifth concerto to Mr. Thomas' accompaniment with truly astonishing effect. The second movement in particular was delightfully done.

Rubinstein's prosperity dated from his American tour, and his later years were filled with honors in Russia until latterly, when the old time antipathy against the Jews came uppermost. He taught and composed for the honor of the art—and for the good of students. While refusing concert offers of the most brilliant description (in 1891 an offer for an American tour of $125,000) and playing only for charity, he nevertheless gave frequent lecture recitals for the benefit of pupils, and played a great series of historic recitals in all the great European capitals, about two years ago. These were in fabulous demand, but the great master repeated each program for students only, free of charge.

As is generally known, Rubinstein was a player of masterful moods. His touch was delightfully expressive, and while he had enormous power and upon occasion could, and did, pound terribly, in his best moments, whether upon the side of delicacy and deep tenderness, or in cyclonic moods like the "raptus" of Beethoven, he was a player without a peer in his way. His enormous memory he often abused, playing as many as five of the greater Beethoven sonatas at a sitting—a feat not colossal for the player, but terrible for the listener. While comparison has no place in art, the question whether Rubinstein was not as great a player as Liszt, or even greater, is one more easily asked than answered. Upon the whole, however, it seems quite certain from the testimony of all the artists who came under the personal influence of Liszt that no one of the younger men possessed a tithe of his powers as pianist. Dr. Mason says that Liszt could do anything upon the piano, whereas all these others were great in provinces only. This appears also certain from the testimony of the works they left. Liszt must have had a far finer intuition of musical effect, and a vastly greater catholicity of taste, than the gifted Russian, as appears in the original compositions for the pianoforte, and still more in the numberless arrangements, which cover so many phases of musical literature, and at times with so colossal a cleverness and so deep an intuition of the capacity of the piano—that they remain equally grateful as technical studies for students and as tone poetry for music lovers. To this class belong Liszt's numberless arrangements of the Beethoven symphonies, the Schubert and Schumann songs, the Bach organ pieces, and the like, not to mention the lighter and more brilliant rhapsodies and operatic arrangements. Nothing of this is found in Rubinstein.

Moreover, it must have been this inner something of cosmopolitan sympathy in Liszt which made his attitude towards the new composers, Berlioz, Wagner, and the others, so different from that of Rubinstein. In this respect Rubinstein was a Hebrew of the Hebrews, trying everything new by the law of Moses. The law, the classical law of form, was to him the end of onward movement.

And so while Rubinstein was a man of positive character, full of ideas, strong and honest, deep in his sympathies, he was also opinionated and resolute and uncompromising. Everything had to go his way, and he did not so much as take the trouble to examine another way, if by chance it might have been better. Mason tells how when he and Mills had to prepare the Bach triple concerto with Rubinstein, Mason, foreseeing differences regarding the mordents, took under his arm the clavier book of Emanuel Bach, in which he carefully illustrates the manner in which his father intended the mordents to be played. When the passage occurred containing the first, the three artists played them each in a different way. Then Mason called a halt and proposed that all play them in the same manner, and in order to settle doubt as to which *was* the manner, he produced his book. Whereupon Rubinstein said, "What is that?" and cast a glance over the examples, but went on immediately "This is how *I* play them," and the other two had to follow his way, and it was not the way of Emanuel Bach nor yet of the great Sebastian himself. *Ex pede Herculem.* This was Rubinstein "from within," as German educators say.

Such a man is more interesting than a smooth and pliant character, and story, like the caressing ivy, loves to twine itself around such a rugged trunk. From a number of sources we have interesting reminiscences of Rubinstein.

W. S. B. M.

DR. MASON ON RUBINSTEIN'S TOUCH.

It is with pleasure that I notice in a late issue of *The Musical Courier*, October 10, that you call renewed attention to the article entitled "Piano Touch," by Alexander McArthur, published in your issue of October 3. This subject is of transcendent importance to piano students, who as a rule, give it but little practical attention, and turn all their efforts in the direction of getting a mechanical technic, neglecting or postponing the cultivation of a habit of musical and emotional touch.

It is never too early to begin to cultivate and persist in the practice of that peculiar manner of touch which leads to the development of beauty, color and singing quality of tone, as this is far more to be desired than mere mechanical technic and finger skill; and really, if it is only properly cultivated and persistently followed up, it brings with it and leads constantly to the acquirement of a technic which at the same time is musical and poetical, thus far above and beyond mere machine effects.

The mechanical pianos, which have recently been brought to such a degree of perfection, are really in their way quite astonishing, and they excite very pleasurable sensations on the part of those who are somewhat superficial in their musical perceptions. They present, too, in perfection—so far as relates to mechanism—certain features which are universally acknowledged by piano players to be of the highest importance. By illustration, in one way only a perfect mechanical legato is attained on these instruments. The adjustment and action of the machinery is so exact and perfect that there can be no other result. It is simply a mathematical problem, so easy of demonstration that there can be no dispute about it. It is perfect as is humanly possible. But this result, although perfectly attained in the machine, is not what the musician longs for. The mechanical legato, being simply and naturally the product of a machine, is entirely devoid of heart qualities and lacks sympathetic and musical tenderness. The musical and emotional legato and tone beauty resulting from the genuine musical temperament is the real thing, the rare thing; the thing beyond all others to be desired, and the serious question is, how is this to be attained? In its highest manifestation it is only possible to a thoroughly musical temperament, such as, for instance, that of Anton Rubinstein, about whose wonderfully beautiful touch Mr. McArthur had so much to say.

It is, however, possible of attainment in degree, provided students will give it a really earnest, diligent and persevering attention, such as implied by these words of Rubinstein, viz.: "Strength and lightness—that is one secret of my touch—the other, assiduous study in my early manhood. I have sat hours trying to imitate the timbre of Rubini's voice in my playing, and it is only with labor and tears bitter as death that the artist arrives at perfection. Few understand this, consequently there are few artists." This language seems extravagant, but it is true, and right here is the secret of the thing. Intensity, determination, assiduity and unceasing perseverance in the direction of the desired end—not in some other direction—and this, too, must not be delayed until after a merely dry, mechanical technic has become so deeply rooted and ingrained as to have formed a stubborn habit of absolute musical negation on the part of the player, and driven all of the poetry out of him. But it must be from the very beginning onward, or as Rubinstein puts it—"In my early manhood." It was my privilege to make the acquaintance of Rubinstein at this period of his life, namely, during the early part of the year 1854, when he was but twenty-four years old, and this happened in a peculiarly pleasant way. He came to Weimar by special invitation to visit Liszt; but at the time of his arrival Liszt, with most of his pupils, who numbered not more than five all told in those days, happened to be absent from home for a few days in attendance on some musical festival, of which he had the charge. For some reason I alone had stayed at home, and under these circumstances it devolved upon me to do the honors, thus affording a most favorable opportunity of forming a very desirable acquaintanceship.

Rubinstein spent several months with Liszt in the latter's own home, and during this period there were many opportunities of becoming thoroughly familiar with his playing under all moods and circumstances. We were constantly delighted with the beauty, power, nobility, ardor and intensity of his touch. His playing was inspired, and thus entirely free from stiffness and conventionality, and it was colored with a peculiar warmth and geniality of tone, so to speak, which was characteristic of him. He showed me many curious and original things which he did in order to cultivate his technic, such as for instance, playing the right hand part of many of Chopin's etudes with the left hand alone, or with both hands in unison, or vice versa, playing the left-hand part with the right hand alone. Of course this manner of playing needed some readjustment or slight change in some of the passages. But throughout all of this practice, be it noted, the poetical part—the musical phrasing, the nuances, the expression and beauty of tone—was ever and always present, and no amount of technic or mechanical effort ever drove this out of his head for a moment. Whatever his special motive or object in practice for the time being, his playing, in mere exercises for technic, was invariably and always poetic, sympathetic, emotional and full of temperament.

WILLIAM MASON.

From *The Musical Courier.*

AUTOGRAPHS OF RUBINSTEIN.

The theme first appears in the major mode and is marked "Allegro." It is vigorous and robust in character, suggesting the energy and ambition of youth and determination of early manhood. This was written in Weimar, Germany in the year 1854. "Nineteen years later in another world," as Rubinstein has written underneath the foregoing, he repeats the theme but this time in the minor mode and marking it "Adagio," thus completely changing its character. It has now lost its brightness and vigor and gives the idea that the top of the hill has been reached and the descent begun, and Rubinstein calls attention to the fact by his words "not the same."

Rubinstein at first strenuously objected to putting in his signature a second time and persisted for quite a while in refusing to write it, but finally took his pen and wrote as just been described.

W. M.

(From Dr. Mason's Book of Autographs. Specially reproduced for Music.)

WILLIAM STEINWAY'S REMINISCENCES OF RUBINSTEIN.

In a recent Sunday's "Herald" there was printed a most interesting interview with Mr. Maurice Grau relating to Mr. Anton Rubinstein's engagement by Mr. Grau's uncle, Jacob Grau, which was perfected during the spring of 1872—the gentleman whom Mr. Grau describes as being too modest to have his name mentioned as having made the necessary deposit in Vienna—I hope that he will not call me immodest when I complete his tale by stating that I am the gentleman in question, having deposited with Mr. Rubinstein's banker there, Herr Biederman, the necessary funds in United States gold bonds. Mr. Maurice Grau took the place of his uncle, who was very ill and, in fact, bed-ridden, and, although barely twenty-one years old at the time, managed Mr. Rubinstein's *tournée* with great skill. Mr. Grau has certainly always been a very hard and successful worker.

On Tuesday, September 10, 1872, Rubinstein and Wieniawski, the celebrated violinist, arrived on the steamer Cuba and immediately called on me, inspected Steinway Hall, and expressed themselves as delighted with its acoustic properties.

His first concert took place on Monday evening, September 23, 1872, and not only was Steinway Hall with its 2,400 seats packed to the doors but people stood upon chairs all through the performance, and many were unable to enter the building at all. It was as hot as midsummer, and all the windows had been thrown open. Never in my life, either before or after that night, have I been privileged to see all the literary and musical artists assembled in such numbers. Artists had come from all over the country in thousands. From one of the boxes leaned Anna Mehlig, the celebrated pianist, who had come expressly all the way from California for the occasion. A magnificent orchestra under the late Karl Bergman's baton assisted. The first number played by Mr. Rubinstein was his own Piano Concerto in D minor, No. 4. The enthusiasm of the audience as they listened to Anton Rubinstein's magnificent composition increased as he progressed, and as he infused his own powerful individuality into his hearers the scene was simply indescribable. At the close of the piece he was recalled again and again. Henry Wieniawski also achieved an immense success. Later in the evening Mr. Rubinstein played his smaller pieces, such as the march from "The Ruins of Athens," his own "Barcarolle" and "Valse Caprice," and the enthusiasm and appreciation of his intelligent audience grew greater and greater. No artist who has appeared since has ever achieved—at least to my knowledge—a success like Rubinstein's. His titanic, overpowering individuality as an executant and as a composer were fully demonstrated before the close of that memorable evening.

One laughable incident of that night I remember well. Just as Rubinstein was playing a pianissimo passage in his concerto, a terrible howl was heard through the open windows of the eastern side of Steinway Hall, while from the western side of the building arose a fearful noise much like the sound of splitting wood. At a beseeching look from the artist I rushed out and sent two trusted employees, who had been in charge of the door, to investigate. The gift of a dollar each to two colored gentlemen—for such the disturbers proved to be, one of whom was endeavoring to teach an old dog new tricks, the other who was effectually splitting his next morning's kindlings promptly caused an immediate cessation of the disturbance, and happiness was once more restored to every one in the hall, including the great artist himself.

The next day Mr. Rubinstein came in to see me, bearing in his arms a large bag full of gold and silver. He then told me that having heard in Europe that the majority of the people in America were "rascals" and that their paper currency in most instances was not good he had exacted in his contract that his money should be paid him in specie semi-monthly in advance. The first two weeks' salary be-was holding in his arms, and did not have the least idea what to do with it. I explained the depreciated currency to him, told him the system was at any rate better than in Russia, where it was at a discount of sixty per cent, and advised him promptly to sell his specie. I eventually did it for him, and opened an account in his name at the Bank of the Metropolis, which has ever been what one might call a musical bank since its establishment. I noticed at the same time that his face was quite puckered and seemed much inflamed, and upon my asking him how he had thus far been impressed with the country, "Well, quite favorably," he replied dolefully, "the people are educated, have musical taste, are hospitable, but these small black flies that bite a man all day and all night, are almost unbearable!" The sequel showed that he had practiced till very late at night at the piano and had left the window open on account of the heat. He was then at the Clarendon Hotel, Seventeenth street and Fourth avenue, and the burning gas, less than the beautiful music, perhaps, had attracted swarms of mosquitoes into his room. On my advice the windows remained closed thereafter and he suffered no more in the future from "those small black flies."

The series of concerts that he gave in New York went on with ever increasing success. It ended on Friday, October 12, 1872, and then the whole troupe which, though numerous, held only pigmies as compared with the giants Rubinstein and Wieniawski, started on a tour through the country, which began at the Boston Music Hall, on Monday evening, October 14, 1872. It scored everywhere a great artistic, and in the larger cities a financial success, as well. Mr. Rubinstein began to suffer intensely under the terms of his American contract, which called upon him to play seven times a week! He became very much downcast, and this mood is reflected in several letters, which I have, and which were written to me at that time; personal conversations held with him later confirmed the fact. Having to play every night and to repeat practically the same program, to travel by night on the primitive affairs then called sleeping cars—all this was simply torture to him, and drove him literally to despair. Not only was Anton Rubinstein one of the greatest artists the world has ever seen—he was at the same time one of the purest, most unselfish and honest men that I ever knew. The value of money did not exist for him, and he was a man of the most generous and noble impulses. His fealty to duty, therefore, made him patiently bear all the toils and trials attendant upon traveling the long distances between our American cities. But all through the remainder of his life, while he bore the kindliest feelings toward the American people, and paid glowing tribute to their enthusiasm for music, he never spoke without a shudder of the tortures he had suffered, not only on the sea voyages but also during this enforced traveling by land, with the primitive railroad conveniences of those days. This is the chief reason why he never made a contract to go to America without inserting the clause that, up to a certain date he might retract, and when the date came he invariably did retract.

Before he left New York for his *tournée* through the country, he called at Steinway Hall one afternoon about five o'clock for his mail. A bulky registered letter had come for him, and it contained letters from his children, a long letter from his wife, and newly-taken photographs of his family. The tears came to his eyes as he said to me, "Friend Steinway, I feel so happy that I must play for you!" Meantime, it had grown late, and everything was closed for the day. Four other musical gentlemen whom he knew personally, had come in, and the doors were closed, when he sat down at the grand Steinway piano to play for us. Twelve o'clock at night still found us there, spell-bound, for such heavenly music we had never heard before. Then and only then, I realized what four celebrated men could do. Goethe, who wrote the poem of the "Erl King;" Franz Schubert, who had composed the melody; Franz Liszt, who had transcribed it for pianoforte, and Anton Rubinstein, who could play it. At the risk of being called sentimental, I must say that on that memorable night it appeared to us as if we heard the voice of the little child, the clattering of the horse's hoofs, the wild entreaties of the Erl King as plainly as if we had witnessed it ourselves. And as I went home that night, I thought that truly that was a day that could never be repeated in all the course of my life. Now, all five of them, including the great artist are dead, and I alone remain. Only the remembrance survives, and that I shall carry to the grave with me.

I became, perhaps, his most trusted friend, and have often rejoiced in the fact that Anton Rubinstein and Theodore Thomas, whom I first brought together, became dearer to each other almost day by day.

On Friday, May 23, the day before his return to Europe, I spent almost all day with Rubinstein, and at 6 p. m., himself, Maurice Grau, my brother Albert, Gustav Schirmer and I, took supper together at the Café Brunswick. It was that day that Rubinstein spoke the following words

"Now, Mr. Steinway, I leave to-morrow. I have found in America something that I least expected to find. While I knew that first-class American pianos stand unexcelled by any in the world, I had no idea that such a new country had an orchestra like Theodore Thomas's. Never in my life, although I have given concerts in St. Petersburg, Vienna, Berlin, Paris, London and other great centres, have I found an orchestra that was as perfect as the organization Theodore Thomas has created and built up. When he accompanies me with his orchestra, it is as though he could divine my thoughts, and then as though his orchestra could divine his. It is as perfect as the work of some gifted pianist accompanying a singer with whom he has often rehearsed. I know of but one orchestra that can compare with that of Theodore Thomas, and that is the orchestra of the Imperial Academy of Paris, which was established by the first Napoleon in the year 1808, into which only artists, when young, are admitted; and they may have any number of rehearsals until they arrive at absolute perfection. It is that orchestra alone which is as perfect as Theodore Thomas's—but, alas, they have no Theodore Thomas to conduct them!"

Rubinstein sailed, as I said before, on Saturday, May 24, 1873, and although I read of his triumphs and exchanged a couple of letters with him, I did not see him again till 1892.

On Wednesday, September 14, 1892, I visited Dresden and received an invitation from him to call and see him at the hotel, the Europaeisches Hof. The twenty years which had elapsed since our last meeting seemed to have made no perceptible inroads upon his appearance. His hair was not yet gray, and he looked in the best of health. He received me in the most friendly manner, congratulated me upon my audience with their Majesties the Emperor and Empress of Germany, which had occurred the Sunday before, and said: "Now, friend Steinway, let us have a chat about America, the great country which I have never forgotten, and from which I receive almost weekly tokens of friendship in the shape of offers of engagements, offers of establishing a Rubinstein Conservatory, etc., etc.; but you see I do not even go to London any more, for the short trip from Calais to Dover means to me during those two hours a hell on earth. And yet I like England, as I like America. In both of these English speaking countries I have met with nothing but greatest liberality and hospitality and acts of friendship." After describing to him the immense progress made in America toward appreciating really good music, and that especially to the refinement and culture of our American ladies was due the high state of art and taste for music, I was staggered by Rubinstein's reply (he had meanwhile by the way, been granted the title of Excellency). "Well, friend Steinway," said he, "I think ladies ought never to study music as an art. At least they ought not to take up the time of teachers who are able to teach and make true artists. And I will tell you why," he added. "There is no question but that there are twenty musical ladies to one musical man, and my own experience is that they learn more quickly, have more poetry, and, in fact, are more diligent pupils than men. But what is the invariable result? When a young lady has become a perfect artist some handsome mustache comes along, and she chooses the handsome mustache in preference to her art." I need hardly say that I demurred somewhat at this, as I do not believe in the policy of relegating musical ladies to becoming old maids. I then learned from him that his favorite pupil, who was but twenty-one years of age, one of the most accomplished artists, and, to his idea, undoubtedly the greatest living lady pianist, had just announced to him her engagement to a handsome Russian officer.

He then informed me that the engagement with Messrs. Abbey, Schoeffel & Grau for $125,000 for fifty concerts had actually been made, but that the saving clause of being able to decline had been made use of by him on the first of July, 1892, and that he had then and there fully made up his mind never to cross the ocean again. I am certain that all rumors to the contrary were without foundation in fact.

On this occasion I also saw young Hoffmann there, who is now a young man between eighteen and nineteen years of age.

In Rubinstein's death the world of music and art has lost the last gigantic figure who could be mentioned in the same breath with the immortal Titans of a century past. He was indeed a great composer having written magnificent large orchestral tone pictures, operas, compositions for the pianoforte and most beautiful songs, and always being very prolific at that. The volume of any great master's compositions may be a matter of taste, but there can be no dissenting voice when I assert, that as an executant artist he has never been excelled, and in that respect, both as composer and executant artist, he stands almost unrivalled. His personal magnetism was almost indescribable. Though somewhat serious in his intercourse with people, he made friends of all whom he met. Add to that his sterling integrity as a man, his purity of character, his never-failing enthusiasm for his art, and the fact that he never broke his word—all these things render his death, at the comparatively early age of 64, a calamity to the world of music and art.

WILLIAM STEINWAY.

(From *Freund's Weekly*.)

THE LAST ILLNESS OF RUBINSTEIN.

"Owing to his sedentary habits combined with an over keen appetite, Rubinstein's disease developed into a general obesity of the system. The advice of physicians he never followed. He used to say, 'I love my physician as a man, but not as a physician.' In the last weeks he was frequently subject to fainting fits. In the second week of November Rubinstein complained of pain in the arm and the chest. His wife took fright and immediately sent for Dr. Vompe, but the composer refused to submit to an examination or to receive drugs. On the nineteenth of November, Dr. Vompe called again, in the evening; Rubinstein was sitting at his writing desk and finally consented to submit to an auscultation of the heart. However he merely removed the left flap of his coat and said: 'Very well, now listen!' 'I cannot hear your heart through your shirt and vest,' his physician protested. Rubinstein arose, buttoned up his coat and said: 'All right, we might as well play whist.' 'What about your heart?' the doctor exclaimed. 'You may hear it some other time,' replied Rubinstein, going. They then played whist until twelve o'clock. Rubinstein then, as was his custom took a glass of Xeres wine and went to bed. At two o'clock he was dead.

"The report of his sudden demise spread over Petergof with lightning speed, and reached St. Petersburg early in the morning. At one o'clock in the afternoon the first requiem mass was said in the conservatory, which remained closed for three days in token of grief. At half past six in the evening a special train of the Baltic railroad, engaged by the Czar's Russian Musical Society, left for Petergof carrying professors and teachers of the conservatory, directors of the musical society and students from the vocal department. The villa of the dead master was fully lighted. In the large white hall in the lower story the body lay on a catafalque draped in black. At the head there lay a group of exotic flowers; at the feet there were piled, on black cushions, all the honorary insignia and decorations of the deceased master. Several wreaths lay on the coffin. Rubinstein's face exhibited a happy smile; the lips were somewhat bluish. His white hands were crossed over his breast. At seven o'clock in the evening the ceremonies commenced, many residents of Petergof being present. The ritual songs were sung by the pupils of the conservatory. Touching was this parting of pupils and colleagues with their former master, as the plaintive chords filled the spacious white hall where the great master of tones lay dead.

"Dissection showed a highly developed brain with numerous convolutions. The master's studio, an octagonal chamber in the second story of the tower, will remain as it was when the master left it. Opposite the door is a writing desk, covered with a cloth of many black stains; on the desk there stand two candlesticks, a single inkstand of marble, and photographs of his children and his brother James. On the right there are two plain music-stands with a Turkish divan between them. In the corner on the left is a piano. In order that his play might not disturb his family, Rubinstein had the floor of his study underlined with sawdust. In one corner of the room stands a fine bronze statuette of the Goddess of Music—once presented to him by the French as a token of gratitude for his historical concerts. Rubinstein loved comfort though he was quite modest in his needs. He left only a small estate for he was of a charitable disposition and most of his concerts were given in the interest of charity."

Translated from a St. Petersburg paper, by

J. J. KRAL.

THE FUTURE OF MUSIC AND THE INNER LIFE OF MAN.

INDICATIONS are not wanting that great as is the importance of the art of music in the present state of civilized mankind, its office will be more important and its ministry more highly prized in the future, and to this progress no bounds can at present be set. It is true that many casual observers have an underlying notion that in all probability the art of music has reached its limits. Just as it is the custom in literary circles to speak of the writings of Shakespeare as beyond comparison with those of any other, and especially beyond comparison with those of the present day, so they speak of the music of Beethoven as beyond everything else, and especially finer than anything that can be produced at the present time, or is likely to be in the future. With this notion they combine another, derived from the general tone or the discussion concerning Wagner and the music of the future; that the continual introduction of discords, the multiplication of sounding apparatus in the orchestra, and the admitted necessity of associating the word with music in order to make it intelligible, when taken together are tantamount to a confession that all the good musical ideas have been written out, and that henceforth it is only a question of adding new instruments to the Beethoven scores, in order to furbish up the old things a little, and of producing new music fitted for extraordinary and spectacular occasions.

In further support of this general position, they point us to the admitted fact that to the ordinary musical amateur the works of Beethoven are still beyond the bounds of the enjoyable, and become intelligible only by
of superior artistic quality or personality in the interpretation. Still more evident appears this notion when we consider the fact that the master universally acknowledged the greatest since Beethoven, in his ability to treat musica

themes, Johannes Brahms, is still so wide of general acceptance that the critics have not yet gotten over talking of his unintelligibility—meaning thereby, as in all art discussions, intelligibility to *them*,—for criticism is always written from a personal standpoint, although the fact is not so generally recognized as it ought to be. If, therefore, this great master Brahms has not found it possible to interest the world in new symphonies, and as a matter of fact has withheld two additional ones which are already finished from his pen, until a time when the taste moderates somewhat from the over sonorous and sensational (of which Tschaikowsky is a magnificent exponent), is it not therefore demonstrated that the art of symphony has been finished, and that there is nothing more to do in this direction?

Plausible as these positions are, there is reason to believe, nay to be certain, that they are entirely wrong. Whereof let us now consider. There are certain activities of man which began to show themselves at a period in history when, according to the hypothesis of the more straightforward development theory, he ought to have been exclusively concerned with matters appertaining to his immediate well-being. Among these are religion, poetry, fiction, and music. Far back in the Vedic times, when perhaps the early Aryans had not broken across the Himalayan barrier, there were hymns to the gods, and there was music. Strong and tonal forms were cultivated and highly prized. They were believed to possess intimate relations with the soul. More than six centuries before our era, Pythagoras, the Greek philosopher, taught that before retiring at night his disciples ought to attune their spirits by singing a hymn to the gods, in order that thus refreshed they might arise to a new day of service and well doing. In this exercise the element of pleasing the gods by offering them a sacrifice of praise and song does not seem to have entered; but solely the effect upon the singer himself, through the attuning influence of music upon his spirit. No doubt the words and the tonal forms made a one, and the latter was not as yet recognized as able to perform this office alone.

All of the four forms of mental activity above mentioned

have something in common, recognizing which, perhaps we will be in position to go farther in our discussion. Religion may be described as the effort of the individual to place himself entirely under control of the ideal—not merely his thought, but also conduct. And the tendency is more and more to reduce it to this concept, and to relegate dogma to a remote position upon the outposts of the camp, where it is very reluctant to stay. Poetry, fiction, and drama, are forms of "the might have been;" the play of imagination, having in it something of delight, but mainly a prophetic element of teaching concerning human life and its relations. Through these forms some of the most important education is now and always has been communicated; and the prospect is brighter for an increase of the influence of this form of art than for its suppression.

There is material for much instructive reflection in the history of our existing art of music, which taken all around offers a very interesting conundrum to the development philosopher, but this would take us too far. Suffice it to mention that from the early Egyptian times, long before the days of Joseph, music had an honored place in life. Twenty centuries or more aided in its development before it blossomed into the classical drama of Greece. Then another ten or fifteen centuries intervened during which music was mastering a vocabulary, and finding its harmony and counterpoint. About A. D. 1600 this part of musical science had reached a creditable point, and here began a fresh exploration of the art in search of means of emotional and dramatic expression, for it was opera where first the relation of music to emotion was thoroughly explored. All along with the progress, through the masterworks of such writers as Monterverde, Scarlatti, Handel, Bach, Gluck, and so on to Mozart, there was a related series of experiments having for their object the projecting of the means of musical expression, instruments, etc. Then with Beethoven came the first greater master who brought together the appealing tenderness and sentiment of opera, the sonority and the emotionally graded tone-colors, and a noble ideality all his own, and incarnated the whole in the Symphony.

The Beethoven symphony is a new work. It is not the Mozart symphony enlarged; it is something different. With Mozart it is generally the pleasing, the agreeable, the clever; but rarely anything of deep feeling. The personality of the man stands before us in the delightful tonal forms, sweet, ready and delightful. But in Beethoven we encounter a different element. This man is not altogether so sweet as Mozart; his ideas often are rugged; and he is not troubled to ask whether we are pleased. Yet we listen all the same, for immediately the world has recognized that in this music, whether it be counted good or not, there is something to say.

Taking the most significant feature first, consider his slow movements. These are as simple as people's songs, in their beginnings, and the principal subject in spite of its elaborations later remains the same lofty and deep spirit, to be enjoyed by every hearer who will retain himself in proper condition, waiting to be moved upon and not stopping his ears by the effort to "understand." In other parts strong contrasts are found, and in the allegros occasional types of a spirit almost or quite tragic. It is impossible to listen to one of these great works without feeling that the composer is saying something to us through these sounding tones. *What is this something?* It is not description, and is not poetic representation. No landscape, no great historical event is here brought to elucidation. Yet there is a something which all feel, but which no one is able satisfactorily to explain. Volumes have been written to tell us what we ought to find in these great and epoch-marking works. And at the end of all the reading, the hearer who with quiet soul will give himself up to the contemplation while the sounding tonal forms roll through his chambers of hearing and around him, will have something in his spirit which neither one nor all the volumes have given him—but which Beethoven himself has said to him through these masterworks of art.

Since Beethoven, instrumental music has explored in various directions the extraordinary and the sensational, and the vocabulary of music and its means of tone color have greatly expanded. The world of the fantastic and the strange has been conquered, so that there is now very little in heaven or earth or hell which a gifted composer might not bring to expression.

And behind all this progress there is one sole purpose. With steady step music has progressed towards the art of saying something to human souls. Out of the vast inner world of the Unseen, the Blest, and the Eternal, the prophetic seer brings in tones his living and moving message. We do not need a story; we do not need an explanation. Simply to hear and hear again, and to be silent and hear again—this is the road and the only road. These great works are written like the messages of inspiration "for those who have ears to hear." The inner message of music like the inner tone of the creation, is for him who listens within.

Nothing that I can say is adequate to characterize the beauty of this musical message, nor its compass and variety. Nor is there as yet any limit in either direction. Higher beauty, greater variety, and manifold forms of inspiration are open to the composer of the future. The common chord of the tonic, which one would say the Italian composers had exhausted a century ago, served Beethoven very well for the first four measures of his great Heroic symphony. It is not a question of chords, nor yet of tone-color. It is merely a question of something to say. Nor when we consider the manner in which musical forms bring soul life to expression or suggestion, does there appear any limitation to its possibilities of development. Every musical idea moves in three planes, to which yet a fourth attaches itself; or we might say that a musical idea, for high art purposes, has four dimensions, being thus removed forever from under what Schopenhauer calls the *Satz vom Grund* (principal of sufficient reason) the conditions of material time, space, and causality. Or rather put under new conditions of this kind peculiar to itself. Rhythm, Melody and Harmony afford three related directions within which countless combinations and shadings can be effected. And all can be intensified and made luminous by the aid of tone color. Under the influence of the latter some of the most biting dissonances assume absolute beauty, and appeal in most significant manner.

Hence in order to have an infinite series of musical works constantly increasing in beauty, significance, and appeal to individual human souls, it is merely a question of an infinite series of great souls, gifted and trained in musical directions, and actuated by the ideal. So much for possibility upon the creative side. What these great souls may in process of time communicate to us through the mystical language of tones, no one can predict. But that every incident as soul life is susceptible of translation into tonal forms, in which it becomes intelligible to all the world, the music of six hundred songs of Schubert, and the instrumental music of Beethoven prove to us. In all probability the composer of the future will pour out his inspirations in tones, with a lavish amplitude like that of Schubert, in whom everything which stirred assumed musical cadence, and sought expression to the ear.

There are certain features in the nature of music itself which are not without bearing upon the present discussion. The composer derives his incitation of his environment, which may be his actual outward environment, as in the case of the realist novelist, or of his inner environment of the ideal, as was the case with Shakespeare and other great masters of imagination and fancy. More than this. The composer will do the same as the novelist does, who invents plausible situations, which might have been actual occurrences, in order through their solution to express his theory of the essential nature of life and its duties. The powers of music, as we have seen, are equal to representing almost any possible state of mind, and it is quite certain that the responsive composer will in every case represent the mood of the moment when the idea of his work overtakes him or is awakened within him.

Music also has within itself not only great potentiality of sorrow and striving, but even a positive liking for them. Just as the soul is most touched by great tragedy, so it is only in the deep minor strains, and the clashing and striving rush of the impassioned *Allegro* that the heart is most stirred, and a ground afforded for the heavenly peace of the noble *Adagio*. And this, in turn, is far from being insensible to the sweep and the fluctuations of the deep world-currents of the soul.

And just here again we come upon one of the strangest contradictions of music. Helmholtz told us that nature gave us the major triad, and some of our recent investigators are telling us that the primitive man follows along the harmonic track in trying to produce melodies; or, as one says it, his musical impulses work off along the line of least resistance, which is through the melodic steps of the common chord. Upon forsaking this one he changes to another, but all the time his melody runs along the line of the major triad. This theory is all very well, but there are two objectors who would like to settle with it. The first one calls attention to the very strange if not inexplicable fact, that while nature is thus holding the ear to the common chord—in the very constitution of tone itself, the primitive man whether advanced or in his most primeval state, makes his music in minor mode, in so far as it has mode at all. And the second objector notes that even in these most advanced states of civilization, and among composers in whom the natural incitation of music is most delicate, the minor chord constitutes more than half our music. An eminent writer upon the purity of musical intonation has lately written this to me from his own standpoint; and after a life of theorizing and investigation, which in his case has taken the practical form of inventing a musical instrument and a practical keyboard for playing in perfect tune up to a division of fifty-three tones in the octave, he finds at last that perfect tune is not what the musical soul desires; and that while slow simple chords in pure harmony sound better upon his improved instrument, the common run of instrumental music is not improved by it, but on the contrary impoverished, the dissonances themselves losing character and the music ceasing to be intelligible to the extent formerly experienced. Moreover, in all periods of history of which I have any knowledge there has been a hiatus between the theory of music and the actual music that men made. While speaking of one kind of effect men have unconsciously made another, and as a rule another which went straight to the heart of the hearers.

Thus by this road we are brought to realize that the science of acoustics fails to account for our art of music, and that its real seat and the motives by which it moves itself are psychical. True the observer is able to trace the roots of much of the psychical expression which music produces upon sensitive subjects, to this that or the other element in its constitution. As for instance, the mode does something, the rhythm something, the tone color something and so on; but when all is counted, there remains over and above a something which is not melody, is not harmony, is not rhythm, nor yet distinctly a definite result of the combination of all—but a something which pleases the ear more than the ear can explain; stirs the blood more than the rhythm can explain; and winds up the consciousness by a sort of cumulative movement until the whole being is alive with the experience—an experience which is too intimate and too near the heart to be classed as mere enjoyment, and too influential upon the soul to be dismissed as mere amusement or a casual act. This is true of much of the music since the time of Bach; and of most of that since Beethoven it is emphatically true. Just at the moment I am thinking of the fifth symphony of Tschaikowsky, the great C major symphony of Schubert, and the second symphony of Brahms; but there are fifty other great and shining examples, in the orchestral repertory, while operatic and chamber music are full of them. Why do our composers fall into the minor so readily, when nothing is farther from their intention than to write a plaint or an elegy? And why do we hear these long successions of minor chords, dissonances suspended, struck free upon the beat, lugged in as passing notes, multiplied in all the parts, crossing one another in a strange and mystical progress, and why the fierce peal of the brass, the sounding impact of the percussion, and the nervous and heartfelt accents of the strings, when everything passes off later and leaves us

refreshed instead of being fatigued, and the ear delighted instead of being tired? Had we but followed a quarter of of the dissonances of the work, we might have been half deaf for a week. Why is this, but because there is in music something else which we get, and getting which we care not how it comes to us, nor what the exercise of mere sense-perception so long as the incoming message is not too long kept waiting at the gates of the outer ear? At least one moral may be safely drawn:—It is that the happiness of our musical future is not bound up with that of the common chord. Men go through great tribulation to gain a heaven in tones nowadays, but it is none the less heaven when we are there, nor does the memory of the way strike us with weariness. And according to all appearance there is no limitation to the future in this direction.

II

Seeing therefore that as yet no limitation appears to the powers of the coming composer to say whatever he may have to say in tones, and by novel combinations or by those of long use to bring to human ears and human hearts messages of the very highest and most ideal import, what is the outlook, we may ask, with references to the intelligibility of these messages? In other words, will the coming hearer be able to receive them, and will he be anxious to receive them? This is an important question, having in it the whole subject of musical education and of popular capacity. And there is ground for optimistic conclusions in this direction, no less than in the one which we have last been considering.

In so far as regards the appetite for music, there is all the encouragement desired. There was never a time in the history of the world when so many young people studied music, nor when they learned so much of playing, singing, and hearing. Whatever the short comings of the present generation of concert hearers and private students may be, their attainments are far in advance of those of any former generation, and they are in vastly greater numbers. This appears not alone in the variety of great musical works performed in all the principal cities, but still more in the material which is taken up and at least partly digested in private study the whole country through. Indeed it is not easy to account for the general hurry to get to a piano or an organ and to take lessons and to learn at least something about playing. No other domestic desire appears so out of proportion to the family purse or the family heredity. In a family where the parents were very little musical, and had perhaps no valid training in any branch of the art, you find an instrument, a desire, an application, and at length respectable often remarkable attainments, and a beginning of real musical enjoyment.

Here we come upon another of the secret things of music. A writer in the Fortnightly Review lately had an article upon "The Religion of the Pianoforte," in which he suggests that the true explanation of the willingness of the average young person to undergo the drudgery of practice, the bondage of lessons, and the work of wrestling with scores of pieces which are certainly caviare to the general is that they find in the tonal forms a new kind of fiction, a new kind of tragedy. As their fingers travel over the keys and their eyes perhaps with some difficulty decipher the notation, the mind is soaring above, and what inner fantasies arise, who shall tell? Surely there must be something of this sort behind the strange devotion to so artificial an ideal—if we judge it from a merely external standpoint. In many a country home the pianoforte opens almost the only door into the ideal. Even the highstrung works of modern composers are by no means tabooed, and many young girls scarcely out of their 'teens play creditably ambitious compositions proper to the concert room or the closet of the advanced tonal connoisseur.

Let it be granted that the education as yet is imperfect, and the general training in music very inadequate. Grant, if you like, that the subject matter of these exercises often fails to reach proper dignity, and more often still the performances fail in important points of technic and of depth; still the phenomenon is none the less remarkable and full of promise. Where there is so well defined an appetite there will surely arise ways of making it more enlightened, and better able to minister to these deep seated longings of the soul.

And supposing the requisite improvements of educational methods to be made, have we not then a public for our promised composers of the future? What other branch of art or literature has so large a one, or so cosmopolitan, or one so well adapted to still further promote the universal brotherhood of man? Is it not something when musical composers and interpretative artists are now by common consent citizens of all countries, equally at home in all, and sought after by high and by low? A new artist comes, he plays once, twice, three times, always to larger and larger houses, and to increasing appreciation, which however, increases exactly in proportion not to the technical skill of the artist, but in proportion to the depth of the impression he makes upon the sympathies of his hearers. It is not a question of playing fast or playing loud, nor yet of performing impossibilities; but always and forever, of *saying something*. And this art passes current all over the world. I once asked the veteran violinist Remenyi how he made out in South Africa where music was so new. He answered that it made no difference. He played just the same as in Berlin, Rome, Vienna, or in Weimar itself. This which takes place in a plane not the highest in the temple of music will sometime take place in the highest plane, and in smaller communities, and all over the land. Just as our lyceum bureaus send their concerts to small villages, in later times the great artists will be heard all over the country. And quite surely the average of private performance will constantly advance, under the facilitation of heredity and early education, and by so much the audiences waiting for our great composers will be more and more willing to hear the highest, the truest, the most ideal message which they have to deliver. All this is quite in the nature of things. It is a question of choosing, of seeding and of tending.

And while it would seem impertinent to suggest that in the future music will not only surpass everything which the best composers have written, and will speak to larger and larger quotas of the civilized peoples, until its place in the popular estimation, and its relation to the inner life of the men and women of the world will be more intimate, more direct, more precious than that of any other form of art whatever, the facts nevertheless point exactly in this direction. And none the less potently from the circumstance that all this music-making, all this music hearing and music study takes place through the free choice of the individual. There is no paid ministry for working up a love for music; there is no public gathering for pushing its cult. The folks make music and hear music because they love it; and they love it not for the sweetness of its sound, nor yet for the cleverness of the fingering by which it played; but solely and first of all for what it says to them. And the successful artist always is he or she who seems to make the music say something. For in all this interpretation it is not a question of hearing exactly what the composer meant to say, but of hearing what he *seems* to say, and the value of the experience is measured by its seeming to say something.

So much appears upon the surface. But the argument has more in it still. For by just so much as music says something to those who give themselves up to it, by just so much it becomes a force with influence upon their lives, and upon their doing and being. And so we may look for a time when this force will be understood and intelligently employed in education, as it sometimes begins to be now; but upon wider and higher scale, until many things which have not yielded to the pulpit nor yet to the press, will soften themselves to music. Who knows? The Pythagorean tuning of mind by means of tones will become a reality; and it will sometime be found that the intellect is sharpened and the imagination kindled by tonal fantasy, not merely for itself, but for great and noble deeds. Such are some of the possibilities open before the art of music, as related to the inner life of man.

Chicago, Dec. 30, 1894. W. S. B. MATHEWS.

EDITORIAL BRIC-A-BRAC.

A FRIEND has sent me a clipping from the *Boston Evening Transcript* of Dec. 31, containing Mr. W. F. Apthorp's article upon the concert of the Boston Symphony orchestra, the previous Saturday evening. Several things in this clipping are interesting. First and foremost the program itself, which was this:

> TSCHAIKOWSKY, Symphony Pathétique, Op. 74 (First time).
> HENRY HOLDEN HUSS, Concerto in B major, for pianoforte. (first time.) Solo part by the Composer.
> BERLIOZ, Overture to "Benvenuto Cellini" opus 23.

The program, as will be seen was concise and strong. It is true that placing the concerto of a young composer directly after the powerful orchestration and intense imagition of Tschaikowsky was a trifle cruel. This, however, was no doubt mitigated by an intermission which came between the two works. Another point of note was the fact of the first performance of the Tschaikowsky work—some months later than the first performance here or in New York.

The main interest of the clipping, of course, lies in the quality of Mr. Apthorp's article, which is masterly to a degree. It has almost all the good qualities which musical criticism can have, being extremely well written, appreciative, and intelligent without being effusive or dyspeptic. Upon this point, however, it is well for envious newspaper men to notice the collocation of dates. The concert was played in public rehearsal on Friday afternoon and again in the evening of Saturday. Mr. Apthorp's article was probably written sometime Sunday, and was put in type Monday forenoon. Therefore his ideas had time to clear up, and he himself the leisure to prepare an article having in it repose and the manysided consideration of opposing ideas, which a program of this character could not but awaken in the mind of so experienced an observer. I am sorry that I have not room for the article in full, or at least for large extracts from it (it is a little over a column long).

Substantially Mr. Apthorp does not find himself in sympathy with the Tschaikowsky symphony. He says:—

"Once reading the score and once hearing the work do not furnish any very sound basis for forming an opinion of so long, varied and exceedingly complex a composition as this symphony. There is much in it which we personally do not like; much of which we hardly know yet whether we like or not; but there is an inflexible seriousness, a deep earnestness of purpose in it throughout such as must be recognized at once. Never has Tschaikowsky shown himself more grimly in earnest. The amount of elaborate work in the score is something stupendous; and yet one can say that only the third movement the *allegro molto vivace*, is in any way over developed. Here to be sure, in spite of a heroic cut made by Mr. Paur, the development does seem considerably in excess over what the material can well bear."

Concerning the Huss concerto for the piano, Mr. Apthorp considers that there is too much thematic material and that the development is undertaken upon too large a scale for the experience and genius of the composer. He makes the further point that if American composers would not try to tell all they know in some one work, but write more and shorter, they would have a much better chance of being heard. This fallacy of young American composers is quite on the same plane as the tendency of young theologues to preach everything they think they know in one sermon. They spread out later.

Mr. Paur's action in venturing to cut so important a work as this of Tschaikowsky at its first hearing is a piece of very questionable judgement. A great series of symphony concerts is like a musical art gallery, in which it is endeavored to afford examples of all noble styles, each in its highest illustration. But to present large works by acknowledged masters in incomplete form, especially for their first hearing, is certainly a mistake—no matter how excessive the development may appear to the conductor or the newspaper hearer. The public is always at this point in position to learn, and it is always possible that the development may *not* be excessive when rightly comprehended. What would be thought of an art gallery which should present a picture by any great artist with some one portion covered up, upon the opinion of the hanging committee that the development of motive had been "excessive?" Would not this be to counteract the very intention of a public gallery of art? On first hearing every work should be given in its entirety; and only later, after several hearings, separate movements, or still more heroic a selection, a movement abridged. Indeed it is questionable whether abridgement is legitimate in case of master works in symphony concerts. From another source I hear that the Boston orchestra is playing as well or better than ever.

* * *

The Chicago orchestra has been playing some very nice programs in a manner better than ever. On Dec. 29th there was a popular program as follows:

Overture, "From the Highlands," (new) Op. 4 — Frederic Lamond
Te Deum Laudamus (new) — G. [illegible]
for string orchestra and organ.
Scherzo, Op. 45 (new) — Goldmark
Ballata, "There was a Prince in olden times," from "Il Guarany."
Miss Electa Gifford. — Gomez
"Siegfried's Rhine Journey," from "Die Gotterdämmerung." — Wagner
March Marocaine, — Berlioz
Suite "L'Arlesienne," — Bizet
Prelude, Minuetto, Adagietto, Carillon
Song, "Nymphs and Fauns," — Bemberg
Miss Electa Gifford.
Waltz, "From the Vienna Woods," — Joh. Strauss
Zither Solo by Mr. Wunderle.
"Danse Cosaque," — Tschaikowsky

January 5th a request program:

Overture, "Academic Festival," — Brahms
Sonata in E Minor — Bach
Largo—Allegro, Adagio, Vivace,
Polonaise Op. 53 — Chopin
Symphony, No. 5, in E minor — Tschaikowsky
Andante; Allegro con anima.
Andante cantabile.
Valse.
Finale.

January 19th, a symphony program, the selection of the symphony having been determined by the second choice of votes for the request program on the 5th.

Suite, No. 3, in D, — Bach
Concerto for Violin, Violoncello and Orchestra — Brahms
Violin, Mr. Becker,
Violoncello, Mr. Steindel
Symphony No. 5 — Beethoven

The popular program was the most tedious of the season. A collection of pieces of this character is like a dinner composed exclusively of bon-bons. It is delightfully sweet in conception; but in execution impracticable and disappointing. The new compositions were interesting, but Lamond's "Highland" overture lacks sustained development and the interest thereunto appertaining; and the "Te Deum" of the genial Italian, Giovanni Sgambati, was one of his earlier works, peculiar and perhaps hardly likely to occupy any other than a somewhat subordinate and quasi popular place upon serious programs. It is a pity we could not hear some of his serious orchestral work, for he is a master of decided individuality and attractive quality.

The singing of Miss Electa Gifford was pleasing but in the "Il Guarany" ballata not sufficiently intense. She was recalled and sang again. Her accompaniments were delightfully played upon the pianoforte by Mr. Clarence Eddy, whereby the concert presented the unwonted spectacle, of Mr. Middleschulte at the great organ and Mr. Eddy in the same program at the piano. Mr. Middleschulte is an excellent player, and there is no intention of reflecting upon him in any way. But when one remembers Clarence Eddy's celebrity as organ virtuoso, one remarks an incident of this kind.

* * *

The best program of the series up to this time was the closing one of the half season, Jan. 5th. Brahms' Academic overture was admirably given. Then came Mr. Thomas' transcription of Bach's Sonata for violin solo, in D minor, which makes a beautiful and almost symphonic work. That there was much of inference in the carrying out of the instrumentation goes without saying, but it was most charmingly done, and nothing could put the musicianship of Mr. Thomas in stronger light—world's fair memories to the contrary notwithstanding. (For it was a favorite idea at that time, with certain ones, that Mr. Thomas was not a musician, but only conductor. A fine and illuminating distinction!) This violin sonata has been a favorite one with Mr. Thomas for many years, and the present transcription was made about fourteen years ago. It deserves to be better known. Then following this came his spirited and highly effective transcription of Chopin's great Polonaise in A flat—played some weeks ago for the first time. This went with splendid verve and made a great effect.

The second part brought us that master work, Tschaikowsky's fifth symphony, played here last season—played now with great fervor and moving effect. Mr. Thomas may reserve it from his list of symphonies, as he did in a conversation which I recounted some months ago, but it is a highly impassioned orchestral tone poem, nevertheless, and it does not so much matter by what name it is designated so long as its tropical luxuriousness of passion flowers and richly intertwined vegetation is preserved.

* * *

Of the value of these concerts as a great educational factor, too much cannot be said. It is a pity that the teachers do not make more effort to induce their students to attend regularly. If this were done it would fill up all the low priced seats, in short order, and be of great advantage to the students themselves. It is also curious how few attend both concerts, the rehearsals and the evening concerts. To hear the same program twice in immediate connection is much more instructive than when a repetition is heard only after an interval of some months, when one has forgotten the main features of the principal works—which very likely he may never have been heard before.

* * *

Among the smaller concerts of the month in Chicago have been a number which for one reason or another deserve attention possibly here only upon a small scale. First of these was a song recital by Mr. Anton Schott, the famous Wagnerian tenor, who gave a very fine program in Kimball hall, Dec. 21st. His voice is strong and well managed, except that when he sings loud his tone is too robust. Doubtless this comes of doing Siegfried against the Wagner instrumentation. He is an artist of fine distinction. Upon this occasion Mr. Robert Goldbeck played several solos—also a noteworthy occurrence.

Another of the smaller affairs was that given by a

talented young pupil of Mr. Liebling, Miss Myrtle Fisher, at Kimball hall, Dec. 27th. I missed the first number, which was the Bach-Liszt organ fantasia and fugue, in G minor; but came just in time to hear most of the fragment of the Waldstein sonata of Beethoven. Her other solo number consisted of a Scherzo from Rubinstein's opus 100, Raff's "La Fileuse," Liebling's "Feu Follet," and the Liszt "Campanella." This playing was admirable in every way. The touch was bright and telling, the playing clear and musical, and all around the girl has exceptional talent—as well as an exceptional teacher. There were several concerted numbers, the Chopin Krakowiak, opus 14, with second pianoforte and string quartet, and the Liszt fantasia on "Don Juan" for two pianos.

* * *

Another of these concerts was that of the child prodigy, little Marie Edwards, in Central Music hall, January 2d. The child is about seven years old. She played a duet with her father, (the overture to "William Tell,") accompanied a violin piece, sang several little pieces and accompanied herself, announced the pitches of notes struck together or in succession in any part of the keyboard (Dr. Ziegfeld presiding) and wrote a melody selected by one of the audience and played for her upon the violin in the ante room. The child has great talent and the present concert had been encouraged by Messrs. Melville E. Stone, of the Associated Press, and James W. Scott, of the Chicago *Herald*. Efforts are to be made to secure a proper education for her.

* * *

Mr. Bruno Oscar Klein has been very successful in performing his own works in Germany, and his opera of "Kenilworth" is to be performed in Hamburg, in February. The story follows Scott's novel. The music is published by Hoffmeister of Leipsic. It is said to be original and interesting. We shall see—or rather we shall hear at long range, for the last place to hear important American works is in America itself.

W. S. B. M.

REVIEWS AND NOTICES.

HANDBOOK OF MECHANICAL EXERCISES, STUDIES FOR THE PIANO A Selection of Indispensable Exercises from the first Rudiments to the Highest Development. Progressively arranged in Strictly Methodical Order with Explanatory Notes, by Julius Handrock. English translation by Dr. Theo. Baker. Music oblong folio. Pp 142. $1.25. G. Schirmer. 1895.

In this work we have exactly what the lengthy title promises, provided only that we grant the author his premises. It is in fact a thesaurus of the old-fashioned material for technic. Beginning with five finger exercises, 23 pages, we come to scales, 7 pages, five finger again 4 pages, broken chords and arpeggios, other exercises in extensions, scales, and all sorts of mechanical figures—all in plain form with a few directions at beginning for applying at least a semblance of rhythmic treatment. Those who like this sort of thing will find the work admirable. If the reviewer is not mistaken, however, the Schirmer collection of similar material by Mr. O. R. Skinner, covers more ground than this, and with a certain proportion of the Tausig element added. The great majority of the exercises in this work are to be found in any of the standard instruction books, such as Richardson, and the like. They have been printed over and over, and it is not easy to discover a reason for repeating them. Nevertheless, here they are, well printed, and no doubt complete after their kind. There was a time, not so very long ago, when this kind of material was considered the foundation for piano playing. That time has past.

IN THE GARDEN. "From Goldmark's Rustic Wedding." Transcribed for organ by Clarence Eddy. 75c. Ditson. A well made and pleasing concert paraphrase, or transcription: with registration marked for a three manual organ of moderate appointment, such as are now found almost everywhere. Not very difficult.

Organ pieces, for Reed or Pipe Organ. By J. W. Simpson

March. Duffield.
Postlude in A. Lemmens. Prelude in A. Hird.
Andantino. Scharwenka. Andante. Agate.
Communion. Marchant. Communion in G. Brown
Romance. Sacred March. G. T. B.

These are all pieces of facility, and nearly all short. There is no pedal part, and no registration. When a piece purports to be adapted to reed and "pipe" organs, it gives itself away as of exceeding provincialism at the start. It is like advertising a new overture as adapted for the reed organ, the mandolin, the banjo, or full orchestra. Those who are looking for very easy organ music, not hampered by disagreeable reminders of inefficiency in the form of an unused and unusable pedal part, will find this about what they are looking for. The reed organist will be no happier with these pieces than the real organist (or ought we say "pipe" organist?) because they have no indications of registration.

CLOUD, FIELD, AND SHOWER, BEING TEN LITTLE SONGS FOR CHILDREN. By Ernest Osgood Hiler, Boston, Miles & Thompson, $1.50.

A charming set of little songs for children, both as poetry and music. While keeping generally within the diatonic contents of the key, Mr. Hiler is fresh in melody and uses modulation so easily as to relieve his pieces of a certain commonplace quality which children's songs find it so difficult to avoid. In some instances the management of form has been very clever, as in the "Cloud Lullaby" where a long sentence has been handled with masterly skill, and the musical form thereby improved. It is one of the best signs of the musical future of this country that students are writing such things as these; for Mr. Hiler is, if we mistake not, still a student in philosophy and music under Professor John K. Paine, at Harvard. And whatever these talented fellows may later do in the way of grand operas, it is of the first importance that they learn how to be intelligible—which is precisely where Mr. Hiler at present appears to be "at." Any mother having musical taste of her own and desiring something to sing to her children, having in it the tendencies towards better taste than she came into in her own childhood (and there are many of this kind in America) will find this collection well worth knowing.

Mention formerly has been made of the beautiful musical magazine which appeared for the first time one year ago, *The Italian Musical Review* (*La Rivista Musicale Italiana.*) It is quarterly of rather larger size and content than the North American Review, (which by the way contains rather less matter than MUSIC), and it is published once a quarter. The fourth number is now at hand, with an index for binding. The total number of pages reaches 804, making an average of about two hundred pages per issue. The present number contains in the literature part four articles. L. Torchi has a very important memoir, extending to about eighty pages, upon "Italian Canzone and Arias for a single voice, in the 17th century;" Alfred Ernst, "The Hero Motives in the Wagner works," 20 pages, in French; A. Sandberger, "Orlando di Lasso," 30 pages; A. Griveau, "The Sense and Expression of Pure Music," French, 30 pages. The International Lyric Theatre, of Milan, 7 pages. All the remainder, nearly fifty pages, is devoted to reviews of musical works. The articles cited above are all important, and the production of experts, who besides being expert are also full of musical faith and enthusiasm, and of a belief in its future and its desirability.

HUNGARIAN MELODIES. Text from the Originals, done into English by J. S. of Dale and F. Korbay. The Music transcribed by Korbay. London, Stanley, Lucas, Weber, & Co. 1893. Quarto, Pp 154.

This elegantly gotten up music book, from last season, makes one of the prettiest presents that one could ask. The retail price is $5.00. The melodies are Hungarian, with all the passion, pathetic yearnings, and the fiery ardor proper to that form of art. Some of them are old, but most of them are from within the present century. The texts fit the unruly rhythms as well as could be expected, where no words could fit perfectly and at the same time be grammatical. In the introduction, Mr. Korbay traces the characteristic rhythms of Hungarian music to the prevailing feet of its poetry, and admits that no other language can do these rhythms as well. Among the melodies are several which will be recognized by piano scholars as the originals of Liszt's rhapsodies. The pianoforte settings here are also very free and masterly, and a lover of Hungarian music could not desire a better prepared volume than this of Mr. Korbay. Much might be said of the melodies individually but this would take us too far.

MATHEWS' GRADED MATERIALS FOR THE PIANOFORTE. Comprising the Required Work in Passage Playing and Expression, from the beginning of the study to the end of the eighth grade. Selected from Standard Sources, classical and modern; progressively arranged and edited for Intelligent Study and Easy Teaching. By W. S. B. Mathews. Four Volumes, two grades in each volume. Vol. I. Grades I and II. Sheet music. 61 pp, 1894. The John Church Company, $1.00.

The foregoing title is so full that perhaps no more is necessary for defining the place intended by the extremely well printed work to which it relates. As is well known, the multiplication of Etudes has long since reached a point where the amount of material offered the piano teacher is simply bewildering, and the amount of good material far exceeding practical bounds of use. Among this material there is a vast amount wholly useless, or of very little value. Many books of Etudes contain one or two useful and musical pieces, while all the remainder is dry and unfruitful. Hence in some quarters there has been a tendency to give up the use of Etudes in favor of pieces, on the ground that the latter if well studied advance the playing more rapidly and more musically. This is quite true with the proviso mentioned, "if well studied," but experience shows that it is highly desirable that a part of the pupil's work be done upon material which while having musical spirit and value is not primarily designed for mere amusement, but will require serious work. The Etude exactly fills this place. So in Europe there have been many series of collected studies brought together, by excellent editors, such as Louis Kohler, Dr. Hugo Riemann, and Kuhner. The latter in particular has made an admirable work, but it is far too large for American use, and besides is too hampered by existing copyrights upon the pieces of the romantic school to be satisfactorily balanced between classical and modern styles. Moreover all the European collections as well as several which have been made in this country contain entirely too many studies of obsolete schools, like that of Cramer, for instance, a comparatively little of which goes a long way.

As an example of the range taken in the present work it may be mentioned that Grade I contains 61 pieces, mainly from Berens, Loeschhorn, Gurlitt, Biehl, Ascher, Le Couppey, Czerny. The same writers are mostly represented in Grade II, and others besides, namely, Reinhold, Krug, Heller, Bertini, S. Bagge, and Streabbog. In all, fourteen writers in 81 pages.

As an agreeable first reader, I fancy teachers generally will find this little volume very handy. The remaining volumes of the series are expected to follow rapidly, Vol. II being already in press. From a typographical point of view this is one of the handsomest specimens of the American music printer's art.

W. S. B. M.

NEW MUSIC.

BARCAROLLE—GREAT SALT LAKE. By C. F. Stayner. 40 cents.

Those who are looking for American music should not overlook this meritorious and unhackneyed composition by Mr. Charles F. Stayner, of Salt Lake City, Utah. For in it we have not alone his idea of the great lake, but also some really clever and admirably conceived music, carefully marked for the pedal (with great intelligence) and well worthy the notice of teachers. The piece impresses one at first as having been conceived for the organ, it is so closely wrought, but upon examination one sees that the organ could never do this with anything like the effect of a good pianoforte, because while the harmonies are closely woven, the voices move in such a way and the pedal adds so much to the effect that the organ could not possibly offer anything adequate in compensation for these peculiar tone colors of the piano. It is about 5th grade, and quite within the ability of any amateur.

ELEGY IN MEMORY OF THE EMPEROR, ALEXANDER III, OF RUSSIA. By V. J. Hlavac. M. Bernard, St. Petersburg, 1895.

From that fine conductor and genial musician, Mr. V. J. Hlavac, we have a copy of his Elegy in memory of the dead Emperor. It is a lovely threnody, in style quasi Italian, beginning in thirds, and keyed chromatically in a manner which would interest a harmonist to unravel. Doubtless there underlies this feature of the work an allusion to some variety of folks song, pertinent to the land over which the great Emperor ruled, or whence the gifted composer was derived. Mr. Hlavac spent nearly the whole time of the fair in Chicago, where he made many friends and many more admirers by his conducting and playing no less than by his services as judge of instruments.

ALL SORTS. (From the John Church Company).

MARCH OF THE BROWNIES. Winthrop. 1st grade, fairly well done. Five finger positions, quarter notes.

MAZURKA. By Moszkowski. Op 38. No. 3 in G. Fourth or fifth grade. Pleasing mazurka, well done with nice phrasing.

SUNSHINE GALOP. Philla Elliott. Key of E flat. Easy 3d grade.

If the young man of the period does not look out, while he is composing impossible operas the young woman of the end of the century will get in her work and capture the ear of the rising generation— which is merely another way of capturing the dollars later.

THE SHEPHERD'S WOOING. Richard Stahl.

A pleasing idylle for piano in which the Shepherd woos quite classically, a la the English Phyllis and Corydon of the Elizabethan epoch. After a certain amount of sentiment in his first two periods the Shepherd subsides into a very fetching länder, which must have done the business. Pleasing for teaching, third grade.

NOCTURNE Opus 13. Raving. A fairly pleasing nocturne in the key of D flat. Reprinted from long ago, since it is opus 13.

POCANETO POLKA. Mandoline and Piano. Charles E. Pratt. Bright and pleasing. Popular.

FOR THE PIANO. (O. Ditson Co.)

REVERIE POETIQUE. For four hands. By Francesco D'Orso. 60c. Third grade, pleasing. With a little sentiment.

COQUETTING AND DISPORTING. Eight variations. L. von Beethoven. Revised and fingered by Ernst Perabo. 75c. Pleasing variations, by Beethoven, fingered and annotated by Ernst Perabo. Well adapted for teaching, despite the fact that the variation form as such has "gone out."

NOCTURNE. By Michael H. Cross. Pleasing fourth grade teaching piece, also capable of use as tone poem.

ADESTE FIDELES. (Portuguese Hymn.) transcribed by J. N. Pattison. 35c. Easy variations or rather transcription. First verse melody in bass; second, in soprano. Third grade.

A LEAF FROM MEMORY. Op. 107, No. 4. Nicolai von Wilm. 35c. A rather tender and sentimental album leaf. Fourth grade.

SUNSET REVERIE. By Richard Goerdeler. 50c. Pleasing and popular style. Melody first time in octaves with third between. At return of theme, repeated octaves. Available for teaching as amusement. 4th grade.

THE OLIVE PRIMROSE. Gavotte. By Frank Wallis Worsley 50c.

GALLANT TROOPERS. Scene Militaire. by Carman. 35c.

THE JOLLY SAILOR BOY, AND SONG OF THE BEGGAR CHILD. By Harold Leston. 25c. each.

OUR NAVY GRAND MARCH. Alfred Obemdorfer. Joseph Flanner Milwaukee, Wis. 50c. A pleasing march. 4th grade.

SONGS. O. Ditson Co.

THE HUM OF BEES. Words by Marion Aaig. Music by L. J. L. Molloy. 50c. A pleasing melody with a gavotte like rhythm. Key of E flat.

A [illegible] NIGHT. [illegible] [illegible] [illegible] English and French words.

[illegible]

[illegible]

[illegible]

[illegible]

[illegible]

[illegible]

He. How clear and [illegible] the heavens.

[illegible] "How clear and [illegible] the heavens" etc. etc.

THE FIRST [illegible]. Ed. Lawes. [illegible] [illegible] of Lawes.

THE NIGHT. La Notte. [illegible] and [illegible] L. M[illegible] [illegible]. A [illegible] with a [illegible] turn of the words, as [illegible].

She. "Ah leave thy sweet little cottage,
 My gondola is here.
We will return together
 Ere morning doth appear.
He. Ah leave thy little cottage,
 My gondola is here. She obligato. "Ah Yes.
We will return together
 Ere morning doth appear. She obligato. "Ah Yes.
He. Hide not thy face enchanting
 From jealous eyes of love.

Music of this sort will never wear out. As long as the world stands it will express the emotions of tender hearts which have reached this point in their experience.

Receipt of the following sheet music is acknowledged: From O. Ditson & Company.

THE SPLENDID GOAL. Notturno, for voice, violin and 'cello with piano accompaniment. By Paolo La Villa.

THE HOPE OF EVERY HEART. Jules Jordan.

THE LEAST OF THESE. Sacred song. Reginald Barrett.

MOORISH SERENADE. Martin Roeder.

THE STREAMLET. Song. Anton Streleski.

FROM THE JOHN CHURCH COMPANY.

AND HAVE YOU TOO. Vittorio Carpi.

AT SPRING TIME. E. Marzo.

I FEAR THY KISSES. Leandro Campanari.

THEN WOULD I DIE. Vittorio Carpi.

SONG OF THE COQUETTE.

MUSIC

MARCH, 1895.

BOSTON MUSIC IN 1851 AND 1852.

AMONG the music students in Boston in the seasons of 1852 and '53 was one named D. P. F. Van der Sande, who later became a piano teacher in Boston. In 1865 he came to Chicago, and established himself. Mr. Van der Sande has remained in Chicago ever since. Among the reminiscences of his early days in Boston is a collection of programs, from which through his kindness MUSIC is enabled to make certain extracts. The collection embraces something like fifty programs of the Germania Musical Society; nine of the Mendelssohn Quintette Club, from their second season in 1851; and ten or twelve of the orchestral concerts of the Musical Fund Society, led at that time by Mr. Geo. James Webb; and a considerable number of program of star concerts, etc, among them being several of the Jenny Lind concerts, and others by Maurice Strakosch, William Mason (in 1854) and others.

Beginning with the older of these programs we are able by their aid to form quite a good idea of the kind of selections which at that time were offered to the musical public. Boston was then far from being fresh ground, musically. The Handel and Haydn Society, organized in 1815, had for some years given oratorios regularly, and at the time immediately in question had given them with a very fair standard of performance. The Harvard Musical Association began about 1845 to give chamber concerts in

Cambridge; and the Boston Academy of Music had been founded in 1831 under the auspices of the late Dr. Lowell Mason, for the general purpose of extending musical knowledge, the objects proposed in the prospectus including orchestral concerts, music in the public schools, a musical journal, etc. Mr. Geo. James Webb had been a life long associate of Dr. Mason, and his prominence in Boston had been attained in the work of the Academy. The Boston Music Hall, where the symphony concerts are still given, was opened to the public in 1852, and many of the concerts to be mentioned hereafter took place in it. The impetus for building it came from the Jenny Lind concerts, which aroused great enthusiasm and gave point to the fact that at the time Boston did not possess any building suitable for first class musical performances. Another important inspiration in American music was the visit of the Jullien orchestra, which numbered some sixty players, or more, and was in fact the first full orchestra ever heard in this country.

The Musical Fund Society was a sort of co-operative orchestra, whose concerts were given for the purpose of collecting a fund for the support of aged and infirm musicians. When the present writer attended their concerts in 1852 the players numbered about fifty. The oldest program of theirs in the present collection is that of Feb. 1, 1851, the concert being given in Tremont Temple. The entire program was this:

Jubel Overture — Von Weber
Aria, "[illegible]" — Donizetti
Miss Borghese. (Piano accompaniment.)
Potpourri for Clarinet, Themes from "Der Freyschutz" — George
Mr. Thomas Ryan. (With orchestra.)
Rondo Brilliant, "[illegible]" from "Don Pasquale" — Donizetti
Miss Borghese. (Orchestral accompaniment.)
Theme and variations for Cello, A. Franchomme — Mr. T. Mass
Chansonette, "[illegible]"
Miss Borghese.
Overture, "Les Mousquetaires de la Reine" — F. Halevy

The second program of this list is from the date Dec. 13, 1851, the location still Tremont Temple. The solo performers are Thomas Ryan, Wulf Fries, and Mme Goria Bothe, who was the star of the occasion. She sang the since famous "Robert toi que j'aime," and an aria from Halvey's "Charles VI." The orchestral numbers of this concert were interesting and notable. Beethoven's "Eroica" symphony was played for the first time in Boston, as also was Berlioz's Overture to "Waverly," the MSS of which, the program states, had been procured for the society by Mr. Jonas Chickering—whose name in all musical annals of Boston stands out clear above others up to about two years later than the time of which we now speak—his death having taken place in 1853.

Our next programme is of a year later, Dec. 4, 1852, and the place is the New Music Hall. The director is now Mr. August Fries, and the star is Miss Caroline Lehmann. Miss Lehmann sang "O mio Fernando," and a romance by Mercadante. The orchestral numbers consisted of Beethoven's 8th symphony, for the first time in Boston, Mendelssohn's "Ruy Blas" overture, and the overture to "Le Roi d'Yvetot" (by request.) The programme also contains a full list of the players from which the personnell and make up of the band can be ascertained. It consisted of seven first violins, seven seconds, six violas, five "cellos and contrabasses," three flutes, two oboes, two clarinets, two bassoons, four horns, four trumpets, three trombones one ophicleide and three for tympani and percussion. Total forty eight besides the director and sub-director.

One week later, Dec. 18, 1852, the programme contained for orchestral numbers Mendelssohn's 3d symphony (in A minor), one of the Beethoven overtures to "Lenore," (number not stated,) and the Donizetti overture to "Roberto Devereux" (first time). The singer of this occasion was Miss Mary Isabella Webb, daughter of Mr. Geo. James Webb, and later wife of Dr. William Mason. Miss Webb, who had a lovely voice and a beautiful style, sang Donizetti's "Regnava nel silenzo" from "Lucia," the ballad "Auld Robin Gray," and Wallace's "Happy Birdling of the Forest," with flute obligato by Mr. A. Werner. Mr. Wulf Fries plays a fantasia for 'cello, by Kummer.

Again Jan. 8, Miss Webb sang, her numbers being

the De Beriot "Air Varie," the Malibran "Le Retour de la Tyrolienne," and Wallace's "The Gypsy Maid." The words are printed in the program, and the director is now again Mr. Geo. James Webb. The orchestral numbers are Mozart's "Jupiter" symphony, Beethoven's overture to "Prometheus," the Berlioz orchestration of Weber's "Invitation to the dance," and Reissiger's overture to "Die Felsenmuhle."

At the concert of Jan 24, 1852 the famous Mme. Anna Thillon was vocal soloist. Alary's "Polka Militaire," and "Her Name" by Puget. Mr. J. E. Goodson played a prelude and five part Fugue in C sharp minor by Bach—probably upon the piano, though the instrument is not stated. The orchestral numbers are the Haydn 11th symphony (presented to the society by the Brothers Fries.) Beetho-

MR. ALFRED JAELL.

ven's overture to "Lenore," probably the third, (presented to the society by C. C. Perkins, Esq.) and Rossini's "Gazza Ladra" overture.

At the concert of Feb. 21st the orchestral numbers

were Beethoven's 7th symphony (the most brilliant of his symphonies, the programme states, "by particular request,") Mozart's Overture to "Titus," and Lindpaintner's Overture "Guerriere," composed for the celebration of the twenty-fifth anniversary of König Wilhelm of Wurtemburg, concerning whom Boston was destined to hear more. The principal solo artist at this concert was Alfred Jaell, who remained in Boston for nearly two years, and was heard over and over again in these concerts and in those of the Germania musical society. On the present occasion he played the Mendelssohn G minor concerto with orchestra, and for solo his own fantasias upon "Rigoletto" and "The Carnival of Venice." Apparently the orchestral numbers made a success, for we find the Lindpaintner overture on the list again, March 6th, and the Mendelssohn symphony in A minor. The singer of this concert was the famous Mrs. Emma G. Bostwick, and her numbers the inevitable "Robert," "Casta Diva," and Wallace's "Happy Birdling," with flute obligato.

The sixth season of the Musical Fund society was directed by Mr. F. Suck, and the present writer heard a large number or all of the concerts. For the concert of Jan. 1, 1853, in Music Hall, "the celebrated Hungarian pianist and vocalist, lately arrived from Europe, has most kindly volunteered her services," which consisted of the grand scene and aria from "Der Freyschuetz," and the Hungarian National Song "The Errant." The orchestral numbers are insignificant, a Haydn symphony, Kalliwoda overture in C, and Cherubini "Les deux Journé," and an arrangement of "Schubert's Serenade" by F. Suck, for orchestra.

At the concert of Jan. 1853 the Schumann symphony, op 38, (1st) was performed for the first time in Boston. This symphony had been sent home to the society from Leipsic, some two or three years before, by Mr. William Mason, who had taken the Schumann fever upon his arrival there. But when first rehearsed the musicians were inclined to regard it as a failure, and it was all this time before courage was mustered up to bring it out. Here also another Schubert song appears arranged for orchestra, "The Elegy of Tears." The overtures are Spohr's "Jessonda," and Rossini's "William Tell." The singer, Mme. Leh-

CARICATURE OF ALFRED JAELL.

mann sang "Une voce poco fa," and "Ernani Involami," and "The Last Rose of Summer." Verily we might be writing of any concert season, and of any date, so uniform are the appearances under certain conditions.

Space does not permit further extracts from this very interesting series of concerts, except to note the ever fresh appearance of arrangement from Schubert songs, for orchestra, always by the director, Mr. F. Suck. The "Ave Maria" seems to have been an immediate favorite. There is however one concert which it would not do to omit.

On Feb. 17th, 1855, there was a cantata given, the music by C. C. Perkins, Esq., and the text curiously enough, by H. F. Chorley, Esq., of the London Athenaeum. "The Pilgrims Cantata," and it is indeed curious that from Boston it should be necessary to go to London to secure a poem on such a subject, with Lowell and Longfellow right there at Cambridge, and the musical author also no unknown young man but a citizen of high standing, and an alumnus of Harvard. The full programme is too long for quoting, but one or two titles are suggestive. For instance there is a choral quartette which the bill describes as "suggestive of a trust in Providence, accompanied by the Organ alone." Mr. H. Millard appears as tenor in this concert. On the whole the showing of the Musical Fund society must be regarded as more than creditable.

The interest in the concerts of the Germania Musical Society is of another kind. This famous orchestra was first composed mainly of students of Berlin university, some of whom were perhaps discredited by sympathy with the revolutionary disturbances of 1848. The society made its first American home in Baltimore, where it nearly starved, and disbanded, after having given some hundreds of orchestral concerts in all parts of the country. Later the the society was called together again in Boston, and for about three seasons it had things very much its own way. It is not possible in the space at present disposal to make an exhaustive list of the performances of this estimable society. At the time now under consideration the leader was Carl Bergmann afterwards of the New York Philharmonic; and the first flute Carl Zerrahn. The players numbered only twenty-four, the first and second violins being four each, and basses two. Yet such was the precision of their playing and the spirit, that they set a higher standard of performance than had ever before been reached

CAMILLA URSO.

in America except in the case of the Jullien orchestra The Germanias were distinctly up with the times. For instance October 22, (1853) in Music Hall, the opening concert of their season (with orchestra enlarged to 50) the programme contained these:

1. Symphony, No. 5 in C minor. Beethoven
2. Aria from "Maria di Rudenz," Donizetti
   Mlle. Caroline Pintard.
3. Invitation to the Dance, instrumented by Berlioz. Weber
4. Overture to the Grand Romantic Drama, "Tannhauser und der Saengerkrieg auf der Wartburg." (FIRST TIME IN AMERICA.) (A description of this Overture as written by the Composer, will be found in "Dwight's Journal of Music," of Oct. 22d.) Richard Wagner
5. Grand Concerto in E major, for flute. Briccialdi
6. Fantasia for Piano, "Don Giovanni." Thalberg
   Performed by Carl Hause.
7. The celebrated Concert Polka, with variations. Alary
   Mlle. Caroline Pintard.

The overture to Tannhauser was repeated on Nov. 5th, the other orchestral numbers being Gade's 1st symphony, the Nocturne from Mendelssohn's "Midsummernight's Dream," and a Reissiger overture. During this same season there was a revival of interest in Beethoven's Ninth symphony, which by the aid of the Handel and Haydn society was given March 12, 1853, and again April 3d, 1853, which date is mentioned at the head of the bill as the "682d Concert in America" a record which deserves to be long remembered to the credit of this highly enterprising body of musicians.

The principal solo pianist of the seasons 1851 and 1852 was Alfred Jaell, who was a clear and most charming player. His usual numbers were operatic fantasias by Thalberg or his own slightly less difficult settings of the same themes. But occasionally he played concertos, particularly those of Mendelssohn, and the E minor of Chopin. Even during this time an occasional break is made in direction of something higher. For instance Jan. 17, 1852, in the Melodeon, the Germanias accompanied Mr. Charles Mueller in Beethoven's 3d concerto for piano. Even in one of the programs containing Beethoven's ninth symphony Jaell played the Thalberg "Semiramis" fantasia. March 26, 1853, he played the Weber Concertstueck. March 5, the Mendelssohn Cappriccio Brilliante with orchestral accompaniment. Feb. 19, the Litolff concerto, in E flat. Jan. 28, 1853, Jaell played the Chopin Ballade in G minor, and the waltz op 64, which ever one it might have been.

In the season of 1851, program music had some attention, a violinist Miska Hauser appearing at several of the Germania concerts, with pieces of his own composition, one of the most favorite being his "Bird on the Tree, Caprice," describing, as the programme states, "the sensations of a bird which after having escaped from its cage flies into the free forest, and hopping from twig to twig and from tree to tree repeats the little airs it has been taught by its mistress." Another program gives the date Nov. 1, 1851, as the first time in Boston for the Berlioz arrangements of Weber's "Invitation to the Dance." It was during the season of 1853 that the afterwards celebrated violinist Camilla Urso made her first appearances. She was then a sallow little girl in short gowns, rather sad looking, the victim of parental driving. The present writer well remembers the fatherly and appreciative manner in which Bergmann used to lead her on for her numbers, and the absorbed way in which she played them. Heaven knows whether the sphynx like face had ideas behind it or not; but the violin under her fingers had ideas in it, and this the public acknowledged with enthusiasm.

In the season of 1854 there was a pianist named Robert Heller, who seems to have had more nerve than Jaell in the selection of program numbers. Among them we find, Feb. 4th, 1854, Beethoven's 4th Concerto for piano. The same program contained Cherubini's overture to "Medea," Mendelssohn's "The Fair Melusina," and Beethoven's 7th symphony, besides William Schultze in Mendelssohn's concerto for violin, op 64. This would be regarded as a strong program at the present time—in fact too strong and too long, but speaking nevertheless volumes for the standard making it possible to offer it as a commercial speculation—for this is exactly what the Germania concerts were. They stood upon their own earnings. On the 4th of March following, Heller played the Beethoven 5th concerto, and the programs contained besides the Overture to "Magic Flute," a Scherzo from Schumann, and the Mendelssohn Symphony in A minor. The singer had the aria from "Der Freyschutz," "Wie nahte wie in Schlummer." On the 18th of March, Heller played again the first, second and third movements of the 5th concerto, and the orchestra had the first three movements of the ninth symphony, and other good numbers. Here also was sung "Earl King" (sic), of Schubert, by Mlle Caroline Lehmann. The ninth symphony seems to have had friends in Boston, for on April 8th we find again the first three movements at the head of the program. Here also Miss Lehmann sang "Hear ye Israel" from "Elijah," and the Mendelssohn Choral society sang "Be not Afraid," and Handel's "Hallelujah."

Schubert's symphony in C, (No. 10) appears several times in these concerts. As for instance Jan. 7th, 1854, and Jan. 8th, 1853, and earlier. It was a rather strong program of Feb. 18, 1854:

1. Grand symphony "Jupiter." — Mozart
(Contains the celebrated Fugue").
2. Concerto for Piano, No. 4, in G major. — Beethoven
Mr. Robert Heller.
3. Overture to "Hebrides" (Fingal's Cave). — Mendelssohn
4. Andante and Variations from the Septette in E flat, op. 20. — Beethoven
(Played by seven solo performers).
5. Adagio Religioso, from the symphony cantata "The Hymn of Praise." — Mendelssohn
6. Overture "Der Freyschutz." — Weber

The program of Jan. 8th, 1853, which opened with the Schubert symphony in C, had the Mendelssohn "Midsummernight's Dream" overture, the last two movements of the Mendelssohn Concerto in G minor for piano (Jaell), and closed with one of Meyerbeer's "Fackeltanze."

The length to which these citations have extended admonishes us that they must stop.

To the Germanias must also be given the honor of probably having taken the lead in offering a "Grand Wagner Night," which they did Dec. 3d, 1853, with the following curious program:

1. Grand Overture to "Tannhauser." — R. Wagner
2. Air from the "Barber of Seville," "Una voce poco fa." — Rossini
Mlle Caroline Pintard.
3. Frauenlied. Zug der Frauen from the opera of "Lohengrin." — R. Wagner
4. Fantasia on Bohemian Airs for violin. — Paganini
Mr. Wm. Schultze.

5. Empfang beim Kayser. (Reception at the Emperor's) from "Lohengrin." R. Wagner

PART SECOND.

6. Overture to "Rienzi." R. Wagner
7. Air from "Sonnambula," "Vi ravviso," Bellini
Sung by F. Rudolph.
8. Ensemble and Chorus from "Tannhauser." R. Wagner
9. Duetto from "Semiramide" for contralto and baritone. Rossini
Mlle. Pintard and Mr. Rudolph.
10. Grand Finale und Waffentanz from "Rienzi." R. Wagner

It is to be remembered that the concert was given in 1853, when as yet "Lohengrin" was the latest performed of Wagner's operas, and these had only been heard a few times each. It is quite likely that the exile of Wagner and the sympathy these young men had with his political opinions may have had something to do with their giving an evening of his music.

Among the treasures of the collection of programs from which the preceding citations have been made is one of Oct. 4, 1853, at the new Music Hall, when Ole Bull was assisted by the musical phenomenon, Adelina Patti, and "Maurice Strakosch, the great pianist, director and conductor"—(the descriptives are probably his own). Strakosch opened the concert with a piano solo, his own fantasia upon themes from "Lucia" and opened the second with his own "Musical Rockets." Ole Bull played his own compositions consisting of operatic reminiscences, and other things. The little Patti sang "O Luce di quest' Anima," "Ah non Giunge," "Comin' thro' the Rye," and Jenny Lind's "Echo Song." At the next of Ole Bull's "farewell concerts in America," (Patti was already in the "farewell" business) the same order of pieces prevailed, the Patti numbers being "Happy Birdling of the Forest," "Ah non Giunge," "Home, Sweet Home," and "Jenny Lind's "Echo Song." Strakosch played his own "La Sylphide," and an imitation of the banjo.

Here also is a program of William Mason's concert in Tremont Temple, Oct. 3d, 1854, when he played Liszt's 2d Hungarian Rhapsody, the Beethoven "Moonlight Sonata," and the Handel E minor Fugue, as well as the Chopin Impromptu in A flat, and a Saltarello by Heller, on a theme of Mendelssohn. He was assisted by the famous

Mollenhauer brothers, of whom one is still living, who gave some very strong violin numbers. The same combination had a second concert a week later, but unfortunately the program is not in the lot.

Another interesting lot of programs are those of the Mendelssohn Quintette Club, of which we have two from the second season, three from the third season, and a few later. In the second season of Feb. 27, 1851, we find such combinations as this:

1. Quintette in E minor. — Spohr
2. Songs. Die Lotus Blume. — Schumann
   On Wings of Song. — Mendelssohn
   Mr. August Kreissmann.
3. Elegy for violin. — Ernst
   August Fries.
4. Sonata for Piano and violoncello. — Mendelssohn
   Messrs. C. C. Perkins and Wulf Fries
5. The Erl King. — Schubert
   Mr. August Kreissmann.
6. Quintette in C, op. 29. — Beethoven

The words of the "Erl King" are printed on the program.

On Feb. 3, 1853, the Club gave a Mendelssohn Birthday Festival, at which the program contained the Ottetto, Variations for piano and 'cello, (Otto Dresel as pianist), Andante and Scherzo from 1st. Quartette, and the 2d Trio for piano and strings.

The general conclusion from reading these programs is that much good seed-sowing has been done in America aside from the work of the New York Philharmonic and the Theodore Thomas concerts, and it is indeed curious to observe how conservative our programs still remain, and how closely these resemble most of those that are given today. Mr. Thomas has succeeded in drawing the line considerably closer with regard to the introduction of vocal numbers not in harmony with the general character of the instrumental music in the same connection. But after all the growth in this direction is less assured than one could wish. The trouble is with missionary work in music as it is in religion. One may do something for the individuals immediately reached, but there are a lots more coming on who are not reached, and who have to be reached again by precisely similar efforts. Thus history repeats itself.

One thing however is quite clear, which is that in his own work Mr. Thomas has evolved for himself, or taken where they left it, many points from the work of the Germanias.

Of course it is not to be supposed that in Boston the Germania musical society reached any such standard of tonal finish as that now regularly maintained by the Boston Symphony Orchestra, the New York Philharmonic or the Theodore Thomas Chicago Orchestra. In completeness, and in tonal finish these organizations are far in advance of the work of the Germania society. But that in its time was equally an advance upon the standard previously set up.

EGBERT SWAYNE.

IS "PERFECT INTONATION" PRACTICABLE?

CERTAINLY.

Certainly not.

And certainly this is a very paradoxical answer needing explanation.

But in order to reconcile this apparent contradiction, something of an "*Apologia pro Vita Sua*" will have to be worked into the treatment at various points.

The "*Vita*" dates back to 1839. Vermont and New Hampshire families, in the early part of the century, emigrated to the Canadian border, cleared farms and peopled towns on the Canadian side. My grandparents pursued their way in 1806, through more than one hundred woody miles, and my father, then four years old, remembered "crossing the line," near which they were to find a life-long habitation. About four miles south of my own parental roof was that Vermont line, which there runs east and west, "Jay Peak" being prominently in view thirty-five miles to the south of west, and a nearer branch of the Green Mountains, including Owl's Head and Orford Mountain, being twenty miles or more to the west of us, on our Canadian side.

An "ear for music" was a family characteristic; and while no piano nor other "equally tempered" instrument was in the house till the children were about grown up, violins and voices and a quartette were not wanting. We were not of the rub-a-dub sort of talent, as were some of the neighboring youngsters, who usually, to my silent displeasure, did not sing nor whistle nor fiddle in time, if indeed they could fiddle at all. I was offered the tempting reward of a three-bladed knife, by a boy twice my size, if I would "learn" him to play one tune on the fiddle. I labored with him for hours, but with such indifferent success that I did not get the knife, and indeed did not deserve it, for I dishonored my profession by giving encouragement where there was no ground of hope that the pupil would ever be able to saw out "Old Dan Tucker" or "Dandy Jim"--I forget which it was—any too melodiously. I do not wish to throw any contempt, even now, upon those and especially much better pieces of music, such as "Fisher's Hornpipe," "The Road to Boston," and the large repertory of others which we played, many of which, however, were less interesting than these two, because they did not admit of such excellent subordinate parts. How I wish I could now hear a specimen of those made-up "second parts" with which I was wont to accompany my seniors in our little string band at home! I held that old yellow fiddle in a reversed position, as they do a 'cello. As for "notes," my older brother used to play "psalm tunes" with my father from the books, but in those earliest years we had no "fiddle books," though when I heard that one of the neighboring boys had a real "book" to play from, it was for the time being something rather awe-inspiring to think of. But that *book* did not and could not cause that boy to play *in tune;* and I used to think it made him play all the more out of tune, because his attention was more taken up with the notes than with the sounds he was making. There *may* be a moral in this remark, but we are only story-telling now.

It must have been about 1845, and not long before I had fiddled my first tune, that I first heard an instrument of fixed tones. It was a "teter" melodeon, or simply a melodeon, for we knew of no other kind at that time. It was several years afterwards that melodeons on legs became popular. The scale of these little lap melodeons—there were three or four of them in town to my knowledge in 1845-50—was perhaps three and a fraction octaves. The instrument was apparently little else than a bellows with the usual ivory and ebony keys on the top, though the keys were very short, and the blowing was done with the arm or wrist of the player, or by another person, by a tetering motion. It was an economical arrangement truly, though the motion, if not actually producing sea-sickness, must have left more or less longing for *terra firma!*

It is impossible for me to tell now in what style of "temperament" those little melodeons were tuned. All reed instruments remain for some time, often a long time, very nearly in tune, that is, in whatever kind of tune they are tuned. Equal temperament tuning in America and Europe was by no means so universal all along through the first half of our century as it became about the middle of it; and organs and reed instruments did not take it so readily as did pianos; for in this system, making all Major Thirds for instance equally sharp and harsh, the instruments of prolonged tones would be thus the greatest sufferers. As for those little melodeons, however, I am pretty sure that some of them at least were *not* tuned in equal temperament, nor so intended. Some of the thirds must have been pure or much more approximately so than the division of the Octave into twelve equal parts allows; while other thirds would consequently be worse than the equal temperament allows, and therefore so bad as to be little used I remember coming across one of those lap melodeons about 1858, after I had become accustomed to the later melodeons on legs, which were tuned equally—though I knew not of any such thing as musical temperament then—and I was surprised to find the chord of A♭ and some others on this lap melodeon very discordant, and am inclined to think this was about as it was tuned where it was manufactured, although some one *might* have tampered with the reeds in trying to tune it more to his satisfaction, as I did myself once and not long after this. But I will come to that by and by. At any rate, some of the triads of some of those little tetering melodeons of my childhood must have been much more harmonious than the triads of our present scale of semitones; for they impressed my ear as something quite heavenly. And yet the tones of a reed are poor in quality, while those of violins are, or can be, far superior to them. But there was something so solid and certain and true about that ancient melodeon harmony, at least in the tonic, the dominant and the sub-dominant chords of one or two keys probably, that it seemed like a revelation in those early years.

Another great event occurred, and it was in 1849, an

event greater even than the lap melodeon harmony! A second-cousin, a girl of fourteen had brought home from Boston a two-dollar accordeon. Oh! ye gods, ye musical gods of earth, forever "shaking" in all your modern chromatic trumpets! look down and pity me, not only as I was then, but as I am now, if you will; but never shall I entirely lose the impression of those blissful moments when I at last stood, mute and statuesque, before that small but most celestial accordeon, while the owner played one of the simplest of tunes! It was then that perfect intonation was dominant in my soul and refused to be subdominant (and indeed there is no real subdominant chord in the accordeon). I received the impression that the people of Boston, whence the instrument came (though it was probably made in Germany), did little else than make and use such beautiful things, and that the city was Paradise! While we, notwithstanding the wealth of mountain air and home-made food, thought ourselves at least fifty miles out of the world, and two hundred and fifty from Boston and happiness, from which *former* place I am trying to make this little retrospect.

I have seen it stated that a reed organ or a melodeon is essentially an accordeon on a larger scale! It is essentially no such thing at all. Besides its peculiarity of producing one set of notes or one harmony by drawing and another by pressing, it has the still more distinctive quality of its peculiar intonation. Its seven-toned scale, which is found complete in the middle at least, is neither any kind of a tempered scale whatever, nor even the untempered diatonic major scale, as usually defined! Then what can it be? Well, it is by far the most musical scale possible for an accordeon, and we had better now understand this scale before going any further; especially as I can hardly expect that many of my readers will be more fortunate than I have been in finding a single book or printed article of any kind that informs us what are the intervals of the diatonic scale which belongs to the accordeon.

This scale and that of the mouth organ or harmonica, these being identical, are doubtless tuned by ear by means of the perfect chords which compose them, and their tuners do not necessarily know much about the arithmetic of these chords either. But they necessarily have very delicate tools and the best facilities for doing their work; and they tune those little reeds so as not to "beat" at all, and thus they are in perfect tune. These "free reeds" or brass vibrators, which are also the sounding material of melodeons and reed organs, the latter, however, being somewhat different in shape from those of the accordeon, and producing a different quality of tone, are about the best kind of sounding body for tuning and remaining in tune, whether it is some kind of tempered tuning which we want—in which case the "beats" can be easily determined and heard, or perfect tune, in which there are no beats.

There is more than one—there are more than two—correct definitions of our untempered diatonic scale major. The one which we usually find in musical and acoustical treatises and cyclopedias—as if this were the only one!—is, that it is composed of three major triads as tonic, dominant, and subdominant all in perfect tune. This is one style of it, and about the only one known to readers. But hardly the simplest melody or harmonious progression could be accounted for by such a scale as that alone. This triad, the most harmonious in music, is vibrationally 4:5:6, in which 4:6, or simply 2:3, is the true fifth, the simplest of all ratios next to that of the octave, 1:2. The ratio 1:3 might indeed be called simpler than the 2:3, but we are speaking of vibrational rates within an octave, for these are about all we need to consider in treating of the numerical laws of intonation. The ratio 1:3 would of course vibrationally form an octave plus a fifth. The 4:5 and the 5:6, which are the true Major and the true Minor Thirds, cannot be reduced to simpler terms. Three such triads consolidated as above result in a major scale whose steps are vibrationally as follows: 8:9, 9:10, 15:16, 8:9, 9:10, 8:9, 15:16. This is well known to musical readers. But readers do not generally know the mathematical art of *measuring ratios*, which is the same as measuring the musical intervals thus formed, —for the very numbers which express the vibration ratios are not those which really measure the intervals, and afford but a dim idea of their relation or specific magnitudes. My *nil* system of measurement, described in this magazine of June, 1893, can be depended upon as the best possible for the present treatment of intonation, perfect and tempered. The system of the late Mr. Ellis, the translator of Helmholtz, which mentally divides the octave interval into twelve-hundred equal parts, each of which he calls a "cent," it being thus a hundredth of an equal semitone, is much better than nothing, and possesses the advantage of the round number, one hundred. But my mental division of six hundred and twelve is more economical and much more exact, much more so than by any possible Octave division without going up into thousands. The number is also, like twelve hundred, divisible by twelve, so that our equal semitone, which is one hundred of Mr. Ellis's cents, is fifty-one nils. Either of course is perfectly mathematical for the tempered intervals; but the nils are much nearer to the mathematical truth for the untempered or perfect intervals than are the cents. Comparisons will have to remain odious to the end of the world, but the truth must be told, and then the heavens may fall!

This is a long--and it may be an "odious"—digression, by which the reader, however, is not invited to "cipher" out these things much, but only to take the most simplified results of my own "ciphering."

In the above usually defined diatonic scale major, consisting of three perfect major triads, the steps measure in nils as follows: 104, 93, 57, 104, 93, 104, 57, the Octave being six hundred and twelve nils. This is of course much nearer the mathematical truth than any one can sing them, or even tune them, even with reeds, but none too near for science.

But this is *not* the diatonic scale of the accordeon.

Indeed if the diatonic scale were tuned in equal temperament for the accordeon—which would be not only entirely unnecessary but destructive of its peculiar harmony of intonation—it would actually be much more tolerable thus, on the whole, than if it were tuned in this "true" scale above described! The tonic chord, produced by blowing in one direction, would be of course true in this scale, but two tones in each complete Octave produced by the *other* motion, would be unendurable. And yet those two tones are the true and harmonious Fourth (3:4) and Sixth (3:5) of the scale! That is, they would harmonize truly with the *first* of the scale. But that tone is never heard by the same motion of the bellows as gives the dominant harmony, and this subdominant fourth and sixth do not belong to the dominant, which has its own true fourth and sixth of the scale, or seventh and ninth from the dominant note.

But it may be thought that the two kinds of Fourths and Sixths are almost the same thing, and that the difference is only a "mathematical subtlety." Well, I wish we could all hear this *subtlety* just now, and then we would know. In the first place, that kind of a sixth, being of the subdominant, makes, as is pretty well known to students, a very false fifth from this Second of the scale, or D—A, in this "true" scale of C, this D belonging to the dominant chord. The fifth is a whole Comma (80:81) flat, this being 11 nils. It sounds enough like a Fifth to make us think it was intended to be a Fifth, but is horribly out of tune. (There is no "mystery" about this. The three component triads of this scale are indeed perfect, but these two tones are so remotely related vibrationally in the consolidation of the triads that the ear cannot recognize that relation, and therefore it is not musical, and we would not consider it musical at all but for an approximate coincidence. The ratio is 27:40: and these large numbers form a ratio too complicated for the ear. Yet this ratio being *measured*, it is found to *approach* in size to that of the simple and very recognizable and musical ratio 2:3, which is the true Fifth. Nature was not at all *obliged* to make it a Fifth! but the approximate coincidence is one of similar cases which render our wonderful tonal system possible.)

This true Fourth, 3:5, which is harmonious and true in the subdominant chord, and even makes a good and musical dissonance with the dominant *tone*, either with or without the tonic tone, makes the four-toned dominant seventh *chord* rough and untuneful, and although, for certain reasons not now to be specified, it is more tolerable thus than is a Fifth 11 nils flat, as aforesaid, still it is even more than that out of its own proper tune in the dominant chord. The difference is indeed a larger Comma (63:64) of 14 nils. Now these facts are going to lead us presently into what may seem incredible to some. We will lower this true Fourth the 14 nils, which may be roughly called a quarter of a semitone; then we will raise the true Sixth (in the subdominant chord) 11 nils, which is the smaller Comma. We shall then have not only the true D—A (Scale of C) but a Fourth on the tonic which, although quite out of tune with that, makes a true Harmonic Seventh from the dominant (4:7). But have we not thus spoiled completely the beautiful interval F—A, the pure Major Third! For we have indeed added 14 nils to one end of it and 11 nils to the other end, and 25 nils is about half our equal semitone, of 51 nils! *No*, though we have certainly made something else of it. Its vibrational ratio is now no longer 4:5, but one a little more complicated, 7:9, yet not so much so as not to make a very perceptible and peculiar harmony, especially as a harmonic continuation of the major triad, thus, 4:5:6:7:9, this being the most harmonious of pentads. But if this very large Third (7:9) were placed in the major triad *instead* of the (4:5), the effect would be intolerable, for it is not far from *half way* in size between the Major Third and the true Fourth. Mr. Ellis calls this the Supermajor Third, and both Ellis and Helmholtz recognize and name the very small Third (6:7) and call it Subminor; and it is exactly as much smaller than the Minor Third (5:6) as the 7:9 is larger than the 4:5, that is, *twenty-five nils*, or the sum of the two Commas 63:64 and 80:81, which make a very large Comma (35:36). This may be called roughly half a semitone, but it is not and cannot (very musically) be used as a melodic or even an enharmonic interval in progressions of perfect chords, but it enharmonically divides into the two lesser Commas. That is, *in principle*; it would never be perfectly so in any attempts at perfect intonation, that is, not as perfectly as the intervals are here measured in nils. The 53-division of the octave, which very well represents perfect harmony, and which I use in a complete instrument of that system, represents the 14-nil and the 11-nil Commas each by 1-53d of an octave, which is about 11½ nils.

Now we have found the accordeon style of the diatonic scale, and find that it is *not* the *trichordal* scale, the one usually defined, but a *dichordal* scale, for it is composed of only *two* harmonics, namely, the same tonic chord as in the other, and a five-toned chord on the dominant. It is indeed perfectly so tuned by the accordeon manufacturers —by ear—whatever they know or do not know about its numerical rationale. The vibration ratios of the steps of this dichordal scale are 8:9, 9:10, 20:21, 7:8, 8:9, 9:10, and 15:16, and they measure 104, 93, 43, 118, 104, 93, and 57 nils. The difference between the two diatonic semitones is the 14-nil Comma, and the "whole tones" differ by either the 14-nil or the 11-nil or their sum.

Now the triad (6:7:9) is *not* a minor triad, at least our well known minor triad which has a Minor Third (5:6) and a Major Third (4:5), like the major triad, but in a reversed order. The 6:7:9 triad has indeed the true Fifth, 6:9 being simply 2:3, but very differently divided.

To make this triad minor the middle tone must go up 25 nils, or to make it substantially our tempered minor triad the middle tone must go up 17 nils (the Fifth being but one nil flat in our tempered scale, which is almost entirely imperceptible).

This triad when not associated with the other two tones of the pentad, one of which is the root, is not very pleasing; and to use it in any such way—in place of the minor triad for instance—would at once show itself very unmusical.

This accordeon scale is perfect where the usually defined diatonic scale is false, and *vice versa*. It frequently requires both, that is, nine tones per octave instead of seven, to render the simplest hymn tunes in true harmony. Moreover the second of the scale has frequently to be lowered an 11 nil Comma in order to get the relative minor chord of the subdominant in true tune. And the minor triad in this relation is very common, so that there are *ten* tones per octave very necessary for playing about any half dozen of the simplest hymn tunes in true harmony, namely those containing no accidentals at all. Where such do exist, as in fact they do in most hymn tunes, corresponding enharmonic changes of a comma occur also.

In our 12-division of the octave, all Fifths are but one nil short; all Major Thirds are seven nils large—and this temperal Third also answers for the (7:9); and the Minor Third, which is shortened 8 nils, does duty for the little (6:7) also; and the Harmonic Seventh (4:7) is lengthened 16 nils, which makes it the same as two other Minor Sevenths, each being made thus 10-12ths of an octave.

In the 53 division, every thing may be called practically perfect except the Septal element, the 4:7 being still between two and three nils large. But a *nil* is next to *nothing* to the ear, and even two or three nils of imperfection, in such a subordinate order of chords as Septals, is not serious.

In the present article, I have attempted to bring out the fact, so little known, that scarcely any music can be rendered in true and full harmony in merely one style of diatonic scale; and I mean music, too, in which there is not a single accidental. There are almost always not seven but eight, very frequently nine, and not at all seldom ten tones per octave, in which latter case the music employs still another style of major scale than the two above defined, namely, one having its Second on the tonic 9:10 instead of the usual 8:9 (93 nils instead of 104). That is, the two first steps would change places.

Without, however, attempting much more in this number, I present here a beautiful little hymn tune of Wm. B. Bradbury's. Like very many hymn and other tunes, it is in *both* kinds of diatonic major scales above defined; for it has the subdominant chord and also the Septal element in the dominant and in one place also the dominant seventh and ninth. It is perfectly beautiful as thus rendered on my instrument, although so simple a piece might also be played in true tune on an instrument of quite limited modulation, while this fifty-three-division is capable of unlimited modulation, like our existing twelve system.

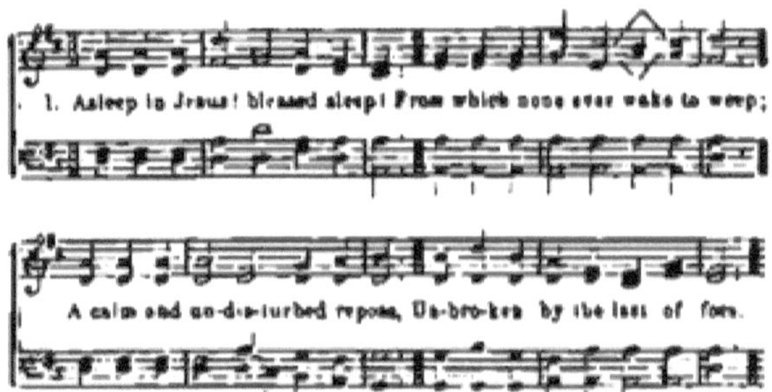

The first line contains nothing but what is common to both styles, but in the second line we have first the Minim Third (6:7), then its inversion the Maxim Sixth (7:12), then the Major Sixth (3:5), *then the Maxim Third* (7:9), then a Septal Fourth (7:10), followed by the tonic chord. The effect is also enhanced by filling up these harmonics with the instrument, though there be not voices enough to do so, especially the pentad of the Ninth, which is here represented only by two radical bass tones and the Maxim Third, vibrationally 2:4:7:9.

In the third line is the true subdominant triad, not in the accordeon scale at all, introduced by a "natural" in the bass, which, however, is *not* the usual C corresponding to this D, but a Septal comma lower, 14 nils, forming the true Harmonic Seventh (4:7) on the D below, or a true dominant Seventh for the key of G. This kind of chromatic semitone, here represented by the "natural," is (14:15), and although the same in the 53-system as the last step of the scale (15:16), is really four nils larger. In the last line the Minim Third again occurs immediately before the last chord. My instrument has not a particularly fine quality of tone, yet this piece is rendered by it much more beautifully than musical people who have never heard such can imagine; although they might sometimes have heard something very near it rendered by good natural singers without an instrument.

I am treating of the nature, the possibilities, and the

impossibilities of "perfect intonation;" I shall also take in by the way the question of the perpetuity of our equally tempered system, or uncial scale. In my own mind there has been no question about it at all for many years, it being believed completely indispensable for a large part of music and therefore immortal—young as it is. My reasons for this belief, however, are mostly different from those usually adduced; for it is generally supposed that the whole argument for the use of the imperfect intonation of the uncial scale is a merely mechanical one, or one of convenience. There is a *musical* reason for it, and one at least *twelve times* stronger than any other, and this I hope will appear incidently in following numbers.

Yet I have also fully realized for many years that immense advantages would accrue to music if something could be done to render it more possible for thoughtful musicians and others to know to some extent the nature of true or untempered intonation; for in that way alone can they know the true and proper uses of the tempered. Our highest musical authorities, doctors of music and all the rest, do not understand these things—do not *begin* to understand them —and here it will be in order to let the heavens fall again !

Next time I may go on further with the accordeons, the old melodeons, and more "egotistigraphy"—the word is truly borrowed—and this will help to view the field of intonation.

The accordeon style of scale belonged intimately to music, vocal at least, long before that instrument was invented, it having been always in the nature and rationale of music, and might have cleared up many a dark point. If Henry Liston for example, early in the century, had known of it, he would never have written such pitiable nonsense about this same chord of the Major Ninth, in connection with his "Enharmonic Organ." (See his article *Music*, in the old Edinburg Encyclopedia.)

[TO BE CONTINUED.]

JAMES PAUL WHITE

THE NATURE OF MUSIC AND ITS RELATION TO THE QUESTION OF WOMEN IN MUSIC.

AMONG the fine arts music is pre-eminent in its dependence upon Form for its expression. To body forth the airy somethings of his brain the painter uses the familiar objects of nature. If he be a realist, form beyond the mere technical knowledge of how to produce an image of the object hardly comes into play. And this would be true were the method that of an impressionist or that of the painfully conscientious limner of every leaf. The aim in both is the same—to depict an image of reality. The idealist may and does give greater range to his imagination in form, yet he is handicapped by the definite nature of whatever objects he may choose for the expression of his idea. The utmost the painter can do is to combine his objects imitated, sometimes perverted from nature as in the case of conventionalized art, in such a way as to make them stand as symbols of some meaning broader than would appear in the objects themselves. William Black may represent the plagues of Egypt by a hideous monster from all over whose body emanate fiendish looking swirls of something which we may imagine with the aid of modern science to be blasting currents of microbes, and though as a whole this monster is not of nature, he is pieced together out of perfectly recognizable natural objects. His shape is in the likeness of a man, his scales those of a fish, his emanations, the conventional representation of wind, for even the unseeable must be represented by the seeable in painting.

The poet also uses words everyone of which brings to the mind a definite image or idea. In constructing his poem, therefore, his devotion to form is limited by the necessity of presenting clearly the idea. Yet his tether is longer than in the case of the painter, for where the painter can raise only to symbolism, the poet scales the heights of metaphor. The painter may give indirect expression by direct means, but the poet can give direct expression by indirect means. A crude illustration will make this point clear. The poet instead of saying "the moon was shining" may say "the lamp of night cast her pale light abroad" but the painter can only say this by painting an image of moonlight, for to paint a student lamp or a piano lamp or any other kind of lamp with which we are familiar suspended in the sky would be utterly meaningless. Or for another example, the poet might speak of the "greening year" and everyone would immediately see the trees with their young green leaves and the grass with the freshness of spring, but if a painter merely daubed his canvas with light green paint, who would know that it meant spring, or admire it if they did know.

With music, however, there are no definite objects nor concrete ideas to exercise the slightest restraint upon the form, and therefore the composer may, indeed must, centralize to the utmost his energies on the form. Even his material has an element of art form in it. The very bottom fact of music is the sensuous pleasure derived from sound and rhythm. It makes no difference whether music originated in emotional cries or whether it originated in rhythm, there was latent in the being who first struggled toward music, a faculty for deriving pleasure from sound and rhythm, otherwise music would never have become an art.

Without going into a discussion as to which element, sound or rhythm, had precedence in the formation of music, before sound could become fit to be used as a material in the production of an art, it had to be subjected to an intellectually formative process. Out of the infinite number of pitches possible, a certain number had to be chosen with certain definite relations to each other, nor was this choice consummated in a single day. Centuries, perhaps, thousands of years elapsed before the final choice was made, as we have it today, in the diatonic major scale. Definite duration had to be given to pitch, and various relations in the durations set up. Now, the guiding principal in all these developments must have been the desire for beauty, and the intellectual perception that greater beauty in the manipulation of sound was attainable by such means, since none of them add one jot or one tithe to the definiteness of the idea to be expressed. Thus, we find that as far back as we can push, music presents us with the phenomenon of formal development. Totally unhampered from the first with any necessity of presenting concrete ideas, appealing in its simplest conceivable form to the sensuous perception of beauty, it has been left free to develop to its furthest confines the beauty of form. In this respect it is somewhat akin to the purely Arabesque in art, but it has qualities which carry it far and away beyond. While the Arabesque is form reduced to its simplest expression, music is form raised to its most complex expression, as I shall explain more fully presently. Yet they are alike in the fact that neither could exist without form, the relation between form and thought in each case being inseparable and constant, differing too from both painting and poetry because the latter are capable of almost infinite variations in the relations of form to thought, sometimes one and sometimes the other being uppermost. Thus it is that of all artists the composer must have the keenest perception of beauty in the abstract. The painter and the poet may do work which passes for art, though possessed of only a modicum of appreciation for the abstractly beautiful, because each is aided by the element of truth which forms part of the material of his art, but the musician who has no such perception simply cannot write music at all. He might be a man capable of the most abstract emotions, or of the deepest passions, but if he have not the supreme faculty of creating beauty of form in sound he must forever be dumb.

This fact which anyone will see with a little thought to be easily demonstrable, seems at first sight to range us on the side of those philosophers and musical æstheticians who claim that music is solely a formal art as Hanslick says "it's only subject matter, forms set in motion by sound." Yet, those who have experienced almost every degree of nervous excitation when listening to music will very justly have it that music has its soul side; but the question is, just what is the nature of this soul side of music? August Wilhelm

Ambros, not satisfied with Hanslick's definition, has attempted to pluck out the heart of the mystery as difficult to get at as the life principle in the fairy tale of Pauchkin. "Far away, far away, hundreds of thousands of miles away from this there lies a desolate country covered with thick jungle. In the midst of the jungle grows a circle of palm trees, and in the center of the jungle stand six jars full of water, piled one above the other; below the sixth jar is a cage which contains a little green parrot, on the life of the parrot depends my life."

He is equally dissatisfied with those who claim that the emotions are the sphere of music. Even emotions are of too definite a nature to form the soul-stuff of music. Its real office is to "convey moods of finished expression; it, as it were, forces them upon the hearer. It conveys them in finished form because it possesses no means for expressing the previous series of ideas which speech can clearly and definitely express." No one will be inclined to decry that music awakens moods but we have only got as far as the cage in the story, the parrot still eludes us. The difficulty with this explanation, as with every other one that has been attempted, is that there is the tendency to separate the expression from that which is expressed in music, leading inevitably to too definitely a bounded realm over which music holds sway.

The nearest to a definite answer that seems possible to the writer, is that the soul of music is the very essence of the beautiful in form, born into it through its exceeding exquisiteness, as beauty gave birth to soul in the myth of Galatea. In other words, the soul of music is the product of the form. The great composer is like the Prometheus of Goethe. He creates beautiful forms and through their beauty they attain life. To the creating of this beautiful form must go first of all æsthetic perception, but this must be indefinitely enriched and deepened by the emotions and the intellect, in fact, mind and heart and soul must be transmuted into the beautiful in form as earth and sunshine and air into flowers. Only thus does music become a vehicle of expression, and reflect mind and heart and soul. Calmly the artistic faculty presides over this most wondrous of chemic changes. Emotion and thought are marshalled by it to the supreme attainment of a work of art. It is as if the composer divided himself in two. As the psychologist makes a scientific diagnosis of his own sensations the composer may be said to make an artistic synthesis of his own sensations. So much is the soul of music a product of its form, that the two are inseparable. We cannot say of a piece of music as we do of a poem that the idea expressed is good but the expression is bad, for the idea to be expressed and the expression of it are absolutely one. Only through the form of the expression can any glimmer of the idea be caught.

Granted, then, that music is the art in which form reaches its most supreme and untrammelled development, what is the faculty of paramount importance to the composer? Clearly, it is the faculty not only of perceiving that which will be most beautiful in form, but, also, the power to create it. Undoubtedly, all great composers are born with this faculty, but the power to realize their conceptions, to make them incarnate in forms of immortal loveliness, comes only with long and patient study.

The bearing of all this upon the hackneyed subject of women in music may not be very evident at first sight when, however, a clever writer assures us as Miss Brower did in a recent article in the *Atlantic* that "music has the emotions for its sphere," and that "few of the great composers had any education to speak of," and argues therefrom that the musical idea must be a divine inspiration, which has fallen to the lot of men, in whose ears alone "God whispers," since women have failed to attain fame as composers, and finally clinches her argument by stripping women of the heritage of emotions allowed her by the most scornful of the opposite sex; is it not time that the voice of one crying in the wilderness should bear witness to the truth, first, that the possession of even abstract emotional power is not of itself sufficient to make a composer, the best modern thought having long ago relegated the "emotions" to their proper place as excellent fertilizers, but by no means the whole world of music. And, furthermore, that all of the great composers, far from being the ignoramuses that some people would have us believe, were thoroughly trained, either through their own efforts, or through the aid of teachers and experience, in all that pertains to the technic of composition, and not a few were educated men in other respects.

Mendelssohn and Schumann are shining examples. Beethoven had more Latin, even if he had less Greek, than Shakespeare, besides a knowledge of French and Italian and a thorough acquaintance with German and English literature. It is not worth while to multiply instances; they can be found in any musical dictionary.

As for their musical education, there is not one from Bach down who did not have it. They were usually taught several instruments, were drilled in the laws of counterpoint, and pored over the scores of the great composers who preceded them. In fact, no art can boast a more continuous record of special training than that of music, and no art requires special training more than music. And to men almost exclusively in the past has fallen the lot of special training. During the middle ages, when modern music came into being, learning was in the hands of the monks and this was true of musical learning as well as of every other branch of knowledge. The names in musical history during this period are St. Ambrose, Bishop of Milan; St. Gregory the Great; Isidore, Archbishop of Seville; the monks Hucbald, and Guido d'Arezzo; and in spite of "God's whisperings" it took these inspired gentlemen nine centuries to discover the very simple fact that two notes could be sounded simultaneously; and in their slavishness to Greek tradition, they even then allowed only perfect fifths and fourths, and eighths, to be sounded together, for had not Pythagoras with all his extraordinary sensitiveness to celestial harmony been deaf to the harmonic relations of any but these intervals?

In the mean time, of course, the people were doing something for music in their folk-song, and no one knows whether these were always the invention of men. Very clever arguments have been adduced to the contrary and the burden of mythical proof is certainly in favor of women.

We must not forget the Gopis of India, who danced and sang with Krishna in scales of their own invention, nor the Goddess Saraswati who gave music to the Hindus, nor Fou Ki, the supernatural female who bestowed music on the Chinese.

Whatever may be the truth as to their invention, when folks-song make a step in development, and first get themselves noticed, women have fallen into the background, and it is entirely reasonable to suppose that it was because of their lack of knowledge of musical form. The Troubadours were among the first developers of folk-song and they were, as Fanny Raymond Ritter says, well acquainted with the laws of composition. The laws of music were then highly complicated and ill classified, yet they were well understood by the best Troubadours.

We do not hear of women being subjected to any such drill in the gradually developing laws of counterpoint and later of harmony. Even within the last decade, the writer has heard of German teachers who absolutely refused to teach women the science of harmony, because, as they declared, no woman could understand it. If such a feeling is possible in this enlightened century, it is easy to picture what might have been the attitude in the past toward the training of women in the direction of creative work in music. This fact needs peculiar emphasis, because in Germany the two tendencies, on the one hand, of musical development, and, on the other, of suppression of women have been most marked.

Against the argument that women have had no opportunities, Miss Brower adduced that woman had a lute put into her hands before the pen. That is just the trouble; she has had so much and no more. She has until comparatively recently been taught to execute but not to create.

Another way in which conditions have been peculiarly favorable for the development of the composing faculty in men is that they have always breathed in the midst of musical environments. When a Bach or a Hayden is discovered to have a voice he immediately becomes a choir boy, and being a boy he knows he may someday become choir master.

so he observes the effects which may be produced from the organ, or the effects in chorus singing—all of which he lays up in his mind and digests as artistic food.

Likewise, when a Handel or a Beethoven plays an instrument ere long he plays in an orchestra, and so has constant opportunity of observing the qualities and capabilities of the instruments, the timbre, the intensity of sound and so on. Only by such means can he hope ever to use instruments effectively. And this artistic expression is no more than artistic diet without which the artistic faculty can no more grow and develop than could a human body develop physically without food.

I repeat, that, considering the peculiarly important part played by form in music, and by form I do not mean necessarily classic form, but form in all its modern developments—more of this artistic diet is needed in the development of a creative talent than in any other art. The priestess of music does not give forth her oracles from the tripod of goodness, truth and beauty. She is an airy sibyl who balances herself upon the pinnacle of beauty alone. All elements else must be transformed into the purely beautiful, and this is why the oracles of this sibyl are the most difficult of all to interpret. I do not intend to argue from these facts that women are great composers. The proof of this must lie alone in her production of great musical works. I think, however, as I have tried to show, that the nature of music is such that certain conditions in the past have militated greatly against her highest development in the art, and notwithstanding the fact that the lute was put into her hand before the pen, these causes are not any innate inferiority of mind or heart, of intellect or emotion, but a lack of that transcendant power of expression in form, which in music, especially, can only come, and has only come even to the greatest of musicians, after the most profound and careful study of the laws of composition and of the masterpieces of the art.

Until women have had the same sort of training, above all, the same musical environments, the same opportunity to devote themselves body and soul to the art of composition, it is manifestly unfair to declare them mentally and emotionally incapable of great work.

The difficulties that women must overcome are far greater than those which meet men at the dawn of their musical career. They must come into competition with all the great works which have preceded them, and they must struggle in the face of a prejudice against their possession of genius so deeprooted and wide spread that even their faith in themselves wavers, and the desire to attain without which no goal can be made is thus shorn of the strong impulse that should "aim at the stars" and is content if it but "hits the moon."

HELEN A. CLARKE.

FLOWER-MAIDENS IN "PARSIFAL."

In every scent a charm to haunt the heart,
In every hue to bind the spirit's eye.
In every glance pierces the will a dart
Hence, youth! there is no life save thou depart!

PHILIP B. GOETZ

THE STORY OF A GENIUS

VI

Alphonse de Sterny! The man at that time exercised a quite mysterious charm on the ear of every one—were he artist or dilletanti—who was interested in music.

Today, in our times, when judgment daily becomes older and more skeptical, we can form no idea of the mad idolatry which in the fifties was shown to the two or three piano virtuosos. De Sterny belonged to the most idolized. The Sterny enthusiasm entered like a devastating disease into all the cities in which he gave concerts. Nevertheless it was hard to solve the riddle of his power. Those of his colleagues who were envious asserted plainly that he owed his triumphs not so much to the artistic rendering of his selections as to the universal attraction of his personality.

He was the perfection of a *homme à succès*. Just dandified enough to pass for elegant, just careless enough to pass for distinguished, sufficiently quick and malicious to be called intellectual, frivolous and profligate enough to be held for genial. He was very handsome, wore his hair always arranged in the modern style, always dressed after the latest fashion, as should a man of good form, with the most sober earnestness without any artistic deviations. His conversation was amusing, his manner blameless. He was the natural son of a French diplomat, called himself De Sterny after his birthplace, and had twenty-five thousand francs income as the world knew—inherited from an Italian princess, which the world did not know.

His piano playing was perfectly beautiful, a rain of pearls, a chain of flowers, masterly even in technique, never a false note, never an ordinary touch.

The great Russian god of the piano, part of whose effect consisted in many false tones, asserted cuttingly: "De

Sterny's playing reminded him of the performance of a countess." But Sterny, to whom naturally this remark was repeated by good friends, smiled at it with his charming politeness, and continued—at least in the beginning of his career—to refinedly caress an instrument, which at that time other virtuosos only genially maltreated, and by his moderation electrified the public, already over satisfied with musical orgies. He moved quite exclusively in the best circles of society, showed himself always ready to do a service to his colleagues.

On the whole, when Gesa learned to know him he was a perfectly shallow, perfectly selfish, unusually talented, very good natured and vain man, who willingly got himself talked about. He became a character later in order to maintain himself upon the pedestal to which the public had raised him. Another would have become dizzy up there.

He liked to patronize, and therefore he did not satisfy himself with pressing the young violinist's hand, but gave him his address and asked him to come to him the next morning in the "Hotel de Flandres" so that "we can speak of your future," he said encouragingly. Then he was still charming to all the others present in the green room, gave his hand to Delilea, whose tears were running down his cheeks, patted the debutante on the shoulder, wished him "Good luck"—and vanished.

At the little artist's supper which the giver of the concert had arranged for those who took part in it, Gesa did not eat a mouthful and spoke not a word. With pale cheeks and staring eyes he gazed before him into the future—a future in which the trees had golden leaves and their fruit sparkled like diamonds—a future in which dust and mould were unknown things, in which houris beaming with beauty and shedding happiness wandered between thornless bushes, and the laurel trees instinctively inclined to him.

At that time Gesa Von Zaylen's eyes were not anxiously squinted, as those of a wild animal dreading the light, but wide open like those of a young eagle for whom no light is too bright—whom even the sun itself does not blind.

No one could receive a gifted but obscure beginner more

heartily than the great De Sterny received the little Von Zuylen. He invited the boy to breakfast, twice, three times in succession. Gesa become an installed piece of furniture, perhaps rather a favorite plaything in the virtuoso's elegant apartment in the hotel. He must bring his violin with him, must improvise for the virtuoso, while De Sterny many times accompanied him on the piano with the sensitive skill which characterised his gifted nature. He drew Gesa into conversation, he laughed, laughed immoderately over the boy's original remarks. Sterny soon could meet none of his acquaintances without calling to him "Have you seen my little gypsy yet? I must make you acquainted with my little gypsy. That is a wonder—but a wonder! He improvises like Chopin—only quite differently. Yesterday he quoted Shakespeare to me, and today he discovered that Marsala was worse than Tokay. And he is pretty—*a croquer*!"

In Brussels society the fable of the "eighth wonder" spread, and Princess L. for love of his patron arranged a *soirée musicale* on which occasion the eighth wonder in the world really for a moment ran the risk of losing his prestige.

Sterny with the most charming pedantry, troubled himself with all the details of his protegé's appearance, had him measured for a pair of patent leather shoes, with his own hand, on the evening of the great event pulled his white cravat straight, and brought him in his own carriage to the L. palace. But already in the vestibule, brilliant with old arms, and with two mysterious coats of mail, Gesa's robust confidence vanished completely. He, who at a public concert had offered himself to the public with the courage of a lion, here clung with quite childish anxiety to Sterny.

"Have you brought the eighth wonder of the world with you?" called the princess to the virtuoso upon his entrance. She was a blonde, unusually friendly lady, very lively, and very near sighted for which reason she incessantly held her *lorgnon* to her eyes. "Have you brought the eighth wonder of the world with you?" she called in a tone as if the eighth wonder of the world were something comical. "Naturally, here it is—it is called Gesa Von Zuylen—Gesa Von Zuylen, *c'est drôle*—is it not princess? May I ask you to treat my wonder carefully, it is sensitive!"

"So—really! That is charming. It pleases me when a young artist feels a certain pride; that is always becoming. What eyes he has!" looking at Gesa through her *longnon*—"my husband has already told me of his eyes. An embodied gypsy—he recently quoted Shakespeare. I laughed over that so." Then as the other guests entered, "I beg you to make the eighth wonder of the world comfortable, De Sterny," she remarked, "you are at home here." This was the princess' manner of treating a sensitive wonder carefully.

De Sterny placed the boy for the present in a corner from which he soon drew him to present him to several ladies and gentlemen. Gesa took on a defiant manner. The ladies especially were very friendly, very patronizing, only it occurred to scarcely one of them to address a word to him. All spoke of him before him as if he were a picture or did not understand French. They were astonished, and praised, while he yet stood before them they forgot him again and spoke with each other of other things.

He felt stranger and stranger; it seemed to him as if he were walking on painfully smooth, dangerously thin ice. He shivered. All about him was so brilliant and so cold. The fine, low, flute-like voices of good society pained him. Light and piercing like snow-flakes the words seemed to strike his glowing cheeks.

He could have cried. He was the eighth wonder of the world; they stared at him through a *lorgnon*, talked about him and—troubled themselves no more about him.

Among others he overheard the words: "He comes from the Rue Ravestein." "What is that! the Rue Ravestein?" "What is that? It is hard to explain to a lady." "*Vraiment?*" "But he makes an astonishing well-bred appearance—*il n'a pas du tout l'air peuple! Mais puis que c'est un tzigane*—" Gesa's throat contracts.

"Shall we hear you today?" ask the ladies, who crowd around De Sterny the virtuoso.

"Me?" replied he "Me? I am only manager today,

and have stage fright—horrible stage fright."

The moment was come! Gesa should play; his heart beat up in his neck. He was not himself, but an awkward fellow staring with fright, who had his fingers on the violin. In the midst of Mendelssohn's violin concerto he stopped, collected himself, hurried over, and only bunglingly completed the piece. One had seldom heard it worse played. De Sterny was beside himself and Gesa would have liked to sink through the floor.

Some people applauded because they had noticed nothing and had scarcely listened. But the most shrugged their shoulders and said: "De Sterny is an enthusiast."

When De Sterny wished to put in a word for the poor little gypsy, begged pardon for him and asserted he had never heard him play so badly, they answered him. "Bah! we do not blame you, Sterny; we know you are an enthusiast!"

Society talked and laughed, and ate refreshments in their fleeting way. Then a deputation of the most beautiful ladies came and begged Sterny to play something, and he seated himself at the piano with his good humored readiness, his smiling consciousness of victory.

After he had finished playing, he stepped up to Gesa and said "My dear boy, collect yourself! Could you forget that any one hears you but me, and improvise something? Try to recall the theme you played for me recently. Your future depends on it, and I would so like to be proud of you!"

These last words worked wonders. "I will play—only—only—so that I will do you no discredit!" murmured Gesa.

The boy was deathly pale, he trembled in his whole frame when he took up his violin, his eyes sparkled, then they hid themselves sadly behind his long dark lashes.

A rain of fire shone before his eyes, a whirlpool raged in his breast, wild, longing melodies rang in his ears.

Had he dreamed the measures, or had a complaining autumn storm borne them to him from his father in a distant country? Were they echoes of songs which his mother had learned from her lover, with which later she had cradled her child in sleep, while she sat on the door sill of the house in the dirty alley, into which the sad crucifix looked down? Who knows?

A singing and sobbing sound from his violin, such as one only hears from Hungarian gypsies, harsh modulations, piercing melodies, a mad storm of passion and music, then a last fierce rejoicing—and he broke off.

Breathless, he stared before him. He knew he had done his best! He listened inquisitively. If he had expected a storm of applause to follow his public production, he was disappointed. Only a little buzz, like dry leaves which an autumn storm has piled up, sounded through the room; as if from a great distance he heard the words: "*Charmant, magnifique, original, tsigane.*" He lowered his head, a black cloud danced before his eyes. Then De Sterny stepped up to him and slapped him on the shoulder. "Bravo, bravo," he said. "We are rehabilitated!" and turning to the company with a triumphant smile—"Now have I exaggerated?"

But Gesa did not hear the answer of the drawing room; he pressed De Sterny's hand to his hot lips and burst into tears. De Sterny was his heaven, his God. "*Mais voyons grand enfant,*" the virtuoso calmed him. And society was charmed, naturally; more by the generosity of the virtuoso than by the geniality of the boy.

VII.

"What is a chimera?" asked the little gypsy once, of his great friend. It was afternoon. Gesa had been turning over the leaves of a book by Baudelaire, "Les Fleurs du mal." The virtuoso had written letters meanwhile. He wore a yellow dressing gown of Japanese silk in which he reminded one of a gigantic candle, yawned and stretched himself, looked pale and worn, and one perceived in him that he had not really slept for fifteen years.

"What is a chimera?" asked Gesa.

"A chimera,—a chimera—it is a siren with wings," defined De Sterny turning round.

"Hm!" Gesa lowered his eyes thoughtfully and then raised them penetratingly. "A noble siren?"

"Yes, as one takes it."

De Sterny sat by the chimney to warm his feet. "Devilish cold, hand me the Chartreuse—so. A refined siren as far as I am concerned," he continued. "The siren has soft human arms with which she cradles us in destructive joys; the chimera has claws with which she tears our hearts. The siren charms us into the mire, the chimera allures us into heaven. We never attain heaven, and sometimes we feel very well in the mire!—devilish well but—*Sapperment!* you do not understand that," and the virtuoso pulled the boy's ear.

Gesa looked somewhat confused, he had really not understood one word of the tirade of his patron. "But still some of us do attain heaven—the heaven of art—Walhalla—the Pantheon," he remarked, with the important bombast of a young man who has read more than he has understood, and willingly airs his little bit of knowledge. "If only one starts soon enough."

"Oh yes, some!" murmured the virtuoso, and smiled peculiarly. "Michel Angelo, Raphael, Beethoven," cited the boy. "Shakespeare, Milton, Mozart and Leonardo da Vinci" the virtuoso continued the strange litany, laughing aloud—"but I assure you one must have quite astonishing strength to attain Heaven, and quite peculiarly constructed lungs in order to feel well therein."

The virtuoso yawned slightly. He belonged to those who amuse themselves with sirens without conceding their power over them, and who usually go out of the way of chimeras.

But Gesa was still dissatisfied. "Have all chimeras wings?" he asked thoughtfully.

"God forbid" said the virtuoso. "Very many of them have no wings—but they do not count, they allure one on the erroneous path of ambition, they stand with their four paws fast in the mud and bay at the moon without stirring."

"But—" "My dear," said the virtuoso laughing, "if you have any thing else to ask, say so. I will ring the bell so that the waiter can bring you a conversation lexicon. I am at an end with my Latin."

VIII

It was about seven years later towards the middle of May. After a long absence Gesa came back to Brussels. Alphonse de Sterny had known how to make practical use of the enthusiasm of Brussels society; Gesa was assisted with a government stipend, and beside that, by the favor of many high patrons, had been sent to Paris in order to study with one of the most famous violinists of the time. He had studied, loitered, loitered a great deal, then studied again, was very much wondered over, very much envied, had learned to empty his champagne glass and to distinguish between those women who are offended if one is impudent to them, and those who are offended if one is not.

He had made his first concert tour with a famous Italian staccato singer, and a still more famous Moravian impressario, had earned many laurels, and finally in Nice, had quarrelled with the 'cellist on account of the singer, had challenged the 'cellist and mortally insulted the impressario.

The impressario however, was a prudent man, who thought nothing of such trifles. When, two months later in Paris, he wished to get together attractions for his American tour, he made Gesa a brilliant offer; but the young violinist, rich in possession of a few thousand francs which were left to him from his last concert tour, refused the offer of the great Mainsky shortly and decidedly with the words: "the virtuoso career bored him; he wished to devote himself entirely to composition."

He was twenty-four years old. At that age many musicians have already finished their immortal masterpieces. Gesa had as yet published nothing but a "Reverie" nearly ten years before, which appeared with a pretty portrait of the youthful composer on the title page, and in the imposing form of a dilletanti composition which was bought by the whole Faubourg St. Germain, but by no one else.

Since that time he had scratched down many things but finished nothing—and yet he felt so rich. Only he had never willed. When he took up his pen one thought pursued another, but he needed rest to compose. Rest in Paris is an article of luxury which only the greatest men can compel.

The recollection of Brussels arose in him— Brussels with its Gothic churches, and crooked streets; its enthusiastic Catholicism, its luxuriant vegetation and its elegant life. A kind of homesickness overcame him— he set out for there.

It was the middle of May. May is wonderfully beautiful in Brussels. No long fight but only a gay conflict between rain and snow purifying the air there. Golden vapors hang in the atmosphere, and weave a fairy like glory around the streets, losing themselves in the distant perspective. Like bright gleams they illuminate the Gothic stone lace work of the St. Sudule, and spread a light veil over the green splendor of the parks. There is something quite strange about their damp light, these sunbeams dissolved in golden mist about all the metallic vibrating and twittering which in spring glorifies sober Brussels like a halo.

The statues in the park have lost their straw wrappings, Through the trees whose fine foliage still exhales the delightful perfume of spring, which it loses in the beginning of June, glide the sunbeams, touching the outline of a knotty black branch with a silver stripe of light, painting broad flecks of brightness on a mighty tree trunk, sliding gaily in the damp grass and playing hide and seek with the shadows of transparent leaves. Around the house of the Prince of Orange luxuriant blooming elder trees wave their white and pale violet clusters dreamily. Before the King's garden grows a sea of violet rhododendrons. And satiated with perfume, mild, enervating, a scarcely perceptible breeze stirs the air ---the sirocco of the north.

Covered with dust, Gesa strides from the *Gare du Midi* across the boulevards to the Rue Ravestein. All interests him. All is homelike. He remains standing, looks around him, smiles, goes a little further, stands still again in his foolish, world-forgetting way. Now he turns from the *Montagne de la cour*, before his eyes the Rue Ravenstein spreads itself out. A strange feeling overcomes him, a feeling of nameless anxiety and oppression. He would have liked to turn around and flee and still something draws him nearer! Misty golden light bathes the distance, the strange alley with its mediaeval architectural adornments. The crucifix leaning against the black church walls, looks like an old picture on a golden ground.

"Is Monsieur Delileo at home?" asked Gesa of a maid at the door of a well known building, who busied herself—unheard of waste of time—in cleaning the door sill. The Flemish words fell unusually haltingly from his lips. The maid looked at him somewhat astonished and nodded. His heart beat, when he entered the door and then quickly climbed the old wooden steps, creaking under his impetuous young feet.

Knocking at the door he received no answer. He entered. The room had still the same green tapestry, at the mere sight of which one could have poisoned himself with arsenic; but it was much neater, much more coquettishly arranged than at the time when Gesa had lived there with his foster father. A peculiar perfume streamed out to him, a narcotic, dreamy perfume! Under the portrait of "the Gualtieri" in the broken delft pitcher stood a large bouquet of seductive, vari-colored poppies—those enchanting, beautiful, gigantic poppies which are known by the name of "*perrots de Nice*."

The door of this first room was open. From the outer wall of the second room opened a balcony enclosed in glass, within which sat at a little round table Delileo and—his daughter.

Gesa started. He looked at the girl silent with wonder. Only in Italy had he seen features with at the same time such regular and yet so peculiarly rounded lines. The girl's small head rested on a pair of classic, strong shoulders; her uniformly pale face was lighted by a pair of strangely dark eyes and deep red lips.

Delileo's daughter although she at that time could be scarcely seventeen, had nothing of the angular prettiness of northern adolescents; her whole form expressed early maturity, strangely luxuriant, entrancing.—Italian beauty!

While Gesa still stood there sunk in the sight of her, Gaston Delileo looked up, stretched his head forward, blinked as if dazzled. The young artist smiled and stepped forward.

"Gesa, you?" and in the next moment the "melancholy

gentleman" held his foster son in his arms. Then both shed a few tears of pleasure, and Delileo pushed "his boy" before him in order to be able to look at him well—then embraced him again. "Are you really going to stay with us for a little? asked he, and his voice shook.

"As long as you will let me, father," replied Gesa. "I would like to work in quiet here, that is to say, I know very well that there is no place for me here. I will hire a room near you. But"—he looked at the young girl—"please make me acquainted with my sister!"

"Ah, truly! now Annette this is Gesa Von Zuylen. I have often told you of him. Bid him welcome, and you, Gesa, give her a kiss as a brother should."

Supper was over; the long gray twilight had obliterated all the golden glory of Brussels. Only a small reddish strip of light fell from a street lamp in the alley, and a second shone in the colored glass of the church window.

Gesa sat comfortably leaning back in the softest arm chair of the whole establishment, in the little green tapestried room, and laid his numerous composition projects before the attentive Gaston. Annette was silent. Her large eyes shone in the twilight.

Gesa talked and talked and the "melancholy man" interrupted him at the most but once or twice to call out "*Cela sera superbe!*"

With regular rhythm and strange dying away the distant noise of the city penetrated to the Rue Ravestein like a monotonous lullaby. The dreamy, sleepy smell of the poppies became stronger with the advancing night, and from time to time one heard the shiver of a petal, which sunk down dying on the cold marble top of the table.

[TO BE CONTINUED]

From the German of Ossip Schubin.

Translated by E. L. LATHROP.

BEETHOVEN'S NOTE-BOOK OF 1803.

II.

THE eighth-note-movement, which is given to the second subordinate subject, in the first greater sketch, is replaced in the variant of this sketch by a movement in quarter notes. In this variant the theme consists of two four-measure sections. In the second greater sketch the sections of the theme are lengthened, and in the third greater sketch the theme is prolonged to three and more sections. An effort toward extension is here evident. In the sketch last mentioned the extension is made principally by repetition. The first four-measure-section of the theme returns in the higher octave as the third section. This repetition is without reason, it is at least unnecessary. This so simple theme with its repeated quarter notes, contains material for transformation, but not for unadorned repetition. Two four-measure sections suffice to express such a content. If given another coloring this theme could be effectively repeated, and such a coloring could be won by the change from the tonic major to the tonic minor. In a variant of the third greater sketch (p. 15) (Figure 7) this was done.

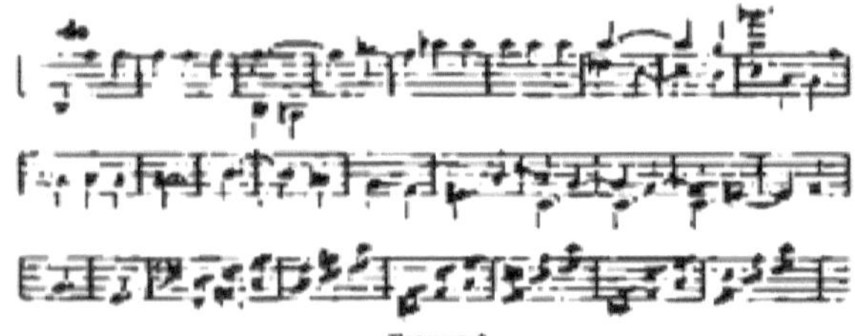

FIGURE 7.

(This excerpt begins in B flat minor, as the context shows.) From this point on the repetition of the theme always occurs in B flat minor, and with this turn of affairs the way was opened for a new version.

Several of the following sketches, (pp. 15 to 18) of which the one which is here given (p. 18) (Figure 8) is the last, are devoted to giving a different turn to the

Figure 8.

feeble and lamenting passage in F minor (into which the B flat minor theme of the second subordinate subject of the variant, measure 12, onward, runs, and which in another place and in a somewhat different version or shape occurs in the third greater sketch), and, furthermore, to gain a

Figure 9.

new starting point. At last Beethoven, as we see in the fourth greater sketch, abandoned this passage altogether and took, for the continuation of the subject, material from the subject itself. By this means, especially by the use of the motive [music notation] taken directly from the theme, the subordinate subject gained in unity and consistence.

There follow now a few more sketches, which rapidly approach the final form. Here (pp. 22 and 23) (Figure 9) the first four measures of the subordinate subject have reached their ultimate shape, and here (p. 26) (Figure 10)

Figure 10.

the theme, which in its former readings deserves to be called a succession of melodic sections rather than a real melody, has been developed into a self existent, periodic formation.

The last sketches offer opportunity for a few remarks. In the variant of the last of the above sketches, the after period (meas 1 to 9), into which the B flat period runs, is made up of two motives taken from the theme of the second subordinate subject (and) and lasts until the beginning of the passage in eighth notes which leads into the final subject. It may be noticed that the first of these motives consists of three primes followed by a descending second. In the score this place looks differently. The regular movement is twice interrupted by a slurred phrase containing notes of different pitches, (Figure 11). This motive is consequently melodically altered. By this abandonment of what may be called strict motive treatment, a fine characteristic trait is gained. The following second motive is made, with its halting rhythm, so much the more effective. We ask: *Is not this sketch a commentary on the printed version?* But this printed version is not to be found in the sketch-book; from which we argue that it must have originated later.

Our second observation leads us back to the second greater sketch. Of all existing sketches this is the one in which we have before us the first conception of this part of the movement, and which gives us the most faithful picture of the composer's original idea. However much the sketch may

FIGURE 11.

differ from the final version, still many a characteristic is there which in another form has been embodied in the score. We only need to recall the two introductory measures which are to be found only in this sketch and which appear again in the score itself, although filled with another content. If one follows the course of modulation, one cannot but see that the most remote key is that of D flat major, and that the digression to this key takes place during the progress of the second subordinate subject. In the sketches immediately following, no effort to reach this key is perceptible, although the effort is easily seen in the later sketches. To prove this point it is only necessary to examine the two sketches last given (after pp. 22, 23, and 26 of the Sketch-Book), in which the digression to D flat major occurs at the place corresponding to that in the first greater sketch, and in which furthermore D flat major is the only remote key which is touched in the first part of the movement. A direct connection between the original and the final reading is thus not demonstrable; but this modulatory coincidence is surely remarkable. If one attaches a prophetic significance to the first sketch, one can find its modulatory idea realized in the score, although in another form.

The nearer we approach to the end of this part of the movement, the greater become the number of the sketches. Those of the final subject are the most numerous, and, from the many phenomena which they present, it is difficult to hold fast to the thread of connection.

In the first greater sketch and its variant, the final subject (we presuppose that one may call by this name the entire part which follows the second subordinate subject) appears as a sequence, and a carrying up and down, of a few motives, from which at last emerges near the end of the part, with clearly defined tonality, the closing phrase itself, and a fragment of the leading subject which follows it. Apart from this material, in the further working out of the final subject, only a short zigzag run in eighth notes and the passage-like continuation of the third measure of the leading subject were found fit to live. (The reader should add to the eighth notes which follow the theme of the second subordinate subject in the variant in question, an accompanying bass figure taken from the third measure of the leading subject). The structure of the second subordinate subject must have influenced that of the final subject. A change may be seen already in the second greater sketch. The second subordinate subject has gained in extension and in precision of expression, and the final subject has gained in extension and in variety of the motives employed. By the chromatic passage with which it terminates, the second

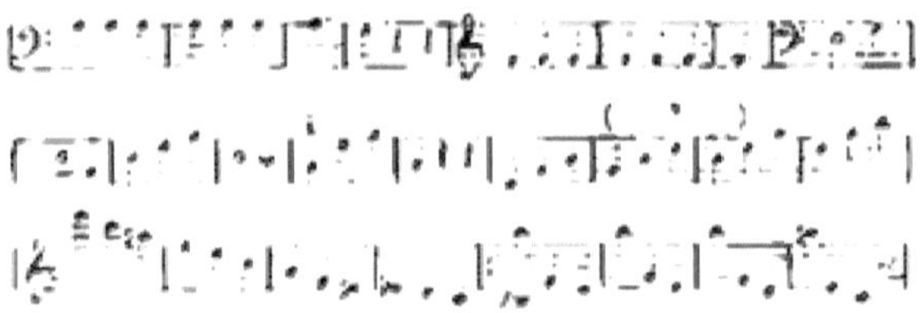

FIGURE 12.

subordinate subject has been given a sad character. Was this to express a mournful recollection of the deceased hero? It almost seems so. The passage pushes on towards a something having firm construction. What better could have been used as a counterpoise than (as happened in the second sketch in question) the leading subject, the Hero-Idea itself, which now enters, *pianissimo*, as if consoling and softly warning?

It is evident that Beethoven spent considerable time in trying to base the final subject principally on the leading subject and on parts of it. One can see this in a few sketches, in which, however, the leading subject is introduced not in B flat major, as in the second sketch, but in E flat major, and first of all in this fragmentary sketch (p. 11) (Figure 12), then in the third greater sketch, and then in this sketch, (p. 16) (Figure 13).

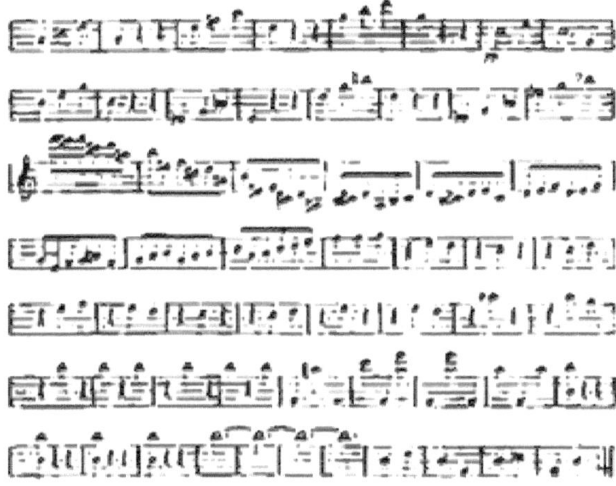

FIGURE 13.

The parts of the leading subject which are made use of in this and the other sketches, and are employed as passages, are in part the third and fourth measures of the leading subject, and in part the third measure alone. (To the syncopated notes in the violin clef, which soon follow the leading subject in the third greater sketch, one must imagine a bass figure formed from the third measure of the leading subject itself).

The sketch last given demands our prolonged consideration. This sketch which the reader may imagine as preceded by the second subordinate subject in the inversion of the second greater sketch, where it runs downward in a chromatic passage—is the first in which there occur three passages—like sections formed of different motives, which one may also find in the score and in the same succession, although in a different reading. These parts or sections, which constantly underwent transformation until they reached their final shape, are:— 1) a falling and rising passage in eighth notes; 2) a passage based principally on the motive ; and 3) repeated chords in the 2-4 rhythm . The figure which is principally the basis of the passage in eighth notes may be found in the first sketch, but does not appear again until in the sketch in question. The motives on which the two other sections are based, appear in this sketch for the first

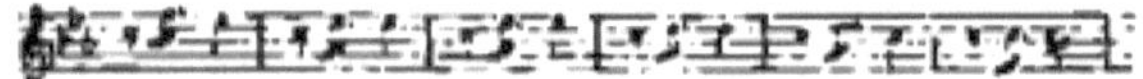

Figure 14

time. The origin of the first of these might be found in the theme of the second subordinate subject, were it not for the presence of a few small sketches; as for instance this (p. 14), (Figure 14) and also in the fact which speaks to the contrary, that the motive employed in the final subject uses the step of a second, while the theme of the second subordinate subject has appeared in all preceding sketches as made up of primes, thus indicating an individual origin. If we consider this sketch, as a whole, and also in its internal connection, we observe the following:- We find in it the

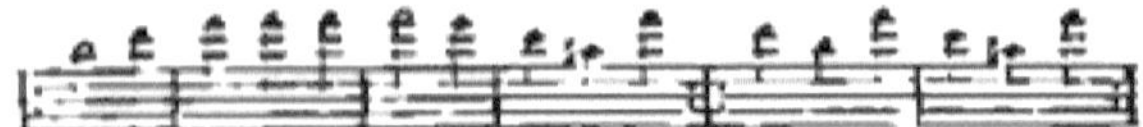

Figure 15

leading subject, interwoven as a passage (in E flat major) and surrounded by transpositions of the third and fourth measures. It passes by the listener like a vision. This transition from the second subordinate to the final subject is not altogether clear. To this sketch, however, must be accorded the power to demonstrate that a transition formed of successive passages, which of themselves are composed of various motives and figures, was not fitted to precede and set off in a favorable light the swing and the variety which mark the final subject, with its own vigorous motives, which in their turn are ranged one after the other; furthermore, it is worthy notice, that only by erecting a separating member between them could the proper relationship, one to the other, be found for these two greater parts, so

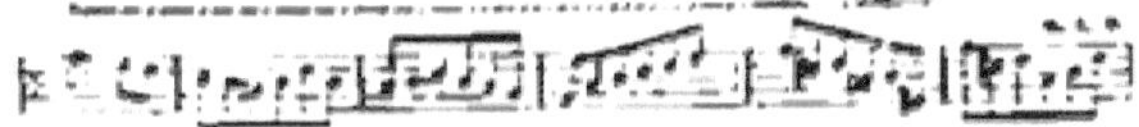

Figure 16.

rich and so different in content. This separating member could be erected only on the basis of some fixed tonality; and this tonality could be no other than that of B flat major; and on this tonal basis belonged neither a passage nor a softly entering theme, but a theme of marked rhythm and of determined entrance.

So at this place a new turn was taken. Beethoven sought for another and independent theme, one which should properly introduce the final subject. In his seeking and trying he approaches the former material only in so far that from amongst the nine or ten different themes

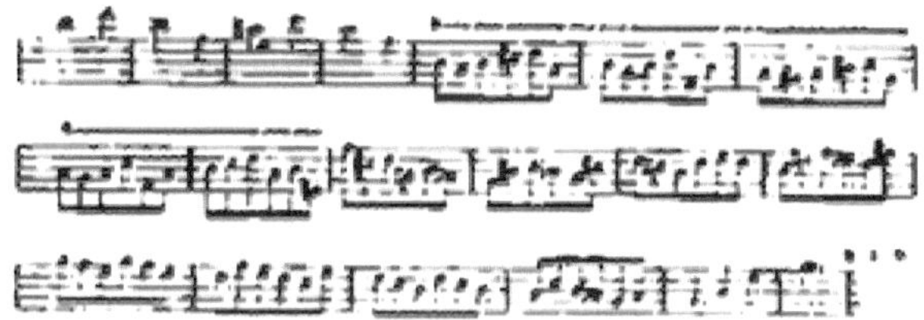

Figure 17.

which he found and of which two of the first are given here (pp. 4 and 18), (Figures 15 and 16), he at last, in a variant (p. 23) (Figure 17) whose beginning we have already given on an earlier page of this exposition, (Figure 10), strikes upon a theme formed from the first two measures of the leading subject. Comparing the theme first originated with the later ones, one observes that the later ones move in general through larger intervals than the earlier, and thus show an energetic character which the others lack.

We find the reason for this in the growth under the composer's pen of the second subordinate subject, which with its dark coloring and the concentrated character it gradually assumed, required as its successor a final subject with a strong and energetic beginning. In holding fast to the idea of beginning the final subject with an independent theme, Beethoven, apart from the considerations due to the constantly changing second subordinate subject, was no doubt upheld by the thought, that an anticipation of the leading subject would lessen the effect of the second part of the movement, upon which he had already begun to work and in which the leading subject was to undergo development.

[TO BE CONTINUED]

From the German of Gustav Nottebohm.

Translated by BENJAMIN CUTTER.

OF SONGS AND SINGING.

IT may be news to the average singer that there was once a composer of songs whose name was Franz Schubert. Mr. Schubert's work was highly esteemed shortly after his death, which took place in 1828, and his songs are generally regarded by those who understand this form of art as peculiarly fortunate in melody, delicate harmony, and easy natural correspondence between the poetry and the music. They suit the voice extremely well, and by reason of all these great and exceptional qualities they are really classic. Moreover, Mr. Schubert was a very prolific writer. Although he came to expression at a very early age, writing at the age of sixteen and seventeen some of the most remarkable compositions which have ever adorned the literature of song, his early works show little or nothing of immaturity or experiment. He seems to have gone to the root of the matter by intuition, and to have made center shots without necessity of rests to aim over, or preliminary practice. There are circles in Germany where the songs of Schubert are still heard, and occasionally in England this takes place. These beautiful compositions have been published in every language, and are cherished (in theory) the world over. But not in Chicago.

There was a later writer of songs who also had talent. His name was Robert Franz, and he died only a year or two ago. I had a letter a few days ago from a would-be composer, who in stating his desires mentioned incidentally that if he could not get higher he thought he might write little things like the songs of Franz. Perhaps he might, and it would be greatly to his credit, for the songs of Franz also form a world of their own. There are still singers in the world who know the songs of Franz. But they do not live in Chicago. Mr. Franz's songs are generally very short, and it is perhaps for this reason that they do not suit the somewhat trying climate of the Chicago concert room. Perhaps they awaken a feeling similar to that which actuated the epitaph of the three months old infant, whose grave lines, conceived in the first person, ran thus:—

"If I so soon was done for,
Pray what was I begun for."

Between these two worthy gentlemen, Messrs. Schubert and Franz, there was still another gentlemen who wrote some very delightful songs. His name was Robert Schumann, and among his productions is one set known as "Woman's Love and Life," which go nearer the very heart of song than any others that I know of, since they deal with the most intimate feelings of a sensitive heart, and with the most ideal and intense moments of an ideal life. They also suit the voice not badly, and, as in cases already mentioned, there are provinces where Schumann's songs are still heard. But not in Chicago.

For a long time it was a mystery to me why all these hundreds of compositions of transcendent excellence were so persistently ignored by our singers. I said to myself that there must be a mistake somewhere. When compositions were so well known (in theory at least), so true musically, so melodious, so poetic, so agreeable upon every account, why is it that we do not hear them?

What do we hear in place of them? Generally arias from operas, occasionally little French songs, not bad in their way—though of the way no one can judge when they are sung only in the original—since an Auditorium full of hearers affords less than a score who are able to understand French words upon hearing, particularly when they are French as she is sung. Sometimes we have an English song. When we happen to have read the poem forming the ostensible reason of its being, we may understand this; but as a rule the text of this also needs a Frenchman to explain it to us.

What is song? Is it voice, poetry or music? Let us try and find out this, and then perhaps we may discover a reason why this department of literature is so persistently ignored. Song is all these, I answer. Music first; poetry behind the music and illuminating it, or music illuminating the poetry, just as you please to have it. In a good song the music and the poetry "make a one," as the new church people so wisely say. Nobody knows which part of this "one" ought to be mentioned first, since in the song they are mutually interdependent and equal. The voice is the minister through which music and text come to hearing. The voice must be satisfactory, or somewhere the music or the text will fail to arrive, as very often happens, even in Chicago.

There are no limitations to the demands upon the singer which a good song will make. Schubert's "Erl King," "Gretchen at the Spinning Wheel," "The Young Nun," and "To be Sung upon the Waters," are songs which take the whole voice, and make grave demands upon the dramatic capacity of the singer. In all our manifold colleges of music, with something like twenty-five hundred pupils, there cannot be found at the present moment ten promising young vocalists equal to the demands of these songs. Even in the faculties, aggregating perhaps a score or two of experienced singers, we can hardly find three who can sing songs of this character creditably.

We are not now speaking of amateur Hamlets among college professors. These gentle spirits of song were no Shakespeares. They were great masters, but their work was lyric and not dramatic. The songs are to a great extent for the closet quite as much as for the stage. Always there is a standpoint which one has to grant them; a poetical concept which the hearer ought to understand, and above all with the singing a text every word of which is hearable, and feelable no less as word than as poetry, all along with and through the melody and phrasing of the song.

Here we begin to come to the root of the matter. If our great unknown of songs requires a combination of well delivered text, well sung melody, and well conceived dramatic situation and musical interpretation, the reason our singers fight somewhat shy of them is not far to seek.

Our singers do not know how to treat language. They generally phrase melody rather badly; and deliver the voice even more poorly than they realize the musical meaning of the songs they operate upon, or "execute," as they very properly call it. Our singers do not care very much for poetry.

What do they like? First of all to get upon the stage. And since getting upon the stage is primarily a matter of personality and good luck, together with a certain minimum of voice and cultivation, and a faculty of appearing to do much better than they really do, this is the point toward which their studies take them. Voices not very well placed; tones not well matured; phrasing which either is imitated from the teacher or else very wooden in its quality; and complete inability to sing any known language so that it goes current in the country where that language happens to be spoken,—this is the outfit from which the provincial critic would expect the songs of Schubert, Franz, Schumann, and whatever other great masters of real song there may be.

What *is* a song? A song, I answer, is a moment. A moment which is first of all representative and ideal, then poetic. Upon this underlying foundation, which the poet furnishes, the musician builds with free musical fantasy, in such wise that the poetry is more poetical, the text more intense and impressive, and the inner spirit of the poem and situation embodied in music which is like a beautiful atmosphere of tone, through which glisten the battlements of celestial cities of the ideal. There is nothing which song may not do for us. It is the ideal brought to us in characteristic moments. Not volumes, not hours of study, not long explanations; but a phrase, a quatrain of text, a minute and a half of melody, and a sympathetic voice and competent treatment, and straightway we find ourselves transported, more pleasingly than by an Aladdin's carpet, to ideal states of pleasure and beauty beside which the tales of the Thousand and One Nights are tame and unprofitable.

When will such songs as these be heard in our concert rooms? Never, I answer, until our good voices give over expecting to step at first start into such impossible extravagances as "Ernani involami," and the like. Never, until our young singers learn that something more than mere tone is needed to make a singer. Never, until they learn that it is something to be able to sing intelligibly in some one language, and that the easiest language for them will be their own mother tongue, as well as the one in which they can measure their success more easily by discovering whether their hearers follow them. Never, until our young singers (and their teachers) remember that good voices are common in America; and ambitious young women the rule, rather than the exception; and that along with natural good qualities it is no disadvantage to a singer to have the support of a motive—to appear to be presenting something which the hearer either desires to hear or else *would* desire to hear if only he knew what he ought to like; and the nerve to decide upon a line of action and persist in it until recognition comes.

Our singers do not learn their songs. Besides the elementary facts of singing them badly, and of ignoring the text, which might be pardonable in singers unable to understand the speech, they do not half master the spirit of the song itself. They do not enter into it, make it a part of themselves, and prepare to give it out with enthusiasm, as a message both precious and desired.

Meanwhile every singer comes before the public with an aria upon which she does not very much rely, for she feels in her inmost heart that she is as yet outside of it; but by the aid of a vigorous squall upon the note before the last she expects to bring down the house, or at least bring down her friends, who have been furnished with complimentary tickets for the purpose. Then after one or two preliminary and coy returns to acknowledge the applause, but not too late (lest the applause die down entirely) back she comes with a song that she really *does* expect to do her business. And what is it? "Sweet Genevieve," "Kiss me, darling when the twilight falls," "In the gloaming," or something of the kind. No poetry, no music to speak of, very little real melody, even the words in rather a questionable state of completeness, but with a soft and melting suggestiveness which brings at last the dear public to her feet. Or if not to her feet—when there are so many more feet than are needed to go around) at least brings her to the heaven of newspaper notice. And this is immortality.

But when you ask me whether I think the present selection of songs for concert performance a greater disrespect to the song-writing art, to the public, or to the art of the singer, I am unable to answer. The question is too hard for me. I merely remember that there are certain great names mentioned in histories of song literature, and a few of us have studied the works of these great masters and find them pre-eminent. Others have heard that there are such works; and a few singers, who from modesty or absence of high notes do not expect to go in grand opera, sing the songs in private. They have not had lessons upon them. Such things are mainly outside the range of the ordinary vocal teacher. But there are people who sing them sometimes. And a small circle of appreciative students who find this inner world worth knowing. But why should not this circle of congenial and appreciative souls be extended? And why should it not include all the singers and many of their friends? Why should the taste in songs be so much lower than it is in the piano, the orchestra, or other departments of music which are studied intelligently?

These are questions which I cannot answer. If I thought it would bring an answer I would offer a prize for a good answer. Why not?

W. S. B. M.

TO YOUNG COMPOSERS.

MANY are the young composers, possessed of a slight theoretic knowledge and much ambition, who are daily submitting manuscripts to leading music publishers, only to have these music publishers return their manuscripts with a polite (condescendingly polite) note of thanks. It is hard in this life to have all your efforts for fame and the laurel wreath come to grief. It is a hard matter, an almost pathetic proceeding, to read or play over a rejected manuscript, and feel that its intrinsic worth is unappreciated. The sensitive aspirant for celebrity mutters over to himself these old lines and they acquire a new meaning.

> "Full many a flower was born to blush unseen,
> And waste its sweetness on the desert air."

The first moments of disappointed ambition are keenly painful. The restless feeling that you are still one of the common throng, the "ignoble crowd," coupled with a burning desire to distinguish yourself, produces a peculiar state of mind that only the artistic nature can fully comprehend. You unroll the neatly tied up music, (which you had all pictured out as printed, with tasteful title cover and exposed for sale in Schirmer's or Ditson's window) and the load of your individual insignificance sinks heavily upon you. The labor spent seems all lost. Of what use is your music unless some one outside of your circle of friends can appreciate it? (You smooth out the creased manuscript all this time). What is the good of having musical talent anyhow? Surely this song, which has been returned, is as well written and conceived as hundreds of songs that are published. Suddenly to the really gifted young composer comes the thought that he could compose a better song than the one before him. This thought contains the vital spark of all true art conception. It is not a merely creditable composition, on a par with many others, but the *best* composition that you can produce, which the publisher will accept. "There is always room at the top." To do your best is to have done all that man can do and though your *best* be far beneath some others *poorest* the truthfulness of the idea remains. Therefore, young composers, do your best. Until you can calmly analyze and direct your own works, weighing their merits with a steady hand, until you can honestly say, "This is the best I can do under the present circumstances, and with my knowledge and experience."—until that time comes beware of casting your half fledged composition-birds on the world's care. In after years should you ever become famous, the critics will not know whether you wrote those pieces recently or not and will judge accordingly. Beware also of the critics, for they are the eyes by which that many headed monster, the public, views the artist. The unprejudiced and honest critic will hold up both your faults and your virtues to the public gaze therefore let the latter outnumber the former by so many, that the faults are lost sight of entirely, just as a tiny fleck on a rose leaf does not impair its beauty. To sum up all, be cautious of publishing early in life and rely mainly on your master's judgement in the matter. Surely he is to be depended on else you should not take lessons of him. Pupils of masters like Mr. Dudley Buck, Dr. Dvorak or Mr. B. J. Lang, soon appreciate their own insignificance by simply comparing their embryo ideas and works with those of their teachers. Let your standard of measurement be high, so will your work be superior. Let not that "itching" to see yourself in print overpower you. Undoubtedly many who are in print would fain be out of it, but the irrevocable step has been taken.

Robert Schumann says in regard to the young composer, "It is well known that most young composers try to do their business too well; that is to say they try to put too much material together, and this, in inexperienced hands, becomes in the after treatment too often a heaped up and awkward conglomeration." This is mainly applicable to students treading the more advanced art paths, and for them it is pregnant with meaning. Simplicity of subject matter, clarity of development, preservation of the essential elements of form should characterize the young composer's efforts. In these days of striving after unique, highly colored, bizarre, startling effects, resembling those bold masses of gorgeous color in certain French paintings, it is refreshing to hear a simple, clearly outlined string quartette by Haydn or Mozart. The absence of strained effects, the purity of harmony, the careful working out of every part, the exquisite imitations, the attention to minute details remind me of the old cathedrals, elaborately finished in each hidden nook and corner by the conscientious artist builder, whose art was religious. "Form" alone can give this symmetrical beauty to a composition. It is only occasionally that a genius arises like Tschaikowsky, who throws "form" to the winds. The student should no more model his style after Liszt or Tschaikowsky than a writer should imitate the style of Carlisle or Hugo. In these men their style is the legitimate outgrowth of their peculiar natures, but copied it becomes absolutely ridiculous.

Let the earnest young composer live upon the works of Bach, Handel, Haydn and Mozart, for in them he finds pure models. Representing as they do, an age of less romantic and complex emotions their productions are healthier than the highly seasoned, overwrought works of the present day and the young minds more easily digests them. To use a rather unusual and a bit inelegant simile, a Mozart symphony is like wholesome roast meat, while a Liszt symphonic poem is like a cleverly concocted French salad, wherein the pleasure of taste lies in the "whole dish" its separate ingredients being not plainly distinguishable. To begin life on musical French salad is to foreshadow a dyspeptic and useless old age. Eschew the salad therefore and choose the meat.

There is another tendency which young composers must beware of, namely the choosing of hackneyed words for songs. Every musical neophyte begins his career, be it glorious or inglorious, by setting "Du bist wie eine Blume" to music. Oh! shade of Heine, little do you dream how your violet song flame has pulsated on the musicians lyre, till its sweetness has become too common to enchant with its primitive charm. Now that universal opinion has pronounced Rubinstein's version of the song to be the best, is it not absurd and foolish for inferior men to essay new treatments? Would there were a fine for every using of this poor worn out lyric!

The trend of the young composer's thought is too frequently toward the shorter songs, those little poem-pictures which to quote the English humorist, George Grossmith, "end before they're fairly begun" and this continual treatment of small themes is not conducive to strength in the more extended art-poems. Guard against expressing frequently the diminutive poems of Heine, who was after all only a great poet in a small way. Seek more virile poems and endeavor to compose longer songs—songs which possess a certain "form" and not mere evanescent tone-sketches. Labor always to surpass your most perfectly executed work, then will your horizon broaden and extend on either side till your unconscious egoism vanishes in contemplation of the yet untravelled tracts of art country. Strive not to win the ephemeral applause, begotten of popular favor; strive not for applause at all; work conscientiously to compose as little poor music as possible and your aim will be high. Travel abroad and view the historic countries there, go to the art exhibitions and see what the sister arts have accomplished, read the best books, seek the most cultivated society where an atmosphere of elegance and culture is found, in short, make for yourself the highest, broadest, and kindest life possible and your music will embody all these lofty sentiments. To conclude, let me give a quotation from Schopenhauer, "Every person has lead with which he attemps to measure the depth of art. The string of some is long, that of others very short; yet each thinks he has reached the bottom, while in reality art is as a bottomless deep, that none have as yet fully explored, and probably none never will. Art is endless."

FRANK E. SAWYER.

CLARENCE EDDY, ORGAN VIRTUOSO.

The career of the distinguished organ virtuoso, Mr. Clarence Eddy, affords an interesting example of rare personal qualities and commanding professional attainments coming to a leading position in the city and the nation, and attaining international fame, with scarcely a set-back or interruption in his onward progress from the beginning to the present time.

Born of good family, at Greenfield, Mass., in 1851, Clarence Eddy early showed a talent for music, and very soon distinguished himself in the direction of the organ. After certain lessons from the best teachers of the vicinity and the attainment of considerable reputation as performer, he was sent in 1868 to Hartford, where for one year he had lessons of Dudley Buck, then just back from his European studies. · Here the talent of the boy was recognized as full of promise, and at the end of the year he was appointed organist of the Bethany Congregational church at Montpelier, Vt. In this position the extraordinary gifts of the young virtuoso were more and more unmistakable, and at the close of a two years engagement there his long cherished wish was gratified, and he departed for Germany, for the thorough training which he craved. He went immediately to Berlin, where under the instruction of the veteran virtuoso and artist, August Haupt, in organ playing and and counterpoint, and of Loeschhorn in piano, he spent two and a half industrious and fruitful years. It is doubtful whether any student in Berlin worked harder than Mr. Eddy. He practiced from nine to ten and even fifteen hours daily upon the organ, the piano, and in counterpoint. His instrumental practice he did upon a pedal pianoforte, which he had to have built for him. This in the slow German fashion required a matter of six months, during which the ambitious young artist performed his practice upon an ordinary piano, playing his pedal passages upon the floor where the pedal keys ought to have been. After this novel kind of "absent treatment" he was able to go to the church and perform his difficult fugues and sonatas to the satisfaction of his master.

Naturally his industry soon made itself felt, and as one stage after another of his development was reached, his teacher, the veteran Haupt, conceived for him a strong affection, and began to take pride in him and in finding hard nuts for him to crack. Among the virtuoso tasks thus created especially for Mr. Eddy, were Haupt's arrangements of the Chopin study in C sharp minor, opus 10, No. 4, the four hand variations in C, of Thiele arranged for two hands, Bach's great six voice fugue for string instruments, "The Musical Offering," arranged for the organ. Haupt was very fond of hearing those things played by the masterly hand of his pupil.

CLARENCE EDDY
(aged 4.)

During his study in Berlin Mr. Eddy played everything of Bach's organ works and most of those for the piano. He explored the whole range of organ literature, and there was nothing in the older and strict organ repertory or in the new one by Best and other later arrangers with which he was not familiar.

When he had finished with Haupt, he took a magnificent letter of introduction from his master, speaking of him as one of the first of living virtuosi, and went upon a concert tour in Germany, in which he played in all the leading cities with great success, receiving commendations from the profession and from the press such as rarely fall to the lot of foreign artists in that idealistic but self-centered country. He laid the foundation of many personal friendships, especially with organ virtuosi. Among these the standing of Clarence Eddy immediately became that of an approved master. It was during this tour that he made his first appearance at an International Exposition, that of Vienna in 1872, where he played as a representative American organist. This part of his career has had three brilliant additions made to it later, for in Philadelphia, in 1876, Mr. Eddy played officially, and again as representative of America at the French exposition of 1889. The latest chapter, and even more brilliant, was that of the Columbian Exposition Chicago, in 1893.

CLARENCE EDDY
(aged 16.)

Although out of place chronologically I may give here a sample program from the Paris exposition, played at the Trocadero August 2d, 1889.

1	Toccata e Fuga en ré mineur.	J. S. Bach (1685-1750)
2	Sonate en sol mineur op. 77 (*Dédiée à M. Clarence Eddy*).	Dudley Buck
	I. Allegro moderato ma energico.	
	II. Adagio molto espressivo.	
	III. Allegro vivace non troppo.	
3	Variations sur un air Américain.	J. V. Flagler
4	Morceau de Concert, op. 24. Introduction, Thème, Variations et Final.	Alex. Guilmant
5	*a* Adagio de la 6 Symphonie.	Ch. M. Widor
	b Cantilène nuptiale.	Th. Dubois
6	Thème, Variations et Final.	Louis Thiele

When he returned to America he came immediately to Chicago, where he had a great success from the very beginning—a success in some degrees facilitated by the warm interest of the late Mr. George W. Lyon, who used his influence in favor of the young man to much good purpose. At that time Mr. Eddy was exactly twenty-three years of age, but as he already had a long beard and his hair was cut in the German student fashion he easily looked to be more than thirty. Hence the impression of youthfulness cut no figure in popular estimation, and it was as master that he took immediate rank.

His organ playing at that time was remarkably easy in all technical respects, and he had what very few organists have, a good metrical accent, whereby such well wrought pieces as Bach's great Prelude in B minor, the Prelude in E minor, and the Fantasia in G minor went with something attractive in them, so that people listened to them with an interest which Bach's organ music had not awakened here previous to that time. Mr. Eddy's programs were somewhat of the strict order. Excepting the great pieces of Thiele and the virtuoso pieces especially arranged for him, his selections were mostly confined to the strict German school. These he played with consummate ease and with great finish. The state of his technic may be judged by organists when I mention that for a year or more he had been in the habit of playing the six trio sonatas of Bach every day—upon the pedal piano, playing the crossing manual voices at their proper pitch, by interlocking his hands, playing the long

CLARENCE EDDY
(Berlin, 1875.)

fingers of one hand through those of the other. In this way, which would be regarded by many as impracticable, he acquired a marvellously perfect technic of pedal and manual, the latter being particularly neat—the legitimate effect of all this practice in pure organ music.

He had not been in Chicago more than a year before he was made director in chief of the Hershey School of Musical Art, of which Mrs. Sara Hershey was director and proprietor. Some time later he married Mrs. Hershey, and thus formed one of those matrimonial alliances which contradict the current aphorism that "two of a trade cannot agree," for the firm of Mr. and Mrs. Clarence Eddy has been a unit in all good activities in music since it was first cemented by the benediction of the Rev. Dr. Ryder in 1879 sixteen years ago.

CLARENCE EDDY
(Berlin, 1876.)

While not strictly germane to the present article a word concerning this distinguished woman may not be out of place. Mrs. Eddy after considerable experience as teacher and singer in America went abroad for further study, and spent five years with the best teachers of Italy, Germany and London, finishing later with some lessons of Mme. Rudersdorf, in Boston. To an active mind, great good sense, and ability of a high order, Mrs. Eddy has united hard study and the art of learning by experience. It is no wonder therefore that her pupils have been so generally recognized as distinguished above others for musical intelligence and well balanced qualifications. This good sense, which so emphatically distinguishes her professional work, extends also to her domestic and private life, and there are few women who have warmer friends or are more admired among their own sex than Mrs. Eddy.

Almost from his first arrival in Chicago Mr. Eddy assumed the rank of a public institution. Coming unknown to a city where organists had found it difficult to secure so much as $800 a year salary, and this only in one or two very exceptional cases, he immediately engaged at a salary of $1,800, and that too in a church which up to that time had never shown special ambition in the matter of music.

All the earlier organ recitals of Mr. Eddy in Chicago were given upon the three manual organ of his church.

Upon the opening of Hershey Hall in 1876, a three manual organ of limited appointment but very convenient and effective, was erected there by Wm. A. Johnson & Son, and upon this Mr. Eddy gave his unparalleled series of one hundred organ recitals without any repetitions of the numbers. Naturally and inevitably, considering the enormous number of compositions required, the programs covered the entire range of organ music. The closing one of the series was given June 23, 1878, most of the numbers having been written expressly for the occasion. The following are given as sample programs of this series:

1st. Recital in Hershey Music Hall, March 3, 1877.

1 Sonata in G minor, No. 2, — Gustav Merkel
2 Rhapsodie, No. 3, — Saint Saens
3 Fugue in G minor, — J. S. Bach
(Peters edition, Book 4, No. 7)
4 Introduction and Concert Variations, — Frederic Archer
5 Cantilene Pastorale — Alex. Guilmant
6 Concert Piece in E flat minor, — Louis Thiele

50th Recital in Hershey Music Hall, April 13, 1878.

1 Prelude and Fugue in B minor, — Adolph Hesse
2 Canonic studies in E Flat and A flat, op. 56 Nos. 3 and 4. — R. Schumann
3 Prelude and Fugue on Bach, — J. S. Bach
4 Grand Sonata in C minor, — Julius Reubke
(Psalm 94.)
5 Overture to Oberon, — Von Weber
(Arranged for the organ by S. P. Warren.)

100th Recital in Hershey Music Hall, June 23, 1879.

1	Overture Triomphale, op. 11,	F. O. Grimm
2	*a* Canon in G,	S. B. Whitney
	b Fugue in E minor,	James H. Rogers
3	Concerto in C, No. 4,	J. S. Bach
4	Prophet Fantasie and Fugue,	Franz Liszt
5	Sonata in D, No. 4,	S. de Lange
6	Andante in A minor,	Immanuel Faisst
7	Pastorale in A,	S. G. Pratt
8	Fantasie in E minor,	Gustav Merkel
9	Festival Prelude and Fugue on "Old Hundred",	Clarence Eddy

This series of programs, given in a small hall, before audiences rarely reaching the number of two hundred hearers, was mentioned from one end of the country to the other. The correspondents of the musical journals followed them, and their result was an important increase of Mr. Eddy's growing reputation. Meanwhile, from his first arrival in Chicago he had been in demand for opening organs in all parts of the country. Almost every considerable organ for twenty years has now been opened by Mr. Eddy or else has been played by him within a very short time after its opening. In this way and as part of his ordinary professional career he has made no less than three trips to the Pacific coast, where his success has been of a high order.

In this relation Mr. Eddy has proven a first class success from a money standpoint, his concerts almost invariably drawing more money than they cost, whereby the churches have found him a profitable artist to engage. This reflects favorably upon all parties concerned. Upon the organist, because it shows how real are his attractive qualities and how reliable his reputation; upon the churches, because it shows that they can appreciate a good thing when it is brought them in a well finished package; and upon the popular ability to appreciate organ music, for Mr. Eddy rarely plays anything but the best.

As a connoisseur of organ construction and voicing, Mr. Eddy is one of the finest living. He has given concerts upon every really large organ in the civilized world—that is to say, in central Europe, England and the United States. All the large and important new organs he knows intimately, their appointment, their tonal gifts and graces, and their mechanical excellencies and defects.

Everywhere treated well himself, he has invariably treated others well. Such composers of strict organ music as Gustav Merkel, A. G. Ritter, Josef Rheinberger, Alex.

CLARENCE EDDY
(Chicago, 1878.)

Guilmant, Th. Salome, Theo. Dubois, C. M. Widor, Eugene Gigout, W. T. Best, Dudley Buck, and the like, owe something to an artist who makes their compositions known over so wide a compass of new country as Mr. Eddy reaches in America. It was Mr. Eddy who endeavored to secure the presence of the leading organists of the world for the World's Fair of Chicago. Owing to the difficulties in the management only one of the great masters came, Alexander Guilmant, and he only because Mr. Eddy, with characteristic generosity, not only secured the great Frenchman a fee for his work at the

CLARENCE EDDY AND ALEXANDER GUILMANT
(A World's Fair reminiscence, Chicago, 1893.)

Fair, but also worked up for him a tour embracing engagements enough to make his American visit profitable. Here again virtue was its own reward, for it was Mr. Eddy's idea that his own fame would only shine the brighter when the qualifications of the greatest players of the world were present in the minds of those who listened to his programs.

In this case, however, I have greatly understated the indebtedness of the Columbian Exposition to Mr. Eddy, for it was entirely through his efforts that a concert organ of first class appointment was procured and placed in position in choral hall, where it could be used for recitals and other proper additions to exposition purposes. The instrument, by the great house of Farrand & Votey of Detroit, was of

CLARENCE EDDY
At the present time

modern appointment, having four manuals, about seventy speaking stops, pneumatic wind-chests, electric action, adjustable combination pistons, etc. Upon this instrument were given all the recitals of visiting organists (the series aggregating fifty recitals or more) Mr. Eddy himself giving twenty, the programs carefully arranged in order to cover as far as possible the whole range of organ music.

Mr. Eddy is one of those rare men of personal character and decision who almost never make enemies. It is very rare indeed that one hears from him an unfriendly comment upon the works of any other, and personally he never mentions his own work but with reserve, and after much persuasion. This is not so much from modesty (for between ourselves, I feel quite sure that he understands the good qualities of Clarence Eddy's playing as well if not better than I do), but from natural gentlemanliness and refinement of disposition. In fact I should say that the most noticable mental peculiarity or gift of Mr. Eddy is his sense of finish and completeness. This combined with the capacity of infinite industry, is what makes him a virtuoso. And the same quality underlies his entire mind, and makes him a man of natural good taste in every relation and capacity. Hence without affecting the brilliant or the blasé, he is a popular man socially and by reason of his simplicity and manly repose, the admiration of women no less than of men.

The city of Chicago owes Mr. Eddy a debt, for the great concert organ in the Auditorium would hardly have been placed there, or at least would not have been made so complete, but for him. No sooner was the Auditorium talked of than Mr. Eddy saw the importance of placing in it an organ of first class modern appointment. Accordingly at the proper moment he wrote to Mr. Crosby, then manager of the great house of Hilbourn Roosevelt, to prepare specifications. Mr. Crosby prepared one for $25,000 which he thought would practically answer needs; and another for $32,000 which he hoped to get accepted. With these he reached Chicago and almost immediately came to a meeting with Mr. Ferdinand W. Peck, who created the Auditorium, Mr. Adler, the architect, and Clarence Eddy. The points of the specifications were explained by Mr. Eddy. Mr. Peck became interested. His infallible disposition to "get the best" asserted itself. He desired to know whether there were not other improvements which would render the organ more complete and monumental. This was a man after Roosevelt's own heart, for the Roosevelt house was nothing in organ building if not ideal. The consequence was that Mr. Crosby went back to New York with a contract for a modern concert organ, practically equal to the very best in the world, and in some respects superior to any other, for $45,000. It is quite true that the cause of organ music did not derive so much benefit from this characteristic liberality as had been expected, for later it was discovered that since the investment of $45,000 represented a certain amount of interest, it was not proper to use the organ but upon condition of its proper expenses being paid. This commercial reasoning has operated thus far to limit the use of the Auditorium organ, beyond what was proper to have been expected; but it was not Mr. Eddy's fault. At the opening of this magnificent instrument Mr. Eddy played a "Triumphal Fantasia," by Theodore Dubois, written expressly for that occasion and dedicated to him.

Few elements in Mr. Eddy's success are more admirable than the progressive breadth of his taste in the matter of programs. At first limiting himself to the strict school of German organ music, he has finally come to the Apostolic condition of recognizing every school as possessing merit, whereby there is not in the world of sincere organ music anything which is "common or unclean." Moreover, Mr. Eddy builds his programs carefully, with due regard to sequence and contrast and climax. Among recent concerts of his perhaps the following are as characteristic illustrations as any:—

Christ M. E. Church, Pittsburgh, Pa., Jan. 3, 1895:—

1 Sonata in C minor, op. 25. Th. Salome
I. Andante maestoso—Allegro risoluto.
II. Andante—Andantino con moto.
III. Allegro con moto—Allegro non troppo ma deciso.

2 *a* In Paradise, (new) Th. Dubois
b Toccata. .. ..

3 *a* Pastorale, op. 26, No. 1 (new). Louis Adolphe Coerne
b Caprice in B flat. Alex. Guilmant

4 *a* Romance, (new), A. Chauvet
b Gavotte in F major. Padre Martini
(Arrangement by Alex. Guilmant.)

5 *a* Shepherds' Farewell to the Holy Family. Berlioz
(Chorus from the "Infancy of Jesus.")
b Funeral March and Seraphic Song. Alex. Guilmant

6 *a* Intermezzo, Mascagni
(From "Cavalleria Rusticana.")
b Grand Processional March, Gounod
(From the "Queen of Sheba.")
(Two new transcriptions for the organ by Clarence Eddy.)

8 Overture to "William Tell" Rossini
(By Request.)

Friday afternoon, Jan. 4, 1895:—

1 Prelude and Fugue in D major. J. S. Bach

2 *a* "Am Meer," (By the sea"), Franz Schubert
b "Spring Song". Mendelssohn
(Arrangements for the organ by Clarence Eddy.)

3 Sonata Pontificale, J. Lemmens
I. Allegro Moderato. II. Adagio.
III. Marche Pontificale. IV. Fugue. Fanfare.

4 *a* Allegretto in D minor. Arthur Foote
b A Royal Procession. Walter Spinney
(Two new compositions dedicated to Clarence Eddy.)

5 *a* Canon in B minor, Robert Schumann
b Fugue in D major. Alex. Guilmant

6 Passacaglia, op. 65, (new). Oskar Wermann
(Dedicated to Clarence Eddy.)

7 Prelude to the opera "Otho Visconti," Frederic Grant Gleason

8 *a* "In the Garden," Carl Goldmark
(From the Symphony. "A Country Wedding.")
b Wedding March, Mendelssohn
(From the "Midsummer Night's Dream.")
(New arrangements for the organ by Clarence Eddy.)

Or we might take his recent programs in the Chicago Auditorium, Tuesday evening, Jan. 22, 1895.

1 Sonata in C Minor, op. 25, Th. Salomé
I. Andante maestoso—Allegro risoluto.
II. Andante—Andantino con moto.
III. Allegro con fuoco—Allegro non troppo ma deciso.

2 Pastorale, op. 28, No. 1, (new) Louis Adolphe Coerne

3 A Royal Procession, Walter Spinney
(Dedicated to Clarence Eddy.)

4 *a* Caprice in B Flat, Alex. Guilmant
b Torchlight March, "

5 *a* Intermezzo, Mascagni
(From "Cavalleria Rusticana.")
b Grand Procession March, Gounod
(From the "Queen of Sheba.")
(Two new transcriptions for the organ by Clarence Eddy.)

6 Prelude to the opera "Otho Visconti," Frederic Grant Gleason

7 Canon in B Minor. Robert Schumann

8 Concert Fugue in G Major. J. L. Krebs

9 Concert Piece in E Flat Minor. Louis Thiele

Tuesday evening, January 29, 1895:

1 Concert piece op. 24. — Alex. Guilmant
(Prelude, Theme, Variation and Finale.)

2 Shepherd's Farewell to the Holy Family. — Berlioz
(Chorus from the "Infancy of Jesus.")

3 Etude in C Sharp Minor, op. 10, No. 4. — Chopin
(Arranged for the Organ by August Haupt.)

4 *a* Romance, "The Evening Star." — Richard Wagner
b Pilgrim's Chorus. — "
(Transcriptions from "Tannhaeuser," by Clarence Eddy.)

5 Scherzo and Finale. — Dudley Buck
(From the First Sonata.)

6 Coronation March from "The Prophet." — Meyerbeer
(Arranged by W. T. Best.)

7 In Paradise (New). — Th. Dubois

8 *a* Romance in B Flat Minor (New). — A. Chauvet
b Gavotte in F Major. — Padre Martini
(Arrangements by Alex. Guilmant.)

9 *a* "Am Meer" (By the Sea). — Franz Schubert
b Wedding March, from the "Midsummer Night's Dream." — Mendelssohn
(New arrangements for the organ by Clarence Eddy.)

And in this connection a word may not be amiss upon his playing. His technic is masterly in all directions—pedal, manual, registration, and interpretation; he is master in all. Amid the pitfalls of the combination pistons of a modern electric action, he is as cool as upon an ordinary instrument. Even upon the treacherous organ of Boston Music hall, Mr. Eddy managed not to come to grief, where so many things were done by combinations which did not show upon the draw stops.

For eighteen years Mr. Eddy has held position as organist and master of the choir in the First Presbyterian church of Chicago. Here his programs are carefully prepared, and given to the printer by Tuesday of each week. The entire service is considered as a whole, and the musical selections have in view not only a desirable sequence among themselves, but also a reference to the character of the expected sermon and the key note of the occasion. The only draw-back to this state of musical consideration between the organist and minister happens when the minister decides to change his sermon late Saturday afternoon. The organist is not always able to change his program to match, where so many things have to be foreseen and prepared in advance.

For eighteen years, or so, Mr. Eddy has been organist

of the Apollo Club, accompanying many important works. sought after more and more as he advances in age.

Speaking of the estimation in which Mr. Eddy is held by the leading composers of organ music throughout the world I may mention that among others the following important organ compositions have been dedicated to him:—Sonata in G minor, No. 2, by Dudley Buck, of Brooklyn, N. Y.; Sonata in D, No. 4, by S. de Lange, of Cologne; Passacaglia, opus 95, by Oskar Wermann, of Dresden; Fantasia in E minor, by Gustav Merkel, of Dresden; Fantasia de Concert, op. 33, by F. de la Tombelle, of Paris; Fantasie triomphale, by Theodore Dubois, of Paris; and Sonata in G minor, No. 5, op. 80, by Alexander Guilmant, of Paris.

The illustrations in the preceding pages are from photographs not previously published. The first picture was an ambro-type, in which the contrast is insufficient for making a good "half tone," but it shows a youngster with an excellent forehead. The early age at which Mr. Eddy's face reached its mature expression is very remarkable, and I do not remember any other case in which a strong face and strong character showed maturity at so early an age as twenty-four, the first Chicago photograph, taken more than eighteen years ago, serving very well as a portrait of Mr. Eddy today.

As for the characterization of the artist and his career I may add that, unlike many sketches of this kind, the present is based upon the personal experience of the writer, and an acquaintance covering the whole of Mr. Eddy's Chicago career. I may also mention that it was begun by a most complimentary letter from Mr. Dudley Buck, introducing the organist and man. The length of the sketch is to be regretted; but facts are sometimes stubborn things, and the principle of doing a thing well if at all is to be held responsible.

W. S. B. M.

AN ODD MUSICAL AFTERNOON.

Having long been haunted by the fear that such bits of sins as I may commit in the body, will be expiated hereafter by my unwilling spirit in listening to amateur performances on the melodeon, and reed organ, the barrel organ and the accordeon, I admit to going to hear the Aeolian organ with a secret bias. "It is," I told myself, "in the nature of machinery to grind with iron (or wooden) precision, and it is in the nature of reeds and reed pipes to squawk whenever opportunity offers." Still, when one has discovered that he can be mistaken, that it is not well to know too much before hand, and has retained the ability usually lost with childhood to admit he has been mistaken, one is not altogether warped past even-handedness. Moreover I sought to put myself in that receptive and impartial frame which alone can learn or judge, and which affords its happy possessor consolation that religion cannot give.

The Aeolian and a piano attached to it like a sort of mechanical Siamese twin were in full swing when I arrived doing the overture to Zampa. "Everything," says Epictetus, "has two handles." This exhibition was no exception to his rule. The eye put in its claim first, and for an instant or two I did not hear for looking at the piano keys moving as if under invisible fingers. Behind the two instruments, (the piano was at the left) were bellows operated by an electric motor. From the Aeolian to the piano ran a cable about the size of an ordinary rubber gas pipe of the kind used for a drop light. This cable was composed of many wires, one for each piano key. Each wire connected at the bottom of the upright piano with a pneumatic valve, which, the electric current on, opened when the same note was struck upon the organ, and set going an apparatus that struck the hammer upon its string. The Aeolian, in appearance like the finest cabinet organ or upright piano, had a sort of cup-board above its long line of registers, and in this opening was a roll of manilla paper on which with square holes for characters, was written in a cypher known only perhaps to the trade, the composition then playing. On the bench before it, sat, not a player, for he did not touch the keys, but a conductor who drew forth now one stop, now another, now made combinations, now compelled the mechanism to *ff*, now to *pp*, now *sf*, and so on, and regulated the tempo quite as if he were doing all the work himself, or rather as if the many voices were so many players whom he was directing with a baton.

This was no common reed organ I speedily discovered, but an instrument possessing a wide range of effects, and capable of giving forth a wide range of orchestral suggestion. I also discovered now that I had gotten hold of the ear handle of the performance, that the accompanying piano was more a curious sight than a musical co-partner, since spite of the proverbial quickness of lightning the piano hammers decended a fraction, an attenuated fraction, but still a fraction of time too late, and what perhaps was more wearing, with remorseless uniformity of touch. All things end. The overture did and rolled upon its one little, slim rolling pin was put away in a box that seemed the twin of a corset box. I then saw that the punctured paper had flowed over a bar of fine hard wood in which were fifty-eight small, square holes. If the bellows was going and a hole in the manilla paper came opposite a hole in that bar, the pneumatic action produced a tone, and if connection were made, sent the news on to the piano. Any sort of motor would do, the conductor explained, gas, water, or coal oil, and the bellows and all appliances could be hidden in a closet, or in the wall.

The next selection, Gounod's Ave Maria was played by the Aeolian alone, and beautifully. Even bias had to admit that this combination of wood, brass and iron was not soulless. The third selection was "Lead kindly light," but for causes unknown it sounded to me quite flat, perhaps another conductor had possession, and this was not his favorite. Liszt's Third Rhapsody was the fourth selection and showed the instrument's full powers and limitations. I then discovered what I had missed was power of differentiation. If the trumpets were pianissimo, so too were the flutes, and the oboes. All the voices of this minature orchestra took on precisely the same shade of tone since machinery cannot do everything.

As I listened the wonder grew that pneumatic wind valves, pipes and wheels could so respond to different conductors as to reveal mind mysteries, and I found myself fancying that it even had a taste of its own and rendered some compositions far better than others because it is so elected, just as the phonograph reproduces some voices and instrumental combinations far better than others. And when I had found all the fault I possibly could with it, its performances seemed to me worlds ahead of the average organist's playing upon the average organ. I do not fancy its warmest advocate will declare of it as Berlioz' trombone prophet did of his instrument, "that it is destined sooner or later to dethrone all other instruments," but there is certainly plenty of room for it, and room where it will be warmly welcomed. The world holds plenty of people who with musical feeling and intelligence have not the time or the fingers to conquer the technic of the key-board. Age, rheumatism, blindness, all the woes that shut one up to solitude do not exclude one from conducting the Aeolian, and I fancy it might offer suggestions to the candid, humble-minded pianist or organist say in the country, who not finding his own rendering of certain compositions all he wishes, hankers to hear them done with at least mechanical correctness. To such a player it would be acutely sensitive, and therein lies its charm to the musician. Drolly enough, like its big cousin the great organ, it can revenge itself upon the indifferent by going through a composition with all the sans-souci callousness of its little poor relation the barrel organ. Clearly it is no toy, but a true instrument come to stay.

From the Aeolian I went to visit the Regina, which despite its Latin name is a music box of American invention. The pretty Swiss toys have always held for me charming, odd hints of August thickets singing with insect orchestras, but possibly because I am an American I never have wanted to hear the best one play its repertoire twice over within an hour, probably because the tunes came in exactly the same order each time. The American inventor of the Regina felt perhaps the same ennui at the old regularity for his box is not only unlimited in repertoire, (save as the pocket-book may limit its possessor in the purchase of tune disks) but permits one to arrange his program in a new order at each new hearing, and to put the Last Rose of Summer first or last or in the middle as he pleases. In place of the old cylinder detachable steel disks are used. These are fifteen and one-half inches in diameter, and are of comparative small cost, about seventy-five cents apiece. In appearance they are very like thin, light buzz saws before the teeth are cut, and it seems to me a round six dozen might be put in a tall hat box. On these disks tiny square holes, and tiny pegs write out the composition be it ever so complex, after some cabalistic recipe. The pegs as the disk revolves strike against star wheels, and they in turn strike the comb which as in the old boxes produces the tones. When a selection has been played the desired number of times and the clock work has run down, the movable bar holding the tune disk is lifted, another disk is set upon the center pivot, the bar let down, the clock-work wound up and a new entertainment begins. A cog wheel walks into holes in the rim of the disk, and so turns it, and tiny wooden supports hold it in place at the sides. A softer and more resonant tone is produced than by the old cylinder, and as I walked away to the strains of "Two little girls in blue, boys," I permitted myself the simple luxury of for a moment cracking the tenth commandment and coveting a Regina.

ELIZABETH CUMINGS.

A MODERN MASTER IN LEIPSIC

Just opposite the old Thomasschule and across the square from the Thomaskirche in Leipsic is No. 17 Thomaskirchof, one of a row of houses and stores having little in common with the musical atmosphere sacred to the memory of Johann Sebastian Bach. At least one would think so until upon entering No. 17 and climbing painfully up four flights of steep German stairs we find a little retreat devoted to the development in music of aims so truly high as to be in harmony even with the spirit of the great Johann Sebastian.

Allow me to introduce to you Herr Robert Teichmuller as he comes forward to greet us with a bow and a cordial "Guten Tag" or if your appearance is unmistakeably transatlantic, in fluent English which will at once put you at ease. You will find in Herr Teichmuller a courteous German gentleman of about thirty-five years, above middle height, slender and dark, with kindly grey eyes and pleasant mouth; his hair is black and bushy, and he has a habit of running his fingers through it till it stands on end rather ferociously. The music room is not large and is quite crowded by two grand pianos standing side by side; the walls are decorated with pictures of musicians, photographs of celebrated people and places, and every available bit of standing room is filled with books, music and bric-a-brac.

Herr Teichmuller is one of the best exponents of the modern German school of pianoforte playing. He was educated in the Royal Conservatorium of Leipsic but the method he teaches bears little resemblance to that known in this country as the "Leipsic Method;" for while the majority of the conservatorium masters are content to jog along teaching as they themselves were taught, Herr Teichmüller has worked out for himself a method which is in every way adapted to the needs of the modern pianist. The most glaring faults usually found in the American students are in slovenly technic, tight arm, wrist and hand

and a consequently hard tone. Two or three years on the old school plan will probably improve the technic, but the tone will remain as unsympathetic as ever and the musical education of the student, as far as his or her own work is concerned, is but slightly advanced. Herr Teichmuller's first step is to give a true idea of tone production; he insists on the entirely loose, devitalized arm, the natural position of hand with curved fingers, and the "letting fall"—*fallen lassen* of the fingers (contrast with the word "strike" so often used). The first few lessons will probably be devoted to nothing but tone work on original exercises which he writes out, adapting them to the needs of each pupil's hand, and gradually taking them in increasing tempo; then follows the study of staccato, scales, arpeggios, chords and other forms of technic. It is a joyful day when one gets the first easy study or Bach's Little Preludes, and the way is made if not smooth always enjoyable to the earnest worker by the never failing patience and the individual interest which our master takes in each pupil. Indeed there is an ideal feeling of good fellowship and camaraderie not often met with between master and pupil which is one of the most delightful memories of our student life.

I have never seen Herr Teichmuller lose his temper with a pupil, but he can make one feel very small. I remember one day feeling particularily diminutive, when, on having expressed a desire to play something which was not only too difficult but did not "lie" for my hands, he said, "Fraulein were you to play that you would remind me of an ant on the back of an elephant." All through the course each piece studied, however easy, must be finished as perfectly as if for concert work; at whatever stage therefore the Teichmuller pupils leave off they have more or less of a repertoire which they can render in finished style. This contrasts favorably with the work of students on the old method. I have known numbers of hard workers, who after two or three years have little to show but increased agility and muscular strength. The last teaching hour of the day is one that is coveted, for then the master will unbend and intersperse the lesson with bright criticisms of current musical doings or reminiscences of his student days. I cannot resist repeating one story which he delights to tell. He and a friend started early one Sunday morning for a day in the country; after walking some miles they came to a village where the pastor was an acquaintance. It being just time for morning service, Herr Teichmuller was invited to play the organ. The friend offered to do the blowing and Herr Teichmuller took his place and waited, but no wind came. Then feeling something must be wrong he looked around and saw to his amazement and that of the congregation, the chandelier in the center of the church rapidly ascending and descending—the friend had got hold of the wrong rope!

Herr Teichmüller is a pedagogue first and a concert pianist second; he teaches too many hours daily for either his nerves or his technic to be in condition for concert work, and it is only when the *Stimmung* is perfect that he can be prevailed upon to play in company. The pupil, however, who has brought an exceptionally good lesson and is rewarded by the master seating himself at the piano and playing a few numbers from perhaps Schumann's "Carnival" or "Kreisleriana" or a Brahms Rhapsodie, is made happy and inspired to still further efforts. Proud indeed is he who can say "Herr Teichmuller played for me to-day." He is looked on with envy not unmixed with respect by less fortunate comrades.

Not the least helpful to the student wishing to make a specialty of teaching are the teaching lessons given in the last few weeks of our course; in them Herr Teichmuller theoretically teaches his method from the first lesson onward, explaining all points with the greatest clearness, and showing the best way of imparting to others what we ourselves have learned. The discussion and hot words often to be heard in Leipsic on the subject of old and new methods of pianoforte teaching bring to mind Schumann and the war he waged against the Philistines, who, if now not quite so stiff necked as in his day might be more cordial in their treatment of the valiant Davidsbundler.

HELEN F. YOUNG.

BOHEMIAN MUSIC IN 1894.

THE last year has witnessed more than one important event in our musical life and furnished more than one important chapter for the history of Bohemian art. Whether we survey the field of original composition—notedly of instrumental music—or look over the year's history of the theatre or concert halls, or study works already finished though not yet performed, or consider musical activity in our smaller country towns, or watch the triumphant march of Bohemian music through foreign countries—everywhere do we see effort, activity and progress.

With the full consciousness of power and evident zeal for work, a new actor has lately appeared on the stage. It is the youngest school of composers, a strong cohort of enthusiastic musicians, numbering among its members some men whose talent is of the highest order, a school which has produced, during the short time of its existence, a respectable amount of noteworthy musical literature. Well may we congratulate ourselves! The public still remembers the recent successes, in the concert hall, of Suk and Novak, the two coryphei of the youngest school whose very débuts at once revealed their strength. What we noticed with especial pleasure was the fact that the enthusiasm was not confined to the critics and the reviewers, that the Bohemian public itself received the young composers with evident sympathy, giving them that encouragement which is absolutely necessary in order that the hopes placed in this new school may be fully realized. This is really a noteworthy fact, and one that has been quite rare in the past, as far as we can remember. Even in the case of artists who enjoy international fame today we have always acted in accord with the proverb which says that no one is a prophet in his own country. The habitual distrust of our public was too well known to us so that we hardly dared to expect, in this particular case, any result so favorable. However, it must be acknowledged here that the true reasons lay in something else. It would be insincerity not to own that the generation which immediately followed Dvorak did not attain to any considerable height, that it was not wholly original. Many were called, but none were chosen. We shall not speak of an actual reaction, but considering that unusual activity of the seventies when Dvorak and Fibich, following in the footsteps of Smetana, were rousing an astonishing activity in the musical life of the nation, the period of the eighties meant inertness, leaning toward foreign models and elements, fatigue, stagnation. The new awakening is the work of the youngest school, and here we may rightly speak of a renascence of Dvorakian ideals inasmuch as most of the youngest composers are pupils of Dvorak's school.

These young men surely have a promising future before them, and their indomitable energy, their culture and industry confirm our belief that their productions will be healthy and vigorous. Of their latest works we shall mention the Compositions for Pianoforte of Josef Suk and Oskar Nedbal, Suk's Overture to the Winter's Tale, for grand orchestra, Vitezslav Novak's Serenade for pianoforte, and impassionate Songs.

The Bohemian opera this time is not as rich as in former years. Only one new work has been performed, Richard Rozkosny's opera in one act, "Stoja," a work of melodic richness and dramatic effectiveness, evidently influenced by the modern Italian words of Mascagni, Leoncavallo, *et consortes*. Two of the older Bohemian operas were resuscitated and very well performed. Fibich's "Blanik," and Dvorak's delightful "Tvrde Palice" (Stubborn Heads). It is only a pity that the resuscitation of both of these works did not meet with the success it deserved. It seems as if the operatic taste of our public had considerably deteriorated under the influence of the crying brutality of Italian verism. And if we finally mention the new version of Dvorak's opera "Dimitrij" which really captured the audience in its new garb, we have recorded everything that deserves mention in the yearly chronicle of dramatic music. The coming year, however, promises full compensation in every respect. The latest opera by Zdenko Fibich, "Boure" (The Tempest—libretto by Jaroslav Vrchlicky, based on Shakespeare's drama) will be performed during the winter season; master Karel Bendl has finished two new compositions, "Mati Mila," (Mother Mila), opera in one act, and a popular ballet, "Ceska Svatba" (A Bohemian Wedding),—and finally, Karel Kovarovic will, we hope, finish his long expected serious opera "Armida."

With far greater eloquence the glory of Bohemian music has been proclaimed in the concert hall where many new works of considerable interest and undoubted value have been performed for the first time. We refer again to our youngest composers; in the first place we must mention that significant concert of the Umelecka Beseda (Society of Artists) given in the hall of Svatovaclavska Zalozna where two great works were performed for the first time, works that at once stamped their authors as eminent artists: the Quintet in G minor by Joseph Suk and Variations on Schumann's Theme by Vitezslav Novak. The success of these two compositions on that occasion served as a creditable introduction of the youngest school before the public and won for it both recognition and popularity. Since then we have had opportunity to listen to several other specimens of work of the youngest school of which we shall only mention a Serenade for stringed instruments by Joseph Suk, Pianoforte Quartet by Vitezslav Novak, "Slavnostni pochod" (Festive March) for grand orchestra by Oskar Nedbal, Sonata for pianoforte and violin by the same author, and smaller compositions, pianoforte and vocal, by Fr. Picka, Ed. Tregler and others.

Of the older composers, master Zdenko Fibich gave us a new valuable Quartet in D major, and a symphonic poem "Vpodvecer" (In the Evening); Josef Klicka furnished additional proof of his skill in chamber composition by his String Quartet, in vocal music he won new fame by his great work "Prichod Cechu na Rip" (The Coming of the Bohemians to the Rip Mountain) for soli, chorus and orchestra; at its first performance by the Hlahol society the work was very warmly received. Karel Weiss, whose individuality is so strongly marked, demonstrated his talents in his symphony in C minor (performed at the National Theatre) whose bold structure and melodic richness have added a new laurel to his wreath. Less effective was the Symphony in F major by Joseph B. Foerster, though it possesses delicacy of expression and the polyphonic work is well and skillfully done. Mr. Foerster's true field is lyric, and for that reason we expect from him valuable contributions in the line of songs. Attention is due furthermore to the new compositions by Hanus Trnecek; a Concerto for pianoforte and orchestra, and his "Slavnostni pochod," both of which—beside a number of new songs—we have heard at the popular concerts of the Umelecka Beseda. It is evidently in the field of instrumental music that we have reaped the richest harvest, and, judging by the industry exhibited by the youngest composers we may expect that, in the coming years, our musical literature will be enriched with many a valuable work in this particular sphere.

The visit of our beloved master Antonin Dvorak to Prague was an event of more than ordinary significance. It did much towards inspiring and encouraging the youngest generation of our composers. On the thirtieth of May the renowned master and his family came to Prague, welcomed by numerous admirers, but staid only a few days, retiring to his favorite Tusculum, Vysoka, where he spent the summer and part of the autumn in almost unceasing work. The long cherished hopes of his friends were satisfied on the thirteenth of October: the master conducted, at the National Theatre of Prague, a concert the most important number of which was Dvorak's fifth symphony, entitled "Znoveho Sveta" (From the New World). This new work which had aroused so many expectations, was received with enthusiasm, and we surely have the right to expect that it will be repeated this winter or in the coming lenten season. This symphony in E minor is not only valuable as a work of absolute music rich in melodic beauties, but also extremely interesting on account of its characteristic melodies and orchestral coloratura. It is evident that in selecting his themes the composer paid especial attention to American

(negro and Indian) songs. Thus, for instance, the secondary theme of the first phrase seems to have been taken, so to say, from the very lips of the people. The individuality and foreign origin of some of these themes, however, does not prevent the master from infusing the whole with that charm of freshness so characteristic of his compositions. A real gem is the second phrase, the impressive Largo in D flat major, the fundamental motive of which is derived from an Irish song. The delightful Scherzo and the lofty Finale, with its imposing gradations, are Dvorak's in every note. The success of the work is the best refutation of all various doubts which had been expressed before its performance, as if Dvorak had abandoned, in the new symphony, all that marked his former compositions; it places in strong light the meanness of a German editor who, though having no grounds to support his assertion, accused Dvorak of having adopted, without any changes, one part of his new symphony from an older one. Of older well known orchestral compositions of our master, performed at that same concert, we mention his Overture to 'Josef Kajetan Tyl' and the Serenade for stringed instruments. In the Bohemian Society for Chamber Music we have also listened to his new Quintet in E flat major, written in America, whose second and fourth parts are built on foreign themes, the Larghetto being particularly spirited and warm. On the sixteenth of October the master left for New York.

With sincere joy do we register another event which has brought about a healthy reaction in our concert life and has already rendered considerable service to Bohemian art. We mean the foundation of a Bohemian "Society for Chamber Music" which owes its origin to the women of Prague, and which is all the more important as, in this important sphere of the musical art, we have heretofore been obliged to look solely to a German society which, we are sorry to say, has always been inimical to Bohemian art. It may seem incredible, and still it is a fact, that the gentlemen who ruled the Kammermusik-Verein, would not allow the compositions of Smetana, Dvorak or Fibich to be performed at a time when the names of these three great composers of

Bohemia have already won the admiration of the entire musical world. In the very heart of Bohemia, in Bohemian Prague, that society possessed impudence enough to ignore Bohemian art. The Bohemian Society for Chamber Music entered upon life under very auspicious circumstances. The idea received immediate recognition and support and in a short time the new society secured such a large and extensive membership that its existence is now secure. Moreover, the society has secured the best executive artists—the Bohemian Quartette—and the wonderful success of its first concert astonished many a one and made him think, Why have we not done this before? The ladies to whom the society owes its existence deserve our heartiest thanks.

Prague, Jan. 1895.

Translated from the Bohemian of Frant K. Hedja, by

J. J. KRAL.

WHAT IS CLASSICAL MUSIC?

MUSIC which through prolonged usage has proved its possession of those qualities which entitle it to be taken as a standard of excellence, and which has come to be acknowledged, first by competent judges, and subsequently by the public generally as representing the highest expression of musical taste and hence authorative as a model. Such music combines in true proportions the qualities of both heart and head or, in other words, it is characterized by the union of the emotional and the intellectual in proper equipoise and through the possession of these qualities in their right adjustment, combination and relationship, it is delightful and instructive,—always fresh and incapable of growing old.

The reason why classical music does not always please at the first hearing is because *all* have not the faculties of perception and reception in an adequate degree. Those who have fine and penetrating discernment and the ability of making nice distinctions, perceive at once. With others it requires time, study and close acquaintanceship in order to duly appreciate.

WILLIAM MASON.

EDITORIAL BRIC-A-BRAC.

THE unwonted space which certain favorite subjects have consumed this month cuts short current topics, and the present is merely a resumé. The concerts of the Chicago orchestra have continued with a constantly increasing standard of perfection. Among the best since last time was that in which Mr. W. C. E. Seeboeck played his new concerto for pianoforte and orchestra. The work contains quite a number of delightful passages and parts, but as a whole it is not quite up to the standard which those who know the genius of Mr. Seeboeck have learned to expect. The trouble seems to be with the radical motives themselves, which do not happen to be such as lend themselves to a graceful and easy development. The interworking of the orchestra and pianoforte is in many respects delightful. Portions of the solo part Mr. Seeboeck has treated very broadly, in passages of full chords and massive effects, which certainly are not so congenial to his talent as softer and more delicate elaborations.

It is stated that Mr. Thomas has promised to play another work of Seeboeck's this season or a little later. Which is well, for Seeboeck is both a pianist of unusual talent and a composer of exceptional grace and elegance.

* * *

Among the attractions of the month have been the visits of the violinist Ysaye (pronounced *ee-sy-eh*, ey having the sound of i in like.) This artist is one of the best violinists ever heard in America, having a beautiful bow and great technic. His numbers in the first appearance were the Saint Saens concerto for violin and orchestra, and Max Bruch's Scotch Fantasia, both of which he played delightfully, and to the great arousing of the audience, which recalled him again and again. He played for encores something from Bach. His latest appearance, Feb. 19th, is too late for this issue, but in general it may be stated that his work is artistic in a high degree. He has certain mannerisms, such as see-sawing with his body, and requiring a high pedestal to stand upon, in order that he may be as high as the orchestral director; but he is none the less a great artist.

* * *

The other Belgian master, Mr. Cesar Thomson has been here for two concerts in Central Music hall, under the direction of that skilled manager, Mr. F. Wight Neumann. The audiences were not too large, but the playing had the same masterly qualities as before, and the hearers were wildly enthusiastic. He was assisted by Miss Fuller, one of the two ensemble pianists who gave a concert late in Dec., in Central Music hall. Miss Fuller is a well taught player, from Moszkowski, of Berlin. She apparently is a fairly good musician, and a good player, but distinctly not a virtuoso.

* * *

Among the chamber concerts mention ought to be made of the Spiering quartette which gave a program with a Brahms Quintette as its last number. While the earlier parts of the program had been rather tiresome and commonplace, the playing in the Brahms number was better, and the piece pleased better, but it was not a success. The audience was appreciative. The concert as a whole lacked that something which has so often been mentioned here, and which careful hearers miss much oftener than concert givers understand, — namely, concentration and artistic faith in the pieces played. The early numbers made little or no effect, and by the time the Brahms piece came on the hearers were too tired to listen with good attention.

* * *

The concerts of the Chicago orchestra are rapidly approaching an end for the present season. After the concerts of March 8th the orchestra will go upon the road for a tour to the Pacific coast. At least seven weeks of concerts will be given during which the orchestra will earn at least

$50,000. This will be well from every point of view, but mainly from the fact that the visits of an organization such as this will be an event in the smaller cities, which under ordinary circumstances could not hope to hear orchestral concerts of the first class at more than extremely rare intervals.

Following are the dates and places of this tour:—

March 13, Grand Rapids, Mich.,—14, Ann Arbor, Mich.,—15, Detroit, Mich.,—16, Toledo, Ohio;—18 Sandusky, Ohio;—19, Cleveland, Ohio;—20, Akron, Ohio;—21, Buffalo, N. Y.,—22, Toronto, Canada;—23, Hamilton, Canada;—25, Rochester, N. Y.,—26, Jamestown, N.Y.,—27 and 28, Pittsburg, Pa.,—29 and 30, Columbus, Ohio; April 1, Delaware, Ohio;—2, Springfield, Ohio;—3, Dayton, Ohio;—4, Indianapolis, Ind.,—5, Champaign, Ill.,—6, Peoria, Ill.,—April 15,—St. Louis,—16 and 17, Kansas City,—18, Lincoln, Nebraska,—19 and 20, Omaha, Nebraska,—22 to 27, Iowa Cities,—29 and 30, Minneapolis, Minn.,—May 1 and 2, St. Paul, Minn.,—3, Madison, Wis.,—4, Milwaukee, Wis.

* * *

I complained last year of the quality of the symphony analytical programs. They have been better this year, but still owing to the absence of musical examples they do not afford the aid to students which they ought. One of the most glaring cases of bad editing which has come to my notice occurred in the program of Jan. 4th, concerning the Bach sonata transcribed for the orchestra. The program has a page or so of matter relating to the Bach family, with some mention of this particular Bach (John Sebastian). But not one word identifying the sonata, telling when it had been transcribed, whether played before or not—or any other information in any way relating to the particular selection. This was the more to be regretted because, owing to his reticence, Mr. Thomas loses a great deal of credit for work of this kind that a smaller man would take care should be tallied in his favor.

* * *

The financial plans for next year are now being arranged. The orchestral association has increased the board of directors to nine, and has made provision for a board of governing directors composed of every one who contributes upwards of $50 apart from tickets and seats, and each subscriber actually donating money in this way without asking seats in the return, is entitled to one vote for each fifty dollars so subscribed.

That this is a great benefit goes without saying; and a respectable number of Chicago citizens willing to subscribe the amounts necessary to make them voting directors is not only to be hoped but to be confidently expected. It is not the Chicago way to let a good thing slip.

It is stated that the success of the present season in spite of the hard times is encouraging. The deficits for the four years now nearly finished have been as follows:—$53,613 for the first season, $51,381 for the second season, $48,972 for the third season, and $31,000 for the present season. Against this record the circular of the board of governors mentions the following figures as those expended by Mr. Higginson of Boston in establishing the orchestra there:—first season, $23,000; second, $44,000; third, $31,-000; fourth, $22,000, fifth $52,000 (orchestra increased and travelled); sixth, $52,000; seventh, $35,000; eighth, $25,000; ninth, $12,000; and since about even. At the present rate the deficit next year will be much smaller. And the receipts at the concerts where Ysaye played were about $2,000 in excess of any former ones in the history of the orchestra, not even excepting the Paderewski concerts —so it is stated.

At present, prices of tickets are too low, or rather there are too many seats at 25 cts. and 50cts., to such an extent that if all were occupied the concerts would not be self supporting. The suggestion has been made that all the main balcony be put at 50 cts. leaving for the 25ct. places only the two upper galleries—which indeed have a very advantageous acoustical position, and are accessible by elevator. Their only disadvantage is that they are not always accessible from the body of the house, and the holders of tickets there are cut off from the foyers of the house. This might be met by opening the gate at the top of the stairs at the intermission, permitting the gallery sitters to come down to other parts of the house. Should they happen to forget to go back after intermission no great harm would be done, since all the seats have coupons, and when wanted the intruder would not be able to hold them. This would probably make a difference of $4,000 in the season; perhaps more.

* * *

We seem to be living in an epoch of improved musical journalism. All the musical journals manifest a marked improvement over the kind that used to be published a few years ago. The *Musical Courier* is a great newspaper, printing a vast amount of musical information from many parts of the world. While the tone of this large journal is not always all that one could wish, it is at least a record which no advancing musician can afford to miss.

All the smaller journals show improvement; *Brainard's Musical World*, which under the editorship of the late Dr. Karl Merz gained such wide acceptance as a friend and guide of musical students, is now containing articles from such pens as those of Emil Liebling, Robert Goldbeck, Wm. H. Sherwood. The number for February contained a lesson from Mr. Liebling upon Schumann's "Bird as Prophet." It is clear and useful, and while there will be dispute concerning his teaching of grace notes, the lesson is none the less likely to do good, inasmuch as it is clearly expressed, and does not attempt to go into the matter too deeply.

The *Vocalist*, by Mr. Frank H. Tubbs, is improving, and is well worth the money. This is in the octavo size, like MUSIC, but with about half the number of pages. *Werner's Voice Magazine*, a specialist of specialists, is also out in the same form, in which it makes an impressive appearance. Our local neighbors the *Indicator*, *Presto* and *Musical Times* conduce to the happiness of the music trade according to their several wonts, week after week, and now and then manage to include quite a little musical news or comment.

The indefatigable John C. Freund is pegging away at the *Music Trades*, and gives not a little trade news together with some attention to politics. His younger brother Harry Freund keeps up his *Musical Weekly* with spirit, and as the quotation we made last time from Steinway's "Reminiscences of Rubinstein" shows, not without excellent matter.

* * *

At a recent afternoon concert of the Chicago Musical College a series of songs were sung which had been composed by one of the pupil graduates, Miss Grace Olcott, pupil in composition of Mr. Adolph Koelling. Of these there have been published, "Swift fly the hours," "The Happiest Heart," and "Life is but a Dream." The others were sung from MSS., the titles being "Slumber Song," "Twere better so," "Good Night," and last and best a Spanish song, "I'll Sing to thee, my guitar." The latter is a song of considerable development, running to five or six pages. The movement is well handled, the musical ideas plenty, the modulations and nuances well and effectively managed, and the whole musicianly to a high degree. The Slumber song is also a very pleasing thing. "Life is but a Dream," is being sung by that popular vocalist, Miss Fanchon Thompson, and it is one of the best. The above are but a small part of Miss Olcott's work. She writes the music as the mood takes her, and later endeavors to procure words. Sometimes she writes the words herself, and in this way she obtained the Spanish song. If she perseveres in the career of composer she will do still better, for the quality of the work is highly creditable to the College and her teacher, no less than to her own talent.

MISS GRACE OLCOTT.

* * *

The Apollo Club gave its second concert of the season Feb. 7, with a program composed of Max Bruch's "Arminius." The work is written very richly for orchestra, and the chorus is employed more for mass effects than for any other purpose. The story appertains to the early history of Germany and its struggle against the Romans, and the treatment is such as to interest Germans more than any others. In fact the work is one of those literary and art works of which so many have been composed within the last twenty years, glorifying German ideas and German spirit at the expense of other nationalities. It is therefore much better suited to a German audience and to German singers than to Americans. On the present occasion the music had not been very well prepared, for which reason some of the difficult choral passages did not go as intended. There had been but one short rehearsal with orchestra, which itself had been much reduced from symphony proportions. The result was a lack of confidence and the rhythmic swing was not fully realized. The work ought to have had at least four full rehearsals with orchestra. Sometime such an idea will be realized even in Chicago.

The solo work on this occasion was done by Mrs. Julia Wyman, Mr. Riedel, and Mr. Max Heinrich. The latter sang splendidly, and with admirable delivery of the text. His work was a model of what such singing ought to be. Mr. Riedel was suffering with a cold, and so was not at his best. Mrs. Wyman was rather over-weighted by the demands of the part. The concert was conducted, of course, by Mr. Wm. L. Tomlins.

* * *

It appears that I was wrong in my statements of the position of Mr. James Paul White concerning Temperament and Perfect Intonation, which I embodied in the "Bulletin" for February. I have a private letter and a supplementary note making the following corrections:—

"My position with regard to the equal temperament scale is and long has been not only very different from, but much stronger than what you have said. It is *not* "good enough for ordinary uses" but it is the only scale that is good and tolerably musical *at all* for nearly all rapid music which is not quite simple in character; and the real reasons for this

I never find in other minds, and I hope to bring them out, as well as possible in the present state of things, in this series. But I am really unable to state this position in a fairly unmistakable manner in one page or perhaps several, and would prefer to attempt it only as readers become somewhat acquainted with facts concerning this phase of music which are almost entirely unknown.

"I must also take exception to your statement of my position (although you do not refer to me by name) in your article on pages 409 and 410 of MUSIC, concerning the effect of dissonances in pure intonation. The real facts upon this point will probably come out later, for which I must beg you and your readers to wait."

* * *

Mr. Wm. H. Sherwood will make an eastern tour during the latter part of March and the first of April, when he will play in most of the leading cities and before various clubs and organizations which are in the habit of having him. He has also played a considerable number of engagements under the auspices of Mr. Derthick's Musical Literary clubs, in which he has proven a very profitable attraction. His Chicago recitals go on in a curiously quiet way, considering the high rank of this leading American artist. The Chicago daily press seems to have fallen into the habit of ignoring recitals by local artists, even the greatest, upon the difficult theory that they are given for advertising purposes. Why not given for educational purposes? This I understand to be the exact state of the case, and I know of no good journalistic reason why an artist playing as important programs, and in so masterly a way as Mr. Sherwood generally shows in his recitals, should not receive the treatment the press bestows so generally upon all other kinds of serious artists. Mr. Sherwood is playing splendidly now, and well deserves his thousands of friends and admirers in all parts of the country.

W. S. B. M.

THE PRACTICAL TEACHER.

HOW TO SECURE A GOOD TONE.

A good and beautiful tone, which is as indispensable to the one as to the other, may be at the command of each if the laws relating to touch are obeyed.

While it is quite a simple thing for any one to strike the keys of a pianoforte, it is not easy to produce a large, full, round and mellow tone, for this involves the proper use of a very complicated mechanism, in which the muscles should habitually be kept in a state of elasticity, with nevertheless sufficient firmness and contraction in parts of the hand, wrist, and finger to give power, support and stability. Too much contraction necessarily causes rigidity, which obviously affects the tone disagreeably, and on the other hand an excess of laxity and flaccidity of the muscles works equally to disadvantage in the opposite direction, resulting in weakness, insipidity and general lack of character. The problem consists in combining and blending the two principles so that the right proportion and relation is established and perfected. This is by no means an easy thing to do, and if the writer is justified in forming conclusions from his own personal experience, it is a fact that a comparatively small number of the multitude engaged in studying and practicing the pianoforte succeed in acquiring a touch which is equal to the demands of fully finished and artistic playing, notwithstanding persevering and long continued work. In seeking the reason for this it will probably be found that the quality of the work is generally at fault; or, if the work is in part well done, there is something omitted which should receive attention—something lacking in practice which should be supplied.

And we think the mischief lies just here, namely, that certain things which belong to the beginning are neglected at that time, or postponed, under the impression that they can be better attended to at a later period. One of the earliest directions to the beginner is to invariably lift the fingers high before striking the keys, and the importance of this act in practice is so constantly emphasized and reiterated from day to day as to exclude from the pupil's mind other things which ought to receive equal and concurrent attention. The object of high-lifted finger is a good one, being to aid in stretching the muscles and to develop strength and promote independence and freedom of muscular action, especially in the metacarpal, or third joints. This kind of practice is important and useful and should receive its daily share of attention, but the time allotted to it should be only in the proportion of, say, one to six, or thereabouts; that is, if three hours be given to daily practice, one sixth of that time, or half an hour will be amply sufficient, and this in the beginning, and while this is done another principle, which relates to rapid motion, should not be forgotten, but should receive equal attention in practice. Because if the touch of high-raised finger is used exclusively or unduly it leads to bad results and establishes modes of finger motion which are in direct conflict with the principles upon which rapid passage playing is based. A mechanic who is constructing a machine in which strength, elasticity and rapidity of movement are equally essential must keep all three principles in view from the outset and work accordingly. Pianoforte playing from the very nature of the instrument, depends in a large measure for its legitimate effects on passage playing. The reason for this is that the pianoforte lacks the power of tone prolongation which is a property of the human voice as well as of the violin and other stringed instruments of the same class. In order to produce a good effect with these passages, which consist of scales, arpeggios, broken chords, or indeed of any series of tones following in rapid succession, it is necessary that the fingers should rise but a short distance above the keys, and the player must be able to produce full tone of adequate and varying power without using the straight up and down hammer-like stroke. This requires attention in rudimentary stages just as much as does any other principle, and its accomplishment will be much facilitated through the agency of another kind of touch, in which not only the metacarpal, but also the first and second finger joints are equally concerned, and the entire mechanism is kept in an extreme state of elasticity and flexibility, with nevertheless sufficient contractile power for reserve strength and to serve as a base and support. A confirmed habit of lifting the fingers high precludes the possibility of swift and facile passage playing, for there is no time for superfluous motion in a degree of rapidity which is hardly exceeded by the quickness of thought. Besides this the tone produced by the blow from high raised finger is not purely musical, as it must be vitiated in some degree by the thud which is a result of the blow. This thud may not be perceptible when accompanied by the musical tone, but it is there nevertheless, as may be quickly demonstrated by drumming on a board with the fingers. In performing rapid passages the fingers must move with the greatest possible freedom and agility, and their motion resembles more the act of skating than of walking. They move in the manner of a glissando, for they glide over the keys with the utmost celerity and smoothness, producing a zephyr-like effect as if the tones were blown or breathed out, rather than resulting from finger percussion. As to this point eminent authority is at hand. Czerny says "The inferior mechanism of the keys is such that the strings will only sound well when before the percussion we do not raise the fingers too high, as otherwise, along with the tone there will be heard the blow on the key." Thalberg says: "We must bring forth the full tone without a hard striking on the keys, but by forcing them—pressing them with vigor, energy and animation, while the fingers are held but a short distance above them." He says further on in the form of a recommendation to young players, "never strike the keys from a great height." In this connection, Liszt's opinion of Czerny's playing is significant. It is forcibly expressed in a letter dated Weimar March 17, 1856, and addressed to Dyonis Pruckner, in Vienna. "I wholly approve of your intention to spend several months in Vienna and its charming suburbs. Also of your familiar association with Master Czerny, whose multiform musical experience will be of great use to you. Of all composers now living who have occupied themselves especially with the pianoforte playing and composing, I know no one whose views and judgement present so fair a standard of what has been accomplished. During the years of 1820-30, when the greater part of Beethoven's creations were a kind of sphinx for most musicians, Czerny played exclusively Beethoven with as excellent judgment as adequate and effective technique, and later on did not ignore and oppose the progress which had been made in technique, but essentially contributed thereto through his instrument and works." This is strong testimony from the highest authority as to the efficiency and conception of Czerny's Beethoven playing, and this too during Beethoven's lifetime.

During an experience of thirty years as a pianoforte teacher the writer has had constant trouble with pupils who had acquired the habit of high raised fingers and confirmed it to such a degree that the fingers could be moved in no other way. He has a lively sympathy for the poor teachers who are called upon by such players for "finishing lessons." The habit of a hard, unyielding, hammer-like and unsympathetic touch has become so ingrained and wrought into the very fibre as to form a second nature, and it must be counteracted by modifying and qualifying influences before any such things as polish or finish is possible. How much better it is to view the end from the beginning, and to avoid this trouble by acting in accordance with proverbial wisdom, viz.: "A stitch in time saves nine," or "An ounce of prevention is worth a pound of cure." For practical application let the practice with high-raised fingers be accompanied by forms of exercise which require a position in which the fingers are held close to the keys, thus favoring velocity or rapid playing, and by other exercises which are adapted to the cultivation of extreme elasticity of muscle in finger, wrist and forearm. By means of this combination the three properties of strength, elasticity and velocity receive simultaneous attention, and the cultivation of technique proceeds and develops systematically in accordance with these principles. One kind of touch supplies what the other lacks, and they work together and mutually assist each other, thus tending in united action to the acquirement of a complete and perfect touch. Different kinds of touch based upon these three principles, separately or combined, can be applied to any form of exercise which the teacher is in the habit of using, and such practice may therefore accompany and supplement any and every pianoforte method or instruction book.

WILLIAM MASON.

(By permission of the John Church Company, from Mason and Mathews PRIMER OF MUSIC.)

COMMONSENSE SUGGESTIONS TO TEACHERS.

(Extracts from a lecture delivered in Kimball Hall, Feb. 8, by Mr. Emil Liebling. Reported for Music by Miss Anna L. Mathews.)

Music teaching is a trade: simply a business. Some of us know very little about it, and then the minority of all the music teachers find out a few facts by the experience of years. It has been my particular endeavor to simplify the work and to reduce it as far as possible to the same basis as that on which we could apply common sense to almost any pursuit. A number of years ago I attended a reception of the Art Club and while there admired a picture. The artist, Mr. Payne, happened to be standing there and I remarked to him that I did not believe I could ever paint a picture. "Why of course you could," said he. "But" said I, "I can't even draw a cat." "A cat is a pretty hard thing to draw," he said. "Now if you will go to work systematically and do what I tell you to for three years, I will enable you to sketch almost anything at sight, to draw a correct picture, and if you have any imagination or inventiveness to furnish quite an artistic production."

Now I honestly think I can make anybody play the piano. I cannot make an artist of every body, but I believe that I can, within a not too long period, say three years. I don't mean three Chicago years, where the pupil commences about the first of October and then goes, at the first of November to attend a wedding down in Indiana; then when she comes back she goes to work on her Christmas presents and takes a vacation. After Christmas she comes back all broken up, and perhaps a neighbor gets sick and she stops a couple of weeks on that account, and by that time spring calcimining commences. Then Easter. The first of May gets pretty warm, no use commencing now. That is a Chicago year, very lucrative to the music teacher. But I mean the year of twelve months at the rate of three or four hours a day.

I believe that anybody can, within three years, learn to play well enough to play a Mendelssohn Song without Words, perhaps one of the easiest of Beethoven's Sonatas, and the Bach Inventions, and that would probably be plenty to most people. The work, however, would have to be very practically done.

* * *

The next couple of methods which really belong together are mechanical appliances. Mechanical appliances, one resembling the keyboard of the piano, the other resembling what we might call a miniature gallows, a very funny looking thing. The keyboard is a dumb instrument; the most extravagant claims are made for it and I really heard a girl play at Saratoga, at the same meeting, who played remarkably well. I couldn't judge whether she wouldn't have played better if she had done all her practice on a real live piano. When I first was introduced to the dumb piano they had a great scheme connected with it. When you pressed the key down there was a click, and when the key went up there was another click. It stood to reason then if one key was pressed down and held until the next was also pressed down, the two clicks would meet and give the effect of one, and it was skillfully argued that this would be the perfect legato, and most alarming statistics were published all over the country showing how many people died every year from the want of a perfect legato. I tried it and couldn't make it do at all. I had indulged in the hope that I played legato: I found that I could not play legato at all. I could hear those two clicks every time and I made up my mind that if I couldn't play a better legato with that I would try to get along the rest of my life with the legato I had been using, and if my legato was good enough for me it might be for my pupils.

The other machine had nothing to do with music. It goes on the principle that music is a matter of muscles; that you can develope high musical activity by developing muscles. If you become conscious of the name of certain muscles in your arms, that will be a very fine thing in playing a piece. The inventor came to see me, wanted my indorsement. You know I am a very tender hearted person. I endorse anything and anybody. We give endorsements for anything. We spent a whole afternoon together, and he said, naming some of the endorsers, "Now these people found it a good thing, why don't you." Well, I told him I would try it. I got one of the machines and tried it; I couldn't make any of those motions he could, but I could play the piano and he couldn't, and that's where I had him. I said, "Now you can beat me very much in working that machine, but I can play you out of town on the piano"—and that ended the machine.

* * *

Now then in regard to practice. I think that each pupil who comes to take lessons wants to learn. I really think so, and the majority do learn. I think that the American girl, (I have taught too few of the American boys to speak in a general way) will learn quicker, will learn what they learn better, than the girls of any other nation; they are more intelligent; they are very quick to learn and they have a most stupendous technical talent, undoubtedly a great technical talent. I was two years in Berlin, and while there taught the advanced classes of Kullak's Conservatory. I had about forty pupils. Now those girls didn't begin to play as well as our girls here. Then I attended a public examination of the Vienna Conservatory and their playing was fair, average, commonplace playing. They played concertos which they had studied during the entire school year, not a bit better than you will hear them here in the Chicago Musical College or any other of our schools. The great point that remains, and the most important is to tell the girl how to practice, what to do.

* * *

Here comes at once the question of scales. Now every pupil has this experience: She goes to a new teacher; first question, "Have you taken scales?" "Yes." "Play one." Sits down and plays the C Major scale, which of course is the most difficult of all scales. Every division of three or four notes distinctly heard. "Well" the teacher says, "that's very bad." He doesn't tell her why it is bad or what she must do to get it better; says, "you must practice scales." "How much must I practice scales?" "The more the better." "Which scales?" "All the major scales." Well, she comes the next time. "Have you practiced scales?" "Yes." Sits down and plays a scale but in another key. "Well," he says, "that's a little better. You must keep on." The third time the scale isn't heard at all and that's the end of it. Now, as a matter of fact, scale playing ought to be done every day. It is, however, only one of many things.

* * *

A pupil must be made to connect a certain idea with a certain kind of work, then having something definite to think of she accomplishes a definite object, whereas if it is all indefinite nothing can be accomplished. Let one pupil practice the scale of C that way ten times, tell her that that is done for the purpose of developing the fourth finger, to guard against pushing from the arm, keep the fingers curved well up among the keys, guard against any excess of force you can carry anything to excess—that excess is very liable to damage the hand. Raise the fingers very slowly, very firmly, then stop a moment. Then let her do the very opposite thing. Instead of raising the fingers high and striking firmly and in the moment of striking exert an appreciable amount of pressure; let her keep close to the keys and not strike heavily. This is a different mode of playing and it stands to reason it will produce a different result. It will develop variety and smoothness.

* * *

The first object of practice is clearness. This can be accomplished by a light staccato touch. Staccato work in scales is very useful, and it is this staccato work which has given to every pianist his technique, from Joseffy down. They all practice that way. It is one of the singular things in piano playing, that in order to play a legato passage clearly and cleanly, you must practice it very slow but staccato. You must take any passage whatever and play it slowly, long enough with a staccato, then play it legato, and all your passage work will have a brilliancy, a clearness, a touch, which nothing else will produce.

We will say that we practice our scales in three different ways and with the average pupil we advise an hour in the morning of scale practice, usually taking major scales, the relative minor and with more advanced pupils double thirds.

I think a good way to practice arpeggios, and a very simple way is to take the first common chord in its three positions. Where pupils have small hands, omit the octave, and so on. Practice the arpeggios in the three positions, also this way. Return in the opposite way. If you will remember how much of all the classical music consists exclusively of scales and arpeggios you will see the importance of this. A person who can play a good scale and a good arpeggio can really play most of the Beethoven sonatas, because there is very little octave work in them. After playing the ordinary common chord in the arpeggios I give to the pupil the diminished chord in its fourth position. There are only twelve positions in all, and then dominant seventh.

* * *

Mr. Liebling then went on to give certain directions regarding the proper method of introducing studies, and much other interesting matter for which unfortunately there is just now not sufficient room. But concerning which he will probably write for us specially later on. The lecture was very interesting and delightfully informal. The usual touches of Liebling sarcasm and wit were not wanting. From time to time musical illustrations were played, a few measures here and a few there, from widely different sources, and this was a very noteworthy feature of the evening. All these extracts were given off hand, of course, without reference to notes, and the ability to do this upon a scale of such magnitude is an important part of the lecturer's practical qualification as Master of the pianoforte.

— —

REVIEWS AND NOTICES.

MUSIC BUREAU FOR COMPOSERS.

In another column will be found information of a new undertaking by the indefatigable publishers, Messrs. J. B. Millet Company, whose epoch-marking "Famous Composers and their Works" has now reached a sale of more than 25,000 copies—something unprecedented in the history of musical works. They now propose to establish a sort of bureau to which young composers can send compositions for critical examination, correction, advice, and if worthy, for sale upon terms which are mutually fair, as will be found by sending for a circular. In a private letter the company says:

"Our intention is to provide that assistance to those who hope to become composers, and to give them just as good advice as they could obtain if they applied to a personal friend. At the present moment there is hardly a teacher in any large city who is not compelled to give up a certain portion of his time to answer questions about compositions submitted by friends or acquaintances. We have found on consultation with a number of these teachers, upon explaining to them the intention of this bureau, that they would be enormously relieved of such obligation, and we have found everywhere a strong desire to assist this undertaking.

It is, of course obvious to everybody that any person beginning to write music has a harder task before him than a beginner in almost any other profession. Nobody wants his music until he has established a reputation, which of course is an impossibility unless it is published, so that any young would-be composer no matter how good his composition may be, is a long time in getting any start at all.

We propose to do what we can to afford anybody who has written a good composition to bring it before the public. We can do this because we have our general agencies established all through the country (in all twenty-one including London, Honolulu, Manitoba and Canada) and can reach our subscribers directly.

We should be glad therefore in writing your notice of the Bureau, if you would recognize the fact that we are not attempting to establish a mill for turning out composers, but we are endeavoring to give that assistance which they cannot obtain elsewhere, namely, the criticism and advice of the best informed. We have made our arrangements to do this, and any applicant will get the same conscientious attention that he would receive if he were personally known to us. If it seems advisable to inform any applicant or any correspondent that he had better give up studying music altogether we shall certainly do so; in other words, we shall carry out the spirit of the undertaking in every particular."

NEW MUSIC.

AD. M. FOERSTER. FANTASY PIECES. Op. 38. H. Kleber & Bro. Pittsburgh.
The Evening Star.
Sylvan Sprites.
Evening Bells.
Canon.
The Sea.
Harlequin.
Pretty Marie.
Triumphal March.
Antique.
Prelude.
Mazurka.
Homage to Rubinstein.

In these twelve pieces a very clever and musical composer has created a valuable set of studies in expression and musical feeling. The earlier number are easier, lying fairly within the resources of the third grade, provided only that a proper emphasis has been put upon touch and tone-quality. The second one in particular is an excellent study in rhythm, the right hand coming in for some measures on the half beat after the left, the counterpoint being of the syncopated variety. The other numbers in the first division of the work (for it is divided into three chapters) are not so good, it seems to the reviewer. The second and third division belong to the fourth grade. Such things as these and the little books of studies published a few years ago by MacDowell are to be welcomed as pleasing signs of the times in America.

WM. D. ARMSTRONG.
Chromatic studies. (Kunkel).
Sonatina in G. (Presser).
Impromptu a la Valse. (Schirmer).
Gondellied. (Schirmer).

The book of second grade studies, first named above, is of less assured value than the other pieces on the list, but all alike show a disposition to fresh and musical thinking, and afford promise of still better things to follow. The Impromptu a la Valse is a pleasing salon piece of the 4th grade. The Gondellied slightly more difficult in every way, 5th grade. The little sonatina a timely addition to 2d grade teaching material, and fortunately for the victims, not at all dry. One would say that very good things might be expected from a composer capable of such pieces as these.

XAVER SCHARWENKA:-

Op. 67, No. 2. Im Zwielicht.

Op. 67, No. 2. Abendfrieden.

Op. 68, No. 3. Zum Andeken.

These three new publications of the John Church Company belong to the set of twelve pieces by Xaver Scharwenka, of which several have been noticed in previous issues. "In the Twilight," is rather less like its title than would be expected, the opening subject being very rapid, and based upon an unusual bass figure. The spirit is like that of an impromptu, rather energetic in character. The middle part is in B flat major (the first being minor), and lying low in the upper bass range of the piano more nearly answers to the name of the piece. 5th grade.

"Evening Repose" is a good study in a broad melody (in octaves with an inner-lying tone) and a moving accompaniment in the "first bass," as the vocal directors would call it. Pleasing when well done. 6th grade.

"A Souvenir" is a sort of romance, or song without words, with moving accompaniment interlocking in figuration. Clever, and excellent practice. 5th grade.

POLKA NAPOLITAINE. Mandoline and Guitar. Louis Tocaben. Designed for two mandolines and guitar.

PARTING, ROMANCE, for Zither Solo. Rev. John B. Bauer. Very pleasing.

"THE TEAR." Song for contralto. Gralen—Hofman. Op. 80, No. 2.

"OUT ON A COLLEGE RAH! RAH!" David Braham. Something for the votaries of learning.

"THE SWEETEST GIRL OF ALL." Waltz Song and Refrain. Richard Stahl. Another song for those who prefer the smiling vein.

"THE ORDER OF NIGHT OWLS." March Song. Words and music by Percy Grant. A galop with words. The words do not matter.

CHURCH MUSIC

RONEY'S PROCESSIONALS.

"Alleluja, Sing Today."

"Stand Up for Jesus."

"In the Light of God."

"O Little town of Bethlehem."

"In the Hour of Trial."

"Lord who at Cana's Wedding Feast."

"Tender Shepherd, Thou Has Stilled."

"The Coming of the King."

"It Came upon the Midnight Clear."

The above are a set of marching hymns, some to standard texts and some, like "In the Light of God" by Mr. Roney's distinguished brother, the dean of the literary faculty at Armour Institute. The music is admirably well adapted for practical use, and in point of contrapuntal quality not insignificant. All the above are published by Mr. Roney at popular rates, (5, 10, and 20 cents each, retail, according to length.)

HERMANN SCHOLTZ

MUSIC.

APRIL, 1896.

THE AMERICAN PEOPLE AND MUSICAL PROGRESS.

THE conviction has long been held and repeatedly advanced that the unexampled prosperity of this country is presently to be accompanied by similar and unparalleled progress in art. The conviction is based, first, upon the characteristic turn of the American mind, which is essentially idealistic and imaginative, rather than mechanically practical as superficial observers are apt to think. The evidences of this strange assertion abound upon every hand. They are plainly to be seen in the omnipresence of romances, poems and magazines and other reading matter, in railway carriages, street-cars, and even in the midst of scenery or life well-worth watching for its own sake; every one of these books, so eagerly and so absorbingly devoured, is an individual evidence of a mind active, and hungry for the ideal.

The brilliancy of American invention, surpassing that of every other nation in variety and in practical result, is testimony to their high qualities of mind, imagination and wit; the latter showing itself in unexampled cleverness, adapting means to ends. When one walks through the over crowded corridors of the Patent Office at Washington, one has before him monuments of the mental life of the people more eloquent than the monuments of Egypt, Assyria, Greece, or Rome. There is hardly one of these machines but represents a life-fashion, high, sincere and self-devoting.

Behind the inventor and his years of discouraging struggle, stood in many cases the capitalist, advancing whole fortunes for waste in experiments which might, and often did, end in nothing. In this manner such men as Gray and Edison have been helped with a liberality more than princely. These are merely examples of a far-reaching activity of mind which has planned and carried out our railway, telegraph, and telephone systems, built our cities and laid the foundations of great educational endowments. The number and elegance of our churches, the complexity of their benevolent and missionary operations, and the free-handed extravagance of our public charities, all grow out of the same seed, namely the mastery of the Ideal.

That the American people will some day cut a great figure in Art, is based, second, upon the remarkable prosperity and consequent leisure for mental growth, which this country as a rule enjoys above that of any other in the civilized world. While there may come periods of economic depression and great individual suffering, America stands at the head of all the nations of the world in the standard of expense and liberality of family life in all its social classes, as measured by comparison with the economic standard of similar classes elsewhere.

The political economist may multiply his statistics and deductions until he has filled volumes, showing that there is only so and so much wealth created in any one year, and that in this army of life we cannot all be major-generals. But so long as our national habit of thinking measures success by its financial results, and while every man can point to this one or that one of his acquaintances who started in life with no better opportunities than his own, yet who now is wealthy and distinguished, it will be impossible to quell the discontent. Supposing we grant that all cannot excel: the exasperating question still remains, Why might it not have been *he* instead of the other man.

The avenues of distinction are too few. Multiply them sufficiently and disappointments in the pursuit of great wealth will be mitigated, entirely concealed, or in many cases, as has always been and still is in Germany, more than compensated by successes in these and other channels. The distinguished athlete has in his personal eminence, as greatest in some one walk of life, compensation for failure in others. So it is with great professional men who do not happen to be in the more lucrative departments, but find in their national or international eminence a compensation for what they cannot but feel as gross inequality in material rewards, as compared with those meted out to some of their college mates who have gone into business.

The desire to excel is deeply rooted in the human heart, and is indeed the germ of that which we call progress, no less than that which we call discontent and unrest—both which are merely disappointments at failure to excel.

Music has the power to occupy the heart and to exercise it pleasantly, whereby the individual forgets these disquieting reflections upon the inequality of his economic state. Take the case of the 20,000 American Germans, collected in Milwaukee a few years ago at the Saengerfest. In these times of anarchy, violence and crankism, here we have these men turned loose in a peaceful city for a whole week, under conditions of lodging and food supply rendering a regular habit of life impossible. Good fellowship reigned. Much beer was drank, and the "wee sma' hours ayant the twa" had a liberality of companionship unprecedented in Wisconsin annals. But not a single arrest for fighting or disorder was made during the week. These were most peaceable and law-abiding citizens, carrying within themselves the power of self-occupation and contentment. Where can the Milwaukee gathering be equalled except under like conditions?

Still more recently we have had at the World's Fair a similar example upon a vastly larger scale, and with people gathered not alone from the musical classes, but from all walks of American life, together with many from foreign countries. Here again the effect of a noble mental preoccupation was seen in the entire absence of disorder or offences against the person and property of the individual.

As to the form of art in which America will excel, it must necessarily be the musical. Music is the art of the present time. If it can be said to have come already to its fullest powers of creation, it can only have been within the memory of men now living. Franz Liszt who died but yesterday, was a boy of fifteen when Beethoven's 9th Symphony was written. He had completed his concert career and returned from it before most of the great works of the Romantic school were written. In one sense certainly, and to how great extent he would be a very bold philosopher who should undertake to tell, Music is the greatest of the arts. Or, if objection be taken to the term "greatest" in this connection, the most *inner*; the art best able to represent the innermost surgings and swellings of feeling, ranging through every kind and grade, from the peaceful, the seraphic, the self-disturbed and morbid, the heroic, the tender, and all these vague states hardly definite enough to be called "longing." It was not by accident that the great productive epoch of this art, covering the first half of the present century, should have fallen *after* rather than before the general deepening of mind indicated by the appearance and reception of such deeply subjective thinkers as Hegel, Schlegel, Goethe, Schiller, and the like. The self-consciousness of the present age is deeper than that of any former one, which being the case the merely outward and imitative arts like sculpture and painting no longer afford it the satisfactory expression.

However the reader may think upon this point, there is no doubt with regard to the aptitude of the American people for appreciating and performing music. They possess three qualifications rarely conjoined: Ideality, as already noticed, a fineness and sensitiveness of nervous organization, and under favorable considerations the capacity for co-operation, that is to say, social aptitude. It is this wealth of aptitudes for musical exercise, comparatively latent until recently, which has given us the rapid development we already have a progress which has come on so quietly that very few not immediately concerned in it are aware of the strength and depth of it. In a decade we have done what it has taken a century to do in the older country. Partly, of course, we have succeeded so well because the egg had already been set on end before the eyes of some of us, but this would not have been sufficient if the conditions here had not been of such unparalleled promise. It is true that the necessary and useful, but not always competent, class of gentlemen called Critics, are continually charging that much of the fine music served up in concerts, operas, and festivals, is "over the heads of the average American." So it is. It is over the heads of the average man everywhere, over the heads of all except a very few of the most gifted, and, as I think sometimes, over the heads of all of us. Who can measure the depth, the far reaching grasp, of such geniuses as Dante, Michael Angelo, Shakespeare, and Beethoven? Just as there are summer schools where earnest souls devote weeks of study to a poem of Dante or a cartoon of Michael Angelo or a play of Shakespeare, so in time there will be schools where weeks will be devoted to a single one of Beethoven's works. But because we ourselves can neither create mountains, glaciers, stars, or a moon, or describe the process or perhaps the intent for which they *were* created, is it any reason why we may not behold them, admire them, wonder at them, love them, and perhaps be raised by them? This is all there is of it in the objection that the music is over their heads.

But this general value of music as a form of culture and a means of self-contained enjoyment, there are other reasons why the practical cultivation of it is advantageous from an educational and a social point of view. I am not now thinking of the bread and butter aspect of the question, except to remind the reader that a salary of twenty five dollars a week for playing in an orchestra is money more easily earned than the salary of the average book-keeper, and the opportunities to rise out of it into something more lucrative are fully as numerous, if watched for with prudence and soberness. But what I mean is the study of music as an art for its own sake, as a recreation, or diversion, opening a door out of the hard realities of mercantile life into a fascinating province of the ideal. The influence of music upon those who perform it in the love of it, or who even listen to it in the love of it, is great both directly and indirectly. As Hegel says of it, its design is "to fill the heart and bring to consciousness everything developed and undeveloped which human feeling can carry, experience and bring forth, in its innermost and most secret parts; whatever the human heart in its manifold possibilities and moods desires to express or excite; and especially whatever the spirit has in its idea of the most Essential and High; the glory of the Honored, the Eternal and the True." But more than this, it quickens the action of the mind in other directions so that oftener and oftener we are being told by eminent lawyers, writers and preachers that nothing so rests and prepares them for their strongest exercise of mind as hearing music. Some prefer one sort and some another, and have not discovered which sort is medicine for which, but that there is an influence here which eventually we shall understand, we have no more doubt than that untold ohms of electrical energy are running to waste which some smart inventor will yet learn how to harness into man's uses.

There are two prevailing evils in the present system of our musical efforts. First we are *buying* our music too much and not earning it enough. To a discriminating hearer there is, of course, a more perfect satisfaction of the auditory sense in hearing a concert than in giving one, tho' I have rarely seen an artist who would not rather produce the music himself. But music stands in an entirely different relation to society from that of any other of the arts. It is *per se* the social art. All its nobler forms are co-operative in a highly curious way. A picture, or a statue, for instance, or even a poem, is created once for all. When it is done there is nothing left for the amateur to do but to stand off and admire it and get out of it as much as ever he can of inspiration and uplifting. With music it is different. What the composer gives us is a written memoranda of such and such effects and tones. Whenever we would realize for our own ears the quality of those effects and take out of them the meaning that they may have been made to contain, we must re-create the work for ourselves—reproduce in sound the effects described in the score. This reproduction may require the co-operation of a great number of persons,

It is not unusual in these days for three thousand singers and players to be concerned in a single performance of a great choral work. But while this is done in one city there is nothing to hinder its being repeated in a dozen, fifty, a hundred or even a thousand others. Musical creations have unlimited capacity for reproduction, each one of which in whatever generation or place may be a perfectly authentic transcript of the composer's conceptions.

There is also social pleasure, and a kind of education, in taking practical part in the preparation of such works. No hearers get so much out of the musical festivals as the singers in the chorus. The long study leads them up to a juster appreciation of their poetry and beauty. This kind of culture cannot possibly be bought.

Music is an excellent harmonizer in the family. The singing of quartettes, or the playing of concerted music exerts a tranquilizing influence upon family differences wholly aside from the aesthetic pleasure to be had from following the pleasing melodies and clever thematic work of a composer. A boy stands a better chance of becoming a good citizen if he studies music. It keeps him at home and renders the saloon powerless to attract him. This value of music is being understood in many quarters, as I have had pleasure in observing, but it needs to be carried much farther.

The second of the chief evils to which I have referred, is that too much of the elementary teaching is in the hands of the incompetents. That the elementary lessons in playing will be given by virtuosi or those in singing by Patti's or Nilsson's I neither expect nor desire. But this at least would be possible, and in fact is absolutely necessary: that the earliest lessons should proceed from teachers who are in love with art and in sympathy with it and have the intuitions of culture. When this is the case the early training is taken out of the dull and cheerless plodding of the usual mechanic, the face of the neophyte is turned towards the glowing east, whereby his baby smiles are made to glisten in the light of heaven. It is not an orthodox start, but a true start.

This defect in our elementary instruction is more and

more in process of rectification through the better qualification of young teachers, as incidental to the greater number of music schools in all parts of the country, and to better methods in all of them. For this reason it is not thought necessary to pursue this part of the subject further. Taking all these considerations together, it is proper to affirm that the cultivation of music in a multitude of ways, and especially in forms requiring the co-operation of several or of many performers, is to be recommended, as profitable not alone for the individuals but also for the community. And for the reasons already stated there is no country in which such cultivation might be expected to reach ultimately a higher or more universal validity than here in America.

WM. L. TOMLINS.

TRISTAN AND ISOLDE.

OF the legends evolved from the first poetic impulses of the race, there are some which appear to contain in their organization an imperishable element and to possess a language for all time. Of these the story of Tristan and Isolde, which had its origin in the twelfth century, is a noteworthy example. Through seven hundred years this "High Song of Love" has lived in one shape or another. As a story of knightly adventure it is found first in the "Morte d'Arthur, or Round Table Tales" by Sir Thomas Malory. After this prose version there followed many different renderings of the legend, each century recasting it in its own manner, for the most part in poetic form, until in our own day and generation it has reached, perhaps, its best expression in the great music-drama of Richard Wagner.

This musical work opens with a short prelude for the orchestra, which is in itself an epitome of the love life of the drama. There the attractive forces of the tragedy, enshrouded in musical phrases, convey unspeakably subtle and psychological meaning. Conditions of mind rather than dramatic situations are presented, but with such intensity as to captivate and enthrall the attention of the hearer. Insidiously and whisperingly the fundamental theme steals in upon the opening bars of the prelude. Yet mark well its threadlike tones, for in this quiet flow there is the hidden strength of raging currents. This deeply concentrated, yet softly breathing melody, is used throughout the opera to symbolize the influence of the love potion, or the working of irresistible passion, and though carried through a variety of harmonic complications never loses its characteristic intensity.

There are two other themes which present themselves in the course of the prelude which are notable in subject matter; these are, the one which suggests the entrance of Tristan, heroic, masterful, and pervasive in tone, and the one which portrays the effect of his glance upon Isolde. "He looked into my eyes," she says, "and lo! resentment dies and love awakes." Like some giant force it springs into life and dominates mercilessly to the end; for "many waters cannot quench love, neither can the floods drown it; if a man would give the substance of his life for love, it would utterly be contemned."

The opening scene of the music drama of Tristan and Isolde presents an animated picture of sea life. The ship, like some large, white-winged creature, has sped over the water as though eager to reach her goal; with dancing expectation she now rides upon the shimmering waves; a sailor in the rigging lilts a lovesong to his absent Irish sweetheart:—

"Frisch weht der Wind, der Heimat zu
Mein Irische Kind wo weilest du?"

In the sunlight the waters sparkle with sheen and shine; heaven's all-embracing gleaming azure curtain enfolds the earth, and all nature smiles. But all too far from smiles are some of her children. For Isolde, she of the blue-black Irish hair and Irish eyes, veils her face from the light of day, not only to shut out from vision the dazzling sunlight radiance, but to screen herself from the horror of the picture that rises before her. For the ship has sailed too swiftly—already the Cornish coast is in sight where, upon its watch towers, the "weary King" awaits his bride. Time passes, and few are the hours in which to act. So Isolde, in the madness of her despair, calls upon the elements for help, the winds to rage and waves to rise, for storm and wreck to splinter and shiver the ship to atoms.

"Destroy this proud ship, she cried to the sea,
Swallow its shattered fragments and all that dwell upon it.
The floating breath I will give to ye, oh winds, as a reward."

Then she bursts into wild imprecations, curses the futile powers of her race, strong in the brewing of balsamic potions and powerful philters, but impotent and weak in the mastery of the elements. Like an angry tide the storm within the breast of Isolde beats and surges and, in its access, rises to a height that seems to touch even the heart of the Universal Mother. The heavens cloud and wild winds whistle as if in unison with the storm-tossed soul of the wrestling woman. With agonizing cries Isolde declares that life must end, that she cannot and will not live, but neither shall he to whom she has given her heart. Then, with hasty resolution, she dispatches a herald for Tristan, to command his immediate presence; to which demand, after some parleying with the messenger, the knight reluctantly accedes, and as he stands before Isolde, filling the entire space of the open door-way with his manly figure, he is not unlike one of the sun-gods in grace of outline and fair proportion. Respectfully he greets Isolde and queries earnestly as to her wishes, but his gracious salutation is met with such a torrent of wild words as to utterly confound his senses. As, however, the meaning of her speech gradually dawns upon his conscience, he begins to comprehend the import of the unrelenting cry that rises from her lips, and to realize that that which she demands is nothing less than blood for blood. For the sin of blood-guilt upon Tristan's shoulders in the murder of Sir Morold, she demands atonement; for not only was Sir Morold the champion of Ireland, but the warrior to whom she was betrothed, and a brave knight of gallant courtesy who would have defended her to the death. With fiery strokes she lashes Tristan with the whip of scorn until, stung to the quick by her cruel words and taunts, he hastily draws his sword and bids her drive it home. But she quickly thrusts back the blade. No; not by that portal shall death enter, rather it is decreed that together they shall drink a draught which shall bring oblivion to the house of clay in which they dwell. With an imperious nod she beckons to Brangane to prepare the cup of poison, and then in solemn silence they drink the fatal potion to its dregs. After which, in hushed and quiet expectation they await the approach of death. But, alas! alas! what is the climbing rapture which steals in through the heart and mounts to the brain with a fine intoxication? It is an inflowing instead of an ebbing tide. Life pouring in, full, rich and abundant. For they have pressed to their lips, not the quiet cordial of death, but that strong elixir which works like madness in the blood. Ah, unhappy ones! caught in the network of Fate whose strong meshes only the hand of Death can unloose. God help and save them!

As life and death crowd hard upon each other, as tragedy and comedy brush and touch, so over and above the rage of this dire conflict, the rollicking, free life of the sailor goes merrily on to an accompaniment of broad harmonies and strong uprising melodies, which have the breeziness and flavor of sea winds and the freedom of open air spaces in their buoyant movement. And, as the ship reaches her goal, the sailors break into a fine chorus of greeting, and with pomp and circumstance King Mark receives his bride.

In the opening scene of the second act, it is a soft summer night and the King's garden is ablaze with beauty. In triumphant challenge the Queen of the Flowers rears her imperial head; tall white lillies nod gently to one another in the silver moonlight as if whispering tender secrets; gentle breezes shake the treetops and waft abroad fragrant and spicey odors. In the distance the sound of horns is heard for the King and his court have gone hunting, and the palace, but for the presence of Isolde and her faithful Brangane, would be almost deserted. Outside the palace door the torch burning in the ring gives warning signal to Tristan to keep far off. With ill-concealed impatience Isolde waits for the moment of its extinguishment. But the ever watchful Brangane knows that the sound of the far distant horns betokens a return from the chase. Therefore she counsels delay, pleads for the light to be allowed to burn through the hours of the night; for she feels there is treachery abroad; she fears that the artful Melot is plotting and watching to betray the lovers to the King. But none are quite so blind as those who will not see, and Isolde alive with the bliss of living, with pulses attuned to the harmonies of Nature, heeds not the far off echoes of the hunting chorus; she hears but the soft rippling murmur of the falling water in the fountain; the gentle rustling of the leaves in the swaying treetops, and the cheerful chirruping chorus of the myriad insect voices in the balmy stillness of the summer night. And finding Brangane deaf to her entreaties, she flings prudence to the winds and runs with headlong speed to snatch the beacon light from its socket and cast it recklessly to the ground. Then, with eager, fluttering signals, she beckons to her waiting lover.

With the entrance of Tristan follows the long dialogue between the lovers, and emotion, perhaps, has never found a richer form of expression than in the musical tones of this great love poem in whose impassioned strains there is the fire and fervor, the strength and sweep of deep on-rolling rhythms, which are maintained first by the one voice, then by the other, and again by the two, in a unison which is portentous. In the white heat of the moment this dual expression reaches a unification of force which is sublime. These rich treasures of the human heart, flung out and heaped upon each other, form a pyramidal structure of song —a monument—as great as the white wonder of the world erected by that Eastern monarch to the memory of an undying love, which is

> "A passion, and a worship, and a faith
> Writ fast in alabaster, so that Earth
> Hath nothing anywhere of mortal toil
> So fine-wrought, so consummate, so supreme,
> So beyond praise, Love's loveliest monument."

But, alas! the wonderful harmony of this impassioned love song is rudely broken by the warning watch cry of Brangane which rings out upon the midnight air with the clearness of a clarion call. Like a sentinel at the gates has she stood through the long hours until the consuming anxiety within her rises to her lips and voices itself in the imperative summons of her warning cry. And almost before her tones have died upon the air, the lovers are surprised by the precipitate entrance of Kurvenal, who in the capacity of vanguard has rushed with arrow-like speed to announce the approach of the King. But his friendly errand proves well-nigh fruitless, for the treacherous Melot is upon his heels, and as the faithful shield-bearer pauses for breath, the King and his courtiers confronted the unhappy lovers. With chivalric impulse, Tristan throws his mantle over the drooping Isolde to shield her from the gaze of the gaping crowd, and then with as fine a resolution as he can command, braces himself to meet the situation. The King does not spare him, but in a long wandering speech, accuses him of having violated all the principles of knightly honor, of having slain all that was fairest and best in life, and having poisoned with viper-like breath, the very atmosphere from which he had drawn breath and substance. And as the King realizes that all the values of life are swept away by this blighting, blasting stroke, he gropes as if smitten with sudden blindness, reaches out searchingly for that which has led to this disastrous result, as totally blind to the inevitable law of cause and effect as are the majority of human beings. In the excess of his self-pity he overlooks the law of revenge, and when Tristan discovers that the King will not attack him, he courts a quarrel with the traitorous Melot, who in an access of fury turns upon Tristan with sudden rage and bestows upon him a murderous and mortal sword thrust.

In the opening scene of the last act of the music-drama there is a change of locality, for the wounded Tristan has been conveyed by his faithful shield-bearer to his ancestral home in Brittany. Stricken with a cruel sickness the gallant knight lies low upon a couch of pain, and as he writhes fever stricken and anguish-tossed, his brain wanders in the land of delirium, and his lips murmur:—

> "Come, let us leave the shadow of this wood,
> Ride down, and bathe my hot brow in the flood.
> Mild shines the cold spring in the moon's clear light
> God! tis *her* face plays in the waters bright.
> 'Fair love' she says, 'canst thou forget so soon.
> At this soft hour, under this sweet moon.'"

Ah, sweet saints! is there then no succoring spirit for this helpless one, no angel of deliverance to release him from his prison hour of agony? In the whole wide world is there not one who can bring balm for his healing and comfort for his breaking heart? Ah, yes! there is one who has all these gifts to bestow, that Irish princess who, in the foretimes proved herself an adept in the art of healing. So Isolde's aid has been invoked, and even now the swift tides of the sea are bearing her to the shores of Brittany. The followers of Tristan are upon coast guard watching for the appearance of the white sails and already they gleam in the distance. Sail swiftly, O ship, thou art running a race with time for the life blood coursing in mortal veins! Sail swiftly! Sail swiftly! As heedful as some conscious prescient creature, the ship rears herself proudly and with a sudden increase of speed, sweeps around the dangerous headland, thereby bringing into nearer range the figure of Isolde standing with outstretched arms upon the prow. As the ship strikes the shore, she speeds with flying steps to the bedside of her waiting lover, only, however, to receive in her arms his dying form as he draws his last mortal breath.

And now what of Isolde, and of that which has been as the breath of life to her, of that which is variously counted as the mortal or immortal part of the sons of men? Does the night of desolation close round and lap her in its sable folds, or is she clothed upon and enveloped in a radiance which is but a presage of that which is to come? Harken! Bend low and incline a listening ear to the notes of the song which rises from Isolde's lips; its opening strains so soft, and low, and clear, are tinged with a sad flavor of reminiscent tone. Then as the rigid bonds of mortal grief begin to slip, and memory asserts itself, a longer, fuller note resounds; a glimpse of ascension appears, as of a voice cleaving through space and mounting in aerial flights. On and on it soars with gathering and strengthening force until as though freed from limits, it bursts into pæan upon pæan of joyful, unrestricted, triumphant melody. Even more joyous it rises, recedes and rises, sinks and falls, accelerates, increases, rushes onward with greatening fullness of tone until all the regions of illimitable space seems to be filled with the story of its song. There is a little ebbing of its mighty flow only that it may gather and break forth again in a more powerful outburst, and then the voice, with a sudden leap, throws itself forward with joyous impetus as if to besiege even the gates of heaven, upon whose portals, in tremendous, o'ermastering waves, the flood of melody seems to surge and beat. Whereupon, as though this were a force sufficient to break even the seal of the Great Mystery itself, all clasping bolts and cleaving bars fall asunder to make entrance for her who, upborne upon the wings of her immortal song, passes through the arched portals of the gates of rest to the eternal harmony of the spheres.

"Life, I repeat, is energy of love
Divine or human; exercised in pain,
In strife, or tribulation; and ordained,
If so approved and sanctified, to pass,
Through shades and silent rest, to endless joy."

ANNE B. MITCHELL.

MY KEYS.

To no crag-crowning castle above the wild main,
To no bower of fair lady, or villa in Spain,
To no deep hidden vaults where the stored jewels shine,
Or the South's ruddy sunlight is prisoned in wine:
To no gardens enchanted where nightingales sing,
And the flowers of all climes breath perpetual spring:
To none of all these
They give access, my keys,
My magical ebon and ivory keys.

But to temples sublime, where music is prayer,
To the bower of a goddess supernally fair,
To the crypts, where the ages their mysteries keep,
Where the sorrows and joys of earth's greatest ones sleep:
Where the wine of emotion a life's thirst may still,
And the jewels of thought gleam to light at my will:
To more than all these
They give access, my keys,
My magical ebon and ivory keys.

To bright dreams of the past in locked cells of the mind,
To the tombs of dead joys in their beauty enshrined,
To the chambers where love's recollections are stored,
And the fanes where devotion's best homage is poured:
To the cloudland of hope, where the dull mist of tears
As the rainbow of promise illumined appears:
To all these, when I please,
They give access, my keys,
My magical ebon and ivory keys.

EDWARD BAXTER PERRY.

On train from Savannah to Atlanta, Jan. 25, 1895.

PROFESSOR HERMANN SCHOLTZ.

IT has been a matter of interest and chagrin to me to know and realize how little our new country knows and thinks of one of the greatest and most useful teachers in the old. I wish it lay in my power to teach all here to appreciate and honor him in the same degree that all who know him do. One of the greatest pleasures during my life, and by far the most interesting period of my musical studies, were the lessons (I should say better hours) I spent with Prof. Hermann Scholtz; for one hardly realized him to be the master: so ever courteous, gentle, and friendly, possessed of so great musical intelligence and feeling, yet so modest with all that it humbled one to think of one's own diminutiveness, and to realize that sometimes we considered ourselves nearly finished musicians. I feel sure all pass through this stage of learning, if unacknowledged. I remember one time very well in a fit of great discouragement when things would not go right, crying out to my teacher "I never can learn to play the piano;" whereupon she smilingly consoled me saying, "My dear, now you will really begin to make progress for you have learned the hard lesson, how little you really do know." I think she was right, but it is a hard climb.

Prof. Scholtz was born the 9th day of June, 1845, at Breslau, where he was a pupil of Brosig's. From 1865 to 1867 he studied in Leipsic, and then upon the advice of Liszt went to Munich where at the royal conservatory he received instruction from Hans von Bulow and in composition from Rheinberger. After graduating he taught for six years there, then went to Dresden where he has lived since 1875, and in 1880 received the title of Sachsischen Kammer-virtuose." (I know no adequate translation of this title. It is the highest honor and signifies aside from that, that at the parlor concerts of the court of Saxony he may play—a favor granted to few.) I do not feel capable of expressing any criticism of his work as a composer, but if one takes time to acquaint himself with them, I feel sure he will not find it to his regret, but much to his enjoyment. Aside from his orchestral Suites, I would make especial mention of his Ballade op. 60, and many enchanting lyrical pieces very sympathetically written—his Albumblätter, Romanze, Liebesgesang and Burleske Op. 71, and many more too numerous to write of here. We all know him best as the reviser of Chopin, and in that rôle he has done excellent work, and devoted much time to it, even to looking up the old instrument of Chopin's, in order to complete some of his ideas, as in a number of Chopin's works, I might mention the Scherzo in B Minor, he claims Chopin would undoubtedly have carried the second arpeggio in the middle phrase, beginning with D sharp, equally high as the first, had his instrument had sufficient range; and he was supported in this theory by finding it fell short many notes of our pianos. And surely we should all feel grateful for the many difficult fingerings which he has in great measure overcome and made easy.

In every way Prof. Scholtz is a most delightful teacher, and his music room where he always gives his lessons is enough to delight a musician's heart so full of mementos of the old masters and music of all kinds; and to crown all two grand pianos, at one of which he always sits with a copy of the pupil's lesson, thus sparing you the nervous feeling of having some one "look over your shoulders," and at times playing with you, imbuing you with his spirit and tempo.

The only time I ever saw him express any resentment or show any sign of anger, was over a considered insult to Hans von Bulow, his old master. Von Bülow had been in Bohemia and in a manner most exasperating to the Germans favored the Bohemians, translating his name into their language and calling himself by it, incensing them more and more, so finally when he was announced to give a concert on a certain night in Dresden everyone expected an outbreak. His piano chair was decorated with laurel—enemies said at his own expense—and finally at the close of the opening symphony, the doors at the rear of the stage opened and Von Bulow stood, arms crossed, defiantly there, waiting for the expected storm of hisses and whistling intermixed with applause, that came from hundreds of people. Finally after waiting a few minutes and finding there was no lull in the fiendish noise that deafened everything and everybody, he advanced through the orchestra to the piano and stood still again, but the noise only increased and it was not until several arrests were made that the concert could have a semblance of beginning but although well guarded by policemen, during some of the solo passages in a softer strain, some irrepressible, overexcited person would send forth a volley of hisses. In fact, I cannot say despite Von Bulow's great virtuosity that I enjoyed the concert very much. I spoke of this event one day to my beloved teacher and he broke forth impetuously, "Shameful, shameful! if one cannot respect the man, let them respect the music, we are not dealing with his character at a concert." Perhaps it is well we do not always have to take this into consideration, but let him rest in peace for he is no more!

I have not spoken of Herr Scholtz yet in one of his most charming qualities, that of a pianist. He plays rather seldom as his time is very fully occupied and of late has had an affection of his hand aside from an injury to one of his fingers that has debarred him from overuse of them, but he is always a most warmly welcomed and a very sympathetic performer, and so generous to all brother artists that one appreciates his greatness the more. Some day I hope he will make a tour of this country as he would much like to do, and I am sure would win many well-deserved laurels, and perhaps vie in favor with one of our great favorites here—he of the land of the Poles and the tousled hair—a great genius certainly.

Prof. Scholtz has a fine face, nothing particularly denoting the musician beyond a dreamy look in his eyes, and a noble head which his scholars all reverence.

MARY Y. MANN.

IX.

The poppies lay in the gutters, and many other fresh pretty bouquets had faded under the portrait of "the Gualtieri." May had given place to June, June to July. Gesa still every evening laid his composition plans before his foster father, played him one melody or another on his violin, or the sketch of an *ensemble* on the old spinet, let Gaston assure him "*cela sera superbe!*" improvised a great deal, dreamily heard the mysterious singing and ringing in his soul and—accomplished nothing.

He had hired an attic room of a washerwoman, but passed the whole day at Gaston Delileo's, made pleasant by Annette's pretty domesticity.

The "melancholy man" had found and accepted a regular position, probably for love of the daughter now dependant upon him. He busied himself as secretary at a theatre, and besides that as writer of *feuilletons* for a paper. That brought him a suitable income. His home did not bear the stamp of misery, but uncommon prosperity—the posperity of the Rue Ravenstein. Gesa felt at home in this place. He always found a comfortable arm chair on the arms of which he could rest his hands while he spoke of his future, and in whose cushions he could lean his head while he discovered the outlines of the splendor awaiting him between the smoke wreaths of his caporal cigarettes. He always found a flask of good Bordeaux on the table when he sat down to dinner.

He loved the long, dallying meals, which took from him the necessity of doing anything, and gave him such a plausible pretext for his favorite idleness; he loved to trifle with his coffee while Annette sat opposite him and sipped hers. He loved to turn over the music of forgotton old masters, and to rummage the works of half forgotten poets. If a verse pleased him his eyes glowed, he thundered on the most colossal adjectives, and read the verse twice, thrice, yea twenty times to little Annette. He might as well have read them to the Flemish maid outside, who did not understand one word of French; only she probably would not have smiled so prettily thereto. Then he took a piece of music paper, and set the verse to music, tried his hastily written composition on the old spinet, which tremblingly gave back the stormy measures of his overflowing youth with a fine, broken voice, like a grandmother who at the edge of the grave sings for the last time a love song. Then Annette must try to sing the verse. Annette had a glorious contralto, she exerted herself to sing very well so as to please him. He was not satisfied. "More expression Annette, more passion!" called he. "Do you feel nothing, nothing at all here?" and with his finger he tapped her heart. She smiled, blushed fiery red and turned her face away from him.

Gaston Delileo had resolved to look upon Annette and Gesa as brother and sister; that cut off all further thought and was very convenient. He did not wish to notice how much Annette busied herself for her "brother," with what flattering little services she spoiled him, with what expressions her great southern eyes hung on him at times.

He only noticed that at first Gesa's bearing was a perfectly cool, hearty, brotherly one. Towards the end of July he began to neglect the Rue Ravestein a little, and entangled himself in an affair with a Parisian actress, who was staying at the Galerie theatre, and was bored in Brussels.

Annette was consumed with jealousy without Gesa guessing the cause of her disturbed manner.

"What is the matter with Annette?" he asked anxiously while he stroked her thin cheeks with his warm caressing hand. "What makes you sad? It is this pestilent city air which is not good for you. Send her to the sea shore for a little, father!"

The old man shrugged his shoulders. "Alas I have not the means," murmured he.

"The means! the means!" said Gesa, "Please permit

me to advance them to you. I lived for so long on your kindness."

Gesa quite forgot how much his little attentions to Mlle. Irma had cost him. When he hurried across to his room to get a couple of bank notes, he found in his purse a single twenty-franc piece. First he scratched his head, then he laughed very heartily, and triumphantly brought his emptied purse over to Delileo. "Now it mocks me, me and my boasting large promises," said he, "for see, that is my whole wealth—but only wait—only wait—I have my head and my hands full of gold. If only I could be in the right mood for working. The little fever! Do you perhaps know where I have laid the libretto of my opera?"

Towards the end of August Mlle. Irma left Brussels. Gesa became irritable; this mood showed itself favorable to his industry.

One morning he felt the "little fever." He spread out his music paper before him, smoothed it with his hands, cut his pen, rested his elbows on the single tottering table of his attic room, wrote a line, crossed it out again—stretched himself; an universal bodily unrest tortured him. He resolved first to go out doors for a little, wandered in the park, remained standing from time to time as if listening to an inner voice, absently ran into the passers by, and thoughtfully sat down on a bench. Suddenly a breeze, at first light, but then loudly howling blew through the tree tops. Gesa started, seized his temples, a flood of music streamed through his soul.

He hurried to his attic room and wrote and wrote.

The hour at which he was accustomed to join Annette for lunch—Delileo seldom returned home for this meal—was past; the late dinner hour had arrived. Gesa still bent over his music paper. Several leaves lay around him on the floor. Some one knocked at his door; he did not hear. Delileo entered. "What are you doing, my boy, that we see nothing of you today? Are you ill?"

Gesa stared at him as if awakened from a wonderful dream. "No," he answered simply "I am working."

He was deathly pale, his hands trembled. Delileo

insisted that he might at least interrupt his activity for an hour in order to take some nourishment.

Gesa followed him unwillingly. He sat at the table, ate nothing, spoke not a word, and looked incessantly at the same point like a seer. After the meal, he wandered up and down in the sitting room humming disconnected melodies to himself, from time to time touched the keys of the old spinet, with closed lips hummed a single tone in which a grand finale should terminate, beat the air, directing an imaginary orchestra, suddenly stamped on the floor and cried "Bravo."

Delileo, who in his time had had much to do with poets and composers, let him quietly alone. He treated him with the consideration which falls to the share of unfortunately mentally ill persons and geniuses. Annette could not understand this strange manner at all, and at last—however thoughtful she had formerly been to Gesa—broke out in a happy laugh.

Strangely enough the violinist was very vexed at this childishness, and hastily murmuring, "good night," left the room. He worked at his opera until gray morning.

Many days passed—days during which Gesa neither ate nor slept, looked disturbed and vexed, and at the same time enjoyed an indescribable, painful happiness, a condition of heavenly exaltation. In vain did Delileo warn him: "Do not overwork yourself. One can over excite one's gift of invention, as one can over strain the voice. Be moderate!"

Gesa only shook his handsome head and half closing his eyes, smiled thoughtfully to himself. Perhaps he did not hear his foster father.

Then suddenly after, with a loud, jubilant hurrah for himself, he had completed the finale of the fifth act—the third and fourth he had not yet begun—his soul became silent. Pegasus threw him off, as an overworked, ill-treated Pegasus does, threw him from the spheres of light into earthly misery. Painful headaches and boundless melancholy tormented him, his own accomplishments suddenly seemed repulsive to him; where formerly he had seen only the beauties of his work, he now saw only its faults, compared it with works of other masters, grated his teeth, and struck his brow with his fist. He pitilessly judged his work as overstrained and ludicrously romantic. He lived upon only the coldest, dryest musical fare. A nocturne of Chopin gave him a nervous attack. He fiddled incessantly the "Chaconne" of Bach. He made the impression of one recovering from a severe illness. With untidy clothes and dragging step he crept around aimlessly, or crouched in the gloomiest corner of the green room, his head in his hand, brooding for hours.

Once, after he had imprudently tried one of his last compositions on his violin, he laid his instrument away with nervous haste, threw himself in the great leather arm chair which the Delileo family respected as Gesa's arm chair, uneasily bit his nails and suddenly broke into convulsive sobs. Then Annette stepped shyly up to him, stroked his hair compassionately and whispered: "Poor Gesa, does it pain one so to be a genius?"

Then he drew her down on his knee and kissed her often and tenderly on the hair, on the eyes, on the mouth, and when half frightened, half happy, she at first let this happen, and then somewhat embarrassed drew back from him, he at first permitted her to escape from his arms, but then took both her hands in his and looking lovingly at her, said gently: "Annette, my good little Annette, can you tolerate me? Will you be my wife? Not now, but when I have become a great artist—I will perhaps yet be one for your sake."

She blushed, and stammered, "What do you want of such a foolish little girl?"

"But if she pleases me?" he jested, touched.

She bent her little head over his hand, which she kissed and then crouched down on a stool at his feet.

When Gaston came home, he found them thus. He gave his blessing to their betrothal.

X.

Gesa's affection for his betrothed became every day more tender and hearty. Her manner to him changed in that she lost something of her shyness, and took a tone of teasing opposition. As it was no longer possible to look upon the children as brother and sister, Delileo resolved to beg Gesa to confine his intercourse with Annette to the evening hours and besides that only to a daily walk.

O those daily walks! Annette loved the gay street, and loved to stand before the displays in the shop windows while she asked her betrothed if he would buy her this or that article of luxury if he became a great artist. Her preferences were not very costly and seldom exceeded a pretty ribbon or a pair of coquettish gold buckled shoes. He laughed at her questions, and usually the next morning sent her the longed for article as a present, with a pretty, tender, expressive little note. A few lessons which he now gave permitted him these loving expenditures.

In opposition to Annette, he had a disinclination for gay streets, and prefered to ramble with her in the park, at this season empty and deserted. Dreamy and world-forgetting, he wandered near her under the trees rustling in the November wind. Here and there great puddles obstructed the path, and if no one could see he carried the girl across. Annette liked to loiter a little, and leaned ever heavier on his arm. Meanwhile, if he walked beside her quite silent and sunk in thought, she gave him a little push to rouse him. "Please wake up, tell me something!" said she. Then he looked happily down at her with moist eyes and murmured: "I love you,"—he knew nothing further. He was boundlessly in love, and tiresomely industrious. He composed diligently at this time, with more collectedness and less exaltation than formerly. The completion of his opera he had put off for the present, but had almost completed a dramatic arrangement of Dante's Inferno.

XI.

"Annette!" called Gesa one evening toward the end of November, while he plunged breathlessly into the green sitting room, "Annette! father!"

"What is it my boy?" asked Delileo.

De Sterny has written to me! He is coming to Brussels next week!"

"Ah!" said Annette, vexed and disappointed—"I really believed you had drawn the great lottery prize, or come to surprise us with an offer of an engagement at five thousand francs a month."

"But Annette!" said Gesa.

"No wonder that you are glad," said Delileo tenderly and sympathetically, and as Gesa's great tragic eyes still rested with an expression of astonished reproof on the face of his betrothed he said excusingly: "Do not be vexed at her indifference. She does not know who de Sterny is."

Gesa passed the evening in explaining to his betrothed what de Sterny had been to him ten years ago, and what his name universally signified.

XII.

She had understood; the nimbus of the virtuoso had become clear to her. Gesa no longer need fear that she would not sufficiently honor his great friend. Why should she not One met his name everywhere. The newest *bonbons*, patent leather shoes, and handkerchiefs—all were called after "de Sterny," and at that time little children played concerts and virtuoso as in the early part of the century they played consul and battle of Marengo.

Annette now took singing lessons. Another little luxury which Gesa had obtained for her, and the girls whom she met at her singing lessons spoke of nothing but De Sterny.

The uncle of one of the scholars was *capell meister* at the *Monnaie* theater. De Sterny had visited him and had forgotten one of his gloves. The above mentioned scholar brought the relic with her to the next singing class. The glove was cut in pieces and divided among all the feminine scholars of Signor Mortini. Many enthusiasts twenty years later still wore their pieces of kid sewed in linen bags next their hearts.

At that time de Sterny had reached the zenith of his fame. His last journey through Russia had resembled a triumphal procession. In Odessa they had received him with discharge of cannon, in Moscow processions had met him, jubilent students had unhitched the horses from his carriage, the most beautiful women had rained down flowers from the windows of the principal streets on his illustrious head; in St. Petersburg a princess had insisted upon entertaining him in her palace; sables, laurel wreaths, diamond rings, tons of caviare and a golden samovar had been humbly laid at his feet by Russian enthusiasm.

All this Gesa told his betrothed. But what he omitted to tell her was that the greatest ladies in Russia had sued in vain for his love, and that a Georgian princess whom he had scorned terribly, had shot herself while he was playing at his last concert at St. Petersburg. This, Annette learned from her friends in the singing school. It interested her more than all de Sterny's other triumphs.

Naturally Gesa went to meet the virtuoso at the railway station. But as, besides him, half Brussels was at the *gare du nord* to receive de Sterny, his old *protégé* had to content himself with a cordial hand shake, and an invitation to visit him next morning at the Hotel de Flandres.

When Gesa entered there at the appointed hour, he found de Sterny, his head resting on one hand, his pen in the other, seated at his writing table before some written music with many corrections. His features were sharpened. In his whole nervous, precise, mechanically polite being was betrayed that mysterious something which one acquires by incessant intercourse, with people of high rank. One perceived in him that he had accustomed himself, so to speak, to sleep with open eyes, as hares and courtiers.

"Well how are you? I am truly glad to see you," he called out to the violinist; "It makes me really young to look you in the eyes. I was very astonished to hear of your prolonged stay in Brussels. What in the devil are you doing here? I thought you had long been far away with Marinsky—the impresario."

"My engagement fell through, that is I had no inclination to bind myself," stammered Gesa, blushing slightly.

"So! hm! and meanwhile you are loitering." De Sterny treated the young violinist still in his old hearty, patronizing manner. "Sapristi! You look splendidly. Too well for a young artist—look at me—skin and bones—and what are you doing really? Projects—what?"

"Oh I am very industrious," Gesa answered him. "I give lessons."

"So! lessons—you—lessons! *Nom d'un chien!* I should think it would certainly be better and more amusing to dig gold in America with Marinsky. Lessons! And besides, so few pretty women learn to play the violin. Well, and besides that—what else are you doing?"

"I am composing. You seem also—"

"Really, really," replied De Sterny, pushing the music paper in his portfolio. "Ah, how can one compose in the life I lead! Bah! I have had enough of squandering my existence in railway carriages and concert halls! Oh! only four weeks rest—beefsteak *aux pommes*, country air, flowers and a friend." There was a knock without—the virtuoso's servant entered. "I am not at home," called De Sterny.

"It is Count S——."

"I am not at home, animal. To anyone, do you hear?"

The familiar disappeared.

"You see how it is" grumbled the virtuoso—"before a quarter of an hour has elapsed, ten people will have been announced. It is an insipid life. Always to perform the same tricks, always to be applauded!"

"Would you perhaps liked to be hissed *for a change*?" asked Gesa laughingly.

At this gay, but still perfectly innocent reply, the virtuoso changed color slightly, and looked distrustfully, first at the young violinist and then at the portfolio in which he had hidden his composition. Gesa's always expressive eyes soon convinced him that he meant no harm.

If De Sterny had a credulous young friend it was Gesa Von Zaylen.

"It is really a shame," remarked the violinist heartily, after a short pause, "that you give yourself so little time for composing. I have never heard anything of yours but transcriptions—perhaps you will confide something to me."

De Sterny frowned. "Hm!" he muttered. "I cannot show such things much. They loose by it. It destroys the impression if one shows them to every possible person."

Gesa colored up to E.'s eyes. "Every possible person," repeated he offended.

But at that De Sterny only laughed heartily. "Still so sensitive," said he. "I did not mean it so. *La langue m'a fourche mon garcon.* We already know that you are an exceptional man. *Sacrebleu!* I am the last to deny it. As soon as I have finished an important work I will show it to you. "That"—with a glance at the writing table—"that is nothing, nothing at all. The sketch of a little ballet music. Princess L.—you still remember her well—besought me—even wrote to me in Vienna about it—you understand I cannot refuse. *C'est assomant!* A countess ballet! And now be so good as to ring the bell so that they will bring us breakfast. During the meal you shall tell me what really keeps you here, for that you remain here merely to be able to compose at your leisure I do not believe."

During the meal Gesa confided his great secret to his friend. De Sterny started up. "So that is it! Now you could not have done anything more stupid," said he. "I suspected something—an unusually prolonged *liaison* from which I would have extricated you. But a betrothal! To marry, to become father of a family at your age! Yes, what are you thinking of? It is ruin, it is the grave! The grave of your capabilities, do you hear, not that of your body. That will thrive in this sober moral atmosphere. You will grow fat as an alderman, will celebrate one baptism after another; with turned up trousers and a roll of music under your arm, you will run from one street to another to give lessons, and your ambition will culminate in being first violinist in an orchestra, or if you are fortunate, in becoming capellmeister. Sapristi! You need the whip of an impressario at your back, and not the feather pillow of a calm domestic life under your head. The pillow that you fill will besides contain few feathers. But that is all the same. You only need a pretext for rest and as far as I am concerned, will sleep on a potato sack."

"You speak like a cynic, like a true love-atheist," said Gesa, who had not quite given up his passion for great words. "Who says," continued he "that I am thinking of marrying day after tomorrow. I will not receive the hand until I have won a position for myself."

"Ah, so! Well that is a consolation. Who is she then? One of your scholars, the blonde daughter of a square citizen—what?"

"She is the daughter of my fosterfather."

"Oh! The daughter of the Gualtieri! And you will marry her—marry?"

"You cannot imagine how charming she is," murmured Gesa.

"That the daughter of Gualtieri is charming, I can easily imagine," said the virtuoso, and in his eyes suddenly shone an expression of longing reverie quite unusual to them—"that one wishes to marry the daughter of Gualtieri, I cannot understand. You perhaps do not know who the Gualtieri was?

Gesa bit his lips. "I only know she made my fosterfather happy."

"So—hm! Made him happy! He was mad like all of us. To be allowed to clean her boots would have made him happy.—Hm! I know the story of Delileo's marriage. It is a legend which is still told in artist circles, only they often make mistakes in the names. I remembered the names—because Delileo interested me on your account and—and—because the Gualtieri—was my first love!"

Gesa started. "Your first love!" said he breathlessly.

The virtuoso passed his hand over his forehead and laughed bitterly. "Yes!—In the salon of d'Agoult I learned to know her. I looked like a girl, was scarcely eighteen years old and in love—but in love! She laughed at me—I wore myself out in vain longing—she never wished to know anything of me! Now after twenty years I cannot hear her name without something sultry creeping through my veins. God, she was beautiful! A face—a smile and hair! Dark hair with reddish lights on her neck and temples. As if strewn with gold dust. And with a certain grand manner—"

The virtuoso interrupted himself and looked thoughtfully

before him. The recollection of the Gualtieri was the one wounded spot in his heart. Touched, Gesa looked in the altered face of his friend.

"How could this woman resolve to marry my poor foster father?" asked he.

"How?—yes how! She had lost her voice, her lovers, her health. She was thirty eight years old. He was of good family and still preserved the remnant of a very fine property, of which he had earlier wasted the greatest part in philanthropic undertakings. He spoiled her and petted her like a princess, and she—she left him a half year after the birth of the child—your betrothed—with a Pole, I believe, a quite obscure adventurer. Delileo discovered her in the deepest misery and a condition of terrible illness, in an attic. He took her to him and cared for her till her death. Hm! poor devil!—He made the alliance against the wishes of his relatives, against the council of his friends. He had spent all his money, so he then buried himself in the Rue Ravestein. His lot is hard, and yet he at least lived a year and a half long at her side."

Alphonse De Sterny was silent and brooded to himself. Gesa laid his hand on his arm. "The remembrance of this woman still lives so powerfully in you," said he, "and do you wonder that I will marry the daughter—her daughter who inherits all the charm of the mother without her sins?"

De Sterny smiled no pleasant smile. "How old is she then—sixteen or seventeen if I reckon rightly, is it not so?" asked he.

Gesa nodded.

"So. Hm! And you will already judge of her temperament?" De Sterny drummed a little musical triumphal march on the table.

Gesa blushed. "De Sterny!" said he after a pause—"however I love you I cannot bear to hear you speak so. Do me the kindness to learn to know the little one, and then judge yourself. Come some evening—drink a cup of tea with us if you are not afraid of the Rue Ravestein.

"When you will, great child—tomorrow—day after tomorrow. You still keep early hours. I can come before

I must go into society.

A few minutes after Gesa took his leave. De Sterny accompanied him out and called to him gaily over the banisters: "So day after tomorrow about eight! I am curious to learn to know your La Rue!"

[TO BE CONTINUED]

From the German of Ossip Schubin.

Translated by E. L. Lathrop.

EDWARD BAXTER PERRY.

We sat within the twilight dim and sweet,
And listened while, from depths unseen, unknown,
Strong melodies which he had made his own
The master drew. No burning passion's heat,
But strength of purpose, life's best end to meet
Though hard the way, breathed forth in every tone:
And winsome cheer for any, sad or lone,
Whom on his journey he should chance to greet.

We call thee blind! but thou hast eyes to see
The length and breadth, the depth, the height of life:
Thou blendest with thy soul's strong majesty
That tenderness, with which true strength is rife.
O that our inner vision might, as thine,
Be keen to penetrate life's truths divine!

Catherine Rossiter Hisbee.

Wellesley College School of Music.

MUSIC IN MYSTICISM.

FROM the midst of our charming but alarming civilization, with its smoky cities and its misty atmosphere, I will carry away the reader on the wings of my Muse to that far remote spot of ages where man first refreshed himself in the fresh perfumed dew of life, inhaling the pure air of divine inspiration. It is the pre-historic primitive forest, the Biblical Eden, where the primitive man lived and loved, not deluded by illusions and vision, and confused in mind as we by a philosophical fog and a misty theology. I will transport my fellowmen to that place where Adam beheld the grandeur of a God not through a microscope, and Eve heard the voice of her creator, not through a pulpit telephone. It was in the golden age of pre-historic time, when a God was more human and man more of a god, when a God could not lie, and a man would not swear. It was at that time when sulphuric acid and phosphoric liquid were not in operation, to materialize the spirit from the unseen space to the seen place, as the great spirit of the universe manifested himself in every nook and corner of the Creation in the shape of the "Rising Sun!" Music was the first revealer to point the simple primitive man on high to that luminous light as the conception of Him, the light and life giver.

In the September and the October numbers of MUSIC I have described in a historical sketch how music was the developer, the elevator and the educator of primitive man in all advanced thought. Here I will confine myself to showing something of the relation of music to mysticism, in a brief historical outline. The primitive forest was nature's music hall wherein daily morning sacred concerts were tendered by the creatures to the Creator. Those concerts attracted the attention of the primitive man, who in his simplicity tried to imitate, began to sing his first natural tones. Ra, Ha, tones so often heard by the uncultured people as well as in our modern scientific sublime music. As his songs were attributes to the most high, the sun, hence the sun-god was called Ra. The word 'hurrah' which is used as a victory cry is very old. It was uttered by the primitive man, when night parted and old father Sol looked out from his heavenly balcony with a golden smile; then he cried out joyfully "Hu Ra" (this is Ra). As music was the first to impress man's mind with divine thoughts, for only music, the language of the soul, is capable of expressing in communication with the universal spirit where philosophy and theology fail to comprehend, hence music and mysticism were going hand in hand on the progressive road of mankind's elevation to the higher and nobler life. In MUSIC, I said: "That a primitive lawgiver need not be imbued with occult power in order to bring the people into submission; a singing bird resting in his breast was the best testimony for his divine inspiration, and as Moses was a stutterer he was afraid that the people would not listen to him." I may venture here to say that in mystic science the relation of Moses with Reuel his father-in-law will be explained in a wonderful way. Reuel means the Semitic Apollo, and his seven daughters are the seven muses. Moses took one of them to wife, her name was Ziporah, which means in Hebrew "bird of Ra," (in Hebrew and in Chaldean tongue bird and morning have the same term,—the former Ziper, the latter Zepar as I explained at length in the September MUSIC). Ziporah may represent the Lyric, one of those seven daughters of Ra or the seven muses, (seven muses corresponding to the intervals of music). King Solomon calls those muses "*Benoth Hashir*" the daughters of song. In taking Ziporah, that singing bird of Ra, before he started on his great misson, the writer of the scripture indicated that Moses was a great poet, as was necessary for one who claimed divine inspiration. In another Hebrew term, a primitive one, we will find another keynote to the Ra cult. The primitive Hebrew seer of the time of Samuel was called Roe, meaning the one who sees Ra, as distinguished from the prophet called Nabi, meaning orator. Here we that see music and mysticism understand each other perfectly, and music was the philosophy of the Hebrew Mosaic ethical cult, and only by and through music was Elisha, the famous Hebrew prophet, able to get inspiration to foretell the battle, and on its wing his spirit was able to reach that unattainable thing which we call the "future."

The Sohar (the Light), that wonderful cabbalistic commentary upon the five books of Moses, whose standard in mystic science is very highly placed, regarded music as the primary atom of the creation, like that of Light. In the same book, a cabbalist tells us that he once saw two stars, one flying from one side, the other from another direction and that their motion indicated that they were praising their Creator. How strange this cabbalistic notion may appear to be; yet it can be confirmed by modern science as its commentary. Those shooting stars, those celestial loafers, who tramp aimless in the vast space of nature, are, according to modern astronomers, planets in their primary evolutionary state, cycling between to be or not to be. Motion, vibration, is the indication of new creations, and in their shootings they denote that they are evolving from their nebular shells to solid planets. Now, what is music? Music is also a vibration and motion; it is produced when any matter or substance is in a vibrating state in a rhythmic order of motion. Here, we see clearly the mystic meaning of that cabbalistic narrator. The church claims that God has created the universe by the word, or the Logos. How much more poetical is the mystic notion; that the Almighty made his creation by the power of music. Indeed, the everlasting vibration of motion in nature, denotes that endless epic song of the Almighty, the sacred music of Creation.

The Cabbala says that there are seven heavens, each with seven palaces and seven gates corresponding to the seven qualities of man and the seven intervals of music. The Sohar remarks that each song in the Scriptures begins with the word *Oz* (then) a word of Aleph and Sain. The Aleph is in number one, while the Sain represents number seven. The songs beginning with that word are the songs of Moses on the red sea, the songs of Jehoshua, the song of David, the song of Deborah, the song of Solomon on the dedication of

the temple. That word represents number eight, which is the full octave of music, the full harmony of creation. (The Chinese say that there are eight different sounds in nature: 1, the sound of the skin; 2, the stone; 3, the metal; 4, the baked earth; 5, the silk; 6, the wood; 7, bamboo; 8, the gourd. It may be that the same notion was thought of by all the ancients). Mystic science says that only we who understand the full octave in the harmony of music, have grasped the wisdom of the Creator, and those who are singing the song in this life, they will sing it in life hereafter also. There is a place in the 7th heaven called Ken Zipor (nest of the bird); it is the place where the Messiah lives and the Shekina (divine woman,) dwells, and celestial maidens are singing before her the sacred song of life. The angels' duty is to sing, and if they fail the hour for singing they are silent sometimes for the Jubilee cycle (fifty years) and sometimes for the duration of a Sabbath year (seven years). The everlasting song of the angels consists of one single half stanza — "Blessed the Glory of God."

From the dwelling place of his Shekina (divine womanhood) the angels are divided into two general divisions, the Erelim (half gods) to sing by day and the Malachim (messengers) to sing at night. All those innumerable hosts of celestials are placed under the control of Mettatron and Sandalphon. The former is called the prince of the Face, and is graced with greatest privilege, not given even to the four archangels, the privilege to sit. From a scientific point of view the Mettatron myth can be explained on the mystic plan of nature; vibration, motion, are the indicators of life, while rest in the full sense of the work means death, or out of life's activity. Now everything which grows and moves has no rest, and every being from the little worm up to the Seraph manifests its existence in its motion and vibratory state. This manifestation is not applied to those beings who by order of the gradation in nature are nearer to the intelligent principle, as to those rest and vibration are one and the same; hence Mettatron, who is regarded in mystic science as the very nearest offspring of the divine principle, has the privilege of sitting, the signification of rest. The second prominent angel is Sandalphon, whose celestial body measures in length five hundred years walk (by foot not by railroad), and whose duty it is to turn the prayers of sincere worshipers into gems, as ornaments in the crown of his Creator. Sandolphon has also another duty, in the capacity of general song master of the heavens, and the angels sing in accordance with his directions. The Sohar tells us of the heavenly concerts as follows: The Almighty has created angels to sing in the day and Seraphim to sing at night, those to the right hand side, the others to the left hand side. The night singers are divided into three sections, corresponding to the three divisions in the night (four hours as a division), those who are the night singers, are the princes of all the musicians, and the more they sing the more they gain strength by the song to understand and to grasp the wisdom that heaven and earth cannot comprehend. Hail to him who knows that song, as by it he will understand the laws and grasp the truth of knowledge with such strength, power and force as to know what was and what will be. David and Solomon gained their knowledge only through that song, and in the psalms are hidden the events to come; and King Solomon's "Song of Songs" was really the same song of love, the mystery of life. In another version the Sohar describes the celestial sacred concert as follows: "Seven planets has God created in each heaven, and in each heaven are many suns serving the Almighty" (what a grand astronomical conception); some are set to control the works of the sons of man, and singers controlling the science of song. There is not a star, planet or host, which does not praise the Almighty; when night comes they are divided into three principal divisions to the three corners of the universe, east, west and north; and in each corner there are thousands of billions of them all controlling music, and upon each section or division a holy beast is placed, to control it, and they sing until morning. When the dawn of morning breaks those who are on the south side, all the bright stars, begin to sing glorifying the Almighty. The angel who experienced an encounter with the patriarch Jacob begged the latter for leave when the morning star shone upon the pugilistic ring, as it was now his time to return to the celestial orchestra to contribute his share to the heavenly concert. There are three palaces where mortal woman control the musical departments; in the first palace is Basje (daughter of God) the daughter of Pharaoh, who brought up Moses; in the second palace there is Sarah the daughter of Asher and grand-daughter of the patriarch Jacob; both, legends claim, were translated into immortality; in the third palace Deborah the woman poet and prophet, has charge of that musical section. When a soul is liberated from its clay prison—the body—the archangel Michael with a host of Seraphim tenders it a reception, and under the strains of a musical march they escort it into the city "Celestial Jerusalem." The resurrection according to Cabbalistic notions will be done by the power of music, when the dry bones of the dead will begin to sing (to vibrate as the sign of life) as those dry bones scattered on the plains of Dura which were resurrected by the prophet. The Sohar says, "The souls and all those in the creation are singing, and the living fools do not hear that sweet music of life." That mystic saying sounds as the saying of Hellas' sage Pythagoras, who claimed to hear the songs of the Spheres.

The Cabbala claims that musical sounds like other forces in nature are of a refined material etherial matter, since they can be seen in the varieties of their colors as the sunrays and moonbeams. No matter how strangely that statement sounds from a modern scientific view, it is a fact; for if it were not matter it could not strike, and its vibratory state is evidence enough that it is something, and in such a case it must have some color too. Even the Talmud, which looks upon mysteries with more scientific spectacles, says that when God gave the laws on Mount Sinai the people heard the sounds of the voices, and the striking force of their motion was so great that they trembled backwards three miles distance. The sound theory, if proven by scientific process, will open to us another door to the mystic chamber of the Cosmos, and many things will be revealed to us of which even an Edison never dreamed. The power of mystical music is known in the folk-lores of all the nations, from the Greek myth of Orpheus, who by the power of music started into Pluto's dominion and achieved through it victory over that gloomy ruler, to the humble fisherman in the Norse lore, who, beguiled by the song of the mermaids, lost his life in the billows of the Rhine. But in no folk-lore is the power of music so forcibly and beautifully described as in the lore of mysticism. The following narrative is a proof of the sublimity of music. When Sennacherib, the Assyrian King, with eighty thousand men besieged Jerusalem, the Scripture tells us that the Angel of the Lord went into the camp at night and smote the encamped soldiers to death. The mystic folk-lore explains how and by what ways and means they died. The Archangel Gabriel went at midnight into the camp, and opened the ears of the soldiers to listen to the song of the Seraphim, and the power of that sweet music drew out their souls from their bodies. What a sublime poetical touch is this legendary picture! Another beautiful legend in mystic folk-lore is to be found in the Talmud, which tells us that when the Egyptians were drowned at night in the Red sea the angels as usual sang their everlasting song, as suddenly the Almighty said unto them, "the works of my hands, my children, are perishing in the waves and you are singing!" What a human expression of a God! What a noble sentiment of love, which is God! It will be a hard task to prove that the Talmudical narrator believed in the Jewish God, who liked so much the killing business without the slightest regard to age, sex, and beast or man. The Cabbala says that the thunderbolt is the sound of a powerful music, and the flash of lighting its color. The children of Korah, who rebelled against Moses and sank into the depth of the ground with all their belongings, have a fortified place in hell, according to Rabbinical lore, where they sing, praising the Almighty (for what ?).

King David, whom I styled in my "Music in the Psalms" the father of Hebrew music, is the only Hebrew personage around whom legend has woven her mythical web, and music has inscribed his immortal fame with a splendid aureole of musical lore. It seems that music was the sole solution of his life, as he himself says in the Psalms: "Songs are to me Thy laws, in the house of my dwelling." King David, says the Cabbala, lives forever through the power of music. Rabbinical lore tells us that King David's sleep resembled that of a horse, which amounts to sixty minutes duration. A harp, says the Talmud, hung over his bed, and at midnight the northwind blew into its strings, invoking sweet strains to awaken the King to rise and praise his Creator with music and songs. To that magic harp, that æolian harp, King David is alluding in the Psalms (chapter 108) when he says: "Awake my glory, awake my harp, I will awaken the morning star." Once, so narrates the Talmud, King David, overpowered by the grandeur of nature in the full inspiration of music, cried out in a fit of self exaltation, "Who in the world praises the maker with such a song as I?" "Not so exalted," replied a frog from the marsh, "are lusty majesty, little creature as I am, I praise the Creator without pause and rest." That reply placed a damper upon the King's temper, and he began to meditate upon his own nothingness. How heart-touching is the Biblical picture in sketching the well-known scene, when David still a shepherd sitting at the post of that crowned lunatic, giant King Saul, playing his magic harp, and through his musical invocation driving out the evil spirit, which took possession of his body, where priests and spirit mediums failed to break the terrible spell. Here is another notion of the ancients, and a right one in demonstrating the mystical power of music. I think that the only remedy for lunacy is not to be found in Gilead's drug stores, but in the sweet strains of an harmonious song, in music! In Cincinnati I lectured at Dr. Kobb's parlor before a select audience of physicians, on the subject of "Lunacy and its Cure," where I proved on a scientific basis, that only music must be applied to a lunatic, as the disease is of a spiritual nature, whence its need to calm his irritations, which can only be effected by music. Philosophy is not a cure for toothache, and castor oil cannot be administered to the soul. King David, in elevating that divine art, became the greatest Educator of his nation, and we should not wonder that his people consider him still alive, as indeed he lives in the body of his race. The death of that crowned musician is told in a wonderful tale the like of which in beauty is not found in all the fairy tales from Hindostan to Lapland. The tale in question runs as follows.

When David grew in age, he knew that the only way to escape the terrible tribute of death, was in absorbing himself in the divine art, praising his Creator in songs without pause. The Angel of Death could not approach him, and he was on the alert for an opportunity to present his demand, but in vain. The grim messenger took to tricks, and, like an Indian magician, began to make a display of illusions before the singing king. First he showed him marching soldiers with bands of music; they passed before the king saluting, cheering, greeting in the customary military manner, but the king did not pay attention to them, his mind still wandering in the spaceless musical spheres. Then, the angel of Death tried a more powerfully impressive illusion, a revolt with all its horror. What a terrible spectacle; the people in arms against this aged king, and what a scene—the trumpet blows, the commander cries, the rebels kill, pillage, and apply the torch to that handsome mansion, where his majesty had enjoyed many a happy hour. All these illusions displayed were in vain, for David sat calmly under the shadow of a fig tree in his garden, deeply fathoming in the secrets of nature, while his lips were murmuring the sweet songs of his own compositions, which were flowing from his mouth like the soft streams of a rivulet through a green lawn in summer. At last a rough northwind broke out in a cyclonic rage, tearing down the ironroofs, felling the mighty cedars, and with a crash the fig tree fell, and turning his head to see what was going on, and diverting his mind from that spiritual joy to which that divine act was transported, the angel of death had the opportunity to fall upon his victim as a robber bird shoots upon his prey, and a moment later, the king lay a corpse. This narrative may be taken by simple minded people as one of the many fairy tales of Arabia's "Thousand and One Nights," but to the enlightened thinkers it will appear as in the reach of a possibility. What nourishes us and prolongs our lives? It is the happy thought of joy, as demonstrated by people who forget for many days to think, to eat, and to sleep, as soon as they are under the spell of a happy thought of joy, and they seem not to suffer hunger or want of sleep as under ordinary circumstances they would. Now is there a happier thought than the thought of a spiritual joy carried and inspired by the divine act of music?

Every sensible thinker, who has his own mind not the mind of his school master, has an opportunity to observe, in the cosmopolitan nature a striking marked individuality and the economic missionary distributions carried in such a harmonious variety, evidence enough for the ungraspable wisdom of divine providence. From the little butterfly to the big planet, the sun, each one has his peculiar individuality, working side-tracked on his own mission in his own way to the benefit of Universalism. On the same principle, the nations are divided and each marked, with its peculiar mission to fulfill the harmonious sound in the cosmic concert. If England's mission on earth is the pioneer work and to rule the waves, the Americans have the mission of agriculture and engineering, the Germans philosophy and morals, the Italians, music and divine arts, while the French are the yeast of the nations. On the same scale and schedule the missions among the ancient nations were distributed, in corresponding circumstances of climate, country and surroundings. The Phoenicians, were like John Bull today, a nation of traders doing pioneer work of a civilizing character. Like John Bull the Moloch worshipper, mammon was his aim in all the directions of life. The Egyptians were like the modern Yankees, an agricultural people, and in the science of engineering and architecture surpassed all the nations at large. The temper of the ancient Hebrews can be compared to that of the French, and their histories resemble each other in a most striking way. Hellas' enlightened people were with their Aristotle, Plato and Socrates, a nation of thinkers, like the Germans with their Kant, Hegel, and Leibnitz. The Chaldeans had the divinest mission, the mission of music, like the Italians of today. It is curious to note that both countries have the same geographical diagram in addition to their delightful sunny clime. Italy, is divided in upper and lower Italy, and in the country of the Chaldeans, Aram was the upper land and Caslim the lower land. The main characteristic quality of the Chaldeans is the musical mark and their elevation in that divine art, which made them the most advanced nation in centuries gone by. The Chaldeans believed in the great Jehovah, ere a Moses thought that a Supreme Being under such a name could reveal Himself in a burning bush. They presented Abraham, charging him with heathen doctrine on account of his belief in a dual God by the name of *Elohim*, so that he was obliged to flee to Canaan where the Elohistic cult was the state religion. Proof of the above statement is the narrative of the Bible, which tells us that Nimrod, the first king of the Chaldeans, was a mighty hunter before Jehovah. The Chaldeans did not search for the Creator in the lower creation like the Egyptians, to find Him as a crocodile in the muddy yellow Nile. They looked on high, above, to that firmament upon which the Great Epic of Creation is written in luminous letters—the stars.

The Tower of Babel was not built by the Chaldeans for the purpose of fighting God as the Bible tells us, or to be a tombstone to a rotten mouldering king. The tower was built by the progressive Chaldeans to emancipate themselves from capricious nature, to live a scientific life free and independent.

NAPHTALI HERZ IMBER.

CHOPIN'S LAST CONCERT.

[The original of the article upon Chopin which appeared in the January number of Music called out the following lines upon the same inexhaustible subject by the distinguished French littérateur and composer, Oscar Comettant.]

THE last occasion upon which Chopin was heard publicly in Paris, as recalled by Madam Berton, was on the 16th of February 1848, eight days before the downfall of King Louis Philippe, and the proclamation of the second French Republic.

I remember it well for I was there. Although a novice at that time in the profession of journalism, I wrote a report of this memorable soirée for the *Siècle*; and it was not without that sweet and feverish emotion which follows in the strain of a circumstance suggesting an event delightful, but remote, that I recently discovered among the autographs preserved by the house of Pleyel, a printed ticket, thrown there by chance, no doubt, of which I give the reproduction:

Soirée de M. Chopin
Dans l'un des salons de M. M. Pleyel
20 Rue Rochechouart.
Le mercredi 16 février, 1848, à 8 heures ½,
Rang Prix: 20 francs Place réservée

This concert ticket did not resemble other concert tickets any more than Chopin resembled other pianists. The letters, in English scrip, were engraved from copper plate upon squares of fine, glazed cardboard, which were very elegant and distinguished in style.

Jules Janin had announced in a manner which seems strange to us at this date, but which was peculiar to him, this concert of the illustrious pianist-composer in the *Journal des Débats*, February the 14th. I quote:

"One word in conclusion. M. Chopin is to give his concert next Tuesday. It is not, however, a farewell, a departure, a halt in the campaign,—far from it; M. Chopin will remain in Paris, and enjoy his relaxation at the scene of his triumphs."

But mark the inaccuracies of those five lines. It was,

in very truth, his farewell concert to the Parisians—this soirée; it was not announced for Tuesday but for Wednesday; and furthermore, shortly after this concert Chopin undertook a voyage to England and Scotland from which he returned to Paris only to die on the seventeenth of October, 1848.

I was present at the last public appearance of Chopin in Paris and I witnessed his obsequies in the Church of the Madeleine on October the thirtieth, and gave an account of the sad and imposing ceremonies.

All his life Chopin had had an almost devout admiration for the genius of Mozart. They rendered the requiem of the sovereign master at the funeral of the sovereign pianist, and Meyerbeer conducted the performance.

The solos were sung by Mesdames Viardot and Castellan, and by Lablache and Alexis Dupons. Lefebvre Urly presided at the great organ.

As I write these lines I can hear again the muffled strains of the celebrated *Marche Funèbre*, tender, full of tears, overflowing with affection and regret.

A low sound like a murmur swept through the church as the coffin appeared and each one rose reverently to pay homage to the dead artist, the incomparable poet of the piano. This sound, which was caused by the simultaneous movement of the figures kneeling in prayer and rising together spontaneously, by the rustling of garments and the displacing of chairs—this tribute of respect at the sight of the coffin I can hear yet, as I can hear the first inexorable chords of the *Marche*.

The cortege passed along the boulevard; the ropes of the funeral car were held by Franchomme, Eugene Delacroix, Meyerbeer and Prince Czartorsyki.

I have read in fetes that when Chopin gave his last concert in Paris, he was so enfeebled and bowed by illness that he could with difficulty walk. I saw nothing of the sort. Each time that he came upon the stage to take his place at the piano he walked erect with no signs of feebleness. His face was pale, it is true, but without appearing greatly altered, and he played that evening as he always played,

While listening to him in meditative admiration I recalled vaguely what Moscheles had written a short time before, concerning the music and the playing of Chopin.

"The *ad libitum* playing which under other interpreters becomes simply a want of rhythm, is with him an element of the most delightful originality. The harshness of certain modulations to which I can never grow accustomed when I play them myself, ceases to shock me when rendered by his poetic fingers, gliding so delicately over the ivory. He manages his *pianos* in such a way that it becomes unnecessary to employ any violent *fortes* to produce the desired contrast. He is unique in the world of pianoforte players."

And now does any one ask why Chopin was so especially fond of the Pleyel piano? A variety of reasons have been given; Liszt fancied he had hit upon the principle one. The passage in which he makes mention of it is rather curious.

"Chopin was particularly fond of the pianos of Pleyel because of their silvery sonority, slightly muffled, and because of their light action which allowed him to elicit tones that we might think pertained to one of those harmonicas of which romantic Germany has preserved the monopoly, and which its ancient masters constructed so ingeniously by the union of crystal and water." Chopin played marvellously that evening upon one of those piano harmonicas, with his magic fingers, with his poetic soul; and I have no need to say that he was recalled, amid resounding applause and acclamations of enthusiasm. Franchomme participated in this great success, the last that they were destined ever to achieve together.

I have heard it said that, having expended all his energy, moral and physical, at this performance, he suffered a reaction then and there and that he fainted away in the artist's foyer. At that time it was known that his malady was deep seated and incurable, and that the days of the great artist were numbered. His voyage to England only rendered them brief and painful.

In a letter which Chopin wrote from Scotland, he says: "I am very weak; I no longer compose, not from lack of will, but from lack of strength."

After Chopin, George Sand. I find among my autographs a letter from the immortal writer whose heart and soul were for a time one with the heart and soul of Chopin; and I do not hesitate to make it public here for it has certainly escaped the notice of those who have recently collected and published the letters of George Sand.

"I received yesterday, my dear sir, the piano resuscitated and more delightful, I think, than it was before. I know not how to thank you for this care and skill which enables me to hear once more the pleasant voice of a dear old friend. But although Madame Viardot has written me of your generous intention, ought I to accept these repairs as a gratuity? Not that the obligation is repugnant to me, but consider the labors of your artistic workman! I fear to seem rash, and I beg you will set my conscience at ease by telling me what I should do in respect to them.

Accept, my dear sir, the assurance of my affectionate and distinguished regards.

Nohant, 29th inst. GEORGE SAND."

Having written these two names, Chopin and George Sand, I cannot resist the temptation to revert to them for a moment.

In the notable rupture between these two, who seemed united forever, on which side was the fault? Liszt has written thus:

"Madame Sand, whose energetic personality and brilliant genius excited the delicate nature of Chopin to an admiration that consumed it, as a too spirituous wine shatters the fragile case in which it is contained."

What appears to be certain is that weariness and disenchantment fell on both and this was fatal. The admiration for their reciprocal talents which had drawn them together, could not suffice to hold them long united; and Madame Audly spoke truly when she said: "To love one another in sickness as in health, to sustain one another, to forgive one another,—neither the attractions of beauty nor genius afford sufficient motive; there is needed the stern sense of duty, and the blessing of heaven to purify the impulses of the heart and to communicate their own incorruptibility. These neither Chopin nor George Sand possessed; nor could they ever hope to attain them."

The last drop of bitterness which caused the overflow of his cup of sorrow long ago filled—since that sad and curious voyage to Majorca—was the romance that George Sand wrote under the title of "Lucrezia Floriani."

In this romance we see a certain Prince Karal, by nature sickly, and of a haughty, nervous temperament, restless and jealous, who conceived a passionate attachment for Lucrezia an artist of renown, already in middle life. They love each other but Lucrezia dies a martyr to the ferociously tender character of Prince Karal.

Whether, as George Sand says in the story of her life, there had been between herself and Chopin misunderstandings which neither knew how to adjust, or whether without taking council of anyone but himself he seized upon a pretext for breaking a chain which had grown too heavy to bear, it is a fact that Chopin recognized or thought he recognized himself in Prince Karal; and the gulf of separation yawned forever more. George Sand protested against any such intention as her disillusioned friend attributed to her. "Certain enemies—I had some, who were near to him, and called themselves friends, as though the torture they inflicted upon a suffering heart were not in very deed murder—certain enemies made him believe that this romance was a revelation of his character. Without doubt, at that moment his memory was impaired, he had forgotten the book. Would that he had not re-read it!"

There was a last interview of which different accounts have been given.

"I saw him once more for a moment in 1848. I pressed his hand, so cold and trembling. I wanted to speak with him but he——It was my turn to say that he no longer loved me. I spared him that pang and I entrusted all to the hands of Providence and to the future. I never saw him again." So ended the memorable friendship.

Translated from the French by

FRANCES A. VAN SANTFORD

VARIATIONS ON THE MOST BEAUTIFUL PHRASE IN "LA TRAVIATA."

(PATTI, singing and thinking:) "A fine house this evening. How lovely "La Traviata" is, but when one has sung it a thousand times one begins to be bored. It even wears on your nerves. No matter how superb the air, when one has repeated it for fifteen years it becomes monotonous. No one has any idea how fatiguing it is, but it must be played. Though why should it be played? no one listens; it is lost time. All the women come to be looked at; the men to look at them. We are only an excuse. There are perhaps five or six simpletons in the house who have an idea of hearing me in my best role, but they are old stupids whom no one pays any attention to. Oh, see, the Marquise in the corner box; she is always pretty; she is even striking in broad day-light. A few steps away one would take her for eighteen. When I first made my debut at the Italiens in 1865, she was already in her prime. She has an artist to make her up for the day. If I only knew where she got her, because a successful makeup for the day needs to be entirely different from the night. One must seek an entirely different effect. They say that to remain eternally young one must not abuse water. Nina l'Anelos washed only with cold cream. How pretty those new plaited gowns are. It is strange there are some women that everything becomes. See, there is Madam X., and with her husband, too. What, has she gone back to conjugal felicity? That is something I'll never do."

(In the wings, Nicolini, humming the air, as he waits for the curtain to rise.) "How lucky; one act less. It is maddening to sing before such a public. Now see, the gas is turned down; hardly a gleam in the hall. It is so mean to lower the gas at the Italiens. It is stingy and small. Of course, I know if they did not turn it down it would cost more; it is economy, wise economy. I think my voice is improving and people come as much to hear me as Adelina, that is providing they come for us at all. The foot-lights are beginning to smoke; I know the signs. I wonder if the audience will notice. Bah! As if this cake-eating people ever notice anything. They come to exhibit themselves. Here are the two best singers in the world before them, and they think of everything but them."

(In a front box a very pretty blonde woman, young and unsophisticated.) "What a lovely phrase; how sweet, tender and expressive. One can see that they feel what they sing—so deeply. She really has a beautiful voice, but the voice is in my opinion but a secondary matter. The acting; the soul; the intelligence is more than all. How unfortunate not to know Italian. The words suit the music so well. Love is great—love like that in "La Traviata," of which one dies. Not that it is really necessary to die. Is such a story possible? Oh, I would love and be loved so. They say such love never exists in marriage; but then is it necessary? As for me, I am determined to know what it is or at least to die. But how dreadful to think; it seems to me every one must know what is passing through my mind. That tenor is not really fascinating; but he is not bad either; only not my style. My ideal is some one immense, with heavenly blue eyes, curly chestnut hair, and a lovely blonde moustache, so blonde it is nearly white. Unfortunately I did not meet my ideal until after. It is always so they say. When we know the man we love, we don't love at all. So my husband; well my husband. I loved him a great deal at first, when he embraced me furtively, in secret. I find that delicious; but that of course, does not last. Is it my fault that I am mistaken? Patti also was mistaken. Who is not mistaken at least once?"

(In the front seat, a practical woman.) "They must make an awful lot of money in these plays; to make all that with one's voice. Oh! if I had a talent like that I would make the most of it and myself too. Why has Patti never gone about by herself? She has always had a manager; at first Strakosch, then the other and now this one. What is the use of it? With so much talent one ought to be sufficient to one's self. I know she is still young, but, *basta!* it is not her they love; it is her voice. She could not be sure of any attachment if she could not sing at all. How foolish these operas are. This gentleman to whom she gives a flower and who replies that his life is bound to hers—at least that is what I suppose he responds, if one can believe this translation. One never sees anything like this in real life; such high strung, ridiculous sentiments. There is a woman who could have lived a charming tranquil life, even to an extreme old age, if she had not fallen in love. With whom, and why? Suddenly she sells her jewels, her horses, then the father comes and sings to encourage her the most tiresome air I ever heard. Then she insults the beloved object at the ball. Afterward she excuses herself, but it is too late. Inevitable result of love, of love as depicted by the poets, painters and musicians."

(A gentleman in a box with two ladies.) "When will they finish this act? What a bore these Italians are. That closing phrase irritates me, and it is not the end, either; it returns all the time. Only to think, that I might be now stretched out in an easy chair enjoying a little gossip; these wretched Italians destroy my whole existence. And Blanche! She will be furious. I have not seen her for more than eight days; not since I was caught in the races. This evening I fear I shall not find her, or may disturb her. Hold! there she is in the second row. I hope she will not motion to me. She has a good deal of tact generally. If my mother-in-law should suspect I had an affair. Misery. I would rather tell my wife everything than have my mother-in-law even suspect. (Nicolini's voice is heard in the wing taking up the same phrase.) Again; again; positively, that devil of an air drives me mad. I would rather hear the trumpets in "Aida," for at least then we have the ballet, but here there is not the slightest recreation. There are lots of pretty women here, but why will they lower the gas between the acts? The subscribers should offer to contribute to keep the gas burning. Then we poor men would have a little reward."

(The gentleman's wife listening attentively.) "The music is admirable; it intoxicates, enthralls one; I can understand one's enthusiasm, even more, for a tenor; when Nicolini repeats from the wing that phrase I adore, a thrill runs over me, clear down my back. It is strange, it is the same sort of a thrill that runs through me when I see that officer who rides so well. You feel as though a little cold snake ran across your shoulders and down your back. It is horrible but fascinating. That officer's moustaches were remarkable, so long, so silken, and soft as one's hair. They blew out in the breeze when he rode; I never saw such moustaches. Oh, there is the Russian I met at Nice, who looked at me always before he played. It would be very easy to fall in love with an actor, especially if he were handsome. How true it is that music elevates the soul; it does more, it makes me better. When I listen to that air so tender, so pure, I feel as if I were so myself. I would I might share the feeling with some one who could understand it." (The same box: mother of the lady, keeping time to the music with her head.) "How soothing that air is. If I don't take care I shall go to sleep. I mustn't do that. I must watch my son-in-law and daughter, especially the latter. If he wishes to go astray, why that is a thing one can repair, but with her when it will be, it will be. I looked at her during the races and it seemed to me that she was more interested in one of the cavaliers than was exactly proper, and one she did not know. She ought to at least have known him, but no, I would rather she were interested in one she did not know. She listens to Nicolini too attentively, her nerves are tense, the least thing makes her tremble; it is very unhealthy. That Nicolini! He is not like the singers of my youth. I used to be in love with Mario. O, but I was smitten. Happily, M. de Lamartine came just in time to make a diversion. I loved Lamartine madly, all the women of my age did, but they were wrong. He was not the man we thought him. I would like to know the opinion of a woman like Patti about singers. What makes my son-in-law so fidgety. He is sleepy. Positively the boy does not hear the music, and his wife hears it too well."

(In an orchestra seat, a bald gentleman, humming the air.) "It is sublime. Tu, tu, tu; Oh, it is ideal. And it is the only opera that is not silly. The Lady of the Camellias. What a work; They should see Bartet in the role, at the Francais, in place of these machines who are playing it. I have not seen it since I saw Pierson. What year was that? O, how thin she was. She is beginning to get fat. Tu, tu, tu, I think X. better begin to watch his wife. She makes eyes at everybody. Well he was foolish to marry a woman of twenty; the imbecile. He is fifty, and poorly preserved. Tu, tu, tu, tu. Nothing is more ridiculous than such a marriage, for the husband. Lord! what a situation! A young wife should have a young husband. That phrase is admirable, admirable. (He continues to hum and look at the people who attract his attention, gradually changing the air to La sire de Framboisy, to the profound amazement of his neighbors.)

(What Verdi thought when he wrote the phrase.) "This shall be a song tender and passionate, expressing the pain of not being loved, and the fear of abandoning oneself to that love. They shall feel at once regret and desire; they shall hear the cry of the woman who sees before her an unknown future, and all the interest of the action of the whole opera shall center in this single motive."

From the French of Gyp.

Translated by FRANCES WHEELOCK TELLER.

JOHANNES BRAHMS.

THERE is a very old saying that "the kingdom of heaven cometh not with observation." Something of this kind occurs to one who happens to remember how Johannes Brahms made his first appearance in the world of music. It was the violinist Remenyi who discovered him. Sometime in 1851 Remenyi appeared at Weimar, bringing to Liszt a young man about eighteen years old, whom he introduced as a coming genius. He was a meagre youth in physique, and not well furnished as to his outer man; but for credentials he had his first trio in B flat, which Liszt proceeded to play and to admire. That fascinating master, then about forty-two years of age, was of all great musicians the one the best and most pleasing for a young aspirant to encounter. Especially if his work gave promise of absolute novelty, or of rare power in any direction. Liszt by the unerring light of genius discerned the divine spark, and just where ordinary criticism breaks down (namely, in the really new, and therefore the unascertained and the uncatalogued) Liszt came out strongest. The young man's trio made an impression. Then happened the one unfortunate incident of the interview—and nobody can tell whether it happened for better or for worse. It was a very hot day, and now late in the afternoon. Remenyi and Brahms had travelled all night, and in the comfortless German third class carriages. They had eaten little.

Liszt was pleased with the trio, and by way of return favor he offered to play to Brahms his new sonata for pianoforte, then just written, and played as a great favor to the most advanced and appreciative only. So the young Brahms seated himself to listen. It was a long sonata and like all of Liszt's works not well joined together in its development. Brahms found himself dreadfully sleepy. He made manful efforts to keep awake, squirmed in his chair, and for a moment seemed to succeed; but fate was too much for him. Nature asserted itself and he dozed off completely. Just then at a particularly tender passage Liszt glanced around to see how his young friend was taking it—and made the discovery. He said nothing, completed the sonata, got up and closed the piano. And Remenyi whispered aside to Brahms: "You might as well pack your things and go; you have done it." So they went.

But the unfortunate incident did not hinder Liszt watching the future career of Brahms with interest; the coterie at Weimar immediately began to play the works of Brahms, and to talk about him as the coming genius. This, it will be remembered was before Schumann had emerged from the obscurity of contemporaneous composers. Schumann also reviewed a work of Brahms in the *Neu Zeitschrift* in 1853, and when Dr. Mason came back to America he brought with him some of the compositions of Brahms, and it was with the Brahms trio that he opened his famous series of chamber concerts in New York, in 1857, Theodore Thomas being first violin. Brahms was a fixed feature of almost every successive year during the twelve that this remarkable series of concerts lasted.

Brahms came of a musical stock. His father was contrabassist at Hamburgh, and it was from him that the boy received his first instruction. When he was about twenty, he was appointed director at Detmold, and there he remained until 1862, when he removed to Vienna, in which city he has lived most of the time since.

It has been very unfortunate for the reputation of Johannes Brahms, that some one told a reporter that his music was hard to understand. This unproductive bit of information, which probably first saw the light somewhere along in the fifties, has gone thundering down the ages ever since whenever anything of Brahms has appeared upon a concert program. I credit the reporter with one item of progress. He has discovered that the "Hungarian Dances," as instrumented by Brahms, are not hard to understand. Why it should not also have occurred to him that the master hand capable of instrumenting a pleasing and piquant score like that of the Hungarian Dances should not happen upon more of the same sort when engaged in putting his own newest and best ideas into instrumental dress, is one of those mysteries which a non-journalist cannot understand. But the record is "news" none the less.

Brahms' music is hard to understand. All new music is hard to understand, in just the proportion that it is new. If Beethoven's fifth symphony were to be brought forward today as a new composition, credited to some young composer, it is altogether likely that it would seem stale—simply from the fact of its progressions having been so much used by the smaller composers since. But when a new composer comes forward with music which shows insight and advance—*new* ideas, new effects, depth and seriousness, this is always hard to realize at first. And for ordinary musicians and critics none the less than for the laity. Indeed harder for them than for the laity. For when a work has real novelty in it, it always shows moments of the blest and intelligible (as Carlyle said of the talk of Coleridge) and the layman, not being preoccupied with his theories, notices these passages and enjoys them. It may be Greek to him between times, but when he strikes a pleasing moment he is not above recognizing it. But the musician having commenced his musical life with a course of miss-nancy sonatinas, and progressed slowly through interminable successions of Haydn and Mozart, with a multitude of thing by Dussek and the other philistines on the side, finds one after another of his most precious prejudices violated and overthrown by the new comer. He is disturbed, distracted, disgusted. Even the moment of sweetness and light, which he might enjoy, is gone before he has ceased to fear that it will too soon give place to some other soul-racking novelty. Just as there are college presidents who in moments of confidence will admit that they do not enjoy Browning, so there are hosts of practical musicians of no small reputation who do not enjoy Brahms. They did not enjoy Schumann when he was new. They did not regard the young Beethoven with his heroic symphony as likely ever to reach the clearness of form of Haydn or the delicious sweetness of Mozart. And it did not occur to them that the new man might have had something to offer better than either.

Brahms is generally credited with having upheld the traditions of classical form—whatever this may mean. He has steadily protested against the modern tendency towards the high strung and the over sonorous—and this quite as vigorously at the very moment when his own latest score has offered numerous examples of elaboration as trying to the unaccustomed as any of the over sonorities of Wagner and Tschaikowski. He has drawn a line; but it has been at a very advanced point, and in a different place. All the same, Brahms is distinctly the child of the later part of the nineteenth century.

Johannes Brahms is unquestionably the greatest master of musical composition since Beethoven; and greater than he. Schumann, himself both musician and a poet, is a child beside Brahms in mastery of the art of developing a musical idea. Whether we take it in harmony, rhythm, form, or in orchestral elaboration, Brahms is a master of first rank—he *is* the first rank, and their are few in the ranks immediately below him. This already showed in his earliest published works. His first trio is vigorous, original, and highly elaborate. It is also poetic—but it took time to find this out.

Brahms and Wagner have something in common. Both had an intense confidence in the ideal. What they felt and what they heard in their musical fantasy, they believed that the world would sometime be glad to hear with them. Wagner judged his generation more accurately than Brahms judged his. But Wagner had an advantage. He worked in the external and showy field of the drama. Building upon myths which appealed to the German heart, he was able to live until the nation had adopted his works as part of that rich and manysided product of the ninetecth century German mind. He not only acquired a place, he acquired *the* place, and everybody else holds position somewhat by sufferance. What Wagner had done in novel musical ways, for illustrating extraordinary emotional states, the action made immediately intelligible, and after a few years of the usual discussion (in which Wagner himself took part with no uncertain hand or fictitious modesty) the new methods commended themselves, and younger composers avail themselves of these rare sonorities for lighter and less significant occasions. But Brahms had no such advantage. He has from the first addressed himself to the realm of pure music. The ideal in tones; the highest, most lofty, the purest, and most poetic. This is the direction of Brahms' thought and aspiration. He does not seek to make an external impression. When one listens to the best symphonies of Beethoven, one thinks of the music and goes with the master, instead of reasoning of instrumentation, and voice *carrying*.

Is it musical?

Is it significant?

Does it carry you with it?

These are the questions, and Brahms has waited until almost the close of a long and active life, in order to receive a valid answer.

In the nature of the case questions of this kind cannot be answered off hand. Even the chamber works had to wait long for frequent performances. They were too difficult for the players, not less than for the hearers and critics. An organization for giving chamber concerts is mortgaged heavily in the direction of the pleasing, for musical influence ceases the moment you get out of touch with your audience. The problem is to get your own way, yet to seem to give them theirs. This is an art and a science.

Theodore Thomas, for example, is past master in both departments.

The orchestral compositions had a very slow rate of progress. With the one exception of the Hungarian Dances, nothing of Brahms' orchestral writing can be said to have begun to be popular (even in the limited sense in which the term applies to serious art-works of this rank) until very recently. Mr. Thomas played a Brahms symphony in Chicago as long ago as 1874 — and the critics came up with the punishment to fit the crime; it was "difficult to understand," "unclear in form," "deeply subjective" — and the whole stock of verbal counters with which the critic opens the Jack-pots of art, and makes or loses as the gods will. Nevertheless Brahms is getting advertised. No matter how difficult a man may write, the very difficulty of his work will excite the ambition of some virtuoso to master his work, and so he gets a hearing. Unfortunately the hearings are very far apart, and the intelligibility which comes from hearing a thing over often enough to understand it thoroughly, only happens when it has become to some degree unnecessary.

The popular apprehension of the inner attitude of a great genius is all wrong. The public thinks of him as a sort of musical clock in solitary meditation, trying with all his might to strike thirteen every time. Well, why not? There are clocks in Italy which strike all the way up to twenty-four. But this is not on account of self-communing ambition, but on account of original excellence of construction. It strains a clock no more to strike twenty-four than to strike ten—provided only that the machine had been originally constructed with reference to the higher potencies. So it is with great poets and great composers. Browning saw something within the situation, within the scene, which his verse brings out, and it is this inner something which makes him at times difficult to understand; and so it is with Brahms. It is the course which his musical thought takes of its own volition, the natural novelties of crystallization in his musical ideas, which makes his music novel to us, and by so much difficult to understand.

Speaking of the attitude of Brahms, I do not know that I have been more surprised than at reading the account of the Strauss Jubilee. Johann Strauss, the waltz king, author of "Prince Mathusalem," "The Poor Jonathan." "The Merry War," and thousands of charming strains which have gladdened all the world, had a jubilee, and all Vienna came to do him honor. This was the jubilee of the very antipodes to Johannes Brahms, and one would have said *a priori* that Brahms would be conspicuous by his absence. But no. It was Brahms that made the speech of congratulation and presented the laurel wreath; for he honestly owned to loving a Strauss waltz as well as the least of his musical or lay brethren. And on his part Johann Strauss is also a friend and a prodigious admirer of the great Brahms, whom he rightly holds for the foremost living composer.

Theodore Thomas says that it is one of the inevitable signs of dilletantism in music to seek to make comparisons. That every artist has his own place and standing, which is not to be compared with that of any other to the detriment of either.

And this may be so for those who happen to be furnished with a sort of high-art thermometer, recording so-and-so many degrees of absolute honor; but when one lacks this scientific guide, this foretoken of immortality, what is he to do but to ask Is it warmer? Or colder? Is it wetter? Or dryer? When there is no absolute at hand, why should we not do our little best with comparison?

And so if it is not proper for us to compare Brahms with any of the great composers who came to maturity and public acceptance a little before him, we may at least ask whether we ought to think of Brahms as a successor of Beethoven, and the creator of works which are likely to live. As an orchestral composer and a writer of tone-poetry of the highest class, I should say that Brahms is one of the greatest that has yet appeared. He is far more master of musical construction, easier in the ramifications of style, and more fluent, than Schumann, if in orchestration not fully up to the latest advances of Wagner.

Deliberately restraining his scores considerably within the instrumental limits of Wagner, he nevertheless uses material in manners which are quite as modern and advanced. He writes his chords full and organ like, handles his strings, wood-wind and brass like contrasting choirs, with only occasional touches of complete ensemble, and knows better than almost any one else what kind of ideas best suit a particular instrument.

One of the most striking illustrations of this is in the beautiful and immensely difficult pianoforte concerto, which Mr. Joseffy lately played with Mr. Thomas and the Chicago orchestra. In every part of the symphony one could see that the idea had first been chosen in a form adapted to the peculiar genius of the pianoforte. Then it had been sufficiently transformed for the instruments. Sometimes it had not been changed, and the instruments followed the piano. This is something which Beethoven never attained. In his concertos there is very little which peculiarly suits the pianoforte. In many other concertos there is nothing which exactly suits the orchestra, as for example in the Chopin concerto in E minor. Schumann, again, in his A minor concerto, writes gloriously for the pianoforte, in the principal subject; but as the work goes on we discover that the orchestra hampers the pianoforte writing, and at the same time the orchestral writing is equally hampered by the pianoforte. This you see the minute you compare the concerto with the great Phantasie in C, or the Etudes Symphoniques. Everything in the concerto sounds distinctly pianoforte-like, yet rarely with the pianoforte at it its best. Brahms on the contrary, while producing in this work an orchestral tone-poem such as might well pass for a symphony (in which position it would be one of the greatest) also writes most charmingly for the pianoforte. While the piano part is full of difficulties, it is nevertheless pianoforte writing, and the peculiar qualities of the instrument are every where taken into account.

It is the same with the violin concerto, which was played with the Chicago orchestra by Mr. Marteau. Here, of course, there is no inherent contradiction of spirit, as exists between the pianoforte and the orchestra. The violin is indeed the head of the orchestral cohort, and all that the concerto does is to bring it out into even more than its usual prominence. But with what grace and beauty is this accomplished! And with what consummate skill are sonorous colorings placed as back-grounds where they will serve only to enrich the effect of the solo part and intensify the charm!

Consider again that colossal task, the double concerto for violin, 'cello and orchestra. This we had in smaller force, the solo artists although gifted with technic lacking that distinction of style and the commanding elements which are necessary to render solo tasks of this caliber intelligible.

But it was delightfully conceived, and one had in the single work an entire concert, so rich was it in orchestral effect, delicate poetry of the solo instruments, and most wise and well-considered in the ensemble.

There are two adventitious aids which the reputation of Brahms might now receive, and the regret is that the order in which they are here mentioned is probably inevitable: First to die, then to be played oftener. Were he to die, the newspapers of all civilized lands would mourn his loss as that of the greatest of living tone-masters—an honor they rarely or never will give him while living, and then but momentarily. To die is the poet's only sufficient advertisement. Alas that it should be so! Were William Shakespeare now living and bringing out of one of his scrap-books tragedies or comedies once a year, the press would treat him with little honor, and probably would pillory him for improper devotion to the scrap-book ideal, in spite of such master inspirations as "To be or not to be," or "The quality of mercy is not strained." The second adventitious aid to the recognition of Brahms is the real one; it is to have his works played oftener. The world has moved. Our ears have become advanced. We retain and compare musical impressions over a wider range of relationship than was the case a generation ago. Handel is antiquated; Bach still lives, but we can enjoy his works only as exceptions to our current diet; Haydn symphonies sound like string quartettes played a trifle large and seasoned with a few notes of trumpets and wood-wind. Mozart in feminine phrase is "too sweet for any use;" and Mendelssohn has departed to the place where good boys go. We have left to us the over-worked immortal nine of Beethoven (now rather shrunk to about five,) and two of Schubert; we tolerate Schumann for the sake of his ideas. We hear Tschaikowski because he is a master in his way. But the greatest of tone poets now living, and the greatest since Beethoven, appears to be Brahms. What is now wanted is plenty of playing and plenty of hearing and sifting. Truth will prevail.

Assertions of this kind are somewhat uncertain and risky.

In every generation there are always poets who write just well enough to leave the average comprehension in a position of doubt. This has been well expressed in the case of Brahms by the musical editor who was requested by a correspondent to give an article upon Brahms. To which the editor, more modest than the generality, and perhaps reprehensibly so, replied that so far as his acquaintance went musicians seemed mostly to be divided into two classes with respect to Brahms: The one thought Brahms too good for them; the other thought him not good enough. It was evident that both alike failed to comprehend the great master, and so the editor waited for a later coming light.

This position is not yet deserted. Nevertheless it is evident upon the face of it that a new composer able at once to gain the attention, and retain it, of all the most advanced artists in the world, is likely later to gain the attention of the ordinary hearers. For we are all of us creatures of our environment; the genius belongs to his generation like all the rest of us. He is simply a puppy who gets his eyes open at the seventh or eighth day instead of coming in squarely with the rest of the litter upon the ninth.

Meanwhile the great composer has not been without honor. Ever since his German Requiem, in 1868, he has occupied a peculiarly honorable standing. He was made doctor of philosophy by the university of Cambridge in England in 1877, and in 1881 the university at Jena repeated the honor. In 1886 he was made Knight of the Order of Merit by the king of Prussia. These tokens count for something, inasmuch as the character of Brahms utterly precludes the idea of his having directly or indirectly sought after them.

It is not the purpose in this article to write exhaustively upon Brahms. There are several provinces of his work which require an article each. Such are his songs, his chamber works, and his compositions for pianoforte. In the latter province it may be noticed that while in point of technic more advanced than any other writer, his works as yet have not begun to be played, except at rare intervals and by the most pronounced virtuosi. Rosenthal played here the variations upon a theme of Handel—a work which in musical handling as far surpasses the technic of Schumann's Etudes Symphoniques as it falls short of that work in genial and manysided freshness of imagination. Yet as musical handling it is masterly to the highest degree. Schumann was like the preacher who forsook his text in order to stick more closely to his congregation; Brahms sticks to his text. The congregation goes out and takes a rest. Enough appears however to show the most careless observer that a master is in question. A writer able to create such works as the symphonies, concertos, and chamber works of Johannes Brahms, must indeed have said something important in his compositions for pianoforte, an instrument of which he is master in the highest sense. But this part of the question we will attack later.

W. S. B. M.

LOHENGRIN.

Strain, strain thine eyes, this parting is for aye!
    Grief have her will of thee! Thy faith confessed
    To his unequal, he must go, the quest
Fulfilled that brought him hither on thy day
Of imminent, direst peril. Now away,
    To other shores bids him the Grail's behest.
    Thou knewest him too late to spare thy breast
This keen remorse, thy soul this dark dismay.

Yet canst thou face not all disconsolate
    The coming years. The horn remains, the sword,
The ring he left thee, and the child whom late
Thou mournedst; while beyond the power of fate
    To dim the memory of that love outpoured
    Upon thee by thy stainless knight and lord.

WILLIAM MORTON PAYNE.

IS PERFECT INTONATION PRACTICABLE?

II.

THE continuation of early personal experiences illustrative of the subject in hand, can wait till a more convenient season. This number is devoted to the Septal element of intonation, which, although the most subordinate, is one of the four constituent elements of the rationale of tune, and is little understood—when not entirely ignored—in nearly all musical philosophies. The scale of the accordeon,* which was truly defined in the former number, shows that the Septal element of tune is not at all new to music. These instruments, as well as mouth harmonicas, which have the same *dichordal* scale, are very musical instruments in a certain way, notwithstanding the objections against them for the general purposes of music. If they should be tuned in the equal temperament of the piano or organ, or, worse yet, in the "true scale" of three perfect major triads, they would not sell. Nobody would want them; they would be pronounced "out of tune," and truly would be. When new and little used, the accordeon—with one set of reeds only, that is, not accompanied by a second set tuned a shade above or below, for a "*vox celeste*" effect—is an instrument of "perfect intonation." That is, the two harmonics which compose its scale, and which it really uses as such, as tonic and dominant—and dominant and tonic forever!—are perfect, the one being the major triad, vibrating as 4:5:6, the other the harmonious pentad, or Major Ninth chord, 4:5:6:7:9. (The lowest tone of this, however, which is here the root, cannot be given by the same motion of the bellows as gives the four other tones of the chord, except from the bass accompaniment, whose reeds are at the opposite end of

*Note. In trying to describe my first impressions on first hearing an accordeon, in the March number, the types made me say a funnier thing than I intended. Interested readers will therefore kindly mark on the margin of page [illegible], [illegible] line triumphs instead of trumpets. And while about it, mark (3:4) instead of (8:5) near bottom of page [illegible].

the bellows. That root tone is in its scale however, for it is the Fifth contained in the tonic triad—opposite motion.

It must have been very generally noticed that the intonation of this instrument, and of its miniature mouth instrument, is peculiar and quite different from that of other instruments of fixed tones. The difference between its scale and others, both tempered and untempered, is indeed much greater than is supposed; and those who care to read this paper are referred to the former one, in which the differences are truly defined. The want of variety and the oddity of the intonation might sometimes suggest that some change in the instrument is desirable. That, however, could not improve its musical quality, but would greatly lessen it unless other tones were *added* to its scale; and the simple working principle of the instrument hardly admits of that, although it is sometimes done to a very limited extent. The simple accordeon, however, is one of the lucky hits in mechanical invention; and the fact that its tuners, where it is made, tune it in that particular way—without necessarily recognizing the Septal element of tune (4:7) or knowing just why they tune it so, only that it *sounds* right thus—is one, but only one, of the abundant proofs of the general recognition, in musical ears, of this element of music.

This popular instrument is incapable of producing a discord, unless the dissonance of a certain Second in one place (9:10) be called thus. And yet it can scarcely render any entire piece of music correctly. Although its two harmonies are the most indispensable two in music, the constant want of the subdominant triad major (of whose three tones it possesses but one, the first of the scale), not to mention the minor triad in its various relations, also diminished and augmented chords, suspensions and dissonances of all kinds—and modulation itself, makes frequent unkind cuts necessary, even in very simple music. "A charm from the skies," in the favorite of favorites, cannot be truly rendered, therefore, on the usual simple instrument; yet on those having a second scale, a scale of G and one of C, for example, the tonic chord of the latter would of course be the required

the bellows. That root tone is in its scale however, for it is the Fifth contained in the tonic triad—opposite motion.

It must have been very generally noticed that the intonation of this instrument, and of its miniature mouth instrument, is peculiar and quite different from that of other instruments of fixed tones. The difference between its scale and others, both tempered and untempered, is indeed much greater than is supposed; and those who care to read this paper are referred to the former one, in which the differences are truly defined. The want of variety and the oddity of the intonation might sometimes suggest that some change in the instrument is desirable. That, [illegible] over, could not improve its musical quality, [illegible] greatly lessen it unless other tones were *added* [illegible] and the simple working principle of the [illegible] admits of that, although it is sometimes [illegible] limited extent. The simple accordeon, however, [illegible] the lucky hits in mechanical invention; and the [illegible] tuners, where it is made, tune it in that [illegible] way—without necessarily recognizing the [illegible] (4:7) or knowing just why they tune it [illegible] that it *sounds* right thus—is one, but only one, of the [illegible] proofs of the general recognition, [illegible] of this element of music.

This popular instrument is incapable [illegible] a discord, unless the dissonance of a certain [illegible] place (9:10) be called thus. And yet it can [illegible] render any entire piece of music correctly. [illegible] two harmonies are the most indispensable [illegible], the constant want of the subdominant triad [illegible] of whose three tones it possesses but one, the first of the scale [illegible] not to mention the minor triad in its various relations, also diminished and augmented chords, suspensions and [illegible] of all kinds—and modulation itself, makes frequent [illegible] cuts necessary, even in very simple music. "A charm from the skies," in the favorite of favorites, cannot be truly rendered, therefore, on the usual simple instrument; yet on those [illegible] ing a second [illegible] a scale of G and one of C, for example, the ton[illegible] latter would of course be the required subdominant, and thus "Sweet Home," as well as other music which is misused by the accordeon, can be played truly.

The tones re, fa, and la, as given on the accordeon, are vibrationally 6:7:9. This is *not* a minor triad, nor anything very near it, although its fifth is just the same as in the minor and the major, the ratio 6:9 being simply 2:3. But the *division* of the Fifth is here more than two-thirds as different from that into a minor triad as that is different from the division of a Fifth into a major triad, so to speak. If we add 25 nils to this Minim Third, 6:7, it becomes the Minor Third, 5:6; and if we add 36 nils (the smallest chromatic semitone) to this, it becomes the Major Third, 4:5. Moreover, and consequently, if we add 25 nils to this last, it becomes the Maxim Third, 7:9. The usual diatonic semitone, which is correctly defined as the difference between a Fourth, 3:4, and a Major Third, 4:5, the result being, 15:16, is 57 nils; and the equal and artificial semitone, or unce (a twelth part of an Octave), is 51 nils. These facts afford a conception.

This triad, 6:7:9, is of course tuned in our uncial scale the same as the minor triad, and the 25 nils of difference between the middle tones of the two triads are divided rather unequally, in order to form the uncial minor triad (whose Thirds, as in the uncial major triad, are three-twelths and four-twelths of an Octave.) This Septal triad very generously and disinterestedly submits to a rise of 17 nils in its middle tone, and the corresponding tone of the minor triad comes down 8 nils, the two triads being thus identified. As for the Fifth, it remains almost exactly the same, it being allowed, however, one nil flat in the uncial scale, although this is almost imperceptible.*

Of triads, the most harmonious is the major, 4:5:6. Were it not for the *reversion* of triads (which can be done in music to a very limited extent), the next most harmonious triad would be 5:6:7—called "diminished." But although this is a very smooth sounding chord, even more

*(Note.—It must not be supposed that tuners of pianos and organs necessarily recognize all these facts in tuning the uncial scale. The Septimal elements can be left out of count entirely, in this tempered tuning; but it is very useful for tuners to know the true nature of the Quintal element [illegible] the Major Third.)

so than the minor triad, we must accord the latter the second harmonious place on the list. The vibration ratio and nature of the minor triad I will take up later. The fourth triad in point of harmony is the 6:7:9. All these, excepting the minor triad, are in the accordeon scale, and in its five-toned harmony, 4:5:6:7:9. The least harmonious of regular and perfect triads, however, is one still more rough than 6:7:9; it is the reversion of the 5:6:7—the same change as takes place in making the major triad into a minor. This reversion of the small trial, however, I will speak of in connection with the Diminished Seventh chord (probably in the next number.) The real rationale of this curious and rough but very effective passing harmony, the Diminished Seventh, is Septal, like the true Dominant Seventh and the Augmented Sixth harmonies.

If it be asked why the triad 6:7:9 should not also be reversed, in music, like the 4:5:6: and the 5:6:7, the answer is, that a triad becomes less harmonious by reversion, and I have found but two which are sufficiently harmonious to begin with to bear the change and still remain musical, even as dissonances. By reversion a chord becomes one which is more complicated vibrationally; hence the loss of harmony to a certain extent. The major chord is so *very* harmonious, belonging as it does to an order of harmony (Quincal) superior to the Septal, can survive the reversion of the order of its Thirds quite well, and becomes *sadder*, if in no respect *wiser*, in the more complicated form of 10:12:15; its Fifth and individual Thirds, however, still pure and simple as ever. But while the little Septal triad, 5:6:7, can make a similar change and still remain musical for a limited use (as a dissonance), I do not find any musical virtue in the reversion of the more complicated but still musical triad, 6:7:9; for it is a little more complicated to begin with than the 5:6:7, and much more than the major, which not only belongs to a more harmonious element than the Septal but is also in smaller ratio numbers. There is another reason why the ear will not accept such a reversion. It would suggest the major triad horribly out of tune, its first Third being 25 nils sharp for a Major Third, while the correct but rather inharmonious uncial Major Third is only 7 nils sharp.

The 6:7:9 triad, however, though not very harmonious as a mere triad, is delightfully so as a continuation of the major, completing the pentad 4:5:6:7:9; and the four kinds of more or less harmonious Thirds measure in nils as follows: 197, 161, 136, and 222; while the four are represented in our uncial scale respectively by those of 204, 153, 153 and 204 nils—apparently two Major and two Minor Thirds. Those who doubt or deny these statements might just as well kick against the pricks. They are among the true matters of this world's knowledge.

Because a set of reeds or pipes is correctly tuned in equal temperament by a very slight and almost imperceptible flattening of every Fifth (one nil), many suppose, therefore, that the variations from real harmony which our uncial scale involves are only some trifling thing like that! But our uncial or equal semitone scale is nearly Pythagorean, and must necessarily be, so far as concerns both the Quincal and Septal elements. The "tempering" of each of the twelve Fifths (alternating by downward Fourths) by one nil, merely uses up the Pythagorean Comma (twelve nils), so as to reach exactly the same tone or its octave as was started with. Both the Quincal and the Septal elements of tune, from which all Thirds arise, are "not in it" at all, or if they are, their rights cannot be respected. It is thought that temperament is a compromise between Fifths and Thirds. Rather poor definition. The true Major Third (4:5) is the representative of the Quincal element. The different elements—four in all—cannot tune into each other perfectly, although they blend together in one and the same harmony. Four perfect Fifths up from C, for example, octaves being eliminated, happen to make something approximating to E, it being 11 nils higher. Flattening each Fifth one nil (an amount fixed upon *not* to accommodate the E but to reach the C again precisely in the whole cycle of twelve) does indeed benefit the E, taking off four nils of its discord, and thus leaving but seven, or seven-elevenths of the comma, 80:81. And so with all the other uncial Major Thirds, which are thus made one third part of an Octave.

But this very slight flattening of the Fifth has a contrary effect upon the Septal element. It thus substitutes a worse thing for the 4:7 interval than real Pythagorean intonation would give; for a true double Fourth—a Pythagorean interval—is only 14 nils larger than the representative Septal, 4:7, while sharpening each Fourth by a nil, as in the uncial scale, increases the difference to sixteen nils, or almost one-third part of an equal semitone (unce).

The almost imperceptible flattening of each Fifth, or sharpening of each Fourth by the same amount, is for just one purpose and no more—to reach the *twelfth* move and arrive squarely on the same pitch as started with; and as for the approximate Quineals and Septals which are passed on the way, the one class are left a little better and the other a little worse, without however, any benevolent designs on either.

Now seven is the largest prime number entering into musical ratios, the next larger being eleven, and this is certainly *not* a musical prime. The simple chord made by vibrations as 5:7, as well as its derivatives the Minim and Maxim Thirds, the little Fifth, 5:7, the Septal semitones 20:21 and 14:15, and the inversions of all these, belong to pure and untempered musical harmony and melody, and have been substantially in use from time immemorial; although little indeed can be learned about them by reading, and that little does not usually interest any one in their favor. The *sense* of the diatonic semitone mi-fa is more often Septal than Quineal—20:21 instead of 15:16; although the latter is *always* the *final* step of the major scale. The simplest *melody*, saying nothing of harmony, could hardly exist truly, neither could its whole rationale be consistently found, without reference to the Septal element; and though Quineal intervals, or even Trial intervals (Pythagorean), can be substituted for the Septals, and still make coarsely approximate intonation, young children, in part singing, will often intone all four of the Thirds much more naturally than the uncial scale gives them. The simple vibration relation of each tone to the root of the duad, triad, tetrad or pentad, is what really shapes or senses the intonation of each tone, and thus we vocally guage the "whole tones" and "semitones." Even a fair hit can be vocally made at the two enharmonic Commas, in part singing, by being allowed to follow nature, that is, singing each successive chord in tune. Those two Commas are 14 and 11 nils (63:64 and 80:81). In practice they can be regarded as identical, and are indeed made so in the 53 system of Octave division, which also identifies many other mathematical distinctions, though with no such amount of sacrifice of harmony as is done in the uncial or 12-division. In fact this practical (practical for certain cases) system of 53 equal intervals per Octave — or tempered Commas is about what is generally supposed to be the approximation of the 12-system to true harmony. This latter is often spoken of as practically true and harmonious (though it is far from it); but the 53-system is.

The twelve system, however, has a great and peculiar and redeeming virtue, of a really musical nature; and I shall find the right place to tell about it eventually. I have not the least quarrel with it.

[TO BE CONTINUED.]

JAMES PAUL WHITE.

———

WHERE IT IS SUMMER IN FEBRUARY.

WHEN we left the twinkling lights of Chicago behind, and plunged off into the darkness and snow towards Monon and Louisville, Nashville and Montgomery it was hard to believe that far ahead of the engine's nose there was neither snow nor north wind, for into the luxurious comfort of our sleeper would every now and then dart in a keen reminder like a stinging little needle of cold, that there was winter outside. Louisville did not seem particularly southern for on its icy streets without warning, and with great emphasis I suddenly sat down. All the beautiful panoramas of mountains that delight the traveler along the L. and N. route were white with snow, and even on the limits of the whilom capital of the Confederacy, I saw patches of snow. But as the day wore on somewhere in the piney woods we struck a different atmosphere, an air in which was no suspicion of chill. Picturesque Mobile smelling of salt-water, and swarming with banana pedlers put winter out of sight, and when we had shot over the miles of bog and bayou between Bay St. Louis and the Crescent city I found myself in a bedroom fifteen feet high, and about thirty feet square, and warmed by a pint basin of coals, and felt as if I had been juggled over four months of the year into June.

We hung up our fur capes in the armoir, the New Orleans wardrobe is always an armoir, and the next morning set out with a vivacious lady from Natchez to "pirouette up and down the banquettes" of the French quarter! There was an odd sensation of remoteness in the very names of the streets, Royal—Chartres—Dauphine—and the quaint architecture, was the antipodes, say of the auditorium. Here a facade was beautiful, with balconies and galleries of ornamental stone work. Some stone cornices were ornamented in ribbon patterns or garlands and suggested that once upon a time their owners had been men of elegant tastes, if now they were given over to bottle men, second hand furniture or ill smelling bird stores. In convenient corners old aunties their heads in neat tignons with wonderfully quilled wings on each side, a bunch of wool in front of each ear in which swung golden hoops, sold pralines and other mysterious sweets. Everywhere fluttered the colors of his majesty, Rex of the Carnival. Through dark passages one had glimpses of red paved courts, and walls washed with yellow ochre, and from them and the steamy earth came faint odors, which made the blooming appearance of the native when young, and his hearty old age amazing. The haunted house which Cable has immortalized was a palace in its day. Over its wide windows, and along its cornice are cut garlands and ribbons and its doorway is superbly carved and colored. On one side is spring on the other autumn. But a saloon smelling of sour beer occupied most of the lower floor, and the rest is a bakery in which we found a redundant and maternal creole, the owner. "All full up stairs of families," she explained with a shrug. "Ghosts! Ah—no. I lief here 18 mont; no see nussing. Nussing in dose story I tell you."

The unusual cold and snow Feb. 11th had burned the violets in the cathedral garden, and turned the stately palms and magnolias brown, and as I lingered within looking at the altar piece St Louis very stiff of leg about to set out on his crusade, I overheard a confidence that two candles had been offered to our Lady of Lourdes that the cold should not quite destroy a cherished lemon tree. Our Lady by the way has a crown said to be of real diamonds, and below her ripples over rock work water said to have come from Lourdes, a superfluity considering the water privileges of New Orleans in the eyes of a doubting Protestant. The Carnival began in earnest Monday morning when his majesty Rex came up the harbor and rode on a wonderful contraption called a float to the city hall to receive the keys of the city. Military companies from home and abroad accompanied him and the small boy was in an ecstacy of enjoyment. King Proteus came with a pageant of 18 floats Monday evening, illustrating the story of Asgard. Probably even in Chicago Scandinavian mythology is not generally well known, and New Orleans received the show with tepid admiration. A young person from Texas stood not far from me during the passing of this spectacle, and her observations were pointed and distinctly audible. "Gee! Asgard and the gods. Who in suds was Asgard! Seems like they might a chose something queerer. But it is puffickly splendid. It sho' is if you can't make nothin' of it" Possibly because evil spirits quite lose their terrors when pictured in form, the procession did not look "puffickly splendid," to your correspondent. Rex's procession Tuesday morning more successfully appealed to the popular heart. After his uneasy rosy-wreathed throne trooped nineteen fairy tales drawn from the pages of Fergus Hume's Chronicles of Fairy-land, and only a cantankerous spirit would deny that they bore the sunlight remarkably well. Nothing could be better than the Wise Owl in his hollow tree, and the Rabbits in the Enchanted Garden. But *the* procession of the Carnival was the Comus procession Monday night. Miss Wilde a local artist, designed it in every detail, and it was what seems impossible, Seventeen Songs of Long Ago. A monster lyre formed King Comus' throne, and behind and about him rayed out two bars of music, a web of twinkling bronze lines. Acanthus leaves formed the pedestal, and before the monarch attendants (inaudibly) played pipes, cymbals and the harp. The second float was "The Songs of Long Ago." A huge mandolin leaned against three half rolled sheets of music. The pendent ends of a bow of golden ribbon encircled the car, and on it was written the title. Two laurel wreaths rested against the mandolin. The great god Pan embowered in reeds, on either side of him fishes and lotus blossoms was on the third float, the "Origin of Song," and after him came the first song which in honor of the occasion, and in deference to the humid climate, and equally humid tastes of the locality was—"Landlord, fill the flowing Bowl." The songs which followed were "The Mistletoe Bough," "Comin' through the Rye," "Listen to the Mocking Bird," "Hunting We will go," "The Indian's Death Song," "Wearin' of the Green," "Spider and the Fly," "Stars of the Summer

Night," "The Last Rose of Summer," "The Shells of the Ocean," "The Merry Month of May," "Gaily the Troubadour," "Dixie," "I'd be a Butterfly," "A Song of Other Days," and "Home Sweet Home."

After my northern eyes had lost a little of the frosty, critical feeling with which a low temperature has caused them to witness anything in the nature of "doings" I found the spectacle charming and every detail carefully worked out. The mocking bird was as big as a condor, and the mistletoe berries as big as cantaloups, but the coloring was beautiful, and only mean spirited folks forever find fault. The big green spider had immeshed three or four victims in her sparkling webs with great cleverness, and save in their green color the clothes of the attendants on the "Wearing of the Green" were exactly like those of the Irishman of the story books; and the angels wings in "Home Sweet Home" were well hung, and if not exactly feathery, were flossy looking. I found myself applauding with the rest, and when the band playing Dixie and the float of that name halted before the Chess and Checkers Club gallery where I was a guest, I rose with the rest of the ladies, though there are traditions against Dixie in my family. Two plantation negroes on cotton bales were at the front of the float, magnolias and orange trees and the dwarf palmetto ornamented it, and around it hung oranges as big as pie pumpkins, a trifle big to be sure, but handsome.

The opening tableau at the Comus ball at the French Opera house was like a water color panorama. But to those present who had not seen Dixie the Sambo and Dinah of the cotton bales were objectionable. "Niggers!" said someone behind me, "I call that bad taste. Anything but niggers!" In New Orleans, as elsewhere, it is impossible to please everybody, but when all the fault has been found that can be—the Comus procession of '93 will remain to all who saw it a charming recollection.

The music in the Jesuit Church is beautiful and well mingled with heavy odors of aloes and myrrh. In the tiny Greek church far down the Esplanade is an American melodeon with a fine American squawk of its own, and a picturesque old pastor, remarkably like the Archbishop of Zante, who visited us during the World's Fair Congress of Religions. New Orleans is a fascinating and many sided city, and the best wish I can make for any overwrought literary worker is—he may travel as I did through the garden spot of Eastern Indiana, and the historic ways of Kentucky, Tennessee, Alabama and Mississippi to this strange home made among the sedges and the reeds, which nature had evidently set apart to polywogs and crocodiles.

New Orleans, Feb. 28, 1895. ELIZABETH CUMINGS.

REGINALD DE KOVEN ON "FALSTAFF."

Had any composer of any country or of any age written "Falstaff" as it stands today, one would have admired and been astonished at his technique, his verastility, his originality and unfailing freshness and variety of musical thought; but when we consider that it was written by a man past 80, "Falstaff" strikes the intelligent auditor as little less than miraculous. "Falstaff" stamps Verdi, long acknowleged as the greatest and most popular melodist of his day and age as the greatest living master of his art.

The first adverse criticism that is usually made in regard to "Falstaff" is that it lacks definite melody or tune. This is to a certain extent true if one allows that melody and tune are synonymous, but there are many different types and kinds of melody, and of melody of the highest type, that which is used to express the more subtle emotions and feelings, there is certainly no lack in "Falstaff." It may well be that had Verdi been a younger man "Falstaff" would have been more melodious in the sense that the term is usually applied, and yet one could never believe from hearing this music that there was any lack of youthful spirit or vigor in the brain that conceived and the hand and mind that executed it.

The music of "Falstaff" is essentially and in every respect modern to a degree, and may be said to have carried on not a little the development of musical art and science, and added to the fund of musical knowledge which we possess today. It has been said that in starting out to write "Falstaff" Verdi had "Die Meistersinger" prominently in mind, and meant to write an Italian replica of that immortal work. If this be so he can hardly have been thought to have succeeded, for where "Die Meistersinger" is indisputably grand opera, "Falstaff" is nothing more or less than what Verdi has called it, namely "a lyric comedy" or comedy set to music. In "Die Meistersinger" Wagner has struck the chords of a far greater variety of human emotions than Verdi has attempted to do as in "Falstaff" the comic note is struck from the first and kept up to the close, the only variation of this, and one which seems almost out of place in the opera, being Ford's strenuous and dramatic soliloquy in the second act, which strikes one as neither from an æsthetic standpoint, in keeping with the general character of the music nor with the general tone and trend of the work.

Upon the answer to the question whether music is or can be in and of itself humorous, i.e., capable of exciting independently our risible faculties, "Falstaff," as a work of art, must stand or fall. It may well be that the general point of view is too subtle, the detail too fine, the insinuation too delicate, for the music to appeal to the average opera-goer, but that the music in and of itself is humorous, even were the text not there to explain and point its meaning, can hardly be denied. Nothing more really comic musically has ever been written, than the clarinet and bassoon with pizzicati bass which accompany Falstaff's answering "No" to his own questions in the great "Honor" soliloquy, or the mock stateliness and sarcastic pomp of Dame Quickly's "Reverenza," and the whole of her scene with Falstaff at the beginning of the second act.

Instances of this sort might be multiplied throughout the opera. Is not the mock penitence of the two servants when they return to their master as full of humor in the music as in the action, and is not Falstaff's "Va Vecchio John" as comically ponderous and rotund as the fat old knight himself? One must in fact be familiar with every word of the book which the composer has so aptly and succinctly illustrated to be in absolute touch and sympathy with the music, which moves in constant accord with the spirit and meaning of the word and situation to a remarkable extent.

It has been said, and the point has undoubtedly well taken, that the opera as such lacks contrast; there is too much bustle, hustle and scurry, and too little repose; while the turmoil and excitement is so insistent and persistent that one often has hardly the breathing space or opportunity to judge of what is going on musically. The loves of Anne and Fenton, which are touched upon in the lightest possible way, might perhaps have been enlarged upon with good artistic results, or, and perhaps better still, the composer might have at least suggested the pathetic side, which undoubtedly to the Anglo-Saxon mind, exists in regard to the "greasy-knight." At any rate, those who are familiar with his death as detailed by Shakespeare, might appreciate this want in the composer's musical characterization and wish that he had thought best to, at any rate, suggest the reverse of the picture.

It is possible because only the humorous side of Falstaff has been touched upon that the opera was not a success in England. In Germany, again, it has not been received with the same favor as in France and Italy, owing to the fact that Nicolai's treatment of the same subject has a hold upon the people which it is difficult to dislodge; but we of this country knowing little of Nicolai, and not having the same reverential affection, perhaps, for Shakespeare as our brethren in England, can look upon "Falstaff" for what it is, an avowed musical farce, meant not to excite deep thought, but to amuse, and wonder at the skill and ingenuity with which the spirit of the comedy has been brought out in the musical setting.

REGINALD DE KOVEN.

THE PRACTICAL TEACHER.

ELEMENTARY RULES OF EXPRESSION IN PIANO-PLAYING.*

1. RHYTHM is the foundation of musical intelligibility. Hence the measure accents are always to be observed unless the composer has rendered it impossible by means of ties and syncopations in both hands at once. In the latter case the composer has probably set up a new measure temporarily, without changing his bars and figures.

2. The bar indicates the place of the strong pulse. Hence the place following the bar invariably takes the strong accent.

3. The secondary accents fall in their proper places. Moreover when pulses are subdivided the half-beat places are stronger than the quarter beats, exactly as in the larger groupings of measure. (It is not necessary to try to compute these degrees of relative force. If the time be counted, and the half-beats in some way indicated, the accentuation will generally adjust itself.)

4. A syncopated tone beginning upon the off beat and holding over across the measure accent anticipates the measure accent. It therefore has *all* of the measure accent and a little something more, expressive of its passionate breaking into the measure rhythm.

5. Meanwhile the true measure accent is generally given by the other hand at the proper time. A syncopation is a clash of accents, and unless the true accent is given by one hand while the other observes the syncopation, there will be no adequate clash.

6. As a rule, any tone beginning upon a half beat and holding across the beat receives an accent. There are exceptions to this however, as in accompaniments chords are sometimes repeated upon the half beat and held across the beats, when only a pulsation is intended and not a syncopated effect. (The left hand chords in Schumann's "Warum" are a case in point.)

7. All melody tones are supposed to be delivered legato unless the contrary is expressed or implied.

8. A tone which concludes an idea and is followed by a rest, if its indicated duration is not more than one pulse, almost invariably takes an elastic touch.

9. Short figures of two, three, or four tones (very seldom four) repeated in forming a larger design, should be defined to the ear. (See Nos. 3, 9, etc.)

10. Ascending passages are almost invariably crescendo.

*

11. Descending passages are generally diminuendo.

12. Dissonant tones falling upon the beat are invariably accented beyond the importance of the rhythmic place they occupy.

13. Resolution tones into which accented dissonances resolve are played less intensely than the dissonances they resolve.

14. By Melody quality is meant the appealing quality in a tone which makes it sound as if someone were addressing you through it. This is the natural quality for melody, and must always be attained. (It is made by earnest touch and pressure.)

15. Accompaniment quality of tone is less intense, and more passive. Whenever the accompaniment has a melodic idea, this in turn takes a melodic quality of touch.

16. As a rule, attack a key with force in proportion to the duration of tone desired. (This rule is almost invariable; but it does not require a long tone in the accompaniment to be made more intense than a shorter tone in the melody. The melody always preponderates.)

17. The rule sometimes given that the first tone in a phrase is to be accented is false. There is nothing in it. Rhythmic and harmonic considerations determine accents. Position within the phrase has nothing whatever to do with it, any more than the numeric position of a syllable in a sentence determines whether it should be accented.

18. The entire time occupied by a piece of music is divided into pulses and measures. These pulses and measures flow continuously from the beginning of a movement to the end. When there is a ritard it is generally prepared by a slight accelerando, and this exactly balances the ritard. in such a way that the entire rhythm of the movement comes out correctly as the sum of the pulses contained within it. Hence, in studying the detail of a piece, you must later make sure of regaining the general sweep of the larger rhythm, and adhere to it, because *even and correct rhythm is the foundation of repose in music.*

W. S. B. M.

*Copyright, 1895 by the John Church Company. Reprinted by permission from "The Beginner in Phrasing," now in press.

THE SCALES IN PIANO TEACHING.

Between the time when a pupil begins the piano at the age of seven, eight, or nine, to the completion of the tenth grade at the age of perhaps sixteen, the entire major scales need to be gone over in about four grand stages, or methods. It is of these that I propose to write. What I have to say is independent of all books of scales, excepting Mason's, which I regard as containing certain principles of scale practice and certain forms of scales for practice, which cannot be dispensed with by any student meaning to arrive at superior scale playing. Or by any teacher meaning to arrive at the best possible performance of scale runs by the shortest possible route. Taking the course of study from the beginning to the attainment of a high degree of skill, I would say that the scales had to be gone over about four times, from different standpoints, and for different purposes. Of these the following are the general conceptions:

First time. 1st and 2d grade. Object, to familiarize the pupil with the keyboard and to form the habit of automatic selection of the proper combination of white and black digitals for the signature. In this grade also the foundation of correct scale fingering is laid. Therefore I begin here by teaching the scale from the chords of which it is composed, according to the illustrations given in the Primer of Music by Dr. Mason and the undersigned. Taking the tonic triad with the left hand we have the right hand play a dominant triad upon the upper tone of the tonic, while the left hand is still holding. Then crossing over, let the right hand play the subdominant triad below the tonic, its upper tone joining with the tonic triad. Then collect the equivalents of all these tones into the right hand within the compass of the octave, and we have from the tonic chord, C E G C, from the subdominant elements F A C, and from the dominant D G B, and after each of these chords has been touched by the right hand and is being held, touch the proper bass softly below. In this way we teach the scale from a harmonic standpoint, as it should be, and at the same time form the perception of the natural harmonic relations of the different tones of the key.

As soon as a group of keys has been formed in this way then proceed to teach the scale fingering according to the classification of Dr. Mason: the first class containing all the scales up to four sharps: the rule requiring the right hand fourth finger upon seven. The second class contains all having five black keys, and the rule gives the fourth finger the upper black key of the group of five black keys. The left hand has the fourth finger on the lower black of the group of three. The third contains all the scales from four flats down to one.

Two points are to be observed in giving these scales. The first is that we give all the scales of a group at one single lesson, in order to associate them for fingering. Second, that the forms of practice be at first only one octave and with one hand at a time. I also deviate here from Mason's directions in two respects, concerning which every teacher must be his own judge, whether he will do better to go with me or with the greater master. Mason, it will be remembered, gives the scales in D flat first, and states that this is the easiest scale for the fingers. So it is. But there is another element here. We are not seeking the easiest key-board form. We are forming the hands to runs such as they are likely to meet in the practice. And so long as all the elementary books begin with the least chromatic keys, and have considerable of this writing before introducing the higher number of flats and sharps, I think it on the whole more convenient to observe the same order with the scale practice. Another point where Mason goes rather fast is in requiring four octaves at the beginning. He says that a beginner can just as well play four octaves as any smaller number. And so he can. But there is this important consideration. In treating these scales I am in the habit of applying rhythm, according to his directions, and the minute you do this the forms resulting from a four octave scale become very long—so long as to over tax the fingers and the attention of beginners. Hence I begin with one octave and carry each scale through every kind of measure up to twelve counts, accenting always on the first count and completing the form until the accent comes out upon the tonic. This already gives forms of nine times up and down the octave. The right and left hand should alternate in the playing, one taking one meter and the other following it with the next. To go through all the major scales in this manner will take about three months or possibly more.

Second time through. Second and third grades. Object, to make the fingering certain, and to begin to get good runs. The general length of the forms will be two octaves, and contrary motion and canon forms will be introduced in the course of the practice. The accentual treatment will continue, and I should carry all forms of measure through two, three, and four tones to a count. Later in the course of this time through, Mason's first Rhythmic Table might be introduced, but only with three grades, until after considerable practice with velocity according to his system, which is to go along with every lesson, beginning with very short forms and gradually extending.

We have to remember that in the early work, with small children, we are dealing with weak attention and with still weaker muscles. It takes a good deal of attention to get strength, and still more to form groups of four tones or more, and keep them along without great mental effort. Note carefully that it is of the utmost importance to proceed from one key to another, changing the scale at every lesson. It is just as easy for the pupil to practice a new scale as to go on with the old one. In case the old one is too imperfect, let it go on with a new one, having both practiced. The ability to change easily and readily from one key to another is one of the very important habits to form as early as possible in the course.

Opposed to this I have been told by certain teachers that having taken up Mason's volume of scales they had attempted to go through all the forms and it had taken them more than six months to go through one key. This, of course, is entirely contrary to the intention of the distinguished author. I have not myself just now read over again the directions there, but I feel safe in saying that the principle of changing frequently, at least with every lesson, from one key to another is insisted upon. Another great importance in this time through the scale is the administration of canon forms. The canon forms of Mason are among the most important pieces of apparatus that piano technic can show. They should best be given in all the distances from one octave up to two, but better I think for each distance at a time, rather than making a continuous exercise and changing the turning point each time. In this treatment observe the directions in the book and take the utmost care to place the proper finger upon the topmost note, and not allow any finger that happens to be handy be put there. The canons conduce to independence of hands, and above all if treated in this way to certainty of fingering, and the student must be perfectly accurate. There is one place to draw a line. It is that never under any circumstances are we to permit improper fingering. We cannot be too careful. What we are trying to do, and what will be of inestimable value to the pupil all the way through, is to form a habit of certain fingering with every combination of white and black keys—in other words, to get the hand formed to the key in such a way that it will apparently of its own accord finger every scale right, without having to stop and think about it.

Third time. Fourth and fifth grades. Four octave forms, and the long continuous canons. Perhaps the double scale in thirds might be begun in this time through. Begin with the four octave first rhythmic table, and carry this and the other rhythmic tables through all the keys. This will require a great deal of new practice in velocity, and it will be necessary to practice quite a little in staccato in order to make the playing crisp and the scale tones distinct ann pearly. Joseffy's scale is perfection in these points. In the course of this time through all the long forms in contrary motion are introduced, and in every way the effort is made to impart to scale playing the quality and distinction which belong to first class work. During this time, too, or rather after having gone through the scale in this way, the double sixths are to be taught.

Thus far I have said nothing about the minor scales. I do not know what to say. Precedent is in favor of teaching them the same as the others. From a finger standpoint the minor scales are nearer to those in the major mode upon the same tonic, and the easiest way of introducing them is to teach them by changing the third and sixth of the major into a minor, leaving the scale in the harmonic form. If the teacher likes he can follow Tomaschek in permitting the ascending sixth to be major when there are no harmonic relations involved. Mason has gone beyond this, permitting the ascending sixth to be major in very fast runs in minor thirds, in this following Chopin at the end of the first Ballade.

Whenever the scales are taken up later than this, it is only necessary to require greater force, greater speed, and so on, and to do this same work over and over again. The length of time needed to go through all the keys in this way and to administer all these long forms, particularly if different meters are applied, will consume all the leisure of the teacher, as well as that of the pupil.

I have been over this matter at this time because I find that teachers very generally fail to understand the scope and variety of scale practice proposed in Touch and Technic Vol II.

———

EDITORIAL BRIC-A-BRAC.

In many respects the appearance of Mr. Rafael Joseffy with the Chicago Orchestra, in Brahms' second concerto for pianoforte and orchestra, was the most important piano playing event of the present season. First, of course, by reason of the magnitude, importance, and wholly exceptional quality of the composition; and second, by reason of the equally unusual and pre-eminent quality of the playing. It seems impossible that we should have had living in America for fourteen years a virtuoso of the very highest rank and yet for three whole years he should not have been heard one single time in concert. Yet this is the remarkable state of the case with regard to Mr. Joseffy. As is known to the well informed, Mr. Joseffy is at the present time at least the equal of any pianist living; and there are many who believe him to be distinctly head and shoulders above any other virtuoso at present living. He has always been a popular player with the public, his lovely tone-quality, exquisite neatness, and apparently easy mastery of all the resources of the pianoforte, rendering his work a pleasure to the ear, the eye and the feelings. Yet for some reason he has not been heard in public for three years. And there were many who offered to wager that he would not appear on this occasion—nor would he but for the privilege of making known here with Mr. Thomas a composition of such wholly exceptional excellence. But he played and the public has reason to be glad.

Everybody says that Joseffy has grown during his absence from the stage, and that he now plays broader and more musically, if possible, yet without losing anything of the exquisite certainty which formerly characterized him. I am not so sure about this. That is, I mean I am not so sure that I credit the growth to his time of absence from the stage. Upon the last two occasions when Mr. Joseffy was in Chicago I noticed that he had gained in breadth and in power of tone. Indeed he has elicited from the piano all the tone it had, in his fortissimo moments, any time this ten years. And so while he is undoubtedly more mature, he is now simply what he was then, an artist of the very highest rank, and not inferior to any other, be he whom he may.

As Mr. Liebling says: "Mr. Joseffy has it all; power, delicacy, sweetness, elasticity, and unrivalled speed combined with expression to any extent." The most beautiful qualities of his work are the refinement and the elastic tone-quality. Nothing reminds one of pounding or striking. Each tone comes out as if drawn from the piano, plucked out, as one plucks a harp-string; coaxed, commanded in extreme fortissimo, but never pounded. This is his great art. It carries with it several other excellences. First the tone-quality promotes ventilation, as one might say. No matter how fast Joseffy is playing (and he can play about twice as fast as any one else) every tone comes out clear, and there is room around it for ventilation; it stands out. And when there are long passages of rapid notes very softly, still every one comes out clearly, yet without delaying the run as a whole. This is the astonishing feature of his technique. Then too the elasticity enables him to play longer and with greater apparent ease, and in more sympathetic rhythm than any one can play using a different system of technic.

Naturally he was helped on the present occasion by his pianoforte, which was a very beautiful instrument with a clear, vital, and elastic tone-quality, such as the best samples of the Steinway manufacture possess.

I think Joseffy's rhythm is something astonishing. It is so easy, so sure, so elastic, and so reposeful. The concerto gave him all he could desire for illustrating this quality. It is full of complications, but a solo artist could not have desired a better opportunity than it gave him nor could he have been more sure and solid than was this great artist.

It is a distinct loss to the musical progress of this country that the exigences of the piano makers do not make it possible for Mr. Joseffy to make every year a concert tour. No doubt the artist refuses many engagements. But then a transient engagement is one thing, and a continued tour of three months is quite another. In the latter case the artist gets in the mood for playing, and the financial returns are greater. Anyhow all teachers and players have something to learn from this artist, who from his first appearance in Vienna, sometime about 1870 has been universally admired for the astonishing beauty of his playing.

* * *

The fourth season of the Chicago orchestra closed in a blaze of good feeling Saturday night, March 9. The program was this:

BEETHOVEN

Symphony, "Pastoral"

Awaking of cheerful feelings on arriving in the country.
Scene by the brook.
Merry gathering of the country people.
Storm.
Herdsman's song; blithe and thankful feelings after the tempest

WAGNER

"Rheingold."

a Introduction and Song of the Rhine-Daughters.
b Wotan Beholds Walhalla.
c Rainbow Scene and the Lament of the Rhine-Daughters.

"Walkyrie,"

Ride of the Valkyries.

"Siegfried," "Waldweben."

a Siegfried Ascending Brunhilde's Rock.

"Götterdämmerung."

b Morning Dawn.
c Siegfried's Rhine Journey.
d Dead March.
e Finale.

The main features were the excerpts from the Wagner Trilogy.

These were so planned as to include some of the most significant passages in the whole four evenings, and serve as a reminder of Mr. Thomas' singularly pre-eminent relation to the Wagner cult in America, and the present state of the orchestra, and at the same time give a fore-taste of the music to be heard later in the Damrosch troupe of German opera. The Ride of the Valkyries has now been played in Chicago some scores of times by Mr. Thomas, during a period of more than twenty years, his first playing of it having occurred early in the '70's, from a copy surreptitiously furnished him by Liszt. The present writer well remembers the impression this stupendous composition produced at its first hearing, which was probably in the Kingsbury Music Hall, where the Olympic theatre now is, early in 1873. The power and sweep of it were sufficiently plain. The balance of the instrumentation was not so evident then, with a force of strings not exceeding about half of that of the Chicago orchestra. The first violins then numbered eight, I believe, and the basses four. In place of this we had about twenty first violins on the present occasion and eleven basses. The total number, of the orchestra this time was towards 120, in place of about 57 upon the early occasion.

The audience found something novel and uncanny in this strange piece from the first, but it did not rise to positive liking until after some seasons of the summer concerts, in the course of which it would be played five or six times or even more in a single season. Thus at last the inherent mastership of the composition appears to every one, and while it evidently represents a strange experience, it nevertheless no longer seems impossible.

Another stupendous composition which repetition has at last placed upon the role of master works of the first order (I speak now from the standpoint of the average hearer), is the Siegfried death march. This piece also Mr. Thomas played several years before it was heard in Europe, the copy having been furnished him direct, by Liszt or Wagner. Upon its first presentation, entirely unprepared, with no indication of what it meant, with no preparatory training of ear in the way of four evenings of events and the same motives in their proper places, the hearer nevertheless immediately felt rather than understood that here was a strange yet a powerful message from some world as yet unknown. The "glimpse into Walhalla" (as Liszt said of his showing Von Bulow the "Valkyrie" soon after Wagner had sent him the score) was indeed dim. At last, however, after fifteen years it has become a classic. And even in the concert room it produces an effect beside which few other pieces can compare. But how much greater does it appear when heard in its connection! After two long evenings we come to the close of the strange career of the hero Siegfried. The magic potion of Gutrune has exhausted its work, and once more his mind turns to his romantic and heroic story; the glory of Brunhilde again fills his being, and after he feels the thrust of Hagen's spear he sings once more in honor of that wife whom he had awakened upon the fire-girt rock. Then he dies. There is a silence. Then a single soft stroke of the tympani: and another; a groan from the orchestra, represented by that figure of the strings. Then when the attendants have placed the body upon the shield of the hero and have raised it to their shoulders to bear it back to Brunhilde, the great funeral march begins with those two mighty crashes. It is chaos come again in music, just as the death of Siegfried ends the story. Yet not such chaos that the incidents of his career cannot come teeming in upon us. We have already earlier had the reminiscences of the bird song, and the awakening of Brunhilde as he tells his story to Gunther und Hagen; and in the dead march we go back to the Volsung motive of sorrow, and even to the great motive of the sword. And so masterly is this managed that even the transition of the strain into the major mode instead of imparting surcease of sorrow marks an increase of it. Great as is this piece in the concert room, where it cannot be surpassed by any other, it is vastly greater in its proper place in the drama.

Another of these great numbers which Mr. Thomas played from advance copies long before Europe had heard them, was the "Waldweben," a sort of concentrated extract from the opera of "Siegfried," leaving out short passages of recitative here and there.

* * *

Mr. W. H. Sherwood's fifth recital of the present season took place March 12th, with an interesting program:

H. W. Parker, Suite in A major. For piano, violin and 'cello,
Prelude, Minuet, Andante, and Finale.
Schumann, The Carnaval. Op. 9.
Chopin, Scherzo in B flat minor.
Wagner-Liszt, Isoldes Liebestod.
Schubert-Tausig, Military March.

Mr. Horatio W. Parker, as our readers may know, is one of the most competent of that much advertised but little heard class, the American composer—so competent that he is good enough to travel simply as composer, without any stilts of Americanism. He is now professor of music at Yale college, where he is expected to do something "for the cause," to use a form of expression current in altruistic circles. Exactly what form this "something" will take or can take beyond giving lessons to a few undergraduates, and teaching musical composition to a few post-graduates, it is not easy to see. But there he is, and perhaps this very trio may be one of the somethings which will benefit the cause even more than much work with that evanescent and uncomely bird, the fleeting undergraduate.

This suite is an extremely well-made work. It opens with a Prelude which is perhaps a trifle more melodious in the string parts than a Prelude has need of being; but it is good music with a soul in it, and not afraid of saying so. Then the tempo di menuetto is pleasing, quite so, and fairly well relieved. The next movement is a Romance, in which the second subject affords a strong contrast with the principal, and the whole reaches a considerable degree of intensity and feeling. The finale is presto, diversified and well done.

it is easy to see that Mr. Parker had in his mind a chamber work in classical form, but purposely deviated from it in the interest of the innocent hearer of the present day. It is a work which will interest an audience anywhere when well played, and whether we class it low in the first rank, or high in the second does not signify. At least one would like to hear it again. For at any rate here is music which requires no apology, and which moves straight forward towards its own goal, with step free and confident.

The playing was very good indeed, having in it at least that quality which takes and retains attention. Mr. Sherwood explained that the instrumental parts had only been at hand the day of performance, the rehearsals having been had from the MSS score, in a hand by no means too plain. The performers entered into the spirit of the work admirably, and Mr. Sherwood played his own part splendidly. Mr. Wilfred Woollet, the violinist, and Mr. Frederic Hess, the 'cellist, played warmly and well.

The Carnaval of Schumann is one of those pieces which recalls the complaint of the good old lady against the dictionary, which she thought changed the subject too often. One is but a little sooner begun in a movement than he is done for, and about to embark upon another of these little land-locked lakes of harmony. Mr. Sherwood played the movements delightfully, with great sympathy and divination of Schumann's humoristic spirit. As for the later numbers, the playing was magnificent. The recital did not have the honor of a careful review in any of the daily newspapers, so far as I observed — a curious example of journalistic valuation, concerning which I have previously spoken, especially as realized in Mr. Sherwood's case.

* * *

The *Musical Courier*, which no one who knows it would suspect of partiality, declares that the Stavenhagen recitals are a failure in consequence of the bad piano he plays. The *Courier* not only says so, but it repeats it and harps upon it. It is a veritable John the Baptist (or perhaps the Tishbite would be nearer the dispensation) crying in the wilderness against this prostitution of art. Its high ideals do it honor and distinguish the "cause." By a good fortune several of the New York critics sympathized with him of the *Courier* concerning Stavenhagen's piano, and mentioned the circumstance. The *Courier* has not ceased to reprint everything of this kind — which of course was purely in the interest of a public in danger of being misled. When Stavenhagen came to Chicago the artistic correspondent of the *Courier* was Mr Walton Perkins, lately critic of the *Chicago Times*, in which medium he has done some excellent work, for he is a pianist himself and a good teacher and knows what is what and withal writes like a gentleman. He received a telegram from the *Courier* desiring him to "roast" Stavenhagen again "on account of Eliza" — to wit, the piano. Mr. Perkins, not bethinking himself of the honorarium at stake immediately resigned, and now journalism knows him no more.

* * *

* * *

Speaking of Stavenhagen, I was much interested in his case, since it illustrates a certain vice in piano teaching which has impaired the public work of many great artists, Eugene D'Albert at the head of the list. Stavenhagen is said to be the most modest virtuoso of all, as well as one of the most accomplished. He has enormous technic, and a large repertory, in spite of his playing his Saturday pieces as encores on Thursday and his Thursday pieces as encores on Saturday. His Liszt playing is as good as any I have ever heard. But between him and Joseffy there is a very great difference, most noticeable at one point, namely, the habitual manner of eliciting tone. Joseffy uses a keen finger-elastic touch, in which the point of the finger draws inwards toward the palm of the hand as it touches the keys, and in a general sense the finger does not lie dead upon the key, but long tones are sustained by means of the pedal. Every tone sounds as if plucked out, as one picks the string of a harp. Consequently the element of pounding is entirely absent from Joseffy's playing, and the tone of the piano is never forced. The musical, the bright and the telling are everywhere in evidence. Joseffy, however, does more things with a rigid hand than any pianist I know, getting his elasticity farther back, namely in the arm. Hence while using the fingers in a very vital sense, he nevertheless has peculiarly solid chords and octaves.

Stavenhagen lacks this delicacy of touch, but makes his tone in in the orthodox way of striking downwards upon the key and remaining there. Consequently when he plays softly he has a lovely tone; but the minute he lets loose for forte effects, he produces the impression of pounding, and very often goes through the tone of his piano, which under a kinder treatment might respond more adequately to his needs. The truth is that his instrument really does seem to lack depth and sonority of tone adequate to the demands of the artist, but the difference remains undetermined whether this is a fault of the piano or of the method of the pianist. And even if the piano should be taken in the fault, it would still prove nothing against the makers of the instrument; for how often do we hear bad pianos of every make—even the Steinway. Bad pianos are not a monopoly at this age of the world, that the firm distinguished as having made one should be publicly pilloried. At this rate where would we all be "at?" Go to, wise critics: let us take a rest!

* * *

Stavenhagen affects the average American hearer much as that great artist D'Albert affects it. The hearer cares very little about the playing. D'Albert they say is a very great virtuoso and a magnificent artist. But he did not draw money in this country. They say this was due to want of tact in advertising him. Nothing of the sort. It is purely a question of the tone-production and the personality of the artist. When the public likes an artist it finds it out and goes. Put Paderewski down anywhere, and no matter if the audience is small, the second is larger, the third larger still, and so it goes on increasing, simply because people who were there say that they liked it and are going again. The minute Stavenhagen produces this impression in any American city his fortune is made. But he will not produce this or any other similar impression until he learns to conceal the art by means of which he obtains the full resonance from his instrument. And especially learns not to force the tone.

* * *

Stavenhagen was accompanied by that genius of the violoncello, the fourteen year old boy, Master Gerardy. He had a lovely instrument, from which he elicited a most beautiful and affecting tone. And his delivery of melody has that nameless something in it which makes an artist the joy of all who hear him. He was called back again and again, and with industry his future is secure. His volume of tone is wonderful for a virtuoso so young, and his divination of passion and deep feeling equally suggestive of genius, to which all wisdom is open by intuition. Behold how pleasant it is for brethren to dwell together in unity. It is like the oil on Aaron's beard—what psalm am I quoting now? I am told that the cellist and the pianist in this company have not spoken for some weeks.

* * *

And this reminds me of a letter that I got the other day from a clever young pianist who found himself some weeks ago at the top of his immediate ambition, engaged for a tour with a celebrated violinist. He was to play the accompaniments and two solos in each concert. Being a gifted young fellow, with a charming touch and the utmost love of music, and nothing mean in his disposition anywhere, well educated and of good address, he was full of pleasant anticipation as to the manner in which he would do himself honor and acquire reputation. The tour has now been going on for about eight weeks, and in only two or three places have the newspapers given them anything but conventional notices, showering the adjectives on the violinist, who has long been known as a great master; but passing over the youngster with a word—always commendable, but still only a word. It happened, however, that in two of the larger places the papers took up the young pianist and commented on the very patent fact of his playing being agreeable to hear—which it is to a rare degree. And behold all is trouble. The veteran finds every word given to the new comer exactly that much subtracted from his own meed of honor.

* * *

The irreproachable Band of Sousa has been making a tour of the south with great success. Among the tributes elicited was a new version of "Dixie" in honor of the stirring visitors. It appeared in the Atlanta *Journal*.

"Sousa's Band recently invaded the south and made a remarkable conquest. The playing of his great band has aroused the wildest enthusiasm everywhere and inspired a well known poet of Atlanta to indite these patriotic lines:"

When Sousa's Band's in de land of cotton,
Work and worry's all forgotten,
Look away! Look away! Look away!
Dixie Land.
When de music plays and de coons am hummin'
It makes 'em feel good times is comin',
Look away! Look away! Look away
Dixie Land.

Chorus.
When Sousa's Band's in Dixie's land,
Hooray! Hooray!
'Longside that band we'll take our stand,
And sing and dance in Dixie.
Away! Away
Away down south in Dixie.

In Sunday clo'es we'll go a-prancin',
Up and down a singin', dancin',
Look away! Look away! Look away!
Dixie Land.
An' we'll bring our gals what'er de wedder,
All hands a-keepin' time togedder.
Look away! Look away! Look away!
Dixie Land.

Chorus.
When Sousa's Band's in Dixie, etc.

He! Music's better a corn or money,
Sweeter'n hoe cake soaked in honey.
Look away! Look away! Look away!
Dixie Land.
And when dat Sousa's Band am playin',
Bet your life right dar we're stayin',
Look away! Look away! Look away!
Dixie Land.

Chorus.
When Sousa's Band's in Dixie, etc.

* * *

I have been much interested in watching the progress of Mr. Wilber M. Derthick's scheme of Musical Literary Clubs, as mentioned in these columns and elsewhere several times back. The publication of the books of programs and analyses of the compositions proposed for performance has been going forward at an encouraging rate. Several of the books first published, such as those relating to Bach and Handel, have been thoroughly revised and greatly enlarged in consequence of which the programs provide for a much greater variety of music and for wider range of choice according to the ability of the performing members of the clubs. Mr. Derthick has been engaged for some time upon a general introduction to the whole plan, beginning with a short treatise upon Aesthetics, and the details of the plan proposed for study. This I understand is now ready for circulation, and I am sure that any intelligent person reading it will be impressed with the high aims of the author.

Mr. John S. Van Cleve has decided to remove to Chicago and devote his whole time to the work of the Clubs, partly in lecturing and organizing new clubs, and partly in filling engagements for lecture recitals before some of the older clubs. Among the places where flourishing clubs have lately been organized by Mr. Van Cleve are Marion, Troy, Lima and Athens, Ohio, and Greenville, Ky. The usual experience is that a considerable addition to the membership of the club is made very soon after its opening. A large number of engagements are being made for recitals and lectures, the favorite candidates in demand being at present Messrs. Sherwood, Hunter Perry and Van Cleve. I am told that applications for recitals from Mr. Liebling have been discouraged, by reason of his hostility to the scheme. This is a pity for both parties, considering that both alike enjoy a good thing. Mr. F. Walker has a number of engagements for song recitals, and other attractions are in consideration. The *modus operandi* of this part of the scheme is for the club to secure a minimum of subscriptions, sufficient to ensure the success of the recital. Then whatever is made above this sum goes in part to the local club and in part to the general treasury.

Naturally the crucial question is as to the success or non-success of the work in the long run, by which is meant during the second year of the course, when it has become an old story. I confess that I have had doubts upon this point. But lately Mr. Derthick has sent out a circular letter to all the clubs asking them to make a report upon the interest, and upon their idea of the value of the work after trial. The responses have been remarkably unanimous and favorable.

One thing appears sure; which is that this work is just now in demand and bids fair to fill a place which as yet was not occupied. At the worst it can only advertise the art of music and afford at least a smattering of information concerning it. That some members will mistake knowing a little about music for knowing *music* is altogether likely; but then a similar miscarriage of purpose is not unknown in church circles, where the apparatus has been so much longer in maturing and the priests who administer it have had the advantage of special training and tradition. The priests of music are a self anointed body, for the most part; and in some cases the supply of ointment has been exhausted before the candidate arrived. Hence a few errors of detail.

Another sure thing of this kind of organization is its affording a nucleus in every town where a club is established, for the support of recitals and lectures about music. The range of the programs will also tend to greatly enlarge the repertory of the local players, while the visits of artists will make an equally distinct impression upon the standard of performances. All of which is confirmatory of the sort of sixth sense of Mr. Derthick as to what was wanted.

* * *

Not long ago I heard some remarkable playing upon two pianos by two St. Louis teachers, Miss Marie Miller and Miss Laura Shafer. It seems that when studying with Professor Barth, in Berlin, they conceived the idea of undertaking some playing upon two pianos, not so much for the sake of performing the usual repertory of pieces expressly written for two pianos as for dividing very difficult pieces written for virtuoso performance, and bringing the playing up to the highest finish and unity. As an illustration of what I mean I mention the first piece which they played. It was Schumann's immensely difficult Toccata. This they had divided between themselves in such a way that every note of the original is played and not a single note doubled. By dint of musical feeling and much practice they have been able to follow each other and maintain a perfect sympathy and unity, so that the performance is a great deal more perfect than such a piece usually is, even when played together so perfectly. And the result was certainly astonishing. Later they played Liszt's "Les Preludes" arranged for two pianos, and in this number it was a question of great brilliancy and sonority. Another piece of the kind first mentioned was the Chopin study in C sharp minor, opus 10 number 4. This also divided sounded like the work of a very reliable and many-fingered player. The repertory of these ladies contained many interesting numbers. They would like to work up a business of recitals and boarding schools, and the like. I would suppose that there would be a considerable demand for such work, if the mechanical difficulty of bringing together two grand pianos in small places could be overcome.

* * *

While this playing was very remarkable indeed, it raises one or two very interesting questions. The first is as to the need of this kind of division. In other words, whether it is sufficiently artistic demand, this of hearing the mere notes of a work like the Schumann Toccata played by two persons when it had been originally written for one. The question underlaying is as to what it is that we desire in this piece. Is it the music, pure and simple? Or is it the bravoura of hearing it played by a single player of extraordinary powers? I believe that the element of astonishment is a legitimate part of the effect of this kind of piece, and that to divide it between two, for the sake of the resulting speed, is not wholly unlike dividing the 2:20 of a good trotter between two, making a half mile each.

* * *

Following is the list of works performed by the Chicago Orchestra during the fourth season (1894-95).

BACH	Suite in D.
	Sonata in F minor (Orchestration by Theodore Thomas.)
BEETHOVEN	Symphony, No. 3, Heroic.
	Symphony, No. 5.
	Symphony, No. 6, Pastoral.
	Symphony, No. 7.
	Overture, Leonore, No. 3.
	Overture, Fidelio.
	Theme and Variations from Op. 18.
BERLIOZ	Overture, Les Francs Juges.
	Love Scene; Queen Mab (Scherzo) from Romeo and Juliet.

	March Marocaine.
BIZET	Suite L'Arlesienne.
BRAHMS	Symphony in D.
	Concerto for Piano in D. (Mr. Rafael Joseffy.)
	Concerto for Violin and Violoncello, Op. 102. (Messrs. [illegible] and Steindel.)
	Overture, Academic Festival.
BRUCH	Concerto for Violin in G minor. (Mr. César Thomson.)
	Scotch Fantasia for Violin. (Mr. Eugene Ysaye.)
CHABRIER	Spanish Rhapsody.
CHADWICK	A Pastoral Prelude.
CHAMINADE	Concertstueck for Piano, Op. 40. (Mr. H. [illegible] Schiller.)
CHERUBINI	Overture, The Water Carrier.
CHOPIN	Polonaise, A Flat. (Orchestration by Theodore Thomas.) (2)
	March Funebre. (Orchestration by Theodore Thomas.)
DVORAK	Symphony, From the New World.
	Symphony, From the New World, Largo.
	Overture, Nature.
	Scherzo Capriccioso.
	Slavonic Dances, Fourth Series.
[illegible]	Concerto for Violoncello in G Minor. (Mr. Bruno Steindel.)
FUCHS	Serenade in D.
GOLDBECK	Forest Devotion.
	Leaping Marionettes.
	Two Mexican Dances.
GOLDMARK	The Country Wedding.
	Overture, Sappho.
	Scherzo, Op. 19.
GOMES	Ballata, from Il Guarany. (Miss Electa Gifford.)
HAYDN	Symphony, in B Flat. (B. & H. 12.)
HANDEL	Concerto in D minor
	(For String Orchestra, Two Solo Violins and Violoncello.
	Messrs. Bendix, Kuhn and Steindel.)
HUMPERDINCK	Vorspiel, Hansel and Gretel.
LACHNER	Introduction and Fugue.
LAMOND	Overture, From the Highlands.
LISZT	Hungarian Rhapsody, No. 1.
	Mephisto Waltz.
MACKENZIE	A Nautical Overture.
MASSENET	Suite, Scenes Alsaciennes.
	Overture, Moorish Rhapsody and March from The Cid.
	Recitative and Aria, Pleurez, mes yeux, from The Cid. (Miss Carlotta Desvignes.)
MOZART	Symphony, G minor (K. 550).

	Symphony in D (K 504).
	Lied and Aria from Entführung. (Mr. Max Heinrich).
PAGANINI	Grand Fantasie for Violin. (Mr. Cesar Thomson.)
RHEINBERGER	Concerto for Organ and Orchestra in G minor. (Mr. Clarence Eddy.)
RUBINSTEIN	Overture, Dimitri Donskoi.
	Overture, Antony and Cleopatra
SAINT-SAENS	Concerto for Violin in B minor. (Mr. Max Bendix).
	Concerto for Violin in B minor. (Mr. Eugene Ysaye.)
	Fantasia for Harp. (Mr. Ed. Schuecker.)
	Aria, Amour! viens aider, from Samson und Delila. (Miss Charlotta Desvignes.)
SCHOLZ, B.	Suite, Wandering.
SCHUBERT	Symphony in C.
SCHUMANN	Symphony in C, No. 2.
	Symphony in D, minor, No. 4.
	Manfred, Selections.
SEEBOECK	Concerto for Piano in D major. (Mr. W. C. E. Seeboeck.)
SELMER, JOH.	Carnival of Flanders.
SGAMBATI	Te Deum Laudamus, for String Orchestra and Organ. (Mr. W. Middelschulte).
SITT, HANS	Concert Piece for Viola. (Mr. A. Yunker).
SMETANA	Symphonic Poem, The Moldau.
SPOHR	Overture, Jessonda.
STRAUSS, J.	Waltz, On the Beautiful Blue Danube.
	Waltz, From the Vienna Woods.
STRAUSS, R.	Death and Transfiguration.
THOMAS, A.	Mad Scene, Hamlet. (Miss Lillian Blauvelt.)
TSCHAIKOWSKY	Symphony, No. 5.
	Fantasia, The Tempest.
	Suite in D.
	Danse Cosaque.
	Theme and Variations and Finale, Op. 55.
	Waltz from Ballet, Dornroschen.
WAGNER	Tannhäuser, Overture.
	Tournament March.
	Bacchanale.
	Lohengrin, Vorspiel.
	Introduction to Act III.
	Die Meistersinger, Vorspiel.
	Tristan and Isolde, Prelude and Closing Scene (2).
	Rheingold.
	Introduction and Song of the Rhine Daughters.
	Wotan Beholds Walhalla.
	Rainbow Scene and the Maiden's Lament
	Walküre.
	Ride of the Valkyries (2).

Wotan's Farewell and Fire Charm. (Mr. Max Heinrich)
Siegfried, Waldweben.
Siegfried Ascending Brunnhilde's Rock.
Götterdämmerung.
Morning Dawn.
Siegfried's Rhine Journey (2).
Dead March.
Finale.
Parsifal, Prelude and Glorification
Kaiser March.
Weber Overture, Euryanthe.

* * *

At the closing recital of the interesting series given by Mr. and Mrs. Bicknell Young, the latter part of the program was occupied by a little operatic skit in one act, for two singers with a chorus in the background. The libretto was by Mr. William A. Lamson, and the subject "The Maid and the Reaper." The reaper comes in with his scythe and is mistaken by the maiden for the grim reaper death. Presently, however, the drawings of nature awaken the inexperienced young woman to a more pleasing conception, and her environment is intensified by two strong manly arms, etc. The music of the plot affords room for several arias somewhat in contrast with each other. The reaper has a strongly marked scythe song, and later a bit of benediction. The maiden has reminiscences of grief and sorrow, and presently the awakening and the fullness of love. The invisible chorus helps out the ensemble. The music is by Madam Mazzucato-Young, who also played the accompaniments. The experiment was interesting, and is a step in the right direction. It appears to me, however, that in working it out the following difficulties had not been fully overcome: The music is not well planned for stage action, leaving too much time to stand around for preludes and afterludes to play themselves out. The musical treatment of the pieces, especially in the accompaniments, is not sufficiently varied. The conception is a little too serious and improbable. In short it is a trifle too much like grand opera with the mystery taken out of it, as it always is when the stage is reduced, and the orchestra taken away. I had thought of something a little more in the comedy line, and with more rapid action, but at the same time affording excuse for varied kinds of song.

The performance was given upon the pretty little stage of the new hall in the building of the Y.M.C.A., which occupies the place of the two or three former Farwell halls. The performers were Mr. Young and his pupil Miss Sadie Loverdale. She has a lovely voice, and with experience would do a part of this kind well. The songs of the work are uncommonly good.

The earlier part of the program was signalized by some pleasing singing by Mrs. E. H. Brush and Mr. William A. Lamson. Mme. Chatterton, the harpist, played a solo.

* * *

Grand opera in French and Italian was given in the Auditorium by the Abbey and Grau company from March 11 to March 29. The list of principal performers included such names as the following: Mmes Melba, Eames-Story, Nordica, Scalchi, Mantelli, Drog, and Miss Bauermeister. Messrs Jean and Edouard De Reszke, Maurel, Plançon, Tamagno, Russitano, Ancona, etc.

It will be seen that the list includes three of the best sopranos in the world, and upon the male side the two De Reszkes, Maurel and Plançon are artists of the highest possible eminence. Add to these the names of Tamagno the vociferous Spanish tenor, and the several honored names of utility people of great versatility, and we have an apparatus of rare worth—which cannot at present be surpassed anywhere in the world, and in fact by reason of its vast expense would be impracticable anywhere but in the United States and England. The chorus is large and as efficient as choruses changing their opera every night can be; and the orchestra under the direction of Messrs Mancinelli and Bevignani, is large and fairly satisfactory. With such a list of principal artists it would of course be expected that there would be no "off nights," since the company had been carefully "braced up" according to the famous recipe of the "Deacon's wonderful one-horse shay." And to an extent this has been true. At least two of the performances, however, were decidedly below the standard. "Aida" in the first week with Mme Drog in the title role and Tamagno as tenor, was boisterous and unpleasing. The same may be said of "Il Trovatore" in the second week, with the same cast. Nevertheless in both these Signor Tamagno made a great effect. On the other hand, however, the cast of the "Huguenots" was phenomenally strong, and to find in one opera two sopranos of so distinguished international reputation as Mmes Nordica and Melba is surely something of which the management has a right to be proud, since it is evidence of managerial nerve in its highest potency. The performance was signalized by at least four features of remarkable artistic value: The Raoul of Mr. Jean De Reszke, the Marcel of Mr. Edouard De Reszke, the Valentine of Mme Nordica, and the Queen of Mme Melba. The other leading roles were also in hands which in any other company would be considered exceptionally strong.

Another phenomenal cast (if carried out according to intention) would have been that of Mozart's "Don Giovanni," which was billed to contain Mmes Nordica, Eames-Story, and Miss De Lussan in the three soprano roles; and Messrs Maurel, Edouard De Reszke, Russitano, Abramoff and Carbone in the principal roles upon the male side. But at the last minute Mme Drog was substituted for Mme Nordica. The remainder of the work was delightfully done, the impersonations of the title role by Mr. Maurel reaching a very high value, while Edouard De Reszke was a stage-cy-looking Leporello. Mme Eames-Story was most charming looking and to the ear. It is not likely that the present generation has seen a more beautiful woman upon the stage than she in this role, or has heard purer and more delightful singing than her work in this music. It was beautiful in the extreme. Miss De Lussan, also, made a lovely Zerlina, voice, manner and experience making her phenomenally suitable to the role. The venerable work itself was delightful, and very fresh. The statue scene in the last act seemed rather long and a good while in arriving. But on the whole we are not likely to find many works of so essentially ephemeral character as opera which after a century of use still retain so much of power to please.

The great feature of the first week was the production of Verdi's "Falstaff" concerning which I have elsewhere copied Mr. Reginald De Koven's sensible and well-considered remarks. At the moment of writing I have not heard the work a second time, nor have been able to study the score. My impression, however, is that it is likely to prove attractive for quite a number of years. It is sprightly and in every way cleverly done. As compared with Wagner's "Meistersinger" for instance, it does not strike so deep notes of any kind. Nowhere in it is there anything approaching the tenderness and charm of the prize song of Walther, or the finale in which Beckmesser gives his serenade. But it is quick, the dialogue is free, and the instrumentation spirited and at the same time delicate. It is a work of very high order, and considering that it comes from a master eighty years of age, it is likely to go down into history for this reason if for no other.

The entire repertory was the following:

"The Huguenots:" Mmes Nordica, Melba, Scalchi; Messrs Edouard De Reszke, Jean De Reszke, Ancona, Plançon, etc.

"Otello:" Mmes Eames-Story, Mantelli; Messrs Tamagno, Ancona, Maurel.

"Romeo and Juliette:" Mmes Melba, Emma Eames, De Vigne, Bauermeister, Messrs Jean De Reszke, Edouard De Reszke, Campanari, etc.

"Falstaff:" Mmes Emma Eames, Scalchi, Miss De Lussan, De Vigne, Messrs Maurel, Russitano, Rinaldini, and Campanari.

"Aida:" Messrs Tamagno, Ancona, Mme Drog, etc.

"Faust:" Mme Emma Eames, Mlle Bauermeister, Mme Scalchi, Jean De Reszke, Edouard De Reszke, etc.

"Rigoletto:" Mmes Melba, Scalchi; Messrs Castelmary, Russitano, and Maurel.

"Lohengrin:" Mmes Nordica and Mantelli; Messrs Plançon, Ancona, Abramoff, and Jean De Reszke.

"Don Giovanni:" Mmes Nordica, Eames, Mlle De Lussan; Messrs Edouard De Reszke, Maurel, and Russitano.

"Il Travatore:" Mmes Drog, Van Cauteren and Mantelli; Messrs Campanari and Tamagno.

"Carmen:" Miss De Lussan, Mauguiere, Edouard de Reszke, etc.

"Cavalleria Rusticana:" Mlle Mira Heller, De Vigne; Messrs Tamagno and Ancona.

"Lucia di Lammermoor," Mme Melba, Mr. Russitano, etc.

"Nozze di Figaro:" Mme Emma Eames, Miss De Lussan, Lucille Hill; Edouard De Reszke, Maurel, etc.

In all twenty-two performances and fourteen operas.

W. S. B. M.

ZELIE DE LUSSAN ON "WOMEN IN MUSIC."

WHEN Zelie de Lussan vanished from American *opera comique*, some six or seven years ago, it was in pursuance of a vacation, which American like she wished to take upon the other side of the water. Her fame had already reached a high standard in her native country, and while as yet she had not appeared in parts more exacting than the Daughter of the Regiment and Carmen, she had shown herself not only a very superior singer but also a highly capable artist, and a most engaging personality upon the stage. Having in her own hand those four aces of a lyric career, voice, presence, youth, and brains, with a good card in reserve, in the way of indomitable industry, the De Lussan future was as well assured as a future can be. But it was not with any especial designs upon the English stage that she embarked from New York. She had in her boxes, however, (by the advice of that astute judge of artists, the late Colonel Mapleson,) taken her "Carmen" costumes along, and she had only been about a week in London when she received a note from Sir Augustus Harris asking her to sing "Carmen" at Covent Garden. She sang it. This was the end of Zelie de Lussan for America for several long years. Immediately after the Covent Garden experience she made an engagement with the Carl Rosa company for English opera, and in this field she worked for five years and lingering during the London season, sang at Covent Garden in Italian.

England is more advanced than America. They actually prefer over there to know what it is all about when opera is given, and so they sing it often in the language of the people; they do this not alone with the light operas expressly adapted to the deficiencies of the native companies, but with grand operas, even with *new* operas, and so the name English opera in England means something quite different from what it means here. Take Miss De Lussan's own case.

She has created the part of Gounod's Juliet, in English, and Desdemona in Verdi's "Othello." She sang Carmen about five hundred times in English and Italian, for she has done it many times at Covent Garden; and the Daughter of the Regiment more than three hundred times, including by special command before the Queen at Windsor. The role of Desdemona she created in English for the celebration of Verdi's seventy-seventh birthday.

One of the most peculiar experiences was that of creating the role of Marguerite in Berlioz's "Damnation of Faust," which was sung in English as an opera, in the royal Court Theatre at Liverpool, under the direction of Sir Charles Halle, in January, 1894. She also created the role of Nedda in "Pagliacci" in English.

MISS ZELIE DE LUSSAN.

What sort of an opera did Berlioz's "Damnation of Faust!" make, asked the visitor.

Beautiful, answered the prima donna. It was a spectacle. There are plenty of dancers, and a large chorus. Then the principals have much beautiful music, and the scenic display and the descriptive music of the orchestra makes a grand entertainment vastly superior to the same work merely as an oratorio. They had a great deal of trouble with the mechanical horses for the Ride to Hell and even at the last the illusion was not quite perfect; but it aided the realism of the music, and the effect was prodigious. The ballet of the "Will-o-the-wisps" was also beautifully done, the dance and the music going together delightfully. It was most splendid, I assure you.

At this point the visitor began to bring the discussion around to a point upon which Miss De Lussan's opinions had been especially sought. He asked: If woman is so gifted musically as her success in certain lines would suggest, how do you account for the fact of her making no mark as composer?

Well, now I think that a woman thinks too much of her own self; has too much to think of for her own self, I do not think a woman is strong minded enough to become a composer.

"You have seen a good deal of composers?

I have.

"Did they strike you as being particularly strong minded?"

I think as a rule a woman composer is much more masculine than any other kind of a woman. Mme Chaminade is a lovely composer. It may also be that I do not think a woman can well devote the time she should, that a man would, I do not think a woman is strong enough, unless she is a wonderfully powerful woman.

"Don't you think you work as hard as a man?"

In my singing capacity yes, but if it came down to composing,—counterpoint, harmony and all that sort of thing, I don't think so. I think that you will always find that as a rule a composer has begun his career as a child of five or six years of age, and a woman has not. Look at that Hoffman boy, for instance. He began at four years of age. It is very seldom, you know, that a girl of five or six knows anything about counterpoint and harmony. Take these choir boys in England, where do you find girls five or six years old singing in choirs? The reason is that a woman doesn't begin early enough. I don't know that she doesn't want to, but I don't think she *could*. As a rule you will find that composers have been very serious children. Beethoven is said to have been most serious as a child. We know Haydn and Mozart were the same. Haydn simply lived in the church.

"When there is so much attention paid to music, why shouldn't there be women composers as well as George Eliot's, Elizabeth Barrett Browning, or Rosa Bonheur's?"

But don't you think it is much easier to write a book than to compose music? You know the language. But look what you have to know besides the language; you have to study a half a dozen things to be a musician. Do you think woman's brain can do so many things? I don't think so.

"Do you think that a woman has the creative capacity?"

That's a very hard thing for me to tell. I am afraid I would have to be excused from that.

"You must have met a good many interesting women in London?

I have, but I never met any women composers; yes I did, I met Maude Valerie White and Hope Temple.

Now you take those women. They have written very charming ballads.

"How do their ballads compare for instance with ballads by Cowen?"

I assure you that Hope Temple has written some of the most beautiful ballads I ever listened to.

"That proves something doesn't it? That here is a woman who has had sufficient amount of musical education to bring her to that point and her creative faculty is all right. Now what's the reason that there shouldn't be a woman who will go further and write operas or symphonies.

Mme Holms of Paris wrote a grand opera, but the music was forced. Saint-Saens himself said she tried to write like a man, and spoiled what might have been very beautiful music. It may be the fact that they knew it was a woman might have caused them to criticize her. If she had called herself Saint Saens or Delibes she might have gotten a much better criticism.

"Take your own case for instance? You commenced music quite young, didn't you?

I was almost, I might say, born in music. I was brought up on it, like other children are brought up on pap I suppose. But I was very well nourished, as you can see, and so it came to me naturally. I shouldn't judge other people by myself at all. But the woman who gets up and writes grand opera is going to be a woman with a history, a woman who has had exceptional advantages and heredity.

I think some people mature much later than others. As a child I had a great deal of talent and improvised on the piano. I could sit down and compose some very beautiful things, but I could not study counterpoint or harmony. I would fall asleep over it. But I would put my teacher at the piano, and he would forget all about the lesson and play and play, and the two hours were up. But music comes to me now easily.

"While singing in opera you have to remember practically the whole of the music. Of course you have to remember all the phrases that come just before your sentences; you must know exactly where you come in. What are you conscious of? You aren't conscious of the chord are you?"

I know exactly what phrase is coming before me, and count my time. That's everything in music, in concerted music. Now, in that fugue in the last act of "Falstaff" if I didn't count I simply wouldn't be in it.

I do all my own counting. It's all a question of arithmetic, and if you don't count you can't sing. I have some very difficult entries in that "Falstaff" music. That little duet with Fenton. There's no tune to help you out, and you have merely got to count, yourself; you must not rely on the conductor; you must have it all in yourself.

"How do you remember your intonation? Do you know the chord or what?"

I don't think I think of it half the time. I have a very good ear. It's all brain work. It's all thought. You have got to be very calm in this business; you can't get flurried. The first instinct is to rush, in doing a new opera. Am I going to be there on time, and especially an opera like "Falstaff" where its all chopped up into bits. That conversation in the first act is like net-work, and if you don't come in you are finished. And to do it well you must be so sure of it that you mustn't rely on the conductor. You can't in that music, because its too quick, it's too rapid ; you haven't time to look.

"How do you know where you are in the chord, or don't you know? You have to be square on time and you have also to be square on the chord, do you know the chord?"

I know exactly what has to come before I sing, but if it happened it didn't come I wouldn't be at all annoyed; I sing it myself. In one place in "Falstaff" the violins have three notes before I come in. The first night they failed to come in, but I went on and sang and Mancinelli smiled at me and told me I was all right. Well now, if I had got rattled I would have said "I am not going to sing until I *hear my* da-da-da." But if it doesn't come in it doesn't bother me, because I know where it *ought* to come. There is always an instrumental cue.

"Well, if a young lady was going to study to become a great prima donna, how would she go to work to do it?"

I should certainly advise her to go to a very good teacher. Let that teacher tell that person if she is going to be a great prima donna ; you can tell pretty well if there's a good voice. You want appearance, you want youth, you want health especially, and you want voice of course; of course you want voice, and then you want the feeling, "I know I am going to work and I want to succeed." You don't want to say "I shall study about a year and become a great singer." You want a lot of things to become a prima donna, and I certainly should say a girl is very brave who wants to go on the stage and has nothing but herself to rely on ; because she doesn't know whether her teacher is going to tell her how to sing well or not. She runs the risk ; she may get with a teacher who doesn't understand her voice at all. I know a young lady who sang at a concert and sang very, very well. Well, she went to England and there one of the first teachers heard her sing and said, 'You have been taught all wrong. You don't know how to sing; you have not the first idea how to sing'—and he made her begin singing all over again. When that happens the student says to herself "Well now is he right or is he not? Is he going to teach me the right way to sing?" It is utterly impossible for her to tell. She has nobody to tell her. The only thing she can do, if she feels that she has been taught wrong, is for her to give herself up to this new teacher; but after studying with this new man she may be still all wrong.

"Who are the best teachers in England?"

I do not know. Shakespeare is *very* good, I believe for oratorio. Garcia is still alive. That man is ninety years old and he gives lessons.

"Does he teach well?"

I believe so, very well. Wonderful; he is the brother of Malibran and of Viardot-Garcia in Paris.

I studied only with my mother. Not another soul. No one offered to teach me in England because I went over there as an artist; there was not even such a suggestion. It has been a great satisfaction. That's one chance in lifetime. You would probably not see another woman who had the opportunity I had. My mother had been a great and beautiful singer and knew how to teach me.

"So on the whole you don't think woman is likely to branch out as a composer?"

I am afraid not; in ballads and all that, yes; but really when it comes to Beethoven's sonatas and grand operas, I doubt it. I am very old fashioned anyway.

Chicago, Mar. 20th. ZELIE DE LUSSAN.

REVIEWS AND NOTICES.

A COMPLETE METHOD OF SINGING. By E. Delle Sadie. A Theoretical and Practical Treatise on the Art of Singing. G. Schirmer, New York. $2.00 net.

This handsomely printed volume of 182 pages is a condensation of the author's large work in seven volumes. It contains a sufficient apparatus of solfegi, together with many admirable explanations of the theory of the different acts entering into the highly complex art of singing. It is for the use of teachers, and of students under care of a teacher. There is no such thing possible as learning to sing except by the direct teaching of a living artist. Everything in direction admits of being done in many ways, with the best of intentions, and the student without direct personal supervision is powerless to determine whether he is on the right road or not. Delle Sadie was the one who formed the voice of Christine Nilsson; he was also for nearly five years the master of that admirable teacher, Miss Clara Munger, of Boston. There are none better than he; but as for the book, again be it said, it is a question of how it is done.

SCIENCE AND ART OF BREATHING. By Frank H. Tubbs. New York, The Vocalist, 35 University Place. 1894. $2.00.

Here we have a reprint of the admirable series of articles in *The Vocalist* upon the science and art of breathing. Inasmuch as this art is to singing what the proper mastery of the bow is to playing the violin, the importance of the book is apparent. The work is designed for the use of teachers and for students in self study. It is possible that specific acts like those directed in this book can be accurately well done from direction, without the criticism of the living teacher, whereas if the author had gone further and furnished certain melodies to be sung, no printed directions could have been devised which would have been adequate. This is the difference between this work and that of Delle Sadie, noticed elsewhere. The latter proposes to form singers, and furnishes an apparatus for doing the greater part of the work, in the course of which the *how* is the central and essential point, yet precisely the point which the student is not able to determine for himself. With Mr. Tubbs' book the case is different. Proposing nothing more than a specific treatment of the art of breathing only, it is not impossible that a careful student may derive material aid from the book.

ADVANCED FOURTH MUSIC READER. For Grammar and High School. By James McLaughlin and George Veazie. Boston, 1895, Ginn & Company.

This elegantly gotten up book adds another to the already considerable number of practical music books of the Ginn company. It opens with a series of lessons in two and three parts, written by Dr. W. W. Gilchrist, of Philadelphia, which are generally well done musically and comparatively modern in matter. They are not only valid examples of part writing, but also not unlike any well written music which the student may encounter later. The remainder of the book is made up of classified songs upon the subjects usual in the later collections of school music, the essential point being to have the songs teach something or inculculate something. On a cursory examination (which is the best possible at the moment) this appears to be a very fortunate collection of school music, and the studies in reading appear to be the best the reviewer has ever examined—musical and pleasant.

The modern idea, however calls for something better in the way of adapting words to music than the association of Dr. Holland's "The Evening was glorious" with a regular four line strain of music. Dr. Holland's first line ends with the partial phrase, "And light and through the trees" which the second completes with "Played the sunshine and rain-drops, the birds and the breeze." The music completes its sense at the word "the trees." A modern composer setting those words would carry the sense of his music through the two lines uninterrupted. Something is also due the realistic spirit in effecting rhyming translations from the German. For instance Hoffman von Fallersleben is made to say (in "Greeting to Spring") "We welcome thee to field and fen." Now fen is an excellent rhyme to again, but it is a very unsatisfactory kind of place for a springtime walk. These and such like, however, are mere details. The book appears to be a rarely good one.

DON'T. Applied to certain terms in Musical Theory, that seem to the writer to be incorrectly used or defined. By Geo. F. Root, Mus. Doc. 16mo, paper, pp 104. John Church Company, Cincinnati.

This little book is the outcome of a series of articles running in the *Musical Visitor* for more than a year past. In each chapter Dr. Root takes up the misuse of a single term and shows the more excellent way. The carelessness of musicians even in high standing is very great. While any one of these gentlemen would answer without a moment's hesitation that music is something which has to be heard, and its peculiarities and entities recognizable by ear and by ear only, and are represented in accordance with the system of notation arrived at empirically as a result of several centuries experiment, they will nevertheless use terms in teaching and in ordinary conversation as if the entities of music were determinable by the manner of their representation, and as if the eye were the final arbiter. This is one result of our faulty method of elementary musical training, in which the eye cuts entirely too large a figure and the ear entirely too small if any at all; it is also due to the force of habit, and so strong is this that even the teachers who know how these things should be yet use terms incorrectly without being aware of it. Mr. Root's work has decided value and it is a pity that it could not reach a still wider circle of teachers than it will. The more prominent teachers of the pianoforte, knowing Dr. Root mainly as writer of popular songs and elementary treatises on singing and class teaching, do not all of them understand the work he has done towards clearing up elementary musical terminology. Beginning as a disciple of the late Dr. Lowell Mason, who first began to set our elementary terminology of music in order, he has devoted many years to simplifying and putting in order.

CELEBRATED PIANISTS OF THE PAST AND PRESENT. A. EHRLICH. Translated by A. L. Manchester. Philadelphia, Theo. Presser. 1895.

This substantial volume of 422 pages contains portraits and short biographical sketches of one hundred and thirty-nine pianists. Among these are quite a number of Americans. The sketches are mostly short, many of them no more than three hundred words. Others, again, as Beethoven and Mozart, are quite extended sketches. The portraits are "processed" from the most available existing ones, which often are indifferent lithographs. It is a book, therefore, which the reader will estimate differently according to his demands. As a handy reference book for the student or journalist it is valuable. As a satisfactory account of the greater number of the pianistic guild it is insufficient. As a handy reference for a multitude of lesser lights, it is particularly strong--for many of these names occur only in the largest dictionaries, and some of them not even there. On the whole therefore it is to be mentioned as a utility volume which no "gentleman's library can afford to do without."

SONGS.

SPRINGTIME OF THE HEART. m.sop. Eb. Fried. von Wickede. Ditson.

An effective song in German style, worth reading.

NO JEWELL'D BEAUTY. Words by Gerald Massey; music by Frank Wallis Worsley. Whitney Marvin Music Co.

For baritone. Concert song.

WHERE ART THOU? Frank Wallis Worsley. Whitney Marvin Music Co.

Beginning with a short recitative, this song rises later to quite a climax of intensity, in the manner first made popular by Gounod. The poetry exercises the imagination perhaps a trifle more than sanitary science would warrant, when it says: "I stand and gaze across earth's fairest sea," and finds the sound of it like a clashing chain binding "my beautiful from thee."

THE GONDOLIER. Venetian Boat Song. Emily Gilmore. Whitney Marvin Co.

For baritone.

CLOUDLESS ACROSS THE HEAVENS. Sop. and alto Duet. Campana. Ditson Co.

Pleasing duet in the Italian style, thirds and so on.

"'TWAS EVE AND MAY." Leopold Godowsky. H. Kleber & Bro.

A very musical song for soprano.

THE PASTOR'S DAUGHTER. T. A. Darby. Ditson.

If some one will ascertain and publish the connection existing between the name of this song and the poem, he will confer a favor upon an anxious inquirer, who may be reached through this office. The music is not especially bad (nor yet especially good) and the entire make up is of the same negative order. Why song? Why pastor's daughter? And why bother the public about them? All these are questions in point.

THOU ART TO ME. Charles Gilbert Spross. Thompson & Spross.

A pleasing and musical song with more in it for public performance than the great majority of such songs that reach this review.

FOR ORGAN.

WM. D. ARMSTRONG. Evening song.
Slumber Song. (Schytte.)

Pleasing pieces of moderate difficulty such as average organists will be glad to get. The registration is marked for moderate two manual organ.

FOR VIOLA.

MICHAEL H. CROSS. Romanza ed Arpeggio, with piano accompaniment. Presser.

Elaborately written for viola. Effective if well done.

JOHN CHURCH COMPANY.

DREAMING. By Winthrop.
THE SWING IN THE WOODS. "

Very easy pieces, 1st grade.

MAZURKA ESPAGNOLE. Tocaben. Two mandolins and guitar.
POLKA NAPOLITAINE. " Three mandolins and guitar.

Pleasing works to fill a long felt want.

VICTOR MARCH. Harry C. Jordan.

3d grade, rather forceful.

DITSON COMPANY.

SCOTCH JOHNNIE. J. L. Molloy.

A pleasing song by a well known and popular writer.

THE MOUNTAIN NYMPHS. Operetta. G. W. Stratton.
DOBBS' FARM. Operetta. G. W. Stratton.

The plot of the first is as follows:

A group of Nymphs on the shores of Echo Lake are surprised by the approach of a city girls' school rusticating in the Pebble house. Concealing themselves in the shrubbery the Nymphs, after shyly performing the part of Echo in answer to the girls' hollow, discover themselves in time to rescue some little Franconia huckleberry girls from the unrelenting treatment of the city misses. In the second act is a *Trial by Nymphs* of all the girls to decide which one merits the magnificent gift awarded this midsummer's day by the "Old Man of the Mountain" to the worthiest. As might be supposed "the last shall be first," and Alice, the humble peasant girl bears off the prize.

The plot of "Dobbs' Farm" is this:

Miss Flowerdew, a vain and affected governess, with her young ladies is spending the summer holidays at "Dobbs' Farm," a rustic boarding house among the mountains. Rose, the daughter of a wealthy southern gentleman, and formerly a great favorite of Miss Flowerdew, being apparently forsaken by her father, is now in disgrace, and treated rather as a servant than a pupil. The young girls nurse, not seen for many years, Matilda, comes, however to the Dobbs farm, disguised as a boy, and after receiving conspicuous attention from the governess disguise herself and carries away Rose to her loving father in triumph. Miss Tabbie, mistress of the farm house, and her maid Molly, with their uncompromising country manners, were a counterpart to the affected and foolish Miss Flowerdew.

These two light operettas are for popular use, and like several highly successful works from the same pen in former years, are well adapted to please, and at the same time are practicable for amateurs. Of the two the former is a trifle more difficult. Mr. Stratton has been very successful with waltz movements, but it is a question whether there are not perhaps too many of them in succession in this work. More of double measure would have relieved the untempered sweetness. This, however is a detail.

INSTRUMENTAL.

SWORD AND SADDLE. Calvary March. P. Wachs. Effective and pleasing. 4th grade.

HARVEST MOON. Schottisch. J. A. Reyder. 3d grade, popular style.

CLUB MARCH. John Lloyd Whitney. 4th grade Common.

GALLANT TROOPERS. Scene Militaire. M. Carman. 3d grade Common.

POLLY POLKA. W. P. Fennimore. 3d grade. Common.

THE JOLLY SAILOR BOY. Harold Leston.

MAY DAY MARCH.

These two belong to a set of five easy pieces. 1st grade.

OLIVIA PRIMROSE GAVOTTE. Entr'act. Frank Wallis Wordley A pleasing quasi antique. 4th grade.

OUR DRUM CORPS MARCH. Behr. 3d grade popular.

LONG LIVE VIENNA MARCH. Carciotti. For three mandolins and piano.

TUTTO FUOCO GALOP. Luigi Cerzi. 3d grade.

ELEVEN SKETCHES FOR PIANO. By J. Lewis Brown. Whaley Royce & Co. Toronto. $1.00.

Spinning Song.
An Album Leaf.
A Dream.
Mazurka.
Two Thoughts Gay and Grave
Humoreske.
Melody.
Moment Musicale.
Hungarian Caprice.
Toccata.
Tempo di Menuetto.

A set of ambitious little pieces for the use of students. They will undoubtedly do good, but candor compels the admission that the author has not fully succeeded in writing in the modern style, the harmonic treatment being not particularly fresh. Melodically, however, with this reservation, they are fairly well done, and at any rate the author is entitled to making a creditable attempt.

www.ingramcontent.com/pod-product-compliance
Lightning Source LLC
Chambersburg PA
CBHW021220300426
44111CB00007B/371